1996 Supplement

to

CONSTITUTIONAL LAW

CASES AND MATERIALS

By

WILLIAM COHEN
C. Wendell and Edith M. Carlsmith
Professor of Law, Stanford University

JONATHAN D. VARAT
Professor of Law,
University of California, Los Angeles

NINTH EDITION

Westbury, New York
THE FOUNDATION PRESS, INC.
1996

TEXT IS PRINTED ON 10% POST
CONSUMER RECYCLED PAPER

TABLE OF CONTENTS

(**Bold** Indicates Principal Cases)

TABLE OF CONTENTS

SECTION 3. CASES AND CONTROVERSIES AND JUSTICIABILITY

B. Standing

1. "Conventional" Standing

3. Taxpayer and Citizen Standing

E. Political Questions

PART II. ALLOCATION OF GOVERNMENTAL POWERS: THE NATION AND THE STATES: THE PRESIDENT, THE CONGRESS AND THE COURTS

CHAPTER 4. THE SCOPE OF NATIONAL POWER

SECTION 2. SOURCES OF NATIONAL POWER: EARLY DEVELOPMENTS

A. The Marshall Court's View

SECTION 3. THE SCOPE OF NATIONAL POWER TODAY

A. The Commerce Power

TABLE OF CONTENTS

TABLE OF CONTENTS

CHAPTER 9. THE DUE PROCESS, CONTRACT AND JUST
COMPENSATION CLAUSES AND THE REVIEW OF THE
REASONABLENESS OF LEGISLATION

SECTION 1. ECONOMIC REGULATORY LEGISLATION

C. The Just Compensation Clause of the Fifth
Amendment—What Does it Add to Due Process?

2. Mandated Access to Property

SECTION 2. PROTECTION OF PERSONAL LIBERTIES

C. Personal Autonomy

CHAPTER 10. THE EQUAL PROTECTION CLAUSE
AND THE REVIEW OF THE REASONABLENESS
OF LEGISLATION

SECTION 1. INTRODUCTION—THE SCOPE OF
EQUAL PROTECTION

SECTION 2. SOCIAL AND ECONOMIC
REGULATORY LEGISLATION

TABLE OF CONTENTS

SECTION 3. SUSPECT CLASSIFICATIONS
B. Racial Segregation in Schools and Other Public Facilities

TABLE OF CONTENTS

PART IV. CONSTITUTIONAL PROTECTION OF EXPRESSION AND CONSCIENCE

CHAPTER 13. GOVERNMENTAL CONTROL OF THE CONTENT OF EXPRESSION

SECTION 2. INTERMEZZO: AN INTRODUCTION TO THE CONCEPTS OF VAGUENESS, OVERBREADTH AND PRIOR RESTRAINT

B. Prior Restraint

TABLE OF CONTENTS

B. Political Fundraising and Expenditures

CHAPTER 16. FREEDOM OF THE PRESS

SECTION 6. SPECIAL PROBLEMS OF THE ELECTRONIC MEDIA

CHAPTER 17. RELIGION AND THE CONSTITUTION

SECTION 1. THE ESTABLISHMENT CLAUSE

B. Government Religious Exercises, Ceremonies and Practices

TABLE OF CONTENTS

C. Financial Aid to Church-Related Schools and Church-Related Instruction

1. Elementary and Secondary Schools

TABLE OF CASES

Principal cases are in italic type. Non-principal cases are in roman type. References are to Pages.

xiii

TABLE OF CASES

1996 Supplement

to

CONSTITUTIONAL LAW

CASES AND MATERIALS

*

Part I

THE CONSTITUTION AND THE COURTS: THE JUDICIAL FUNCTION IN CONSTITUTIONAL CASES

Chapter 2

JUDICIAL REVIEW

SECTION 1. THE LEGITIMACY OF JUDICIAL REVIEW

Pages 37–38. Replace last two paragraphs of note, "Prospective and Retroactive Constitutional Decisions," with the following:

Despite the concern that prospective application of new constitutional decisions is inconsistent with the "integrity of judicial review," a footnote in *Griffith* referred to earlier civil cases that applied new rules of constitutional law prospectively only. Chevron Oil Co. v. Huson, 404 U.S. 97 (1971), had described a three-part inquiry: (1) whether the decision announced a new principle of law; (2) whether retrospective operation of the rule would further or retard the purpose of the rule; (3) whether retrospective application would produce substantial inequitable results. In Harper v. Virginia Department of Taxation, 509 U.S. 86 (1993), however, the Court held that the *Griffith* principle was fully applicable to civil cases. Justice Thomas' opinion for the Court said:

"When this Court applies a rule of federal law to the parties before it, that rule is the controlling interpretation of federal law and must be given full retroactive effect in all cases still open on direct review and as to all events, regardless of whether such events predate or postdate our announcement of the rule. This rule extends *Griffith*'s ban against 'selective application of new rules.' ... Mindful of the 'basic norms of constitutional adjudication' that animated our view of retroactivity in the criminal context, ... we now prohibit the erection of selective temporal barriers to the application of federal law in noncriminal cases. In both civil and criminal cases, we can scarcely permit 'the substantive law [to] shift and spring' according to 'the particular equities of [individual parties'] claims' of actual reliance on an old rule and of harm from a retroactive application of the new rule.... Our approach to retroactivity heeds the admonition that '[t]he Court has no more constitutional authority in civil cases than in criminal cases to disregard current law or to treat similarly situated litigants differently.' "

1

In Reynoldsville Casket Co. v. Hyde, 115 S.Ct. 1745 (1995), the Court summarized the holding in *Harper*:

> "[W]hen (1) the Court decides a case and applies the (new) legal rule of that case to the parties before it, then (2) it and other courts must treat that same (new) legal rule as 'retroactive,' applying it, for example, to all pending cases, whether or not those cases involve predecision events."

SECTION 2. CONGRESSIONAL CONTROL OF JUDICIAL REVIEW BY THE FEDERAL COURTS

Page 42. Add as a footnote to Ex Parte Yerger in Note (3):

[1] The Court relied on Ex Parte Yerger in Felker v. Turpin, 116 S.Ct. 2333 (1996). The Antiterrorism and Effective Death Penalty Act of 1996 provided that a state prisoner's second or successive petition for a writ of habeas corpus in a federal district court must be dismissed unless a court of appeals makes a determination that certain conditions apply. A denial of authorization to file "shall not be appealable and shall not be the subject of a petition for ... writ of certiorari." The Court held that the quoted provision did not deprive the Supreme Court of jurisdiction to entertain an original habeas corpus petition.

Chapter 3

THE JURISDICTION OF FEDERAL COURTS IN CONSTITUTIONAL CASES

SECTION 2. CONSTITUTIONAL LITIGATION INITIATED IN THE FEDERAL COURTS

B. ENFORCEMENT OF FEDERAL RIGHTS IN SUITS AGAINST STATE OFFICERS: THE ELEVENTH AMENDMENT

Page 71. Replace Pennsylvania v. Union Gas with the following:

SEMINOLE TRIBE OF FLORIDA v. FLORIDA

___ U.S. ___, 116 S.Ct. 1114, 134 L.Ed.2d 252 (1996)

Chief Justice Rehnquist delivered the opinion of the Court.

The Indian Gaming Regulatory Act provides that an Indian tribe may conduct certain gaming activities only in conformance with a valid compact between the tribe and the State in which the gaming activities are located. ... 25 U.S.C. § 2710(d)(1)(C). The Act, passed by Congress under the Indian Commerce Clause, U.S. Const., Art. I, § 10, cl. 3, imposes upon the States a duty to negotiate in good faith with an Indian tribe toward the formation of a compact, § 2710(d)(3)(A), and authorizes a tribe to bring suit in federal court against a State in order to compel performance of that duty, § 2710(d)(7). We hold that notwithstanding Congress' clear intent to abrogate the States' sovereign immunity, the Indian Commerce Clause does not grant Congress that power, and therefore § 2710(d)(7) cannot grant jurisdiction over a State that does not consent to be sued. We further hold that the doctrine of Ex parte Young, 209 U.S. 123 (1908), may not be used to enforce § 2710(d)(3) against a state official.

I

. . .

In September 1991, the Seminole Tribe of Indians, petitioner, sued the State of Florida and its Governor, Lawton Chiles, respondents. Invoking jurisdiction under 25 U.S.C. § 2710(d)(7)(A), as well as 28 U.S.C. §§ 1331 and 1362, petitioner alleged that respondents had "refused to enter into any negotiation for inclusion of [certain gaming activities] in a tribal-state compact," thereby violating the "requirement of good faith negotiation" contained in § 2710(d)(3). Respondents moved to dismiss the complaint, arguing that the suit violated the

3

State's sovereign immunity from suit in federal court. The District Court denied respondents' motion ...

The Court of Appeals for the Eleventh Circuit reversed the decision of the District Court, holding that the Eleventh Amendment barred petitioner's suit against respondents. ...

... [W]e granted certiorari ... in order to consider two questions: (1) Does the Eleventh Amendment prevent Congress from authorizing suits by Indian tribes against States for prospective injunctive relief to enforce legislation enacted pursuant to the Indian Commerce Clause?; and (2) Does the doctrine of Ex parte Young permit suits against a State's governor for prospective injunctive relief to enforce the good faith bargaining requirement of the Act? We answer the first question in the affirmative, the second in the negative, and we therefore affirm the Eleventh Circuit's dismissal of petitioner's suit.

The Eleventh Amendment provides: "The Judicial power of the United States shall not be construed to extend to any suit in law or equity, commenced or prosecuted against one of the United States by Citizens of another State, or by Citizens or Subjects of any Foreign State." Although the text of the Amendment would appear to restrict only the Article III diversity jurisdiction of the federal courts, "we have understood the Eleventh Amendment to stand not so much for what it says, but for the presupposition ... which it confirms." ... That presupposition, first observed over a century ago in Hans v. Louisiana, 134 U.S. 1 (1890), has two parts: first, that each State is a sovereign entity in our federal system; and second, that " '[i]t is inherent in the nature of sovereignty not to be amenable to the suit of an individual without its consent.' " Id., at 13 ..., quoting The Federalist No. 81 ... (A.Hamilton). ... For over a century we have reaffirmed that federal jurisdiction over suits against unconsenting States "was not contemplated by the Constitution when establishing the judicial power of the United States." *Hans*, supra, at 15.

Here, petitioner has sued the State of Florida and it is undisputed that Florida has not consented to the suit. ... Petitioner nevertheless contends that its suit is not barred by state sovereign immunity. First, it argues that Congress through the Act abrogated the States' sovereign immunity. Alternatively, petitioner maintains that its suit against the Governor may go forward under Ex parte Young, *supra*. We consider each of those arguments in turn.

II

... In order to determine whether Congress has abrogated the States' sovereign immunity, we ask two questions: first, whether Congress has "unequivocally expresse[d] its intent to abrogate the immunity," ... and second, whether Congress has acted "pursuant to a valid exercise of power." ...

A

Congress' intent to abrogate the States' immunity from suit must be obvious from "a clear legislative statement." ... This rule arises from a recognition of the important role played by the Eleventh Amendment and the broader principles that it reflects. . . . In *Atascadero*, we held that "[a] general authorization for suit in federal court is not the kind of unequivocal statutory language sufficient to abrogate the Eleventh Amendment." . . .

Here, . . . Congress has in § 2710(d)(7) provided an "unmistakably clear" statement of its intent to abrogate. Section 2710(d)(7)(A)(i) vests jurisdiction in "[t]he United States district courts . . . over any cause of action . . . arising from the failure of a State to enter into negotiations . . . or to conduct such negotiations in good faith." . . . [T]he numerous references to the "State" in the text of § 2710(d)(7)(B) make it indubitable that Congress intended through the Act to abrogate the States' sovereign immunity from suit.

B

. . . [W]e turn now to consider whether the Act was passed "pursuant to a valid exercise of power." . . .

Petitioner suggests that one consideration weighing in favor of finding the power to abrogate here is that the Act authorizes only prospective injunctive relief rather than retroactive monetary relief. But we have often made it clear that the relief sought by a plaintiff suing a State is irrelevant to the question whether the suit is barred by the Eleventh Amendment. . . .

Similarly, petitioner argues that the abrogation power is validly exercised here because the Act grants the States a power that they would not otherwise have, viz., some measure of authority over gaming on Indian lands. It is true enough that the Act extends to the States a power withheld from them by the Constitution. . . . Nevertheless, we do not see how that consideration is relevant to the question whether Congress may abrogate state sovereign immunity. The Eleventh Amendment immunity may not be lifted by Congress unilaterally deciding that it will be replaced by grant of some other authority. . . .

Thus our inquiry into whether Congress has the power to abrogate unilaterally the States' immunity from suit is narrowly focused on one question: Was the Act in question passed pursuant to a constitutional provision granting Congress the power to abrogate? See, e.g., Fitzpatrick v. Bitzer, 427 U.S. 445, 452–456 (1976). Previously, in conducting that inquiry, we have found authority to abrogate under only two provisions of the Constitution. In *Fitzpatrick*, we recognized that the Fourteenth Amendment, by expanding federal power at the expense of state autonomy, had fundamentally altered the balance of state and federal power struck by the Constitution. . . . We noted that § 1 of the Fourteenth Amendment contained prohibitions expressly directed at the States and that § 5 of the Amendment expressly provided that "The Congress shall have the power to enforce, by appropriate legislation, the provisions of this article." . . . We held that through the Fourteenth Amendment, federal power extended to intrude upon the province of the Eleventh Amendment and therefore that § 5 of the Fourteenth Amendment allowed Congress to abrogate the immunity from suit guaranteed by that Amendment.

In only one other case has congressional abrogation of the States' Eleventh Amendment immunity been upheld. In Pennsylvania v. Union Gas Co., 491 U.S. 1 (1989), a plurality of the Court found that the Interstate Commerce Clause, Art. I, § 8, cl. 3, granted Congress the power to abrogate state sovereign immunity, stating that the power to regulate interstate commerce would be "incomplete without the authority to render States liable in damages." ... Justice White added the fifth vote necessary to the result in that case, but wrote separately in order to express that he "[did] not agree with much of [the plurality's] reasoning." ...

  . . .

... [T]he plurality opinion in *Union Gas* allows no principled distinction in favor of the States to be drawn between the Indian Commerce Clause and the Interstate Commerce Clause.

... Generally, the principle of *stare decisis*, and the interests that it serves, ... counsel strongly against reconsideration of our precedent. Nevertheless, we always have treated *stare decisis* as a "principle of policy," ... and not as an "inexorable command,".... "[W]hen governing decisions are unworkable or are badly reasoned, 'this Court has never felt constrained to follow precedent.'" ... Our willingness to reconsider our earlier decisions has been "particularly true in constitutional cases, because in such cases 'correction through legislative action is practically impossible.'" ...

The Court in *Union Gas* reached a result without an expressed rationale agreed upon by a majority of the Court. ...

The plurality's rationale also deviated sharply from our established federalism jurisprudence and essentially eviscerated our decision in *Hans*. ....It was well established in 1989 when *Union Gas* was decided that the Eleventh Amendment stood for the constitutional principle that state sovereign immunity limited the federal courts' jurisdiction under Article III. ...

Never before the decision in *Union Gas* had we suggested that the bounds of Article III could be expanded by Congress operating pursuant to any constitutional provision other than the Fourteenth Amendment. Indeed, it had seemed fundamental that Congress could not expand the jurisdiction of the federal courts beyond the bounds of Article III. Marbury v. Madison, 1 Cranch 137 (1803). ...

The plurality's extended reliance upon our decision in Fitzpatrick v. Bitzer, 427 U.S. 445 (1976), that Congress could under the Fourteenth Amendment abrogate the States' sovereign immunity was also, we believe, misplaced. *Fitzpatrick* was based upon a rationale wholly inapplicable to the Interstate Commerce Clause, viz., that the Fourteenth Amendment, adopted well after the adoption of the Eleventh Amendment and the ratification of the Constitution, operated to alter the pre-existing balance between state and federal power achieved by Article III and the Eleventh Amendment. ...*Fitzpatrick* cannot be read to justify "limitation of the principle embodied in the Eleventh Amendment through appeal to antecedent provisions of the Constitution." ...

... Reconsidering the decision in *Union Gas*, we conclude that none of the policies underlying *stare decisis* require our continuing adherence to its holding. ... The case involved the interpretation of the Constitution and therefore may be altered only by constitutional amendment or revision by this Court. ...

. . .

In overruling *Union Gas* today, we reconfirm that the background principle of state sovereign immunity embodied in the Eleventh Amendment is not so ephemeral as to dissipate when the subject of the suit is an area, like the regulation of Indian commerce, that is under the exclusive control of the Federal Government. Even when the Constitution vests in Congress complete law-making authority over a particular area, the Eleventh Amendment prevents congressional authorization of suits by private parties against unconsenting States. The Eleventh Amendment restricts the judicial power under Article III, and Article I cannot be used to circumvent the constitutional limitations placed upon federal jurisdiction. Petitioner's suit against the State of Florida must be dismissed for a lack of jurisdiction.

III

Petitioner argues that we may exercise jurisdiction over its suit to enforce § 2710(d)(3) against the Governor notwithstanding the jurisdictional bar of the Eleventh Amendment. Petitioner notes that since our decision in Ex parte Young, 209 U.S. 123 (1908), we often have found federal jurisdiction over a suit against a state official when that suit seeks only prospective injunctive relief in order to "end a continuing violation of federal law." ... The situation presented here, however, is sufficiently different from that giving rise to the traditional Ex parte Young action so as to preclude the availability of that doctrine.

Here, the "continuing violation of federal law" alleged by petitioner is the Governor's failure to bring the State into compliance with § 2710(d)(3). But the duty to negotiate imposed upon the State by that statutory provision does not stand alone. Rather, ... Congress passed § 2710(d)(3) in conjunction with the carefully crafted and intricate remedial scheme set forth in § 2710(d)(7).

Where Congress has created a remedial scheme for the enforcement of a particular federal right, we have, in suits against federal officers, refused to supplement that scheme with one created by the judiciary. ...

Here, Congress intended § 2710(d)(3) to be enforced against the State in an action brought under § 2710(d)(7); the intricate procedures set forth in that provision show that Congress intended therein not only to define, but also significantly to limit, the duty imposed by § 2710(d)(3). For example, where the court finds that the State has failed to negotiate in good faith, the only remedy prescribed is an order directing the State and the Indian tribe to conclude a compact within 60 days. And if the parties disregard the court's order and fail to conclude a compact within the 60–day period, the only sanction is that each party then must submit a proposed compact to a mediator who selects the one which best embodies the terms of the Act. Finally, if the State fails to accept the compact selected by the mediator, the only sanction against it is that the mediator shall notify the Secretary of the Interior who then must prescribe regulations governing Class III gaming on the tribal lands at issue. By contrast with this quite modest set of sanctions, an action brought against a state official under Ex parte Young would expose that official to the full remedial powers of a federal court, including, presumably, contempt sanctions. If § 2710(d)(3) could be enforced in a suit under Ex parte Young, § 2710(d)(7) would have been superfluous; it is difficult to see why an Indian tribe would suffer through the intricate scheme of § 2710(d)(7) when more complete and more immediate relief would be available under Ex parte Young.

Here, of course, we have found that Congress does not have authority under the Constitution to make the State suable in federal court under § 2710(d)(7). Nevertheless, the fact that Congress chose to impose upon the State a liability which is significantly more limited than would be the liability imposed upon the state officer under Ex parte Young strongly indicates that Congress had no wish to create the latter under § 2710(d)(3). Nor are we free to rewrite the statutory scheme in order to approximate what we think Congress might have wanted had it known that § 2710(d)(7) was beyond its authority. If that effort is to be made, it should be made by Congress, and not by the federal courts. We hold that Ex parte Young is inapplicable to petitioner's suit against the Governor of Florida, and therefore that suit is barred by the Eleventh Amendment and must be dismissed for a lack of jurisdiction.

IV

The Eleventh Amendment prohibits Congress from making the State of Florida capable of being sued in federal court. The narrow exception to the Eleventh Amendment provided by the Ex parte Young doctrine cannot be used to enforce § 2710(d)(3) because Congress enacted a remedial scheme, § 2710(d)(7), specifically designed for the enforcement of that right. The Eleventh Circuit's dismissal of petitioner's suit is hereby affirmed.

It is so ordered.

Justice Stevens, dissenting.

This case is about power—the power of the Congress of the United States to create a private federal cause of action against a State, or its Governor, for the violation of a federal right. ... [I]n a sharp break with the past, today the Court holds that with the narrow and illogical exception of statutes enacted pursuant to the Enforcement Clause of the Fourteenth Amendment, Congress has no such power.

The importance of the majority's decision to overrule the Court's holding in Pennsylvania v. Union Gas Co. cannot be overstated. The majority's opinion does not simply preclude Congress from establishing the rather curious statutory scheme under which Indian tribes may seek the aid of a federal court to secure a State's good faith negotiations over gaming regulations. Rather, it prevents Congress from providing a federal forum for a broad range of actions against States, from those sounding in copyright and patent law, to those concerning bankruptcy, environmental law, and the regulation of our vast national economy.

There may be room for debate over whether, in light of the Eleventh Amendment, Congress has the power to ensure that such a cause of action may be enforced in federal court by a citizen of another State or a foreign citizen. There can be no serious debate, however, over whether Congress has the power to ensure that such a cause of action may be brought by a citizen of the State being sued. Congress' authority in that regard is clear.

. . .

For these reasons, as well as those set forth in Justice Souter's opinion, I respectfully dissent.

Justice Souter, with whom Justice Ginsburg and Justice Breyer join, dissenting.

. . .

The fault I find with the majority today is not in its decision to reexamine *Union Gas*, for the Court in that case produced no majority for a single rationale supporting congressional authority. Instead, I part company from the Court because I am convinced that its decision is fundamentally mistaken, and for that reason I respectfully dissent.

. . .

It is useful to separate three questions: (1) whether the States enjoyed sovereign immunity if sued in their own courts in the period prior to ratification of the National Constitution; (2) if so, whether after ratification the States were entitled to claim some such immunity when sued in a federal court exercising jurisdiction either because the suit was between a State and a non-state litigant who was not its citizen, or because the issue in the case raised a federal question; and (3) whether any state sovereign immunity recognized in federal court may be abrogated by Congress.

The answer to the first question is not clear, although some of the Framers assumed that States did enjoy immunity in their own courts. The second question was not debated at the time of ratification, except as to citizen-state diversity jurisdiction; there was no unanimity, but in due course the Court in Chisholm v. Georgia, 2 Dall. 419 (1793), answered that a state defendant enjoyed no such immunity. As to federal question jurisdiction, state sovereign immunity seems not to have been debated prior to ratification, the silence probably showing a general understanding at the time that the States would have no immunity in such cases.

The adoption of the Eleventh Amendment soon changed the result in *Chisholm*, not by mentioning sovereign immunity, but by eliminating citizen-state diversity jurisdiction over cases with state defendants. . . .

The *Hans* Court erroneously assumed that a State could plead sovereign immunity against a noncitizen suing under federal question jurisdiction, and for that reason held that a State must enjoy the same protection in a suit by one of its citizens. ...

The Court's answer today to the third question is likewise at odds with the Founders' view that common law, when it was received into the new American legal systems, was always subject to legislative amendment. ...

. . .

The *Hans* doctrine was erroneous, but it has not previously proven to be unworkable.... I would therefore treat *Hans* as it has always been treated in fact until today, as a doctrine of federal common law. For, as so understood, it has formed one of the strands of the federal relationship for over a century now, and the stability of that relationship is itself a value that *stare decisis* aims to respect.

In being ready to hold that the relationship may still be altered, not by the Court but by Congress, I would tread the course laid out elsewhere in our cases. ... The plain statement rule, which "assures that the legislature has in fact faced, and intended to bring into issue, the critical matters involved in the judicial decision," ... is particularly appropriate in light of our primary reliance on "[t]he effectiveness of the federal political process in preserving the States' interests." Garcia v. San Antonio Metropolitan Transit Authority, 469 U.S. 528, 552 (1985). . . .

When judging legislation passed under unmistakable Article I powers, no further restriction could be required. Nor does the Court explain why more could be demanded. In the past, we have assumed that a plain statement requirement is sufficient to protect the States from undue federal encroachments upon their traditional immunity from suit. ... It is hard to contend that this rule has set the bar too low, for (except in *Union Gas*) we have never found the requirement to be met outside the context of laws passed under § 5 of the Fourteenth Amendment. The exception I would recognize today proves the rule, moreover, because the federal abrogation of state immunity comes as part of a regulatory scheme which is itself designed to invest the States with regulatory powers that Congress need not extend to them. This fact suggests to me that the political safeguards of federalism are working, that a plain statement rule is an adequate check on congressional overreaching, and that today's abandonment of that approach is wholly unwarranted.

. . .

SECTION 3. CASES AND CONTROVERSIES AND JUSTICIABILITY

B. STANDING

1. "CONVENTIONAL" STANDING

Page 107. Add to end of note, "Standing and the Requirement of 'Injury in Fact.'":

Northeastern Florida Chapter of Associated General Contractors v. City of Jacksonville, 508 U.S. 656 (1993). Non-minority contractors who alleged that they would have bid on construction work set aside for minority contractors had standing to challenge the requirement that 10% of city contracts be awarded to minority-owned businesses. It was not necessary that plaintiffs allege or prove that they would have been awarded contracts but for the challenged program. In equal protection cases, the injury in fact is not the denial of the benefit itself but the denial of equal treatment imposed by a barrier to obtaining a benefit—here the inability to compete on an equal footing in the bidding process.

United States v. Hays, 115 S.Ct. 1311 (1995). Voters attacking an alleged racial gerrymander lack standing unless they show that they, personally, have been subject to racial discrimination. White voters who neither reside in the challenged predominantly-Black district, nor prove that they were excluded from that district because they were White, have only a "generalized grievance" and have not suffered "individualized harm."

---

3. TAXPAYER AND CITIZEN STANDING

Page 114. Add footnote "a" to the end of the Court's opinion in Lujan v. Defenders of Wildlife:

a Justice Scalia's position in *Lujan* was originally propounded in Scalia, The Doctrine of Standing as an Essential Element of the Separation of Powers, 17 SUFFOLK U.L.REV. 831 (1983). For a critique, see Sunstein, What's Standing After Lujan? Of Citizen Suits, "Injuries," and Article III, 91 MICH.L.REV. 163 (1992).

E. POLITICAL QUESTIONS

Page 139. Replace Gilligan v. Morgan with the following:

NIXON v. UNITED STATES
506 U.S. 224, 113 S.Ct. 732, 122 L.Ed.2d 1 (1993).

Chief Justice Rehnquist delivered the opinion of the Court.

Petitioner Walter L. Nixon, Jr., asks this court to decide whether Senate Rule XI, which allows a committee of Senators to hear evidence against an individual who has been impeached and to report that evidence to the full Senate, violates the Impeachment Trial Clause, Art. I, § 3, cl. 6. That Clause provides that the "Senate shall have the sole Power to try all Impeachments." But before we reach the merits of such a claim, we must decide whether it is "justiciable," that is, whether it is a claim that may be resolved by the courts. We conclude that it is not.

Nixon, a former Chief Judge of the United States District Court for the Southern District of Mississippi, was convicted by a jury of two counts of making false statements before a federal grand jury and sentenced to prison....

On May 10, 1989, the House of Representatives adopted three articles of impeachment for high crimes and misdemeanors....

After the House presented the articles to the Senate, the Senate voted to invoke its own Impeachment Rule XI, under which the presiding officer appoints a committee of Senators to "receive evidence and take testimony." ... The Senate committee held four days of hearings ... Pursuant to Rule XI, the committee presented the full Senate with a complete transcript of the proceeding and a report stating the uncontested facts and summarizing the evidence on the contested facts. Nixon and the House impeachment managers submitted extensive final briefs to the full Senate and delivered arguments from the Senate floor during the three hours set aside for oral argument in front of that body. Nixon himself gave a personal appeal, and several Senators posed questions directly to both parties.... The Senate voted by more than the constitutionally required two-thirds majority to convict Nixon on the first two articles.... The presiding officer then entered judgment removing Nixon from his office as United States District Judge.

Nixon thereafter commenced the present suit, arguing that Senate Rule XI violates the constitutional grant of authority to the Senate to "try" all impeachments because it prohibits the whole Senate from taking part in the evidentiary hearings.... The District Court held that his claim was nonjusticiable, and the Court of Appeals for the District of Columbia Circuit agreed. A controversy is nonjusticiable—i.e., involves a political question—where there is "a textually demonstrable constitutional commitment of the issue to a coordinate political department; or a lack of judicially discoverable and manageable standards for resolving it...." Baker v. Carr, 369 U.S. 186, 217 (1962). But the courts must, in the first instance, interpret the text in question and determine whether and to what extent the issue is textually committed.... As the discussion that follows makes clear, the concept of a textual commitment to a coordinate political department is not completely separate from the concept of a lack of judicially discoverable and manageable standards for resolving it; the lack of judicially manageable standards may strengthen the conclusion that there is a textually demonstrable commitment to a coordinate branch.

In this case, we must examine Art. I, § 3, cl. 6, to determine the scope of authority conferred upon the Senate by the Framers regarding impeachment. It provides:

"The Senate shall have the sole Power to try all Impeachments. When sitting for that Purpose, they shall be on Oath or Affirmation. When the President of the United States is tried, the Chief Justice shall preside: And no Person shall be convicted without the Concurrence of two thirds of the Members present."

The language and structure of this Clause are revealing. The first sentence is a grant of authority to the Senate, and the word "sole" indicates that this authority is reposed in the Senate and nowhere else. The next two sentences specify requirements to which the Senate proceedings shall conform: the Senate shall be on oath or affirmation, a two-thirds vote is required to convict, and when the President is tried the Chief Justice shall preside.

Petitioner argues that the word "try" in the first sentence imposes by implication an additional requirement on the Senate in that the proceedings must be in the nature of a judicial trial. From there petitioner goes on to argue that this limitation precludes the Senate from delegating to a select committee the task of hearing the testimony of witnesses, as was done pursuant to Senate Rule XI. . . .

There are several difficulties with this position which lead us ultimately to reject it. The word "try," both in 1787 and later, has considerably broader meanings than those to which petitioner would limit it. . . . [W]e cannot say that the Framers used the word "try" as an implied limitation on the method by which the Senate might proceed in trying impeachments. "As a rule the Constitution speaks in general terms, leaving Congress to deal with subsidiary matters of detail as the public interests and changing conditions may require. . . ." Dillon v. Gloss, 256 U.S. 368, 376 (1921).

The conclusion that the use of the word "try" in the first sentence of the Impeachment Trial Clause lacks sufficient precision to afford any judicially manageable standard of review of the Senate's actions is fortified by the existence of the three very specific requirements that the Constitution does impose on the Senate when trying impeachments: the members must be under oath, a two-thirds vote is required to convict, and the Chief Justice presides when the President is tried. These limitations are quite precise, and their nature suggests that the Framers did not intend to impose additional limitations on the form of the Senate proceedings by the use of the word "try" in the first sentence.

. . . [The first sentence of Clause 6] provides that "[t]he Senate shall have the sole Power to try all Impeachments." We think that the word "sole" is of considerable significance. Indeed, the word "sole" appears only one other time in the Constitution—with respect to the House of Representatives' "*sole* Power of Impeachment." Art. I, § 2, cl. 5 (emphasis added). The common sense meaning of the work "sole" is that the Senate alone shall have authority to determine whether an individual should be acquitted or convicted. . . .

. . .

Petitioner . . . argues that even if significance be attributed to the word "sole" in the first sentence of the clause, the authority granted is to the Senate, and this means that "the Senate—not the courts, not a lay jury, not a Senate Committee—shall try impeachments." It would be possible to read the first sentence of the Clause this way, but it is not a natural reading. Petitioner's interpretation would bring into judicial purview not merely the sort of claim made by petitioner, but other similar claims based on the conclusion that the word "Senate" has imposed by implication limitations on procedures which the Senate might adopt. Such limitations would be inconsistent with the construction of the Clause as a whole, which, as we have noted, sets out three express limitations in separate sentences.

The history and contemporary understanding of the impeachment provisions support our reading of the constitutional language. The parties do not offer evidence of a single word in the history of the Constitutional Convention or in contemporary commentary that even alludes to the possibility of judicial review in the context of the impeachment powers. R. Berger, Impeachment: The Constitutional Problems 116 (1973). This silence is quite meaningful in light of the several explicit references to the availability of judicial review as a check on the Legislature's power with respect to bills of attainder, ex post facto laws, and statutes. . . .

The Framers labored over the question of where the impeachment power should lie. Significantly, in at least two considered scenarios the power was placed with the Federal Judiciary. See 1 Farrand 21–22 (Virginia Plan); id., at 244 (New Jersey Plan). Indeed, Madison and the Committee of Detail proposed that the Supreme Court should have the power to determine impeachments. See 2 id., at 551 (Madison); id., at 178–179, 186 (Committee of Detail). Despite these proposals, the Convention ultimately decided that the Senate would have "the sole Power to Try all Impeachments." Art. I, § 3, cl. 6. According to Alexander Hamilton, the Senate was the "most fit depositary of this important trust" because its members are representatives of the people. See The Federalist No. 65, p. 440 (J. Cooke ed. 1961). The Supreme Court was not the proper body because the Framers "doubted whether the members of that tribunal would, at all times, be endowed with so eminent a portion of fortitude as would be called for in the execution of so difficult a task" or whether the Court "would possess the degree of credit and authority" to carry out its judgment if it conflicted with the accusation brought by the Legislature—the people's representative. See id., at 441. In addition, the Framers believed the Court was too small in number: "The awful discretion, which a court of impeachments must necessarily have, to doom to honor or to infamy the most confidential and the most distinguished characters of the community, forbids the commitment of the trust to a small number of persons." Id., at 441–442.

There are two additional reasons why the Judiciary, and the Supreme Court in particular, were not chosen to have any role in impeachments. First, the Framers recognized that most likely there would be two sets of proceedings for individuals who commit impeachable offenses—the impeachment trial and a separate criminal trial. In fact, the Constitution explicitly provides for two separate proceedings. See Art. I, § 3, cl. 7. The Framers deliberately separated the two forums to avoid

raising the specter of bias and to ensure independent judgments ...
Certainly judicial review of the Senate's "trial" would introduce the
same risk of bias as would participation in the trial itself.

Second, judicial review would be inconsistent with the Framers'
insistence that our system be one of checks and balances. In our
constitutional system, impeachment was designed to be the only check
on the Judicial Branch by the Legislature.... Judicial involvement in
impeachment proceedings, even if only for purposes of judicial review, is
counterintuitive because it would eviscerate the "important constitutional check" placed on the Judiciary by the Framers.... Nixon's argument would place final reviewing authority with respect to impeachments in the hands of the same body that the impeachment process is
meant to regulate.

Nevertheless, Nixon argues that judicial review is necessary in order
to place a check on the Legislature. Nixon fears that if the Senate is
given unreviewable authority to interpret the Impeachment Trial Clause,
there is a grave risk that the Senate will usurp judicial power. The
Framers anticipated this objection and created two constitutional safeguards to keep the Senate in check. The first safeguard is that the
whole of the impeachment power is divided between the two legislative
bodies, with the House given the right to accuse and the Senate given
the right to judge.... This split of authority "avoids the inconvenience
of making the same persons both accusers and judges; and guards
against the danger of persecution from the prevalency of a factious spirit
in either of those branches." The second safeguard is the two-thirds
supermajority vote requirement....

In addition to the textual commitment argument, we are persuaded
that the lack of finality and the difficulty of fashioning relief counsel
against justiciability. See Baker v. Carr, 369 U.S., at 210.... This lack
of finality would manifest itself most dramatically if the President were
impeached. The legitimacy of any successor, and hence his effectiveness,
would be impaired severely, not merely while the judicial process was
running its course, but during any retrial that a differently constituted
Senate might conduct if its first judgment of conviction were invalidated.
Equally uncertain is the question of what relief a court may give other
than simply setting aside the judgment of conviction. Could it order the
reinstatement of a convicted federal judge, or order Congress to create
an additional judgeship if the seat had been filled in the interim?

Petitioner finally contends that a holding of nonjusticiability cannot
be reconciled with our opinion in Powell v. McCormack, 395 U.S. 486
(1969)....

Our conclusion in *Powell* was based on the fixed meaning of "[q]ual-
ifications" set forth in Art. I, § 2.... The decision as to whether a
member satisfied these qualifications was placed with the House, but the
decision as to what these qualifications consisted of was not.

In the case before us, there is no separate provision of the Constitution which could be defeated by allowing the Senate final authority to
determine the meaning of the word "try" in the Impeachment Trial
Clause. We agree with Nixon that courts possess power to review either

legislative or executive action that transgresses identifiable textual limits.... But we conclude ... that the word "try" in the Impeachment Clause does not provide an identifiable textual limit on the authority which is committed to the Senate.

For the foregoing reasons, the judgment of the Court of Appeals is

Affirmed.

Justice Stevens, concurring.

For me, the debate about the strength of the inferences to be drawn from the use of the words "sole" and "try" is far less significant than the central fact that the Framers decided to assign the impeachment power to the Legislative Branch.... Respect for a coordinate Branch of the Government forecloses any assumption that improbable hypotheticals like those mentioned by Justice ... Souter will ever occur....

Justice White, with whom Justice Blackmun joins, concurring in the judgment.

Petitioner contends that the method by which the Senate convicted him on two articles of impeachment violates Art. I, § 3, cl. 6 of the Constitution ... The Court is of the view that the Constitution forbids us even to consider his contention. I find no such prohibition and would therefore reach the merits of the claim. I concur in the judgment because the Senate fulfilled its constitutional obligation to "try" petitioner.

I

It should be said at the outset that, as a practical matter, it will likely make little difference whether the Court's or my view controls this case. This is so because the Senate has very wide discretion in specifying impeachment trial procedures and because it is extremely unlikely that the Senate would abuse its discretion and insist on a procedure that could not be deemed a trial by reasonable judges. Even taking a wholly practical approach, I would prefer not to announce an unreviewable discretion in the Senate to ignore completely the constitutional direction to "try" impeachment cases....

II

. . .

Of course the issue in the political question doctrine is not whether the Constitutional text commits exclusive responsibility for a particular governmental function to one of the political branches. There are numerous instances of this sort of textual commitment, e.g., Art. I, § 8, and it is not thought that disputes implicating these provisions are nonjusticiable. Rather, the issue is whether the Constitution has given one of the political branches final responsibility for interpreting the scope and nature of such a power.

. . .

The historical evidence reveals above all else that the Framers were deeply concerned about placing in any branch the "awful discretion, which a court of impeachments must necessarily have." ... Viewed against this history, the discord between the majority's position and the basic principles of checks and balances underlying the Constitution's separation of powers is clear. In essence, the majority suggests that the Framers conferred upon Congress a potential tool of legislative dominance yet at the same time rendered Congress' exercise of that power one of the very few areas of legislative authority immune from any judicial review.... In a truly balanced system, impeachments tried by the Senate would serve as a means of controlling the largely unaccountable judiciary, even as judicial review would ensure that the Senate adhered to a minimal set of procedural standards in conducting impeachment trials.

. . .

III

. . .

In short, textual and historical evidence reveals that the Impeachment Trial Clause was not meant to bind the hands of the Senate beyond establishing a set of minimal procedures. Without identifying the exact contours of these procedures, it is sufficient to say that the Senate's use of a factfinding committee under Rule XI is entirely compatible with the Constitution's command that the Senate "try all impeachments." Petitioner's challenge to his conviction must therefore fail.

. . .

Justice Souter, concurring in the judgment.

I agree with the Court that this case presents a nonjusticiable political question. Because my analysis differs somewhat from the Court's, however, I concur in its judgment by this separate opinion.

. . .

Whatever considerations feature most prominently in a particular case, the political question doctrine is "essentially a function of the separation of powers," ... existing to restrain courts "from inappropriate interference in the business of the other branches of Government," United States v. Munoz–Flores, 495 U.S. 385, 394 (1990), and deriving in large part from prudential concerns about the respect we owe the political departments.... Not all interference is inappropriate or disrespectful, however, and application of the doctrine ultimately turns, as Learned Hand put it, on "how importunately the occasion demands an answer." L. Hand, The Bill of Rights 15 (1958).

This occasion does not demand an answer. It seems fair to conclude that the [Impeachment Trial] Clause contemplates that the Senate may determine, within broad boundaries, such subsidiary issues as the procedures for receipt and consideration of evidence necessary to satisfy its duty to "try" impeachments. Other significant considerations confirm a conclusion that this case presents a nonjusticiable political question ...

As the Court observes, judicial review of an impeachment trial would under the best of circumstances entail significant disruption of government.

One can, nevertheless, envision different and unusual circumstances that might justify a more searching review of impeachment proceedings. If the Senate were to act in a manner seriously threatening the integrity of its results, convicting, say, upon a coin-toss, or upon a summary determination that an officer of the United States was simply " 'a bad guy,' " ... judicial interference might well be appropriate. In such circumstances, the Senate's action might be so far beyond the scope of its constitutional authority, and the consequent impact on the Republic so great, as to merit a judicial response despite the prudential concerns that would ordinarily counsel silence....

Part II

ALLOCATION OF GOVERNMENTAL POWERS: THE NATION AND THE STATES; THE PRESIDENT, THE CONGRESS, AND THE COURTS

Chapter 4

THE SCOPE OF NATIONAL POWER

SECTION 2. SOURCES OF NATIONAL POWER: EARLY DEVELOPMENTS

A. THE MARSHALL COURT'S VIEW

Page 170. Add before Gibbons v. Ogden:

McCULLOCH AND STATE POWER TO CONTROL THE SELECTION OF MEMBERS OF CONGRESS

McCulloch concluded "that the states have no power, by taxation or otherwise, to retard, impede, burden, or in any manner control the operations of the constitutional laws enacted by Congress." Powell v. McCormack, 395 U.S. 486 (1969), held that Congress has no power to alter the qualifications set forth in the text of the Constitution for election to Congress. Where Congress has no power to act and the Constitution is silent regarding state power, does *McCulloch* speak to whether the States possess any power to control who may be elected to Congress to exercise federal power?

In U.S. Term Limits, Inc. v. Thornton, 115 S.Ct. 1842 (1995), the Court concluded that the States, like the Congress, lack the power to add to the "exclusive qualifications" of age, citizenship and residency prescribed for members of Congress by the text of the Constitution. Thus, the Court held invalid a voter-adopted Arkansas constitutional amendment that prohibited the name of an otherwise-eligible candidate for Congress from appearing on the general election ballot if that candidate had already served three terms in the House of Representatives or two terms in the Senate. Justice Stevens' opinion for the Court relied on *McCulloch* in rejecting the argument that the absence of an express constitutional prohibition against state-added qualifications left the State's voters with a "reserved power" to impose term limit qualifications on candidates for Congress from their State.

19

McCulloch was deemed relevant both with respect to the Court's conclusion "that the power to add qualifications is not within the 'original power' of the States, and thus is not reserved to the States by the Tenth Amendment[,]" and to its conclusion that even if the States' original power embraced some control over congressional qualifications, "the Qualifications Clauses were intended to preclude the States from exercising any such power." On the issue of whether the power to add to congressional qualifications was included among the original powers of state sovereignty, Justice Stevens noted that *McCulloch* had "rejected the argument that the Constitution's silence on the subject of state power to tax corporations chartered by Congress implies that the States have 'reserved' power to tax such federal instrumentalities." He pointed to Chief Justice Marshall's conclusion that the decision in *McCulloch* "does not deprive the States of any resources which they originally possessed" and maintained that thus "the principle that certain powers are not reserved to the States despite constitutional silence ... has been a part of our jurisprudence for over 175 years." Likewise, "electing representatives to the National Legislature was a new right, arising from the Constitution itself ...[, and] any state power to set the qualifications for membership in Congress must derive not from the reserved powers of state sovereignty, but rather from the delegated powers of national sovereignty."

On the issue of whether the States were precluded from adding qualifications in any event, Justice Stevens reasoned in part that recognizing such state power would violate the "fundamental principle of our representative democracy" that "the people should choose whom they please to govern them." One central element of that basic principle, he argued, is "that the right to choose representatives belongs not to the States, but to the people"—a proposition for which he drew support from *McCulloch*'s statement that the government of the Union is a government of the people, it "emanates from them. Its powers are granted by them, and are to be exercised directly on them, and for their benefit." Justice Stevens concluded on this point:

> "Permitting individual States to formulate diverse qualifications for their representatives would result in a patchwork of state qualifications, undermining the uniformity and the national character that the Framers envisioned and sought to ensure. Cf. McCulloch v. Maryland, 4 Wheat., at 428–429 (1819)("Those means are not given by the people of a particular State, not given by the constituents of the legislature, ... but by the people of all the States. They are given by all, for the benefit of all—and upon theory should be subjected to that government only which belongs to all"). Such a patchwork would also sever the direct link that the Framers found so critical between the National Government and the people of the United States."

In a separate concurring opinion, Justice Kennedy also emphasized *McCulloch* in support of his view that a "distinctive character of the National Government ... is that it owes its existence to the act of the whole people who created it" and that there "can be no doubt, if we are to respect the republican origins of the Nation and preserve its federal character, that there exists a federal right of citizenship, a relationship between the people of the Nation and their National Government, with which the States may not interfere." Insisting "that the people of the United States ... have a political identity ... independent of, though consistent with, their identity as citizens of the State of their residence[,]" Justice Kennedy stated:

"It might be objected that because the States ratified the Constitution, the people can delegate power only through the States or by acting in their capacities as citizens of particular States. But in *McCulloch v. Maryland*, the Court set forth its authoritative rejection of this idea: 'The Convention which framed the constitution was indeed elected by the State legislatures. But the instrument ... was submitted to the people.... It is true, they assembled in their several States—and where else should they have assembled? No political dreamer was ever wild enough to think of breaking down the lines which separate the States, and of compounding the American people into one common mass. Of consequence, when they act, they act in their States. But the measures they adopt do not, on that account, cease to be the measures of the people themselves, or become the measures of the State governments.' ...

"The political identity of the entire people of the Union is reinforced by the proposition, which I take to be beyond dispute, that, though limited as to its objects, the National Government is and must be controlled by the people without collateral interference by the States. *McCulloch* affirmed this proposition as well, when the Court rejected the suggestion that States could interfere with federal powers. 'This was not intended by the American people. They did not design to make their government dependent on the States.' ... The States have no power, reserved or otherwise, over the exercise of federal authority within its proper sphere. See id., at 430 (where there is an attempt at 'usurpation of a power which the people of a single State cannot give,' there can be no question whether the power 'has been surrendered' by the people of a single State because '[t]he right never existed')...."

Justice Thomas, joined by Chief Justice Rehnquist and Justices O'Connor and Scalia, dissented. Stressing that the "ultimate source of the Constitution's authority is the consent of the people of each individual State, not the consent of the undifferentiated people of the Nation as a whole[,]" he found nothing in *McCulloch* that denied "*the people* of the States" a reserved power under the Tenth Amendment to prescribe eligibility requirements for the candidates who seek to represent them in Congress, given the Constitution's silence on the question. The majority misunderstood *McCulloch*, he argued:

" ... *McCulloch* did make clear that a power need not be 'expressly' delegated to the United States or prohibited to the States in order to fall outside the Tenth Amendment's reservation; delegations and prohibitions can also arise by necessary implication. True to the text of the Tenth Amendment, however, *McCulloch* indicated that all powers as to which the Constitution does not speak (whether expressly or by necessary implication) are 'reserved' to the state level. Thus, in its only discussion of the Tenth Amendment, *McCulloch* observed that the Amendment 'leav[es] the question, whether the particular power which may become the subject of contest has been delegated to the one government, or prohibited to the other, to depend on a fair construction of the whole [Constitution].' . . . *McCulloch* did not qualify this observation by indicating that the question also turned on whether the States had enjoyed the power before the framing. To the contrary, *McCulloch* seemed to assume that the people had 'conferred on the general government the power contained in the constitution, and on the States the whole residuum of power.' . . .

"The structure of *McCulloch*'s analysis also refutes the majority's position. . . . Chief Justice Marshall's opinion began by upholding the federal statute incorporating the Bank. . . . It then held that the Constitution affirmatively prohibited Maryland's tax on the Bank created by this statute[,] rel[ying] principally on concepts that it deemed inherent in the Supremacy Clause of Article VI. . . .

"For the past 175 years, *McCulloch* has been understood to rest on the proposition that the Constitution affirmatively barred Maryland from imposing its tax on the Bank's operations. . . . For the majority, however, *McCulloch* apparently turned on the fact that before the Constitution was adopted, the States had possessed no power to tax the instrumentalities of the governmental institutions that the Constitution created. This understanding of *McCulloch* makes most of Chief Justice Marshall's opinion irrelevant; according to the majority, there was no need to inquire into whether federal law deprived Maryland of the power in question, because the power could not fall into the category of 'reserved' powers anyway."

Justice Thomas also found Marshall's argument "that the power to tax the operations of the Bank of the United States simply was not susceptible to control by the people of a single State "to be "perfectly consistent with my position." He elaborated:

"Marshall reasoned that the people of a single State may not tax the instrumentalities employed by the people of all the States through the National Government, because such taxation would effectively subject the people of the several States to the taxing power of a single State. . . . This sort of argument proves that the people of a single State may not prescribe qualifications for the President of the United States; the selection of the President, like the operation of the Bank of the United States, is not up to the people of any single State. . . . It does not follow, however, that the people of a single State may not prescribe qualifications for their own representatives in Congress."

[The full report in *Thornton* appears, infra at p. 294]

SECTION 3.   THE SCOPE OF NATIONAL POWER TODAY

A.   THE COMMERCE POWER

Page 221.   Delete Perez v. United States and the following Note, "The Role of the Courts, If Any, in Limiting the Regulatory Power of Congress under the Commerce Clause"

Page 227.   Add at end of subsection:

UNITED STATES v. LOPEZ
—— U.S. ——, 115 S.Ct. 1624, 131 L.Ed.2d 626(1995).

Chief Justice Rehnquist delivered the opinion of the Court.

In the Gun–Free School Zones Act of 1990, Congress made it a federal offense "for any individual knowingly to possess a firearm at a place that the individual knows, or has reasonable cause to believe, is a school zone." 18 U.S.C. § 922(q)(1)(A).... The Act neither regulates a commercial activity nor contains a requirement that the possession be connected in any way to interstate commerce. We hold that the Act exceeds the authority of Congress "[t]o regulate Commerce ... among the several States...." U.S. Const., Art. I, § 8, cl. 3.

[Lopez, a 12th grade student, was convicted in federal district court of violating the Act for knowingly possessing a concealed handgun and bullets at his high school in San Antonio. (The Act defines "school zone" as "in, or on the grounds of, a public, parochial or private school" or "within a distance of 1,000 feet from the grounds of a public, parochial or private school." § 921(a)(25).) The Fifth Circuit reversed, holding the Act beyond the power of Congress under the Commerce Clause "in light of what it characterized as insufficient congressional findings and legislative history."] [W]e now affirm.

We start with first principles. The Constitution creates a Federal Government of enumerated powers. See U.S. Const., Art. I, § 8. As James Madison wrote, "[t]he powers delegated by the proposed Constitution to the federal government are few and defined. Those which are to remain in the State governments are numerous and indefinite." The Federalist No. 45, pp. 292–293 (C. Rossiter ed. 1961). This constitutionally mandated division of authority "was adopted by the Framers to ensure protection of our fundamental liberties." Gregory v. Ashcroft, 501 U.S. 452, 458 ... (1991).... "Just as the separation and independence of the coordinate branches of the Federal Government serves to prevent the accumulation of excessive power in any one branch, a healthy balance of power between the States and the Federal Government will reduce the risk of tyranny and abuse from either front." Ibid.

[The Chief Justice reviewed the Court's major commerce power precedents from *Gibbons v. Ogden* through *Wickard v. Filburn* and continued as follows:]

Jones & Laughlin Steel, Darby, and *Wickard* ushered in an era of Commerce Clause jurisprudence that greatly expanded the previously defined authority of Congress under that Clause. In part, this was a recognition of the great changes that had occurred in the way business was carried on in this country. Enterprises that had once been local or at most regional in nature had become national in scope. But the doctrinal change also reflected a view that earlier Commerce Clause cases artificially had constrained the authority of Congress to regulate interstate commerce.

But even these modern-era precedents which have expanded congressional power under the Commerce Clause confirm that this power is subject to outer limits. In *Jones & Laughlin Steel,* the Court warned that the scope of the interstate commerce power "must be considered in the light of our dual system of government and may not be extended so as to embrace effects upon interstate commerce so indirect and remote that to embrace them, in view of our complex society, would effectually obliterate the distinction between what is national and what is local and create a completely centralized government." 301 U.S., at 37; see also *Darby,* 312 U.S., at 119–120 (Congress may regulate intrastate activity that has a "substantial effect" on interstate commerce); *Wickard,* at 125 (Congress may regulate activity that "exerts a substantial economic effect on interstate commerce"). Since that time, the Court has heeded that warning and undertaken to decide whether a rational basis existed for concluding that a regulated activity sufficiently affected interstate commerce. See, e.g., Hodel v. Virginia Surface Mining & Reclamation Assn., Inc., 452 U.S. 264, 276–280 (1981); Perez v. United States, 402 U.S. 146, 155–156 (1971); Katzenbach v. McClung, 379 U.S. 294, 299–301 (1964); Heart of Atlanta Motel, Inc. v. United States, 379 U.S. 241, 252–253 (1964).

Similarly, in Maryland v. Wirtz, 392 U.S. 183 (1968), the Court reaffirmed that "the power to regulate commerce, though broad indeed, has limits" that "[t]he Court has ample power" to enforce. . . . In response to the dissent's warnings that the Court was powerless to enforce the limitations on Congress' commerce powers because "[a]ll activities affecting commerce, even in the minutest degree, [*Wickard*], may be regulated and controlled by Congress," 392 U.S., at 204 (Douglas, J., dissenting), the *Wirtz* Court replied that the dissent had misread precedent as "[n]either here nor in *Wickard* has the Court declared that Congress may use a relatively trivial impact on commerce as an excuse for broad general regulation of state or private activities," id., at 197, n. 27. Rather, "[t]he Court has said only that where *a general regulatory statute bears a substantial relation to commerce,* the *de minimis* character of individual instances arising under that statute is of no consequence." Ibid. (first emphasis added).

Consistent with this structure, we have identified three broad categories of activity that Congress may regulate under its commerce power. . . . First, Congress may regulate the use of the channels of interstate commerce. . . . Second, Congress is empowered to regulate and protect the instrumentalities of interstate commerce, or persons or things in interstate commerce, even though the threat may come only from intrastate activities.... Finally, Congress' commerce authority includes the power to regulate those activities having a substantial relation to interstate commerce, ... i.e., those activities that substantially affect interstate commerce....

Within this final category, admittedly, our case law has not been clear whether an activity must "affect" or "substantially affect" interstate commerce in order to be within Congress' power to regulate it under the Commerce Clause.... We conclude, consistent with the great weight of our case law, that the proper test requires an analysis of whether the regulated activity "substantially affects" interstate commerce.

We now turn to consider the power of Congress, in the light of this framework, to enact § 922(q). The first two categories of authority may be quickly disposed of: § 922(q) is not a regulation of the use of the channels of interstate commerce, nor is it an attempt to prohibit the interstate transportation of a commodity through the channels of commerce; nor can § 922(q) be justified as a regulation by which Congress has sought to protect an instrumentality of interstate commerce or a thing in interstate commerce. Thus, if § 922(q) is to be sustained, it must be under the third category as a regulation of an activity that substantially affects interstate commerce.

First, we have upheld a wide variety of congressional Acts regulating intrastate economic activity where we have concluded that the activity substantially affected interstate commerce. Examples include the regulation of intrastate coal mining; ... intrastate extortionate credit transactions, ... restaurants utilizing substantial interstate supplies, ... inns and hotels catering to interstate guests, ... and production and consumption of home-grown wheat, Wickard v. Filburn, 317 U.S. 111 (1942).... Where economic activity substantially affects interstate commerce, legislation regulating that activity will be sustained.

Even *Wickard*, which is perhaps the most far reaching example of Commerce Clause authority over intrastate activity, involved economic activity in a way that the possession of a gun in a school zone does not....

Section 922(q) is a criminal statute that by its terms has nothing to do with "commerce" or any sort of economic enterprise, however broadly one might define those terms.[3] Section 922(q) is not an essential part of a larger regulation of economic activity, in which the regulatory scheme could be undercut unless the intrastate activity were regulated. It cannot, therefore, be sustained under our cases upholding regulations of activities that arise out of or are connected with a commercial transac-

---

[3] Under our federal system, the " 'States possess primary authority for defining and enforcing the criminal law.' " ... When Congress criminalizes conduct already denounced as criminal by the States, it effects a " 'change in the sensitive relation between federal and state criminal jurisdiction.' " ... [S]ee also Statement of President George Bush on Signing the Crime Control Act of 1990, 26 Weekly Comp. of Pres. Doc. 1944, 1945 (Nov. 29, 1990)("Most egregiously, section [922(q)] inappropriately overrides legitimate state firearms laws with a new and unnecessary Federal law. The policies reflected in these provisions could legitimately be adopted by the States, but they should not be imposed upon the States by Congress").

tion, which viewed in the aggregate, substantially affects interstate commerce.

Second, § 922(q) contains no jurisdictional element which would ensure, through case-by-case inquiry, that the firearm possession in question affects interstate commerce. For example, in United States v. Bass, 404 U.S. 336 (1971), the Court interpreted [the possession component of] former 18 U.S.C. § 1202(a), which made it a crime for a felon to "receiv[e], posses[s], or transpor[t] in commerce or affecting commerce ... any firearm[ ]" to require an additional nexus to interstate commerce both because the statute was ambiguous and because "unless Congress conveys its purpose clearly, it will not be deemed to have significantly changed the federal-state balance." ... The Court thus interpreted the statute to reserve the constitutional question whether Congress could regulate, without more, the "mere possession" of firearms.... Unlike the statute in *Bass*, § 922(q) has no express jurisdictional element which might limit its reach to a discrete set of firearm possessions that additionally have an explicit connection with or effect on interstate commerce.

Although as part of our independent evaluation of constitutionality under the Commerce Clause we of course consider legislative findings, and indeed even congressional committee findings, regarding effect on interstate commerce, ... the Government concedes that "[n]either the statute nor its legislative history contain[s] express congressional findings regarding the effects upon interstate commerce of gun possession in a school zone." ... We agree with the Government that Congress normally is not required to make formal findings as to the substantial burdens that an activity has on interstate commerce.... But to the extent that congressional findings would enable us to evaluate the legislative judgment that the activity in question substantially affected interstate commerce, even though no such substantial effect was visible to the naked eye, they are lacking here.[4]

The Government argues that Congress has accumulated institutional expertise regarding the regulation of firearms through previous enactments.... We agree, however, with the Fifth Circuit that importation of previous findings to justify § 922(q) is especially inappropriate here because the "prior federal enactments or Congressional findings [do not] speak to the subject matter of section 922(q) or its relationship to interstate commerce. Indeed, section 922(q) plows thoroughly new ground and represents a sharp break with the long-standing pattern of federal firearms legislation." ...

The Government's essential contention, *in fine*, is that we may determine here that § 922(q) is valid because possession of a firearm in a local school zone does indeed substantially affect interstate commerce.... The Government argues that possession of a firearm in a school zone may result in violent crime and that violent crime can be

---

[4] ... [T]he Violent Crime Control and Law Enforcement Act of 1994 ... amends § 922(q) to include congressional findings regarding the effects of firearm possession in and around schools upon interstate and foreign commerce. The Government does not rely upon these subsequent findings as a substitute for the absence of findings in the first instance....

expected to affect the functioning of the national economy in two ways. First, the costs of violent crime are substantial, and, through the mechanism of insurance, those costs are spread throughout the population. . . . Second, violent crime reduces the willingness of individuals to travel to areas within the country that are perceived to be unsafe. Cf. *Heart of Atlanta Motel*. . . . The Government also argues that the presence of guns in schools poses a substantial threat to the educational process by threatening the learning environment. A handicapped educational process, in turn, will result in a less productive citizenry. That, in turn, would have an adverse effect on the Nation's economic well-being. As a result, the Government argues that Congress could rationally have concluded that § 922(q) substantially affects interstate commerce.

We pause to consider the implications of the Government's arguments. The Government admits, under its "costs of crime" reasoning, that Congress could regulate not only all violent crime, but all activities that might lead to violent crime, regardless of how tenuously they relate to interstate commerce. . . . Similarly, under the Government's "national productivity" reasoning, Congress could regulate any activity that it found was related to the economic productivity of individual citizens: family law (including marriage, divorce, and child custody), for example. Under the theories that the Government presents in support of § 922(q), it is difficult to perceive any limitation on federal power, even in areas such as criminal law enforcement or education where States historically have been sovereign. Thus, if we were to accept the Government's arguments, we are hard-pressed to posit any activity by an individual that Congress is without power to regulate.

Although Justice Breyer argues that acceptance of the Government's rationales would not authorize a general federal police power, he is unable to identify any activity that the States may regulate but Congress may not. Justice Breyer posits that there might be some limitations on Congress' commerce power such as family law or certain aspects of education. These suggested limitations, when viewed in light of the dissent's expansive analysis, are devoid of substance.

Justice Breyer focuses, for the most part, on the threat that firearm possession in and near schools poses to the educational process and the potential economic consequences flowing from that threat. Specifically, the dissent reasons that (1) gun-related violence is a serious problem; (2) that problem, in turn, has an adverse effect on classroom learning; and (3) that adverse effect on classroom learning, in turn, represents a substantial threat to trade and commerce. This analysis would be equally applicable, if not more so, to subjects such as family law and direct regulation of education.

[I]f Congress can . . . regulate activities that adversely affect the learning environment, then, *a fortiori*, it also can regulate the educational process directly. Congress could determine that a school's curriculum has a "significant" effect on the extent of classroom learning [and] mandate a federal curriculum for local elementary and secondary schools because what is taught in local schools has a significant "effect on classroom learning," and that, in turn, has a substantial effect on interstate commerce.

Justice Breyer rejects our reading of precedent and argues that "Congress ... could rationally conclude that schools fall on the commercial side of the line." Again, Justice Breyer's rationale lacks any real limits because, depending on the level of generality, any activity can be looked upon as commercial. Under the dissent's rationale, Congress could just as easily look at child rearing as "fall[ing] on the commercial side of the line" because it provides a "valuable service—namely, to equip [children] with the skills they need to survive in life and, more specifically, in the workplace." ... We do not doubt that Congress has authority under the Commerce Clause to regulate numerous commercial activities that substantially affect interstate commerce and also affect the educational process. That authority, though broad, does not include the authority to regulate each and every aspect of local schools.

Admittedly, a determination whether an intrastate activity is commercial or noncommercial may in some cases result in legal uncertainty. But, so long as Congress' authority is limited to those powers enumerated in the Constitution, and so long as those enumerated powers are interpreted as having judicially enforceable outer limits, congressional legislation under the Commerce Clause always will engender "legal uncertainty." ...

. . .

... The possession of a gun in a local school zone is in no sense an economic activity that might, through repetition elsewhere, substantially affect any sort of interstate commerce. Respondent was a local student at a local school; there is no indication that he had recently moved in interstate commerce, and there is no requirement that his possession of the firearm have any concrete tie to interstate commerce.

To uphold the Government's contentions here, we would have to pile inference upon inference in a manner that would bid fair to convert congressional authority under the Commerce Clause to a general police power of the sort retained by the States. Admittedly, some of our prior cases have taken long steps down that road, giving great deference to congressional action.... The broad language in these opinions has suggested the possibility of additional expansion, but we decline here to proceed any further. To do so would require us to conclude that the Constitution's enumeration of powers does not presuppose something not enumerated ... and that there never will be a distinction between what is truly national and what is truly local.... This we are unwilling to do.

. . .

Justice Kennedy, with whom Justice O'Connor joins, concurring.

The history of the judicial struggle to interpret the Commerce Clause during the transition from the economic system the Founders knew to the single, national market still emergent in our own era counsels great restraint before the Court determines that the Clause is insufficient to support an exercise of the national power. That history gives me some pause about today's decision, but I join the Court's opinion with these observations on what I conceive to be its necessary though limited holding.

. . .

The history of our Commerce Clause decisions contains at least two lessons of relevance to this case. The first ... is the imprecision of content-based boundaries used without more to define the limits of the Commerce Clause. The second ... is that the Court as an institution and the legal system as a whole have an immense stake in the stability of our Commerce Clause jurisprudence as it has evolved to this point. Stare decisis operates with great force in counseling us not to call in question the essential principles now in place respecting the congressional power to regulate transactions of a commercial nature.... Congress can regulate in the commercial sphere on the assumption that we have a single market and a unified purpose to build a stable national economy.

... This case requires us to consider our place in the design of the Government and to appreciate the significance of federalism in the whole structure of the Constitution.

Of the various structural elements in the Constitution, separation of powers, checks and balances, judicial review, and federalism, only concerning the last does there seem to be much uncertainty respecting the existence, and the content, of standards that allow the judiciary to play a significant role in maintaining the design contemplated by the Framers....

There is irony in this, because of the four structural elements in the Constitution just mentioned, federalism was the unique contribution of the Framers to political science and political theory.... Though on the surface the idea may seem counterintuitive, it was the insight of the Framers that freedom was enhanced by the creation of two governments, not one....

The theory that two governments accord more liberty than one requires for its realization two distinct and discernable lines of political accountability: one between the citizens and the Federal Government; the second between the citizens and the States. If, as Madison expected, the federal and state governments are to control each other, see The Federalist No. 51, and hold each other in check by competing for the affections of the people, see The Federalist No. 46, those citizens must have some means of knowing which of the two governments to hold accountable for the failure to perform a given function.... Were the Federal Government to take over the regulation of entire areas of traditional state concern, areas having nothing to do with the regulation of commercial activities, the boundaries between the spheres of federal and state authority would blur and political responsibility would become illusory. See New York v. United States.... The resultant inability to hold either branch of the government answerable to the citizens is more dangerous even than devolving too much authority to the remote central power.

. . .

[I]t would be mistaken and mischievous for the political branches to forget that the sworn obligation to preserve and protect the Constitution in maintaining the federal balance is their own in the first and primary instance. . . .

At the same time, the absence of structural mechanisms to require those officials to undertake this principled task, and the momentary political convenience often attendant upon their failure to do so, argue against a complete renunciation of the judicial role. . . .

. . . The substantial element of political judgment in Commerce Clause matters leaves our institutional capacity to intervene more in doubt than when we decide cases, for instance, under the Bill of Rights even though clear and bright lines are often absent in the latter class of disputes. . . . But our cases do not teach that we have no role at all in determining the meaning of the Commerce Clause.

Our position in enforcing the dormant Commerce Clause is instructive. . . . [I]n contrast to the prevailing skepticism that surrounds our ability to give meaning to the explicit text of the Commerce Clause, there is widespread acceptance of our authority to enforce the dormant Commerce Clause, which we have but inferred from the constitutional structure as a limitation on the power of the States. . . . True, if we invalidate a state law, Congress can in effect overturn our judgment, whereas in a case announcing that Congress has transgressed its authority, the decision is more consequential, for it stands unless Congress can revise its law to demonstrate its commercial character. This difference no doubt informs the circumspection with which we invalidate an Act of Congress, but it does not mitigate our duty to recognize meaningful limits on the commerce power of Congress.

The statute before us upsets the federal balance to a degree that renders it an unconstitutional assertion of the commerce power, and our intervention is required. . . . In a sense any conduct in this interdependent world of ours has an ultimate commercial origin or consequence, but we have not yet said the commerce power may reach so far. If Congress attempts that extension, then at the least we must inquire whether the exercise of national power seeks to intrude upon an area of traditional state concern.

An interference of these dimensions occurs here, for it is well established that education is a traditional concern of the States. . . . The proximity to schools, including of course schools owned and operated by the States or their subdivisions, is the very premise for making the conduct criminal. In these circumstances, we have a particular duty to insure that the federal-state balance is not destroyed. . . .

The statute now before us forecloses the States from experimenting and exercising their own judgment in an area to which States lay claim by right of history and expertise, and it does so by regulating an activity beyond the realm of commerce in the ordinary and usual sense of that term. . . . [S]chool officials would find their own programs for the prohibition of guns in danger of displacement by the federal authority unless the State chooses to enact a parallel rule.

. . . While the intrusion on state sovereignty may not be as severe in this instance as in some of our recent Tenth Amendment cases, the intrusion is nonetheless significant. Absent a stronger connection or identification with commercial concerns that are central to the Commerce Clause, that interference contradicts the federal balance the Framers designed and that this Court is obliged to enforce.

For these reasons, I join in the opinion and judgment of the Court.

Justice Thomas, concurring.

. . . I write separately to observe that our case law has drifted far from the original understanding of the Commerce Clause. . . .

. . .

In an appropriate case, I believe that we must further reconsider our "substantial effects" test with an eye toward constructing a standard that reflects the text and history of the Commerce Clause without totally rejecting our more recent Commerce Clause jurisprudence.

. . .

I

At the time the original Constitution was ratified, "commerce" consisted of selling, buying, and bartering, as well as transporting for these purposes. . . .

[T]he term "commerce" was used in contradistinction to productive activities such as manufacturing and agriculture. . . .

. . .

The Constitution not only uses the word "commerce" in a narrower sense than our case law might suggest, it also does not support the proposition that Congress has authority over all activities that "substantially affect" interstate commerce. . . .

In addition to its powers under the Commerce Clause, Congress has the authority to enact such laws as are "necessary and proper" to carry into execution its power to regulate commerce among the several States. U.S. Const., Art. I, § 8, cl. 18. But on this Court's understanding of congressional power under these two Clauses, many of Congress' other enumerated powers under Art. I, § 8 are wholly superfluous. After all, if Congress may regulate all matters that substantially affect commerce, there is no need for the Constitution to specify that Congress may enact bankruptcy laws, cl. 4, or coin money and fix the standard of weights and measures, cl. 5, or punish counterfeiters of United States coin and securities, cl. 6. Likewise, Congress would not need the separate authority to establish post offices and post roads, cl. 7, or to grant patents and copyrights, cl. 8, or to "punish Piracies and Felonies committed on the high Seas," cl. 10. . . . Indeed, if Congress could regulate matters that substantially affect interstate commerce, there would have been no need to specify that Congress can regulate international trade and commerce with the Indians. As the Framers surely understood, these other branches of trade substantially affect interstate commerce.

Put simply, much if not all of Art. I, § 8 (including portions of the Commerce Clause itself) would be surplusage if Congress had been given authority over matters that substantially affect interstate commerce.... [T]he power we have accorded Congress has swallowed Art. I, § 8.

    . . .

    ... [F]undamental textual problems should, at the very least, convince us that the "substantial effects" test should be reexamined.

II

The exchanges during the ratification campaign reveal the relatively limited reach of the Commerce Clause and of federal power generally. The Founding Fathers confirmed that most areas of life (even many matters that would have substantial effects on commerce) would remain outside the reach of the Federal Government [and] under the exclusive control of the States.

    . . .

[D]espite being well aware that agriculture, manufacturing, and other matters substantially affected commerce, the founding generation did not cede authority over all these activities to Congress....

Where the Constitution was meant to grant federal authority over an activity substantially affecting interstate commerce, the Constitution contains an enumerated power over that particular activity. Indeed, the Framers knew that many of the other enumerated powers in § 8 dealt with matters that substantially affected interstate commerce. Madison, for instance, spoke of the bankruptcy power as being "intimately connected with the regulation of commerce." The Federalist No. 42, at 287....

    ... Even though the boundary between commerce and other matters may ignore "economic reality" and thus seem arbitrary or artificial to some, we must nevertheless respect a constitutional line that does not grant Congress power over all that substantially affects interstate commerce.

III

If the principal dissent's understanding of our early case law were correct, there might be some reason to doubt this view of the original understanding of the Constitution. According to that dissent, Chief Justice Marshall's opinion in Gibbons v. Ogden, 9 Wheat. 1 (1824) established that Congress may control all local activities that "significantly affect interstate commerce." ...

In my view, the dissent is wrong about the holding and reasoning of Gibbons....

A

. . .

[In *Gibbons*,] the Court took great pains to make clear that Congress could not regulate commerce "which is completely internal, which is carried on between man and man in a State, or between different parts of the same State, and which does not extend to or affect other States." . . .

. . .

. . . From this statement, the principal dissent infers that whenever an activity affects interstate commerce, it necessarily follows that Congress can regulate such activities. Of course, Chief Justice Marshall said no such thing and the inference the dissent makes cannot be drawn.

There is a much better interpretation of the "affect[s]" language: because the Court had earlier noted that the commerce power did not extend to wholly intrastate commerce, the Court was acknowledging that although the line between intrastate and interstate/foreign commerce would be difficult to draw, federal authority could not be construed to cover purely intrastate commerce. Commerce that did not affect another State could *never* be said to be commerce "among the several States."

But even if one were to adopt the dissent's reading, the "affect[s]" language, at most, permits Congress to regulate only intrastate *commerce* that substantially affects interstate and foreign commerce. There is no reason to believe that Chief Justice Marshall was asserting that Congress could regulate all activities that affect interstate commerce. . . .

. . .

B

I am aware of no cases prior to the New Deal that characterized the power flowing from the Commerce Clause as sweepingly as does our substantial effects test. . . .

. . .

As recently as 1936, the Court continued to insist that the Commerce Clause did not reach the wholly internal business of the States. . . .

[F]rom the time of the ratification of the Constitution to the mid–1930's, it was widely understood that the Constitution granted Congress only limited powers, notwithstanding the Commerce Clause. Moreover, there was no question that activities wholly separated from business, such as gun possession, were beyond the reach of the commerce power. If anything, the "wrong turn" was the Court's dramatic departure in the 1930's from a century and a half of precedent.

IV

Apart from its recent vintage and its corresponding lack of any grounding in the original understanding of the Constitution, the substantial effects test suffers from the further flaw that it appears to grant

Congress a police power over the Nation.... The one advantage of the dissent's standard is certainty: it is certain that under its analysis everything may be regulated under the guise of the Commerce Clause.

The substantial effects test suffers from this flaw, in part, because of its "aggregation principle." Under so-called "class of activities" statutes, Congress can regulate whole categories of activities that are not themselves either "interstate" or "commerce." In applying the effects test, we ask whether the class of activities as a whole substantially affects interstate commerce, not whether any specific activity within the class has such effects when considered in isolation....

The aggregation principle is clever, but has no stopping point.... [O]ne always can draw the circle broadly enough to cover an activity that, when taken in isolation, would not have substantial effects on commerce. Under our jurisprudence, if Congress passed an omnibus "substantially affects interstate commerce" statute, purporting to regulate every aspect of human existence, the Act apparently would be constitutional. Even though particular sections may govern only trivial activities, the statute in the aggregate regulates matters that substantially affect commerce.

V

This extended discussion of the original understanding and our first century and a half of case law does not necessarily require a wholesale abandonment of our more recent opinions.[8] It simply reveals that our substantial effects test is far removed from both the Constitution and from our early case law and that the Court's opinion should not be viewed as "radical" or another "wrong turn" that must be corrected in the future. The analysis also suggests that we ought to temper our Commerce Clause jurisprudence.

Unless the dissenting Justices are willing to repudiate our long-held understanding of the limited nature of federal power, I would think that they too must be willing to reconsider the substantial effects test in a future case....

. . .

Justice Stevens, dissenting.

The welfare of our future "Commerce with foreign Nations, and among the several States," U.S. Const., Art. I, § 8, cl. 3, is vitally dependent on the character of the education of our children. I therefore agree entirely with Justice Breyer's explanation of why Congress has ample power to prohibit the possession of firearms in or near schools— just as it may protect the school environment from harms posed by controlled substances such as asbestos or alcohol. I also agree with Justice Souter's exposition of the radical character of the Court's holding and its kinship with the discredited, pre-Depression version of substan-

---

[8] Although I might be willing to return to the original understanding, I recognize that many believe that it is too late in the day to undertake a fundamental reexamination of the past 60 years. Consideration of stare decisis and reliance interests may convince us that we cannot wipe the slate clean.

tive due process.... I believe, however, that the Court's extraordinary decision merits this additional comment.

Guns are both articles of commerce and articles that can be used to restrain commerce. Their possession is the consequence, either directly or indirectly, of commercial activity. In my judgment, Congress' power to regulate commerce in firearms includes the power to prohibit possession of guns at any location because of their potentially harmful use; it necessarily follows that Congress may also prohibit their possession in particular markets. The market for the possession of handguns by school-age children is, distressingly, substantial. Whether or not the national interest in eliminating that market would have justified federal legislation in 1789, it surely does today.

Justice Souter, dissenting.

In reviewing congressional legislation under the Commerce Clause, we defer to what is often a merely implicit congressional judgment that its regulation addresses a subject substantially affecting interstate commerce "if there is any rational basis for such a finding." Hodel v. Virginia Surface Mining & Reclamation Assn., Inc., 452 U.S. 264, 276 (1981)....

The practice of deferring to rationally based legislative judgments "is a paradigm of judicial restraint." FCC v. Beach Communications, Inc., 508 U.S. ___, ___ (1993). In judicial review under the Commerce Clause, it reflects our respect for the institutional competence of the Congress on a subject expressly assigned to it by the Constitution and our appreciation of the legitimacy that comes from Congress's political accountability in dealing with matters open to a wide range of possible choices....

... The modern respect for the competence and primacy of Congress in matters affecting commerce developed only after one of this Court's most chastening experiences, when it perforce repudiated an earlier and untenably expansive conception of judicial review in derogation of congressional commerce power. A look at history's sequence will serve to show how today's decision tugs the Court off course, leading it to suggest opportunities for further developments that would be at odds with the rule of restraint to which the Court still wisely states adherence.

I

... [T]he period from the turn of the century to 1937 is ... noted for a series of cases applying highly formalistic notions of "commerce" to invalidate federal social and economic legislation....

... [D]uring this same period the Court routinely invalidated state social and economic legislation under an expansive conception of Fourteenth Amendment substantive due process....

... [S]ea changes in the Court's conceptions of its authority under the Due Process and Commerce Clauses occurred virtually together, in 1937, with West Coast Hotel Co. v. Parrish, 300 U.S. 379 and NLRB v. Jones & Laughlin Steel Corp., 301 U.S. 1....

In the years following these decisions, deference to legislative policy judgments on commercial regulation became the powerful theme under both the Due Process and Commerce Clauses.... Thus, under commerce, as under due process, adoption of rational basis review expressed the recognition that the Court had no sustainable basis for subjecting economic regulation as such to judicial policy judgments, and for the past half-century the Court has no more turned back in the direction of formalistic Commerce Clause review (as in deciding whether regulation of commerce was sufficiently direct) than it has inclined toward reasserting the substantive authority of *Lochner* due process (as in the inflated protection of contractual autonomy)....

II

There is today, however, a backward glance at both the old pitfalls, as the Court treats deference under the rationality rule as subject to gradation according to the commercial or noncommercial nature of the immediate subject of the challenged regulation.... Thus, it seems fair to ask whether the step taken by the Court today does anything but portend a return to the untenable jurisprudence from which the Court extricated itself almost 60 years ago. The answer is not reassuring.... [I]f it seems anomalous that the Congress of the United States has taken to regulating school yards, the act in question is still probably no more remarkable than state regulation of bake shops 90 years ago. In any event, there is no reason to hope that the Court's qualification of rational basis review will be any more successful than the efforts at substantive economic review made by our predecessors as the century began....

Further glosses on rationality review, moreover, may be in the offing. Although this case turns on commercial character, the Court gestures toward two other considerations that it might sometime entertain in applying rational basis scrutiny (apart from a statutory obligation to supply independent proof of a jurisdictional element): does the congressional statute deal with subjects of traditional state regulation, and does the statute contain explicit factual findings supporting the otherwise implicit determination that the regulated activity substantially affects interstate commerce? Once again, any appeal these considerations may have depends on ignoring the painful lesson learned in 1937, for neither of the Court's suggestions would square with rational basis scrutiny.

A

... [A]s for the notion that the commerce power diminishes the closer it gets to customary state concerns, that idea has been flatly rejected, and not long ago....

Nor is there any contrary authority in the reasoning of our cases imposing clear statement rules in some instances of legislation that would significantly alter the state-national balance....

These clear statement rules ... are merely rules of statutory interpretation, to be relied upon only when the terms of a statute allow, ...

and in cases implicating Congress's historical reluctance to trench on state legislative prerogatives or to enter into spheres already occupied by the States.... But our hesitance to presume that Congress has acted to alter the state-federal status quo (when presented with a plausible alternative) has no relevance whatever to the enquiry whether it has the commerce power to do so or to the standard of judicial review when Congress has definitely meant to exercise that power....

B

There remain questions about legislative findings. The Court of Appeals expressed the view ... that the result in this case might well have been different if Congress had made explicit findings that guns in schools have a substantial effect on interstate commerce, and the Court today does not repudiate that position. Might a court aided by such findings have subjected this legislation to less exacting scrutiny (or, put another way, should a court have deferred to such findings if Congress had made them)? The answer to either question must be no, although as a general matter findings are important and to be hoped for in the difficult cases.

The question for the courts, as all agree, is not whether as a predicate to legislation Congress in fact found that a particular activity substantially affects interstate commerce. The legislation implies such a finding.... Nor is the question whether Congress was correct in so finding. The only question is whether the legislative judgment is within the realm of reason.... If ... the Court were to make the existence of explicit congressional findings dispositive in some close or difficult cases something other than rationality review would be afoot. The resulting congressional obligation to justify its policy choices on the merits would imply either a judicial authority to review the justification (and, hence, the wisdom) of those choices, or authority to require Congress to act with some high degree of deliberateness, of which express findings would be evidence. But review for congressional wisdom would just be the old judicial pretension discredited and abandoned in 1937, and review for deliberateness would be as patently unconstitutional as an Act of Congress mandating long opinions from this Court.... [T]he rationality standard of review would be a thing of the past.

... I would not allow for the possibility, as the Court's opinion may, that the addition of congressional findings could in principle have affected the fate of the statute here.

III

Because Justice Breyer's opinion demonstrates beyond any doubt that the Act in question passes the rationality review that the Court continues to espouse, today's decision may be seen as only a misstep, its reasoning and its suggestions not quite in gear with the prevailing standard, but hardly an epochal case. I would not argue otherwise, but I would raise a caveat. Not every epochal case has come in epochal trappings. *Jones & Laughlin* did not reject the direct-indirect standard in so many words; it just said the relation of the regulated subject matter to commerce was direct enough.... But we know what happened.

I respectfully dissent.

Justice Breyer, with whom Justice Stevens, Justice Souter, and Justice Ginsburg join, dissenting.

... In my view, the statute falls well within the scope of the commerce power as this Court has understood that power over the last half-century.

I

In reaching this conclusion, I apply three basic principles of Commerce Clause interpretation. First, the power to "regulate Commerce ... among the several States," U.S. Const., Art. I, § 8, cl. 3, encompasses the power to regulate local activities insofar as they significantly affect interstate commerce....

Second, in determining whether a local activity will likely have a significant effect upon interstate commerce, a court must consider, not the effect of an individual act (a single instance of gun possession), but rather the cumulative effect of all similar instances (i.e., the effect of all guns possessed in or near schools)....

Third, the Constitution requires us to judge the connection between a regulated activity and interstate commerce, not directly, but at one remove. Courts must give Congress a degree of leeway in determining the existence of a significant factual connection between the regulated activity and interstate commerce—both because the Constitution delegates the commerce power directly to Congress and because the determination requires an empirical judgment of a kind that a legislature is more likely than a court to make with accuracy. The traditional words "rational basis" capture this leeway.... Thus, the specific question before us, as the Court recognizes, is not whether the "regulated activity sufficiently affected interstate commerce," but, rather, whether Congress could have had "a rational basis" for so concluding.

I recognize that we must judge this matter independently.... I also recognize that Congress did not write specific "interstate commerce" findings into the law under which Lopez was convicted. Nonetheless, ... the matter that we review independently (i.e., whether there is a "rational basis") already has considerable leeway built into it. And, the absence of findings, at most, deprives a statute of the benefit of some *extra* leeway....

II

Applying these principles to the case at hand, we must ask whether Congress could have had a *rational basis* for finding a significant (or substantial) connection between gun-related school violence and interstate commerce. Or, to put the question in the language of the explicit finding that Congress made when it amended this law in 1994: Could Congress rationally have found that "violent crime in school zones," through its effect on the "quality of education," significantly (or substantially) affects "interstate" or "foreign commerce"? . . . As long as one views the commerce connection, not as a "technical legal conception," but as "a practical one," Swift & Co. v. United States, 196 U.S. 375, 398 (1905)(Holmes, J.), the answer to this question must be yes. Numerous reports and studies—generated both inside and outside government—make clear that Congress could reasonably have found the empirical connection that its law, implicitly or explicitly, asserts. . . .

For one thing, reports, hearings, and other readily available literature make clear that the problem of guns in and around schools is widespread and extremely serious. . . . And, they report that this widespread violence in schools throughout the Nation significantly interferes with the quality of education in those schools. See, e.g., House Judiciary Committee Hearing 44 (1990)(linking school violence to dropout rate); U.S. Dept. of Health 118–119 (1978)(school-violence victims suffer academically); compare U.S. Dept. of Justice 1 (1991)(gun violence worst in inner city schools), with National Center 47 (dropout rates highest in inner cities). . . . Congress could therefore have found a substantial educational problem—teachers unable to teach, students unable to learn—and concluded that guns near schools contribute substantially to the size and scope of that problem.

Having found that guns in schools significantly undermine the quality of education in our Nation's classrooms, Congress could also have found, given the effect of education upon interstate and foreign commerce, that gun-related violence in and around schools is a commercial, as well as a human, problem. Education, although far more than a matter of economics, has long been inextricably intertwined with the Nation's economy. . . .

In recent years the link between secondary education and business has strengthened, becoming both more direct and more important. Scholars on the subject report that technological changes and innovations in management techniques have altered the nature of the workplace so that more jobs now demand greater educational skills. . . .

Increasing global competition also has made primary and secondary education economically more important. . . .

Finally, there is evidence that, today more than ever, many firms base their location decisions upon the presence, or absence, of a work force with a basic education. . . . In light of this increased importance of education to individual firms, it is no surprise that half of the Nation's manufacturers have become involved with setting standards and shaping curricula for local schools, . . . that 88 percent think this kind of involvement is important, . . . that more than 20 States have recently passed educational reforms to attract new business, . . . and that business magazines have begun to rank cities according to the quality of their schools. . . .

The economic links I have just sketched seem fairly obvious. Why then is it not equally obvious, in light of those links, that a widespread, serious, and substantial physical threat to teaching and learning *also* substantially threatens the commerce to which that teaching and learning is inextricably tied? That is to say, guns in the hands of six percent of inner-city high school students and gun-related violence throughout a city's schools must threaten the trade and commerce that those schools support. The only question, then, is whether the latter threat is (to use the majority's terminology) "substantial." And, the evidence of (1) the *extent* of the gun-related violence problem, (2) the *extent* of the resulting negative effect on classroom learning, and (3) the *extent* of the consequent negative commercial effects, when taken together, indicate a threat to trade and commerce that is "substantial." At the very least, Congress could rationally have concluded that the links are "substantial."

Specifically, Congress could have found that gun-related violence near the classroom poses a serious economic threat (1) to consequently inadequately educated workers who must endure low paying jobs ... and (2) to communities and businesses that might (in today's "information society") otherwise gain, from a well-educated work force, an important commercial advantage ... of a kind that location near a railhead or harbor provided in the past. Congress might also have found these threats to be no different in kind from other threats that this Court has found within the commerce power, such as the threat that loan sharking poses to the "funds" of "numerous localities," Perez v. United States....

To hold this statute constitutional is not to "obliterate" the "distinction of what is national and what is local"; nor is it to hold that the Commerce Clause permits the Federal Government to "regulate any activity that it found was related to the economic productivity of individual citizens," to regulate "marriage, divorce, and child custody," or to regulate any and all aspects of education. For one thing, this statute is aimed at curbing a particularly acute threat to the educational process— the possession (and use) of life-threatening firearms in, or near, the classroom.... For another thing, the immediacy of the connection between education and the national economic well-being is documented by scholars and accepted by society at large in a way and to a degree that may not hold true for other social institutions. It must surely be the rare case, then, that a statute strikes at conduct that (when considered in the abstract) seems so removed from commerce, but which (practically speaking) has so significant an impact upon commerce.

In sum, a holding that the particular statute before us falls within the commerce power would not expand the scope of that Clause. Rather, it simply would apply preexisting law to changing economic circumstances....

III

The majority's holding ... creates three serious legal problems. First, [it] runs contrary to modern Supreme Court cases that have upheld congressional actions despite connections to interstate or foreign commerce that are less significant than the effect of school violence. In Perez v. United States, [402 U.S. 146 (1971)], the Court held that the Commerce Clause authorized a federal statute that makes it a crime to engage in loan sharking ("'[e]xtortionate credit transactions'") at a local level. The Court said that Congress may judge that such transactions, "though purely intrastate, ... affect interstate commerce." ... Presumably, Congress reasoned that threatening or using force, say with a gun on a street corner, to collect a debt occurs sufficiently often so that the activity (by helping organized crime) affects commerce among the States. But, why then cannot Congress also reason that the threat or use of force—the frequent consequence of possessing a gun—in or near a school occurs sufficiently often so that such activity (by inhibiting basic education) affects commerce among the States? The negative impact upon the national economy of an inability to teach basic skills seems no smaller (nor less significant) than that of organized crime.

. . .

The second legal problem the Court creates comes from its apparent belief that it can reconcile its holding with earlier cases by making a critical distinction between "commercial" and noncommercial "transaction[s]." That is to say, the Court believes the Constitution would distinguish between two local activities, each of which has an identical effect upon interstate commerce, if one, but not the other, is "commercial" in nature.... Although the majority today attempts to categorize *Perez, McClung,* and *Wickard* as involving intrastate "economic activity," the Courts that decided each of those cases did *not* focus upon the economic nature of the activity regulated. Rather, they focused upon whether that activity *affected* interstate or foreign commerce. In fact, the *Wickard* Court expressly held that *Wickard*'s consumption of home grown wheat, *"though it may not be regarded as commerce,"* could nevertheless be regulated—*"whatever its nature "*—so long as "it exerts a substantial economic effect on interstate commerce." ...

More importantly, if a distinction between commercial and noncommercial activities is to be made, this is not the case in which to make it.... Schools that teach reading, writing, mathematics, and related basic skills serve *both* social and commercial purposes, and one cannot easily separate the one from the other....

[I]f there is a principled distinction that could work both here and in future cases, Congress (even in the absence of vocational classes, industry involvement, and private management) could rationally conclude that schools fall on the commercial side of the line. In 1990, the year Congress enacted the statute before us, primary and secondary schools spent $230 billion.... Why could Congress, for Commerce Clause purposes, not consider schools as roughly analogous to commercial investments from which the Nation derives the benefit of an educated work force?

The third legal problem created by the Court's holding is that it threatens legal uncertainty in an area of law that, until this case, seemed reasonably well settled.... [T]he legal uncertainty now created will restrict Congress' ability to enact criminal laws aimed at criminal behavior that, considered problem by problem rather than instance by instance, seriously threatens the economic, as well as social, well-being of Americans.

IV

In sum, to find this legislation within the scope of the Commerce Clause would permit "Congress . . . to act in terms of economic . . . realities."   . . . It would interpret the Clause as this Court has traditionally interpreted it, with the exception of one wrong turn subsequently corrected.   See Gibbons v. Ogden, 9 Wheat., at 195 (holding that the commerce power extends "to all the external concerns of the nation, and to those internal concerns which affect the States generally"); United States v. Darby, 312 U.S., at 116–117 ("The conclusion is inescapable that Hammer v. Dagenhart [the child labor case], was a departure from the principles which have prevailed in the interpretation of the Commerce Clause both before and since the decision. . . .   It should be and now is overruled").   Upholding this legislation would do no more than simply recognize that Congress had a "rational basis" for finding a significant connection between guns in or near schools and (through their effect on education) the interstate and foreign commerce they threaten. . . .

Chapter 5

THE SCOPE OF STATE POWER

SECTION 4. IMPLIED RESTRICTIONS OF THE COMMERCE CLAUSE—PRODUCTION AND TRADE

A. RESTRICTING IMPORTATION AND INSULATING IN–STATE BUSINESS FROM OUT–OF–STATE COMPETITION

Page 291. Add after Brown–Forman Distillers Corporation v. New York State Liquor Authority:

WEST LYNN CREAMERY v. HEALY

__ U.S. __, 114 S.Ct. 2205, 129 L.Ed.2d 157 (1994).

Justice Stevens delivered the opinion of the Court.

A Massachusetts pricing order imposes an assessment on all fluid milk sold by dealers to Massachusetts retailers. About two-thirds of that milk is produced out of State. The entire assessment, however, is distributed to Massachusetts dairy farmers. The question presented is whether the pricing order unconstitutionally discriminates against interstate commerce. We hold that it does.

I

Petitioner West Lynn Creamery, Inc., is a milk dealer licensed to do business in Massachusetts. It purchases raw milk, which it processes, packages, and sells to wholesalers, retailers, and other milk dealers. About 97% of the raw milk it purchases is produced by out-of-state farmers. Petitioner LeComte's Dairy, Inc., is also a licensed Massachusetts milk dealer. It purchases all of its milk from West Lynn and distributes it to retail outlets in Massachusetts.

Since 1937, the Agricultural Marketing Agreement Act, 50 Stat. 246, as amended, 7 U.S.C. § 601 et seq., has authorized the Secretary of Agriculture to regulate the minimum prices paid to producers of raw milk by issuing marketing orders for particular geographic areas. While the Federal Government sets minimum prices based on local conditions, those prices have not been so high as to prevent substantial competition among producers in different States. In the 1980's and early 1990's, Massachusetts dairy farmers began to lose market share to lower cost producers in neighboring States. In response, the Governor of Massachusetts appointed a Special Commission to study the dairy industry. The Commission found that many producers had sold their dairy farms during the past decade and that if prices paid to farmers for their milk were not significantly increased, a majority of the remaining farmers in Massachusetts would be "forced out of business within the year." App. 13. On January 28, 1992, relying on the Commission's Report, the Commissioner of the Massachusetts Department of Food and Agriculture (respondent) declared a State of Emergency ... [and promptly] issued the pricing order that is challenged in this proceeding.

The order requires every "dealer" in Massachusetts to make a monthly "premium payment" [based on the amount of its fluid milk product sales] into the "Massachusetts Dairy Equalization Fund." ... Each month the fund is distributed to Massachusetts producers[; i.e., dairy farmers]. Each Massachusetts producer receives a share of the total fund equal to his proportionate contribution to the State's total production of raw milk.

Petitioners ... [sued] in state court seeking an injunction against enforcement of the order on the ground that it violated the Commerce Clause of the Federal Constitution. The state court[s] denied relief....

... We ... reverse.

II

   . . .

   ... Massachusetts' pricing order is clearly unconstitutional. Its avowed purpose and its undisputed effect are to enable higher cost Massachusetts dairy farmers to compete with lower cost dairy farmers in other States. The "premium payments" are effectively a tax which makes milk produced out of State more expensive. Although the tax also applies to milk produced in Massachusetts, its effect on Massachusetts producers is entirely (indeed more than) offset by the subsidy provided exclusively to Massachusetts dairy farmers. Like an ordinary tariff, the tax is thus effectively imposed only on out-of-state products. The pricing order thus allows Massachusetts dairy farmers who produce at higher cost to sell at or below the price charged by lower cost out-of-state producers.[10] If there were no federal minimum prices for milk, out-of-state producers might still be able to retain their market share by lowering their prices. Nevertheless, out-of-staters' ability to remain competitive by lowering their prices would not immunize a discriminatory measure. New Energy Co. of Indiana v. Limbach, 486 U.S., at 275. In this case, because the Federal Government sets minimum prices, out-of-state producers may not even have the option of reducing prices in order to retain market share. The Massachusetts pricing order thus will almost certainly "cause local goods to constitute a larger share, and goods with an out-of-state source to constitute a smaller share, of the total sales in the market."[12] Exxon Corp. v. Governor of Maryland, 437 U.S. 117, 126, n. 16 (1978). In fact, this effect was the motive behind

10 ... The net effect of the tax and subsidy, like that of a tariff, is to raise the after-tax price paid by the dealers....

12 ... For Commerce Clause purposes, it does not matter whether the challenged regulation actually increases the market share of local producers or whether it merely mitigates a projected decline....

the promulgation of the pricing order. This effect renders the program unconstitutional, because it, like a tariff, "neutralize[s] advantages belonging to the place of origin." Baldwin, 294 U.S., at 527.

In some ways, the Massachusetts pricing order is most similar to the law at issue in Bacchus Imports, Ltd. v. Dias, 468 U.S. 263 (1984). Both involve a broad-based tax on a single kind of good and special provisions for in-state producers. *Bacchus* involved a 20% excise tax on all liquor sales, coupled with an exemption for fruit wine manufactured in Hawaii and for okolehao, a brandy distilled from the root of a shrub indigenous to Hawaii. The Court held that Hawaii's law was unconstitutional because it "had both the purpose and effect of discriminating in favor of local products." ... By granting a tax exemption for local products, Hawaii in effect created a protective tariff. Goods produced out of State were taxed, but those produced in State were subject to no net tax. It is obvious that the result in *Bacchus* would have been the same if instead of exempting certain Hawaiian liquors from tax, Hawaii had rebated the amount of tax collected from the sale of those liquors. See New Energy Co. of Indiana v. Limbach, 486 U.S. 269 (1988)(discriminatory tax credit). And if a discriminatory tax rebate is unconstitutional, Massachusetts' pricing order is surely invalid; for Massachusetts not only rebates to domestic milk producers the tax paid on the sale of Massachusetts milk, but also the tax paid on the sale of milk produced elsewhere. The additional rebate of the tax paid on the sale of milk produced elsewhere in no way reduces the danger to the national market posed by tariff-like barriers, but instead exacerbates the danger by giving domestic producers an additional tool with which to shore up their competitive position.[14]

III

Respondent advances four arguments against the conclusion that its pricing order imposes an unconstitutional burden on interstate commerce: (A) Because each component of the program—a local subsidy and a non-discriminatory tax—is valid, the combination of the two is equally valid; (B) The dealers who pay the order premiums (the tax) are not competitors of the farmers who receive disbursements from the Dairy Equalization Fund, so the pricing order is not discriminatory; (C) The pricing order is not protectionist, because the costs of the program are borne only by Massachusetts dealers and consumers, and the benefits are distributed exclusively to Massachusetts farmers; and (D) the order's incidental burden on commerce is justified by the local benefit of

---

[14] One might attempt to distinguish *Bacchus* by noting that the rebate in this case goes not to the entity which pays the tax (milk dealers) but to the dairy farmers themselves. Rebating the taxes directly to producers rather than to the dealers, however, merely reinforces the conclusion that the pricing order will favor local producers. If the taxes were refunded only to the dealers, there might be no impact on interstate commerce, because the dealers might not use the funds to increase the price or quantity of milk purchased from Massachusetts dairy farmers. The refund to the dealers might, therefore, result in no advantage to in-state producers. On the other hand, by refunding monies directly to the dairy farmers, the pricing order ensures that Massachusetts producers will benefit.

saving the dairy industry from collapse. We discuss each of these arguments in turn.

A

Respondent's principal argument is that ... if the State may impose a valid tax on dealers, it is free to use the proceeds of the tax as it chooses; and if it may independently subsidize its farmers, it is free to finance the subsidy by means of any legitimate tax.

Even granting respondent's assertion that both components of the pricing order would be constitutional standing alone,[15] the pricing order nevertheless must fall. A pure subsidy funded out of general revenue ordinarily imposes no burden on interstate commerce, but merely assists local business. The pricing order in this case, however, is funded principally from taxes on the sale of milk produced in other States.[16] By so funding the subsidy, respondent not only assists local farmers, but burdens interstate commerce. The pricing order thus violates the cardinal principle that a State may not "benefit in-state economic interests by burdening out-of-state competitors." New Energy Co. of Indiana v. Limbach, 486 U.S., at 273–274....

More fundamentally, respondent errs in assuming that the constitutionality of the pricing order follows logically from the constitutionality of its component parts. By conjoining a tax and a subsidy, Massachusetts has created a program more dangerous to interstate commerce than either part alone. Nondiscriminatory measures, like the evenhanded tax at issue here, are generally upheld, in spite of any adverse effects on interstate commerce, in part because "[t]he existence of major in-state interests adversely affected ... is a powerful safeguard against legislative abuse." Minnesota v. Clover Leaf Creamery Co., 449 U.S. 456, 473, n. 17 (1981).... However, when a nondiscriminatory tax is coupled with a subsidy to one of the groups hurt by the tax, a state's political processes can no longer be relied upon to prevent legislative abuse, because one of the in-state interests which would otherwise lobby against the tax has been mollified by the subsidy. So, in this case, one would ordinarily have expected at least three groups to lobby against the order premium, which, as a tax, raises the price (and hence lowers demand) for milk: dairy farmers, milk dealers, and consumers. But

---

[15] We have never squarely confronted the constitutionality of subsidies, and we need not do so now. We have, however, noted that "[d]irect subsidization of domestic industry does not ordinarily run afoul" of the negative Commerce Clause. New Energy Co. of Indiana v. Limbach, 486 U.S., at 278; see also Hughes v. Alexandria Scrap Corp., 426 U.S. 794, 815 (1976)(Stevens, J., concurring). In addition, it is undisputed that States may try to attract business by creating an environment conducive to economic activity, as by maintaining good roads, sound public education, or low taxes. Zobel v. Williams, 457 U.S. 55, 67 (1982)(Brennan, J., concurring); Bacchus Imports, Ltd. v. Dias, 468 U.S., at 271; Metropolitan Life Ins. Co. v. Ward, 470 U.S. 869, 876–878 (1985).

[16] It is undisputed that an overwhelming majority of the milk sold in Massachusetts is produced elsewhere. Thus, even though the tax is applied even-handedly to milk produced in State and out of State, most of the tax collected comes from taxes on milk from other States. In addition, the tax on in-state milk, unlike that imposed on out-of-state milk, does not impose any burden on in-state producers, because in-state dairy farmers can be confident that the taxes paid on their milk will be returned to them via the Dairy Stabilization Fund.

because the tax was coupled with a subsidy, one of the most powerful of these groups, Massachusetts dairy farmers, instead of exerting their influence against the tax, were in fact its primary supporters.[18]

Respondent's argument would require us to analyze separately two parts of an integrated regulation, but we cannot divorce the premium payments from the use to which the payments are put. [T]he entire program ... simultaneously burdens interstate commerce and discriminates in favor of local producers. The choice of constitutional means—nondiscriminatory tax and local subsidy—cannot guarantee the constitutionality of the program as a whole. New York's minimum price order also used constitutional means—a State's power to regulate prices—but was held unconstitutional because of its deleterious effects. Baldwin v. G.A.F. Seelig, Inc., 294 U.S. 511 (1935). Similarly, the law held unconstitutional in Bacchus, 468 U.S. 263 (1984), involved the exercise of Hawaii's undisputed power to tax and to grant tax exemptions.

Our Commerce Clause jurisprudence is not so rigid as to be controlled by the form by which a State erects barriers to commerce. Rather our cases have eschewed formalism for a sensitive, case-by-case analysis of purposes and effects....

B

Respondent['s argument] that since the Massachusetts milk dealers who pay the order premiums are not competitors of the Massachusetts farmers, the pricing order imposes no discriminatory burden on commerce ... cannot withstand scrutiny. Is it possible to doubt that if Massachusetts imposed a higher sales tax on milk produced in Maine than milk produced in Massachusetts that the tax would be struck down, in spite of the fact that the sales tax was imposed on consumers, and consumers do not compete with dairy farmers? For over 150 years, our cases have rightly concluded that the imposition of a differential burden on any part of the stream of commerce—from wholesaler to retailer to consumer—is invalid, because a burden placed at any point will result in a disadvantage to the out-of-state producer....

C

Respondent also argues that "the operation of the Order disproves any claim of protectionism," because "only in-state consumers feel the effect of any retail price increase ... [and] [t]he dealers themselves ... have a substantial in-state presence." ... This argument, if accepted, would undermine almost every discriminatory tax case. State taxes are ordinarily paid by in-state businesses and consumers, yet if they discriminate against out-of-state products, they are unconstitutional.... The cost of a tariff is also borne primarily by local consumers, yet a tariff is the paradigmatic Commerce Clause violation.

---

[18] As the Governor's Special Commission ... realized, consumers would be unlikely to organize effectively to oppose the pricing order. The Commission's report remarked, "the estimated two cent increase per quart of milk would not be noticed by the consuming public," App. 18, because the price of milk varies so often and for so many reasons that consumers would be unlikely to feel the price increases or to attribute them to the pricing order.

More fundamentally, ... the purpose and effect of the pricing order are to divert market share to Massachusetts dairy farmers. This diversion necessarily injures the dairy farmers in neighboring States.... The obvious impact of the order on out-of-state production demonstrates that it is simply wrong to assume that the pricing order burdens only Massachusetts consumers and dealers.

D

Finally, respondent argues that any incidental burden on interstate commerce "is outweighed by the 'local benefits' of preserving the Massachusetts dairy industry." ... In a closely related argument, respondent urges that "the purpose of the order, to save an industry from collapse, is not protectionist." ... If we were to accept these arguments, we would make a virtue of the vice that the rule against discrimination condemns. Preservation of local industry by protecting it from the rigors of interstate competition is the hallmark of the economic protectionism that the Commerce Clause prohibits....

The judgment ... is reversed.

Justice Scalia, with whom Justice Thomas joins, concurring in the judgment.

. . .

I

... [W]e have never held, that every state law which obstructs a national market violates the Commerce Clause. Yet that is what the Court says today. It seems to have canvassed the entire corpus of negative–Commerce–Clause opinions, culled out every free-market snippet of reasoning, and melded them into the sweeping principle that the Constitution is violated by any state law or regulation that "artificially encourag[es] in-state production even when the same goods could be produced at lower cost in other States." ...

As the Court seems to appreciate by its eagerness expressly to reserve the question of the constitutionality of subsidies for in-state industry, this expansive view of the Commerce Clause calls into question a wide variety of state laws that have hitherto been thought permissible. It seems to me that a State subsidy would clearly be invalid under any formulation of the Court's guiding principle identified above.... [E]ven where the funding does not come in any part from taxes on out-of-state goods, "merely assist[ing]" in-state businesses unquestionably neutralizes advantages possessed by out-of-state enterprises. Such subsidies ... are often admitted to have as their purpose—indeed, are nationally advertised as having as their purpose—making it more profitable to conduct business in-state than elsewhere, i.e., distorting normal market incentives.

The Court's guiding principle also appears to call into question many garden-variety state laws heretofore permissible under the negative Commerce Clause. A state law, for example, which requires, contrary to the industry practice, the use of recyclable packaging materials, favors local non-exporting producers, who do not have to establish an additional, separate packaging operation for in-state sales. If the Court's analysis is to be believed, such a law would be unconstitutional without regard to whether disruption of the "national market" is the real purpose of the restriction, and without the need to "balance" the importance of the state interests thereby pursued, see Pike v. Bruce Church, Inc., 397 U.S. 137 (1970). These results would greatly extend the negative Commerce Clause beyond its current scope. If the Court does not intend these consequences, and does not want to foster needless litigation concerning them, it should not have adopted its expansive rationale....

II

... I will, on *stare decisis* grounds, enforce a self-executing "negative" Commerce Clause in two situations: (1) against a state law that facially discriminates against interstate commerce, and (2) against a state law that is indistinguishable from a type of law previously held unconstitutional by this Court....

There are at least four possible devices that would enable a State to produce the economic effect that Massachusetts has produced here: (1) a discriminatory tax upon the industry, imposing a higher liability on out-of-state members than on their in-state competitors; (2) a tax upon the industry that is nondiscriminatory in its assessment, but that has an "exemption" or "credit" for in-state members; (3) a nondiscriminatory tax upon the industry, the revenues from which are placed into a segregated fund, which fund is disbursed as "rebates" or "subsidies" to in-state members of the industry (the situation at issue in this case); and (4) with or without nondiscriminatory taxation of the industry, a subsidy for the in-state members of the industry, funded from the State's general revenues. It is long settled that the first of these methodologies is unconstitutional under the negative Commerce Clause.... The second ... is no different in principle from the first, and has likewise been held invalid.... The fourth methodology, application of a state subsidy from general revenues, is so far removed from what we have hitherto held to be unconstitutional, that prohibiting it must be regarded as an extension of our negative–Commerce–Clause jurisprudence and therefore, to me, unacceptable. See New Energy Co. of Indiana v. Limbach, 486 U.S. 269, 278 (1988). Indeed, in my view our negative-Commerce-Clause cases have already approved the use of such subsidies. See Hughes v. Alexandria Scrap Corp., 426 U.S. 794, 809–810 (1976).

The issue before us in the present case is whether the third of these methodologies must fall. Although the question is close, I conclude it would not be a principled point at which to disembark from the negative–Commerce–Clause train. The only difference between methodology (2)(discriminatory "exemption" from nondiscriminatory tax) and methodology (3)(discriminatory refund of nondiscriminatory tax) is that the money is taken and returned rather than simply left with the favored in-state taxpayer in the first place. The difference between (3) and (4), on the other hand, is the difference between assisting in-state industry through discriminatory taxation, and assisting in-state industry by other means. I would therefore allow a State to subsidize its domestic industry so long as it does so from nondiscriminatory taxes that go into the State's general revenue fund. Perhaps, as some commentators contend, that line comports with an important economic reality: a State is less likely to maintain a subsidy when its citizens perceive that the money (in the general fund) is available for any number of competing, non-protectionist, purposes.... That is not, however, the basis for my position, for as The Chief Justice explains, "[a]nalysis of interest group participation in the political process may serve many useful purposes, but serving as a basis for interpreting the dormant Commerce Clause is not one of them." Instead, I draw the line where I do because it is a clear, rational line at the limits of our extant negative-Commerce-Clause jurisprudence.

Chief Justice Rehnquist, with whom Justice Blackmun joins, dissenting.

. . .

Massachusetts has ... provid[ed] a subsidy to aid its beleaguered dairy farmers. In case after case, we have approved the validity under the Commerce Clause of such enactments.... "Direct subsidization of domestic industry does not ordinarily run afoul of the [dormant Commerce Clause]; discriminatory taxation of out-of-state manufacturers does." New Energy Co. of Indiana v. Limbach, 486 U.S. 269, 278 (1988). But today the Court relegates these well-established principles to a footnote and, at the same time, gratuitously casts doubt on the validity of state subsidies, observing that "[w]e have never squarely confronted" their constitutionality....

... The State has not acted to strong-arm sister States as in *Limbach* ; rather, its motives are purely local....

Consistent with precedent, the Court observes: "A pure subsidy funded out of general revenue ordinarily imposes no burden on interstate commerce, but merely assists local business." ... But the Court strikes down this method of state subsidization because the non-discriminatory tax levied against all milk dealers is coupled with a subsidy to milk producers. The Court does this because of its view that the method of imposing the tax and subsidy distorts the State's political process: the dairy farmers, who would otherwise lobby against the tax, have been mollified by the subsidy. But as the Court itself points out, there are still at least two strong interest groups opposed to the milk order—consumers and milk dealers. More importantly, nothing in the dormant Commerce Clause suggests that the fate of state regulation should turn upon the particular lawful manner in which the state subsidy is enacted or promulgated. Analysis of interest group participation in the political process may serve many useful purposes, but serving as a basis for interpreting the dormant Commerce Clause is not one of them.

... [B]oth *Baldwin* and *Bacchus* are a far cry from this case.

... [Unlike the adverse effect on out-of-state milk producers from the minimum price regulation in *Baldwin,* here m]ilk dealers have the same incentives to purchase lower priced milk from out-of-state farmers; dealers of all milk are taxed equally....

... [And] the milk order does not produce the same effect on interstate commerce as the tax exemption in *Bacchus*. I agree with the Court's statement that *Bacchus* can be distinguished "by noting that the rebate in this case goes not to the entity which pays the tax (milk dealers) but to the dairy farmers themselves." This is not only a distinction, but a significant difference. No decided case supports the Court's conclusion that the negative Commerce Clause prohibits the State from using money that it has lawfully obtained through a neutral tax on milk dealers and distributing it as a subsidy to dairy farmers. Indeed, the case which comes closest to supporting the result the Court reaches is the ill-starred opinion in United States v. Butler, 297 U.S. 1 (1936), in which the Court held unconstitutional what would have been an otherwise valid tax on the processing of agricultural products because of the use to which the revenue raised by the tax was put.

... The wisdom of a messianic insistence on a grim sink-or-swim policy of laissez-faire economics would be debatable had Congress chosen to enact it; but Congress has done nothing of the kind. It is the Court which has imposed the policy under the dormant Commerce Clause, a policy which bodes ill for the values of federalism which have long animated our constitutional jurisprudence.

———————

Page 298.   Add at end of subsection:

ASSOCIATED INDUSTRIES OF MISSOURI v. LOHMAN, 114 S.Ct. 1815 (1994). To "compensate" for local sales taxes, Missouri passed a uniform, statewide use tax on all goods purchased out-of-state but used in-state. Although the sum of sales taxes collected by Missouri's many local jurisdictions on intrastate trade may have exceeded the use taxes collected from interstate trade, the Court held the tax system impermissibly discriminatory against interstate commerce as to those local jurisdictions with sales taxes lower than the statewide use tax. The Court refused, however, to invalidate the use tax entirely. Writing for all but Justice Blackmun, who concurred in the judgment without explanation, Justice Thomas said in relevant part:

"... Under the compensatory tax doctrine, a facially discriminatory tax that imposes on interstate commerce the equivalent of an 'identifiable and substantially similar tax on intrastate commerce does not offend the negative Commerce Clause.' ... To ensure that the State is indeed merely imposing countervailing burdens on comparable transactions, we have required that the taxes on interstate and intrastate commerce be imposed on 'substantially equivalent event[s].' ... The end result under the theory of the compensatory tax is that, '[w]hen the account is made up, the stranger from afar is subject to no greater burdens ... than the dweller within the gates. The one pays upon one activity or incident, and the other upon another, but the sum is the same when the reckoning is closed.' Henneford v. Silas Mason Co., 300 U.S. 577, 584, 57 S.Ct. 524, 527, 81 L.Ed. 814 (1937).

"... Respondents urge that the local sales taxes imposed by over a thousand political subdivisions within the State provide the burden on intrastate commerce that Missouri seeks to counterbalance through the use tax in this case. There is no dispute that sales taxes and use taxes such as those at issue here are imposed on 'substantially equivalent event[s].' ...

"Missouri's use tax scheme, however, runs afoul of the basic requirement that, for a tax system to be 'compensatory,' the burdens imposed on interstate and intrastate commerce must be equal.... Where a State imposes equivalent sales and use taxes, we have upheld the system under the Commerce Clause. See Silas Mason, supra, 300 U.S., at 584–587, 57 S.Ct., at 527–529. But in Missouri, whether the 1.5% use tax is equal to (or lower than) the local sales tax is a matter of fortuity, depending entirely upon the locality in which the Missouri purchaser happens to reside. Where the use tax exceeds the sales tax, the discrepancy imposes a discriminatory burden on interstate commerce. Out-of-state goods brought into such a jurisdiction are subjected to a higher levy than are goods sold locally....

"Respondents contend that ... discrimination in some parts of a state tax system may be permissible under the Commerce Clause as long as it is of a sufficiently limited magnitude to be offset by preferential treatment for interstate trade in other portions of the tax scheme....

"... [A]s a general matter we have rejected reliance on any calculus that requires a quantification of discrimination as a preliminary step to determining whether the discrimination is valid. Under our cases, unless one of several narrow bases of justification is shown, ... actual discrimination, wherever it is found, is impermissible, and the magnitude and scope of the discrimination have no bearing on the determinative question whether discrimination has occurred....

"... [D]iscrimination is appropriately assessed with reference to the specific subdivision in which applicable laws reveal differential treatment.

"... Under respondents' view, the Commerce Clause would interpose no bar to the systematic subdivision of the national market through discriminatory taxes as long as the taxes were imposed by counties, rather than by States—and provided, of course, that on balance each State as a whole did not discriminate against interstate trade. Such a rule 'would invite a multiplication of preferential trade areas destructive of the very purpose of the Commerce Clause.'" Dean Milk Co. v. Madison, 340 U.S. 349, 356, 71 S.Ct. 295, 299, 95 L.Ed. 329 (1951). We have never suggested that the Commerce Clause will tolerate such discrimination....

" ...

"... [S]trict parity is demanded by the compensatory tax doctrine as we have explained that a compensatory tax leaves a consumer free to make choices 'without regard to the tax consequences'; if he purchases within the State he may pay a tax, but if he purchases from outside the State he will pay a 'tax of the same amount.' Boston Stock Exchange. . . .

"Respondents' final defense of the use tax is an appeal to Missouri's pure motives: that is, its lack of any intent to discriminate. As the product of a decentralized decisionmaking process that relies on the independent judgment of hundreds of local jurisdictions, the use tax scheme, in respondents' view, cannot reveal any overall design on the part of the State or any other governmental entity to disfavor interstate trade. . . .

". . . [A] State may not . . . appeal to decentralized decisionmaking to augment its powers: it may not grant its political subdivisions a power to discriminate against interstate commerce that State lacked in the first instance.

" . . .

". . . Missouri's use tax scheme impermissibly discriminates against interstate commerce only in those localities where the local sales tax is less than 1.5%. . . . [Petitioners] urge us to hold that the tax is facially invalid in every jurisdiction because there is no countervailing statewide sales tax and no legislation ensuring that local sales taxes will always equal or exceed the use tax. The evil of the system, under this view, is not merely the actual discrimination that results in some localities, but the potential for discrimination in every locality. . . .

"But . . . we repeatedly have focused our Commerce Clause analysis on whether a challenged scheme is discriminatory in 'effect,'. . . .

"For similar reasons, the mere fact that determining the compensatory character of the use tax in this case requires consideration of the sales taxes levied by hundreds of local jurisdictions does not mean that the use tax should be rejected in toto as facially discriminatory. A compensatory tax and the tax for which it compensates need not be promulgated in the same provision of state law, or even through the same governmental entity, to survive Commerce Clause scrutiny. Such matters of form do not determine in substance whether the tax merely requires interstate commerce to 'pay its way,' Complete Auto Transit, Inc. v. Brady, 430 U.S. 274, 281 (1977)(internal quotation marks omitted), or discriminates against interstate trade. . . ."

FULTON CORP. v. FAULKNER, 116 S.Ct. 848 (1996). North Carolina levied an "intangibles tax" on the fair market value of corporate stock owned by its residents, but allowed a percentage deduction (up to 100%) based on the fraction of the issuing corporation's income subject to the State's corporate income tax. A unanimous Court had "no doubt that the intangibles tax facially discriminates against interstate commerce[, because a] regime that taxes stock only to the degree that its issuing corporation participates in interstate commerce favors domestic corporations over their foreign competitors in raising capital among North Carolina residents and tends, at least, to discourage domestic corporations from plying their trades in interstate commerce."

The Court rejected the State's main defense that the deduction provision was a valid "compensatory tax" to make up "for the burden of the general corporate income tax paid by corporations doing business in North Carolina." None of the criteria for a valid compensatory tax were met. First, the State had not adequately identified the intrastate tax burden for which it was trying to compensate. Warning "of the danger of treating general revenue measures as relevant intrastate burdens for purposes of the compensatory tax doctrine[,]" the Court rejected the theory that companies escaping the income tax to the extent they did business in other states were not paying, as were those that did business in-state, for the privilege of access to the State's capital markets. The Court was "unpersuaded that North Carolina's corporate income tax is designed to support the maintenance of an intrastate capital market" rather than for other uses. Second, the State had not shown that the tax on interstate commerce did not exceed the tax on intrastate commerce, because it was impossible to ascertain "what proportion of the corporate income tax goes to support the capital market, or whether that proportion represents a burden greater than the one imposed on interstate commerce by the intangibles tax." Finally, the intangibles tax and the corporate income tax did not "fall on substantially equivalent events." The "objective of the equivalent-event requirement ... is to enable in-state and out-of-state businesses to compete on a footing of equality" and "equality of treatment does not appear when the allegedly compensating taxes fall respectively on taxpayers who are differently described, as, for example, resident shareholders and corporations doing business out of state." Even if a State theoretically might prove that the actual incidence of two taxes would allow "a finding of combined neutrality on interstate competition[,]" here the "doubts" were "dispositive." More broadly, the "general difficulty of comparing the economic incidence of state taxes paid by different taxpayers upon different transactions goes a long way toward explaining why we have so seldom recognized a valid compensatory tax outside the context of sales and use taxes." In fact, "courts will ordinarily be unable to evaluate the economic equivalence of allegedly compensatory tax schemes that go beyond traditional sales/use taxes."

B. REQUIRING BUSINESS OPERATIONS TO BE PERFORMED IN THE HOME STATE

Page 300. Add at end of subsection:

C & A CARBONE v. TOWN OF CLARKSTOWN

511 U.S. 383, 114 S.Ct. 1677, 128 L.Ed.2d 399 (1994).

Justice Kennedy delivered the opinion of the Court.

. . .

We consider a so-called flow control ordinance, which requires all solid waste to be processed at a designated transfer station before leaving the municipality. The avowed purpose of the ordinance is to retain the processing fees charged at the transfer station to amortize the cost of the facility. Because it attains this goal by depriving competitors, including out-of-state firms, of access to a local market, we hold that the flow control ordinance violates the Commerce Clause.

[To finance construction of a solid waste transfer station that would receive bulk solid waste and separate recyclable from nonrecyclable items for shipment and further processing, the Town arranged for a private contractor to build it, operate it for five years with the Town guaranteeing a minimum waste flow and the right to charge haulers an $81 per ton "tipping fee" (a processing cost higher than charged on the private market), and then sell it to the Town for one dollar. To meet the annual guarantee, the town adopted a flow control ordinance requiring all nonhazardous solid waste within the town, whatever its origin, to be deposited at the new transfer station.]

... Carbone operates a recycling center in Clarkstown, where it receives bulk solid waste, sorts and bales it, and then ships it to other processing facilities—much as occurs at the town's new transfer station. While the flow control ordinance permits recyclers like Carbone to continue receiving solid waste, ... it requires them to bring the nonrecyclable residue from that waste to the Route 303 station. It thus forbids Carbone to ship the nonrecyclable waste itself, and it requires Carbone to pay a tipping fee on trash that Carbone has already sorted.

[When the Town discovered that Carbone had shipped nonrecyclable waste to other states, it sought an injunction to force compliance with the flow control ordinance. The state courts sustained the ordinance's constitutionality and issued the injunction.] We ... reverse.

At the outset we confirm that the flow control ordinance does regulate interstate commerce, despite the town's position to the contrary. The town says that its ordinance reaches only waste within its jurisdiction and is in practical effect a quarantine: It prevents garbage from entering the stream of interstate commerce until it is made safe. This reasoning is premised, however, on an outdated and mistaken concept of what constitutes interstate commerce.

While the immediate effect of the ordinance is to direct local transport of solid waste to a designated site within the local jurisdiction, its economic effects are interstate in reach. The Carbone facility in Clarkstown receives and processes waste from places other than Clarkstown, including from out of State. By requiring Carbone to send the nonrecyclable portion of this waste to the Route 303 transfer station at an additional cost, the flow control ordinance drives up the cost for out-of-state interests to dispose of their solid waste. Furthermore, even as to waste originant in Clarkstown, the ordinance prevents everyone except the favored local operator from performing the initial processing step. The ordinance thus deprives out-of-state businesses of access to a local market. These economic effects are more than enough to bring the Clarkstown ordinance within the purview of the Commerce Clause....

The real question is whether the flow control ordinance is valid despite its undoubted effect on interstate commerce. For this inquiry, our case law yields two lines of analysis: first, whether the ordinance discriminates against interstate commerce ...; and second, whether the ordinance imposes a burden on interstate commerce that is "clearly excessive in relation to the putative local benefits," Pike v. Bruce Church, Inc., 397 U.S. 137, 142 (1970). As we find that the ordinance discriminates against interstate commerce, we need not resort to the *Pike* test.

. . .

Clarkstown protests that its ordinance does not discriminate because it does not differentiate solid waste on the basis of its geographic origin. All solid waste, regardless of origin, must be processed at the designated transfer station before it leaves the town....

Our initial discussion of the effects of the ordinance on interstate commerce goes far toward refuting the town's contention that there is no discrimination in its regulatory scheme. The town's own arguments go the rest of the way. As the town itself points out, what makes garbage a profitable business is not its own worth but the fact that its possessor must pay to get rid of it. In other words, the article of commerce is not so much the solid waste itself, but rather the service of processing and disposing of it.

With respect to this stream of commerce, the flow control ordinance discriminates, for it allows only the favored operator to process waste that is within the limits of the town. The ordinance is no less discriminatory because in-state or in-town processors are also covered by the prohibition. In Dean Milk Co. v. Madison, 340 U.S. 349 (1951), we struck down a city ordinance that required all milk sold in the city to be pasteurized within five miles of the city lines. We found it "immaterial that Wisconsin milk from outside the Madison area is subjected to the same proscription as that moving in interstate commerce." ...

In this light, the flow control ordinance is just one more instance of local processing requirements that we long have held invalid.... The essential vice in laws of this sort is that they bar the import of the processing service. Out-of-state meat inspectors, or shrimp hullers, or milk pasteurizers, are deprived of access to local demand for their services. Put another way, the offending local laws hoard a local resource—be it meat, shrimp, or milk—for the benefit of local businesses that treat it.

The flow control ordinance has the same design and effect. It hoards solid waste, and the demand to get rid of it, for the benefit of the preferred processing facility. The only conceivable distinction from the cases cited above is that the flow control ordinance favors a single local proprietor. But this difference just makes the protectionist effect of the ordinance more acute. In *Dean Milk,* the local processing requirement at least permitted pasteurizers within five miles of the city to compete. An out-of-state pasteurizer who wanted access to that market might have built a pasteurizing facility within the radius. The flow control ordinance at issue here squelches competition in the waste-processing service altogether, leaving no room for investment from outside.

Discrimination against interstate commerce in favor of local business or investment is per se invalid, save in a narrow class of cases in which the municipality can demonstrate, under rigorous scrutiny, that it has no other means to advance a legitimate local interest.... A number of amici contend that the flow control ordinance fits into this narrow class. They suggest that as landfill space diminishes and environmental cleanup costs escalate, measures like flow control become necessary to ensure the safe handling and proper treatment of solid waste.

The teaching of our cases is that these arguments must be rejected absent the clearest showing that the unobstructed flow of interstate commerce itself is unable to solve the local problem. The Commerce Clause presumes a national market free from local legislation that discriminates in favor of local interests. Here Clarkstown has any number of nondiscriminatory alternatives for addressing the health and environmental problems alleged to justify the ordinance in question. The most obvious would be uniform safety regulations enacted without the object to discriminate. These regulations would ensure that competitors like Carbone do not underprice the market by cutting corners on environmental safety.

Nor may Clarkstown justify the flow control ordinance as a way to steer solid waste away from out-of-town disposal sites that it might deem harmful to the environment. To do so would extend the town's police power beyond its jurisdictional bounds. States and localities may not attach restrictions to exports or imports in order to control commerce in other states....

The flow control ordinance does serve a central purpose that a nonprotectionist regulation would not: It ensures that the town-sponsored facility will be profitable, so that the local contractor can build it and Clarkstown can buy it back at nominal cost in five years. In other words, ... the flow control ordinance is a financing measure. By itself, of course, revenue generation is not a local interest that can justify discrimination against interstate commerce. Otherwise States could impose discriminatory taxes against solid waste originating outside the State....

Clarkstown maintains that special financing is necessary to ensure the long-term survival of the designated facility. If so, the town may subsidize the facility through general taxes or municipal bonds.... But having elected to use the open market to earn revenues for its project, the town may not employ discriminatory regulation to give that project an advantage over rival businesses from out of State.

. . .

State and local governments may not use their regulatory power to favor local enterprise by prohibiting patronage of out-of-state competitors or their facilities....

Justice O'Connor, concurring in the judgment.

... In my view, ... the town's ordinance is unconstitutional not because of facial or effective discrimination against interstate commerce, but rather because it imposes an excessive burden on interstate commerce. I also write separately to address the contention that flow control ordinances of this sort have been expressly authorized by Congress, and are thus outside the purview of the dormant Commerce Clause.

I

. . .

Local Law 9 prohibits anyone except the town-authorized transfer station operator from processing discarded waste and shipping it out of town. In effect, the town has given a waste processing monopoly to the transfer station. The majority concludes that this processing monopoly facially discriminates against interstate commerce. In support of this conclusion, the majority cites previous decisions of this Court striking down regulatory enactments requiring that a particular economic activity be performed within the jurisdiction....

Local Law 9, however, lacks an important feature common to the regulations at issue in these cases—namely, discrimination on the basis of geographic origin. In each of the cited cases, the challenged enactment gave a competitive advantage to local business *as a group* vis-a-vis their out-of-state or nonlocal competitors *as a group*. In effect, the regulating jurisdiction—be it a State (*Pike*), a county (Fort Gratiot Sanitary Landfill, Inc. v. Michigan Dept. of Natural Resources, 504 U.S. (1992)), or a city (*Dean Milk*)—drew a line around itself and treated those inside the line more favorably than those outside the line. Thus, in *Pike*, the Court held that an Arizona law requiring that Arizona cantaloupes be packaged in Arizona before being shipped out of state facially discriminated against interstate commerce: the benefits of the discriminatory scheme benefited the Arizona packaging industry, at the expense of its competition in California. Similarly, in *Dean Milk,* on which the majority heavily relies, the city of Madison drew a line around its perimeter and required that all milk sold in the City be pasteurized only by dairies located inside the line. This type of geographic distinction, which confers an economic advantage on local interests in general, is common to all the local processing cases cited by the majority. And the Court has, I believe, correctly concluded that these arrangements are protectionist either in purpose or practical effect, and thus amount to virtually per se discrimination.

... Unlike the regulations we have previously struck down, Local Law 9 does not give more favorable treatment to local interests as a group as compared to out-of-state or out-of-town economic interests. Rather, the garbage sorting monopoly is achieved at the expense of all competitors, be they local or nonlocal. That the ordinance does not discriminate on the basis of geographic origin is vividly illustrated by the identity of the plaintiff in this very action: petitioner is a local recycler, physically located in Clarkstown, that desires to process waste itself, and thus bypass the town's designated transfer facility. Because in-town processors—like petitioner—and out-of-town processors are treated equally, I cannot agree that Local Law 9 "discriminates" against inter-state commerce. Rather, Local Law 9 "discriminates" evenhandedly against all potential participants in the waste processing business, while benefiting only the chosen operator of the transfer facility.

I believe this distinction has more doctrinal significance than the majority acknowledges. In considering state health and safety regula-tions such as Local Law 9, we have consistently recognized that the fact that interests within the regulating jurisdiction are equally affected by the challenged enactment counsels against a finding of discrimination. And for good reason. The existence of substantial in-state interests harmed by a regulation is "a powerful safeguard" against legislative discrimination. Minnesota v. Clover Leaf Creamery Co., 449 U.S. 456, 473, n. 17 (1981).... [W]hile there is no bright line separating those enactments which are virtually per se invalid and those which are not, the fact that in-town competitors of the transfer facility are equally burdened by Local Law 9 leads me to conclude that Local Law 9 does not discriminate against interstate commerce.

II

... Even a nondiscriminatory regulation may nonetheless impose an excessive burden on interstate trade when considered in relation to the local benefits conferred....

The local interest in proper disposal of waste is obviously significant. But this interest could be achieved by simply requiring that all waste disposed of in the town be properly processed somewhere. For example, the town could ensure proper processing by setting specific standards with which all town processors must comply.

In fact, however, the town's purpose is narrower than merely ensuring proper disposal. Local Law 9 is intended to ensure the finan-cial viability of the transfer facility. I agree with the majority that this purpose can be achieved by other means that would have a less dramatic impact on the flow of goods....

In addition, "[t]he practical effect of [Local Law 9] must be evaluat-ed not only by considering the consequences of the statute itself, but also by considering how the challenged statute may interact with the legiti-mate regulatory regimes of the other States and what effect would arise if not one, but many or every, [jurisdiction] adopted similar legislation." Wyoming v. Oklahoma, ... (quoting Healy v. Beer Institute, 491 U.S. 324, 336 (1989)).... Over 20 states have enacted statutes authorizing local governments to adopt flow control laws. If the localities in these States impose the type of restriction on the movement of waste that Clarkstown has adopted, the free movement of solid waste in the stream of commerce will be severely impaired. Indeed, pervasive flow control would result in the type of balkanization the Clause is primarily intended to prevent. See H.P. Hood & Sons, 336 U.S., at 537–538.

... The increasing number of flow control regimes virtually ensures some inconsistency between jurisdictions, with the effect of eliminating the movement of waste between jurisdictions. I therefore conclude that the burden Local Law 9 imposes on interstate commerce is excessive in relation to Clarkstown's interest in ensuring a fixed supply of waste to supply its project.

III

[Justice O'Connor here rejected the argument that the Resource Conservation and Recovery Act of 1976 (RCRA) and its amendments authorized local flow control ordinances. Statutory provisions and legislative history may] indicate that Congress expected local governments to implement some form of flow control. Nonetheless, they neither individually nor cumulatively rise to the level of the "explicit" authorization required by our dormant Commerce Clause decisions....

... Should Congress revisit this area, and enact legislation providing a clear indication that it intends States and localities to implement flow control, we will, of course, defer to that legislative judgment. Until then, however, Local Law 9 cannot survive constitutional scrutiny....

Justice Souter, with whom The Chief Justice and Justice Blackmun join, dissenting.

... [T]he majority ignores ... the differences between our local processing cases and this one: the exclusion worked by Clarkstown's Local Law 9 bestows no benefit on a class of local private actors, but instead directly aids the government in satisfying a traditional governmental responsibility. The law does not differentiate between all local and all out-of-town providers of a service, but instead between the one entity responsible for ensuring that the job gets done and all other enterprises, regardless of their location. The ordinance thus falls outside that class of tariff or protectionist measures that the Commerce Clause has traditionally been thought to bar States from enacting against each other....

... There is no indication in the record that any out-of-state trash processor has been harmed, or that the interstate movement or disposition of trash will be affected one whit. To the degree Local Law 9 affects the market for trash processing services, it does so only by subjecting Clarkstown residents and businesses to burdens far different from the burdens of local favoritism that dormant Commerce Clause jurisprudence seeks to root out. The town has found a way to finance a public improvement, not by transferring its cost to out-of-state economic interests, but by spreading it among the local generators of trash, an equitable result with tendencies that should not disturb the Commerce Clause and should not be disturbed by us.

. . .

II

. . .

B

There are ... both analytical and practical differences between this and the earlier processing cases, ... which ... should prevent this case from being decided the same way. First, the terms of Clarkstown's ordinance favor a single processor, not the class of all such businesses located in Clarkstown. Second, the one proprietor so favored is essentially an agent of the municipal government, which (unlike Carbone or other private trash processors) must ensure the removal of waste according to acceptable standards of public health. Any discrimination worked by Local Law 9 thus fails to produce the sort of entrepreneurial favoritism we have previously defined and condemned as protectionist.

1

The outstanding feature of the statutes reviewed in the local processing cases is their distinction between two classes of private economic actors according to location.... [T]he out-of-town processors were not excluded as part and parcel of a general exclusion of private firms from the market, but as a result of discrimination among such firms according to geography alone. It was because of that discrimination in favor of local businesses, preferred at the expense of their out-of-town or out-of-state competitors, that the Court struck down those local processing laws as classic examples of the economic protectionism the dormant Commerce Clause jurisprudence aims to prevent.... The Commerce Clause does not otherwise protect access to local markets....

The majority recognizes, but discounts, this difference between laws favoring all local actors and this law favoring a single municipal one. According to the majority, "this difference just makes the protectionist effect of the ordinance more acute" because outside investors cannot even build competing facilities within Clarkstown. But of course Clarkstown investors face the same prohibition, which is to say that Local Law 9's exclusion of outside capital is part of a broader exclusion of private capital, not a discrimination against out-of-state investors as such.... Thus, while these differences may underscore the ordinance's anticompetitive effect, they substantially mitigate any protectionist effect, for subjecting out-of-town investors and facilities to the same constraints as local ones is not economic protectionism....

2

Nor is the monopolist created by Local Law 9 just another private company successfully enlisting local government to protect the jobs and profits of local citizens.... Clarkstown's transfer station is essentially a municipal facility, built and operated under a contract with the municipality and soon to revert entirely to municipal ownership. This, of course, is no mere coincidence, since the facility performs a municipal function that tradition as well as state and federal law recognize as the domain of local government....

The majority ignores this distinction between public and private enterprise, equating Local Law 9's "hoard[ing]" of solid waste for the municipal transfer station with the design and effect of ordinances that restrict access to local markets for the benefit of local private firms. But private businesses, whether local or out of State, first serve the private interests of their owners, and there is therefore only rarely a reason other than economic protectionism for favoring local businesses over their out-of-town competitors. The local government itself occupies a very different market position, however, being the one entity that enters the market to serve the public interest of local citizens quite apart from private interest in private gain. Reasons other than economic protectionism are accordingly more likely to explain the design and effect of an ordinance that favors a public facility. The facility as constructed might, for example, be one that private economic actors, left to their own devices, would not have built, but which the locality needs in order to abate (or guarantee against creating) a public nuisance.... An ordinance that favors a municipal facility, in any event, is one that favors the public sector, and if "we continue to recognize that the States occupy a special and specific position in our constitutional system and that the scope of Congress' authority under the Commerce Clause must reflect that position," Garcia v. San Antonio Metropolitan Transit Authority, 469 U.S. 528, 556 (1985), then surely this Court's dormant Commerce Clause jurisprudence must itself see that favoring state-sponsored facilities differs from discriminating among private economic actors, and is much less likely to be protectionist.

3

. . .

... The justification for subjecting the local processing laws and the broader class of clearly discriminatory commercial regulation to near-fatal scrutiny is the virtual certainty that such laws, at least in their discriminatory aspect, serve no legitimate, nonprotectionist purpose.... [T]he discriminatory scheme is almost always designed either to favor local industry, as such, or to achieve some other goal while exporting a disproportionate share of the burden of attaining it, which is merely a subtler form of local favoritism.... On the other hand, in a market served by a municipal facility, a law that favors that single facility over all others is a law that favors the public sector over all private-sector processors, whether local or out of State. Because the favor does not go to local private competitors of out-of-state firms, out-of-state governments will at the least lack a motive to favor their own firms in order to equalize the positions of private competitors. While a preference in favor of the government may incidentally function as local favoritism as well, a more particularized enquiry is necessary before a court can say whether such a law does in fact smack too strongly of economic protectionism. If Local Law 9 is to be struck down, ... it must be under that test most readily identified with Pike v. Bruce Church, Inc., 397 U.S. 137 (1970).

III

... Although ... sometimes ... called a "balancing test," it is not so much an open-ended weighing of an ordinance's pros and cons, as an assessment of whether an ordinance discriminates in practice or otherwise unjustifiably operates to isolate a State's economy from the national common market.... "[T]he question becomes one of degree," and its answer depends on the nature of the burden on interstate commerce, the nature of the local interest, and the availability of alternative methods for advancing the local interest without hindering the national one. Id., at 142, 145.

. . .

[T]he dollar cost of the burden need not be pinpointed, its nature being more significant than its economic extent. ... [T]he monopolistic character of Local Law 9's effects is not itself suspicious for purposes of the Commerce Clause.... The only right to compete that it protects is the right to compete on terms independent of one's location.

While the monopolistic nature of the burden may be disregarded, any geographically discriminatory elements must be assessed with care.... There is, to be sure, an incidental local economic benefit, for the need to process Clarkstown's trash in Clarkstown will create local jobs. But this local boon is mitigated by another feature of the ordinance, in that it finances whatever benefits it confers on the town from the pockets of the very citizens who passed it into law. On the reasonable assumption that no one can avoid producing some trash, every resident of Clarkstown must bear a portion of the burden Local Law 9 imposes to support the municipal monopoly, an uncharacteristic feature of statutes claimed to violate the Commerce Clause.

[M]ost of the local processing statutes we have previously invalidated imposed requirements that made local goods more expensive as they headed into the national market, so that out-of-state economies bore the bulk of any burden.... Here, in contrast, every voter in Clarkstown pays to fund the benefits of flow control, however high the tipping fee is set. Since, indeed, the mandate to use the town facility will only make a difference when the tipping fee raises the cost of using the facility above what the market would otherwise set, the Clarkstown voters are funding their benefit by assessing themselves and paying an economic penalty. Any whiff of economic protectionism is far from obvious.

An examination of the record ... shows that the burden falls entirely on Clarkstown residents. If the record contained evidence that Clarkstown's ordinance burdened out-of-town providers of garbage sorting and baling services, rather than just the local business that is a party in this case, that fact might be significant. But petitioner has presented no evidence that there are transfer stations outside Clarkstown capable of handling the town's business, and the record is devoid of evidence that such enterprises have lost business as a result of this ordinance.... Similarly, if the record supported an inference that above-market pricing at the Clarkstown transfer station caused less trash to flow to out-of-state landfills and incinerators, that, too, might have constitutional significance.   There is, however, no evidence of any disruption in the flow of trash from curbsides in Clarkstown to landfills in Florida and Ohio.[16]   Here we can confidently say that the only business lost as a result of this ordinance is business lost in Clarkstown, as customers who had used Carbone's facility drift away in response to any higher fees Carbone may have to institute to afford its share of city services; but business lost in Clarkstown as a result of a Clarkstown ordinance is not a burden that offends the Constitution.

This skepticism that protectionism is afoot here is confirmed again when we examine the governmental interests apparently served by the local law.   [T]he State and its municipalities need prompt, sanitary trash processing, which is imperative whether or not the private market sees fit to serve this need at an affordable price and to continue doing so dependably into the future.   The state and local governments also have a substantial interest in the flow-control feature to minimize the risk of financing this service, . . . [and] there is no question that a "put or pay" contract of the type Clarkstown signed will be a significant inducement to accept municipal responsibility to guarantee efficiency and sanitation in trash processing.   [T]here are limits on any municipality's ability to incur debt or to finance facilities out of tax revenues.   Protection of the public fisc is a legitimate local benefit directly advanced by the ordinance and quite unlike the generalized advantage to local businesses that we have condemned as protectionist in the past. . . .

. . . In proportioning each resident's burden to the amount of trash generated, the ordinance has the added virtue of providing a direct and measurable deterrent to the generation of unnecessary waste in the first place.   And . . . it is far from clear that the alternative to flow control (i.e., subsidies from general tax revenues or municipal bonds) would be less disruptive of interstate commerce than flow control, since a subsidized competitor can effectively squelch competition by underbidding it.

There is, in short, no evidence that Local Law 9 causes discrimination against out-of-town processors, because there is no evidence in the record that such processors have lost business as a result of it.   Instead, we know only that the ordinance causes the local residents who adopted it to pay more for trash disposal services.   But local burdens are not the focus of the dormant Commerce Clause, and this imposition is in any event readily justified by the ordinance's legitimate benefits in reliable and sanitary trash processing.

* * *

The Commerce Clause was not passed to save the citizens of Clarkstown from themselves.   It should not be wielded to prevent them from attacking their local garbage problems with an ordinance that does not discriminate between local and out-of-town participants in the pri-

---

[16] In this context, note that the conflict Justice O'Connor hypothesizes between multiple flow control laws is not one that occurs in this case. . . .   But more fundamentally, even if a nondiscriminatory ordinance conflicts with the law of some other jurisdiction, that fact would not, in itself, lead to its invalidation. . . .   [T]he municipality's interests are substantial and . . . the alternative means for advancing them are less desirable and potentially as disruptive of interstate commerce. . . .

vate market for trash disposal services and that is not protectionist in its purpose or effect. Local Law 9 conveys a privilege on the municipal government alone, the only market participant that bears responsibility for ensuring that adequate trash processing services continue to be available to Clarkstown residents. Because the Court's decision today is neither compelled by our local processing cases nor consistent with this Court's reason for inferring a dormant or negative aspect to the Commerce Clause in the first place, I respectfully dissent.

Chapter 7

SEPARATION OF POWERS

Page 460. Add at end of Section 2:

SECTION 2A. CONGRESSIONAL INTERFERENCE WITH JUDICIAL DECISIONS

PLAUT v. SPENDTHRIFT FARM, INC.

___ U.S. ___, 115 S.Ct. 1447, 131 L.Ed.2d 328 (1995).

Justice Scalia delivered the opinion of the Court.

The question presented in this case is whether § 27A(b) of the Securities Exchange Act of 1934, to the extent that it requires federal courts to reopen final judgments in private civil actions under § 10(b) of the Act, contravenes the Constitution's separation of powers or the Due Process Clause of the Fifth Amendment.

I

In 1987, petitioners brought a civil action against respondents in the United States District Court for the Eastern District of Kentucky. The complaint alleged that in 1983 and 1984 respondents had committed fraud and deceit in the sale of stock in violation of § 10(b) of the Securities Exchange Act of 1934 and Rule 10b–5 of the Securities and Exchange Commission.... [On] June 20, 1991 we decided Lampf, Pleva, Lipkind, Prupis & Petigrow v. Gilbertson, 501 U.S. 350 (1991). *Lampf* held that "[l]itigation instituted pursuant to § 10(b) and Rule 10b–5 ... must be commenced within one year after the discovery of the facts constituting the violation and within three years after such violation." ... We applied that holding to the plaintiff-respondents in *Lampf* itself ... On the same day we decided James B. Beam Distilling Co. v. Georgia, 501 U.S. 529 (1991), in which a majority of the Court held, albeit in different opinions, that a new rule of federal law that is applied to the parties in the case announcing the rule must be applied as well to all cases pending on direct review.... The joint effect of *Lampf* and *Beam* was to mandate application of the 1–year/3–year limitations period to petitioners' suit. The District Court, finding that petitioners' claims were untimely under the *Lampf* rule, dismissed their action with prejudice on August 13, 1991. Petitioners filed no appeal; the judgment accordingly became final 30 days later....

On December 19, 1991, the President signed the Federal Deposit Insurance Corporation Improvement Act of 1991, 105 Stat. 2236. Section 476 of the Act ... provides:

"(a) Effect on pending causes of action

"The limitation period for any private civil action implied under section 78j(b) of this title [§ 10(b) of the Securities Exchange Act of 1934] that was commenced on or before June 19, 1991, shall be the limitation period provided by the laws applicable in the jurisdiction, including principles of retroactivity, as such laws existed on June 19, 1991.

"(b) Effect on dismissed causes of action

"Any private civil action implied under section 78j(b) of this title that was commenced on or before June 19, 1991–

"(1) which was dismissed as time barred subsequent to June 19, 1991, and

"(2) which would have been timely filed under the limitation period provided by the laws applicable in the jurisdiction, including principles of retroactivity, as such laws existed on June 19, 1991, shall be reinstated on motion by the plaintiff not later than 60 days after December 19, 1991."

On February 11, 1992, petitioners returned to the District Court and filed a motion to reinstate the action previously dismissed with prejudice. The District Court found that the conditions set out in §§ 27A(b)(1) and (2) were met, so that petitioners' motion was required to be granted by the terms of the statute. It nonetheless denied the motion, agreeing with respondents that § 27A(b) is unconstitutional. The United States Court of Appeals for the Sixth Circuit affirmed....

. . .

III

... We conclude that in § 27A(b) Congress has exceeded its authority by requiring the federal courts to exercise "the judicial Power of the United States," U.S. Const., Art. III, § 1, in a manner repugnant to the text, structure and traditions of Article III.

Our decisions to date have identified two types of legislation that require federal courts to exercise the judicial power in a manner that Article III forbids. The first appears in United States v. Klein, 13 Wall. 128 (1872), where we refused to give effect to a statute that was said "[t]o prescribe rules of decision to the Judicial Department of the government in cases pending before it." Id., at 146. Whatever the precise scope of *Klein*, however, later decisions have made clear that its prohibition does not take hold when Congress "amend[s] applicable law." ... Section 27A(b) indisputably does set out substantive legal standards for the Judiciary to apply, and in that sense changes the law (even if solely retroactively). The second type of unconstitutional restriction upon the exercise of judicial power identified by past cases is exemplified by Hayburn's Case, 2 Dall. 409 (1792), which stands for the principle that Congress cannot vest review of the decisions of Article III courts in officials of the Executive Branch.... Yet under any application of § 27A(b) only courts are involved; no officials of other departments sit in direct review of their decisions. Section 27A(b) therefore offends neither of these previously established prohibitions.

We think, however, that § 27A(b) offends a postulate of Article III just as deeply rooted in our law as those we have mentioned. Article III establishes a "judicial department" with the "province and duty ... to say what the law is" in particular cases and controversies. Marbury v. Madison, 1 Cranch 137, 177 (1803). The record of history shows that the Framers crafted this charter of the judicial department with an expressed understanding that it gives the Federal Judiciary the power, not merely to rule on cases, but to decide them, subject to review only by superior courts in the Article III hierarchy—with an understanding, in short, that "a judgment conclusively resolves the case" because "a 'judicial Power' is one to render dispositive judgments." Easterbrook, Presidential Review, 40 Case W. Res. L. Rev. 905, 926 (1990). By retroactively commanding the federal courts to reopen final judgments, Congress has violated this fundamental principle.

A

The Framers of our Constitution lived among the ruins of a system of intermingled legislative and judicial powers, which had been prevalent in the colonies long before the Revolution, and which after the Revolution had produced factional strife and partisan oppression. In the 17th and 18th centuries colonial assemblies and legislatures functioned as courts of equity of last resort, hearing original actions or providing appellate review of judicial judgments.... Often, however, they chose to correct the judicial process through special bills or other enacted legislation. It was common for such legislation not to prescribe a resolution of the dispute, but rather simply to set aside the judgment and order a new trial or appeal.... Thus, as described in our discussion of Hayburn's Case, such legislation bears not on the problem of inter-branch review but on the problem of finality of judicial judgments.

The vigorous, indeed often radical, populism of the revolutionary legislatures and assemblies increased the frequency of legislative correction of judgments.... Voices from many quarters, official as well as private, decried the increasing legislative interference with the private-law judgments of the courts. In 1786 the Vermont Council of Censors issued an "Address of the Council of Censors to the Freemen of the State of Vermont," to fulfill the Council's duty, under the State Constitution of 1784, to report to the people " 'whether the legislative and executive branches of government have assumed to themselves, or exercised, other or greater powers than they are entitled to by the Constitution.' " ... A principal method of usurpation identified by the Censors was "[t]he instances ... of judgments being vacated by legislative acts." ...

So too, the famous report of the Pennsylvania Council of Censors in 1784 detailed the abuses of legislative interference with the courts at the behest of private interests and factions. As the General Assembly had (they wrote) made a custom of "extending their deliberations to the cases of individuals," the people had "been taught to consider an application to the legislature, as a shorter and more certain mode of obtaining relief from hardships and losses, than the usual process of law." ...

This sense of a sharp necessity to separate the legislative from the judicial power, prompted by the crescendo of legislative interference with private judgments of the courts, triumphed among the Framers of the new Federal Constitution.... The Convention made the critical decision to establish a judicial department independent of the Legislative Branch by providing that "the judicial Power of the United States shall be vested in one supreme Court, and in such inferior Courts as the Congress may from time to time ordain and establish." Before and during the debates on ratification, Madison, Jefferson, and Hamilton each wrote of the factional disorders and disarray that the system of legislative equity had produced in the years before the framing; and each thought that the separation of the legislative from the judicial power in the new Constitution would cure them....

. . .

Judicial decisions in the period immediately after ratification of the Constitution confirm the understanding that it forbade interference with the final judgments of courts. In Calder v. Bull, 3 Dall. 386 (1798), the Legislature of Connecticut had enacted a statute that set aside the final judgment of a state court in a civil case. Although the issue before this Court was the construction of the Ex Post Facto Clause, Art. I, § 10, Justice Iredell (a leading Federalist who had guided the Constitution to ratification in North Carolina) noted that "the Legislature of [Connecticut] has been in the uniform, uninterrupted, habit of exercising a general superintending power over its courts of law, by granting new trials. It may, indeed, appear strange to some of us, that in any form, there should exist a power to grant, with respect to suits depending or adjudged, new rights of trial, new privileges of proceeding, not previously recognized and regulated by positive institutions.... The power ... is judicial in its nature; and whenever it is exercised, as in the present instance, it is an exercise of judicial, not of legislative, authority." Id., at 398. The state courts of the era showed a similar understanding of the separation of powers, in decisions that drew little distinction between the federal and state constitutions....

By the middle of the 19th century, the constitutional equilibrium created by the separation of the legislative power to make general law from the judicial power to apply that law in particular cases was so well understood and accepted that it could survive even Dred Scott v. Sandford, 19 How. 393 (1857). In his First Inaugural Address, President Lincoln explained why the political branches could not, and need not, interfere with even that infamous judgment: "I do not forget the position assumed by some, that constitutional questions are to be decided by the Supreme Court; nor do I deny that such decisions must be binding in any case, upon the parties to a suit, as to the object of that suit.... And while it is obviously possible that such decision may be erroneous in any given case, still the evil effect following it, being limited to that particular case, with the chance that it may be over-ruled, and

never become a precedent for other cases, can better be borne than could
the evils of a different practice." ...

B

Section 27A(b) effects a clear violation of the separation-of-powers
principle we have just discussed. It is, of course, retroactive legislation
.... When retroactive legislation requires its own application in a case
already finally adjudicated, it does no more and no less than "reverse a
determination once made, in a particular case." The Federalist No. 81,
p. 545 (J. Cooke ed. 1961). Our decisions stemming from Hayburn's
Case ... have uniformly provided fair warning that such an act exceeds
the powers of Congress....

It is true, as petitioners contend, that Congress can always revise
the judgments of Article III courts in one sense: When a new law makes
clear that it is retroactive, an appellate court must apply that law in
reviewing judgments still on appeal that were rendered before the law
was enacted, and must alter the outcome accordingly.... Since that is
so, petitioners argue, federal courts must apply the "new" law created by
§ 27A(b) in finally adjudicated cases as well; for the line that separates
lower court judgments that are pending on appeal (or may still be
appealed), from lower court judgments that are final, is determined by
statute ... and so cannot possibly be a constitutional line. But a
distinction between judgments from which all appeals have been forgone
or completed, and judgments that remain on appeal (or subject to being
appealed), is implicit in what Article III creates: not a batch of unconnected courts, but a judicial department composed of "inferior Courts"
and "one supreme Court." Within that hierarchy, the decision of an
inferior court is not (unless the time for appeal has expired) the final
word of the department as a whole. It is the obligation of the last court
in the hierarchy that rules on the case to give effect to Congress's latest
enactment, even when that has the effect of overturning the judgment of
an inferior court, since each court, at every level, must "decide according
to existing laws." ... Having achieved finality, however, a judicial
decision becomes the last word of the judicial department with regard to
a particular case or controversy, and Congress may not declare by
retroactive legislation that the law applicable to that very case was
something other than what the courts said it was. Finality of a legal
judgment is determined by statute, just as entitlement to a government
benefit is a statutory creation; but that no more deprives the former of
its constitutional significance for separation-of-powers analysis than it
deprives the latter of its significance for due process purposes....

To be sure, § 27A(b) reopens (or directs the reopening of) final
judgments in a whole class of cases rather than in a particular suit. We
do not see how that makes any difference. The separation-of-powers
violation here, if there is any, consists of depriving judicial judgments of
the conclusive effect that they had when they were announced, not of
acting in a manner—viz., with particular rather than general effect—
that is unusual (though, we must note, not impossible) for a legislature.
To be sure, a general statute such as this one may reduce the perception
that legislative interference with judicial judgments was prompted by

individual favoritism; but it is legislative interference with judicial judgments nonetheless. Not favoritism, nor even corruption, but power is the object of the separation-of-powers prohibition. The prohibition is violated when an individual final judgment is legislatively rescinded for even the very best of reasons, such as the legislature's genuine conviction (supported by all the law professors in the land) that the judgment was wrong; and it is violated 40 times over when 40 final judgments are legislatively dissolved.

It is irrelevant as well that the final judgments reopened by § 27A(b) rested on the bar of a statute of limitations. The rules of finality, both statutory and judge-made, treat a dismissal on statute-of-limitations grounds the same way they treat a dismissal for failure to state a claim, for failure to prove substantive liability, or for failure to prosecute: as a judgment on the merits.... Petitioners suggest, directly or by implication, two reasons why a merits judgment based on this particular ground may be uniquely subject to congressional nullification. First, there is the fact that the length and indeed even the very existence of a statute of limitations upon a federal cause of action is entirely subject to congressional control. But virtually all of the reasons why a final judgment on the merits is rendered on a federal claim are subject to congressional control. Congress can eliminate, for example, a particular element of a cause of action that plaintiffs have found it difficult to establish; or an evidentiary rule that has often excluded essential testimony; or a rule of offsetting wrong (such as contributory negligence) that has often prevented recovery. To distinguish statutes of limitations on the ground that they are mere creatures of Congress is to distinguish them not at all. The second supposedly distinguishing characteristic of a statute of limitations is that it can be extended, without violating the Due Process Clause, after the cause of the action arose and even after the statute itself has expired.... But that also does not set statutes of limitations apart. To mention only one other broad category of judgment-producing legal rule: rules of pleading and proof can similarly be altered after the cause of action arises, ... and even, if the statute clearly so requires, after they have been applied in a case but before final judgment has been entered. Petitioners' principle would therefore lead to the conclusion that final judgments rendered on the basis of a stringent (or, alternatively, liberal) rule of pleading or proof may be set aside for retrial under a new liberal (or, alternatively, stringent) rule of pleading or proof. This alone provides massive scope for undoing final judgments and would substantially subvert the doctrine of separation of powers.

The central theme of the dissent is a variant on these arguments. The dissent maintains that *Lampf* "announced" a new statute of limitations in an act of "judicial ... lawmaking," that "changed the law." ... *Lampf* as such is irrelevant to this case. The dissent itself perceives that "[w]e would have the same issue to decide had Congress enacted the *Lampf* rule," and that the *Lampf* rule's genesis in judicial lawmaking rather than, shall we say, legislative lawmaking, "should not affect the separation-of-powers analysis." Just so. The issue here is not the validity or even the source of the legal rule that produced the Article III judgments, but rather the immunity from legislative abrogation of those judgments themselves....

C

Apart from the statute we review today, we know of no instance in which Congress has attempted to set aside the final judgment of an Article III court by retroactive legislation. That prolonged reticence would be amazing if such interference were not understood to be constitutionally proscribed. The closest analogue that the Government has been able to put forward is the statute at issue in United States v. Sioux Nation, 448 U.S. 371 (1980). That law required the Court of Claims, " '[n]otwithstanding any other provision of law ... to review on the merits, without regard to the defense of res judicata or collateral estoppel,' "a Sioux claim for just compensation from the United States— even though the Court of Claims had previously heard and rejected that very claim. We considered and rejected separation-of-powers objections to the statute based upon Hayburn's Case and United States v. Klein.... The basis for our rejection was a line of precedent ... that stood, we said, for the proposition that "Congress has the power to waive the res judicata effect of a prior judgment entered in the Government's favor on a claim against the United States." ...

The Solicitor General suggests that even if *Sioux Nation* is read in accord with its holding, it nonetheless establishes that Congress may require Article III courts to reopen their final judgments, since "if res judicata were compelled by Article III to safeguard the structural independence of the courts, the doctrine would not be subject to waiver by any party litigant." But the proposition that legal defenses based upon doctrines central to the courts' structural independence can never be waived simply does not accord with our cases. Certainly one such doctrine consists of the "judicial Power" to disregard an unconstitutional statute, see *Marbury*, 1 Cranch, at 177; yet none would suggest that a litigant may never waive the defense that a statute is unconstitutional.... What may follow from our holding that the judicial power unalterably includes the power to render final judgments, is not that waivers of res judicata are always impermissible, but rather that, as many federal Courts of Appeals have held, waivers of res judicata need not always be accepted—that trial courts may in appropriate cases raise the res judicata bar on their own motion.... Waiver subject to the control of the courts themselves would obviously raise no issue of separation of powers, and would be precisely in accord with the language of the decision that the Solicitor General relies upon....

. . .

The dissent promises to provide "[a] few contemporary examples" of statutes retroactively requiring final judgments to be reopened, "to demonstrate that [such statutes] are ordinary products of the exercise of legislative power." That promise is not kept. The relevant retroactivity, of course, consists not of the requirement that there be set aside a judgment that has been rendered prior to its being setting aside—for example, a statute passed today which says that all default judgments rendered in the future may be reopened within 90 days after their entry. In that sense, all requirements to reopen are "retroactive," and the designation is superfluous. Nothing we say today precludes a law such as that. The finality that a court can pronounce is no more than what the law in existence at the time of judgment will permit it to pronounce. If the law then applicable says that the judgment may be reopened for certain reasons, that limitation is built into the judgment itself, and its finality is so conditioned. The present case, however, involves a judgment that Congress subjected to a reopening requirement which did not exist when the judgment was pronounced. The dissent provides not a single clear prior instance of such congressional action.

. . .

Finally, we may respond to the suggestion of the concurrence that this case should be decided more narrowly. The concurrence is willing to acknowledge only that "sometimes Congress lacks the power under Article I to reopen an otherwise closed court judgment". In the present context, what it considers critical is that § 27A(b) is "exclusively retroactive" and "appli[es] to a limited number of individuals." If Congress had only "provid[ed] some of the assurances against 'singling out' that ordinary legislative activity normally provides—say, prospectivity and general applicability—we might have a different case."

This seems to us wrong in both fact and law. In point of fact, § 27A(b) does not "single out" any defendant for adverse treatment (or any plaintiff for favorable treatment). Rather, it identifies a class of actions (those filed pre-*Lampf*, timely under applicable state law, but dismissed as time barred post-*Lampf*) which embraces many plaintiffs and defendants, the precise number and identities of whom we even now do not know. The concurrence's contention that the number of covered defendants "is too small (compared with the number of similar, uncovered firms) to distinguish meaningfully the law before us from a similar law aimed at a single closed case," renders the concept of "singling out" meaningless.

More importantly, however, the concurrence's point seems to us wrong in law. To be sure, the class of actions identified by § 27A(b) could have been more expansive (e.g., all actions that were or could have been filed pre-*Lampf*) and the provision could have been written to have prospective as well as retroactive effect (e.g., "all post-*Lampf* dismissed actions, plus all future actions under Rule 10b–5, shall be timely if brought within 30 years of the injury"). But it escapes us how this could in any way cause the statute to be any less an infringement upon the judicial power. The nub of that infringement consists not of the Legislature's acting in a particularized and hence (according to the concur rence) nonlegislative fashion; but rather of the Legislature's nullifying prior, authoritative judicial action. It makes no difference whatever to that separation-of-powers violation that it is in gross rather than particularized (e.g., "we hereby set aside all hitherto entered judicial orders"), or that it is not accompanied by an "almost" violation of the Bill of Attainder Clause, or an "almost" violation of any other constitutional provision.

... The delphic alternative suggested by the concurrence (the setting aside of judgments is all right so long as Congress does not "impermissibly tr[y] to apply, as well as make, the law") simply prolongs doubt and multiplies confrontation. Separation of powers, a distinctively American political doctrine, profits from the advice authored by a distinctively American poet: Good fences make good neighbors.

* * *

We know of no previous instance in which Congress has enacted retroactive legislation requiring an Article III court to set aside a final judgment, and for good reason. The Constitution's separation of legislative and judicial powers denies it the authority to do so. Section 27A(b) is unconstitutional to the extent that it requires federal courts to reopen final judgments entered before its enactment. The judgment of the Court of Appeals is affirmed.

It is so ordered.

Justice Breyer, concurring in the judgment.

[I]t is ... unnecessary for the purposes of this case to decide, that separation of powers "is violated" whenever an "individual final judgment is legislatively rescinded" or that it is "violated 40 times over when 40 final judgments are legislatively dissolved." I therefore write separately.

The majority provides strong historical evidence that Congress lacks the power simply to reopen, and to revise, final judgments in individual cases.... For one thing, the authoritative application of a general law to a particular case by an independent judge, rather than by the legislature itself, provides an assurance that even an unfair law at least will be applied evenhandedly according to its terms.... For another thing, as Justice Powell has pointed out, the Constitution's "separation of powers" principles reflect, in part, the Framers' "concern that a legislature should not be able unilaterally to impose a substantial deprivation on one person." INS v. Chadha, 462 U.S. 919, 962 (1983) (Powell, J., concurring in judgment)....

Despite these two important "separation of powers" concerns, sometimes Congress can enact legislation that focuses upon a small group, or even a single individual.... Statutes that apply prospectively and (in part because of that prospectivity) to an open-ended class of persons, however, are more than simply an effort to apply, person by person, a previously-enacted law, or to single out for oppressive treatment one, or a handful, of particular individuals. Thus, it seems to me, if Congress enacted legislation that reopened an otherwise closed judgment but in a way that mitigated some of the here relevant "separation of powers" concerns, by also providing some of the assurances against "singling out" that ordinary legislative activity normally provides—say, prospectivity and general applicability—we might have a different case.... Because such legislation, in light of those mitigating circumstances, might well present a different constitutional question, I do not subscribe to the Court's more absolute statement.

The statute before us, however, has no such mitigating features. It reopens previously closed judgments. It is entirely retroactive, applying only to those Rule 10b–5 actions actually filed, on or before (but on which final judgments were entered after) June 19, 1991.... It lacks generality, for it applies only to a few individual instances. And, it is underinclusive, for it excludes from its coverage others who, relying upon pre-*Lampf* limitations law, may have failed to bring timely securities fraud actions against any other of the Nation's hundreds of thousands of businesses....

The upshot is that, viewed in light of the relevant, liberty-protecting objectives of the "separation of powers," this case falls directly within the scope of language in this Court's cases suggesting a restriction on Congress' power to reopen closed court judgments....

At the same time, because the law before us both reopens final judgments and lacks the liberty-protecting assurances that prospectivity and greater generality would have provided, we need not, and we should not, go further—to make of the reopening itself, an absolute, always determinative distinction, a "prophylactic device," or a foundation for the building of a new "high wal[l]" between the branches. Indeed, the unnecessary building of such walls is, in itself, dangerous, because the Constitution blends, as well as separates, powers in its effort to create a government that will work for, as well as protect the liberties of, its citizens.... As the majority invokes the advice of an American poet, one might consider as well that poet's caution, for he not only notes that "Something there is that doesn't love a wall," but also writes, "Before I built a wall I'd ask to know/ What I was walling in or walling out." R. Frost, Mending Wall, The New Oxford Book of American Verse 395–396 (R. Ellmann ed. 1976).

. . .

Justice Stevens, with whom Justice Ginsburg joins, dissenting.

. . .

A large class of investors reasonably and in good faith thought they possessed rights of action before the surprising announcement of the *Lampf* rule on June 20, 1991. When it enacted the 1991 amendment, Congress clearly expressed its intent to restore the rights *Lampf* had denied the aggrieved class....

... [H]istory and precedent demonstrate that Congress may enact laws that establish both substantive rules and procedures for reopening final judgments. When it enacted the 1991 amendment to the *Lampf* rule, Congress did not encroach on the judicial power. It decided neither the merits of any 10b–5 claim nor even whether any such claim should proceed to decision on the merits. It did provide that the rule governing the timeliness of 10b–5 actions pending on June 19, 1991, should be the pre-*Lampf* statute of limitations, and it also established a procedure for Article III courts to apply in determining whether any dismissed case should be reinstated. Congress' decision to extend that rule and procedure to 10b–5 actions dismissed during the brief period between this

Court's law-changing decision in *Lampf* and Congress' remedial action is not a sufficient reason to hold the statute unconstitutional.

. . .

. . . [I]n the examples of colonial legislatures' review of trial courts' judgments on which today's holding rests, the legislatures issued directives in individual cases without purporting either to set forth or to apply any legal standard. . . .   The Framers' disapproval of such a system of ad hoc legislative review of individual trial court judgments has no bearing on . . . the 1991 amendment at issue today. The history on which the Court relies provides no support for its holding.

III

The lack of precedent for the Court's holding is not, of course, a sufficient reason to reject it. Correct application of separation-of-powers principles, however, confirms that the Court has reached the wrong result. As our most recent major pronouncement on the separation of powers noted, "we have never held that the Constitution requires that the three branches of Government 'operate with absolute independence.'"   Morrison v. Olson, 487 U.S. 654, 693–694 (1988) (quoting United States v. Nixon, 418 U.S. 683, 707 (1974)). Rather, our jurisprudence reflects "Madison's flexible approach to separation of powers." Mistretta v. United States, 488 U.S. 361, 380 (1989). In accepting Madison's conception rather than any "hermetic division among the Branches," id., at 381, "we have upheld statutory provisions that to some degree commingle the functions of the Branches, but that pose no danger of either aggrandizement or encroachment."   Id., at 382. Today's holding does not comport with these ideals.

. . .

The majority's rigid holding unnecessarily hinders the Government from addressing difficult issues that inevitably arise in a complex society. . . .

. . .

The Court has drawn the wrong lesson from the Framers' disapproval of colonial legislatures' appellate review of judicial decisions. The Framers rejected that practice, not out of a mechanistic solicitude for "final judgments," but because they believed the impartial application of rules of law, rather than the will of the majority, must govern the disposition of individual cases and controversies. Any legislative interference in the adjudication of the merits of a particular case carries the risk that political power will supplant evenhanded justice, whether the interference occurs before or after the entry of final judgment. Cf. United States v. Klein, 13 Wall. 128 (1872); Hayburn's Case, 2 Dall. 408 (1792). Section 27A(b) neither commands the reinstatement of any particular case nor directs any result on the merits. Congress recently granted a special benefit to a single litigant in a pending civil rights case, but the Court saw no need even to grant certiorari to review that disturbing legislative favor. In an ironic counterpoint, the Court today places a higher priority on protecting the Republic from the restoration to a large class of litigants of the opportunity to have Article III courts resolve the merits of their claims.

"We must remember that the machinery of government would not work if it were not allowed a little play in its joints." Bain Peanut Co. of Texas v. Pinson, 282 U.S. 499, 501 (1931)(Holmes, J.).   The three Branches must cooperate in order to govern. We should regard favorably, rather than with suspicious hostility, legislation that enables the judiciary to overcome impediments to the performance of its mission of administering justice impartially, even when, as here, this Court has created the impediment. Rigid rules often make good law, but judgments in areas such as the review of potential conflicts among the three coequal Branches of the Federal Government partake of art as well as science. . . .

Accordingly, I respectfully dissent.

Part III

GOVERNMENT AND THE INDIVIDUAL: THE PROTECTION OF LIBERTY AND PROPERTY UNDER THE DUE PROCESS AND EQUAL PROTECTION CLAUSES

Chapter 8

THE BILL OF RIGHTS, THE CIVIL WAR AMENDMENTS AND THEIR INTERRELATIONSHIP

SECTION 3. APPLICATION OF THE BILL OF RIGHTS TO THE STATES

Page 510.   Add footnote "a" to the end of the first indented paragraph:

a   Compare with *Haslip* the Court's subsequent decision in Honda Motor Co. v. Oberg, 114 S.Ct. 2331 (1994), invalidating under due process Oregon's denial of judicial review of the size of punitive damage awards. Noting that "[o]ur recent cases have recognized a substantive limit on the size of punitive damage awards" and that judicial review as a safeguard against excessive verdicts was a well-established common law tradition from which Oregon alone had deviated (and had done so without providing a substitute procedure), Justice Stevens observed for the majority in pertinent part:

"Oregon's abrogation of a well-established common law protection against arbitrary deprivations of property raises a presumption that its procedures violate the Due Process Clause. . . . [T]raditional practice provides a touchstone for constitutional analysis. . . . Because the basic procedural protections of the common law have been regarded as so fundamental, very few cases have arisen in which a party has complained of their denial. In fact, most of our Due Process decisions involve arguments that traditional protections provide too little protection and that additional safeguards are necessary to ensure compliance with the Constitution. . . .   Pacific Mut. Life Ins. v. Haslip. . . ."

Chapter 9

THE DUE PROCESS, CONTRACT, AND JUST COMPENSATION CLAUSES AND THE REVIEW OF THE REASONABLENESS OF LEGISLATION

SECTION 1. ECONOMIC REGULATORY LEGISLATION

C. THE JUST COMPENSATION CLAUSE OF THE FIFTH AMENDMENT—WHAT DOES IT ADD TO DUE PROCESS?

2. MANDATED ACCESS TO PROPERTY

Page 569. Replace Nollan v. California Coastal Commission with the following:

DOLAN v. CITY OF TIGARD
___ U.S. ___, 114 S.Ct. 2309, 129 L.Ed.2d 304 (1994).

Chief Justice Rehnquist delivered the opinion of the Court.

Petitioner challenges the decision of the Oregon Supreme Court which held that the city of Tigard could condition the approval of her building permit on the dedication of a portion of her property for flood control and traffic improvements.... We granted certiorari to resolve a question left open by our decision in Nollan v. California Coastal Comm'n, 483 U.S. 825 (1987), of what is the required degree of connection between the exactions imposed by the city and the projected impacts of the proposed development.

I

... [The City's] Community Development Code (CDC) ... requires property owners in the area zoned Central Business District to comply with a 15% open space and landscaping requirement [and also] requires that new development facilitate [the city's plan for a pedestrian/bicycle pathway intended to encourage alternatives to automobile transportation for short trips] by dedicating land ... where provided for in the ... plan.

The city['s] ... Master Drainage Plan ... noted that flooding occurred in several areas along Fanno Creek, including areas near petitioner's property[, and] established that the increase in impervious surfaces associated with continued urbanization would exacerbate these flooding problems. To combat these risks, the Drainage Plan suggested a series of improvements to the Fanno Creek Basin, including channel excavation in the area next to petitioner's property.... Other recommendations included ensuring that the floodplain remains free of structures and that it be preserved as greenways to minimize flood damage to structures....

Petitioner Florence Dolan owns a plumbing and electric supply store ... in the Central Business District ... [on a 1.67–acre lot, through and along part of which Fanno Creek flows.] The year-round flow of the creek renders the area within the creek's 100–year floodplain virtually unusable for commercial development. The city's comprehensive plan includes the Fanno Creek floodplain as part of the city's greenway system.

Petitioner applied to the city for a permit to ... nearly doubl[e] the size of the store to 17,600 square feet, ... pav[e] a 39–space parking lot[, and in a] second phase of the project, ... to build an additional structure ... for complementary businesses, and to provide more parking. The proposed expansion and intensified use are consistent with the city's zoning scheme in the Central Business District....

The City Planning Commission granted petitioner's permit application subject to conditions imposed by the city's CDC[, including requirements] that petitioner dedicate the portion of her property lying within the 100–year floodplain for improvement of a storm drainage system along Fanno Creek and that she dedicate an additional 15–foot strip of land adjacent to the floodplain as a pedestrian/bicycle pathway. The dedication required ... encompasses approximately 7,000 square feet, or roughly 10% of the property. In accordance with city practice, petitioner could rely on the dedicated property to meet the 15% open space and landscaping requirement mandated by the city's zoning scheme....

Petitioner requested variances from the CDC standards[,] ... argu[ing] that her proposed development would not conflict with the policies of the comprehensive plan.... The Commission denied the request.

The Commission made a series of findings concerning the relationship between the dedicated conditions and the projected impacts of petitioner's project. First, the Commission noted that "[i]t is reasonable to assume that customers and employees of the future uses of this site could utilize a pedestrian/bicycle pathway adjacent to this development for their transportation and recreational needs." ... The Commission noted that the site plan has provided for bicycle parking in a rack in front of the proposed building and "[i]t is reasonable to expect that some of the users of the bicycle parking provided for by the site plan will use the pathway adjacent to Fanno Creek if it is constructed." ... In addition, the Commission found that creation of a convenient, safe pedestrian/bicycle pathway system as an alternative means of transportation "could offset some of the traffic demand on [nearby] streets and lessen the increase in traffic congestion." ...

The Commission went on to note that the required floodplain dedication would be reasonably related to petitioner's request to intensify the use of the site given the increase in the impervious surface. The Commission stated that the "anticipated increased storm water flow from the subject property to an already strained creek and drainage basin can only add to the public need to manage the stream channel and floodplain for drainage purposes." ... Based on this anticipated increased storm water flow, the Commission concluded that "the requirement of dedication of the floodplain area on the site is related to the applicant's plan to intensify development on the site." ...

[Petitioner's administrative and state court appeals were unsuccessful.]

II

The Takings Clause of the Fifth Amendment of the United States Constitution, made applicable to the States through the Fourteenth Amendment, Chicago, B. & Q.R. Co. v. Chicago, 166 U.S. 226, 239 (1897), provides: "[N]or shall private property be taken for public use, without just compensation." [5] One of the principal purposes of the Takings Clause is "to bar Government from forcing some people alone to bear public burdens which, in all fairness and justice, should be borne by the public as a whole." Armstrong v. United States, 364 U.S. 40, 49 (1960). Without question, had the city simply required petitioner to dedicate a strip of land along Fanno Creek for public use, rather than conditioning the grant of her permit to redevelop her property on such a dedication, a taking would have occurred. Nollan, supra, at 831. Such public access would deprive petitioner of the right to exclude others, "one of the most essential sticks in the bundle of rights that are commonly characterized as property." Kaiser Aetna v. United States, 444 U.S. 164, 176 (1979).

On the other side of the ledger, the authority of state and local governments to engage in land use planning has been sustained against constitutional challenge as long ago as our decision in Euclid v. Ambler Realty Co., 272 U.S. 365 (1926). "Government hardly could go on if to some extent values incident to property could not be diminished without paying for every such change in the general law." Pennsylvania Coal Co. v. Mahon, 260 U.S. 393, 413 (1922). A land use regulation does not effect a taking if it "substantially advance[s] legitimate state interests" and does not "den[y] an owner economically viable use of his land." Agins v. Tiburon, 447 U.S. 255, 260 (1980).

The sort of land use regulations discussed in the cases just cited, however, differ in two relevant particulars from the present case. First, they involved essentially legislative determinations classifying entire areas of the city, whereas here the city made an adjudicative decision to condition petitioner's application for a building permit on an individual parcel. Second, the conditions imposed were not simply a limitation on the use petitioner might make of her own parcel, but a requirement that

---

[5] Justice Stevens' dissent suggests that this case is actually grounded in "substantive" due process, rather than in the view that the Takings Clause of the Fifth Amendment was made applicable to the States by the Fourteenth Amendment. But there is no doubt that later cases have held that the Fourteenth Amendment does make the Takings Clause of the Fifth Amendment applicable to the States, see Penn Central Transp. Co. v. New York City, 438 U.S. 104, 122 (1978); Nollan v. California Coastal Comm'n, 483 U.S. 825, 827 (1987)....

she deed portions of the property to the city. In *Nollan,* supra, we held that governmental authority to exact such a condition was circumscribed by the Fifth and Fourteenth Amendments. Under the well-settled doctrine of "unconstitutional conditions," the government may not require a person to give up a constitutional right—here the right to receive just compensation when property is taken for a public use—in exchange for a discretionary benefit conferred by the government where the property sought has little or no relationship to the benefit. See Perry v. Sindermann, 408 U.S. 593 (1972); Pickering v. Board of Ed. of Township High School Dist., 391 U.S. 563, 568 (1968).

Petitioner contends that the city has forced her to choose between the building permit and her right under the Fifth Amendment to just compensation for the public easements. Petitioner does not quarrel with the city's authority to exact some forms of dedication as a condition for the grant of a building permit, but challenges the showing made by the city to justify these exactions. She argues that the city has identified "no special benefits" conferred on her, and has not identified any "special quantifiable burdens" created by her new store that would justify the particular dedications required from her which are not required from the public at large.

III

In evaluating petitioner's claim, we must first determine whether the "essential nexus" exists between the "legitimate state interest" and the permit condition exacted by the city. Nollan, 483 U.S., at 837. If we find that a nexus exists, we must then decide the required degree of connection between the exactions and the projected impact of the proposed development. We were not required to reach this question in *Nollan,* because we concluded that the connection did not meet even the loosest standard. 483 U.S., at 838. Here, however, we must decide this question.

A

We addressed the essential nexus question in *Nollan.* The California Coastal Commission demanded a lateral public easement across the Nollan's beachfront lot in exchange for a permit to demolish an existing bungalow and replace it with a three-bedroom house.... The public easement was designed to connect two public beaches that were separated by the Nollan's property. The Coastal Commission had asserted that the public easement condition was imposed to promote the legitimate state interest of diminishing the "blockage of the view of the ocean" caused by construction of the larger house.

We agreed that the Coastal Commission's concern with protecting visual access to the ocean constituted a legitimate public interest.... We also agreed that the permit condition would have been constitutional "even if it consisted of the requirement that the Nollans provide a viewing spot on their property for passersby with whose sighting of the ocean their new house would interfere." ... We resolved, however, that the Coastal Commission's regulatory authority was set completely adrift from its constitutional moorings when it claimed that a nexus existed between visual access to the ocean and a permit condition requiring lateral public access along the Nollan's beachfront lot. . . . How enhancing the public's ability to "traverse to and along the shorefront" served the same governmental purpose of "visual access to the ocean" from the roadway was beyond our ability to countenance. The absence of a nexus left the Coastal Commission in the position of simply trying to obtain an easement through gimmickry, which converted a valid regulation of land use into "an out-and-out plan of extortion." . . .

No such gimmicks are associated with the permit conditions imposed by the city in this case. Undoubtedly, the prevention of flooding along Fanno Creek and the reduction of traffic congestion in the Central Business District qualify as the type of legitimate public purposes we have upheld. . . . It seems equally obvious that a nexus exists between preventing flooding along Fanno Creek and limiting development within the creek's 100–year floodplain. Petitioner proposes to . . . expand[ ] the impervious surface on the property and [thus] increas[e] the amount of stormwater run-off into Fanno Creek.

The same may be said for the city's attempt to reduce traffic congestion by providing for alternative means of transportation. In theory, a pedestrian/bicycle pathway provides a useful alternative means of transportation for workers and shoppers. . . .

B

The second part of our analysis requires us to determine whether the degree of the exactions demanded by the city's permit conditions bear the required relationship to the projected impact of petitioner's proposed development. Nollan, supra, at 834, quoting Penn Central, 438 U.S. 104, 127 (1978)(" '[A] use restriction may constitute a taking if not reasonably necessary to the effectuation of a substantial government purpose' "). Here the Oregon Supreme Court deferred to what it termed the "city's unchallenged factual findings" supporting the dedication conditions and found them to be reasonably related to the impact of the expansion of petitioner's business. . . .

. . . The city relies on the Commission's rather tentative findings that increased stormwater flow from petitioner's property "can only add to the public need to manage the [floodplain] for drainage purposes" to support its conclusion that the "requirement of dedication of the floodplain area on the site is related to the applicant's plan to intensify development on the site." . . .

The city made the following specific findings relevant to the pedestrian/bicycle pathway: "In addition, the proposed expanded use of this site is anticipated to generate additional vehicular traffic thereby increasing congestion on nearby collector and arterial streets. Creation of a convenient, safe pedestrian/bicycle pathway system as an alternative means of transportation could offset some of the traffic demand on these nearby streets and lessen the increase in traffic congestion." . . .

The question for us is whether these findings are constitutionally sufficient to justify the conditions imposed by the city on petitioner's building permit. Since state courts have been dealing with this question a good deal longer than we have, we turn to representative decisions made by them.

In some States, very generalized statements as to the necessary connection between the required dedication and the proposed development seem to suffice.... We think this standard is too lax to adequately protect petitioner's right to just compensation if her property is taken for a public purpose.

Other state courts require a very exacting correspondence, described as the "specifi[c] and uniquely attributable" test.... Under this standard, if the local government cannot demonstrate that its exaction is directly proportional to the specifically created need, the exaction becomes "a veiled exercise of the power of eminent domain and a confiscation of private property behind the defense of police regulations." ... We do not think the Federal Constitution requires such exacting scrutiny, given the nature of the interests involved.

A number of state courts have taken an intermediate position, requiring the municipality to show a "reasonable relationship" between the required dedication and the impact of the proposed development....

. . .

We think the "reasonable relationship" test adopted by a majority of the state courts is closer to the federal constitutional norm than either of those previously discussed. But we do not adopt it as such, partly because the term "reasonable relationship" seems confusingly similar to the term "rational basis" which describes the minimal level of scrutiny under the Equal Protection Clause of the Fourteenth Amendment. We think a term such as "rough proportionality" best encapsulates what we hold to be the requirement of the Fifth Amendment. No precise mathematical calculation is required, but the city must make some sort of individualized determination that the required dedication is related both in nature and extent to the impact of the proposed development.[8]

Justice Stevens' dissent relies upon a law review article for the proposition that the city's conditional demands for part of petitioner's property are "a species of business regulation that heretofore warranted a strong presumption of constitutional validity." But simply denominating a governmental measure as a "business regulation" does not immunize it from constitutional challenge on the grounds that it violates a provision of the Bill of Rights. In Marshall v. Barlow's, Inc., 436 U.S. 307 (1978), we held that a statute authorizing a warrantless search of business premises in order to detect OSHA violations violated the Fourth Amendment.... And in Central Hudson Gas & Electric Corp. v. Public Service Comm'n of N.Y., 447 U.S. 557 (1980), we held that an order of the New York Public Service Commission, designed to cut down the use

---

[8] Justice Stevens' dissent takes us to task for placing the burden on the city to justify the required dedication. He is correct in arguing that in evaluating most generally applicable zoning regulations, the burden properly rests on the party challenging the regulation to prove that it constitutes an arbitrary regulation of property rights. See, e.g., Euclid v. Ambler Realty Co., 272 U.S. 365 (1926). Here, by contrast, the city made an adjudicative decision to condition petitioner's application for a building permit on an individual parcel. In this situation, the burden properly rests on the city. See Nollan, 483 U.S., at 836....

of electricity because of a fuel shortage, violated the First Amendment insofar as it prohibited advertising by a utility company to promote the use of electricity. We see no reason why the Takings Clause of the Fifth Amendment, as much a part of the Bill of Rights as the First Amendment or Fourth Amendment, should be relegated to the status of a poor relation in these comparable circumstances. We turn now to analysis of whether the findings relied upon by the city here, first with respect to the floodplain easement, and second with respect to the pedestrian/bicycle path, satisfied these requirements.

It is axiomatic that increasing the amount of impervious surface will increase the quantity and rate of storm-water flow from petitioner's property.... Therefore, keeping the floodplain open and free from development would likely confine the pressures on Fanno Creek created by petitioner's development. In fact, because petitioner's property lies within the Central Business District, the Community Development Code already required that petitioner leave 15% of it as open space and the undeveloped floodplain would have nearly satisfied that requirement.... But the city demanded more—it not only wanted petitioner not to build in the floodplain, but it also wanted petitioner's property along Fanno Creek for its Greenway system. The city has never said why a public greenway, as opposed to a private one, was required in the interest of flood control.

The difference to petitioner, of course, is the loss of her ability to exclude others. As we have noted, this right to exclude others is "one of the most essential sticks in the bundle of rights that are commonly characterized as property." *Kaiser Aetna*, 444 U.S., at 176. It is difficult to see why recreational visitors trampling along petitioner's floodplain easement are sufficiently related to the city's legitimate interest in reducing flooding problems along Fanno Creek, and the city has not attempted to make any individualized determination to support this part of its request.

The city contends that recreational easement along the Greenway is only ancillary to the city's chief purpose in controlling flood hazards. It further asserts that unlike the residential property at issue in *Nollan*, petitioner's property is commercial in character and therefore, her right to exclude others is compromised.... The city maintains that "[t]here is nothing to suggest that preventing [petitioner] from prohibiting [the easements] will unreasonably impair the value of [her] property as a [retail store]." PruneYard Shopping Center v. Robins, 447 U.S. 74, 83 (1980).

Admittedly, petitioner wants to build a bigger store to attract members of the public to her property. She also wants, however, to be able to control the time and manner in which they enter. The recreational easement on the Greenway is different in character from the exercise of state-protected rights of free expression and petition that we permitted in *PruneYard*. In *PruneYard*, we held that a major private shopping center that attracted more than 25,000 daily patrons had to provide access to persons exercising their state constitutional rights to distribute pamphlets and ask passersby to sign their petitions.... We based our decision, in part, on the fact that the shopping center "may

restrict expressive activity by adopting time, place, and manner regulations that will minimize any interference with its commercial functions."
... By contrast, the city wants to impose a permanent recreational easement upon petitioner's property that borders Fanno Creek. Petitioner would lose all rights to regulate the time in which the public entered onto the Greenway, regardless of any interference it might pose with her retail store. Her right to exclude would not be regulated, it would be eviscerated.

If petitioner's proposed development had somehow encroached on existing greenway space in the city, it would have been reasonable to require petitioner to provide some alternative greenway space for the public either on her property or elsewhere. See Nollan, 483 U.S., at 836 ("Although such a requirement, constituting a permanent grant of continuous access to the property, would have to be considered a taking if it were not attached to a development permit, the Commission's assumed power to forbid construction of the house in order to protect the public's view of the beach must surely include the power to condition construction upon some concession by the owner, even a concession of property rights, that serves the same end"). But that is not the case here. We conclude that the findings upon which the city relies do not show the required reasonable relationship between the floodplain easement and the petitioner's proposed new building.

With respect to the pedestrian/bicycle pathway, we have no doubt that the city was correct in finding that the larger retail sales facility proposed by petitioner will increase traffic on the streets of the Central Business District. The city estimates that the proposed development would generate roughly 435 additional trips per day. Dedications for streets, sidewalks, and other public ways are generally reasonable exactions to avoid excessive congestion from a proposed property use. But on the record before us, the city has not met its burden of demonstrating that the additional number of vehicle and bicycle trips generated by the petitioner's development reasonably relate to the city's requirement for a dedication of the pedestrian/bicycle pathway easement. The city simply found that the creation of the pathway "could offset some of the traffic demand ... and lessen the increase in traffic congestion."

As Justice Peterson of the Supreme Court of Oregon explained in his dissenting opinion, however, "[t]he findings of fact that the bicycle pathway system 'could offset some of the traffic demand' is a far cry from a finding that the bicycle pathway system will, or is likely to, offset some of the traffic demand." ... No precise mathematical calculation is required, but the city must make some effort to quantify its findings in support of the dedication for the pedestrian/bicycle pathway beyond the conclusory statement that it could offset some of the traffic demand generated.

. . .

The judgment of the Supreme Court of Oregon is reversed, and the case is remanded for further proceedings consistent with this opinion.

Justice Stevens, with whom Justice Blackmun and Justice Ginsburg join, dissenting.

. . .

... The Court is correct in concluding that the city may not attach arbitrary conditions to a building permit or to a variance even when it can rightfully deny the application outright. ... Yet the Court's description of the doctrinal underpinnings of its decision, the phrasing of its fledgling test of "rough proportionality," and the application of that test to this case run contrary to the traditional treatment of these cases and break considerable and unpropitious new ground.

I

... The state cases the Court consults ... either fail to support or decidedly undermine the Court's conclusions in key respects.

. . .

Not one of the state cases cited by the Court announces anything akin to a "rough proportionality" requirement.... [A]lthough the[y] do lend support to the Court's reaffirmance of *Nollan*'s reasonable nexus requirement, the role the Court accords them in the announcement of its newly minted second phase of the constitutional inquiry is remarkably inventive.

In addition, the Court ignores the state courts' willingness to consider what the property owner gains from the exchange in question.... In this case, moreover, Dolan's acceptance of the permit, with its attached conditions, would provide her with benefits that may well go beyond any advantage she gets from expanding her business. As the United States pointed out at oral argument, the improvement that the city's drainage plan contemplates would widen the channel and reinforce the slopes to increase the carrying capacity during serious floods, "confer[ring] considerable benefits on the property owners immediately adjacent to the creek." ...

The state court decisions also are enlightening in the extent to which they required that the entire parcel be given controlling importance.... None of the decisions identified the surrender of the fee owner's "power to exclude" as having any special significance. Instead, the courts uniformly examined the character of the entire economic transaction.

II

It is not merely state cases, but our own cases as well, that require the analysis to focus on the impact of the city's action on the entire parcel of private property.... Although limitation of the right to exclude others undoubtedly constitutes a significant infringement upon property ownership, Kaiser Aetna v. United States, 444 U.S. 164, 179–180 (1979), restrictions on that right do not alone constitute a taking, and do not do so in any event unless they "unreasonably impair the value or use" of the property. PruneYard Shopping Center v. Robins, 447 U.S. 74, 82–84 (1980).

The Court's narrow focus on one strand in the property owner's bundle of rights is particularly misguided in a case involving the development of commercial property.... The exactions associated with the development of a retail business are ... a species of business regulation that heretofore warranted a strong presumption of constitutional validity.

... The city of Tigard has demonstrated that its plan is rational and impartial and that the conditions at issue are "conducive to fulfillment of authorized planning objectives." Dolan, on the other hand, has offered no evidence that her burden of compliance has any impact at all on the value or profitability of her planned development. Following the teaching of the cases on which it purports to rely, the Court should not isolate the burden associated with the loss of the power to exclude from an evaluation of the benefit to be derived from the permit to enlarge the store and the parking lot.

... Under the Court's approach, a city must not only "quantify its findings," and make "individualized determination[s]" with respect to the nature and the extent of the relationship between the conditions and the impact, but also demonstrate "proportionality." The correct inquiry should instead concentrate on whether the required nexus is present and venture beyond considerations of a condition's nature or germaneness only if the developer establishes that a concededly germane condition is so grossly disproportionate to the proposed development's adverse effects that it manifests motives other than land use regulation on the part of the city....

III

Applying its new standard, the Court finds two defects in the city's case.... Even under the Court's new rule, both defects are, at most, nothing more than harmless error.

In her objections to the floodplain condition, Dolan made no effort to demonstrate that the dedication of that portion of her property would be any more onerous than a simple prohibition against any development on that portion of her property. Given the commercial character of both the existing and the proposed use of the property as a retail store, it seems likely that potential customers "trampling along petitioner's floodplain," are more valuable than a useless parcel of vacant land. Moreover, the duty to pay taxes and the responsibility for potential tort liability may well make ownership of the fee interest in useless land a liability rather than an asset. That may explain why Dolan never conceded that she could be prevented from building on the floodplain....

The Court's rejection of the bike path condition amounts to nothing more than a play on words. Everyone agrees that the bike path "could" offset some of the increased traffic flow that the larger store will generate, but the findings do not unequivocally state that it will do so, or tell us just how many cyclists will replace motorists. Predictions on such matters are inherently nothing more than estimates. Certainly the assumption that there will be an offsetting benefit here is entirely reasonable and should suffice whether it amounts to 100 percent, 35 percent, or only 5 percent of the increase in automobile traffic that would otherwise occur. If the Court proposes to have the federal judiciary micromanage state decisions of this kind, it is indeed extending its welcome mat to a significant new class of litigants. . . . [P]roperty owners have surely found a new friend today.

IV

The Court has made a serious error by abandoning the traditional presumption of constitutionality and imposing a novel burden of proof on a city implementing an admittedly valid comprehensive land use plan. Even more consequential than its incorrect disposition of this case, however, is the Court's resurrection of a species of substantive due process analysis that it firmly rejected decades ago.

. . . Chicago, B. & Q.R. Co. v. Chicago, 166 U.S. 226, 239 (1897), . . . contains no mention of either the Takings Clause or the Fifth Amendment; it held that the protection afforded by the Due Process Clause of the Fourteenth Amendment extends to matters of substance as well as procedure, and that the substance of "the due process of law enjoined by the Fourteenth Amendment requires compensation to be made or adequately secured to the owner of private property taken for public use under the authority of a State." . . . It applied the same kind of substantive due process analysis more frequently identified with a better known case that accorded similar substantive protection to a baker's liberty interest in working 60 hours a week and 10 hours a day. See Lochner v. New York, 198 U.S. 45 (1905). Later cases have interpreted the Fourteenth Amendment's substantive protection against uncompensated deprivations of private property by the States as though it incorporated the text of the Fifth Amendment's Takings Clause. See, e.g., Keystone Bituminous Coal Assn. v. DeBenedictis, 480 U.S. 470, 481, n. 10 (1987). There was nothing problematic about that interpretation in cases enforcing the Fourteenth Amendment against state action that involved the actual physical invasion of private property. See Loretto v. Teleprompter Manhattan CATV Corp., 458 U.S. 419, 427–433 (1982); Kaiser Aetna v. United States, 444 U.S. 164, 178–180 (1979). Justice Holmes charted a significant new course, however, when he opined that a state law making it "commercially impracticable to mine certain coal" had "very nearly the same effect for constitutional purposes as appropriating or destroying it." Pennsylvania Coal Co. v. Mahon, 260 U.S. 393, 414 (1922). The so-called "regulatory takings" doctrine that the Holmes dictum kindled has an obvious kinship with the line of substantive due process cases that *Lochner* exemplified. Besides having similar ancestry, both doctrines are potentially open-ended sources of judicial power to invalidate state economic regulations that Members of this Court view as unwise or unfair.

This case inaugurates an even more recent judicial innovation than the regulatory takings doctrine: the application of the "unconstitutional conditions" label to a mutually beneficial transaction between a property owner and a city. . . . Dolan has no right to be compensated for a taking unless the city acquires the property interests that she has refused to surrender. Since no taking has yet occurred, there has not been any infringement of her constitutional right to compensation. . . .

Even if Dolan should accept the city's conditions in exchange for the benefit that she seeks, it would not necessarily follow that she had been denied "just compensation" since it would be appropriate to consider the receipt of that benefit in any calculation of "just compensation." . . . Particularly in the absence of any evidence on the point, we should not presume that the discretionary benefit the city has offered is less valuable than the property interests that Dolan can retain or surrender at her option. But even if that discretionary benefit were so trifling that it could not be considered just compensation when it has "little or no relationship" to the property, the Court fails to explain why the same value would suffice when the required nexus is present. In this respect, the Court's reliance on the "unconstitutional conditions" doctrine is assuredly novel, and arguably incoherent. The city's conditions are by no means immune from constitutional scrutiny. The level of scrutiny, however, does not approximate the kind of review that would apply if the city had insisted on a surrender of Dolan's First Amendment rights in exchange for a building permit. One can only hope that the Court's reliance today on First Amendment cases, and its candid disavowal of the term "rational basis" to describe its new standard of review, do not signify a reassertion of the kind of superlegislative power the Court exercised during the *Lochner* era.

. . .

In our changing world one thing is certain: uncertainty will characterize predictions about the impact of new urban developments on the risks of floods, earthquakes, traffic congestion, or environmental harms. When there is doubt concerning the magnitude of those impacts, the public interest in averting them must outweigh the private interest of the commercial entrepreneur. If the government can demonstrate that the conditions it has imposed in a land-use permit are rational, impartial and conducive to fulfilling the aims of a valid land-use plan, a strong presumption of validity should attach to those conditions. The burden of demonstrating that those conditions have unreasonably impaired the economic value of the proposed improvement belongs squarely on the shoulders of the party challenging the state action's constitutionality. That allocation of burdens has served us well in the past. The Court has stumbled badly today by reversing it.

I respectfully dissent.

Justice Souter, dissenting.

. . . *Nollan* declared the need for a nexus between the nature of an exaction of an interest in land (a beach easement) and the nature of governmental interests. The Court treats this case as raising a further question, not about the nature, but about the degree, of connection required between such an exaction and the adverse effects of development. The Court's opinion announces a test to address this question, but as I read the opinion, the Court does not apply that test to these facts, which do not raise the question the Court addresses.

First, as to the floodplain and Greenway, the Court acknowledges that an easement of this land for open space (and presumably including the five feet required for needed creek channel improvements) is reasonably related to flood control, but argues that the "permanent recreational easement" for the public on the Greenway is not so related. If that is so, it is not because of any lack of proportionality between permit condition and adverse effect, but because of a lack of any rational connection at all between exaction of a public recreational area and the governmental interest in providing for the effect of increased water runoff. That is merely an application of *Nollan's* nexus analysis.... But ... the city of Tigard never sought to justify the public access portion of the dedication as related to flood control. It merely argued that whatever recreational uses were made of the bicycle path and the one foot edge on either side, were incidental to the permit condition requiring dedication of the 15–foot easement for an 8–foot–wide bicycle path and for flood control, including open space requirements and relocation of the bank of the river by some five feet. It seems to me such incidental recreational use can stand or fall with the bicycle path, which the city justified by reference to traffic congestion. As to the relationship the Court examines, between the recreational easement and a purpose never put forth as a justification by the city, the Court unsurprisingly finds a recreation area to be unrelated to flood control.

Second, as to the bicycle path, the Court ... only faults the city for saying that the bicycle path "could" rather than "would" offset the increased traffic from the store. That again, as far as I can tell, is an application of *Nollan,* for the Court holds that the stated connection ("could offset") between traffic congestion and bicycle paths is too tenuous; only if the bicycle path "would" offset the increased traffic by some amount, could the bicycle path be said to be related to the city's legitimate interest in reducing traffic congestion.

I cannot agree that the application of *Nollan* is a sound one here, since it appears that the Court has placed the burden of producing evidence of relationship on the city, despite the usual rule in cases involving the police power that the government is presumed to have acted constitutionally. Having thus assigned the burden, the Court concludes that the City loses based on one word ("could" instead of "would"), and despite the fact that this record shows the connection the Court looks for. Dolan has put forward no evidence that the burden of granting a dedication for the bicycle path is unrelated in kind to the anticipated increase in traffic congestion, nor, if there exists a requirement that the relationship be related in degree, has Dolan shown that the exaction fails any such test. The city, by contrast, calculated the increased traffic flow that would result from Dolan's proposed development to be 435 trips per day, and its Comprehensive Plan, applied here, relied on studies showing the link between alternative modes of transportation, including bicycle paths, and reduced street traffic congestion.... *Nollan,* therefore, is satisfied, and on that assumption the city's conditions should not be held to fail a further rough proportionality test or any other that might be devised to give meaning to the constitutional limits....

In any event, on my reading, the Court's conclusions about the city's vulnerability carry the Court no further than *Nollan* has gone already, and I do not view this case as a suitable vehicle for taking the law beyond that point....

SECTION 2.   PROTECTION OF PERSONAL LIBERTIES

C.   PERSONAL AUTONOMY

Page 664.   Add after Bowers v. Hardwick:

ROMER v. EVANS, 116 S.Ct. 1620 (1996).   Without citation to Bowers v. Hardwick, the Court invalidated as a denial of equal protection an amendment to the Colorado Constitution precluding any level of state government from protecting the status of persons on the basis of their "homosexual, lesbian or bisexual orientation, conduct, practices, or relationships."   The amendment had "the peculiar property of imposing a broad and undifferentiated disability on a single named group, an exceptional and ... invalid form of legislation[,]" and "[s]econd, its sheer breadth is so discontinuous with the reasons offered for it that the amendment seems inexplicable by anything but animus toward the class that it affects; it lacks a rational relationship to legitimate state interests."

Justice Scalia's dissent, joined by the Chief Justice and Justice Thomas, complained that the Court had contradicted *Bowers*, which had not been challenged.   He thought it obvious that, given *Bowers*, the amendment, understood as a "prohibition of special protection for homosexuals," rested on a "legitimate rational basis":

" ... If it is constitutionally permissible for a State to make homosexual conduct criminal, surely it is constitutionally permissible for a State to enact other laws merely disfavoring homosexual conduct....   And *a fortiori* it is constitutionally permissible for a State to adopt a provision not even disfavoring homosexual conduct, but merely prohibiting all levels of state government from bestowing special protections upon homosexual conduct....

"[Even] assuming that, in Amendment 2, a person of homosexual 'orientation' is someone who does not engage in homosexual conduct but merely has a tendency or desire to do so, *Bowers* still suffices to establish a rational basis for the provision.   If it is rational to criminalize the conduct, surely it is rational to deny special favor and protection to those with a self-avowed tendency or desire to engage in the conduct.   Indeed, where criminal sanctions are not involved, homosexual 'orientation' is an acceptable stand-in for homosexual conduct....

"Surely ... the only sort of 'animus' at issue here [is] moral disapproval of homosexual conduct, the same sort of moral disapproval that produced the centuries-old criminal laws that we held constitutional in *Bowers* . . . . ''

In a footnote, Justice Scalia remarked that ''the Court's suggestion that . . . Amendment 2 [denies] rights on account of 'status' (rather than conduct) opens up a broader debate involving the significance of *Bowers* to this case, a debate which the Court is otherwise unwilling to join.''

For a full report of this case, see infra p. 157.

Chapter 10

THE EQUAL PROTECTION CLAUSE AND THE REVIEW OF THE REASONABLENESS OF LEGISLATION

SECTION 1. INTRODUCTION—THE SCOPE OF EQUAL PROTECTION

Page 684. Replace last sentence of note, "Application of the Equal Protection Limitation to the Federal Government Through the Due Process Clause of the Fifth Amendment," with the following:

That portion of *Metro Broadcasting* was specifically overruled in Adarand Constructors, Inc. v. Pena, 115 S.Ct. 2097, 2115 (1995), however, where the Court declared "that the Constitution imposes upon federal, state, and local government actors the same obligation to respect the personal right to equal protection of the laws."

SECTION 2. SOCIAL AND ECONOMIC REGULATORY LEGISLATION

Page 698. Add ahead of Note, "Modern Rational Basis Review":

FEDERAL COMMUNICATIONS COMMISSION v. BEACH COMMUNICATIONS, INC.

508 U.S. 307, 113 S.Ct. 2096, 124 L.Ed.2d 211 (1993).

Justice Thomas delivered the opinion of the Court.

In providing for the regulation of cable television facilities, Congress has drawn a distinction between facilities that serve separately owned and managed buildings and those that serve one or more buildings under common ownership or management. Cable facilities in the latter category are exempt from regulation as long as they provide services without using public rights-of-way. The question before us is whether there is any conceivable rational basis justifying this distinction for purposes of the Due Process Clause of the Fifth Amendment.

I

The Cable Communications Policy Act of 1984 (Cable Act) . . . provided for the franchising of cable systems by local governmental authorities. . . . Section 602(7) . . . determines the reach of the franchise

94

defined

requirement by defining the operative term "cable system." A cable system means any facility designed to provide video programming to multiple subscribers through "closed transmission paths," but does not include, inter alia,

"a facility that serves only subscribers in 1 or more multiple unit dwellings under common ownership, control, or management, unless such facility or facilities us[e] any public right-of-way." § 602(7)(B)....

In part, this provision tracks a regulatory "private cable" exemption previously promulgated by the Federal Communications Commission (FCC or Commission) pursuant to pre-existing authority under the Communications Act....

This case arises out of an FCC proceeding clarifying the agency's interpretation of the term "cable system" as it is used in the Cable Act.... In this proceeding, the Commission addressed the application of the exemption codified in § 602(7)(B) to satellite master antenna television (SMATV) facilities. Unlike a traditional cable television system, which delivers video programming to a large community of subscribers through coaxial cables laid under city streets or along utility lines, an SMATV system typically receives a signal from a satellite through a small satellite dish located on a rooftop and then retransmits the signal by wire to units within a building or complex of buildings.... The Commission ruled that an SMATV system that serves multiple buildings via a network of interconnected physical transmission lines is a cable system, unless it falls within the § 602(7)(B) exemption.... Consistent with the plain terms of the statutory exemption, the Commission concluded that such an SMATV system is subject to the franchise requirement if its transmission lines interconnect separately owned and managed buildings or if its lines use or cross any public right-of-way....

Respondents ...—SMATV operators that would be subject to franchising under the Cable Act as construed by the Commission—petitioned the Court of Appeals for review.... [A] majority of the court found merit in the claim that § 602(7) violates the implied equal protection guarantee of the Due Process Clause.... In the absence of what it termed "the predominant rationale for local franchising" (use of public rights-of-way), the court saw no rational basis "[o]n the record," and was "unable to imagine" any conceivable basis, for distinguishing between those facilities exempted by the statute and those SMATV cable systems that link separately owned and managed buildings....

Because the Court of Appeals held an Act of Congress unconstitutional, we granted certiorari.... We now reverse.

II

Whether embodied in the Fourteenth Amendment or inferred from the Fifth, equal protection is not a license for courts to judge the wisdom, fairness, or logic of legislative choices. In areas of social and economic policy, a statutory classification that neither proceeds along suspect lines nor infringes fundamental constitutional rights must be upheld against equal protection challenge if there is any reasonably

standard R.R.

conceivable state of facts that could provide a rational basis for the classification. See Sullivan v. Stroop, 496 U.S. 478, 485 (1990); Bowen v. Gilliard, 483 U.S. 587, 600–603 (1987); United States Railroad Retirement Bd. v. Fritz, 449 U.S. 166, 174–179 (1980); Dandridge v. Williams, 397 U.S. 471, 484–485 (1970). Where there are "plausible reasons" for Congress' action, "our inquiry is at an end." United States Railroad Retirement Bd. v. Fritz, supra, at 179. This standard of review is a paradigm of judicial restraint. "The Constitution presumes that, absent some reason to infer antipathy, even improvident decisions will eventually be rectified by the democratic process and that judicial intervention is generally unwarranted no matter how unwisely we may think a political branch has acted." Vance v. Bradley, 440 U.S. 93, 97 (1979) (footnote omitted).

On rational-basis review, a classification in a statute such as the Cable Act comes to us bearing a strong presumption of validity, see Lyng v. Automobile Workers, 485 U.S. 360, 370 (1988), and those attacking the rationality of the legislative classification have the burden "to negative every conceivable basis which might support it," Lehnhausen v. Lake Shore Auto Parts Co., 410 U.S. 356, 364 (1973).... Moreover, because we never require a legislature to articulate its reasons for enacting a statute, it is entirely irrelevant for constitutional purposes whether the conceived reason for the challenged distinction actually motivated the legislature. United States Railroad Retirement Bd. v. Fritz, supra, at 179. See Flemming v. Nestor, 363 U.S. 603, 612 (1960). Thus, the absence of " 'legislative facts' " explaining the distinction "[o]n the record," ... has no significance in rational-basis analysis. See Nordlinger v. Hahn, 505 U.S. 1 (1992)(slip op., at 13)(equal protection "does not demand for purposes of rational-basis review that a legislature or governing decisionmaker actually articulate at any time the purpose or rationale supporting its classification"). In other words, a legislative choice is not subject to courtroom fact-finding and may be based on rational speculation unsupported by evidence or empirical data. See Vance v. Bradley, supra, at 111. See also Minnesota v. Clover Leaf Creamery Co., 449 U.S. 456, 464 (1981). ... Lehnhausen, supra, at 365 (quoting Carmichael v. Southern Coal & Coke Co., 301 U.S. 495, 510 (1937)).

These restraints on judicial review have added force "where the legislature must necessarily engage in a process of line-drawing." United States Railroad Retirement Bd. v. Fritz, 449 U.S., at 179. Defining the class of persons subject to a regulatory requirement—much like classifying governmental beneficiaries—"inevitably requires that some persons who have an almost equally strong claim to favored treatment be placed on different sides of the line, and the fact [that] the line might have been drawn differently at some points is a matter for legislative, rather than judicial, consideration." ... The distinction at issue here represents such a line: By excluding from the definition of "cable system" those facilities that serve commonly owned or managed buildings without using public rights-of-way, § 602(7)(B) delineates the bounds of the regulatory field. Such scope-of-coverage provisions are unavoidable components of most economic or social legislation. In establishing the franchise requirement, Congress had to draw the line somewhere; it had to choose which facilities to franchise. This necessity renders the precise coordinates of the resulting legislative judgment virtually unreviewable, since the legislature must be allowed leeway to approach a perceived problem incrementally. See, e.g., Williamson v. Lee Optical of Okla., Inc., 348 U.S. 483 (1955):

> "The problem of legislative classification is a perennial one, admitting of no doctrinaire definition. Evils in the same field may be of different dimensions and proportions, requiring different remedies. Or so the legislature may think. Or the reform may take one step at a time, addressing itself to the phase of the problem which seems most acute to the legislative mind. The legislature may select one phase of one field and apply a remedy there, neglecting the others. The prohibition of the Equal Protection Clause goes no further than the invidious discrimination." Id., at 489 (citations omitted).

Applying these principles, we conclude that the common-ownership distinction is constitutional. There are at least two possible bases for the distinction; either one suffices. First, ... it is plausible that Congress ... adopted the FCC's earlier rationale[, under which] common ownership was thought to be indicative of those systems for which the costs of regulation would outweigh the benefits to consumers. Because the number of subscribers was a similar indicator, the Commission also exempted cable facilities that served fewer than 50 subscribers....

This regulatory-efficiency model ... provides a conceivable basis for the common-ownership exemption. A legislator might rationally assume that systems serving only commonly owned or managed buildings without crossing public rights-of-way would typically be limited in size or would share some other attribute affecting their impact on the welfare of cable viewers such that regulators could "safely ignor[e]" these systems.

Respondents argue that Congress did not intend common ownership to be a surrogate for small size, since Congress simultaneously rejected the FCC's 50–subscriber exemption by omitting it from the Cable Act.... Whether the posited reason for the challenged distinction actually motivated Congress is "constitutionally irrelevant," United States Railroad Retirement Bd. v. Fritz, supra, ... and, in any event, the FCC's explanation indicates that both common ownership and number of subscribers were considered indicia of "very small" cable systems. Respondents also contend that an SMATV operator could increase his subscription base and still qualify for the exemption simply by installing a separate satellite dish on each building served.... The additional cost of multiple dishes and associated transmission equipment, however, would impose an independent constraint on system size.

Furthermore, small size is only one plausible ownership-related factor contributing to consumer welfare. Subscriber influence is another. Where an SMATV system serves a complex of buildings under common ownership or management, individual subscribers could conceivably have greater bargaining power vis-a-vis the cable operator (even if the number of dwelling units were large), since all the subscribers could negotiate with one voice through the common owner or manager.

Such an owner might have substantial leverage, because he could withhold permission to operate the SMATV system on his property. He would also have an incentive to guard the interests of his tenants. Thus, there could be less need to establish regulatory safeguards for subscribers in commonly owned complexes. Respondents acknowledge such possibilities, ... and we certainly cannot say that these assumptions would be irrational.

There is a second conceivable basis for the statutory distinction. Suppose competing SMATV operators wish to sell video programming to subscribers in a group of contiguous buildings, such as a single city block, which can be interconnected by wire without crossing a public right-of-way. If all the buildings belong to one owner or are commonly managed, that owner or manager could freely negotiate a deal for all subscribers on a competitive basis. But if the buildings are separately owned and managed, the first SMATV operator who gains a foothold by signing a contract and installing a satellite dish and associated transmission equipment on one of the buildings would enjoy a powerful cost advantage in competing for the remaining subscribers: he could connect additional buildings for the cost of a few feet of cable, whereas any competitor would have to recover the cost of his own satellite headend facility. Thus, the first operator could charge rates well above his cost and still undercut the competition. This potential for effective monopoly power might theoretically justify regulating the latter class of SMATV systems and not the former.

III

... [T]here are plausible rationales unrelated to the use of public rights-of-way for regulating cable facilities serving separately owned and managed buildings. The assumptions underlying these rationales may be erroneous, but the very fact that they are "arguable" is sufficient, on rational-basis review, to "immuniz[e]" the congressional choice from constitutional challenge. Vance v. Bradley, 440 U.S., at 112.

The judgment of the Court of Appeals is reversed. . . .

Justice Stevens, concurring in the judgment.

Freedom is a blessing. Regulation is sometimes necessary, but it is always burdensome. A decision not to regulate the way in which an owner chooses to enjoy the benefits of an improvement to his own property is adequately justified by a presumption in favor of freedom.

. . .

... In my opinion the interest in the free use of one's own property provides adequate support for an exception from burdensome regulation and franchising requirements even when the property is occupied not only by family members and guests, but by lessees and co-owners as well, and even when the property complex encompasses multiple buildings.

The master antenna serving multiple units in an apartment building is less unsightly than a forest of individual antennas, each serving a separate apartment. It was surely sensible to allow owners to make use of such an improvement without incurring the costs of franchising and economic regulation. Even though regulation might have been justified ... a justification for nonregulation would nevertheless remain: Whenever possible, property owners should be free to use improvements to their property as they see fit.

That brings us to the "private cable" exemption as applied to Satellite Master Antenna Television (SMATV) systems. A justification for the "private cable" exemption that rests on the presumption that an owner of property should be allowed to use an improvement on his own property as he sees fit unless there is a sufficient public interest in denying him that right simply does not apply to the situation in which the improvement—here, the satellite antenna—is being used to distribute signals to subscribers on other people's property. In that situation, the property owner, or the SMATV operator, has reached out beyond the property line and is seeking to employ the satellite antenna in the broader market for television programming. While the crossing of that line need not trigger regulatory intervention, and the absence of such a crossing may not prevent such intervention, it certainly cannot be said that government is disabled, by the Constitution, from regulating in the case of the former and abstaining in the case of the latter. Such a policy is adequately justified by the presumption in favor of freedom.

Thus, while I am not fully persuaded that the "private cable" exemption is justified by the size of the market which it encompasses,[1] or by the Court's "monopoly" rationale,[2] I agree with its ultimate conclusion. In my judgment, it is reasonable to presume[3] that Congress was motivated by an interest in allowing property owners to exercise freedom in the use of their own property. Legislation so motivated surely does not violate the sovereign's duty to govern impartially. See Hampton v.

[1] Approximately 25% of all multiple dwellings units are in complexes large enough to support an SMATV system.... Furthermore, whereas the FCC had, prior to [the Cable Act], exempted from regulation cable systems of less than 50 subscribers as well as those serving commonly owned multiple unit dwellings, Congress exempted only the latter when it passed the Cable Act, leaving out the exemption based on system size. Respondent thus makes a strong argument that Congress may have rejected the very rationale upon which the FCC, and the Court, rely.

[2] The Court's theory assumes a great deal about the nature of what is essentially a hypothetical market. Moreover, the Court's analysis overlooks the competitive presence of traditional cable as a potential constraint on an SMATV operator's capacity to extract monopoly rents from landlords.

[3] The Court states that a legislative classification must be upheld "if there is any reasonably conceivable state of facts that could provide a rational basis for the classification," and that "[w]here there are 'plausible reasons' for Congress' action, 'our inquiry is at an end.'" In my view, this formulation sweeps too broadly, for it is difficult to imagine a legislative classification that could not be supported by a "reasonably conceivable state of facts." Judicial review under the "conceivable set of facts" test is tantamount to no review at all.

I continue to believe that when Congress imposes a burden on one group, but leaves unaffected another that is similarly, though not identically, situated, "the Constitution requires something more than merely a 'conceivable' or 'plausible' explanation for the unequal treatment." United States Railroad Retirement Bd. v. Fritz, 449 U.S. 166, 180 (1980) (Stevens, J., concurring in judgment). In my view, when the actual rationale for the legislative classification is unclear, we should inquire whether the classification is rationally related to "a legitimate purpose that we may reasonably presume to have motivated an impartial legislature." Id., at 181 (emphasis added).

Mow Sun Wong, 426 U.S. 88, 100 (1976). Accordingly, I concur in the judgment of the Court.

HELLER v. DOE, 506 U.S. 312 (1993). The Court rejected an equal protection challenge by adult mentally retarded people to Kentucky statutes (1) authorizing their involuntary civil commitment on a clear and convincing standard of proof, while requiring proof beyond a reasonable doubt for involuntary commitment of mentally ill persons, and (2) allowing close relatives and guardians of the mentally retarded, but not the mentally ill, to participate in commitment proceedings as parties entitled to present evidence and appeal. Confining itself to "rational-basis review" because that is how the case had been litigated, the Court, per Justice Kennedy, cited much of its discussion of that standard in *Beach Communications* and noted that in neither City of Cleburne v. Cleburne Living Center, infra, page 926, nor Schweiker v. Wilson, supra, page 697, "did we purport to apply a different standard of rational-basis review from that just described." Although "even the standard of rationality ... must find some footing in the realities of the subject addressed by the legislation ... Kentucky has proffered more than adequate justifications for the differences in treatment between the mentally retarded and the mentally ill."

The lower standard of proof for involuntary commitment of the mentally retarded "follows from the fact that mental retardation is easier to diagnose than is mental illness[,]" because it "tends to equalize the risks of an erroneous determination that the subject of a commitment proceeding has the condition in question." Moreover, there is a "reasonably conceivable state of facts ... from which Kentucky could conclude that the second prerequisite to commitment"—dangerousness to self or others—"is established more easily, as a general rule, in the case of the mentally retarded." That is so, because "retardation is a permanent, relatively stable condition," allowing reliance on the record of previous behavior, whereas "[m]anifestations of mental illness may be sudden, and past behavior may not be an adequate predictor of future actions" and prediction is "complicated as well by the difficulties inherent in diagnosis of mental illness." Finally, a "more far-reaching rationale justifying the different burdens of proof" is that the "prevailing methods of treatment for the mentally retarded, as a general rule, are much less invasive than are those given the mentally ill." Whereas the ill typically receive psychotropic drugs and psychiatric treatment involving "intrusive inquiries into the patient's innermost thoughts," the retarded more typically receive training for self-care and self-sufficiency. Although "the loss of liberty ... may be similar in many respects" for both groups, and "some persons committed for mental retardation are subjected to more intrusive treatments ...," it would have been plausible for the Kentucky legislature to believe that most mentally retarded individuals who are committed receive treatment which is different from, and less invasive than, that to which the mentally ill are subjected." The question being "at least debatable, ...

rational-basis review permits a legislature to use just this sort of general-ization." In sum, "[e]ach of these rationales, standing on its own, would suffice to establish a rational basis" for the differential burden of proof.

As for the differential rights of close relatives and guardians to participate in the commitment proceeding, retardation "has its onset during a person's developmental period" and mental illness "may arise or manifest itself ... only after minority when the afflicted person's immediate family members have no knowledge of the medical condition and have long ceased to provide care and support." Moreover, adults diagnosed as mentally ill "may have a need for privacy that justifies ... confining a commitment proceeding to the smallest group compatible with due process." Hence, "Kentucky may have concluded that close relatives and guardians, both of whom likely have intimate knowledge of a mentally retarded person's abilities and experiences, have valuable insights which should be considered during the involuntary commitment process." By contrast, Kentucky also "may have concluded that partic-ipation as parties by relatives and guardians of the mentally ill would not in most cases have been of sufficient help to the trier of fact to justify the additional burden and complications of granting party sta-tus."

Justice Souter's dissent, joined in full by Justices Blackmun and Stevens, found both distinctions "not supported by any rational justifica-tion." [a] He, too, declined to address whether "heightened scrutiny" should apply, but only because it was unnecessary since the distinctions failed "rational-basis scrutiny, ... which we have previously applied to a classification on the basis of mental disability, see Cleburne v. Cleburne Living Center." He "would follow *Cleburne* here" and thought the Court's opinion left "*Cleburne*'s status ... uncertain." [b]

With respect to the burden of proof differential, Justice Souter first argued that rationality is not satisfied "if burdens of proof rise simply with difficulties of proof," because "burdens of proof are assigned and risks of error are allocated not to reflect the mere difficulty of avoiding error, but the importance of avoiding it as judged after a thorough consideration of those respective interests of the parties that will be affected by the allocation"—in this case the State's "interests of protect-ing society from those posing dangers and protecting the ill or helpless individual from his own incapacities" and the individual's interests in "freedom from restraint and freedom from the stigma that restraint and its justifications impose on an institutionalized person." Justice Souter could find no "differences in the respective interests of the public and the subjects of the commitment proceedings" that provided a rational basis for differentiating between the ill and the retarded:

[a] Justice O'Connor also joined the dissent insofar as it found the differential standard of proof for commitment "irrational," but she agreed with the Court that "there are sufficiently plausible and legitimate reasons for the legislative determination" to differenti-ate regarding party status for close relatives and guardians.

[b] Justice Blackmun added a separate dissenting statement to express his "continuing adherence to the view that laws that discriminate against individuals with mental retarda-tion," City of Cleburne v. Cleburne Living Center, Inc., 473 U.S. 432, 455 (1985)(opinion of Marshall, J., joined by Brennan and Blackmun, JJ.) ... are subject to heightened review.

"... Both the ill and the retarded may be dangerous, each may require care, and the State's interest is seemingly of equal strength in each category of cases. No one has or would argue that the value of liberty varies somehow depending on whether one is alleged to be ill or retarded, and a mentally retarded person has as much to lose by civil commitment to an institution as a mentally ill counterpart ... Even assuming, then, that the assertion of different degrees of difficulty of proof both of mental illness and mental retardation and of the dangerousness inherent in each condition is true (an assertion for which there is no support in the record), it lends not a shred of rational support to the decision to discriminate against the retarded in allocating the risk of erroneous curtailment of liberty."

He also disagreed with the Court that "it would have been plausible for the Kentucky legislature to believe that most mentally retarded individuals who are committed receive treatment which is ... less invasive tha[n] that to which the mentally ill are subjected." Studies conducted nationally and in neighboring states indicated widespread use—and frequent abuse—of "mind-altering medication" and "intrusive psychiatric therapy" with respect to the mentally retarded as well as the mentally ill, and "[t]here being nothing in the record to suggest that Kentucky's institutions are free from these practices, and no reason whatever to assume so, there simply is no plausible basis for the Court's assumption that the institutional response to mental retardation is in the main less intrusive ... than treatment of mental illness." Based on the "available literature ... there are no apparent differences of therapeutic regimes that would plausibly explain less rigorous commitment standards for those alleged to be mentally retarded than for those alleged to be mentally ill."

As for the involvement of family members and guardians in the commitment proceeding, Justice Souter thought that although the differences cited by the Court "might justify a scheme in which immediate relatives and guardians were automatically called as witnesses in cases seeking institutionalization on the basis of mental retardation, they are completely unrelated to ... permitting these immediate relatives and guardians to be involved 'as parties' so as to give them, among other things, the right to appeal as 'adverse' a decision not to institutionalize the individual...." Virtually all the State's involuntary commitments of the retarded are promoted by relatives or guardians, and making them parties subjects "someone ... alleged to be retarded" to "a second prosecutor." The import of this was clear to Justice Souter:

"The Court simply points to no characteristic of mental retardation that could rationally justify imposing this burden of a second prosecutor on those alleged to be mentally retarded where the State has decided not to impose it upon those alleged to be mentally ill. Even if we assumed a generally more regular connection between the relatives and guardians of those alleged to be retarded than those said to be mentally ill, it would not explain why the former should be subject to a second prosecutor when the latter are not.

"The same may be said about the Court's second suggested justification, that the mentally ill may have a need for privacy not shown by the retarded. Even assuming the ill need some additional privacy, and that participation of others in the commitment proceeding should therefore be limited 'to the smallest group compatible with due process,' why should the retarded be subject to a second prosecutor? The Court provides no answer.

"Without plausible justification, Kentucky is being allowed to draw a distinction that is difficult to see as resting on anything other than the stereotypical assumption that the retarded are 'perpetual children,' an assumption that has historically been taken to justify the disrespect and 'grotesque mistreatment' to which the retarded have been subjected. See Cleburne ... (Stevens, J., concurring)...."

Page 699. Add after third sentence of the second paragraph:

Of like import but without reference to *Cleburne*, the Court later invalidated an amendment to the Colorado Constitution precluding any level of state government from protecting the status of persons on the basis of their "homosexual, lesbian or bisexual orientation, conduct, practices or relationships," because "its sheer breadth is so discontinuous with the reasons offered for it that the amendment seems inexplicable by anything but animus toward the class that it affects; it lacks a rational relationship to legitimate state interests." Romer v. Evans, 116 S.Ct. 1620, 1627 (1996), infra p. 157.

SECTION 3. SUSPECT CLASSIFICATIONS

B. RACIAL SEGREGATION IN SCHOOLS AND OTHER PUBLIC FACILITIES

Page 756. Add after Missouri v. Jenkins:

MISSOURI V. JENKINS (JENKINS III), 115 S.Ct. 2038 (1995). The Court had denied review of the State's challenge to the scope of the district court's remedial order when it agreed in the preceding case (*Jenkins II*) to address the validity of the district court's taxation orders for financing the remedies required. In *Jenkins III*, the Court nonetheless reached the merits of the State's claim that the district court had exceeded its constitutional remedial authority by ordering the State (1) to fund salary increases for nearly all of KCMSD's instructional and noninstructional employees and (2) to continue to fund remedial quality education programs because student achievement levels remained "at or below national norms at many grade levels." The Court ruled in the State's favor, emphasizing that the district court's "admittedly broad discretion" still had to be confined to eliminating "to the extent practicable the vestiges of prior de jure segregation within the KCMSD: a systemwide reduction in student achievement and the existence of 25 racially identifiable schools with a population of over 90% black students," and also emphasizing that the district court's additional "end purpose" is to restore state and local control of a school system operating in compliance with the Constitution.

Scrutinizing the district court's grounding of the salary orders on improving the "desegregative attractiveness" of KCMSD as a means of remedying the vestiges of segregation, Chief Justice Rehnquist noted that the district court's remedial objective was to create an entire school district equal or superior to surrounding suburban districts rather than just to address the racial identifiability of some of KCMSD's schools. The purpose of creating a "magnet district" was "not only to remedy the system-wide reduction in student achievement, but also to attract non-minority students not presently enrolled in the KCMSD." The lower courts having found no interdistrict constitutional violations, however, no interdistrict relief was warranted under *Milliken I.* The Court now ruled that those remedies designed to induce interdistrict transfer of nonminority students for redistribution within KCMSD exceeded the scope of the district court's broad remedial authority, because the district court had "devised a remedy to accomplish indirectly what it admittedly lacks the remedial authority to mandate directly." Nor, in light of the district court's record findings of no significant interdistrict effects of the de jure segregation within KCMSD and "the typical supposition ... that 'white flight' may result from desegregation, not de jure segregation," could the reliance on desegregative attractiveness be justified by claiming that de jure segregation had "led to white flight from the KCMSD to suburban districts." In short, "[a] district court seeking to remedy an intradistrict violation that has not 'directly caused' significant interdistrict effects ... exceeds its remedial authority if it orders a remedy with an interdistrict purpose." Finally, concerned that the district court's pursuit of "desegregative attractiveness" would justify remedial orders limitless in expenditure and duration, involve "many imponderables," and be "far removed from the task of eliminating the racial identifiability of the schools within the KCMSD," the Court concluded that the salary increase order "is simply too far removed from an acceptable implementation of a permissible means to remedy previous legally mandated segregation."

As for the State's challenge to "the requirement of indefinite funding of a quality education program until national norms are met," the Court noted that the district court's authority extended no further than to remedy to the extent practicable "the incremental effect that segregation has had on minority student achievement." Because not just de jure segregation, but "external factors beyond the control of the KCMSD and the State affect minority student achievement," and because all the parties agreed that "improved achievement on test scores is not necessarily required for the State to achieve partial unitary status as to the quality education programs[—a status the State had not yet requested—]the District Court [on remand] should sharply limit, if not dispense with, its reliance on" the test scores. The Court's underlying concern was that "[i]nsistence upon academic goals unrelated to the effects of legal segregation unwarrantably postpones the day when the KCMSD will be able to operate on its own."

In one concurring opinion Justice O'Connor noted that attracting whites into the school district as an "incidental" benefit of restoring KCMSD to unitary status "would be of no legal consequence[,]" but that here the district court's finding of no interdistrict violation or significant interdistrict segregative effects disallowed "remedies seeking to rectify regional demographic trends that go beyond the scope and nature of the constitutional violation." In another concurring opinion of some length, Justice Thomas questioned whether continuing high black enrollments in KCMSD schools were vestiges of pre–1954 de jure segregation and sharply criticized the district court's finding "that racial imbalances constituted an ongoing constitutional violation that continued to inflict harm on black students" as premised on "the idea that any school that is black is inferior, and that blacks cannot succeed without the benefit of the company of whites." Justice Thomas also urged that the equitable powers of the federal courts be more circumscribed by precise federalism and separation of powers restraints than they previously have been, lest "the institutional ability to set effective educational, budgetary, or administrative policy ... transform the least dangerous branch into the most dangerous one." Specifically, he argued that "absen[t] special circumstances, the remedy for de jure segregation ordinarily should not include educational programs for students who were not in school (or were even alive) during the period of segregation."

Justice Souter authored a dissenting opinion for four Justices. He argued that the Court improperly had addressed "the soundness of the magnet element of the District Court's underlying remedial scheme" in light of the history of this litigation and the State's concession that the salary and test-score questions could be answered without doing so. He contended that the salary orders were designed not only to draw students into the district's schools but to raise the level of student achievement in the KCMSD and thus that "to the extent that the District Court concludes on remand that its salary orders are justified by reference to the quality of education alone, nothing in the Court's opinion precludes those orders from remaining in effect." He understood the district court's findings of no significant interdistrict segregative effects to leave open the possibility that the de jure segregation of KCMSD "produced significant non-segregative effects outside the KCMSD that led to greater segregation within it." On that view, the Court was "rash to reverse the concurrent factual findings" of the two lower courts that the intradistrict segregation had sufficient consequences outside the district to justify the "magnet concept." Finally, Justice Souter interpreted *Milliken I* not to preclude remedial orders whose purpose is to induce interdistrict student transfers as such, but only to prevent remedies that bind "the authorities of other governmental units that are free of violations and segregative effects." Because the "District Court's remedial measures go only to the operation and quality of schools within the KCMSD, and the burden of those measures accordingly falls only on the two proven constitutional wrongdoers in this case, the KCMSD and the State," the district court had not exceeded its authority under *Milliken I.*

C. CLASSIFICATIONS BASED ON GENDER

Page 799. Add after Mississippi University for Women v. Hogan:

J.E.B. v. ALABAMA EX REL. T.B.

511 U.S. 127, 114 S.Ct. 1419, 128 L.Ed.2d 89 (1994).

Justice Blackmun delivered the opinion of the Court.

In Batson v. Kentucky, 476 U.S. 79 (1986), this Court held that the Equal Protection Clause of the Fourteenth Amendment governs the exercise of peremptory challenges by a prosecutor in a criminal trial. The Court explained that although a defendant has "no right to a 'petit jury composed in whole or in part of persons of his own race,' " ... the "defendant does have the right to be tried by a jury whose members are selected pursuant to nondiscriminatory criteria." ... Since *Batson,* we ... have recognized that whether the trial is criminal or civil, potential jurors, as well as litigants, have an equal protection right to jury selection procedures that are free from state-sponsored group stereotypes rooted in, and reflective of, historical prejudice. See Powers v. Ohio, 499 U.S. 400 (1991); Edmonson v. Leesville Concrete Co., 500 U.S. 614 (1991); Georgia v. McCollum, 505 U.S. 42 (1992).

Although premised on equal protection principles that apply equally to gender discrimination, all our recent cases defining the scope of *Batson* involved alleged racial discrimination in the exercise of peremptory challenges. Today we ... hold that gender, like race, is an unconstitutional proxy for juror competence and impartiality.

I

On behalf of relator T.B., the mother of a minor child, respondent State of Alabama filed a complaint for paternity and child support against petitioner J.E.B. in the District Court of Jackson County, Alabama. [During jury selection] the State ... used 9 of its 10 peremptory strikes to remove male jurors; petitioner used all but one of his strikes to remove female jurors. [Given the predominantly female panel,] all the selected jurors were female.

... The court rejected petitioner's [*Batson*] claim and empaneled the all-female jury.... The jury found petitioner to be the father of the child and the court entered an order directing him to pay child support.... The Alabama Court of Civil Appeals affirmed [and t]he Supreme Court of Alabama denied certiorari....

We granted certiorari ... to resolve ... whether the Equal Protection Clause forbids peremptory challenges on the basis of gender as well as on the basis of race. Today we reaffirm what, by now, should be axiomatic: Intentional discrimination on the basis of gender by state actors violates the Equal Protection Clause, particularly where, as here, the discrimination serves to ratify and perpetuate invidious, archaic, and overbroad stereotypes about the relative abilities of men and women.

II

... Gender-based peremptory strikes were hardly practicable for most of our country's existence, since, until the 19th century, women were completely excluded from jury service....

Many States continued to exclude women from jury service well into the present century, despite the fact that women attained suffrage upon ratification of the Nineteenth Amendment in 1920. States that did permit women to serve on juries often erected other barriers, such as registration requirements and automatic exemptions, designed to deter women from exercising their right to jury service....

The prohibition of women on juries was derived from the English common law which, according to Blackstone, rightfully excluded women from juries under "the doctrine of *propter defectum sexus,* literally, the 'defect of sex.' " ... In this country, supporters of the exclusion of women from juries tended to couch their objections in terms of the ostensible need to protect women from the ugliness and depravity of trials. Women were thought to be too fragile and virginal to withstand the polluted courtroom atmosphere....

. . .

... [As late as 1961, i]n Hoyt v. Florida, 368 U.S., at 61, the Court found it reasonable, "despite the enlightened emancipation of women," to exempt women from mandatory jury service by statute, allowing women to serve on juries only if they volunteered to serve. The Court justified the differential exemption policy on the ground that women, unlike men, occupied a unique position "as the center of home and family life." ...

In 1975, the Court finally repudiated the reasoning of *Hoyt* and struck down, under the Sixth Amendment, an affirmative registration statute nearly identical to the one at issue in Hoyt. See Taylor v. Louisiana, 419 U.S. 522 (1975). We explained [that t]he diverse and representative character of the jury must be maintained "partly as assurance of a diffused impartiality and partly because sharing in the administration of justice is a phase of civic responsibility." ...

III

Taylor relied on Sixth Amendment principles, but the opinion's approach is consistent with the heightened equal protection scrutiny afforded gender-based classifications. Since Reed v. Reed, 404 U.S. 71 (1971), this Court consistently has subjected gender-based classifications to heightened scrutiny in recognition of the real danger that government policies that professedly are based on reasonable considerations in fact may be reflective of "archaic and overbroad" generalizations about gender, see Schlesinger v. Ballard, 419 U.S. 498, 506–507 (1975), or based on "outdated misconceptions concerning the role of females in the home rather than in the 'marketplace and world of ideas.'" Craig v. Boren, 429 U.S. 190, 198–199 (1976)....

Despite the heightened scrutiny afforded distinctions based on gender, respondent argues that gender discrimination in the selection of the petit jury should be permitted, though discrimination on the basis of race is not. Respondent suggests that "gender discrimination in this country ... has never reached the level of discrimination" against African–Americans, and therefore gender discrimination, unlike racial discrimination, is tolerable in the courtroom. Brief for Respondent 9.

While the prejudicial attitudes toward women in this country have not been identical to those held toward racial minorities, the similarities between the experiences of racial minorities and women, in some contexts, "overpower those differences." Note, Beyond *Batson*: Eliminating Gender–Based Peremptory Challenges, 105 Harv.L.Rev. 1920, 1921 (1992).... Certainly, with respect to jury service, African–Americans and women share a history of total exclusion, a history which came to an end for women many years after the embarrassing chapter in our history came to an end for African–Americans.

We need not determine, however, whether women or racial minorities have suffered more at the hands of discriminatory state actors during the decades of our Nation's history. It is necessary only to acknowledge that "our Nation has had a long and unfortunate history of sex discrimination," ... a history which warrants the heightened scrutiny we afford all gender-based classifications today. Under our equal protection jurisprudence, gender-based classifications require "an exceedingly persuasive justification" in order to survive constitutional scrutiny.... Thus, the only question is whether discrimination on the basis of gender in jury selection substantially furthers the State's legitimate interest in achieving a fair and impartial trial.[6] In making this assessment, we do not weigh the value of peremptory challenges as an institution against our asserted commitment to eradicate invidious discrimination from the courtroom. Instead, we consider whether peremptory challenges based on gender stereotypes provide substantial aid to a litigant's effort to secure a fair and impartial jury.

Far from proffering an exceptionally persuasive justification for its gender-based peremptory challenges, respondent maintains that its decision to strike virtually all the males from the jury in this case "may reasonably have been based upon the perception, supported by history, that men otherwise totally qualified to serve upon a jury might be more sympathetic and receptive to the arguments of a man alleged in a paternity action to be the father of an out-of-wedlock child, while women equally qualified to serve upon a jury might be more sympathetic and receptive to the arguments of the complaining witness who bore the child." ...

We shall not accept as a defense to gender-based peremptory challenges "the very stereotype the law condemns." Powers v. Ohio, 499

---

[6] Because we conclude that gender-based peremptory challenges are not substantially related to an important government objective, we once again need not decide whether classifications based on gender are inherently suspect....

U.S. 400, 410 (1991). Respondent's rationale, not unlike those regularly expressed for gender-based strikes, is reminiscent of the arguments advanced to justify the total exclusion of women from juries. Respondent offers virtually no support for the conclusion that gender alone is an accurate predictor of juror's attitudes; yet it urges this Court to condone the same stereotypes that justified the wholesale exclusion of women from juries and the ballot box.[11] Respondent seems to assume that gross generalizations that would be deemed impermissible if made on the basis of race are somehow permissible when made on the basis of gender.

Discrimination in jury selection, whether based on race or on gender, causes harm to the litigants, the community, and the individual jurors who are wrongfully excluded from participation in the judicial process. The litigants are harmed by the risk that the prejudice which motivated the discriminatory selection of the jury will infect the entire proceedings.... The community is harmed by the State's participation in the perpetuation of invidious group stereotypes and the inevitable loss of confidence in our judicial system that state-sanctioned discrimination in the courtroom engenders.

When state actors exercise peremptory challenges in reliance on gender stereotypes, they ratify and reinforce prejudicial views of the relative abilities of men and women. Because these stereotypes have wreaked injustice in so many other spheres of our country's public life, active discrimination by litigants on the basis of gender during jury selection "invites cynicism respecting the jury's neutrality and its obligation to adhere to the law." Powers v. Ohio, 499 U.S., at 412. The potential for cynicism is particularly acute in cases where gender-related issues are prominent, such as cases involving rape, sexual harassment, or paternity. Discriminatory use of peremptory challenges may create the impression that the judicial system has acquiesced in suppressing full participation by one gender or that the "deck has been stacked" in favor of one side....

In recent cases we have emphasized that individual jurors themselves have a right to nondiscriminatory jury selection procedures.... Contrary to respondent's suggestion, this right extends to both men and women.... All persons, when granted the opportunity to serve on a jury, have the right not to be excluded summarily because of discrimina-

---

[11] Even if a measure of truth can be found in some of the gender stereotypes used to justify gender-based peremptory challenges, that fact alone cannot support discrimination on the basis of gender in jury selection. We have made abundantly clear in past cases that gender classifications that rest on impermissible stereotypes violate the Equal Protection Clause, even when some statistical support can be conjured up for the generalization.... The generalization advanced by Alabama in support of its asserted right to discriminate on the basis of gender is, at the least, overbroad, and serves only to perpetuate the same "outmoded notions of the relative capabilities of men and women," Cleburne v. Cleburne Living Center, Inc., 473 U.S. 432, 441 (1985), that we have invalidated in other contexts. See Frontiero v. Richardson, 411 U.S. 677 (1973); Stanton v. Stanton, 421 U.S. 7 (1975); Craig v. Boren, 429 U.S. 190 (1976); Mississippi University for Women v. Hogan, 458 U.S. 718 (1982). The Equal Protection Clause, as interpreted by decisions of this Court, acknowledges that a shred of truth may be contained in some stereotypes, but requires that state actors look beyond the surface before making judgments about people that are likely to stigmatize as well as to perpetuate historical patterns of discrimination.

tory and stereotypical presumptions that reflect and reinforce patterns of historical discrimination.[13] Striking individual jurors on the assumption that they hold particular views simply because of their gender is "practically a brand upon them, affixed by law, an assertion of their inferiority." Strauder v. West Virginia, 100 U.S. 303, 308 (1880). It denigrates the dignity of the excluded juror, and, for a woman, reinvokes a history of exclusion from political participation.[14] The message it sends to all those in the courtroom, and all those who may later learn of the discriminatory act, is that certain individuals, for no reason other than gender, are presumed unqualified by state actors to decide important questions upon which reasonable persons could disagree.

IV

Our conclusion that litigants may not strike potential jurors solely on the basis of gender does not imply the elimination of all peremptory challenges. Neither does it conflict with a State's legitimate interest in using such challenges in its effort to secure a fair and impartial jury. Parties still may remove jurors whom they feel might be less acceptable than others on the panel; gender simply may not serve as a proxy for bias. Parties may also exercise their peremptory challenges to remove from the venire any group or class of individuals normally subject to "rational basis" review. See Cleburne v. Cleburne Living Center, Inc., 473 U.S. 432, 439–442 (1985); Clark v. Jeter, 486 U.S. 456, 461 (1988). Even strikes based on characteristics that are disproportionately associated with one gender could be appropriate, absent a showing of pretext.

If conducted properly, voir dire can inform litigants about potential jurors, making reliance upon stereotypical and pejorative notions about a particular gender or race both unnecessary and unwise. Voir dire provides a means of discovering actual or implied bias and a firmer basis upon which the parties may exercise their peremptory challenges intelligently....

The experience in the many jurisdictions that have barred gender-based challenges belies the claim that litigants and trial courts are incapable of complying with a rule barring strikes based on gender. As with race-based *Batson* claims, a party alleging gender discrimination must make a prima facie showing of intentional discrimination before the party exercising the challenge is required to explain the basis for the

[13] It is irrelevant that women, unlike African–Americans, are not a numerical minority and therefore are likely to remain on the jury if each side uses its peremptory challenges in an equally discriminatory fashion.... Because the right to nondiscriminatory jury selection procedures belongs to the potential jurors, as well as to the litigants, the possibility that members of both genders will get on the jury despite the intentional discrimination is beside the point. The exclusion of even one juror for impermissible reasons harms that juror and undermines public confidence in the fairness of the system.

[14] The popular refrain is that all peremptory challenges are based on stereotypes of some kind, expressing various intuitive and frequently erroneous biases. But where peremptory challenges are made on the basis of group characteristics other than race or gender (like occupation, for example), they do not reinforce the same stereotypes about the group's competence or predispositions that have been used to prevent them from voting, participating on juries, pursuing their chosen professions, or otherwise contributing to civic life. See B. Babcock, A Place in the Palladium, Women's Rights and Jury Service, 61 U.Cinn.L.Rev. 1139, 1173 (1993).

strike.... When an explanation is required, it need not rise to the level of a "for cause" challenge; rather, it merely must be based on a juror characteristic other than gender, and the proffered explanation may not be pretextual. See Hernandez v. New York, 500 U.S. 352 (1991).

Failing to provide jurors the same protection against gender discrimination as race discrimination could frustrate the purpose of *Batson* itself. Because gender and race are overlapping categories, gender can be used as a pretext for racial discrimination. Allowing parties to remove racial minorities from the jury not because of their race, but because of their gender, contravenes well-established equal protection principles and could insulate effectively racial discrimination from judicial scrutiny.

V

Equal opportunity to participate in the fair administration of justice is fundamental to our democratic system. It not only furthers the goals of the jury system. It reaffirms the promise of equality under the law— that all citizens, regardless of race, ethnicity, or gender, have the chance to take part directly in our democracy. Powers v. Ohio, 499 U.S., at 407 ("Indeed, with the exception of voting, for most citizens the honor and privilege of jury duty is their most significant opportunity to participate in the democratic process"). When persons are excluded from participation in our democratic processes solely because of race or gender, this promise of equality dims, and the integrity of our judicial system is jeopardized.

In view of these concerns, the Equal Protection Clause prohibits discrimination in jury selection on the basis of gender, or on the assumption that an individual will be biased in a particular case for no reason other than the fact that the person happens to be a woman or happens to be a man....

The judgment ... is reversed and the case is remanded ... for further proceedings not inconsistent with this opinion.

. . .

Justice O'Connor, concurring.

I agree with the Court that the Equal Protection Clause prohibits the government from excluding a person from jury service on account of that person's gender.... But today's important blow against gender discrimination is not costless. I write separately to discuss some of these costs, and to express my belief that today's holding should be limited to the government's use of gender-based peremptory strikes.

... In further constitutionalizing jury selection procedures, the Court increases the number of cases in which jury selection—once a sideshow—will become part of the main event.

For this same reason, today's decision further erodes the role of the peremptory challenge.... The principal value of the peremptory is that it helps produce fair and impartial juries.... "Peremptory challenges, by enabling each side to exclude those jurors it believes will be most partial toward the other side, are a means of eliminat[ing] extremes of partiality on both sides, thereby assuring the selection of a qualified and unbiased jury." Holland v. Illinois, 493 U.S. 474, 484 (1990)....

Moreover, "[t]he essential nature of the peremptory challenge is that it is one exercised without a reason stated, without inquiry and without being subject to the court's control." Swain, 380 U.S., at 220.... Our belief that experienced lawyers will often correctly intuit which jurors are likely to be the least sympathetic, and our understanding that the lawyer will often be unable to explain the intuition, are the very reason we cherish the peremptory challenge. But, as we add, layer by layer, additional constitutional restraints on the use of the peremptory, we force lawyers to articulate what we know is often inarticulable.

In so doing we make the peremptory challenge less discretionary and more like a challenge for cause. We also increase the possibility that biased jurors will be allowed onto the jury, because sometimes a lawyer will be unable to provide an acceptable gender-neutral explanation even though the lawyer is in fact correct that the juror is unsympathetic.... Because I believe the peremptory remains an important litigator's tool and a fundamental part of the process of selecting impartial juries, our increasing limitation of it gives me pause.

Nor is the value of the peremptory challenge to the litigant diminished when the peremptory is exercised in a gender-based manner. We know that like race, gender matters. A plethora of studies make clear that in rape cases, for example, female jurors are somewhat more likely to vote to convict than male jurors. See R. Hastie, S. Penrod, & N. Pennington, Inside the Jury 140–141 (1983)(collecting and summarizing empirical studies). Moreover, though there have been no similarly definitive studies regarding, for example, sexual harassment, child custody, or spousal or child abuse, one need not be a sexist to share the intuition that in certain cases a person's gender and resulting life experience will be relevant to his or her view of the case....

Today's decision severely limits a litigant's ability to act on this intuition, for the import of our holding is that any correlation between a juror's gender and attitudes is irrelevant as a matter of constitutional law. But to say that gender makes no difference as a matter of law is not to say that gender makes no difference as a matter of fact. I previously have said with regard to *Batson:* "That the Court will not tolerate prosecutors' racially discriminatory use of the peremptory challenge, in effect, is a special rule of relevance, a statement about what this Nation stands for, rather than a statement of fact." Brown v. North Carolina, 479 U.S. 940, 941–942 (1986)(O'Connor, J., concurring in denial of certiorari). Today's decision is a statement that, in an effort to eliminate the potential discriminatory use of the peremptory, ... gender is now governed by the special rule of relevance formerly reserved for race. Though we gain much from this statement, we cannot ignore what we lose. In extending *Batson* to gender we have added an additional burden to the state and federal trial process, taken a step closer to eliminating the peremptory challenge, and diminished the ability of litigants to act on sometimes accurate gender-based assumptions about juror attitudes.

These concerns reinforce my conviction that today's decision should be limited to a prohibition on the government's use of gender-based peremptory challenges....

. . .

Accordingly, I adhere to my position that the Equal Protection Clause does not limit the exercise of peremptory challenges by private civil litigants and criminal defendants. This case itself presents no state action dilemma, for here the State of Alabama itself filed the paternity suit on behalf of petitioner. But what of the next case? Will we, in the name of fighting gender discrimination, hold that the battered wife—on trial for wounding her abusive husband—is a state actor? Will we preclude her from using her peremptory challenges to ensure that the jury of her peers contains as many women members as possible? I assume we will, but I hope we will not.

Justice Kennedy, concurring in the judgment.

. . .

There is no doubt under our precedents ... that the Equal Protection Clause prohibits sex discrimination in the selection of jurors. Duren v. Missouri, 439 U.S. 357 (1979); Taylor v. Louisiana, 419 U.S. 522 (1975). The only question is whether the Clause also prohibits peremptory challenges based on sex. The Court is correct to hold that it does. The Equal Protection Clause and our constitutional tradition are based on the theory that an individual possesses rights that are protected against lawless action by the government. The neutral phrasing of the Equal Protection Clause, extending its guarantee to "any person," reveals its concern with rights of individuals, not groups (though group disabilities are sometimes the mechanism by which the State violates the individual right in question).... For purposes of the Equal Protection Clause, an individual denied jury service because of a peremptory challenge exercised against her on account of her sex is no less injured than the individual denied jury service because of a law banning members of her sex from serving as jurors.... The injury is to personal dignity and to the individual's right to participate in the political process.... The neutrality of the Fourteenth Amendment's guarantee is confirmed by the fact that the Court has no difficulty in finding a constitutional wrong in this case, which involves males excluded from jury service because of their gender.

. . .

[I]t is important to recognize that a juror sits not as a representative of a racial or sexual group but as an individual citizen. Nothing would be more pernicious to the jury system than for society to presume that persons of different backgrounds go to the jury room to voice prejudice.... The jury pool must be representative of the community, but that is a structural mechanism for preventing bias, not enfranchising it....

Chief Justice Rehnquist, dissenting.

... Accepting Batson v. Kentucky, 476 U.S. 79 (1986), as correctly decided, there are sufficient differences between race and gender discrimination such that the principle of *Batson* should not be extended to peremptory challenges to potential jurors based on sex.

That race and sex discrimination are different is acknowledged by our equal protection jurisprudence, which accords different levels of protection to the two groups. Classifications based on race are inherently suspect, triggering "strict scrutiny," while gender-based classifications are judged under a heightened, but less searching standard of review. Mississippi Univ. for Women v. Hogan, 458 U.S. 718, 724 (1982). Racial groups comprise numerical minorities in our society, warranting in some situations a greater need for protection, whereas the population is divided almost equally between men and women. Furthermore, while substantial discrimination against both groups still lingers in our society, racial equality has proved a more challenging goal to achieve on many fronts than gender equality. See, e.g., D. Kirp, M. Yudof, M. Franks, Gender Justice 137 (1986).

Batson, which involved a black defendant challenging the removal of black jurors, announced a sea-change in the jury selection process. In balancing the dictates of equal protection and the historical practice of peremptory challenges, long recognized as securing fairness in trials, the Court concluded that the command of the Equal Protection Clause was superior. But the Court was careful that its rule not "undermine the contribution the challenge generally makes to the administration of justice." 476 U.S., at 98–99. *Batson* is best understood as a recognition that race lies at the core of the commands of the Fourteenth Amendment....

Under the Equal Protection Clause, these differences mean that the balance should tilt in favor of peremptory challenges when sex, not race, is the issue. Unlike the Court, I think the State has shown that jury strikes on the basis of gender "substantially further" the State's legitimate interest in achieving a fair and impartial trial through the venerable practice of peremptory challenges.... The two sexes differ, both biologically and, to a diminishing extent, in experience. It is not merely "stereotyping" to say that these differences may produce a difference in outlook which is brought to the jury room. Accordingly, use of peremptory challenges on the basis of sex is generally not the sort of derogatory and invidious act which peremptory challenges directed at black jurors may be.

. . .

Justice Scalia, with whom The Chief Justice and Justice Thomas join, dissenting.

. . .

The Court ... spends time establishing that the use of sex as a proxy for particular views or sympathies is unwise and perhaps irrational. The opinion stresses the lack of statistical evidence to support the widely held belief that, at least in certain types of cases, a juror's sex has some statistically significant predictive value as to how the juror will behave. This assertion seems to place the Court in opposition to its earlier Sixth Amendment "fair cross-section" cases. See, e.g., Taylor v. Louisiana, 419 U.S. 522, 532, n. 12 (1975)("Controlled studies ... have concluded that women bring to juries their own perspectives and values that influence both jury deliberation and result"). But times and trends do change, and unisex is unquestionably in fashion.... Even if sex was a remarkably good predictor in certain cases, the Court would find its use in peremptories unconstitutional.... Of course the relationship of sex to partiality would have been relevant if the Court had demanded in this case what it ordinarily demands: that the complaining party have suffered some injury. Leaving aside for the moment the reality that the defendant himself had the opportunity to strike women from the jury, the defendant would have some cause to complain about the prosecutor's striking male jurors if male jurors tend to be more favorable towards defendants in paternity suits. But if men and women jurors are (as the Court thinks) fungible, then the only arguable injury from the prosecutor's "impermissible" use of male sex as the basis for his peremptories is injury to the stricken juror, not to the defendant.

Indeed, far from having suffered harm, petitioner, a state actor under our precedents, see Georgia v. McCollum ..., has himself actually inflicted harm on female jurors.[2] ...

The core of the Court's reasoning is that peremptory challenges on the basis of any group characteristic subject to heightened scrutiny are inconsistent with the guarantee of the Equal Protection Clause. That conclusion can be reached only by focusing unrealistically upon individual exercises of the peremptory challenge, and ignoring the totality of the practice. Since all groups are subject to the peremptory challenge (and will be made the object of it, depending upon the nature of the particular case) it is hard to see how any group is denied equal protection.... That explains why peremptory challenges coexisted with the Equal Protection Clause for 120 years. This case is a perfect example of how the system as a whole is even-handed. While the only claim before the Court is petitioner's complaint that the prosecutor struck male jurors, for every man struck by the government petitioner's own lawyer struck a woman. To say that men were singled out for discriminatory treatment in this process is preposterous. The situation would be different if both sides systematically struck individuals of one group, so that the strikes evinced group-based animus and served as a proxy for segregated venire lists. See Swain v. Alabama, 380 U.S. 202, 223–224 (1965). The pattern here, however, displays not a systemic sex-based animus but each side's desire to get a jury favorably disposed to its case. That is why the Court's characterization of respondent's argument as "reminiscent of

[2] I continue to agree with Justice O'Connor that *McCollum* and *Edmonson* erred in making civil litigants and criminal defendants state actors for purposes of the Equal Protection Clause. I do not, however, share her belief that correcting that error while continuing to consider the exercise of peremptories by prosecutors a denial of equal protection will make things right. If, in accordance with common perception but contrary to the Court's unisex creed, women really will decide some cases differently from men, allowing defendants alone to strike jurors on the basis of sex will produce—and will be seen to produce—juries intentionally weighted in the defendant's favor: no women jurors, for example, in a rape prosecution. That is not a desirable outcome.

the arguments advanced to justify the total exclusion of women from juries," is patently false. Women were categorically excluded from juries because of doubt that they were competent; women are stricken from juries by peremptory challenge because of doubt that they are well disposed to the striking party's case.... There is discrimination and dishonor in the former, and not in the latter—which explains the 106–year interlude between our holding that exclusion from juries on the basis of race was unconstitutional, Strauder v. West Virginia, 100 U.S. 303 (1880), and our holding that peremptory challenges on the basis of race were unconstitutional, Batson v. Kentucky, supra.

. . .

Even if the line of our later cases guaranteed by today's decision limits the theoretically boundless *Batson* principle to race, sex, and perhaps other classifications subject to heightened scrutiny (which presumably would include religious belief, see Larson v. Valente, 456 U.S. 228, 244–246 (1982)), much damage has been done. It has been done, first and foremost, to the peremptory challenge system, which loses its whole character when (in order to defend against "impermissible stereotyping" claims) "reasons" for strikes must be given....

And damage has been done, secondarily, to the entire justice system, which will bear the burden of the expanded quest for "reasoned peremptories" that the Court demands. The extension of *Batson* to sex, and almost certainly beyond, ... will provide the basis for extensive collateral litigation, which especially the criminal defendant (who litigates full-time and cost-free) can be expected to pursue. While demographic reality places some limit on the number of cases in which race-based challenges will be an issue, every case contains a potential sex-based claim. Another consequence ... is a lengthening of the voir dire process that already burdens trial courts.

The irrationality of today's strike-by-strike approach to equal protection is evident from the consequences of extending it to its logical conclusion. If a fair and impartial trial is a prosecutor's only legitimate goal; if adversarial trial stratagems must be tested against that goal in abstraction from their role within the system as a whole; and if, so tested, sex-based strategems do not survive heightened scrutiny—then the prosecutor presumably violates the Constitution when he selects a male or female police officer to testify because he believes one or the other sex might be more convincing in the context of the particular case, or because he believes one or the other might be more appealing to a predominantly male or female jury. A decision to stress one line of argument or present certain witnesses before a mostly female jury—for example, to stress that the defendant victimized women—becomes, under the Court's reasoning, intentional discrimination by a state actor on the basis of gender.

. . .

UNITED STATES v. VIRGINIA

___ U.S. ___, 116 S.Ct. 2264, ___ L.Ed.2d ___ (1996).

Justice Ginsburg delivered the opinion of the Court.

Virginia's public institutions of higher learning include an incomparable military college, Virginia Military Institute (VMI). The United States maintains that the Constitution's equal protection guarantee precludes Virginia from reserving exclusively to men the unique educational opportunities VMI affords. We agree.

I

Founded in 1839, VMI is today the sole single-sex school among Virginia's 15 public institutions of higher learning. VMI's distinctive mission is to produce "citizen-soldiers," men prepared for leadership in civilian life and in military service. VMI pursues this mission through pervasive training of a kind not available anywhere else in Virginia[—] ... an "adversative method" [that] constantly endeavors to instill physical and mental discipline in its cadets and impart to them a strong moral code....

. . .

Neither the goal of producing citizen-soldiers nor VMI's implementing methodology is inherently unsuitable to women. And the school's impressive record in producing leaders has made admission desirable to some women....

II

. . .

VMI today enrolls about 1,300 men as cadets....

VMI['s] ... " ... adversative, or doubting, model of education" ... features "[p]hysical rigor, mental stress, absolute equality of treatment, absence of privacy, minute regulation of behavior, and indoctrination in desirable values." ...

VMI cadets live in spartan barracks where surveillance is constant and privacy nonexistent; they wear uniforms, eat together in the mess hall, and regularly participate in drills.... Entering students are incessantly exposed to the rat line, "an extreme form of the adversative model," comparable in intensity to Marine Corps boot camp....

. . .

[The United States, prompted by a female applicant's complaint, sued Virginia and VMI in 1990. The District Court ruled in favor of VMI but the Fourth Circuit reversed and remanded,] suggest[ing] these options for the State: Admit women to VMI; establish parallel institutions or programs; or abandon state support, leaving VMI free to pursue its policies as a private institution....

... Virginia proposed a parallel program for women: Virginia Women's Institute for Leadership (VWIL). The 4-year, state-sponsored undergraduate program would be located at Mary Baldwin College, a private liberal arts school for women, and would be open, initially, to

about 25 to 30 students. Although VWIL would share VMI's mission—
to produce "citizen-soldiers"—the VWIL program would differ, as does
Mary Baldwin College, from VMI in academic offerings, methods of
education, and financial resources....

. . .

[T]he District Court ... decided the plan met the requirements of
the Equal Protection Clause....

A divided Court of Appeals affirmed....

. . .

III

[T]his case present[s] two ultimate issues. First, does Virginia's
exclusion of women from the educational opportunities provided by
VMI—extraordinary opportunities for military training and civilian leadership development—deny to women "capable of all of the individual
activities required of VMI cadets," ... the equal protection of the laws
guaranteed by the Fourteenth Amendment? Second, if VMI's "unique"
situation ...—as Virginia's sole single-sex public institution of higher
education—offends the Constitution's equal protection principle, what is
the remedial requirement?

IV

We note, once again, the core instruction of this Court's pathmark-
ing decisions in J.E.B. v. Alabama ex rel. T. B., ... and *Mississippi
Univ. for Women*, ...: Parties who seek to defend gender-based government action must demonstrate an "exceedingly persuasive justification"
for that action.

Today's skeptical scrutiny of official action denying rights or opportunities based on sex responds to volumes of history....

... Since *Reed*, the Court has repeatedly recognized that neither
federal nor state government acts compatibly with the equal protection
principle when a law or official policy denies to women, simply because
they are women, full citizenship stature—equal opportunity to aspire,
achieve, participate in and contribute to society based on their individual
talents and capacities....

... To summarize the Court's current directions for cases of official
classification based on gender: Focusing on the differential treatment or
denial of opportunity for which relief is sought, the reviewing court must
determine whether the proffered justification is "exceedingly persuasive." The burden of justification is demanding and it rests entirely on
the State.... The State must show "at least that the [challenged]
classification serves 'important governmental objectives and that the
discriminatory means employed' are 'substantially related to the achievement of those objectives.'" ... The justification must be genuine, not
hypothesized or invented *post hoc* in response to litigation. And it must
not rely on overbroad generalizations about the different talents, capacities, or preferences of males and females....

The heightened review standard our precedent establishes does not make sex a proscribed classification.... Physical differences between men and women ... are enduring....

"Inherent differences" between men and women ... remain cause for celebration, but not for denigration of the members of either sex or for artificial constraints on an individual's opportunity. Sex classifications may be used to compensate women "for particular economic disabilities [they have] suffered," ... to "promot[e] equal employment opportunity," ... to advance full development of the talent and capacities of our Nation's people.[7] ... But such classifications may not be used, as they once were, ... to create or perpetuate the legal, social, and economic inferiority of women.

[W]e conclude that Virginia has shown no "exceedingly persuasive justification" for excluding all women from the citizen-soldier training afforded by VMI.... Because the remedy proffered by Virginia—the Mary Baldwin VWIL program—does not cure the constitutional violation, i.e., it does not provide equal opportunity, we reverse....

V

... Virginia ... asserts two justifications in defense of VMI's exclusion of women. First, ... "single-sex education provides important educational benefits," ... and the option of single-sex education contributes to "diversity in educational approaches,".... Second, ... "the unique VMI method of character development and leadership training," the school's adversative approach, would have to be modified were VMI to admit women....

A

Single-sex education affords pedagogical benefits to at least some students, ... and that reality is uncontested in this litigation. Similarly, it is not disputed that diversity among public educational institutions can serve the public good. But Virginia has not shown that VMI was established, or has been maintained, with a view to diversifying, by its categorical exclusion of women, educational opportunities within the State. In cases of this genre, our precedent instructs that "benign" justifications proffered in defense of categorical exclusions will not be accepted automatically; a tenable justification must describe actual state purposes, not rationalizations for actions in fact differently grounded....

. . .

[7] Several *amici* have urged that diversity in educational opportunities is an altogether appropriate governmental pursuit and that single-sex schools can contribute importantly to such diversity. Indeed, it is the mission of some single-sex schools "to dissipate, rather than perpetuate, traditional gender classifications." See Brief for Twenty–Six Private Women's Colleges.... We do not question the State's prerogative evenhandedly to support diverse educational opportunities. We address specifically and only an educational opportunity recognized by the District Court and the Court of Appeals as "unique," ... an opportunity available only at Virginia's premier military institute, the State's sole single-sex public university or college....

Neither recent nor distant history bears out Virginia's alleged pursuit of diversity through single-sex educational options. In 1839, when the State established VMI, a range of educational opportunities for men and women was scarcely contemplated. Higher education at the time was considered dangerous for women. . . .

Virginia eventually provided for . . . women's seminaries and colleges. . . . By the mid–1970's, all four schools had become coeducational. . . .

Debate concerning women's admission as undergraduates at the main university continued well past the century's midpoint. . . .

Ultimately, in 1970, . . . the University of Virginia . . . introduced coeducation and, in 1972, began to admit women on an equal basis with men. . . .

Virginia describes the current absence of public single-sex higher education for women as "an historical anomaly." . . . But the historical record indicates action more deliberate than anomalous: First, protection of women against higher education; next, schools for women far from equal in resources and stature to schools for men; finally, conversion of the separate schools to coeducation. . . . [I]n 1990, . . . the Virginia Commission on the University of the 21st Century . . . reported: " 'Because colleges and universities provide opportunities for students to develop values and learn from role models, it is extremely important that they deal with faculty, staff, and students without regard to sex, race, or ethnic origin.' " . . . This statement, the Court of Appeals observed, "is the only explicit one that we have found in the record in which the Commonwealth has expressed itself with respect to gender distinctions."
. . .

Our 1982 decision in *Mississippi Univ. for Women* prompted VMI to reexamine its male-only admission policy. . . . A Mission Study Committee . . . studied the problem from October 1983 until May 1986, and in that month counseled against "change of VMI status as a single-sex college." . . . Whatever internal purpose the Mission Study Committee served—and however well-meaning the framers of the report—we can hardly extract from that effort any state policy evenhandedly to advance diverse educational options. As the District Court observed, the Committee's analysis "primarily focuse[d] on anticipated difficulties in attracting females to VMI," and the report, overall, supplied "very little indication of how th[e] conclusion was reached."

In sum, we find no persuasive evidence in this record that VMI's male-only admission policy "is in furtherance of a state policy of 'diversity.' " . . . A purpose genuinely to advance an array of educational options . . . is not served by VMI's historic and constant plan—a plan to "affor[d] a unique educational benefit only to males." . . . However "liberally" this plan serves the State's sons, it makes no provision whatever for her daughters. That is not equal protection.

B

Virginia next argues that VMI's adversative method of training provides educational benefits that cannot be made available, unmodified, to women. Alterations to accommodate women would necessarily be ... so "drastic," ... as to transform, indeed "destroy," VMI's program.... Neither sex would be favored ...: Men would be deprived of the unique opportunity currently available to them; women would not gain that opportunity because their participation would "eliminat[e] the very aspects of [the] program that distinguish [VMI] ..." ...

The District Court forecast from expert witness testimony, and the Court of Appeals accepted, that coeducation would materially affect "at least these three aspects of VMI's program—physical training, the absence of privacy, and the adversative approach." ... And it is uncontested that women's admission would require accommodations, primarily in arranging housing assignments and physical training programs for female cadets.... It is also undisputed, however, that "the VMI methodology could be used to educate women." ... The District Court even allowed that some women may prefer it to the methodology a women's college might pursue.... ["S]ome women," the expert testimony established, "are capable of all of the individual activities required of VMI cadets," [and t]he parties ... agree that "some women can meet the physical standards [VMI] now impose[s] on men." ... In sum, as the Court of Appeals stated, "neither the goal of producing citizen soldiers," VMI's *raison d'etre*, "nor VMI's implementing methodology is inherently unsuitable to women." ...

... [T]he District Court made "findings" on "gender-based developmental differences[,]" [that] restate the opinions of Virginia's expert witnesses, opinions about typically male or typically female "tendencies." ... For example, "[m]ales tend to need an atmosphere of adversativeness," while "[f]emales tend to thrive in a cooperative atmosphere." ...

The United States does not challenge any expert witness estimation on average capacities or preferences of men and women. Instead, the United States emphasizes that ... we have cautioned reviewing courts to take a "hard look" at generalizations or "tendencies" of the kind pressed by Virginia, and relied upon by the District Court.... State actors controlling gates to opportunity, we have instructed, may not exclude qualified individuals based on "fixed notions concerning the roles and abilities of males and females." ...

It may be assumed ... that most women would not choose VMI's adversative method.... [H]owever, ... it is also probable that "many men would not want to be educated in such an environment." ... The issue, however, is not whether "women—or men—should be forced to attend VMI" [but] whether the State can constitutionally deny to women who have the will and capacity, the training and attendant opportunities that VMI uniquely affords....

The notion that admission of women would downgrade VMI's stature, destroy the adversative system and, with it, even the school, is a judgment hardly proved, a prediction hardly different from other "self-fulfilling prophec[ies]," ... once routinely used to deny rights or opportunities. When women first sought admission to the bar and access to legal education, concerns of the same order were expressed....

Medical faculties similarly resisted men and women as partners in the study of medicine. . . .

Women's successful entry into the federal military academies, and their participation in the Nation's military forces, indicate that Virginia's fears for the future of VMI may not be solidly grounded. . . . The State's justification for excluding all women from "citizen-soldier" training for which some are qualified, in any event, cannot rank as "exceedingly persuasive," as we have explained and applied that standard.

. . .

. . . Surely . . . the State's great goal is not substantially advanced by women's categorical exclusion, in total disregard of their individual merit, from the State's premier "citizen-soldier" corps. Virginia, in sum, "has fallen far short of establishing the 'exceedingly persuasive justification,'" . . . that must be the solid base for any gender-defined classification.

VI

In the second phase of the litigation, Virginia presented its remedial plan—maintain VMI as a male-only college and create VWIL as a separate program for women. The plan met District Court approval. The Fourth Circuit . . . deferentially reviewed the State's proposal and decided that the two single-sex programs directly served Virginia's reasserted purposes: single-gender education, and "achieving the results of an adversative method in a military environment." . . . Inspecting the VMI and VWIL educational programs to determine whether they "afford[ed] to both genders benefits comparable in substance, [if] not in form and detail," . . . the Court of Appeals concluded that Virginia had arranged for men and women opportunities "sufficiently comparable" to survive equal protection evaluation. . . .

A

A remedial decree . . . must closely fit the constitutional violation; it must be shaped to place persons unconstitutionally denied an opportunity or advantage in "the position they would have occupied in the absence of [discrimination]." See Milliken v. Bradley, 433 U.S. 267, 280 (1977). . . . The constitutional violation in this case is the categorical exclusion of women from an extraordinary educational opportunity afforded men. A proper remedy for an unconstitutional exclusion, we have explained, aims to "eliminate [so far as possible] the discriminatory effects of the past" and to "bar like discrimination in the future." . . .

Virginia chose not to eliminate, but to leave untouched, VMI's exclusionary policy. For women only, however, Virginia proposed a separate program, different in kind from VMI and unequal in tangible and intangible facilities. . . .

VWIL affords women no opportunity to experience the rigorous military training for which VMI is famed. . . . Instead, the VWIL program "deemphasize[s]" military education, . . . and uses a "cooperative method" of education "which reinforces self-esteem,". . . .

VWIL students participate in ROTC and a "largely ceremonial" Virginia Corps of Cadets, ... but Virginia deliberately did not make VWIL a military institute. The VWIL House is not a military-style residence and VWIL students need not live together throughout the 4–year program, eat meals together, or wear uniforms during the school day.... VWIL students thus do not experience the "barracks" life "crucial to the VMI experience," the spartan living arrangements designed to foster an "egalitarian ethic." ... Virginia deemed that core experience nonessential, indeed inappropriate, for training its female citizen-soldiers.

VWIL students ... [are k]ept away from the pressures, hazards, and psychological bonding characteristic of VMI's adversative training, [and thus] will not know the "feeling of tremendous accomplishment" commonly experienced by VMI's successful cadets....

Virginia maintains that these methodological differences are "justified pedagogically," based on "important differences between men and women in learning and developmental needs," "psychological and sociological differences" Virginia describes as "real" and "not stereotypes." ...

... [G]eneralizations about "the way women are," estimates of what is appropriate for most women, no longer justify denying opportunity to women whose talent and capacity place them outside the average description. Notably, Virginia never asserted that VMI's method of education suits most men. It is also revealing that Virginia accounted for its failure to make the VWIL experience "the entirely militaristic experience of VMI" on the ground that VWIL "is planned for women who do not necessarily expect to pursue military careers." ... By that reasoning, VMI's "entirely militaristic" program would be inappropriate for men in general or as a group, for "[o]nly about 15% of VMI cadets enter career military service." ...

In contrast to the generalizations about women on which Virginia rests, we note again these dispositive realties: VMI's "implementing methodology" is not "inherently unsuitable to women," ...; "some women ... do well under [the] adversative model," ...; "some women, at least, would want to attend [VMI] if they had the opportunity," ...; "some women are capable of all of the individual activities required of VMI cadets," ... and "can meet the physical standards [VMI] now impose[s] on men,".... It is on behalf of these women that the United States has instituted this suit, and it is for them that a remedy must be crafted,[19] a remedy that will end their exclusion from a state-supplied educational opportunity for which they are fit, a decree that will "bar like discrimination in the future." ...

[19] Admitting women to VMI would undoubtedly require alterations necessary to afford members of each sex privacy from the other sex in living arrangements, and to adjust aspects of the physical training programs.... Experience shows such adjustments are manageable. See U.S. Military Academy, ... Report of Admission of Women ... (1977–1980)(4–year longitudinal study of the admission of women to West Point)....

B

In myriad respects other than military training, VWIL does not qualify as VMI's equal. VWIL's student body, faculty, course offerings, and facilities hardly match VMI's. Nor can the VWIL graduate anticipate the benefits associated with VMI's 157–year history, the school's prestige, and its influential alumni network.

. . .

. . . [T]he . . . VWIL program [is] fairly appraised as a "pale shadow" of VMI in terms of the range of curricular choices and faculty stature, funding, prestige, alumni support and influence. . . .

Virginia's VWIL solution is reminiscent of . . . Sweatt v. Painter, 339 U.S. 629 (1950). Reluctant to admit African Americans to its flagship University of Texas Law School, the State set up a separate school for Herman Sweatt and other black law students. . . .

. . . This Court contrasted resources at the new school with those at the school from which Sweatt had been excluded. . . .

More important than the tangible features, the Court emphasized, are "those qualities which are incapable of objective measurement but which make for greatness" in a school, including "reputation of the faculty, experience of the administration, position and influence of the alumni, standing in the community, traditions and prestige." . . . [T]he Court unanimously ruled that Texas had not shown "substantial equality in the [separate] educational opportunities" the State offered. . . . In line with *Sweatt*, we rule here that Virginia has not shown substantial equality in the separate educational opportunities the State supports at VWIL and VMI.

C

. . .

The Fourth Circuit plainly erred in exposing Virginia's VWIL plan to a deferential analysis, for "all gender-based classifications today" warrant "heightened scrutiny." . . . Valuable as VWIL may prove for students who seek the program offered, Virginia's remedy affords no cure at all for the opportunities and advantages withheld from women who want a VMI education and can make the grade. . . . In sum, Virginia's remedy does not match the constitutional violation; the State has shown no "exceedingly persuasive justification" for withholding from women qualified for the experience premier training of the kind VMI affords.

VII

. . .

A prime part of the history of our Constitution . . . is the story of the extension of constitutional rights and protections to people once ignored or excluded. VMI's story continued as our comprehension of "We the People" expanded. . . . There is no reason to believe that the admission of women capable of all the activities required of VMI cadets would destroy the Institute rather than enhance its capacity to serve the "more perfect Union."

. . .

Justice Thomas took no part in the consideration or decision of this case.

Chief Justice Rehnquist, concurring in the judgment.

. . .

I

Two decades ago in Craig v. Boren, 429 U.S. 190, 197 (1976), we announced that "[t]o withstand constitutional challenge, . . . classifications by gender must serve important governmental objectives and must be substantially related to achievement of those objectives." We have adhered to that standard of scrutiny ever since. . . . While the majority adheres to this test today, it also says that the State must demonstrate an " 'exceedingly persuasive justification' " to support a gender-based classification. It is unfortunate that the Court thereby introduces an element of uncertainty respecting the appropriate test.

While terms like "important governmental objective" and "substantially related" are hardly models of precision, they have more content and specificity than does the phrase "exceedingly persuasive justification." That phrase is best confined, as it was first used, as an observation on the difficulty of meeting the applicable test, not as a formulation of the test itself. . . .

Our cases dealing with gender discrimination also require that the proffered purpose for the challenged law be the actual purpose. [O]n this ground . . . the Court rejects the first of two justifications Virginia offers[—]the goal of diversity among its public educational institutions. While I ultimately agree that the State has not carried the day with this justification, I disagree with the Court's method of analyzing the issue.

. . .

. . . [Not until the 1982 *Mississippi University for Women* decision was] Virginia [placed] on notice that VMI's men-only admissions policy was open to serious question.

The VMI Board of Visitors, in response, appointed a Mission Study Committee [that] ended up cryptically recommending against changing VMI's status as a single-sex college . . . [because of] the changes that admission of women to VMI would require, and the likely effect of those changes on the institution. That VMI would have to change is simply not helpful in addressing the constitutionality of the status after *Hogan*.

. . . I agree with the Court that there is scant evidence in the record that [diversity in education with room for single-sex institutions] was the real reason that Virginia decided to maintain VMI as men only.* But,

---

* The dissent equates our conclusion that VMI's "asserted interest in promoting diversity" is not " 'genuine,' " with a "charge" that the diversity rationale is "a pretext for

unlike the majority, I would consider only evidence that postdates . . .
Hogan, and would draw no negative inferences from the State's actions
before that time. [A]fter *Hogan*, the State was entitled to reconsider its
policy with respect to VMI, and to not have earlier justifications, or lack
thereof, held against it.

Even if diversity in educational opportunity were the State's actual
objective, the State's position would still be problematic[, because] . . .
the diversity benefited only one sex; there was single-sex public education available for men at VMI, but no corresponding single-sex public
education available for women. . . .

I do not think, however, that the State's options were as limited as
the majority may imply. . . . Had Virginia made a genuine effort to
devote comparable public resources to a facility for women, and followed
through on such a plan, it might well have avoided an equal protection
violation. I do not believe the State was faced with the stark choice of
either admitting women to VMI . . . or abandoning VMI and starting
from scratch for both men and women. . . .

But . . . neither the governing board of VMI nor the State took any
action after 1982. If diversity in the form of single-sex, as well as
coeducational, institutions of higher learning were to be available to
Virginians, that diversity had to be available to women as well as to men.

The dissent criticizes me for "disregarding the four all-women's
private colleges in Virginia (generously assisted by public funds)." The
private women's colleges are treated by the State exactly as all other
private schools are treated, which includes the provision of tuition-
assistance grants to Virginia residents. Virginia gives no special support
to the women's single-sex education. But obviously, the same is not true
for men's education. Had the State provided the kind of support for the
private women's schools that it provides for VMI, this may have been a
very different case. For in so doing, the State would have demonstrated
that its interest in providing a single-sex education for men, was to some
measure matched by an interest in providing the same opportunity for
women.

Virginia offers a second justification for the single-sex admissions
policy: maintenance of the adversative method. I agree with the Court
that this justification does not serve an important governmental objective. A State does not have substantial interest in the adversative
methodology unless it is pedagogically beneficial[, and] . . . there is no
. . . evidence in the record that an adversative method is pedagogically
beneficial or is any more likely to produce character traits than other
methodologies.

discriminating against women." Of course, those are not the same thing. I do not read
the Court as saying that the diversity rationale is a pretext for discrimination, and I would
not endorse such a proposition. We may find that diversity was not the State's real reason
without suggesting, or having to show, that the real reason was "antifeminism." Our
cases simply require that the proffered purpose . . . be the actual purpose, although not
necessarily recorded. The dissent also says that the interest in diversity is so transparent
that having to articulate it is "absurd on its face." Apparently, that rationale was not
obvious to the Mission Study Committee which failed to list it among its reasons for
maintaining VMI's all-men admission policy.

II

... [I]t is not the "exclusion of women" that violates the Equal Protection Clause, but the maintenance of an all-men school without providing any—much less a comparable—institution for women.

Accordingly, the remedy should not necessarily require either the admission of women to VMI, or the creation of a VMI clone for women. An adequate remedy ... might be a demonstration by Virginia that its interest in educating men in a single-sex environment is matched by its interest in educating women in a single-sex institution.... It would ... suffic[e] if the two institutions offered the same quality of education and were of the same overall calibre.

If a state decides to create single-sex programs, [it] would, I expect, consider the public's interest and demand in designing curricula. And rightfully so. But the state should avoid assuming demand based on stereotypes; it must not assume *a priori*, without evidence, that there would be no interest in a women's school of civil engineering, or in a men's school of nursing.

In the end, ... VWIL ... fails as a remedy, because it is distinctly inferior to the existing men's institution and will continue to be for the foreseeable future. VWIL simply is not, in any sense, the institution that VMI is. In particular, VWIL is ... appended to a private college, not a self-standing institution; and VWIL is substantially underfunded as compared to VMI. I therefore ultimately agree with the Court that Virginia has not provided an adequate remedy.

Justice Scalia, dissenting.

Today the Court shuts down an institution that has served the people of the Commonwealth of Virginia with pride and distinction for over a century and a half. To achieve that desired result, it rejects ... the factual findings of two courts below, sweeps aside the precedents of this Court, and ignores the history of our people. As to facts: it explicitly rejects the finding that there exist "gender-based developmental differences" supporting Virginia's restriction of the "adversative" method to only a men's institution, and the finding that the all-male composition of ... VMI is essential to [its] character. As to precedent: it drastically revises our established standards for reviewing sex-based classifications. And as to history: it counts for nothing the long tradition ... of men's military colleges supported by both States and the Federal Government.

Much of the Court's opinion is devoted to deprecating the closed-mindedness of our forebears with regard to women's education, and even with regard to the treatment of women in areas that have nothing to do with education. Closed-minded they were—as every age is, including our own, with regard to matters it cannot guess, because it simply does not consider them debatable. The virtue of a democratic system with a First Amendment is that it readily enables the people, over time, to be persuaded that what they took for granted is not so, and to change their laws accordingly. That system is destroyed if the smug assurances of each age are removed from the democratic process and written into the Constitution. . . .

I

. . .

I have no problem with a system of abstract tests such as rational-basis, intermediate, and strict scrutiny (though I think we can do better than applying strict scrutiny and intermediate scrutiny whenever we feel like it). . . .   But . . . the function of this Court is to preserve our society's values . . . , not to revise them; to prevent backsliding from the degree of restriction the Constitution imposed upon democratic government, not to prescribe, on our own authority, progressively higher degrees. . . .   [The] abstract tests . . . cannot supersede—and indeed ought to be crafted so as to reflect—those constant and unbroken national traditions that embody the people's understanding of ambiguous constitutional texts. . . .

. . . [T]he tradition of having government-funded military schools for men is as well rooted in the traditions of this country as the tradition of sending only men into military combat.   The people may decide to change the one tradition, like the other, through democratic processes; but the assertion that either tradition has been unconstitutional through the centuries is not law, but politics-smuggled-into-law.

And the same applies, more broadly, to single-sex education in general, which . . . is threatened by today's decision with the cut-off of all state and federal support. . . .

Today, . . . single-sex education is prohibited nationwide, not by democratic processes but by order of this Court. Even while bemoaning the sorry, bygone days of "fixed notions" concerning women's education, the Court favors current notions so fixedly that it is willing to write them into the Constitution . . . by application of custom-built "tests." This is not the interpretation of a Constitution, but the creation of one.

II

To reject the Court's disposition today, however, it is not necessary to accept my view that the Court's made-up tests cannot displace longstanding national traditions as the primary determinant of what the Constitution means. It is only necessary to apply honestly the test the Court has been applying to sex-based classifications for the past two decades. . . .

. . . [T]he United States urged us to hold in this case "that strict scrutiny is the correct constitutional standard for evaluating classifications that deny opportunities to individuals based on their sex."   . . . The Court, while making no reference to the Government's argument, effectively accepts it.

. . . [T]he Court . . . interpret[s] "exceedingly persuasive justification" in a fashion that contradicts the reasoning of *Hogan* and our other precedents.

That is essential to the Court's result, which can only be achieved by establishing that intermediate scrutiny is not survived if there are some women interested in attending VMI, capable of undertaking its activities, and able to meet its physical demands....

Only the amorphous "exceedingly persuasive justification" phrase, and not the standard elaboration of intermediate scrutiny, can be made to yield th[e] conclusion that VMI's single-sex composition is unconstitutional because there exist several women (or, one would have to conclude under the Court's reasoning, a single woman) willing and able to undertake VMI's program. Intermediate scrutiny has never required a least-restrictive-means analysis, but only a "substantial relation" between the classification and the state interests that it serves.... There is simply no support in our cases for the notion that a sex-based classification is invalid unless it relates to characteristics that hold true in every instance.

Not content to execute a de facto abandonment of the intermediate scrutiny that has been our standard for sex-based classifications for some two decades, the Court purports to reserve the question whether, even in principle, a higher standard (i.e., strict scrutiny) should apply....

[I]f the question of the applicable standard of review for sex-based classifications were ... reconsider[ed], the stronger argument would be not for elevating the standard to strict scrutiny, but for reducing it to rational-basis review. The latter certainly has a firmer foundation in our past jurisprudence: Whereas no majority of the Court has ever applied strict scrutiny in a case involving sex-based classifications, we routinely applied rational-basis review until the 1970's.... And of course normal, rational-basis review of sex-based classifications would be much more in accord with the genesis of heightened standards of judicial review, the famous footnote in United States v. Carolene Products Co., 304 U.S. 144 (1938).... It is hard to consider women a "discrete and insular minorit[y]" unable to employ the "political processes ordinarily to be relied upon," when they constitute a majority of the electorate. And the suggestion that they are incapable of exerting that political power smacks of the same paternalism that the Court so roundly condemns. Moreover, a long list of legislation proves the proposition false. See, e.g., Equal Pay Act of 1963 ...; Title VII of the Civil Rights Act of 1964 ...; Title IX of the Education Amendments of 1972....; Women's Business Ownership Act of 1988.... ; Violence Against Women Act of 1994....

III

... [T]he question ... is whether the exclusion of women from VMI is "substantially related to an important governmental objective."

A

It is beyond question that Virginia has an important state interest in providing effective college education for its citizens. That single-sex instruction is an approach substantially related to that interest should be evident enough from the long and continuing history in this country of men's and women's colleges....

The evidence establishing that fact was overwhelming—indeed, "virtually uncontradicted".... This finding alone ... should be sufficient to demonstrate the constitutionality of VMI's all-male composition.

But besides its single-sex constitution, VMI is different from other colleges in ... employ[ing] a "distinctive educational method[.]" ... [A] State's decision to maintain within its system one school that provides the adversative method is "substantially related" to its goal of good education. Moreover, it was uncontested that "if the state were to establish a women's VMI-type [i.e., adversative] program, the program would attract an insufficient number of participants to make the program work," ...; and it was found by the District Court that if Virginia were to include women in VMI, the school "would eventually find it necessary to drop the adversative system altogether,".... Thus, Virginia's options were an adversative method that excludes women or no adversative method at all.

There can be no serious dispute that, as the District Court found, single-sex education and a distinctive educational method "represent legitimate contributions to diversity in the Virginia higher education system." ...

... Substantial evidence in the District Court demonstrated that the Commonwealth has long proceeded on the principle that " '[h]igher education resources should be viewed as a whole—public and private' "—because such an approach enhances diversity and because " 'it is academic and economic waste to permit unwarranted duplication.' " ... (quoting 1974 Report of the General Assembly Commission on Higher Education to the General Assembly of Virginia). It is thus significant that, whereas there are "four all-female private [colleges] in Virginia," there is only "one private all-male college," which "indicates that the private sector is providing for th[e] [former] form of education to a much greater extent that it provides for all-male education." ... In these circumstances, Virginia's election to fund one public all-male institution and one on the adversative model—and to concentrate its resources in a single entity that serves both these interests in diversity— is substantially related to the State's important educational interests.

B

The Court ... relies on ... contentions that are irrelevant or erroneous as a matter of law, foreclosed by the record ..., or both.

. . .

... The Court suggests that Virginia's ... asserted interest in promoting diversity of educational options ... is not "genuin[e]," but is a pretext for discriminating against women.... The relevance of the Mission Study Committee is that its very creation, its sober 3–year study, and the analysis it produced, utterly refute the claim that VMI has elected to maintain its all-male student-body composition for some misogynistic reason.

The Court ... is wrong ... in its implication that ... an explicit statement of "actual purposes" is needed....

It is, moreover, not true that Virginia's contemporary reasons for maintaining VMI are not explicitly recorded.... As the parties stipulated, th[e 1990 Commission R]eport "notes that the hallmarks of Virginia's educational policy are 'diversity and autonomy.' " ...

. . .

... [T]he Court [also] finds fault with Virginia's failure to offer education based on the adversative training method to women[,] dismiss[ing] the District Court's " 'findings' on 'gender-based developmental differences' " ...

Ultimately, in fact, the Court does not deny the evidence supporting these findings ... [but] simply dispenses with the evidence submitted at trial—it never says that a single finding of the District Court is clearly erroneous—in favor of the Justices' own view of the world....

... But treating the evidence as irrelevant is absolutely necessary for the Court to reach its conclusion....

. . .

The Court's analysis ... [, a]pplied generally, ... means that whenever a State's ultimate objective is "great enough to accommodate women" (as it always will be), then the State will be held to have violated the Equal Protection Clause if it restricts to men even one means by which it pursues that objective—no matter how few women are interested in pursuing the objective by that means, no matter how much the single-sex program will have to be changed if both sexes are admitted, and no matter how beneficial that program has theretofore been to its participants.

... [T]hat VMI would not have to change very much if it were to admit women ... is irrelevant: If VMI's single-sex status is substantially related to the government's important educational objectives, as I have demonstrated above and as the Court refuses to discuss, that concludes the inquiry....

But if such a debate were relevant, the Court would certainly be on the losing side[, given] ... findings by two courts below, amply supported by the evidence, ... that VMI would be fundamentally altered if it admitted women.... [5]

... Finally, the absence of a precise "all-women's analogue" to VMI is irrelevant. In Mississippi Univ. for Women v. Hogan, 458 U.S. 718 (1982), we attached no constitutional significance to the absence of an all-male nursing school. As Virginia notes, if a program restricted to one sex is necessarily unconstitutional unless there is a parallel program

---

[5] The Court's do-it-yourself approach to factfinding ... is exemplified by its invocation of the experience of the federal military academies to prove that not much change would occur. In fact, the District Court noted that "the West Point experience" supported the theory that a coeducational VMI would have to "adopt a [different] system," for West Point found it necessary upon becoming coeducational to "move away" from its adversative system....

restricted to the other sex, "the opinion in *Hogan* could have ended with its first footnote, which observed that 'Mississippi maintains no other single-sex public university or college.' " ...

... I have thus far said nothing about VWIL because it is, under our established test, irrelevant, so long as VMI's all-male character is "substantially related" to an important state goal. But VWIL now exists, and the Court's treatment of it shows how far-reaching today's decision is.

... Even though VWIL was carefully designed by professional educators who have tremendous experience in the area, and survived the test of adversarial litigation, the Court simply declares, with no basis in the evidence, that these professionals acted on " 'overbroad' generalizations."

C

[T]he concurrence ... finds VMI unconstitutional on a basis that is more moderate than the Court's but only at the expense of being even more implausible. The concurrence offers three reasons: First, that there is "scant evidence in the record" that diversity of educational offering was the real reason for Virginia's maintaining VMI.... I have cited the clearest statements of diversity as a goal for higher education in [several reports.] There is no evidence to the contrary, once one rejects (as the concurrence rightly does) the relevance of VMI's founding in days when attitudes towards the education of women were different.... [I]t is absurd on its face even to demand "evidence" to prove that the Commonwealth's reason for maintaining a men's military academy is that a men's military academy provides a distinctive type of educational experience (i.e., fosters diversity). What other purpose would the Commonwealth have? One may argue, as the Court does, that this type of diversity is designed only to indulge hostility towards women- -but that is a separate point, explicitly rejected by the concurrence, and amply refuted by the evidence I have mentioned in discussing the Court's opinion.[6] ...

Second, the ... pedagogical benefits of VMI's adversative approach were not only proved, but were a given in this litigation. The reason the woman applicant who prompted this suit wanted to enter VMI was ... [that s]he wanted the distinctive adversative education that VMI provided....

A third reason the concurrence offers ... is ... that after our decision in *Hogan* ... the Commonwealth should have known that what this Court expected of it was ... the creation of a state all-women's program. Any lawyer who gave that advice ... ought to have been either disbarred or committed....

[6] The concurrence ... "read[s] the Court" not "as saying that the diversity rationale is a pretext" for discriminating against women, but as saying merely that the diversity rationale is not genuine. The Court itself makes no such disclaimer, which would be difficult to credit inasmuch as the foundation for its conclusion that the diversity rationale is not "genuin[e]" is its antecedent discussion of Virginia's "deliberate" actions over the past century and a half, based on "[f]amiliar arguments," that sought to enforce once "widely held views about women's proper place."

In any event, "diversity in the form of single-sex, as well as coeducational, institutions of higher learning," *is* "available to women as well as to men" in Virginia. The concurrence is able to assert the contrary only by disregarding the four all-women's private colleges in Virginia (generously assisted by public funds) and the Commonwealth's longstanding policy of coordinating public with private educational offerings. According to the concurrence, the reason Virginia's assistance to its four all-women's private colleges does not count is that "[t]he private women's colleges are treated by the State exactly as all other private schools are treated." But if Virginia cannot get credit for assisting women's education if it only treats women's private schools as it does all other private schools, then why should it get blame for assisting men's education if it only treats VMI as it does all other public schools? ...

IV

. . .

Under the constitutional principles announced and applied today, single-sex public education is unconstitutional. By going through the motions of applying a balancing test—asking whether the State has adduced an "exceedingly persuasive justification" for its sex-based classification—the Court creates the illusion that government officials in some future case will have a clear shot at justifying some sort of single-sex public education. Indeed, the Court ... purports to have said nothing of relevance to other public schools at all. . . .

. . .

[Yet] the rationale of today's decision is sweeping: for sex-based classifications, a redefinition of intermediate scrutiny that makes it indistinguishable from strict scrutiny. Indeed, the Court indicates that if any program restricted to one sex is "uniqu[e]," it must be opened to members of the opposite sex "who have the will and capacity" to participate in it. [T]he single-sex program [in]capable of being characterized as "unique" is ... nonexistent.

[R]egardless of whether the Court's rationale leaves some small amount of room for lawyers to argue, it ensures that single-sex public education is functionally dead. The costs of litigating the constitutionality of a single-sex education program, and the risks of ultimately losing that litigation, are simply too high to be embraced by public officials. . . . The enemies of single-sex education have won. . . .

. . .

There are few extant single-sex public educational programs. The potential of today's decision for widespread disruption of existing institutions lies in its application to private single-sex education. . . .

... The Government ... contends that private colleges which are the direct or indirect beneficiaries of government funding are not thereby necessarily converted into state actors to which the Equal Protection Clause is then applicable. . . . That is true. It is also virtually meaningless.

The issue will be not whether government assistance turns private colleges into state actors, but whether the government itself would be violating the Constitution by providing state support to single-sex colleges....

The only hope for state-assisted single-sex private schools is that the Court will not apply in the future the principles of law it has applied today. That is a substantial hope, I am happy and ashamed to say.... It will certainly be possible for this Court to write a future opinion that ignores the broad principles of law set forth today, and that characterizes as utterly dispositive the opinion's perceptions that VMI was a uniquely prestigious all-male institution, conceived in chauvinism, etc., etc. I will not join that opinion.

. . .

E. "BENIGN" DISCRIMINATION: AFFIRMATIVE ACTION, QUOTAS, PREFERENCES BASED ON GENDER OR RACE

---

2. CLASSIFICATIONS ADVANTAGING RACIAL MINORITIES

Page 887. Replace Metro Broadcasting, Inc. v. Federal Communications Commission with the following:

ADARAND CONSTRUCTORS, INC. v. PENA
___ U.S. ___, 115 S.Ct. 2097, 132 L.Ed.2d 158 (1995).

Justice O'Connor announced the judgment of the Court and delivered an opinion with respect to Parts I, II, III–A, III–B, III–D, and IV, which is for the Court except insofar as it might be inconsistent with the views expressed in Justice Scalia's concurrence, and an opinion with respect to Part III–C in which Justice Kennedy joins.

Petitioner Adarand Constructors, Inc., claims that the Federal Government's practice of giving general contractors on government projects a financial incentive to hire subcontractors controlled by "socially and economically disadvantaged individuals," and in particular, the Government's use of race-based presumptions in identifying such individuals, violates the equal protection component of the Fifth Amendment's Due Process Clause. The Court of Appeals rejected Adarand's claim. We conclude, however, that courts should analyze cases of this kind under a different standard of review than the one the Court of Appeals applied. We therefore vacate the Court of Appeals' judgment and remand the case for further proceedings.

I

[In 1989 an agency of the United States Department of Transportation (DOT) awarded the prime contract for a highway construction project in Colorado to Mountain Gravel & Construction Company. Mountain Gravel subcontracted the guardrail portion of the contract to Gonzales Construction Company rather than to Adarand, the low bidder, because the prime contract authorized additional compensation for hiring subcontractors certified as small businesses controlled by "socially and economically disadvantaged individuals."] Federal law requires [such] a subcontracting clause . . . in most federal agency contracts, and it also requires the clause to state that "[t]he contractor shall presume that socially and economically disadvantaged individuals include Black Americans, Hispanic Americans, Native Americans, Asian Pacific Americans, and other minorities, or any other individual found to be disadvantaged by the [Small Business] Administration [SBA] pursuant to section 8(a) of the Small Business Act." 15 U.S.C. §§ 637(d)(2), (3). Adarand claims that the presumption set forth in that statute discriminates on the basis of race in violation of the Federal Government's Fifth Amendment obligation not to deny anyone equal protection of the laws.

These fairly straightforward facts implicate a complex scheme of federal statutes and regulations. The Small Business Act . . . defines "socially disadvantaged individuals" as "those who have been subjected to racial or ethnic prejudice or cultural bias because of their identity as a member of a group without regard to their individual qualities," § 8(a)(5), . . . and it defines "economically disadvantaged individuals" as "those socially disadvantaged individuals whose ability to compete in the free enterprise system has been impaired due to diminished capital and credit opportunities as compared to others in the same business area who are not socially disadvantaged." § 8(a)(6)(A) . . . .

. . .

[Two SBA programs were relevant. The "8(a) program" confers numerous benefits, including automatic eligibility for the challenged subcontractor compensation provisions, on small businesses 51% owned by individuals who qualify as "socially and economically disadvantaged." The SBA presumes that Black, Hispanic, Asian Pacific, Subcontinent Asian, and Native Americans, as well as "members of other groups designated from time to time by SBA," are "socially disadvantaged," but it allows any other individual to prove social disadvantage. Every 8(a) participant must also prove "economic disadvantage." The "8(d) subcontracting program" is limited to eligibility for such subcontracting provisions, and it operates like the 8(a) program, except that the Court felt "some uncertainty . . . whether participation in the 8(d) subcontracting program requires an individualized showing of economic disadvantage." For particular participants in both the 8(a) and 8(d) programs, third parties can rebut the presumptions of economic or social disadvantage.

[Funds for the highway project were appropriated in the Surface Transportation and Uniform Relocation Assistance Act of 1987 (STURAA), which required no less than 10% of those funds to be spent with certified disadvantaged small businesses. STURAA incorporated the Small Business Act's definitions, including the race-based presumptions, and required the Transportation Secretary to set minimum criteria for

State governments to use in certifying eligible businesses. The Secretary's regulations required certifying authorities to use rebuttable race-based presumptions of both social and economic disadvantage. The record did not reveal whether Gonzales had been certified under these regulations or under either the SBA's 8(a) or 8(d) program.]

Adarand [sued] various federal officials ..., claiming that the race-based presumptions involved in the use of subcontracting compensation clauses violate Adarand's right to equal protection. The District Court granted the Government's motion for summary judgment.... The ... Tenth Circuit affirmed.... It understood our decision in Fullilove v. Klutznick, 448 U.S. 448 (1980), to have adopted "a lenient standard, resembling intermediate scrutiny, in assessing" the constitutionality of federal race-based action.... Applying that "lenient standard," as further developed in Metro Broadcasting, Inc. v. FCC, 497 U.S. 547 (1990), the Court of Appeals upheld the use of subcontractor compensation clauses....

. . .

III

The Government urges that "[t]he Subcontracting Compensation Clause program is ... a program based on disadvantage, not on race," and thus that it is subject only to "the most relaxed judicial scrutiny." ... To the extent that the statutes and regulations involved in this case are race neutral, we agree. The Government concedes, however, that "the race-based rebuttable presumption used in some certification determinations under the Subcontracting Compensation Clause" is subject to some heightened level of scrutiny....

Adarand's claim arises under the Fifth Amendment [Due Process Clause.] Although this Court has always understood that Clause to provide some measure of protection against arbitrary treatment by the Federal Government, it is not as explicit a guarantee of equal treatment as the Fourteenth Amendment [Equal Protection Clause].... Our cases have accorded varying degrees of significance to the difference in the language of those two Clauses....

A

Through the 1940s, this Court had routinely taken the view in non-race-related cases that, "[u]nlike the Fourteenth Amendment, the Fifth contains no equal protection clause and it provides no guaranty against discriminatory legislation by Congress." Detroit Bank v. United States, 317 U.S. 329, 337 (1943).... When the Court first faced a Fifth Amendment equal protection challenge to a federal racial classification, it adopted a similar approach, with most unfortunate results. In Hirabayashi v. United States, 320 U.S. 81 (1943), the Court considered a curfew applicable only to persons of Japanese ancestry. The Court observed—correctly—that "[d]istinctions between citizens solely because of their ancestry are by their very nature odious to a free people whose institutions are founded upon the doctrine of equality," and that "racial discriminations are in most circumstances irrelevant and therefore prohibited." ... But it also cited *Detroit Bank* for the proposition that the

Fifth Amendment "restrains only such discriminatory legislation by Congress as amounts to a denial of due process," ... and upheld the curfew....

... Korematsu v. United States, 323 U.S. 214 (1944), ... did not address the view ... that the Federal Government's obligation to provide equal protection differs significantly from that of the States. Instead, it began by noting that "all legal restrictions which curtail the civil rights of a single racial group are immediately suspect ... [and] courts must subject them to the most rigid scrutiny." ... That promising dictum might be read to undermine the view that the Federal Government is under a lesser obligation to avoid injurious racial classifications than are the States.... But ... the Court ... inexplicably relied on "the principles we announced in the *Hirabayashi* case" ... to conclude that, although "exclusion from the area in which one's home is located is a far greater deprivation than constant confinement to the home from 8 p. m. to 6 a. m.," ... the racially discriminatory order was nonetheless within the Federal Government's power.

In Bolling v. Sharpe, 347 U.S. 497 (1954), the Court for the first time explicitly questioned the existence of any difference between the obligations of the Federal Government and the States to avoid racial classifications....

Bolling's facts concerned school desegregation, but its reasoning was not so limited....

Later cases in contexts other than school desegregation did not distinguish between the duties of the States and the Federal Government to avoid racial classifications....

... Thus, in 1975, the Court stated explicitly that "[t]his Court's approach to Fifth Amendment equal protection claims has always been precisely the same as to equal protection claims under the Fourteenth Amendment." Weinberger v. Wiesenfeld, 420 U.S. 636, 638, n. 2 (1975).... We do not understand a few contrary suggestions appearing in cases in which we found special deference to the political branches of the Federal Government to be appropriate, e. g., Hampton v. Mow Sun Wong ... (1976)(federal power over immigration), to detract from this general rule.

B

Most of the cases discussed above involved classifications burdening groups that have suffered discrimination in our society. In 1978, the Court confronted the question whether race-based governmental action designed to benefit such groups should also be subject to "the most rigid scrutiny." Regents of Univ. of California v. Bakke ... did not produce an opinion for the Court....

Two years after *Bakke*, the Court faced another challenge to remedial race-based action, this time involving action undertaken by the Federal Government. In Fullilove v. Klutznick, 448 U.S. 448 (1980), the Court upheld Congress' inclusion of a 10% set-aside for minority-owned businesses in the Public Works Employment Act of 1977. As in *Bakke*, there was no opinion for the Court. Chief Justice Burger, in an opinion joined by Justices White and Powell, observed that "[a]ny preference based on racial or ethnic criteria must necessarily receive a most searching examination to make sure that it does not conflict with constitutional guarantees." ... That opinion, however, "d[id] not adopt, either expressly or implicitly, the formulas of analysis articulated in such cases as [Bakke]." ... It employed instead a two-part test which asked, first, "whether the objectives of th[e] legislation are within the power of Congress," and second, "whether the limited use of racial and ethnic criteria, in the context presented, is a constitutionally permissible means for achieving the congressional objectives." ... It then upheld the program under that test, adding at the end of the opinion that the program also "would survive judicial review under either 'test' articulated in the several Bakke opinions." ... Justice Powell wrote separately to express his view that the plurality opinion had essentially applied "strict scrutiny" as described in his Bakke opinion—i. e., it had determined that the set-aside was "a necessary means of advancing a compelling governmental interest"—and had done so correctly.... Justice Stewart (joined by then-Justice Rehnquist) dissented, arguing that the Constitution required the Federal Government to meet the same strict standard as the States when enacting racial classifications, ... and that the program before the Court failed that standard. Justice Stevens also dissented, arguing that "[r]acial classifications are simply too pernicious to permit any but the most exact connection between justification and classification," ... and that the program before the Court could not be characterized "as a 'narrowly tailored' remedial measure." ... Justice Marshall (joined by Justices Brennan and Blackmun) concurred in the judgment, reiterating the view of four Justices in Bakke that any race-based governmental action designed to "remed[y] the present effects of past racial discrimination" should be upheld if it was "substantially related" to the achievement of an "important governmental objective"—i. e., such action should be subjected only to what we now call "intermediate scrutiny." ...

In Wygant v. Jackson Board of Ed., 476 U.S. 267 (1986), the Court considered ... whether a school board could adopt race-based preferences in determining which teachers to lay off....

The Court's failure to produce a majority opinion in Bakke, Fullilove, and Wygant left unresolved the proper analysis for remedial race-based governmental action....

The Court resolved the issue, at least in part, in 1989. Richmond v. J.A. Croson Co., 488 U.S. 469 (1989), concerned a city's determination that 30% of its contracting work should go to minority-owned businesses. A majority of the Court in Croson held that "the standard of review under the Equal Protection Clause is not dependent on the race of those burdened or benefited by a particular classification," and that the single standard of review for racial classifications should be "strict scrutiny." ...

With Croson, the Court finally agreed that the Fourteenth Amendment requires strict scrutiny of all race-based action by state and local governments. But Croson of course had no occasion to declare what standard of review the Fifth Amendment requires for such action taken by the Federal Government. *Croson* observed simply that the Court's "treatment of an exercise of congressional power in *Fullilove* cannot be dispositive here," because *Croson*'s facts did not implicate Congress' broad power under § 5 of the Fourteenth Amendment....

Despite lingering uncertainty in the details, however, the Court's cases through *Croson* had established three general propositions with respect to governmental racial classifications. First, skepticism: " '[a]ny preference based on racial or ethnic criteria must necessarily receive a most searching examination,' " .... Second, consistency: "the standard of review under the Equal Protection Clause is not dependent on the race of those burdened or benefited by a particular classification," *Croson* ..., i. e., all racial classifications reviewable under the Equal Protection Clause must be strictly scrutinized. And third, congruence: "[e]qual protection analysis in the Fifth Amendment area is the same as that under the Fourteenth Amendment,".... Taken together, these three propositions lead to the conclusion that any person, of whatever race, has the right to demand that any governmental actor subject to the Constitution justify any racial classification subjecting that person to unequal treatment under the strictest judicial scrutiny....

A year later, however, the Court took a surprising turn. Metro Broadcasting, Inc. v. FCC, 497 U.S. 547 (1990), involved a Fifth Amendment challenge to two race-based policies of the Federal Communications Commission. In *Metro Broadcasting*, the Court repudiated the long-held notion that "it would be unthinkable that the same Constitution would impose a lesser duty on the Federal Government" than it does on a State to afford equal protection of the laws.... by holding that "benign" federal racial classifications need only satisfy intermediate scrutiny, even though *Croson* had recently concluded that such classifications enacted by a State must satisfy strict scrutiny. "[B]enign" federal racial classifications, the Court said, "—even if those measures are not 'remedial' in the sense of being designed to compensate victims of past governmental or societal discrimination—are constitutionally permissible to the extent that they serve important governmental objectives within the power of Congress and are substantially related to achievement of those objectives." ... The Court did not explain how to tell whether a racial classification should be deemed "benign," other than to express "confiden[ce] that an 'examination of the legislative scheme and its history' will separate benign measures from other types of racial classifications." ...

Applying this test, the Court first noted that the FCC policies at issue did not serve as a remedy for past discrimination.... Proceeding on the assumption that the policies were nonetheless "benign," it concluded that they served the "important governmental objective" of "enhancing broadcast diversity," ... and that they were "substantially related" to that objective.... It therefore upheld the policies.

By adopting intermediate scrutiny as the standard of review for congressionally mandated "benign" racial classifications, *Metro Broadcasting* departed from prior cases in two significant respects. First, it turned its back on *Croson*'s explanation of why strict scrutiny of all governmental racial classifications is essential:

"Absent searching judicial inquiry into the justification for such race-based measures, there is simply no way of determining what classifications are 'benign' or 'remedial' and what classifications are in fact motivated by illegitimate notions of racial inferiority or simple racial politics. Indeed, the purpose of strict scrutiny is to 'smoke out' illegitimate uses of race by assuring that the legislative body is pursuing a goal important enough to warrant use of a highly suspect tool. The test also ensures that the means chosen 'fit' this compelling goal so closely that there is little or no possibility that the motive for the classification was illegitimate racial prejudice or stereotype." ... We adhere to that view today, despite the surface appeal of holding "benign" racial classifications to a lower standard, because "it may not always be clear that a so-called preference is in fact benign," *Bakke* ... (opinion of Powell, J.)....

Second, *Metro Broadcasting* squarely rejected one of the three propositions established by the Court's earlier equal protection cases, namely, congruence between the standards applicable to federal and state racial classifications, and in so doing also undermined the other two—skepticism of all racial classifications, and consistency of treatment irrespective of the race of the burdened or benefited group.... Under *Metro Broadcasting*, certain racial classifications ("benign" ones enacted by the Federal Government) should be treated less skeptically than others; and the race of the benefited group is critical to the determination of which standard of review to apply. *Metro Broadcasting* was thus a significant departure from much of what had come before it.

The three propositions undermined by *Metro Broadcasting* all derive from the basic principle that the Fifth and Fourteenth Amendments to the Constitution protect persons, not groups. It follows from that principle that all governmental action based on race—a group classification long recognized as "in most circumstances irrelevant and therefore prohibited," *Hirabayashi* ...—should be subjected to detailed judicial inquiry to ensure that the personal right to equal protection of the laws has not been infringed. These ideas have long been central to this Court's understanding of equal protection, and holding "benign" state and federal racial classifications to different standards does not square with them. "[A] free people whose institutions are founded upon the doctrine of equality," ibid., should tolerate no retreat from the principle that government may treat people differently because of their race only for the most compelling reasons. Accordingly, we hold today that all racial classifications, imposed by whatever federal, state, or local governmental actor, must be analyzed by a reviewing court under strict scrutiny. In other words, such classifications are constitutional only if they are narrowly tailored measures that further compelling governmental interests. To the extent that *Metro Broadcasting* is inconsistent with that holding, it is overruled.

In dissent, Justice Stevens['s] ... criticisms reflect a serious misunderstanding of our opinion.

... What he fails to recognize is that strict scrutiny does take "relevant differences" into account—indeed, that is its fundamental purpose. The point of carefully examining the interest asserted by the government in support of a racial classification, and the evidence offered to show that the classification is needed, is precisely to distinguish legitimate from illegitimate uses of race in governmental decisionmaking. And Justice Stevens concedes that "some cases may be difficult to classify"; all the more reason, in our view, to examine all racial classifications carefully. Strict scrutiny does not "trea[t] dissimilar race-based decisions as though they were equally objectionable"; to the contrary, it evaluates carefully all governmental race-based decisions in order to decide which are constitutionally objectionable and which are not. By requiring strict scrutiny of racial classifications, we require courts to make sure that a governmental classification based on race ... is legitimate, before permitting unequal treatment based on race to proceed.

Justice Stevens chides us for our "supposed inability to differentiate between 'invidious' and 'benign' discrimination," because it is in his view sufficient that "people understand the difference between good intentions and bad." But ... the point of strict scrutiny is to "differentiate between" permissible and impermissible governmental use of race. And Justice Stevens himself has already explained in his dissent in *Fullilove* why "good intentions" alone are not enough ...: "[E]ven though it is not the actual predicate for this legislation, a statute of this kind inevitably is perceived by many as resting on an assumption that those who are granted this special preference are less qualified in some respect that is identified purely by their race. Because that perception—especially when fostered by the Congress of the United States—can only exacerbate rather than reduce racial prejudice, it will delay the time when race will become a truly irrelevant, or at least insignificant, factor...."; see also id., at 537 ("Racial classifications are simply too pernicious to permit any but the most exact connection between justification and classification"); *Croson*, supra, at 516–517 (Stevens, J., concurring in part and concurring in judgment)("Although [the legislation at issue] stigmatizes the disadvantaged class with the unproven charge of past racial discrimination, it actually imposes a greater stigma on its supposed beneficiaries").... These passages make a persuasive case for requiring strict scrutiny of congressional racial classifications.

Perhaps it is not the standard of strict scrutiny itself, but our use of the concepts of "consistency" and "congruence" in conjunction with it, that leads Justice Stevens to dissent. According to Justice Stevens, our view of consistency "equate[s] remedial preferences with invidious discrimination," and ignores the difference between "an engine of oppression" and an effort "to foster equality in society," or, more colorfully, "between a 'No Trespassing' sign and a welcome mat." It does nothing of the kind. The principle of consistency simply means that whenever the government treats any person unequally because of his or her race, that person has suffered an injury that falls squarely within the language and spirit of the Constitution's guarantee of equal protection. It says nothing about the ultimate validity of any particular law; that determination is the job of the court applying strict scrutiny. The principle of consistency explains the circumstances in which the injury requiring strict scrutiny occurs. The application of strict scrutiny, in turn, determines whether a compelling governmental interest justifies the infliction of that injury.

Consistency does recognize that any individual suffers an injury when he or she is disadvantaged by the government because of his or her race, whatever that race may be. This Court clearly stated that principle in *Croson* ... Justice Stevens does not explain how his views square with *Croson*, or with the long line of cases understanding equal protection as a personal right.

Justice Stevens also claims that we have ignored any difference between federal and state legislatures. But requiring that Congress, like the States, enact racial classifications only when doing so is necessary to further a "compelling interest" does not contravene any principle of appropriate respect for a co-equal Branch of the Government. [T]rue[,] various Members of this Court have taken different views of the authority § 5 of the Fourteenth Amendment confers upon Congress to deal with the problem of racial discrimination, and the extent to which courts should defer to Congress' exercise of that authority.... We need not, and do not, address these differences today. For now, it is enough to observe that Justice Stevens' suggestion that any Member of this Court has repudiated in this case his or her previously expressed views on the subject is incorrect.

C

. . .

... *Metro Broadcasting* undermined important principles of this Court's equal protection jurisprudence, established in a line of cases stretching back over fifty years. Those principles together stood for an "embracing" and "intrinsically soun[d]" understanding of equal protection "verified by experience," namely, that the Constitution imposes upon federal, state, and local governmental actors the same obligation to respect the personal right to equal protection of the laws.... [W]e cannot adhere to our most recent decision without colliding with an accepted and established doctrine....

. . .

It is worth pointing out the difference between the applications of stare decisis in this case and in Planned Parenthood of Southeastern Pa. v. Casey, 505 U.S. ___ (1992). *Casey* explained how considerations of stare decisis inform the decision whether to overrule a long-established precedent that has become integrated into the fabric of the law. Overruling precedent of that kind naturally may have consequences for "the ideal of the rule of law".... In addition, such precedent is likely to have engendered substantial reliance, as was true in *Casey* itself.... But in this case ... we do not face a precedent of that kind, because *Metro Broadcasting* itself departed from our prior cases—and did so quite recently. By refusing to follow *Metro Broadcasting*, then, we do not depart from the fabric of the law; we restore it. We also note that reliance on a case that has recently departed from precedent is likely to be minimal, particularly where, as here, the rule set forth in that case is unlikely to affect primary conduct in any event....

... [W]e think that well-settled legal principles pointed toward a conclusion different from that reached in *Metro Broadcasting*, and we therefore disagree with Justice Stevens that "the law at the time of that decision was entirely open to the result the Court reached." ... There is nothing new about the notion that Congress, like the States, may treat people differently because of their race only for compelling reasons.

"The real problem ... is whether a principle shall prevail over its later misapplications." ... *Metro Broadcasting*'s untenable distinction between state and federal racial classifications lacks support in our precedent, and undermines the fundamental principle of equal protection as a personal right. In this case, as between that principle and "its later misapplications," the principle must prevail.

D

Our action today makes explicit what Justice Powell thought implicit in the *Fullilove* lead opinion: federal racial classifications, like those of a State, must serve a compelling governmental interest, and must be narrowly tailored to further that interest.... [I]t follows that to the extent (if any) that *Fullilove* held federal racial classifications to be subject to a less rigorous standard, it is no longer controlling. But we need not decide today whether the program upheld in *Fullilove* would survive strict scrutiny as our more recent cases have defined it.

Some have questioned the importance of debating the proper standard of review of race-based legislation.... But we agree with Justice Stevens that, "[b]ecause racial characteristics so seldom provide a relevant basis for disparate treatment, and because classifications based on race are potentially so harmful to the entire body politic, it is especially important that the reasons for any such classification be clearly identified and unquestionably legitimate," and that "[r]acial classifications are simply too pernicious to permit any but the most exact connection between justification and classification." *Fullilove* ... (dissenting opinion).... We think that requiring strict scrutiny is the best way to ensure that courts will consistently give racial classifications that kind of detailed examination, both as to ends and as to means. *Korematsu* demonstrates vividly that even "the most rigid scrutiny" can sometimes fail to detect an illegitimate racial classification.... Any retreat from the most searching judicial inquiry can only increase the risk of another such error occurring in the future.

Finally, we wish to dispel the notion that strict scrutiny is "strict in theory, but fatal in fact." ... The unhappy persistence of both the practice and the lingering effects of racial discrimination against minority groups in this country is an unfortunate reality, and government is not disqualified from acting in response to it. As recently as 1987, for example, every Justice of this Court agreed that the Alabama Department of Public Safety's "pervasive, systematic, and obstinate discriminatory conduct" justified a narrowly tailored race-based remedy. See United States v. Paradise, 480 U.S., at 167 (plurality opinion of Brennan,

J.); id., at 190 (Stevens, J., concurring in judgment); id., at 196 (O'Connor, J., dissenting). When race-based action is necessary to further a compelling interest, such action is within constitutional constraints if it satisfies the "narrow tailoring" test this Court has set out in previous cases.

IV

Because our decision today alters the playing field in some important respects, we think it best to remand . . . for further consideration in light of the principles we have announced. The Court of Appeals, following *Metro Broadcasting* and *Fullilove*, analyzed the case in terms of intermediate scrutiny. It . . . did not decide . . . whether the interests served by the use of subcontractor compensation clauses are properly described as "compelling." It also did not address the question of narrow tailoring in terms of our strict scrutiny cases, by asking, for example, whether there was "any consideration of the use of race-neutral means to increase minority business participation" in government contracting, *Croson* . . . , or whether the program was appropriately limited such that it "will not last longer than the discriminatory effects it is designed to eliminate," *Fullilove* . . . (Powell, J., concurring).

Moreover, unresolved questions remain concerning the details of the complex regulatory regimes implicated by the use of subcontractor compensation clauses. For example, the SBA's 8(a) program requires an individualized inquiry into the economic disadvantage of every participant, . . . whereas the DOT's regulations implementing STURAA § 106(c) do not. . . . And the regulations seem unclear as to whether 8(d) subcontractors must make individualized showings, or instead whether the race-based presumption applies both to social and economic disadvantage. . . . We also note an apparent discrepancy between the definitions of which socially disadvantaged individuals qualify as economically disadvantaged for the 8(a) and 8(d) programs; the former requires a showing that such individuals' ability to compete has been impaired "as compared to others in the same or similar line of business who are not socially disadvantaged," . . . while the latter requires that showing only "as compared to others in the same or similar line of business," . . . . The question whether any of the ways in which the Government uses subcontractor compensation clauses can survive strict scrutiny, and any relevance distinctions such as these may have to that question, should be addressed in the first instance by the lower courts.

. . .

Justice Scalia, concurring in part and concurring in the judgment.

I join the opinion of the Court, except Part III–C, and except insofar as it may be inconsistent with the following: In my view, government can never have a "compelling interest" in discriminating on the basis of race in order to "make up" for past racial discrimination in the opposite direction. . . . Individuals who have been wronged by unlawful racial discrimination should be made whole; but under our Constitution there can be no such thing as either a creditor or a debtor race. That concept is alien to the Constitution's focus upon the individual ... and its rejection of dispositions based on race, see Amdt. 15, § 1 (prohibiting abridgment of the right to vote "on account of race") or based on blood, see Art. III, § 3 ("[N]o Attainder of Treason shall work Corruption of Blood"); Art. I, § 9 ("No Title of Nobility shall be granted by the United States"). To pursue the concept of racial entitlement—even for the most admirable and benign of purposes—is to reinforce and preserve for future mischief the way of thinking that produced race slavery, race privilege and race hatred. In the eyes of government, we are just one race here. It is American.

It is unlikely, if not impossible, that the challenged program would survive under this understanding of strict scrutiny, but I am content to leave that to be decided on remand.

Justice Thomas, concurring in part and concurring in the judgment.

I agree with the majority's conclusion that strict scrutiny applies to all government classifications based on race. I write separately, however, to express my disagreement with the premise underlying Justice Stevens' and Justice Ginsburg's dissents: that there is a racial paternalism exception to the principle of equal protection. I believe that there is a "moral [and] constitutional equivalence" (Stevens, J., dissenting) between laws designed to subjugate a race and those that distribute benefits on the basis of race in order to foster some current notion of equality. Government cannot make us equal; it can only recognize, respect, and protect us as equal before the law.

That these programs may have been motivated, in part, by good intentions cannot provide refuge from the principle that under our Constitution, the government may not make distinctions on the basis of race. As far as the Constitution is concerned, it is irrelevant whether a government's racial classifications are drawn by those who wish to oppress a race or by those who have a sincere desire to help those thought to be disadvantaged. There can be no doubt that the paternalism that appears to lie at the heart of this program is at war with the principle of inherent equality that underlies and infuses our Constitution. . . .

These programs ... also undermine the moral basis of the equal protection principle. Purchased at the price of immeasurable human suffering, the equal protection principle reflects our Nation's understanding that such classifications ultimately have a destructive impact on the individual and our society. . . . [T]here can be no doubt that racial paternalism and its unintended consequences can be as poisonous and pernicious as any other form of discrimination. So-called "benign" discrimination teaches many that because of chronic and apparently immutable handicaps, minorities cannot compete with them without their patronizing indulgence. Inevitably, such programs engender attitudes of superiority or, alternatively, provoke resentment among those who believe that they have been wronged by the government's use of race. These programs stamp minorities with a badge of inferiority and may cause them to develop dependencies or to adopt an attitude that they are "entitled" to preferences....

In my mind, government-sponsored racial discrimination based on benign prejudice is just as noxious as discrimination inspired by malicious prejudice. In each instance, it is racial discrimination, plain and simple.

Justice Stevens, with whom Justice Ginsburg joins, dissenting.

Instead of deciding this case in accordance with controlling precedent, the Court today delivers a disconcerting lecture about the evils of governmental racial classifications.... I believe this Court has a duty to affirm....

I

The Court's concept of skepticism is, at least in principle, a good statement of law and of common sense. Undoubtedly, a court should be wary of a governmental decision that relies upon a racial classification.... [B]ecause uniform standards are often anything but uniform, we should evaluate the Court's comments on "consistency," "congruence," and stare decisis with the same type of skepticism that the Court advocates for the underlying issue.

II

The Court's concept of "consistency" assumes that there is no significant difference between a decision by the majority to impose a special burden on the members of a minority race and a decision by the majority to provide a benefit to certain members of that minority notwithstanding its incidental burden on some members of the majority. [T]hat assumption is untenable. There is no moral or constitutional equivalence between a policy that is designed to perpetuate a caste system and one that seeks to eradicate racial subordination. Invidious discrimination is an engine of oppression, subjugating a disfavored group to enhance or maintain the power of the majority. Remedial race-based preferences reflect the opposite impulse: a desire to foster equality in society. No sensible conception of the Government's constitutional obligation to "govern impartially" ... should ignore this distinction.[1]

. . .

The consistency that the Court espouses would disregard the difference between a "No Trespassing" sign and a welcome mat. It would

---

[1] As Justice Ginsburg observes, the majority's "flexible" approach to "strict scrutiny" may well take into account differences between benign and invidious programs.... Even if ... so, ... it is unfortunate that the majority insists on applying the label "strict scrutiny" to benign race-based programs. That label has usually been understood to spell the death of any governmental action to which a court may apply it. The Court suggests today that "strict scrutiny" means something different—something less strict—when applied to benign racial classifications. Although I agree that benign programs deserve different treatment than invidious programs, there is a danger that the fatal language of "strict scrutiny" will skew the analysis and place well-crafted benign programs at unnecessary risk.

treat a Dixiecrat Senator's decision to vote against Thurgood Marshall's confirmation in order to keep African Americans off the Supreme Court as on a par with President Johnson's evaluation of his nominee's race as a positive factor. It would equate a law that made black citizens ineligible for military service with a program aimed at recruiting black soldiers. An attempt by the majority to exclude members of a minority race from a regulated market is fundamentally different from a subsidy that enables a relatively small group of newcomers to enter that market. An interest in "consistency" does not justify treating differences as though they were similarities.

The Court's explanation for treating dissimilar race-based decisions as though they were equally objectionable is a supposed inability to differentiate between "invidious" and "benign" discrimination. But the term "affirmative action" is common and well understood. Its presence in everyday parlance shows that people understand the difference between good intentions and bad. As with any legal concept, some cases may be difficult to classify, but our equal protection jurisprudence has identified a critical difference between state action that imposes burdens on a disfavored few and state action that benefits the few "in spite of" its adverse effects on the many. *Feeney*, 442 U.S., at 279.

Indeed, our jurisprudence has made the standard to be applied in cases of invidious discrimination turn on whether the discrimination is "intentional," or whether, by contrast, it merely has a discriminatory "effect." Washington v. Davis, 426 U.S. 229 (1976). Surely this distinction is at least as subtle, and at least as difficult to apply ... as the usually obvious distinction between a measure intended to benefit members of a particular minority race and a measure intended to burden a minority race. A state actor inclined to subvert the Constitution might easily hide bad intentions in the guise of unintended "effects"; but I should think it far more difficult to enact a law intending to preserve the majority's hegemony while casting it plausibly in the guise of affirmative action for minorities.

Nothing is inherently wrong with applying a single standard to fundamentally different situations, as long as that standard takes relevant differences into account. For example, if the Court in all equal protection cases were to insist that differential treatment be justified by relevant characteristics of the members of the favored and disfavored classes that provide a legitimate basis for disparate treatment, such a standard would treat dissimilar cases differently while still recognizing that there is, after all, only one Equal Protection Clause.... Under such a standard, subsidies for disadvantaged businesses may be constitutional though special taxes on such businesses would be invalid. But a single standard that purports to equate remedial preferences with invidious discrimination cannot be defended in the name of "equal protection."

Moreover, the Court may find that its new "consistency" approach to race-based classifications is difficult to square with its insistence upon rigidly separate categories for discrimination against different classes of individuals. For example, as the law currently stands, the Court will apply "intermediate scrutiny" to cases of invidious gender discrimination and "strict scrutiny" to cases of invidious race discrimination, while applying the same standard for benign classifications as for invidious ones. If this remains the law, then today's lecture about "consistency" will produce the anomalous result that the Government can more easily enact affirmative-action programs to remedy discrimination against women than it can enact affirmative-action programs to remedy discrimination against African Americans—even though the primary purpose of the Equal Protection Clause was to end discrimination against the former slaves.... When a court becomes preoccupied with abstract standards, it risks sacrificing common sense at the altar of formal consistency.

As a matter of constitutional and democratic principle, a decision by representatives of the majority to discriminate against the members of a minority race is fundamentally different from those same representatives' decision to impose incidental costs on the majority of their constituents in order to provide a benefit to a disadvantaged minority.[5] Indeed, ... the former is virtually always repugnant to the principles of a free and democratic society, whereas the latter is, in some circumstances, entirely consistent with the ideal of equality....

III

The Court's concept of "congruence" assumes that there is no significant difference between a decision by the Congress of the United States to adopt an affirmative-action program and such a decision by a State or a municipality. [T]hat assumption ... ignores important practical and legal differences between federal and state or local decisionmakers.

[5] ... Justice Thomas argues that the most significant cost associated with an affirmative-action program is its adverse stigmatic effect on its intended beneficiaries. Although I agree that this cost may be more significant than many people realize, ... I do not think it applies to the facts of this case. First, ... [n]o beneficiaries of the specific program under attack today have challenged its constitutionality—perhaps because they do not find the preferences stigmatizing, or perhaps because their ability to opt out of the program provides them all the relief they would need. Second, even if ... a minority-owned business challeng[ed] the stigmatizing effect of this program, I would not find Justice Thomas' extreme proposition—that there is a moral and constitutional equivalence between an attempt to subjugate and an attempt to redress the effects of a caste system—at all persuasive. It is one thing to question the wisdom of affirmative-action programs: there are many responsible arguments against them, including the one based upon stigma, that Congress might find persuasive when it decides whether to enact or retain race-based preferences. It is another thing altogether to equate the many well-meaning and intelligent lawmakers and their constituents—whether members of majority or minority races— who have supported affirmative action over the years, to segregationists and bigots. Finally, although Justice Thomas is more concerned about the potential effects of these programs than the intent of those who enacted them ..., I am not persuaded that the psychological damage brought on by affirmative action is as severe as that engendered by racial subordination. That, in any event, is a judgment the political branches can be trusted to make. In enacting affirmative action programs, a legislature intends to remove obstacles that have unfairly placed individuals of equal qualifications at a competitive disadvantage.... I do not believe such action, whether wise or unwise, deserves such an invidious label as "racial paternalism." If the legislature is persuaded that its program is doing more harm than good to the individuals it is designed to benefit, then we can expect the legislature to remedy the problem. Significantly, this is not true of a government action based on invidious discrimination.

These differences have been identified repeatedly and consistently both in opinions of the Court and in separate opinions authored by members of today's majority. Thus, in Metro Broadcasting, Inc. v. FCC, 497 U.S. 547 (1990), ... we identified the special "institutional competence" of our National Legislature. . . . We recalled the several opinions in *Fullilove* that admonished this Court to " 'approach our task with appropriate deference to the Congress, a co-equal branch charged by the Constitution with the power to "provide for the . . . general Welfare of the United States" and "to enforce, by appropriate legislation," the equal protection guarantees of the Fourteenth Amendment.' . . ." . . .

The majority in *Metro Broadcasting* and the plurality in *Fullilove* were not alone in relying upon a critical distinction between federal and state programs. In his separate opinion in Richmond v. J.A. Croson Co., 488 U.S. 469, 520–524 (1989), Justice Scalia discussed the basis for this distinction. . . .

In her plurality opinion in *Croson*, Justice O'Connor also emphasized the importance of this distinction when she responded to the City's argument that *Fullilove* was controlling. She wrote: "What appellant ignores is that Congress, unlike any State or political subdivision, has a specific constitutional mandate to enforce the dictates of the Fourteenth Amendment. The power to 'enforce' may at times also include the power to define situations which Congress determines threaten principles of equality and to adopt prophylactic rules to deal with those situations. The Civil War Amendments themselves worked a dramatic change in the balance between congressional and state power over matters of race." . . .

An additional reason for giving greater deference to the National Legislature than to a local law-making body is that federal affirmative-action programs represent the will of our entire Nation's elected representatives, whereas a state or local program may have an impact on nonresident entities who played no part in the decision to enact it. Thus, in the state or local context, individuals who were unable to vote for the local representatives who enacted a race-conscious program may nonetheless feel the effects of that program. This difference recalls the goals of the Commerce Clause, U.S. Const., Art. I, § 8, cl. 3, which permits Congress to legislate on certain matters of national importance while denying power to the States in this area for fear of undue impact upon out-of-state residents. . . .

Ironically, after all of the time, effort, and paper this Court has expended in differentiating between federal and state affirmative action, the majority today virtually ignores the issue. It provides not a word of direct explanation for its sudden and enormous departure from the reasoning in past cases. Such silence, however, cannot erase the difference between Congress' institutional competence and constitutional authority to overcome historic racial subjugation and the States' lesser power to do so.

Presumably, the majority is now satisfied that its theory of "congruence" between the substantive rights provided by the Fifth and Fourteenth Amendments disposes of the objection based upon divided constitutional powers. But it is one thing to say (as no one seems to dispute) that the Fifth Amendment encompasses a general guarantee of equal protection as broad as that contained within the Fourteenth Amendment. It is another thing entirely to say that Congress' institutional competence and constitutional authority entitles it to no greater deference when it enacts a program designed to foster equality than the deference due a State legislature. The latter is an extraordinary proposition; ... our precedents have rejected it explicitly and repeatedly.

Our opinion in *Metro Broadcasting* relied on several constitutional provisions to justify the greater deference we owe to Congress when it acts with respect to private individuals.... In the programs challenged in this case, Congress has acted both with respect to private individuals and, as in *Fullilove*, with respect to the States themselves.[9] When Congress does this, it draws its power directly from § 5 of the Fourteenth Amendment.... The Fourteenth Amendment directly empowers Congress at the same time it expressly limits the States.[11] This is no accident. It represents our Nation's consensus, achieved after hard experience throughout our sorry history of race relations, that the Federal Government must be the primary defender of racial minorities against the States, some of which may be inclined to oppress such minorities. A rule of "congruence" that ignores a purposeful "incongruity" so fundamental to our system of government is unacceptable.

. . .

IV

The Court's concept of stare decisis treats some of the language we have used in explaining our decisions as though it were more important than our actual holdings....

[9] The funding for the preferences challenged in this case comes from ... STURAA ..., in which Congress has granted funds to the States in exchange for a commitment to foster subcontracting by disadvantaged business enterprises, or "DBE's." STURAA is also the source of funding for DBE preferences in federal highway contracting. Approximately 98% of STURAA's funding is allocated to the States.... Moreover, under STURAA States are empowered to certify businesses as "disadvantaged" for purposes of receiving subcontracting preferences in both state and federal contracts.... In this case, Adarand has sued only the federal officials responsible for implementing federal highway contracting policy; it has not directly challenged DBE preferences granted in state contracts funded by STURAA. It is not entirely clear, then, whether the majority's "congruence" rationale would apply to federally regulated state contracts, which may conceivably be within the majority's view of Congress' § 5 authority even if the federal contracts are not. See Metro Broadcasting, 497 U.S., at 603–604 (O'Connor, J., dissenting). As I read the majority's opinion, however, it draws no distinctions between direct federal preferences and federal preferences achieved through subsidies to States. The extent to which STURAA intertwines elements of direct federal regulations with elements of federal conditions on grants to the States would make such a distinction difficult to sustain.

[11] We have read § 5 as a positive grant of authority to Congress, not just to punish violations, but also to define and expand the scope of the Equal Protection Clause. Katzenbach v. Morgan, 384 U.S. 641 (1966). In *Katzenbach*, this meant that Congress under § 5 could require the States to allow non-English-speaking citizens to vote, even if denying such citizens a vote would not have been an independent violation of § 1.... Congress, then, can expand the coverage of § 1 by exercising its power under § 5 when it acts to foster equality. Congress has done just that here; it has decided that granting certain preferences to minorities best serves the goals of equal protection.

This is the third time in the Court's entire history that it has considered the constitutionality of a federal affirmative-action program. On each of the two prior occasions, the first in 1980, Fullilove v. Klutznick, 448 U.S. 448, and the second in 1990, Metro Broadcasting, Inc. v. FCC, 497 U.S. 547, the Court upheld the program.....

In the Court's view, our decision in *Metro Broadcasting* was inconsistent with the rule announced in Richmond v. J.A. Croson Co., 488 U.S. 469 (1989). But two decisive distinctions separate those two cases. First, *Metro Broadcasting* involved a federal program, whereas *Croson* involved a city ordinance. *Metro Broadcasting* thus drew primary support from *Fullilove*, which predated *Croson* and which *Croson* distinguished on the grounds of the federal-state dichotomy that the majority today discredits. Although members of today's majority trumpeted the importance of that distinction in *Croson*, they now reject it in the name of "congruence." It is therefore quite wrong for the Court to suggest today that overruling *Metro Broadcasting* merely restores the status quo ante, for the law at the time of that decision was entirely open to the result the Court reached. Today's decision is an unjustified departure from settled law.

Second, *Metro Broadcasting*'s holding rested on more than its application of "intermediate scrutiny." ... What truly distinguishes *Metro Broadcasting* from our other affirmative-action precedents is the distinctive goal of the federal program in that case. Instead of merely seeking to remedy past discrimination, the FCC program was intended to achieve future benefits in the form of broadcast diversity....

[P]rior to *Metro Broadcasting*, the interest in diversity had been mentioned in a few opinions, but it is perfectly clear that the Court had not yet decided whether that interest had sufficient magnitude to justify a racial classification. *Metro Broadcasting*, of course, answered that question in the affirmative. The majority today overrules *Metro Broadcasting* only insofar as it is "inconsistent with [the] holding" that strict scrutiny applies to "benign" racial classifications promulgated by the Federal Government. The proposition that fostering diversity may provide a sufficient interest to justify such a program is not inconsistent with the Court's holding today—indeed, the question is not remotely presented in this case—and I do not take the Court's opinion to diminish that aspect of our decision in *Metro Broadcasting*.

The Court's suggestion that it may be necessary in the future to overrule *Fullilove* in order to restore the fabric of the law is even more disingenuous than its treatment of *Metro Broadcasting*. For the Court endorses the "strict scrutiny" standard that Justice Powell applied in *Bakke* and acknowledges that he applied that standard in *Fullilove* as well. Moreover, Chief Justice Burger also expressly concluded that the program we considered in *Fullilove* was valid under any of the tests articulated in *Bakke*, which of course included Justice Powell's.... The Court thus adopts a standard applied in *Fullilove* at the same time it questions that case's continued vitality and accuses it of departing from prior law.... As was true of *Metro Broadcasting*, the Court in *Fullilove* decided an important, novel, and difficult question. Providing a different answer to a similar question today cannot fairly be characterized as merely "restoring" previously settled law.

V

The Court's holding in *Fullilove* surely governs the result in this case. The Public Works Employment Act of 1977 (1977 Act) ... is different in several critical respects from the portions of the Small Business Act (SBA) ... and STURAA ... challenged in this case. Each of those differences makes the current program ... significantly less objectionable than the 1977 categorical grant of $400 million in exchange for a 10% set-aside in public contracts to "a class of investors defined solely by racial characteristics." *Fullilove*, 448 U.S., at 532 (Stevens, J., dissenting). In no meaningful respect is the current scheme more objectionable than the 1977 Act. Thus, if the 1977 Act was constitutional, then so must be the SBA and STURAA. Indeed, even if my dissenting views in *Fullilove* had prevailed, this program would be valid.

Unlike the 1977 Act, the present statutory scheme does not make race the sole criterion of eligibility for participation in the program. Race does give rise to a rebuttable presumption of social disadvantage which, at least under STURAA, gives rise to a second rebuttable presumption of economic disadvantage.... But a small business may qualify as a DBE, by showing that it is both socially and economically disadvantaged, even if it receives neither of these presumptions.... Thus, the current preference is more inclusive than the 1977 Act because it does not make race a necessary qualification.

More importantly, race is not a sufficient qualification. Whereas a millionaire with a long history of financial successes ... would have qualified for a preference under the 1977 Act merely because he was an Asian American or an African American, ... neither the SBA nor STURAA creates any such anomaly. The DBE program excludes members of minority races who are not, in fact, socially or economically disadvantaged.... The presumption of social disadvantage reflects the unfortunate fact that irrational racial prejudice—along with its lingering effects—still survives. The presumption of economic disadvantage embodies a recognition that success in the private sector of the economy is often attributable, in part, to social skills and relationships. Unlike the 1977 set-asides, the current preference is designed to overcome the social and economic disadvantages that are often associated with racial characteristics. If, in a particular case, these disadvantages are not present, the presumptions can be rebutted.... The program is thus designed to allow race to play a part in the decisional process only when there is a meaningful basis for assuming its relevance.

[I]t is particularly significant that the current program targets the negotiation of subcontracts between private firms. The 1977 Act applied entirely to the award of public contracts, an area of the economy in which social relationships should be irrelevant and in which proper supervision of government contracting officers should preclude any discrimination against particular bidders on account of their race. [Here], the program seeks to overcome barriers of prejudice between private parties—specifically, between general contractors and subcontractors.

The SBA and STURAA embody Congress' recognition that such barriers may actually handicap minority firms seeking business as subcontractors from established leaders in the industry that have a history of doing business with their golfing partners. Indeed, minority subcontractors may face more obstacles than direct, intentional racial prejudice: they may face particular barriers simply because they are more likely to be new in the business and less likely to know others in the business. Given such difficulties, Congress could reasonably find that a minority subcontractor is less likely to receive favors from the entrenched businesspersons who award subcontracts only to people with whom—or with whose friends—they have an existing relationship. This program, then, if in part a remedy for past discrimination, is most importantly a forward-looking response to practical problems faced by minority subcontractors.

The current program contains another forward-looking component that the 1977 set-asides did not share. Section 8(a) of the SBA provides for periodic review of the status of DBE's, ... and DBE status can be challenged by a competitor at any time under any of the routes to certification.... Such review prevents ineligible firms from taking part in the program solely because of their minority ownership, even when those firms were once disadvantaged but have since become successful. The emphasis on review also indicates the Administration's anticipation that after their presumed disadvantages have been overcome, firms will "graduate" into a status in which they will be able to compete for business, including prime contracts, on an equal basis.... As with other phases of the statutory policy of encouraging the formation and growth of small business enterprises, this program is intended to facilitate entry and increase competition in the free market.

Significantly, the current program, unlike the 1977 set-aside, does not establish any requirement—numerical or otherwise—that a general contractor must hire DBE subcontractors. The program we upheld in *Fullilove* required that 10% of the federal grant for every federally funded project be expended on minority business enterprises. In contrast, the current program contains no quota. Although it provides monetary incentives to general contractors to hire DBE subcontractors, it does not require them to hire DBE's, and they do not lose their contracts if they fail to do so. The importance of this incentive to general contractors (who always seek to offer the lowest bid) should not be underestimated; but the preference here is far less rigid, and thus more narrowly tailored, than the 1977 Act. Cf. *Bakke*, 438 U.S., at 319–320 (opinion of Powell, J.) (distinguishing between numerical set-asides and consideration of race as a factor).

Finally, the record shows a dramatic contrast between the sparse deliberations that preceded the 1977 Act ... and the extensive hearings conducted in several Congresses before the current program was developed.... If the 1977 program of race-based set-asides satisfied the strict scrutiny dictated by Justice Powell's vision of the Constitution—a vision the Court expressly endorses today—it must follow as night follows the day that the Court of Appeals' judgment upholding this more carefully crafted program should be affirmed.

. . .

Justice Souter, with whom Justice Ginsburg and Justice Breyer join, dissenting.

. . .

... The statutory scheme must be treated as constitutional if *Fullilove* v. *Klutznick,* 448 U.S. 448 (1980), is applied, and petitioners did not identify any of the factual premises on which *Fullilove* rested as having disappeared since that case was decided.

. . .

In these circumstances, I agree with Justice Stevens's conclusion that stare decisis compels the application of *Fullilove....   Fullilove ...* produced a result on shared grounds that petitioner does not attack: that discrimination in the construction industry had been subject to government acquiescence, with effects that remain and that may be addressed by some preferential treatment falling within the congressional power under § 5 of the Fourteenth Amendment.[1] ... Once *Fullilove* is applied, as Justice Stevens points out, it follows that the statutes in question here (which are substantially better tailored to the harm being remedied than the statute endorsed in *Fullilove ...*) pass muster under Fifth Amendment due process and Fourteenth Amendment equal protection.

The Court ... does not reach the application of *Fullilove ...*, and on remand ... the Government and petitioner [must] address anew the facts upon which statutes like these must be judged on the Government's remedial theory of justification: facts about the current effects of past discrimination, the necessity for a preferential remedy, and the suitability of this particular preferential scheme.... [I]t seems fair to ask whether the statutes will meet a different fate from what *Fullilove* would have decreed. The answer is, quite probably not, though of course there will be some interpretive forks in the road before the significance of strict scrutiny for congressional remedial statutes becomes entirely clear.

... Indeed, the Court's very recognition today that strict scrutiny can be compatible with the survival of a classification so reviewed demonstrates that our concepts of equal protection enjoy a greater elasticity than the standard categories might suggest....

In assessing the degree to which today's holding portends a departure from past practice, it is also worth noting that nothing in today's opinion implies any view of Congress's § 5 power and the deference due its exercise that differs from the views expressed by the *Fullilove*

---

[1] If the statutes are within the § 5 power, they are just as enforceable when the national government makes a construction contract directly as when it funnels construction money through the states. In any event, as Justice Stevens has noted, it is not clear whether the current challenge implicates only Fifth Amendment due process or Fourteenth Amendment equal protection as well.

plurality. . . . Thus, today's decision should leave § 5 exactly where it is as the source of an interest of the national government sufficiently important to satisfy the corresponding requirement of the strict scrutiny test.

Finally, . . . I do not understand that today's decision will necessarily have any effect on the . . . long accepted . . . view that constitutional authority to remedy past discrimination is not limited to the power to forbid its continuation, but extends to eliminating those effects that would otherwise persist and skew the operation of public systems even in the absence of current intent to practice any discrimination. . . . This is so whether the remedial authority is exercised by a court, . . . the Congress, . . . or some other legislature. . . . Indeed, a majority of the Court today reiterates that there are circumstances in which Government may, consistently with the Constitution, adopt programs aimed at remedying the effects of past invidious discrimination. . . .

When the extirpation of lingering discriminatory effects is thought to require a catch-up mechanism, like the racially preferential inducement under the statutes considered here, the result may be that some members of the historically favored race are hurt by that remedial mechanism, however innocent they may be of any personal responsibility for any discriminatory conduct. When this price is considered reasonable, it is in part because it is a price to be paid only temporarily; if the justification for the preference is eliminating the effects of a past practice, the assumption is that the effects will themselves recede into the past, becoming attenuated and finally disappearing. . . .

Surely the transition from the *Fullilove* plurality view (in which Justice Powell joined) to today's strict scrutiny (which will presumably be applied as Justice Powell employed it) does not signal a change in the standard by which the burden of a remedial racial preference is to be judged as reasonable or not at any given time. If in the District Court Adarand had chosen to press a challenge to the reasonableness of the burden of these statutes, more than a decade after *Fullilove* had examined such a burden, I doubt that the claim would have fared any differently from the way it will now be treated on remand from this Court.

Justice Ginsburg, with whom Justice Breyer joins, dissenting.

For the reasons stated by Justice Souter, and in view of the attention the political branches are currently giving the matter of affirmative action, I see no compelling cause for the intervention the Court has made in this case. I further agree with Justice Stevens that . . . large deference is owed by the Judiciary to "Congress' institutional competence and constitutional authority to overcome historic racial subjugation." I write separately to underscore . . . the considerable field of agreement . . . revealed in opinions that together speak for a majority of the Court.

I

. . .

The divisions in this difficult case should not obscure the Court's recognition of the persistence of racial inequality and a majority's acknowledgement of Congress' authority to act affirmatively, not only to end discrimination, but also to counteract discrimination's lingering effects.... Those effects, reflective of a system of racial caste only recently ended, are evident in our workplaces, markets, and neighborhoods. Job applicants with identical resumes, qualifications, and interview styles still experience different receptions, depending on their race. White and African–American consumers still encounter different deals. People of color looking for housing still face discriminatory treatment by landlords, real estate agents, and mortgage lenders. Minority entrepreneurs sometimes fail to gain contracts though they are the low bidders, and they are sometimes refused work even after winning contracts. Bias both conscious and unconscious, reflecting traditional and unexamined habits of thought, keeps up barriers that must come down if equal opportunity and nondiscrimination are ever genuinely to become this country's law and practice.

Given this history and its practical consequences, Congress surely can conclude that a carefully designed affirmative action program may help to realize, finally, the "equal protection of the laws" the Fourteenth Amendment has promised since 1868.

II

The lead opinion uses one term, "strict scrutiny," to describe the standard of judicial review for all governmental classifications by race. But that opinion's elaboration strongly suggests that the strict standard announced is indeed "fatal" for classifications burdening groups that have suffered discrimination in our society. That seems to me, and, I believe, to the Court, the enduring lesson one should draw from Korematsu v. United States, 323 U.S. 214 (1944).... A *Korematsu*-type classification, as I read the opinions in this case, will never again survive scrutiny....

For a classification made to hasten the day when "we are just one race," (Scalia, J., concurring in part and concurring in judgment), however, the lead opinion has dispelled the notion that "strict scrutiny" is " 'fatal in fact.' " ... Properly, a majority of the Court calls for review that is searching, in order to ferret out classifications in reality malign, but masquerading as benign. The Court's once lax review of sex-based classifications demonstrates the need for such suspicion. See, e.g., Hoyt v. Florida, 368 U.S. 57, 60 (1961)(upholding women's "privilege" of automatic exemption from jury service)....

Close review also is in order for this further reason.... [S]ome members of the historically favored race can be hurt by catch-up mechanisms designed to cope with the lingering effects of entrenched racial subjugation. Court review can ensure that preferences are not so large as to trammel unduly upon the opportunities of others or interfere too harshly with legitimate expectations of persons in once-preferred groups....

* * *

While I would not disturb the programs challenged in this case, and would leave their improvement to the political branches, I see today's decision as one that allows our precedent to evolve, still to be informed by and responsive to changing conditions.

———

Page 906. Add at end of subsection:

MILLER v. JOHNSON

___ U.S. ___, 115 S.Ct. 2475, 132 L.Ed.2d 762 (1995).

[The report in this case appears, infra at p. 170]

———

RACIAL GERRYMANDERING AND THE VOTING RIGHTS ACT

[This Note appears, infra at p. 189]

———

G. WHAT OTHER CLASSIFICATIONS WILL PROVOKE HEIGHTENED SCRUTINY?

———

2. CLASSIFICATIONS DISADVANTAGING THE RETARDED, THE ELDERLY, THE POOR, ETC.

———

Page 938. Add after City of Cleburne v. Cleburne Living Center:

HELLER v. DOE, 506 U.S. 312 (1993). The summary report of this case appears, supra at p. 100.

———

ROMER v. EVANS

___ U.S. ___, 116 S.Ct. 1620, 134 L.Ed.2d 855 (1996).

Justice Kennedy delivered the opinion of the Court.

One century ago, the first Justice Harlan admonished this Court that the Constitution "neither knows nor tolerates classes among citizens." Plessy v. Ferguson, 163 U.S. 537, 559 (1896)(dissenting opinion). Unheeded then, those words now are understood to state a commitment to the law's neutrality where the rights of persons are at stake. The Equal Protection Clause enforces this principle and today requires us to hold invalid a provision of Colorado's Constitution.

I

[A]n amendment to the Constitution of the State of Colorado, adopted in a 1992 statewide referendum ... as "Amendment 2," ... [stemmed] in large part from ordinances that had been passed in various Colorado municipalities[,] bann[ing] discrimination in many transactions and activities, including housing, employment, education, public accommodations, and health and welfare services. ...What gave rise to the statewide controversy was the protection the ordinances afforded to persons discriminated against by reason of their sexual orientation....

Yet Amendment 2, in explicit terms, does more than repeal or rescind these provisions. It prohibits all legislative, executive or judicial action at any level of state or local government designed to protect the named class, a class we shall refer to as homosexual persons or gays and lesbians. The amendment reads:

"No Protected Status Based on Homosexual, Lesbian, or Bisexual Orientation. Neither the State of Colorado, through any of its branches or departments, nor any of its agencies, political subdivisions, municipalities or school districts, shall enact, adopt or enforce any statute, regulation, ordinance or policy whereby homosexual, lesbian or bisexual orientation, conduct, practices or relationships shall constitute or otherwise be the basis of or entitle any person or class of persons to have or claim any minority status, quota preferences, protected status or claim of discrimination. This Section of the Constitution shall be in all respects self-executing." ...

Soon after Amendment 2 was adopted, this litigation to declare its invalidity and enjoin its enforcement was commenced in [state court by] homosexual persons, some of them government employees[, and by] governmental entities which had acted earlier to protect homosexuals from discrimination but would be prevented by Amendment 2 from continuing to do so. Although Governor Romer had been on record opposing the adoption of Amendment 2, he was named in his official capacity as a defendant, together with the Colorado Attorney General and the State of Colorado.

The trial court granted a preliminary injunction. ...[On appeal, s]ustaining the interim injunction and remanding the case for further proceedings, the State Supreme Court held that Amendment 2 was subject to strict scrutiny under the Fourteenth Amendment because it infringed the fundamental right of gays and lesbians to participate in the political process. ... To reach this conclusion, the state court relied on our voting rights cases, e.g., Reynolds v. Sims, 377 U.S. 533 (1964); Carrington v. Rash, 380 U.S. 89 (1965); Harper v. Virginia Bd. of Elections, 383 U.S. 663 (1966); Williams v. Rhodes, 393 U.S. 23 (1968), and on our precedents involving discriminatory restructuring of governmental decisionmaking, see, e.g., Hunter v. Erickson, 393 U.S. 385 (1969); Reitman v. Mulkey, 387 U.S. 369 (1967); Washington v. Seattle School Dist. No. 1, 458 U.S. 457 (1982); Gordon v. Lance, 403 U.S. 1 (1971). On remand, the State advanced various arguments in an effort to show that Amendment 2 was narrowly tailored to serve compelling interests, but the trial court found none sufficient. It enjoined enforcement of Amendment 2, and the Supreme Court of Colorado ... affirmed. ... We ... affirm ..., but on a rationale different from that adopted by the State Supreme Court.

II

The State's principal argument in defense of Amendment 2 is that it puts gays and lesbians in the same position as all other persons. So, the State says, the measure does no more than deny homosexuals special rights. This reading of the amendment's language is implausible. We rely ... upon the authoritative construction of Colorado's Supreme Court[, which] ... found it invalid even on a modest reading of its implications. ...

> "The immediate objective of Amendment 2 is, at a minimum, to repeal existing statutes, regulations, ordinances, and policies of state and local entities that barred discrimination based on sexual orientation. ...

> "The 'ultimate effect' of Amendment 2 is to prohibit any governmental entity from adopting similar, or more protective statutes, regulations, ordinances, or policies in the future unless the state constitution is first amended to permit such measures." ...

Sweeping and comprehensive is the change in legal status effected by this law. So much is evident from the ordinances that the Colorado Supreme Court declared would be void by operation of Amendment 2. Homosexuals, by state decree, are put in a solitary class with respect to transactions and relations in both the private and governmental spheres. The amendment withdraws from homosexuals, but no others, specific legal protection from the injuries caused by discrimination, and it forbids reinstatement of these laws and policies.

The change that Amendment 2 works in the legal status of gays and lesbians in the private sphere is far-reaching, both on its own terms and when considered in light of the structure and operation of modern anti-discrimination laws. ... [M]ost States have chosen to counter discrimination by enacting detailed statutory schemes. ...

Colorado's state and municipal laws typify this emerging tradition of statutory protection. ... The laws first enumerate the persons or entities subject to a duty not to discriminate. ... The Boulder ordinance, for example, has a comprehensive definition of entities deemed places of "public accommodation." ... The Denver ordinance is of similar breadth, applying, for example, to hotels, restaurants, hospitals, dental clinics, theaters, banks, common carriers, travel and insurance agencies, and "shops and stores dealing with goods or services of any kind," ....

These statutes and ordinances also depart from the common law by enumerating the groups or persons within their ambit of protection. ...Colorado's state and local governments have not limited anti-discrimination laws to groups that have so far been given the protection of heightened equal protection scrutiny under our cases. ... Rather, they set forth an extensive catalogue of traits which cannot be the basis for discrimination, including age, military status, marital status, pregnancy, parenthood, custody of a minor child, political affiliation, physical or mental disability of an individual or of his or her associates—and, in recent times, sexual orientation. . . .

Amendment 2 bars homosexuals from securing protection against the injuries that these public-accommodations laws address. That in itself is a severe consequence, but there is more. Amendment 2, in addition, nullifies specific legal protections for this targeted class in all transactions in housing, sale of real estate, insurance, health and welfare services, private education, and employment. . . .

Not confined to the private sphere, Amendment 2 also operates to repeal and forbid all laws or policies providing specific protection for gays or lesbians from discrimination by every level of Colorado government. The State Supreme Court cited two examples of protections in the governmental sphere that are now rescinded and may not be reintroduced. The first is Colorado Executive Order D0035 (1990), which forbids employment discrimination against "'all state employees, classified and exempt' on the basis of sexual orientation." . . . Also repealed, and now forbidden, are "various provisions prohibiting discrimination based on sexual orientation at state colleges." . . . The repeal of these measures and the prohibition against their future reenactment demonstrates that Amendment 2 has the same force and effect in Colorado's governmental sector as it does elsewhere and that it applies to policies as well as ordinary legislation.

Amendment 2's reach may not be limited to specific laws passed for the benefit of gays and lesbians. It is a fair, if not necessary, inference from the broad language of the amendment that it deprives gays and lesbians even of the protection of general laws and policies that prohibit arbitrary discrimination in governmental and private settings. . . .At some point in the systematic administration of these laws, an official must determine whether homosexuality is an arbitrary and thus forbidden basis for decision. Yet a decision to that effect would itself amount to a policy prohibiting discrimination on the basis of homosexuality, and so would appear to be no more valid under Amendment 2 than the specific prohibitions against discrimination the state court held invalid.

If this consequence follows from Amendment 2, as its broad language suggests, it would compound the constitutional difficulties the law creates. The state court did not decide whether the amendment has this effect, however, and neither need we. In the course of rejecting the argument that Amendment 2 is intended to conserve resources to fight discrimination against suspect classes, the Colorado Supreme Court made the limited observation that the amendment is not intended to affect many anti-discrimination laws protecting non-suspect classes. . . .In our view that does not resolve the issue. In any event, even if, as we doubt, homosexuals could find some safe harbor in laws of general application, we cannot accept the view that Amendment 2's prohibition on specific legal protections does no more than deprive homosexuals of special rights. To the contrary, the amendment imposes a special disability upon those persons alone. Homosexuals are forbidden the safeguards that others enjoy or may seek without constraint. They can obtain specific protection against discrimination only by enlisting the citizenry of Colorado to amend the state constitution or perhaps, on the State's view, by trying to pass helpful laws of general applicability. This is so no matter how local or discrete the harm, no matter how public and widespread the injury. We find nothing special in the protections Amendment 2 withholds. These are protections taken for granted by most people either because they already have them or do not need them; these are protections against exclusion from an almost limitless number of transactions and endeavors that constitute ordinary civic life in a free society.

III

The Fourteenth Amendment's promise that no person shall be denied the equal protection of the laws must co-exist with the practical necessity that most legislation classifies for one purpose or another, with resulting disadvantage to various groups or persons. ... We have attempted to reconcile the principle with the reality by stating that, if a law neither burdens a fundamental right nor targets a suspect class, we will uphold the legislative classification so long as it bears a rational relation to some legitimate end. See, e.g., Heller v. Doe, 509 U.S. ___, ___ (1993).

Amendment 2 fails, indeed defies, even this conventional inquiry. First, the amendment has the peculiar property of imposing a broad and undifferentiated disability on a single named group, an exceptional and, as we shall explain, invalid form of legislation. Second, its sheer breadth is so discontinuous with the reasons offered for it that the amendment seems inexplicable by anything but animus toward the class that it affects; it lacks a rational relationship to legitimate state interests.

Taking the first point, even in the ordinary equal protection case calling for the most deferential of standards, we insist on knowing the relation between the classification adopted and the object to be attained. The search for the link between classification and objective gives substance to the Equal Protection Clause; it provides guidance and discipline for the legislature, which is entitled to know what sorts of laws it can pass; and it marks the limits of our own authority. In the ordinary case, a law will be sustained if it can be said to advance a legitimate government interest, even if the law seems unwise or works to the disadvantage of a particular group, or if the rationale for it seems tenuous. See New Orleans v. Dukes, 427 U.S. 297 (1976) ...; Williamson v. Lee Optical of Okla., Inc., 348 U.S. 483 (1955) ...; Railway Express Agency, Inc. v. New York, 336 U.S. 106 (1949). ... The laws challenged in the cases just cited were narrow enough in scope and grounded in a sufficient factual context for us to ascertain that there existed some relation between the classification and the purpose it served. By requiring that the classification bear a rational relationship to an independent and legitimate legislative end, we ensure that classifications are not drawn for the purpose of disadvantaging the group burdened by the law. ...

Amendment 2 confounds this normal process of judicial review. It is at once too narrow and too broad. It identifies persons by a single trait and then denies them protection across the board. The resulting disqualification of a class of persons from the right to seek specific protection from the law is unprecedented in our jurisprudence.   ...

It is not within our constitutional tradition to enact laws of this sort. Central both to the idea of the rule of law and to our own Constitution's guarantee of equal protection is the principle that government and each of its parts remain open on impartial terms to all who seek its assistance. ... Respect for this principle explains why laws singling out a certain class of citizens for disfavored legal status or general hardships are rare. A law declaring that in general it shall be more difficult for one group of citizens than for all others to seek aid from the government is itself a denial of equal protection of the laws in the most literal sense.   ...

Davis v. Beason, 133 U.S. 333 (1890), not cited by the parties but relied upon by the dissent, is not evidence that Amendment 2 is within our constitutional tradition, and any reliance upon it as authority for sustaining the amendment is misplaced.   In *Davis*, the Court approved an Idaho territorial statute denying Mormons, polygamists, and advocates of polygamy the right to vote and to hold office because, as the Court construed the statute, it "simply excludes from the privilege of voting, or of holding any office of honor, trust or profit, those who have been convicted of certain offences, and those who advocate a practical resistance to the laws of the Territory and justify and approve the commission of crimes forbidden by it."   ...   To the extent *Davis* held that persons advocating a certain practice may be denied the right to vote, it is no longer good law.   Brandenburg v. Ohio, 395 U.S. 444 (1969) (per curiam).   To the extent it held that the groups designated in the statute may be deprived of the right to vote because of their status, its ruling could not stand without surviving strict scrutiny, a most doubtful outcome.   ...   To the extent *Davis* held that a convicted felon may be denied the right to vote, its holding is not implicated by our decision and is unexceptionable.   See Richardson v. Ramirez, 418 U.S. 24 (1974).

A second and related point is that laws of the kind now before us raise the inevitable inference that the disadvantage imposed is born of animosity toward the class of persons affected.   "[I]f the constitutional conception of 'equal protection of the laws' means anything, it must at the very least mean that a bare ... desire to harm a politically unpopular group cannot constitute a legitimate governmental interest."   Department of Agriculture v. Moreno, 413 U.S. 528, 534 (1973).   Even laws enacted for broad and ambitious purposes often can be explained by reference to legitimate public policies which justify the incidental disadvantages they impose on certain persons. Amendment 2, however, in making a general announcement that gays and lesbians shall not have any particular protections from the law, inflicts on them immediate, continuing, and real injuries that outrun and belie any legitimate justifications that may be claimed for it.   We conclude that, in addition to the far-reaching deficiencies of Amendment 2 that we have noted, the principles it offends, in another sense, are conventional and venerable; a law must bear a rational relationship to a legitimate governmental purpose, ... and Amendment 2 does not.

The primary rationale the State offers for Amendment 2 is respect for other citizens' freedom of association, and in particular the liberties of landlords or employers who have personal or religious objections to homosexuality. Colorado also cites its interest in conserving resources to fight discrimination against other groups. The breadth of the Amendment is so far removed from these particular justifications that we find it impossible to credit them. We cannot say that Amendment 2 is directed to any identifiable legitimate purpose or discrete objective. It is a status-based enactment divorced from any factual context from which we could discern a relationship to legitimate state interests; it is a classification of persons undertaken for its own sake, something the Equal Protection Clause does not permit. ...

We must conclude that Amendment 2 classifies homosexuals not to further a proper legislative end but to make them unequal to everyone else. This Colorado cannot do. A State cannot so deem a class of persons a stranger to its laws. Amendment 2 violates the Equal Protection Clause, and the judgment of the Supreme Court of Colorado is affirmed.

. . .

Justice Scalia, with whom The Chief Justice and Justice Thomas join, dissenting.

The Court has mistaken a Kulturkampf for a fit of spite. The constitutional amendment before us here is not the manifestation of a " 'bare ... desire to harm' " homosexuals, but is rather a modest attempt by seemingly tolerant Coloradans to preserve traditional sexual mores against the efforts of a politically powerful minority to revise those mores through use of the laws. That objective, and the means chosen to achieve it, are not only unimpeachable under any constitutional doctrine hitherto pronounced ...; they have been specifically approved by the Congress of the United States and by this Court.

In holding that homosexuality cannot be singled out for disfavorable treatment, the Court contradicts a decision, unchallenged here, pronounced only 10 years ago, see Bowers v. Hardwick, 478 U.S. 186 (1986), and places the prestige of this institution behind the proposition that opposition to homosexuality is as reprehensible as racial or religious bias. Whether it is or not is precisely the cultural debate that gave rise to the Colorado constitutional amendment (and to the preferential laws against which the amendment was directed). Since the Constitution of the United States says nothing about this subject, it is left to be resolved by normal democratic means, including the democratic adoption of provisions in state constitutions. This Court has no business imposing upon all Americans the resolution favored by the elite class from which the Members of this institution are selected, pronouncing that "animosity" toward homosexuality is evil. I vigorously dissent.

I

. . .

[T]he Court considers it unnecessary to decide the validity of the State's argument that Amendment 2 does not deprive homosexuals of the "protection [afforded by] general laws and policies that prohibit

arbitrary discrimination in governmental and private settings." I agree
that we need not resolve that dispute, because the Supreme Court of
Colorado has resolved it for us. ... The clear import of the Colorado
court's [decision] is that "general laws and policies that prohibit arbitrary discrimination" would continue to prohibit discrimination on the
basis of homosexual conduct as well. ... The amendment prohibits
special treatment of homosexuals, and nothing more. It would not
affect, for example, a requirement of state law that pensions be paid to
all retiring state employees with a certain length of service; homosexual
employees, as well as others, would be entitled to that benefit. But it
would prevent the State or any municipality from making death-benefit
payments to the "life partner" of a homosexual when it does not make
such payments to the long-time roommate of a nonhomosexual employee.
Or again, it does not affect the requirement of the State's general
insurance laws that customers be afforded coverage without discrimination unrelated to anticipated risk. Thus, homosexuals could not be
denied coverage, or charged a greater premium, with respect to auto
collision insurance; but neither the State nor any municipality could
require that distinctive health insurance risks associated with homosexuality (if there are any) be ignored.

[T]he Court's opinion ultimately does not dispute all this, but
assumes it to be true. The only denial of equal treatment it contends
homosexuals have suffered is this: They may not obtain preferential
treatment without amending the state constitution. That is to say, the
principle underlying the Court's opinion is that one who is accorded
equal treatment under the laws, but cannot as readily as others obtain
preferential treatment under the laws, has been denied equal protection
of the laws. If merely stating this alleged "equal protection" violation
does not suffice to refute it, our constitutional jurisprudence has
achieved terminal silliness.

The central thesis of the Court's reasoning is that any group is
denied equal protection when, to obtain advantage (or, presumably, to
avoid disadvantage), it must have recourse to a more general and hence
more difficult level of political decisionmaking than others. The world
has never heard of such a principle. ... And it seems to me most
unlikely that any multilevel democracy can function under such a
principle. For whenever a disadvantage is imposed, or conferral of a
benefit is prohibited, at one of the higher levels of democratic decisionmaking (i.e., by the state legislature rather than local government, or by
the people at large in the state constitution rather than the legislature),
the affected group has (under this theory) been denied equal protection.
To take the simplest of examples, consider a state law prohibiting the
award of municipal contracts to relatives of mayors or city councilmen.
Once such a law is passed, the group composed of such relatives must, in
order to get the benefit of city contracts, persuade the state legislature—
unlike all other citizens, who need only persuade the municipality. It is
ridiculous to consider this a denial of equal protection. ...

The Court might reply that the example I have given is not a denial
of equal protection only because the same "rational basis" (avoidance of
corruption) which renders constitutional the substantive discrimination

against relatives (i.e., the fact that they alone cannot obtain city contracts) also automatically suffices to sustain what might be called the electoral-procedural discrimination against them (i.e., the fact that they must go to the state level to get this changed). This is of course a perfectly reasonable response, and would explain why "electoral-procedural discrimination" has not hitherto been heard of: a law that is valid in its substance is automatically valid in its level of enactment. But the Court cannot afford to make this argument, for as I shall discuss next, there is no doubt of a rational basis for the substance of the prohibition at issue here. The Court's entire novel theory rests upon the proposition that there is something special—something that cannot be justified by normal "rational basis" analysis—in making a disadvantaged group (or a nonpreferred group) resort to a higher decisionmaking level. That proposition finds no support in law or logic.

II

I turn next to whether there was a legitimate rational basis for the substance of the constitutional amendment—for the prohibition of special protection for homosexuals.[1] It is unsurprising that the Court avoids discussion of this question, since the answer is so obviously yes. The case most relevant to the issue before us today is not even mentioned in the Court's opinion: In Bowers v. Hardwick, 478 U.S. 186 (1986), we held that the Constitution does not prohibit what virtually all States had done from the founding of the Republic until very recent years—making homosexual conduct a crime. ... If it is constitutionally permissible for a State to make homosexual conduct criminal, surely it is constitutionally permissible for a State to enact other laws merely disfavoring homosexual conduct. ... And *a fortiori* it is constitutionally permissible for a State to adopt a provision not even disfavoring homosexual conduct, but merely prohibiting all levels of state government from bestowing special protections upon homosexual conduct. Respondents ... counter *Bowers* with the argument that a greater-includes-the-lesser rationale cannot justify Amendment 2's application to individuals who do not engage in homosexual acts, but are merely of homosexual "orientation." ...

But assuming that, in Amendment 2, a person of homosexual "orientation" is someone who does not engage in homosexual conduct but merely has a tendency or desire to do so, *Bowers* still suffices to establish a rational basis for the provision. If it is rational to criminalize the conduct, surely it is rational to deny special favor and protection to those with a self-avowed tendency or desire to engage in the conduct. Indeed, where criminal sanctions are not involved, homosexual "orientation" is an acceptable stand-in for homosexual conduct. A State "does not violate the Equal Protection Clause merely because the classifications made by its laws are imperfect," Dandridge v. Williams, 397 U.S.

---

[1] The Court evidently agrees that "rational basis" ... is the governing standard. The trial court rejected respondents' argument that homosexuals constitute a "suspect" or "quasi-suspect" class, and respondents elected not to appeal that ruling to the Supreme Court of Colorado.... And the Court implicitly rejects the Supreme Court of Colorado's holding ... that Amendment 2 infringes upon a "fundamental right" of "independently identifiable class[es]" to "participate equally in the political process."

471, 485 (1970). Just as a policy barring the hiring of methadone users as transit employees does not violate equal protection simply because some methadone users pose no threat to passenger safety, see New York City Transit Authority v. Beazer, 440 U.S. 568 (1979), and just as a mandatory retirement age of 50 for police officers does not violate equal protection even though it prematurely ends the careers of many policemen over 50 who still have the capacity to do the job, see Massachusetts Bd. of Retirement v. Murgia, 427 U.S. 307 (1976)(per curiam), Amendment 2 is not constitutionally invalid simply because it could have been drawn more precisely so as to withdraw special antidiscrimination protections only from those of homosexual "orientation" who actually engage in homosexual conduct. . . .

Moreover, even if the provision regarding homosexual "orientation" were invalid, respondents' challenge to Amendment 2—which is a facial challenge—must fail. . . . It would not be enough for respondents to establish (if they could) that Amendment 2 is unconstitutional as applied to those of homosexual "orientation"; since, under *Bowers*, Amendment 2 is unquestionably constitutional as applied to those who engage in homosexual conduct, the facial challenge cannot succeed. . . .

III

. . . What [Colorado] has done is not only unprohibited, but eminently reasonable, with close, congressionally approved precedent in earlier constitutional practice.

First, as to its eminent reasonableness. The Court's opinion contains grim, disapproving hints that Coloradans have been guilty of "animus" or "animosity" toward homosexuality, as though that has been established as Unamerican. Of course it is our moral heritage that one should not hate any human being or class of human beings. But I had thought that one could consider certain conduct reprehensible—murder, for example, or polygamy, or cruelty to animals—and could exhibit even "animus" toward such conduct. Surely that is the only sort of "animus" at issue here: moral disapproval of homosexual conduct, the same sort of moral disapproval that produced the centuries-old criminal laws that we held constitutional in *Bowers*. The Colorado amendment does not, to speak entirely precisely, prohibit giving favored status to people who are homosexuals; they can be favored for many reasons—for example, because they are senior citizens or members of racial minorities. But it prohibits giving them favored status because of their homosexual conduct—that is, it prohibits favored status for homosexuality.

But though Coloradans are, as I say, entitled to be hostile toward homosexual conduct, the fact is that the degree of hostility reflected by Amendment 2 is the smallest conceivable. The Court's portrayal of Coloradans as a society fallen victim to pointless, hate-filled "gay-bashing" is so false as to be comical. Colorado not only is one of the 25 States that have repealed their antisodomy laws, but was among the first to do so. . . . But the society that eliminates criminal punishment for homosexual acts does not necessarily abandon the view that homosexuality is morally wrong and socially harmful; often, abolition simply reflects the view that enforcement of such criminal laws involves unseemly intrusion into the intimate lives of citizens. . . .

There is a problem, however, which arises when criminal sanction of homosexuality is eliminated but moral and social disapprobation of homosexuality is meant to be retained. . . . The problem (a problem, that is, for those who wish to retain social disapprobation of homosexuality) is that, because those who engage in homosexual conduct tend to reside in disproportionate numbers in certain communities, . . . have high disposable income, . . . and of course care about homosexual-rights issues much more ardently than the public at large, they possess political power much greater than their numbers, both locally and statewide. Quite understandably, they devote this political power to achieving not merely a grudging social toleration, but full social acceptance, of homosexuality. . . .

By the time Coloradans were asked to vote on Amendment 2, their exposure to homosexuals' quest for social endorsement was not limited to newspaper accounts of happenings in places such as New York, Los Angeles, San Francisco, and Key West. Three Colorado cities—Aspen, Boulder, and Denver—had enacted ordinances that listed "sexual orientation" as an impermissible ground for discrimination, equating the moral disapproval of homosexual conduct with racial and religious bigotry. . . . The phenomenon had even appeared statewide: the Governor of Colorado had signed an executive order pronouncing that "in the State of Colorado we recognize the diversity in our pluralistic society and strive to bring an end to discrimination in any form," and directing state agency-heads to "ensure non-discrimination" in hiring and promotion based on, among other things, "sexual orientation." . . . I do not mean to be critical of these legislative successes; homosexuals are as entitled to use the legal system for reinforcement of their moral sentiments as are the rest of society. But they are subject to being countered by lawful, democratic countermeasures as well.

That is where Amendment 2 came in. It sought to counter both the geographic concentration and the disproportionate political power of homosexuals by (1) resolving the controversy at the statewide level, and (2) making the election a single-issue contest for both sides. It put directly, to all the citizens of the State, the question: Should homosexuality be given special protection? They answered no. The Court today asserts that this most democratic of procedures is unconstitutional. Lacking any cases to establish that facially absurd proposition, it simply asserts that it must be unconstitutional, because it has never happened before. . . . As I have noted above, this is proved false every time a state law prohibiting or disfavoring certain conduct is passed, because such a law prevents the adversely affected group—whether drug addicts, or smokers, or gun owners, or motorcyclists—from changing the policy thus established in "each of [the] parts" of the State. What the Court says is even demonstrably false at the constitutional level. The Eighteenth Amendment to the Federal Constitution, for example, deprived those who drank alcohol not only of the power to alter the policy of prohibition locally or through state legislation, but even of the power to alter it through state constitutional amendment or federal legislation. The

Establishment Clause of the First Amendment prevents theocrats from having their way by converting their fellow citizens at the local, state, or federal statutory level; as does the Republican Form of Government Clause prevent monarchists.

But there is a much closer analogy, one that involves precisely the effort by the majority of citizens to preserve its view of sexual morality statewide, against the efforts of a geographically concentrated and politically powerful minority to undermine it. The constitutions of the States of Arizona, Idaho, New Mexico, Oklahoma, and Utah to this day contain provisions stating that polygamy is "forever prohibited." . . . Polygamists, and those who have a polygamous "orientation," have been "singled out" by these provisions for much more severe treatment than merely denial of favored status; and that treatment can only be changed by achieving amendment of the state constitutions. The Court's disposition today suggests that these provisions are unconstitutional, and that polygamy must be permitted in these States on a state-legislated, or perhaps even local-option, basis—unless, of course, polygamists for some reason have fewer constitutional rights than homosexuals.

The United States Congress, by the way, required the inclusion of these antipolygamy provisions in the constitutions of Arizona, New Mexico, Oklahoma, and Utah, as a condition of their admission to statehood. . . . Thus, this "singling out" of the sexual practices of a single group for statewide, democratic vote . . . has not only happened, but has received the explicit approval of the United States Congress.

I cannot say that this Court has explicitly approved any of these state constitutional provisions; but it has approved a territorial statutory provision that went even further, depriving polygamists of the ability even to achieve a constitutional amendment, by depriving them of the power to vote. In Davis v. Beason, 133 U.S. 333 (1890), Justice Field wrote for a unanimous Court. . . . [T]he proposition that polygamy can be criminalized, and those engaging in that crime deprived of the vote, remains good law. See Richardson v. Ramirez, 418 U.S. 24, 53 (1974). *Beason* rejected the argument that "such discrimination is a denial of the equal protection of the laws." Brief for Appellant in Davis v. Beason, O.T. 1889. . . .[3]

---

[3] The Court labors mightily to get around *Beason*, but cannot escape the central fact that this Court found the statute at issue—which went much further than Amendment 2, denying polygamists not merely special treatment but the right to vote—"not open to any constitutional or legal objection," rejecting the appellant's argument (much like the argument of respondents today) that the statute impermissibly "single[d] him out," Brief for Appellant in Davis v. Beason, O.T. 1889. . . . The Court . . . [makes] the claim that "[t]o the extent [*Beason*] held that the groups designated in the statute may be deprived of the right to vote because of their status, its ruling could not stand without surviving strict scrutiny, a most doubtful outcome." But if that is so, it is only because we have declared the right to vote to be a "fundamental political right," see, e.g., Dunn v. Blumstein, 405 U.S. 330, 336 (1972), deprivation of which triggers strict scrutiny. Amendment 2, of course, does not deny the fundamental right to vote, and the Court rejects the Colorado court's view that there exists a fundamental right to participate in the political process. Strict scrutiny is thus not in play here. Finally, the Court's suggestion that § 501 of the Revised Statutes of Idaho, and Amendment 2, deny rights on account of "status" (rather than conduct) opens up a broader debate involving the significance of *Bowers* to this case, a debate which the Court is otherwise unwilling to join.

This Court cited *Beason* with approval as recently as 1993, in an opinion authored by the same Justice who writes for the Court today. That opinion said: "[A]dverse impact will not always lead to a finding of impermissible targeting. For example, a social harm may have been a legitimate concern of government for reasons quite apart from discrimination.... See, e.g., ... Davis v. Beason, 133 U.S. 333 (1890)." Church of Lukumi Babalu Aye, Inc. v. Hialeah, 508 U.S. 520, 535 (1993). It remains to be explained how § 501 of the Idaho Revised Statutes was not an "impermissible targeting" of polygamists, but (the much more mild) Amendment 2 is an "impermissible targeting" of homosexuals. Has the Court concluded that the perceived social harm of polygamy is a "legitimate concern of government," and the perceived social harm of homosexuality is not?

IV

I strongly suspect that the answer to the last question is yes, which leads me to the last point I wish to make: The Court today ... employs a constitutional theory heretofore unknown to frustrate Colorado's reasonable effort to preserve traditional American moral values. The Court's stern disapproval of "animosity" towards homosexuality might be compared with what an earlier Court (including the revered Justices Harlan and Bradley) said in Murphy v. Ramsey, 114 U.S. 15 (1885), rejecting a constitutional challenge to a United States statute that denied the franchise in federal territories to those who engaged in polygamous cohabitation: "[C]ertainly no legislation can be supposed more wholesome and necessary in the founding of a free, self-governing commonwealth, fit to take rank as one of the co-ordinate States of the Union, than that which seeks to establish it on the basis of the idea of the family, as consisting in and springing from the union for life of one man and one woman in the holy estate of matrimony; the sure foundation of all that is stable and noble in our civilization; the best guaranty of that reverent morality which is the source of all beneficent progress in social and political improvement." ... I would not myself indulge in such official praise for heterosexual monogamy, because I think it no business of the courts (as opposed to the political branches) to take sides in this culture war.

But the Court today has done so, not only by inventing a novel and extravagant constitutional doctrine to take the victory away from traditional forces, but even by verbally disparaging as bigotry adherence to traditional attitudes. To suggest, for example, that this constitutional amendment springs from nothing more than " 'a bare ... desire to harm a politically unpopular group,' " is nothing short of insulting. (It is also nothing short of preposterous to call "politically unpopular" a group which enjoys enormous influence in American media and politics, and which, as the trial court here noted, though composing no more than 4% of the population had the support of 46% of the voters on Amendment 2 ...)

When the Court takes sides in the culture wars, it tends to be with the knights rather than the villeins—and more specifically with the Templars, reflecting the views and values of the lawyer class from which the Court's Members are drawn. How that class feels about homosexuality will be evident to anyone who wishes to interview job applicants at virtually any of the Nation's law schools. . . . [I]f the interviewer should wish not to be an associate or partner of an applicant because he disapproves of the applicant's homosexuality, then he will have violated the pledge which the Association of American Law Schools requires all its member-schools to exact from job interviewers: "assurance of the employer's willingness" to hire homosexuals. . . . This law-school view of what "prejudices" must be stamped out may be contrasted with the more plebeian attitudes that apparently still prevail in the United States Congress, which has been unresponsive to repeated attempts to extend to homosexuals the protections of federal civil rights laws, see, e.g., Employment Non–Discrimination Act of 1994, S. 2238, 103d Cong., 2d Sess. (1994); Civil Rights Amendments of 1975, H.R. 5452, 94th Cong., 1st Sess. (1975), and which took the pains to exclude them specifically from the Americans With Disabilities Act of 1990, see 42 U.S.C. § 12211(a) (1988 ed., Supp. V).

* * *

Today's opinion has no foundation in American constitutional law, and barely pretends to. The people of Colorado have adopted an entirely reasonable provision which does not even disfavor homosexuals in any substantive sense, but merely denies them preferential treatment. Amendment 2 is designed to prevent piecemeal deterioration of the sexual morality favored by a majority of Coloradans, and is not only an appropriate means to that legitimate end, but a means that Americans have employed before. Striking it down is an act, not of judicial judgment, but of political will. I dissent.

SECTION 4. PROTECTION OF PERSONAL LIBERTIES

B. VOTING AND ELECTIONS

-----

2. LEGISLATIVE DISTRICTING

Page 973. Add after Davis v. Bandemer:

MILLER v. JOHNSON

___ U.S. ___, 115 S.Ct. 2475, 132 L.Ed.2d 762 (1995).

Justice Kennedy delivered the opinion of the Court.

The constitutionality of Georgia's congressional redistricting plan is at issue here. In Shaw v. Reno, 509 U.S. ___ (1993), we held that a plaintiff states a claim under the Equal Protection Clause by alleging that a state redistricting plan, on its face, has no rational explanation save as an effort to separate voters on the basis of race. The question we now decide is whether Georgia's new Eleventh District gives rise to a valid equal protection claim under the principles announced in *Shaw*, and, if so, whether it can be sustained nonetheless as narrowly tailored to serve a compelling governmental interest.

I

A

The Equal Protection Clause['s] ... central mandate is racial neutrality in governmental decisionmaking. See, e.g., Loving v. Virginia, 388 U.S. 1, 11 (1967); McLaughlin v. Florida, 379 U.S. 184, 191–192 (1964); see also Brown v. Board of Education, 347 U.S. 483 (1954).... Laws classifying citizens on the basis of race cannot be upheld unless they are narrowly tailored to achieving a compelling state interest. See, e.g., Adarand ...; Croson ... (plurality opinion); Wygant v. Jackson Bd. of Ed., 476 U.S. 267, 274, 280, and n. 6 (1986)(plurality opinion).

In Shaw v. Reno ... we recognized that these equal protection principles govern a State's drawing of congressional districts, though, as our cautious approach there discloses, application of these principles to electoral districting is a most delicate task. Our analysis began from the premise that "[l]aws that explicitly distinguish between individuals on racial grounds fall within the core of [the Equal Protection Clause's] prohibition." ... This prohibition extends not just to explicit racial classifications, but also to laws neutral on their face but " 'unexplainable on grounds other than race.' " ... (quoting Arlington Heights v. Metropolitan Housing Development Corp., 429 U.S. 252, 266 (1977)). Applying this basic Equal Protection analysis in the voting rights context, we held that "redistricting legislation that is so bizarre on its face that it is 'unexplainable on grounds other than race,' ... demands the same close scrutiny that we give other state laws that classify citizens by race." ...

This case requires us to apply the principles articulated in *Shaw* to the most recent congressional redistricting plan enacted by the State of Georgia.

B

In 1965, the Attorney General designated Georgia a covered jurisdiction under § 4(b) of the Voting Rights Act.... In consequence, § 5 of the Act requires Georgia to obtain either administrative preclearance by the Attorney General or approval by the United States District Court for the District of Columbia of any change in a "standard, practice, or procedure with respect to voting" made after November 1, 1964.... The preclearance mechanism applies to congressional redistricting plans, see, e.g., Beer v. United States, 425 U.S. 130, 133 (1976), and requires that the proposed change "not have the purpose and will not have the effect of denying or abridging the right to vote on account of race or color." ... "[T]he purpose of § 5 has always been to insure that no voting-procedure changes would be made that would lead to a retrogression in the position of racial minorities with respect to their effective exercise of the electoral franchise." ...

Between 1980 and 1990, one of Georgia's 10 congressional districts was a majority-black district, that is, a majority of the district's voters were black. The 1990 Decennial Census indicated that Georgia's population of 6,478,216 persons, 27% of whom are black, entitled it to an additional eleventh congressional seat, ... prompting Georgia's General Assembly to redraw the State's congressional districts. Both the House and the Senate adopted redistricting guidelines which, among other things, required single-member districts of equal population, contiguous geography, nondilution of minority voting strength, fidelity to precinct lines where possible, and compliance with §§ 2 and 5 of the Act.... Only after these requirements were met did the guidelines permit drafters to consider other ends, such as maintaining the integrity of political subdivisions, preserving the core of existing districts, and avoiding contests between incumbents....

[Two successive redistricting plans submitted to the Attorney General for preclearance, each containing two majority-minority districts, were rejected because the Justice Department, "relying on alternative plans proposing three majority-minority districts"—one alternative being "the so-called 'max-black' plan ... drafted by the American Civil Liberties Union (ACLU) for the General Assembly's black caucus"— "concluded that Georgia had 'failed to explain adequately' its failure to create a third majority-minority district."] The State did not seek a declaratory judgment from the District Court for the District of Columbia....

Twice spurned, the General Assembly set out to create three majority-minority districts to gain preclearance.... Using the ACLU's "max-black" plan as its benchmark, ... the General Assembly enacted a plan that "bore all the signs of [the Justice Department's] involvement...." The Eleventh District lost the black population of Macon, but picked up Savannah, thereby connecting the black neighborhoods of metropolitan Atlanta and the poor black populace of coastal Chatham County, though 260 miles apart in distance and worlds apart in culture. In short, the social, political and economic makeup of the Eleventh District tells a tale of disparity, not community.... As the attached appendices attest,

> "[t]he populations of the Eleventh are centered around four discrete, widely spaced urban centers that have absolutely nothing to do with each other, and stretch the district hundreds of miles across rural counties and narrow swamp corridors." ...

> "The dense population centers ... were all majority-black, all at the periphery of the district, and in the case of Atlanta, Augusta and Savannah, all tied to a sparsely populated rural core by even less populated land bridges. Extending from Atlanta to the Atlantic, the Eleventh covered 6,748.2 square miles, splitting eight counties and five municipalities along the way." ...

Georgia's plan included three majority-black districts, though, and received Justice Department preclearance....

Elections were held under the new congressional redistricting plan on November 4, 1992, and black candidates were elected to Congress from all three majority-black districts.... [F]ive white voters from the

Eleventh District [sued,] . . . alleg[ing] that Georgia's Eleventh District was a racial gerrymander and so a violation of the Equal Protection Clause as interpreted in Shaw v. Reno. A three-judge [federal district] court was convened [and held] the Eleventh District . . . invalid under *Shaw*, with one judge dissenting. . . .

II

A

Finding that the "evidence of the General Assembly's intent to racially gerrymander the Eleventh District is overwhelming, and practically stipulated by the parties involved," the District Court held that race was the predominant, overriding factor in drawing the Eleventh District. . . . Appellants do not take issue with the court's factual finding of this racial motivation. Rather, they contend that evidence of a legislature's deliberate classification of voters on the basis of race cannot alone suffice to state a claim under *Shaw*. They argue that, regardless of the legislature's purposes, a plaintiff must demonstrate that a district's shape is so bizarre that it is unexplainable other than on the basis of race, and that appellees failed to make that showing here. Appellants' conception of the constitutional violation misapprehends our holding in *Shaw* and the Equal Protection precedent upon which *Shaw* relied.

Shaw recognized a claim "analytically distinct" from a vote dilution claim. . . . Whereas a vote dilution claim alleges that the State has enacted a particular voting scheme as a purposeful device "to minimize or cancel out the voting potential of racial or ethnic minorities," Mobile v. Bolden, 446 U.S. 55, 66 (1980) . . ., an action disadvantaging voters of a particular race, the essence of the equal protection claim recognized in *Shaw* is that the State has used race as a basis for separating voters into districts. Just as the State may not, absent extraordinary justification, segregate citizens on the basis of race in its public parks, New Orleans City Park Improvement Assn. v. Detiege, 358 U.S. 54 (1958)(per curiam), buses, Gayle v. Browder, 352 U.S. 903 (1956)(per curiam), golf courses, Holmes v. Atlanta, 350 U.S. 879 (1955)(per curiam), beaches, Mayor and City Council of Baltimore v. Dawson, 350 U.S. 877 (1955)(per curiam), and schools, *Brown, supra,* so did we recognize in *Shaw* that it may not separate its citizens into different voting districts on the basis of race. The idea is a simple one: "At the heart of the Constitution's guarantee of equal protection lies the simple command that the Government must treat citizens 'as individuals, not "as simply components of a racial, religious, sexual or national class." ' " Metro Broadcasting, Inc. v. FCC, 497 U.S. 547, 602 (1990)(O'Connor, J., dissenting) . . . When the State assigns voters on the basis of race, it engages in the offensive and demeaning assumption that voters of a particular race, because of their race, "think alike, share the same political interests, and will prefer the same candidates at the polls." *Shaw* . . .; see *Metro Broadcasting* . . . (Kennedy, J., dissenting). Race-based assignments "embody stereotypes that treat individuals as the product of their race, evaluating their thoughts and efforts—their very worth as citizens—according to a criterion barred to the Government by history and the Constitution." *Metro*

Broadcasting . . . (O'Connor, J., dissenting) . . .; see Powers v. Ohio, 499 U.S. 400, 410 (1991)("Race cannot be a proxy for determining juror bias or competence"); Palmore v. Sidoti, 466 U.S. 429, 432 (1984)("Classifying persons according to their race is more likely to reflect racial prejudice than legitimate public concerns; the race, not the person, dictates the category"). They also cause society serious harm. As we concluded in *Shaw*: "Racial classifications with respect to voting carry particular dangers. Racial gerrymandering, even for remedial purposes, may balkanize us into competing racial factions; it threatens to carry us further from the goal of a political system in which race no longer matters—a goal that the Fourteenth and Fifteenth Amendments embody, and to which the Nation continues to aspire. It is for these reasons that race-based districting by our state legislatures demands close judicial scrutiny." . . .

Our observation in *Shaw* of the consequences of racial stereotyping was not meant to suggest that a district must be bizarre on its face before there is a constitutional violation. Nor was our conclusion in *Shaw* that in certain instances a district's appearance (or, to be more precise, its appearance in combination with certain demographic evidence) can give rise to an equal protection claim, . . . a holding that bizarreness was a threshold showing. . . . Our circumspect approach and narrow holding in *Shaw* did not erect an artificial rule barring accepted equal protection analysis in other redistricting cases. Shape is relevant not because bizarreness is a necessary element of the constitutional wrong or a threshold requirement of proof, but because it may be persuasive circumstantial evidence that race for its own sake, and not other districting principles, was the legislature's dominant and controlling rationale in drawing its district lines. The logical implication . . . is that parties may rely on evidence other than bizarreness to establish race-based districting. . . .

Our reasoning in *Shaw* compels this conclusion. We recognized in *Shaw* that, outside the districting context, statutes are subject to strict scrutiny under the Equal Protection Clause not just when they contain express racial classifications, but also when, though race neutral on their face, they are motivated by a racial purpose or object. . . . [In prior cases,] the presumed racial purpose of state action, not its stark manifestation, [was] the constitutional violation. . . .

Shaw applied these same principles to redistricting. "In some exceptional cases, a reapportionment plan may be so highly irregular that, on its face, it rationally cannot be understood as anything other than an effort to 'segregat[e] . . . voters' on the basis of race." . . . In other cases, where the district is not so bizarre on its face that it discloses a racial design, the proof will be more "difficul[t]." . . . Although it was not necessary in *Shaw* to consider further the proof required in these more difficult cases, the logical import of our reasoning is that evidence other than a district's bizarre shape can be used to support the claim.

Appellants and some of their amici argue that the Equal Protection Clause's general proscription on race-based decisionmaking does not obtain in the districting context because redistricting by definition involves racial considerations. Underlying their argument are the very stereotypical assumptions the Equal Protection Clause forbids. It is true that redistricting in most cases will implicate a political calculus in which various interests compete for recognition, but it does not follow from this that individuals of the same race share a single political interest. The view that they do is "based on the demeaning notion that members of the defined racial groups ascribe to certain 'minority views' that must be different from those of other citizens," *Metro Broadcasting* . . . (Kennedy, J., dissenting), the precise use of race as a proxy the Constitution prohibits. Nor can the argument that districting cases are excepted from standard equal protection precepts be resuscitated by United Jewish Organizations of Williamsburgh, Inc. v. Carey, 430 U.S. 144 (1977), where the Court addressed a claim that New York violated the Constitution by splitting a Hasidic Jewish community in order to include additional majority-minority districts. As we explained in *Shaw*, a majority of the Justices in *UJO* construed the complaint as stating a vote dilution claim, so their analysis does not apply to a claim that the State has separated voters on the basis of race. . . . To the extent any of the opinions in that "highly fractured decision" . . . can be interpreted as suggesting that a State's assignment of voters on the basis of race would be subject to anything but our strictest scrutiny, those views ought not be deemed controlling.

In sum, we make clear that parties alleging that a State has assigned voters on the basis of race are neither confined in their proof to evidence regarding the district's geometry and makeup nor required to make a threshold showing of bizarreness. Today's case requires us further to consider the requirements of the proof necessary to sustain this equal protection challenge.

B

Federal court review of districting legislation represents a serious intrusion on the most vital of local functions. . . . Electoral districting is a most difficult subject for legislatures, and so the States must have discretion to exercise the political judgment necessary to balance competing interests. Although race-based decisionmaking is inherently suspect, e.g., *Adarand* . . . , until a claimant makes a showing sufficient to support that allegation the good faith of a state legislature must be presumed. . . . The courts, in assessing the sufficiency of a challenge to a districting plan, must be sensitive to the complex interplay of forces that enter a legislature's redistricting calculus. Redistricting legislatures will, for example, almost always be aware of racial demographics; but it does not follow that race predominates in the redistricting process. . . . The distinction between being aware of racial considerations and being motivated by them may be difficult to make. This evidentiary difficulty, together with the sensitive nature of redistricting and the presumption of good faith that must be accorded legislative enactments, requires courts to exercise extraordinary caution in adjudicating claims that a state has drawn district lines on the basis of race. The plaintiff's burden is to show, either through circumstantial evidence of a district's shape and demographics or more direct evidence going to legislative purpose, that race was the predominant factor motivating the legislature's decision to place a significant number of voters within or without a particular district. To make this showing, a plaintiff must prove that the legislature subordinated traditional race-neutral districting principles, including but not limited to compactness, contiguity, respect for political subdivisions or communities defined by actual shared interests, to racial considerations. Where these or other race-neutral considerations are the basis for redistricting legislation, and are not subordinated to race, a state can "defeat a claim that a district has been gerrymandered on racial lines." *Shaw* . . . .

In our view, the District Court applied the correct analysis, and its finding that race was the predominant factor motivating the drawing of the Eleventh District was not clearly erroneous. The court found it was "exceedingly obvious" from the shape of the Eleventh District, together with the relevant racial demographics, that the drawing of narrow land bridges to incorporate within the District outlying appendages containing nearly 80% of the district's total black population was a deliberate attempt to bring black populations into the district . . . . Although by comparison with other districts the geometric shape of the Eleventh District may not seem bizarre on its face, when its shape is considered in conjunction with its racial and population densities, the story of racial gerrymandering seen by the District Court becomes much clearer . . . . Although this evidence is quite compelling, we need not determine whether it was, standing alone, sufficient to establish a *Shaw* claim that the Eleventh District is unexplainable other than by race. The District Court had before it considerable additional evidence showing that the General Assembly was motivated by a predominant, overriding desire to assign black populations to the Eleventh District and thereby permit the creation of a third majority-black district in the Second . . . .

The court found that "it became obvious," both from the Justice Department's objection letters and the three preclearance rounds in general, "that [the Justice Department] would accept nothing less than abject surrender to its maximization agenda." . . . It further found that the General Assembly acquiesced and as a consequence was driven by its overriding desire to comply with the Department's maximization demands. The court supported its conclusion . . . with the State's own concessions . . . . [I]n its brief to this Court, the State concedes that "[i]t is undisputed that Georgia's eleventh is the product of a desire by the General Assembly to create a majority black district." . . . On this record, we fail to see how the District Court could have reached any conclusion other than that race was the predominant factor in drawing Georgia's Eleventh District; and in any event we conclude the court's finding is not clearly erroneous . . . .

In light of its well-supported finding, the District Court was justified in rejecting the various alternative explanations offered for the District. Although a legislature's compliance with "traditional districting principles such as compactness, contiguity, and respect for political subdivisions" may well suffice to refute a claim of racial gerrymandering, *Shaw* . . ., appellants cannot make such a refutation where, as here, those factors were subordinated to racial objectives. Georgia's Attorney General objected to the Justice Department's demand for three majority-black districts on the ground that to do so the State would have to "violate all reasonable standards of compactness and contiguity." ... This statement from a state official is powerful evidence that the legislature subordinated traditional districting principles to race when it ultimately enacted a plan creating three majority-black districts, and justified the District Court's finding that "every [objective districting] factor that could realistically be subordinated to racial tinkering in fact suffered that fate." ...

Nor can the State's districting legislation be rescued by mere recitation of purported communities of interest. The evidence was compelling "that there are no tangible 'communities of interest' spanning the hundreds of miles of the Eleventh District." ... A comprehensive report demonstrated the fractured political, social, and economic interests within the Eleventh District's black population.... It is apparent that it was not alleged shared interests but rather the object of maximizing the District's black population and obtaining Justice Department approval that in fact explained the General Assembly's actions.... A State is free to recognize communities that have a particular racial makeup, provided its action is directed toward some common thread of relevant interests. "[W]hen members of a racial group live together in one community, a reapportionment plan that concentrates members of the group in one district and excludes them from others may reflect wholly legitimate purposes." *Shaw*.... But where the State assumes from a group of voters' race that they "think alike, share the same political interests, and will prefer the same candidates at the polls," it engages in racial stereotyping at odds with equal protection mandates. *Id*....; cf. Powers v. Ohio, 499 U.S., at 410 ("We may not accept as a defense to racial discrimination the very stereotype the law condemns").

Race was, as the District Court found, the predominant, overriding factor explaining the General Assembly's decision to attach to the Eleventh District various appendages containing dense majority-black populations.... As a result, Georgia's congressional redistricting plan cannot be upheld unless it satisfies strict scrutiny, our most rigorous and exacting standard of constitutional review.

III

To satisfy strict scrutiny, the State must demonstrate that its districting legislation is narrowly tailored to achieve a compelling interest.... There is a "significant state interest in eradicating the effects of past racial discrimination." *Shaw*.... The State does not argue, however, that it created the Eleventh District to remedy past discrimination, and with good reason: there is little doubt that the State's true interest in designing the Eleventh District was creating a third majority-black district to satisfy the Justice Department's preclearance demands.... Whether or not in some cases compliance with the Voting Rights Act, standing alone, can provide a compelling interest independent of any interest in remedying past discrimination, it cannot do so here. As we suggested in *Shaw*, compliance with federal antidiscrimination laws cannot justify race-based districting where the challenged district was not reasonably necessary under a constitutional reading and application of those laws.... The congressional plan challenged here was not required by the Voting Rights Act under a correct reading of the statute.

The Justice Department refused to preclear both of Georgia's first two submitted redistricting plans.... It is ... safe to say that the congressional plan enacted in the end was required in order to obtain preclearance. It does not follow, however, that the plan was required by the substantive provisions of the Voting Rights Act.

We do not accept the contention that the State has a compelling interest in complying with whatever preclearance mandates the Justice Department issues. When a state governmental entity seeks to justify race-based remedies to cure the effects of past discrimination, we do not accept the government's mere assertion that the remedial action is required. Rather, we insist on a strong basis in evidence of the harm being remedied.... "The history of racial classifications in this country suggests that blind judicial deference to legislative or executive pronouncements of necessity has no place in equal protection analysis." *Croson*.... Our presumptive skepticism of all racial classifications, see *Adarand* ..., prohibits us as well from accepting on its face the Justice Department's conclusion that racial districting is necessary under the Voting Rights Act. Where a State relies on the Department's determination that race-based districting is necessary to comply with the Voting Rights Act, the judiciary retains an independent obligation in adjudicating consequent equal protection challenges to ensure that the State's actions are narrowly tailored to achieve a compelling interest.... Were we to accept the Justice Department's objection itself as a compelling interest adequate to insulate racial districting from constitutional review, we would be surrendering to the Executive Branch our role in enforcing the constitutional limits on race-based official action. We may not do so....

For the same reasons, we think it inappropriate for a court engaged in constitutional scrutiny to accord deference to the Justice Department's interpretation of the Act. Although we have deferred to the Department's interpretation in certain statutory cases, ... we have rejected agency interpretations to which we would otherwise defer where they raise serious constitutional questions.... When the Justice Department's interpretation of the Act compels race-based districting, it by definition raises a serious constitutional question, ... and should not receive deference.

Georgia's drawing of the Eleventh District was not required under the Act because there was no reasonable basis to believe that Georgia's earlier enacted plans violated § 5. Wherever a plan is "ameliorative," a term we have used to describe plans increasing the number of majority-minority districts, it "cannot violate § 5 unless the new apportionment itself so discriminates on the basis of race or color as to violate the Constitution." *Beer*.... Georgia's first and second proposed plans increased the number of majority-black districts from 1 out of 10 (10%) to 2 out of 11 (18.18%). These plans were "ameliorative" and could not have violated § 5's non-retrogression principle.... Acknowledging as much, ... the United States [objects] that Georgia failed to proffer a nondiscriminatory purpose for its refusal in the first two submissions to take the steps necessary to create a third majority-minority district.

The Government's position is insupportable.... Although it is true we have held that the State has the burden to prove a nondiscriminatory purpose under § 5, ... Georgia's Attorney General provided a detailed explanation for the State's initial decision not to enact the max-black plan.... The District Court accepted this explanation ... and found an absence of any discriminatory intent.... The State's policy of adhering to other districting principles instead of creating as many majority-minority districts as possible does not support an inference that the plan "so discriminates on the basis of race or color as to violate the Constitution," *Beer* ..., and thus cannot provide any basis under § 5 for the Justice Department's objection.

Instead of grounding its objections on evidence of a discriminatory purpose, it would appear the Government was driven by its policy of maximizing majority-black districts. Although the Government now disavows having had that policy, ... and seems to concede its impropriety, see Tr. of Oral Arg. 32–33, the District Court's well-documented factual finding was that the Department did adopt a maximization policy and followed it in objecting to Georgia's first two plans.... In utilizing § 5 to require States to create majority-minority districts wherever possible, the Department of Justice expanded its authority under the statute beyond what Congress intended and we have upheld.

Section 5 was directed at preventing a particular set of invidious practices which had the effect of "undo[ing] or defeat[ing] the rights recently won by nonwhite voters." H.R. Rep. No. 91–397, p. 8 (1969)....

Based on this historical understanding, we recognized in *Beer* that "the purpose of § 5 has always been to insure that no voting-procedure changes would be made that would lead to a retrogression in the position of racial minorities with respect to their effective exercise of the electoral franchise." ... The Justice Department's maximization policy seems quite far removed from this purpose. We are especially reluctant to conclude that § 5 justifies that policy given the serious constitutional concerns it raises. In South Carolina v. Katzenbach, 383 U.S. 301 (1966), we upheld § 5 as a necessary and constitutional response to some states' "extraordinary stratagem[s] of contriving new rules of various kinds for the sole purpose of perpetuating voting discrimination in the face of adverse federal court decrees." ... But our belief in *Katzenbach* that the federalism costs exacted by § 5 preclearance could be justified by those extraordinary circumstances does not mean they can be justified in the circumstances of this case. And the Justice Department's implicit command that States engage in presumptively unconstitutional race-based districting brings the Voting Rights Act, once upheld as a proper exercise of Congress' authority under § 2 of the Fifteenth Amendment, *Katzenbach* ..., into tension with the Fourteenth Amendment. As we recalled in *Katzenbach* itself, Congress' exercise of its Fifteenth Amendment authority even when otherwise proper still must " 'consist with the letter and spirit of the constitution.' " 383 U.S., at

326 (quoting McCulloch v. Maryland, 4 Wheat. 316, 421 (1819)).   We need not, however, resolve these troubling and difficult constitutional questions today.   There is no indication Congress intended such a far-reaching application of § 5, so we reject the Justice Department's interpretation of the statute and avoid the constitutional problems that interpretation raises. . . .

IV

The Voting Rights Act, and its grant of authority to the federal courts to uncover official efforts to abridge minorities' right to vote, has been of vital importance in eradicating invidious discrimination from the electoral process and enhancing the legitimacy of our political institutions.   Only if our political system and our society cleanse themselves of that discrimination will all members of the polity share an equal opportunity to gain public office regardless of race.   As a Nation we share both the obligation and the aspiration of working toward this end.   The end is neither assured nor well served, however, by carving electorates into racial blocs.   "If our society is to continue to progress as a multiracial democracy, it must recognize that the automatic invocation of race stereotypes retards that progress and causes continued hurt and injury."   Edmonson v. Leesville Concrete Co., 500 U.S. 614, 630–631 (1991).   It takes a shortsighted and unauthorized view of the Voting Rights Act to invoke that statute, which has played a decisive role in redressing some of our worst forms of discrimination, to demand the very racial stereotyping the Fourteenth Amendment forbids.

* * *

The judgment of the District Court is affirmed, and the case is remanded for further proceedings consistent with this decision.

It is so ordered.

Justice O'Connor, concurring.

I understand the threshold standard the Court adopts—"that the legislature subordinated traditional race-neutral districting principles . . . to racial considerations"—to be a demanding one.   To invoke strict scrutiny, a plaintiff must show that the State has relied on race in substantial disregard of customary and traditional districting practices. Those practices provide a crucial frame of reference and therefore constitute a significant governing principle in cases of this kind.   The standard would be no different if a legislature had drawn the boundaries to favor some other ethnic group; certainly the standard does not treat efforts to create majority-minority districts less favorably than similar efforts on behalf of other groups.   Indeed, the driving force behind the adoption of the Fourteenth Amendment was the desire to end legal discrimination against blacks.

Application of the Court's standard does not throw into doubt the vast majority of the Nation's 435 congressional districts, where presumably the States have drawn the boundaries in accordance with their customary districting principles.   That is so even though race may well have been considered in the redistricting process.   See Shaw v. Reno. . . .

But application of the Court's standard helps achieve *Shaw*'s basic objective of making extreme instances of gerrymandering subject to meaningful judicial review. I therefore join the Court's opinion.

Justice Stevens, dissenting.

... I add these comments because I believe the respondents in these cases ... have not suffered any legally cognizable injury.

In Shaw v. Reno, 509 U.S. ___ (1993), the Court crafted a new cause of action with two novel, troubling features. First, the Court misapplied the term "gerrymander," previously used to describe grotesque line-drawing by a dominant group to maintain or enhance its political power at a minority's expense, to condemn the efforts of a majority (whites) to share its power with a minority (African Americans). Second, the Court dispensed with its previous insistence in vote dilution cases on a showing of injury to an identifiable group of voters, but it failed to explain adequately what showing a plaintiff must make to establish standing to litigate the newly minted *Shaw* claim. Neither in *Shaw* itself nor in the cases decided today has the Court coherently articulated what injury this cause of action is designed to redress....

Even assuming the validity of *Shaw*, I cannot see how respondents in these cases could assert the injury the Court attributes to them.... The Court's conclusion that they have standing to maintain a *Shaw* claim appears to rest on a theory that their placement in the Eleventh District caused them " 'representational harms.' " ... The *Shaw* Court explained the concept of "representational harms" as follows: "When a district obviously is created solely to effectuate the perceived common interests of one racial group, elected officials are more likely to believe that their primary obligation is to represent only the members of that group, rather than their constituency as a whole." ... [R]epresentational harms ... can only come about ... first, if all or most black voters support the same candidate, and, second, if the successful candidate ignores the interests of her white constituents. Respondents' standing, in other words, ultimately depends on the very premise the Court purports to abhor: that voters of a particular race " 'think alike, share the same political interests, and will prefer the same candidates at the polls.' " ... This generalization, as the Court recognizes, is "offensive and demeaning."

In particular instances, of course, members of one race may vote by an overwhelming margin for one candidate, and in some cases that candidate will be of the same race. "Racially polarized voting" is one of the circumstances plaintiffs must prove to advance a vote dilution claim. Thornburg v. Gingles, 478 U.S. 30, 56–58 (1986). Such a claim allows voters to allege that gerrymandered district lines have impaired their ability to elect a candidate of their own race. The Court emphasizes, however, that a so-called *Shaw* claim is " 'analytically distinct' from a vote dilution claim." [But] the Court [has not] answered the question its analytic distinction raises: If the *Shaw* injury does not flow from an increased probability that white candidates will lose, then how can the increased probability that black candidates will win cause white voters, such as respondents, cognizable harm?

The Court attempts an explanation ... by equating the injury it imagines respondents have suffered with the injuries African Americans suffered under segregation.... This equation, however, fails to elucidate the elusive *Shaw* injury. Our desegregation cases redressed the exclusion of black citizens from public facilities reserved for whites. In this case, in contrast, any voter, black or white, may live in the Eleventh District. What respondents contest is the inclusion of too many black voters in the District as drawn. In my view, if respondents allege no vote dilution, that inclusion can cause them no conceivable injury.

The Court's equation of *Shaw* claims with our desegregation decisions is inappropriate for another reason. In each of those cases, legal segregation frustrated the public interest in diversity and tolerance by barring African Americans from joining whites in the activities at issue. The districting plan here, in contrast, serves the interest in diversity and tolerance by increasing the likelihood that a meaningful number of black representatives will add their voices to legislative debates.... That racial integration of the sort attempted by Georgia now appears more vulnerable to judicial challenge than some policies alleged to perpetuate racial bias, cf. Allen v. Wright, 468 U.S. 737 (1984), is anomalous, to say the least.

Equally distressing is the Court's equation of traditional gerrymanders, designed to maintain or enhance a dominant group's power, with a dominant group's decision to share its power with a previously underrepresented group. In my view, districting plans violate the Equal Protection Clause when they "serve no purpose other than to favor one segment—whether racial, ethnic, religious, economic, or political—that may occupy a position of strength at a particular point in time, or to disadvantage a politically weak segment of the community." Karcher v. Daggett, 462 U.S. 725, 748 (1983)(Stevens, J., concurring). In contrast, I do not see how a districting plan that favors a politically weak group can violate equal protection. The Constitution does not mandate any form of proportional representation, but it certainly permits a State to adopt a policy that promotes fair representation of different groups....

The Court's refusal to distinguish an enactment that helps a minority group from enactments that cause it harm is especially unfortunate at the intersection of race and voting, given that African Americans and other disadvantaged groups have struggled so long and so hard for inclusion in that most central exercise of our democracy.... I have long believed that treating racial groups differently from other identifiable groups of voters, as the Court does today, is itself an invidious racial classification. Racial minorities should receive neither more nor less protection than other groups against gerrymanders. A fortiori, racial minorities should not be less eligible than other groups to benefit from districting plans the majority designs to aid them.

I respectfully dissent.

Justice Ginsburg, with whom Justices Stevens and Breyer join, and with whom Justice Souter joins except as to Part III–B, dissenting.

. . .

... Because I do not endorse the Court's new standard and would not upset Georgia's plan, I dissent.

I

At the outset, it may be useful to note points on which the Court does not divide. First, we agree that federalism and the slim judicial competence to draw district lines weigh heavily against judicial intervention in apportionment decisions; as a rule, the task should remain within the domain of state legislatures.... Second, for most of our Nation's history, the franchise has not been enjoyed equally by black citizens and white voters. To redress past wrongs and to avert any recurrence of exclusion of blacks from political processes, federal courts now respond to Equal Protection Clause and Voting Rights Act complaints of state action that dilutes minority voting strength.... Third, to meet statutory requirements, state legislatures must sometimes consider race as a factor highly relevant to the drawing of district lines.... Finally, state legislatures may recognize communities that have a particular racial or ethnic makeup, even in the absence of any compulsion to do so, in order to account for interests common to or shared by the persons grouped together....

Therefore, the fact that the Georgia General Assembly took account of race in drawing district lines—a fact not in dispute—does not render the State's plan invalid. To offend the Equal Protection Clause, all agree, the legislature had to do more than consider race. How much more, is the issue that divides the Court today.

A

. . .

... District lines are drawn to accommodate a myriad of factors— geographic, economic, historical, and political—and state legislatures, as arenas of compromise and electoral accountability, are best positioned to mediate competing claims; courts, with a mandate to adjudicate, are ill equipped for the task.

B

Federal courts have ventured into the political thicket of apportionment when necessary to secure to members of racial minorities equal voting rights—rights denied in many States, including Georgia, until not long ago.

. . .

It was against this backdrop that the Court, construing the Equal Protection Clause, undertook to ensure that apportionment plans do not dilute minority voting strength. See, e.g., Rogers v. Lodge, 458 U.S. 613, 617 (1982); Regester, 412 U.S., at 765; Wright v. Rockefeller, 376 U.S. 52, 57 (1964). By enacting the Voting Rights Act of 1965, Congress heightened federal judicial involvement in apportionment, and also fashioned a role for the Attorney General. Section 2 creates a federal right of action to challenge vote dilution. Section 5 requires States with a history of discrimination to preclear any changes in voting practices with either a federal court (a three-judge United States District Court for the District of Columbia) or the Attorney General.

These Court decisions and congressional directions significantly reduced voting discrimination against minorities. In the 1972 election, Georgia gained its first black Member of Congress since Reconstruction, and the 1981 apportionment created the State's first majority-minority district. . . .

II

A

Before Shaw v. Reno, 509 U.S. ___ (1993), this Court invoked the Equal Protection Clause to justify intervention in the quintessentially political task of legislative districting in two circumstances: to enforce the one-person-one-vote requirement, see Reynolds v. Sims, 377 U.S. 533 (1964); and to prevent dilution of a minority group's voting strength. . . .

In *Shaw*, the Court recognized a third basis for an equal protection challenge to a State's apportionment plan. The Court wrote cautiously, emphasizing that judicial intervention is exceptional: "[S]trict [judicial] scrutiny" is in order, the Court declared, if a district is "so extremely irregular on its face that it rationally can be viewed only as an effort to segregate the races for purposes of voting." . . . The problem in *Shaw* was not the plan architects' consideration of race as relevant in redistricting. Rather, in the Court's estimation, it was the virtual exclusion of other factors from the calculus. Traditional districting practices were cast aside, the Court concluded, with race alone steering placement of district lines.

B

The record before us does not show that race similarly overwhelmed traditional districting practices in Georgia. Although the Georgia General Assembly prominently considered race in shaping the Eleventh District, race did not crowd out all other factors, as the Court found it did in North Carolina's delineation of the *Shaw* district.

In contrast to the snake-like North Carolina district inspected in *Shaw*, Georgia's Eleventh District is hardly "bizarre," "extremely irregular," or "irrational on its face." . . . Instead, the Eleventh District's design reflects significant consideration of "traditional districting factors (such as keeping political subdivisions intact) and the usual political process of compromise and trades for a variety of nonracial reasons." 864 F.Supp. 1354, 1397, n. 5 (S.D.Ga.1994)(Edmondson, J., dissenting). . . . The District covers a core area in central and eastern Georgia, and its total land area of 6,780 square miles is about average for the State. . . .

Nor does the Eleventh District disrespect the boundaries of political subdivisions. Of the 22 counties in the District, 14 are intact and 8 are divided[—]about the state average in divided counties. . . . Seventy-one percent of the Eleventh District's boundaries track the borders of political subdivisions. . . . Of the State's 11 districts, 5 score worse than the Eleventh District on this criterion, and 5 score better.... Eighty-three percent of the Eleventh District's geographic area is composed of intact counties, above average for the State's congressional districts.... And notably, the Eleventh District's boundaries largely follow precinct lines.

Evidence at trial similarly shows that considerations other than race went into determining the Eleventh District's boundaries. For a "political reason" ... the DeKalb County portion of the Eleventh District was drawn to include a particular (largely white) precinct.... The corridor through Effingham County was substantially narrowed at the request of a (white) State Representative.... In Chatham County, the District was trimmed to exclude a heavily black community in Garden City because a State Representative wanted to keep the city intact inside the neighboring First District.... The Savannah extension was configured by "the narrowest means possible" to avoid splitting the city of Port Wentworth....

Georgia's Eleventh District, in sum, is not an outlier district shaped without reference to familiar districting techniques. Tellingly, the District that the Court's decision today unsettles is not among those on a statistically calculated list of the 28 most bizarre districts in the United States, a study prepared in the wake of our decision in *Shaw*....

C

The Court suggests that it was not Georgia's legislature, but the U.S. Department of Justice, that effectively drew the lines, and that Department officers did so with nothing but race in mind. Yet the "Max–Black" plan advanced by the Attorney General was not the plan passed by the Georgia General Assembly....

And ... Georgia could have demanded relief from the Department's objections by instituting a civil action in the United States District Court for the District of Columbia, with ultimate review in this Court. Instead of pursuing that avenue, the State chose to adopt the plan here in controversy—a plan the State forcefully defends before us....

D

Along with attention to size, shape, and political subdivisions, the Court recognizes as an appropriate districting principle, "respect for ... communities defined by actual shared interests." The Court finds no community here, however, because a report in the record showed "fractured political, social, and economic interests within the Eleventh District's black population."

But ethnicity itself can tie people together, as volumes of social science literature have documented—even people with divergent economic interests. For this reason, ethnicity is a significant force in political life....

To accommodate the reality of ethnic bonds, legislatures have long drawn voting districts along ethnic lines. Our Nation's cities are full of districts identified by their ethnic character—Chinese, Irish, Italian, Jewish, Polish, Russian, for example.... The creation of ethnic districts reflecting felt identity is not ordinarily viewed as offensive or demeaning to those included in the delineation.

III

To separate permissible and impermissible use of race in legislative apportionment, the Court orders strict scrutiny for districting plans "predominantly motivated" by race. No longer can a State avoid judicial oversight by giving—as in this case—genuine and measurable consideration to traditional districting practices. Instead, a federal case can be mounted whenever plaintiffs plausibly allege that other factors carried less weight than race. This invitation to litigate against the State seems to me neither necessary nor proper.

A

The Court derives its test from diverse opinions on the relevance of race in contexts distinctly unlike apportionment. . . . [11]

In adopting districting plans, however, States do not treat people as individuals. Apportionment schemes, by their very nature, assemble people in groups. States do not assign voters to districts based on merit or achievement, standards States might use in hiring employees or engaging contractors. Rather, legislators classify voters in groups—by economic, geographical, political, or social characteristics—and then "reconcile the competing claims of [these] groups." Davis v. Bandemer, 478 U.S. 109, 147 (1986)(O'Connor, J., concurring in judgment).

That ethnicity defines some of these groups is a political reality. . . . Until now, no constitutional infirmity has been seen in districting Irish or Italian voters together, for example, so long as the delineation does not abandon familiar apportionment practices. . . . If Chinese–Americans and Russian–Americans may seek and secure group recognition in the delineation of voting districts, then African–Americans should not be dissimilarly treated. Otherwise, in the name of equal protection, we would shut out "the very minority group whose history in the United States gave birth to the Equal Protection Clause." See *Shaw* . . . (Stevens, J., dissenting).[12]

---

[11] I would follow precedent directly on point. In United Jewish Organizations of Williamsburgh, Inc. v. Carey, 430 U.S. 144 (1977)(UJO), even though the State "deliberately used race in a purposeful manner" to create majority-minority districts, . . . seven of eight Justices participating voted to uphold the State's plan without subjecting it to strict scrutiny. Five Justices specifically agreed that the intentional creation of majority-minority districts does not give rise to an equal protection claim, absent proof that the districting diluted the majority's voting strength. See ibid. (opinion of White, J., joined by Rehnquist and Stevens, JJ.); id., at 179–180 (Stewart, J., concurring in judgment, joined by Powell, J.). Nor is *UJO* best understood as a vote dilution case. Petitioners' claim in *UJO* was that the State had "violated the Fourteenth and Fifteenth Amendments by deliberately revising its reapportionment plan along racial lines." . . . Though much like the claim in *Shaw*, the *UJO* claim failed because the *UJO* district adhered to traditional districting practices. . . .

[12] Race-conscious practices a State may elect to pursue, of course, are not as limited as those it may be required to pursue. See Voinovich v. Quilter, 507 U.S. __, __ (1993)("[F]ederal courts may not order the creation of majority-minority districts unless necessary to remedy a violation of federal law. But that does not mean that the State's powers are similarly limited. Quite the opposite is true. . . .").

B

Under the Court's approach, judicial review of the same intensity, i.e., strict scrutiny, is in order once it is determined that an apportionment is predominantly motivated by race. It matters not at all, in this new regime, whether the apportionment dilutes or enhances minority voting strength. As very recently observed, however, "[t]here is no moral or constitutional equivalence between a policy that is designed to perpetuate a caste system and one that seeks to eradicate racial subordination." Adarand Constructors, Inc. v. Pena, ... (Stevens, J., dissenting).

Special circumstances justify vigilant judicial inspection to protect minority voters—circumstances that do not apply to majority voters. A history of exclusion from state politics left racial minorities without clout to extract provisions for fair representation in the lawmaking forum.... The equal protection rights of minority voters thus could have remained unrealized absent the Judiciary's close surveillance. Cf. United States v. Carolene Products Co., 304 U.S. 144, 153, n. 4 (1938)(referring to the "more searching judicial inquiry" that may properly attend classifications adversely affecting "discrete and insular minorities"). The majority, by definition, encounters no such blockage. White voters in Georgia do not lack means to exert strong pressure on their state legislators. The force of their numbers is itself a powerful determiner of what the legislature will do that does not coincide with perceived majority interests.

State legislatures like Georgia's today operate under federal constraints imposed by the Voting Rights Act—constraints justified by history and designed by Congress to make once-subordinated people free and equal citizens. But these federal constraints do not leave majority voters in need of extraordinary judicial solicitude. The Attorney General, who administers the Voting Rights Act's preclearance requirements, is herself a political actor. She has a duty to enforce the law Congress passed, and she is no doubt aware of the political cost of venturing too far to the detriment of majority voters. Majority voters, furthermore, can press the State to seek judicial review if the Attorney General refuses to preclear a plan that the voters favor. Finally, the Act is itself a political measure, subject to modification in the political process.

C

The Court's disposition renders redistricting perilous work for state legislatures. Statutory mandates and political realities may require States to consider race when drawing district lines.... But today's decision is a counterforce; it opens the way for federal litigation if "traditional ... districting principles" arguably were accorded less weight than race.... Genuine attention to traditional districting practices and avoidance of bizarre configurations seemed, under *Shaw*, to provide a safe harbor.... In view of today's decision, that is no longer the case.

Only after litigation—under either the Voting Rights Act, the Court's new *Miller* standard, or both—will States now be assured that plans conscious of race are safe. Federal judges in large numbers may be drawn into the fray. This enlargement of the judicial role is unwarranted. The reapportionment plan that resulted from Georgia's political process merited this Court's approbation, not its condemnation. Accordingly, I dissent.

UNITED STATES v. HAYS, 115 S.Ct. 2431 (1995). In this companion case to Miller v. Johnson, the Court declined to rule on the merits of an equal protection, "racial gerrymander" challenge to a Louisiana congressional districting plan, because the challengers lacked standing to raise it: they do not live in the majority-minority district that was the "primary focus of their racial gerrymandering claim, and they have not otherwise demonstrated that they, personally, have been subjected to a racial classification." Justice O'Connor's opinion for the Court applied the "rule against generalized grievances" and "therefore reject[ed the challengers] position that 'anybody in the State has a claim[.]' " The opinion also contained the following observations:

"We discussed the harms caused by racial classifications in *Shaw*. We noted that, in general, '[t]hey threaten to stigmatize individuals by reason of their membership in a racial group and to incite racial hostility.' ... We also noted 'representational harms' the particular type of racial classification at issue in *Shaw* may cause: 'When a district obviously is created solely to effectuate the perceived common interests of one racial group, elected officials are more likely to believe that their primary obligation is to represent only the members of that group, rather than their constituency as a whole.' ... Any citizen able to demonstrate that he or she, personally, has been injured by that kind of racial classification has standing to challenge the classification in federal court.

"Demonstrating the individualized harm our standing doctrine requires may not be easy in the racial gerrymandering context, as it will frequently be difficult to discern why a particular citizen was put in one district or another.... Where a plaintiff resides in a racially gerrymandered district, however, the plaintiff has been denied equal treatment because of the legislature's reliance on racial criteria, and therefore has standing to challenge the legislature's action.... Voters in such districts may suffer the special representational harms racial classifications can cause in the voting context. On the other hand, where a plaintiff does not live in such a district, he or she does not suffer those special harms, and any inference that the plaintiff has personally been subjected to a racial classification would not be justified absent specific evidence tending to support that inference...."

Justice Breyer, joined by Justice Souter "join[ed] the Court's opinion to the extent that it discusses voters ... who do not reside within the district that they challenge." Justice Ginsburg concurred in the judgment without comment, and Justice Stevens did so in an opinion objecting to the Court's willingness to recognize that residents of racially gerrymandered districts may suffer individualized harms:

"... The majority fails to explain coherently how a State discriminates invidiously by deliberately joining members of different races in the same district; why such placement amounts to an injury to members of any race; and, assuming it does, to whom.

"... What I do not understand is the majority's view that these racially diverse respondents should fare better if they resided in black-majority districts instead of white-majority districts. Respondents have not alleged or proved that the State's districting has substantially disadvantaged any group of voters in their opportunity to influence the political process. They therefore lack standing to argue that Louisiana has adopted an unconstitutional gerrymander...."

RACIAL GERRYMANDERING AND THE VOTING RIGHTS ACT

A year after Miller v. Johnson, *supra*, the Court, by the same 5–4 alignment, invalidated four more majority-minority districts—three from Texas and one from North Carolina—constructed after the 1990 census with attention to the perceived requirements of the Voting Rights Act ("VRA") and the Justice Department's ("DOJ") enforcement of it. The new companion cases again addressed issues of the nature of the cause of action first recognized in Shaw v. Reno, 509 U.S. 630 (1993)(*Shaw I*); the threshold showing required to trigger strict scrutiny of congressional districts configured in race-conscious fashion; compliance with the Voting Rights Act as a compelling state interest; and the elements of narrow tailoring necessary to satisfy strict scrutiny.

The North Carolina case, Shaw v. Hunt, 116 S.Ct. 1894 (1996)(*Shaw II*), reversed a decision of the District Court, on remand of *Shaw I*, that the State's two majority-minority districts, though deliberately drawn to produce a certain racial composition, were "constitutional, nonetheless, because ... narrowly tailored to further the State's compelling interests in complying with §§ 2 and 5 of the Voting Rights Act...." Refusing to address the challenge to one of the majority-minority districts, because no plaintiffs resided within it nor "provided specific evidence that they personally were assigned to their voting districts on the basis of race[,]" the Court held the other district unconstitutional as "not narrowly tailored to serve a compelling state interest."

The State's initial districting plan had included only one majority-minority district, but when DOJ refused preclearance under VRA § 5 for failure "to give effect to black and Native American voting strength" in a southern part of the State for reasons DOJ considered "pretextual," the State submitted, and received preclearance for, a revised plan with a second majority-black district (District 12) in a northern part of the State. Applying *Miller*, Chief Justice Rehnquist's majority opinion first found race to be the "predominant factor in drawing" District 12 given the bizarre shape and racial demographics of the serpentine district ("dubbed the least geographically compact district in the Nation"); the

State's express acknowledgement in its preclearance submission that the "*overriding* purpose" was to comply with DOJ "dictates ... and to create two congressional districts with effective black voting majorities[;]" the principal draftsman's testimony that creating two majority-black districts was the "principal reason" for the shape of District 12; and the State's initial similar concession to the District Court. That "in shaping District 12, the State effectuated its interest in creating one rural and one urban district, and that partisan politicking was actively at work in the districting process ... does not in any way refute the fact that race was the legislature's predominant consideration. Race was the criterion ... that could not be compromised; respecting communities of interest and protecting Democratic incumbents came into play only after the race-based decision had been made." Hence, District 12 had to satisfy strict scrutiny.

The State could not rely on a compelling interest in remedying past or present racial discrimination, because the District Court had found that such an interest "did not actually precipitate the use of race in the redistricting plan." As for the claim "that the race-based redistricting was constitutionally justified by the State's duty to comply with the Voting Rights Act[,]" the Court "once again" did "not reach" the "question whether under the proper circumstances compliance with the Voting Rights Act, on its own, could be a compelling interest[,] ... because we find that creating an additional majority-black district was not required under a correct reading of § 5 and that District 12, as drawn, is not a remedy narrowly tailored to the State's professed interest in avoiding § 2 liability." Since the State's "first plan ... was ameliorative, having created the first majority-black district in recent history[,]" *Miller* made clear that the plan would not violate § 5 and its "nonretrogression" standard, unless it independently manifested unconstitutional racial discrimination. The nonracial reasons the State initially gave for declining to draw a second majority-black district precluded a finding of any such purpose to discriminate, and, as in *Miller*, the DOJ's pursuit of the "policy of maximizing the number of majority-black districts ... is not properly grounded in § 5 and the Department's authority thereunder."

The argument in favor of District 12 based on avoiding § 2 liability elicited this response:

> " ... Our precedent establishes that a plaintiff may allege a § 2 violation in a single-member district if the manipulation of districting lines fragments politically cohesive minority voters among several districts or packs them into one district or a small number of districts, and thereby dilutes the voting strength of members of the minority population. ... To prevail on such a claim, a plaintiff must prove that the minority group 'is sufficiently large and geographically compact to constitute a majority in a single-member district'; that the minority group 'is politically cohesive'; and that 'the white majority votes sufficiently as a bloc to enable it ... usually to defeat the minority's preferred candidate.' Thornburg v. Gingles, 478 U.S. 30, 50–51 (1986); Growe v. Emison, 507 U.S. 25 (1993)(recognizing that the three *Gingles* preconditions would apply

to a § 2 challenge to a single-member district). A court must also consider all other relevant circumstances and must ultimately find based on the totality of those circumstances that members of a protected class 'have less opportunity than other members of the electorate to participate in the political process and to elect representatives of their choice.' [§ 2(b)]. ...

"We assume, *arguendo*, for the purpose of resolving this case, that compliance with § 2 could be a compelling interest, and we likewise assume, *arguendo*, that the General Assembly believed a second majority-minority district was needed in order not to violate § 2, and that the legislature at the time it acted had a strong basis in evidence to support that conclusion. We hold that even with the benefit of these assumptions, the North Carolina plan does not survive strict scrutiny because the remedy—the creation of District 12—is not narrowly tailored to the asserted end.

"[T]he legislative action [must] substantially address, if not achieve, the avowed purpose. ... [H]ere, ... the legislative action must, at a minimum, remedy the anticipated [§ 2] violation or achieve compliance to be narrowly tailored.[7]

"District 12 could not remedy any potential § 2 violation. ... No one looking at District 12 could reasonably suggest that the district contains a 'geographically compact' population of any race. ... Therefore where that district sits, 'there neither has been a wrong nor can be a remedy.' ...

"Appellees ..., however[,] ... contend, and a majority of the District Court agreed, ... that once a legislature has a strong basis in evidence for concluding that a § 2 violation exists in the State, it may draw a majority-minority district anywhere, even if the district is in no way coincident with the compact *Gingles* district, as long as racially polarized voting exists where the district is ultimately drawn. ...

"We find this position singularly unpersuasive. ... The vote dilution injuries suffered by [people in one area of the State] are not remedied by creating a safe majority-black district somewhere else in the State. [I]f a geographically compact, cohesive minority population lives in south-central to southeastern North Carolina, as the Justice Department's objection letter suggested, District 12 ... would not address that § 2 violation. The black voters of the south-central to southeastern region would still be suffering precisely the same injury that they suffered before District 12 was drawn. District 12 would not address the professed interest of relieving the vote dilution, much less be narrowly tailored to accomplish the goal.

"[The argument] ... derives from a misconception of the vote-dilution claim. To accept that the district may be placed anywhere implies that the claim, and hence the coordinate right to an undilut-

---

[7] We do not suggest that where the governmental interest is eradicating the effects of past discrimination the race-based action necessarily would have to achieve fully its task to be narrowly tailored.

ed vote (to cast a ballot equal among voters), belongs to the minority as a group and not to its individual members. It does not. ...."

"[Finally, that a portion] of the concentration of minority voters that would have given rise to a § 2 claim [may have resided in] not more than 20% of the district [was an insufficient] degree of incorporation [to] mean that District 12 substantially addresses the § 2 violation. We hold, therefore, that District 12 is not narrowly tailored to the State's asserted interest in complying with § 2 of the Voting Rights Act."

Unlike *Shaw II*, the companion Texas case, Bush v. Vera, 116 S.Ct. 1941 (1996), revealed important disagreements among the five majority Justices regarding the level of race-consciousness in districting that will provoke strict scrutiny and their willingness to announce that compliance with the results test of § 2 is a compelling state interest—even though they agreed that under *Shaw I* and *Miller* the District Court was correct to invalidate all three districts. A plurality opinion by Justice O'Connor, joined by Chief Justice Rehnquist and Justice Kennedy, expressly noted that "[s]trict scrutiny does not apply merely because redistricting is performed with consciousness of race ... [nor] to all cases of intentional creation of majority-minority districts[, but only where] ... legitimate districting principles were 'subordinated' to race." Justice Kennedy concurred to note:

"I join the plurality opinion, but the statements ... that strict scrutiny would not apply to all cases of intentional creation of majority-minority districts require comment. I do not consider these dicta to commit me to any position on ... whether race is predominant whenever a State ... foreordains that one race be the majority in a certain number of districts or in a certain part of the State. In my view, we would no doubt apply strict scrutiny if a State decreed that certain districts had to be at least 50 percent white, and our analysis should be no different if the State so favors minority races."

And Justice Thomas, joined by Justice Scalia, concurred only in the judgment to disagree "with Justice O'Connor's assertion that strict scrutiny is not invoked by the intentional creation of majority-minority districts":

" ... [T]he intentional creation of a majority-minority district certainly means more than mere awareness that application of traditional, race-neutral districting principles will result in the creation of a district in which a majority of the district's residents are members of a particular minority group. See Personnel Administrator of Mass. v. Feeney, 442 U.S. 256, 279 (1979)(distinguishing discriminatory intent from 'intent as volition' or 'intent as awareness of consequences'). In my view, it means that the legislature affirmatively undertakes to create a majority-minority district that would not have existed but for the express use of racial classifications—in other words, that a majority-minority district is created 'because of,' and not merely 'in spite of,' racial demographics. See ibid. When that occurs, traditional race-neutral districting principles are necessarily subordinated (and race necessarily predominates), and the legislature has classified persons on the basis of race. The resulting redistricting must be viewed as a racial gerrymander.

" . . .

" . . . Texas readily admits that it intentionally created majority-minority districts and that those districts would not have existed but for its affirmative use of racial demographics. . . . That is enough to require application of strict scrutiny in this case."

The plurality, "differ[ing] from Justice Thomas, who would apparently hold that it suffices that racial considerations be *a* motivation for the drawing of a majority-minority district[,]" thought further inquiry was necessary, as it found the "present case . . . a mixed motive case" in that, besides the conceded goal of producing majority-minority districts, "other goals, particularly incumbency protection . . . also played a role in the drawing of the district lines." Nonetheless, the combination of the District Court's "findings—that the State substantially neglected traditional districting criteria such as compactness, that it was committed from the outset to creating majority-minority districts, and that it manipulated district lines to exploit unprecedentedly detailed racial data—together weigh in favor of the application of strict scrutiny[, although w]e do not hold that any one of these factors is independently sufficient to require strict scrutiny." The District Court also had "found that incumbency protection influenced the redistricting plan to an unprecedented extent[,]" however, compelling scrutiny of "each challenged district to determine whether the District Court's conclusion that race predominated over legitimate districting considerations, including incumbency, can be sustained."

Undertaking this individualized examination, the plurality ultimately concluded that race predominated in the drawing of each of the three districts' "bizarre shapes." With respect to the majority-black District 30 in Dallas County, the plurality acknowledged that "[i]n some circumstances, incumbency protection might explain as well as, or better than, race a State's decision to depart from other traditional districting principles, such as compactness, in the drawing of bizarre district lines[,]" but it emphasized that "to the extent that race is used as a proxy for political characteristics [i.e., assuming that to include blacks is to include Democrats], a racial stereotype requiring strict scrutiny is in operation." In a disagreement with Justice Stevens' dissent that the plurality regarded as "largely factual," they concluded:

"The record discloses intensive and pervasive use of race both as a proxy to protect the political fortunes of adjacent incumbents, and for its own sake in maximizing the minority population of District 30 regardless of traditional districting principles. District 30's combination of a bizarre, noncompact shape and overwhelming evidence that that shape was essentially dictated by racial considerations of one form or another is exceptional [and] leads us to conclude that District 30 is subject to strict scrutiny."

With respect to the interlocking majority-black and majority-Hispanic districts in the Houston area—"two of the three least regular districts in the country"—the influence of incumbency protection was "over-whelmed ... by the State's efforts to maximize racial divisions"—especially since "the district lines correlate almost perfectly with race, ... while both districts are similarly solidly Democratic[,]" and given "the intricacy of the lines drawn, separating Hispanic voters from African–American voters on a block-by-block basis, betray[ing] the critical impact of the block-by-block racial data available on the [computer software] program."

As in *Shaw II*, each of the districts was "not narrowly tailored" to a compelling state interest. The plurality again assumed without deciding that compliance with the results test of § 2 "can be a compelling state interest[,]" though Justice O'Connor separately concurred in her own plurality opinion to join the dissenters in affirming for a different Court majority that "the States have a compelling interest in complying with the results test as this Court has interpreted it." The plurality "also reaffirm[ed] that the 'narrow tailoring' requirement of strict scrutiny allows the States a limited degree of leeway" and leaves the States "flexibility that federal courts enforcing § 2 lack, ... insofar as deference is due to their reasonable fears of, and to their reasonable efforts to avoid, § 2 liability." Indeed, a "§ 2 district that is reasonably compact and regular, taking into account traditional districting principles ... may pass strict scrutiny without having to defeat rival compact districts designed by plaintiffs' experts in endless 'beauty contests.'" Here, however,

> " the districts are [not] narrowly tailored to serve the State's interest in avoiding liability under § 2, because § 2 does not require a State to create, on predominantly racial lines, a district that is not 'reasonably compact.' ... If, because of the dispersion of the minority population, a reasonably compact majority-minority district cannot be created, § 2 does not require a majority-minority district; if a reasonably compact district can be created, nothing in § 2 requires the race-based creation of a district that is far from compact.

> " ... Significant deviations from traditional districting principles, such as the bizarre shape and noncompactness demonstrated by the districts here, cause constitutional harm insofar as they convey the message that political identity is, or should be, predominantly racial. For example, the bizarre shaping of Districts 18 and 29, cutting across pre-existing precinct lines and other natural or traditional divisions, is not merely evidentially significant; it is part of the constitutional problem insofar as it disrupts nonracial bases of political identity and thus intensifies the emphasis on race.[a]

---

[a] Justice Kennedy's concurring opinion noted, with respect to these two districts, that "[a]lthough the State could have drawn either a majority-African–American or majority-Hispanic district in Harris County without difficulty, there is no evidence that two reasonably compact majority-minority districts could have been drawn there.... Section 2 does not require the State to create two noncompact majority-minority districts just because a compact district could be drawn for either minority independently."

" ... The districts before us exhibit a level of racial manipulation that exceeds what § 2 could justify."[b]

The plurality concluded by rejecting the dissenters' calls for reconsidering the *Shaw I* cause of action, stating in part:

"Legislators and district courts nationwide have modified their practices—or, rather, reembraced the traditional districting practices that were almost universally followed before the 1990 census—in response to *Shaw I*. Those practices and our precedents, which acknowledge voters as more than mere racial statistics, play an important role in defining the political identity of the American voter. Our Fourteenth Amendment jurisprudence evinces a commitment to eliminate unnecessary and excessive governmental use and reinforcement of racial stereotypes. ... We decline to retreat from that commitment today."

Justice O'Connor's separate opinion also addressed the dissenters:

"Although I agree with the dissenters about § 2's role as part of our national commitment to racial equality, I differ from them in my belief that that commitment can and must be reconciled with the complementary commitment of our Fourteenth Amendment jurisprudence to eliminate the unjustified use of racial stereotypes. At the same time that we combat the symptoms of racial polarization in politics, we must strive to eliminate unnecessary race-based state action that appears to endorse the disease.

" ... The Voting Rights Act requires the States and the courts to take action to remedy the reality of racial inequality in our political system, sometimes necessitating race-based action, while the Fourteenth Amendment requires us to look with suspicion on the excessive use of racial considerations by the government. But I believe that the States, playing a primary role, and the courts, in their secondary role, are capable of distinguishing the appropriate and reasonably necessary uses of race from its unjustified and excessive uses."

Justice Stevens, joined by Justices Ginsburg and Breyer, filed separate, extended dissents in *Shaw II* and *Vera* that both elaborated previous objections to *Shaw I*'s " 'analytically distinct' jurisprudence of racial gerrymandering" and criticized the Court's application of that jurisprudence "even on its own terms."[c] Justice Souter's lengthy dis-

---

[b] Nor, for the same reasons, were the Districts narrowly tailored to serve the State's compelling interest in remedying the "effects of racially polarized voting attributable to past and present racial discrimination." And the claim that the Houston majority-black district was justified by a compelling interest in complying with VRA § 5 was rejected because the argument sought "to justify not maintenance, but substantial augmentation, of the African–American population percentage"—a result "beyond what was reasonably necessary to avoid retrogression."

[c] Justices Ginsburg and Breyer did not join that portion of Justice Stevens' dissent in *Shaw II* elaborating his criticism in *Miller* and *Hays* that the Court's conception of "standing" and "injury" in its "emerging and misguided race-based districting jurisprudence" was fundamentally flawed. Justice Stevens wrote in part:

"[I]t appears that no individual has been burdened more than any other. The supposedly insidious messages that *Shaw I* contends will follow from extremely irregular

sent, filed in *Vera* but applicable to both cases, was also joined by Justices Ginsburg and Breyer. It called on the Court "to admit *Shaw*'s failure" and abandon the *Shaw* cause of action altogether.

Justice Stevens thought strict scrutiny inappropriate in both cases. He interpreted the Court's precedents to allow States to avoid strict scrutiny unless challengers proved "that the State did not respect traditional districting principles in drawing majority-minority districts." In *Shaw II* he emphasized that precisely because North Carolina had chosen "the winding contours of District 12 over the more cartographically pleasant boundaries [of the alternative majority-black district] proposed by the Attorney General[,]" its "noncompact appearance ... fails to show that North Carolina engaged in suspect race-based districting." Instead, "the record reveals that two race-neutral, traditional districting criteria determined District 12's shape: the interest in ensuring that incumbents would remain residents of the districts they have previously represented; and the interest in placing predominantly rural voters in one district and predominantly urban voters in another." In any event, insofar as the majority assumed that the State had drawn District 12 to avoid § 2 liability,

> "it cannot be correct to say that a racially discriminatory purpose controlled its line-drawing. A more accurate conclusion would be that the State took race into account only to the extent necessary to meet the requirements of a carefully thought out federal statute. ... The majority's implicit equation of the intentional consideration of race in order to comply with the Voting Rights Act with intentional racial discrimination reveals the inadequacy of the framework it

race-based districting will presumably be received in equal measure by all State residents. For that reason, the claimed violation of a shared right to a color-blind districting process would not seem to implicate the Equal Protection Clause at all precisely because it rests neither on a challenge to the State's decision to distribute burdens and benefits unequally, nor on a claim that the State's formally equal treatment of its citizens in fact stamps persons of one race with a badge of inferiority.

" ... [T]he Court's decision to entertain the claim of these plaintiffs would seem to emanate less from the Equal Protection Clause's bar against racial discrimination than from the Court's unarticulated recognition of a new substantive due process right to 'color-blind' districting itself. ... [T]he constitutional claim ... ultimately depends for its success on little more than speculative judicial suppositions about the societal message that is to be gleaned from race-based districting. I know of no workable constitutional principle, however, that can discern whether the message conveyed is a distressing endorsement of racial separatism, or an inspiring call to integrate the political process.

"The fact that our Equal Protection jurisprudence requires strict scrutiny of a claim that the State has used race as a criterion for imposing burdens on some persons but not others does not mean that the Constitution demands that a similar level of review obtain for a claim that the State has used race to impose equal burdens on the polity as a whole, or upon some nonracially defined portion thereof. ...

"If under *Hays* the so-called 'stigmatic' harms which result from extreme race-based districting suffice to secure standing, then I fail to see why it matters whether the litigants live within the 'gerrymandered' district or were placed in a district as a result of their race. ... [A]ll voters in North Carolina would seem to be equally affected by the messages of 'balkanization' or 'racial apartheid' that racially gerrymandered maps supposedly convey. ..."

adopts for considering the constitutionality of race-based districting."

In *Vera*, he argued that "the fair implications of the District Court's findings" were "that Texas' entire map is a political, not a racial gerrymander"—even though it was "clear that race also played a role...." He noted and reinforced the Court's endorsement of the view that a State constitutionally may consider race in the deliberate creation of majority-minority districts, reasoning that "when the state action (i) has neither the intent nor effect of harming any particular group, (ii) is not designed to give effect to irrational prejudices held by its citizens but to break them down, and (iii) uses race as a classification because race is 'relevant' to the benign goal of the classification, ... we need not view the action with the typically fatal skepticism that we have used to strike down the most pernicious forms of state behavior."

Particularly with respect to District 30, Justice Stevens objected that none of the factors relied on by the majority "either singly or in combination ... suggests that racial considerations 'subordinated' race-neutral districting principles."[d] Instead, he found "overwhelming evidence that incumbency protection was the critical motivating factor in the creation of the bizarre Texas districts," and explained that "[a]lthough aspects of our dispute with the plurality are 'largely factual,' they arise not out of our disagreement with the District Court's credibility assessments, but out of that court's erroneous conclusion that the state's overwhelming reliance on this race-neutral factor was illegitimate and irrelevant to its evaluation of the factors involved in the shifting of this District's lines." As to the plurality's "fall-back position ... that even if the predominant reason for the bizarre features of the majority-minority districts was incumbency protection, the State impermissibly used race as a proxy for determining the likely political affiliation of blocks of voters[,]" Justice Stevens found the "demographic calculus far more complex than simple racial stereotyping[,]" doubted its impact compared to the nonracial reasons for forcing the district lines "away from its core[,]" and thought it "neither irrational, nor invidious ... to assume that a black resident of a particular community is a Democrat if reliable statistical evidence discloses that 97% of the blacks in that community vote in Democratic primary elections."

Even assuming the applicability of strict scrutiny, Justice Stevens thought the challenged districts were narrowly tailored to the compelling interest of compliance with the VRA. In *Shaw II*, he thought it irrelevant that District 12 "did not 'remedy' any potential violation of § 2" in southern North Carolina, because a second majority-minority district anywhere in the State would have precluded § 2 liability, and "if a State's new plan successfully avoids the potential litigation entirely, there is no reason why it must also take the form of a 'remedy' for an

---

[d] He found the two Houston districts "a closer question on the application of strict scrutiny[,]" because besides evidence of the "same race-neutral factors motivating the zigzags of District 30[,]" there was "also evidence that the interlocking shapes of the Houston districts were specifically, and almost exclusively, the result of an effort to create, out of largely integrated communities, both a majority-black and a majority-Hispanic district."

unproven violation." He thought the "Court's analysis g[ave] rise to the unfortunate suggestion that a State which fears a § 2 lawsuit must draw the precise district that it believes a federal court would have the power to impose." As for the Texas districts in *Vera*, Justice Stevens, for similar reasons, objected to the Court's "insist[ence] that the lack of compactness in the districts prevent them from being 'narrowly tailored'. . . .":

> " ... While a State can be liable for a § 2 violation only if it could have drawn a compact district and failed to do so, it does not follow that creating such a district is the only way to avoid a § 2 violation. ... The plurality admits that a State retains 'a limited degree of leeway' in drawing a district to alleviate fears of § 2 liability, but if there is no independent constitutional duty to create compact districts in the first place, and the Court suggests none, there is no reason why noncompact districts should not be a permissible method of avoiding violations of law. The fact that they might be unacceptable judicial remedies does not speak to the question whether they may be acceptable when adopted by a state legislature. . . ."

Justice Stevens also noted the

> "great irony that by requiring the State to place the majority-minority district in a particular place and with a particular shape, the district may stand out as a stark, placid island in a sea of oddly shaped majority-white neighbors. ...The Court-imposed barriers limiting the shape of the district will interfere more directly with the ability of minority voters to participate in the political process than did the oddly shaped districts that the Court has struck down in recent cases. Unaffected by the new racial jurisprudence, majority-white communities will be able to participate in the districting process by requesting that they be placed into certain districts, divided between districts in an effort to maximize representation, or grouped with more distant communities that might nonetheless match their interests better than communities next door. By contrast, none of this political maneuvering will be permissible for majority-minority districts, thereby segregating and balkanizing them far more effectively than the Districts at issue here, in which they were manipulated in the political process as easily as white voters. This result ... involves 'discrimination' in a far more concrete manner than did the odd shapes that so offended the Court's sensibilities in *Miller*, *Shaw II*, and *Bush*."

He concluded with these statements:

> "... Perhaps minority candidates, forced to run in majority-white districts, will be able to overcome the long history of stereotyping and discrimination that has heretofore led the vast majority of majority-white districts to reject minority candidacies. Perhaps not. I am certain only that bodies of elected federal and state officials are in a far better position than anyone on this Court to assess whether the Nation's long history of discrimination has been overcome, and that nothing in the Constitution requires this unnec-

essary intrusion into the ability of States to negotiate solutions to political differences while providing long-excluded groups the opportunity to participate effectively in the democratic process...."

Justice Souter's dissent complained that the Court had not yet succeeded in "describ[ing] the elements and defin[ing] the contours of the *Shaw* cause of action ... for reasons that go to the conceptual bone." Moreover, "to the extent that some clarity follows from the knowledge that race may be considered when reasonably necessary to conform to the Voting Rights Act, today's opinions raise the specter that this ostensible progress may come with a heavy constitutional price [—] ... the practical elimination of a State's discretion to apply traditional districting principles...." He urged the Court "to recognize that *Shaw*'s problems result from a basic misconception about the relation between race and districting principles ... that no amount of case-by-case tinkering can eliminate."

He emphasized that the Court, in "assum[ing] over the years that traditional districting principles widely accepted among States represent[] an informal baseline of acceptable districting practices[,] ... has recognized the basically associational character of voting rights in a representative democracy." And in a footnote he observed that the Court had "never disagreed in principle" that "to recognize that racial groups, like all other groups, play a real and legitimate role in political decisionmaking ... involves nothing more than an acknowledgement of the reality that our concepts of common interest, geography, and personal allegiances are in many places simply too bound up with race to deny some room for a theory of representative democracy allowing for the consideration of racially conceived interests."

Like Justice Stevens, he found "the logic of traditional equal protection analysis ... at odds with *Shaw*'s concept of injury": the "expressive" harm *Shaw I* is supposed to address "is not confined to any identifiable class singled out for disadvantage ... [but] would seem ... to fall on every citizen and every representative alike"; there is no objection "to segregation but to the particular racial proportions of the district"; and "this use of race conveys no message about the inferiority or outsider status of members of the white majority excluded from a district ... [and] implies nothing about the capacity or value of the minority to which it gives the chance of electoral success." Moreover, *Shaw* has the "further conceptual inadequacy [that w]hereas it defines injury as the reinforcement of the notion that members of a racial group will prefer the same candidates at the polls, the immediate object of the constitutional prohibition against the intentional dilution of minority voting strength is to protect the right of minority voters to make just such a preference effective":

> "Indeed, if there were no correlation between race and candidate preference, it would make no sense to say that minority voters had less opportunity than others to elect whom they would. When voting is ... racially polarized, ... majority-minority districts provide the only practical means of avoiding dilution or remedying the dilution injury that has occurred already. ... So it is that the Court's definition of injury is so broad as to cover constitutionally

necessary efforts to prevent or remedy a violation of the Fourteenth and Fifteenth Amendments and of § 2 of the Voting Rights Act."

Justice Souter raised special objection to the unmanageability of *Miller*'s "predominant motive" standard, "not merely" because "the very nature of districting decisions makes it difficult to identify whether any particular consideration, racial or otherwise," predominated, but "more fundamental[ly,]" because "in the political environment in which race can affect election results, many of these traditional districting principles cannot be applied without taking race into account and are thus, as a practical matter, inseparable from the supposedly illegitimate racial considerations":

"If ... a legislature may draw district lines to preserve the integrity of a given community, ... this objective is inseparable from preserving the community's racial identity when the community is characterized, or even self-defined, by the race of the majority of those who live there. This is an old truth, having been recognized every time the political process produced an Irish or Italian or Polish ward.

"Or take the traditional principle of providing protection for incumbents. The plurality seems to assume that incumbents may always be protected by drawing lines on the basis of data about political parties. But what if the incumbent has drawn support largely for racial reasons? What, indeed, if the incumbent was elected in a majority-minority district created to remedy vote dilution that resulted from racial bloc voting? It would be sheer fantasy to assume that consideration of race in these circumstances is somehow separable from application of the traditional principle of incumbency protection, and sheer incoherence to think that the consideration of race that is constitutionally required to remedy Fourteenth and Fifteenth Amendment vote dilution somehow becomes unconstitutional when aimed at protecting the incumbent the next time the census requires redistricting. Thus, it is as impossible in theory as in practice to untangle racial consideration from the application of traditional districting principles in a society plagued by racial-bloc voting with a racial minority population of political significance, or at least the unrealized potential for achieving it. And it is for just this fundamental reason that a test turning on predominant purpose is incapable of producing any answer when traditional districting principles are applied in the political environment in which *Shaw I* actions are brought."

According to Justice Souter, *Shaw*'s "basic deficiencies" entail "endemic unpredictability" and "the destruction of any clear incentive for the States with substantial minority populations to take action to avoid vote dilution." The "developments" in these cases "fall short of curing *Shaw*'s unworkability" and corrective "options ... are few." To "impos[e] a principle of colorblindness ... would be [to] submerg[e] the votes of those whom the Fourteenth and Fifteenth Amendments were adopted to protect, ... unless the attitudes that produce racial bloc voting were eliminated along with traditional districting principles[,] ... [and] the Court has repeatedly made it plain that *Shaw* was in no way intended to effect a revolution by eliminating traditional districting practice for the sake of colorblindness." Hence, the options are "to confine the cause of action by adopting a quantifiable shape test or to eliminate the cause of action entirely." Despite taking "the commands of *stare decisis* very seriously," Justice Souter urged complete withdrawal "from the presently untenable state of the law."

––––––

Page 980. Add footnote "a" at the end of line two:

a The Court subsequently held that even more deference was due decisions concerning "the Federal Government's conduct of the census—a context even further removed from intrastate districting than is congressional apportionment." Wisconsin v. City of New York, 116 S.Ct. 1091, 1100 (1996). The Court unanimously rejected a claim that the Secretary of Commerce acted unconstitutionally when he decided not to use a particular statistical adjustment designed to correct an undercount (and the accompanying differential undercount of racial minorities) in the initial 1990 census enumeration. The Secretary had concluded that since the primary purpose of the census was to apportion political representation among the States, it was more important to achieve "distributive accuracy"—having the proportions of people in different areas most accurate—than to achieve the best "numerical accuracy." The Court found "no constitutional basis ... for preferring numerical accuracy to distributive accuracy, or for preferring gross accuracy to some particular measure of accuracy." Given "the Constitution's broad grant of authority to Congress, the Secretary's decision not to adjust need bear only a reasonable relationship to the accomplishment of an actual enumeration of the population, keeping in mind the constitutional purpose of the census"—a standard the Secretary had met by his focus on distributive accuracy.

Chapter 11

DEFINING THE SCOPE OF "LIBERTY" AND "PROP-ERTY" PROTECTED BY THE DUE PROCESS CLAUSE—THE PROCEDURAL DUE PROCESS CASES

SECTION 1. WHEN DOES DUE PROCESS MANDATE CONSTITUTIONAL PROCEDURES?

A. WHAT "PROPERTY" AND "LIBERTY" IS PROTECTED?

Page 1083. Replace Kentucky Department of Corrections v. Thompson with the following:

SANDIN v. CONNER

___ U.S. ___, 115 S.Ct. 2293, 132 L.Ed.2d 418 (1995).

Chief Justice Rehnquist delivered the opinion of the Court.

We granted certiorari to reexamine the circumstances under which state prison regulations afford inmates a liberty interest protected by the Due Process Clause.

I

[While serving an indeterminate sentence of 30 years to life in a Hawaii prison, Conner reacted angrily to a strip-search and was charged with "high misconduct" for physical interference with a correctional function and "low moderate misconduct" for using abusive or obscene language and for harassing employees. An adjustment committee held a hearing at which Conner appeared but was not allowed to present witnesses. The committee found him guilty and sentenced him, inter alia, to 30 days disciplinary segregation for the physical obstruction charge. On appeal, months after serving this punishment, the deputy administrator found unsupported, and so expunged, the high misconduct charge. In the interim, Conner had sued in federal court, claiming that the refusal to allow him to present witnesses deprived him of procedural due process.] The District Court granted summary judgment in favor of the prison officials.

The Court of Appeals ... reversed.... It concluded that Conner had a liberty interest in remaining free from disciplinary segregation ... based ... on a prison regulation that instructs the committee to find guilt when a charge of misconduct is supported by substantial evi-

dence. . . .   [It] reasoned from Kentucky Department of Corrections v.
Thompson, 490 U.S. 454 (1989), that the committee's duty to find guilt
was nondiscretionary.   From the language of the regulation, it drew a
negative inference that the committee may not impose segregation if it
does not find substantial evidence of misconduct. . . .   It viewed this as a
state-created liberty interest. . . .   We . . . reverse.

II

Our due process analysis begins with Wolff [v. McDonnell, 418 U.S.
539 (1974), where] Nebraska inmates challenged the decision of prison
officials to revoke good time credits without adequate procedures. . . .
Inmates earned good time credits under a state statute that bestowed
mandatory sentence reductions for good behavior, . . . revocable only for
" 'flagrant or serious misconduct[.]' "   . . . We held that the Due Process
Clause itself does not create a liberty interest in credit for good behavior,
but that the statutory provision created a liberty interest in a "short-
ened prison sentence" which resulted from good time credits, credits
which were revocable only if the prisoner was guilty of serious misconduct. . . .   The Court characterized this liberty interest as one of "real
substance". . . .

Inmates in Meachum [v. Fano, 427 U.S. 215 (1976), challenged]
transfers from a Massachusetts medium security prison to a maximum
security facility with substantially less favorable conditions. . . .   The
Court began with the proposition that the Due Process Clause does not
protect every change in the conditions of confinement having a substantial adverse impact on the prisoner.   It then held that the Due Process
Clause did not itself create a liberty interest in prisoners to be free from
intrastate prison transfers. . . .   It reasoned that transfer to a maximum
security facility, albeit one with more burdensome conditions, was "within the normal limits or range of custody which the conviction has
authorized the State to impose."   . . . The Court distinguished *Wolff* by
noting that there the protected liberty interest in good time credit had
been created by state law; here no comparable Massachusetts law
stripped officials of the discretion to transfer prisoners to alternate
facilities "for whatever reason or for no reason at all."   . . .

Shortly after *Meachum*, the Court embarked on a different approach
to defining state-created liberty interests.   Because dictum in *Meachum*
distinguished *Wolff* by focusing on whether state action was mandatory
or discretionary, the Court in later cases laid ever greater emphasis on
this somewhat mechanical dichotomy. . . .

[In Hewitt v. Helms, 459 U.S. 460 (1983), the Court] evaluat[ed] the
claims of inmates who had been confined to administrative segregation[.
I]t first rejected the inmates' claim of a right to remain in the general
population. . . .   The Due Process Clause standing alone confers no
liberty interest in freedom from state action taken " 'within the sentence
imposed[.]' "   It then concluded that the transfer to less amenable
quarters for nonpunitive reasons was "ordinarily contemplated by a
prison sentence."   . . . Examination of the possibility that the State had
created a liberty interest by virtue of its prison regulations followed.
Instead of looking to whether the State created an interest of "real

substance" comparable to the good time credit scheme of *Wolff*, the Court asked whether the State had gone beyond issuing mere procedural guidelines and had used "language of an unmistakably mandatory character" such that the incursion on liberty would not occur "absent specified substantive predicates." ... Finding such mandatory directives in the regulations before it, the Court decided that the State had created a protected liberty interest....

As this methodology took hold, no longer did inmates need to rely on a showing that they had suffered a " 'grievous loss' " of liberty retained even after sentenced to terms of imprisonment. Morrissey v. Brewer, 408 U.S. 471, 481 (1972).... For the Court had ceased to examine the "nature" of the interest with respect to interests allegedly created by the State.... In a series of cases since *Hewitt*, the Court has wrestled with the language of intricate, often rather routine prison guidelines to determine whether mandatory language and substantive predicates created an enforceable expectation that the state would produce a particular outcome with respect to the prisoner's conditions of confinement.

. . .

By shifting the focus of the liberty interest inquiry to one based on the language of a particular regulation, and not the nature of the deprivation, the Court encouraged prisoners to comb regulations in search of mandatory language on which to base entitlements to various state-conferred privileges. Courts have, in response, and not altogether illogically, drawn negative inferences from mandatory language in the text of prison regulations. The Court of Appeals' approach in this case is typical: it inferred from the mandatory directive that a finding of guilt "shall" be imposed under certain conditions the conclusion that the absence of such conditions prevents a finding of guilt.

Such a conclusion may be entirely sensible in the ordinary task of construing a statute defining rights and remedies available to the general public. It is a good deal less sensible in the case of a prison regulation primarily designed to guide correctional officials in the administration of a prison....

Hewitt has produced at least two undesirable effects. First, it creates disincentives for States to codify prison management procedures in the interest of uniform treatment.... States may avoid creation of "liberty" interests by having scarcely any regulations, or by conferring standardless discretion on correctional personnel.

Second, the *Hewitt* approach has led to the involvement of federal courts in the day-to-day management of prisons, often squandering judicial resources with little offsetting benefit to anyone....

[W]e believe that the search for a negative implication from mandatory language in prisoner regulations has strayed from the real concerns undergirding the liberty protected by the Due Process Clause. The time has come to return to the due process principles ... in *Wolff* and

Meachum.[5] Following *Wolff*, we recognize that States may under certain circumstances create liberty interests which are protected by the Due Process Clause.... But these interests will be generally limited to freedom from restraint which, while not exceeding the sentence in such an unexpected manner as to give rise to protection by the Due Process Clause of its own force, see, e.g., Vitek, 445 U.S., at 493 (transfer to mental hospital), and Washington, 494 U.S., at 221–222 (involuntary administration of psychotropic drugs), nonetheless imposes atypical and significant hardship on the inmate in relation to the ordinary incidents of prison life.

Conner asserts, incorrectly, that any state action taken for a punitive reason encroaches upon a liberty interest under the Due Process Clause even in the absence of any state regulation. Neither Bell v. Wolfish, 441 U.S. 520 (1979), nor Ingraham v. Wright, 430 U.S. 651 (1977), requires such a rule. *Bell* dealt with the interests of pretrial detainees and not convicted prisoners....

... *Ingraham* ... addressed the rights of schoolchildren to remain free from arbitrary corporal punishment. The Court noted that the Due Process Clause historically encompassed the notion that the state could not "physically punish an individual except in accordance with due process of law" and so found schoolchildren sheltered....

The punishment of incarcerated prisoners, on the other hand, serves different aims than those found invalid in *Bell* and *Ingraham*. The process does not impose retribution in lieu of a valid conviction, nor does it maintain physical control over free citizens forced by law to subject themselves to state control over the educational mission. It effectuates prison management and prisoner rehabilitative goals.... Admittedly, prisoners do not shed all constitutional rights at the prison gate, ... but " '[l]awful incarceration brings about the necessary withdrawal or limitation of many privileges and rights, a retraction justified by the considerations underlying our penal system.' " ... Discipline by prison officials in response to a wide range of misconduct falls within the expected parameters of the sentence imposed by a court of law.

This case, though concededly punitive, does not present a dramatic departure from the basic conditions of Conner's indeterminate sentence. Although Conner points to dicta in cases implying that solitary confinement automatically triggers due process protection, ... this Court has not had the opportunity to address in an argued case the question whether disciplinary confinement of inmates itself implicates constitutional liberty interests. We hold that Conner's discipline in segregated confinement did not present the type of atypical, significant deprivation in which a state might conceivably create a liberty interest. The record shows that, at the time of Conner's punishment, disciplinary segrega-

---

[5] Such abandonment of *Hewitt*'s methodology does not technically require us to overrule any holding of this Court.... Although it did locate a liberty interest in *Hewitt*, it concluded that due process required no additional procedural guarantees for the inmate. As such, its answer to the anterior question of whether the inmate possessed a liberty interest at all was unnecessary to the disposition of the case. Our decision today only abandons an approach that in practice is difficult to administer and which produces anomalous results.

tion, with insignificant exceptions, mirrored those conditions imposed upon inmates in administrative segregation and protective custody. We note also that the State expunged Conner's disciplinary record with respect to the "high misconduct" charge 9 months after Conner served time in segregation. Thus, Conner's confinement did not exceed similar, but totally discretionary confinement in either duration or degree of restriction.... Based on a comparison between inmates inside and outside disciplinary segregation, the State's actions in placing him there for 30 days did not work a major disruption in his environment.

Nor does Conner's situation present a case where the State's action will inevitably affect the duration of his sentence. Nothing in Hawaii's code requires the parole board to deny parole in the face of a misconduct record or to grant parole in its absence.... The decision to release a prisoner rests on a myriad of considerations. And, the prisoner is afforded procedural protection at his parole hearing in order to explain the circumstances behind his misconduct record.... The chance that a finding of misconduct will alter the balance is simply too attenuated to invoke the procedural guarantees of the Due Process Clause....

We hold, therefore, that neither the Hawaii prison regulation in question, nor the Due Process Clause itself, afforded Conner a protected liberty interest that would entitle him to the procedural protections set forth in *Wolff*. The regime to which he was subjected as a result of the misconduct hearing was within the range of confinement to be normally expected for one serving an indeterminate term of 30 years to life.

The judgment of the Court of Appeals is accordingly

Reversed.

Justice Ginsburg, with whom Justice Stevens joins, dissenting.

. . .

Unlike the Court, I conclude that Conner had a liberty interest, protected by the Fourteenth Amendment's Due Process Clause, in avoiding the disciplinary confinement he endured. As Justice Breyer details, Conner's prison punishment effected a severe alteration in the conditions of his incarceration. Disciplinary confinement as punishment for "high misconduct" not only deprives prisoners of privileges for protracted periods; unlike administrative segregation and protective custody, disciplinary confinement also stigmatizes them and diminishes parole prospects. Those immediate and lingering consequences should suffice to qualify such confinement as liberty-depriving for purposes of Due Process Clause protection....[1]

I see the Due Process Clause itself, not Hawaii's prison code, as the wellspring of the protection due Conner. Deriving protected liberty interests from mandatory language in local prison codes would make of

---

[1] .... The Court notes ... that the State eventually expunged Conner's disciplinary record as a result of his successful administrative appeal. But hindsight cannot tell us whether a liberty interest existed at the outset. One must ... know at the start the character of the interest at stake in order to determine then what process, if any, is constitutionally due....

the fundamental right something more in certain States, something less in others....[2]

Deriving the prisoner's due process right from the code for his prison, moreover, yields this practical anomaly: a State that scarcely attempts to control the behavior of its prison guards may, for that very laxity, escape constitutional accountability; a State that tightly cabins the discretion of its prison workers may, for that attentiveness, become vulnerable to constitutional claims. An incentive for ruleless prison management disserves the State's penological goals and jeopardizes the welfare of prisoners.

. . .

Justice Breyer, with whom Justice Souter joins, dissenting.

... The majority, asking whether [Conner's] punishment "imposes atypical and significant hardship on the inmate in relation to the ordinary incidents of prison life" concludes that it does not do so. The majority's reasoning, however, particularly when read in light of this Court's precedents, seems to me to lead to the opposite conclusion. And, for that reason, I dissent.

. . .

II

... In determining whether state officials have deprived an inmate ... of a procedurally protected "liberty," this Court traditionally has looked either (1) to the nature of the deprivation (how severe, in degree or kind) or (2) to the State's rules governing the imposition of that deprivation (whether they, in effect, give the inmate a "right" to avoid it). See, e.g., Kentucky Department of Corrections v. Thompson, 490 U.S. 454, 460–461, 464–465 (1989). Thus, this Court has said that certain changes in conditions may be so severe or so different from ordinary conditions of confinement that, whether or not state law gives state authorities broad discretionary power to impose them, the state authorities may not do so "without complying with minimum requirements of due process." Vitek v. Jones, 445 U.S. 480, 491–494 (1980)("involuntary commitment to a mental hospital"); Washington v. Harper, 494 U.S. 210, 221–222 (1990)("unwanted administration of antipsychotic drugs"). The Court has also said that deprivations that are less severe or more closely related to the original terms of confinement nonetheless will amount to deprivations of procedurally protected liberty, provided that state law (including prison regulations) narrowly cabins the legal power of authorities to impose the deprivation (thereby giving the inmate a kind of right to avoid it). See Hewitt v. Helms....

---

[2] The Court describes a category of liberty interest that is something less than the one the Due Process Clause itself shields, something more than anything a prison code provides. The State may create a liberty interest, the Court tells us, when "atypical and significant hardship [would be borne by] the inmate in relation to the ordinary incidents of prison life." What design lies beneath these key words? The Court ventures no examples, leaving consumers of the Court's work at sea, unable to fathom what would constitute an "atypical, significant deprivation" and yet not trigger protection under the Due Process Clause directly.

If we apply these general pre-existing principles to the relevant facts before us, it seems fairly clear ... that the prison punishment ... deprived Conner of constitutionally protected "liberty." For one thing, the punishment worked a fairly major change in Conner's conditions....

Moreover, irrespective of whether this punishment amounts to a deprivation of liberty independent of state law, here the prison's own disciplinary rules severely cabin the authority of prison officials to impose this kind of punishment. They ... (1) impose a punishment that is substantial, (2) restrict its imposition as a punishment to instances in which an inmate has committed a defined offense, and (3) prescribe nondiscretionary standards for determining whether or not an inmate committed that offense.

Accordingly, under this Court's liberty-defining standards, imposing the punishment would "deprive" Conner of "liberty" within the meaning of the Due Process Clause....

III

The majority, while not disagreeing with this summary of pre-existing law, seeks to change, or to clarify, that law's "liberty" defining standards in one important respect. The majority believes that the Court's present "cabining of discretion" standard reads the Constitution as providing procedural protection for trivial "rights," as, for example, where prison rules set forth specific standards for the content of prison meals. It adds that this approach involves courts too deeply in routine matters of prison administration, all without sufficient justification.... It therefore imposes a minimum standard, namely that a deprivation falls within the Fourteenth Amendment's definition of "liberty" only if it "imposes atypical and significant hardship on the inmate in relation to the ordinary incidents of prison life."

I am not certain whether or not the Court means this standard to change prior law radically.... There is no need, however, for ... significant change ... to achieve the majority's basic objective, namely to read the Constitution's Due Process Clause to protect inmates against deprivations of freedom that are important, not comparatively insignificant. Rather, ... this concern simply requires elaborating, and explaining, the Court's present standards (without radical revision) [so as] not [to] create procedurally protected "liberty" interests where only minor matters are at stake.

Three sets of considerations, taken together, support my conclusion.... First, although this Court ... continues to say, that some deprivations of an inmate's freedom are so severe in kind or degree (or so far removed from the original terms of confinement) that they amount to deprivations of liberty, irrespective of whether state law (or prison rules) "cabin discretion," ... it is not easy to specify just when, or how much of, a loss triggers this protection. There is a broad middle category of imposed restraints or deprivations that, considered by themselves, are neither obviously so serious as to fall within, nor obviously so insignificant as to fall without, the Clause's protection.

Second, the difficult line-drawing task that this middle category implies helps to explain why this Court developed its additional liberty-defining standard, which looks to local law (examining whether that local law creates a "liberty" by significantly limiting the discretion of local authorities to impose a restraint).... Despite its similarity to the way in which the Court determines the existence, or nonexistence, of "property" for Due Process Clause purposes, the justification for looking at local law is not the same in the prisoner liberty context. In protecting property, the Due Process Clause often aims to protect reliance, say, reliance upon an "entitlement" that local (i.e., nonconstitutional) law itself has created or helped to define.... In protecting liberty, however, the Due Process Clause protects ... an absence of government restraint, the very absence of restraint that we call freedom....

Nevertheless, there are several other important reasons, in the prison context, to consider the provisions of state law. The fact that a further deprivation of an inmate's freedom takes place under local rules that cabin the authorities' discretionary power to impose the restraint suggests, other things being equal, that the matter is more likely to have played an important role in the life of the inmate.... It suggests, other things being equal, that the matter is more likely of a kind to which procedural protections historically have applied, and where they normally prove useful, for such rules often single out an inmate and condition a deprivation upon the existence, or nonexistence, of particular facts.... It suggests, other things being equal, that the matter will not involve highly judgmental administrative matters that call for the wise exercise of discretion—matters where courts reasonably should hesitate to second-guess prison administrators.... It suggests, other things being equal, that the inmate will have thought that he himself, through control of his own behavior, could have avoided the deprivation, and thereby have believed that (in the absence of his misbehavior) the restraint fell outside the "sentence imposed" upon him.... Finally, courts can identify the presence or absence of cabined discretion fairly easily and objectively, at least much of the time.... These characteristics of "cabined discretion" mean that courts can use it as a kind of touchstone that can help them, when they consider the broad middle category of prisoner restraints, to separate those kinds of restraints that, in general, are more likely to call for constitutionally guaranteed procedural protection, from those that more likely do not.... I believe courts will continue to find this touchstone helpful as they seek to apply the majority's middle category standard.

Third, there is, therefore, no need to apply the "discretion-cabining" approach—the basic purpose of which is to provide a somewhat more objective method for identifying deprivations of protected "liberty" within a broad middle-range of prisoner restraints—where a deprivation is unimportant enough (or so similar in nature to ordinary imprisonment) that it rather clearly falls outside that middle category. Prison, by design, restricts the inmates' freedom. And, one cannot properly view unimportant matters that happen to be the subject of prison regulations as substantially aggravating a loss that has already occurred. Indeed, a regulation about a minor matter ... may amount simply to an instruction to the administrator about how to do his job, rather than a guarantee to the inmate of a "right" to the status quo.... Thus, this Court has never held that comparatively unimportant prisoner "depriva- tions" fall within the scope of the Due Process Clause even if local law limits the authority of prison administrators to impose such minor deprivations.... And, in my view, it should now simply specify that they do not.

I recognize that, as a consequence, courts must separate the unim- portant from the potentially significant, without the help of the more objective "discretion-cabining" test. Yet, making that judicial judgment seems no more difficult than many other judicial tasks. See Goss v. Lopez, 419 U.S. 565, 576 (1975)("de minimis" line defining property interests under the Due Process Clause). It seems to me possible to separate less significant matters such as television privileges ... from more significant matters, such as the solitary confinement at issue here. Indeed, prison regulations themselves may help in this respect, such as the regulations here which separate (from more serious matters) "low moderate" and "minor" misconduct....

The upshot is the following: the problems that the majority identi- fies suggest that this Court should make explicit the lower definitional limit, in the prison context, of "liberty" under the Due Process Clause— a limit that is already implicit in this Court's precedent.... Those problems do not require abandoning that precedent....

IV

The Court today reaffirms that the "liberty" protected by the Fourteenth Amendment includes interests that state law may create. It excludes relatively minor matters from that protection.... And, it does not question the vast body of case law ... recognizing that segregation can deprive an inmate of constitutionally-protected "liberty." ... That being so, it is difficult to see why the Court reverses, rather than affirms, the Court of Appeals in this case.

. . .

I agree [that the] conditions in administrative and disciplinary segregation are relatively similar in Hawaii [and that] the rules govern- ing administrative segregation do, indeed, provide prison officials with broad leeway. But, I disagree with the majority's assertion about the relevance of the expungement. How can a later decision of prison authorities transform Conner's segregation for a violation of a specific disciplinary rule into a term of segregation under the administrative rules? How can a later expungement restore to Conner the liberty that, in fact, he had already lost? ...

In sum, expungement or no, Conner suffered a deprivation that was significant, not insignificant. And, that deprivation took place under disciplinary rules that ... do cabin official discretion sufficiently. I would therefore hold that Conner was deprived of "liberty" within the meaning of the Due Process Clause.

V

Other related legal principles ... should further alleviate the majority's fear that application of the Due Process Clause to significant prison disciplinary action ... will lead federal courts to intervene improperly.... [T]he "process" that is "due" in the context of prison discipline is not the full blown procedure that accompanies criminal trials [but is] flexible [and] must take account of the legitimate needs of prison administration....

More importantly for present purposes, ... the Due Process Clause does not require process unless, in the individual case, there is a relevant factual dispute between the parties.... [It] does not entitle an inmate to additional disciplinary hearing procedure (such as the calling of a witness) unless there is a factual dispute (relevant to guilt) that the additional procedure might help to resolve....

... [T]he record before us indicates that ... if we were to affirm, it would pose an important obstacle to Conner's eventual success. The ... adjustment committee's report ... says that its finding of guilt rests upon Conner's own admissions.... [and] contains no explanation ... of how the witnesses he wanted to call ... could have led to any evidence relevant to the facts at issue.

. . .

Chapter 12

APPLICATION OF THE POST CIVIL WAR AMENDMENTS TO PRIVATE CONDUCT: CONGRESSIONAL POWER TO ENFORCE THE AMENDMENTS

SECTION 2. APPLICATION OF THE CONSTITUTION TO PRIVATE CONDUCT

C. GOVERNMENT FINANCING, REGULATION AND AUTHORIZATION OF PRIVATE CONDUCT

4. GOVERNMENT APPROVAL OF PRIVATE ACTIVITY

Page 1151. Add to end of Note:

In Romer v. Evans, 116 S.Ct. 1620 (1996), the Court dealt with an amendment to the Colorado Constitution that precluded any level of state government from protecting the status of persons based on their "homosexual, lesbian or bisexual orientation, conduct, practices or relationships." The Colorado Supreme Court held the measure unconstitutional, relying in part on Hunter v. Erickson, supra. The Supreme Court affirmed, but did not rely upon or cite any of the preceding cases, nor did the Court advert to the issue of state action. The full report of this case appears supra, p. 157.

SECTION 4. FEDERAL POWER TO REGULATE PRIVATE CONDUCT UNDER THE THIRTEENTH AMENDMENT

Page 1160. Add to note, "(4) Redress of private racial violence under 42 U.S.C. § 1985(3)":

In Bray v. Alexandria Women's Health Clinic, 506 U.S. 263 (1993), the Court held that § 1985(3) did not provide a federal cause of action against defendants who obstructed access to abortion clinics. Defendants' opposition to abortion was not "class-based invidiously discriminatory animus" because it did not focus on women "by reason of their sex." (The Court did not decide the question left open in Griffin— whether § 1985(3) was limited to cases involving racial animus.)

Part IV

CONSTITUTIONAL PROTECTION OF EXPRESSION AND CONSCIENCE

Chapter 13

GOVERNMENTAL CONTROL OF THE CONTENT OF EXPRESSION

SECTION 2. INTERMEZZO: AN INTRODUCTION TO THE CONCEPTS OF VAGUENESS, OVERBREADTH AND PRIOR RESTRAINT

B. PRIOR RESTRAINT

Page 1253. Add after Near v. Minnesota:

ALEXANDER v. UNITED STATES, 509 U.S. 544 (1993). Alexander received a prison sentence and fine after being convicted of federal obscenity charges and of operating an illegal racketeering (RICO) enterprise based on the distribution of the obscene books and films through a chain of retail stores and theaters he owned. In a separate proceeding authorized by RICO, the assets of all his wholesale and retail businesses, including the expressive materials, were forfeited to the Government, which decided to destroy rather than to sell to the public "pornographic materials—regardless of whether they were legally obscene." The Court rejected the argument that "forfeiture of expressive materials and the assets of businesses engaged in expressive activity, when predicated solely upon previous obscenity violations, operates as a prior restraint because it prohibits future presumptively protected expression in retaliation for prior unprotected speech."

Chief Justice Rehnquist wrote for the majority that to equate "the forfeiture imposed in this case after a full criminal trial with an injunction enjoining future speech"—as in *Near*—"would virtually obliterate the distinction, solidly grounded in our cases, between prior restraints and subsequent punishments." He elaborated:

> "[T]he RICO forfeiture order in this case does not forbid petitioner from engaging in any expressive activities in the future, nor does it require him to obtain prior approval for any expressive activities. It only deprives him of specific assets that were found to be related to

his previous racketeering violations. Assuming, of course, that he has sufficient untainted assets to open new stores, restock his inventory, and hire staff, petitioner can go back into the adult entertainment business tomorrow, and sell as many sexually explicit magazines and videotapes as he likes, without any risk of being held in contempt for violating a court order. Unlike the injunctions in *Near, Keefe,* and *Vance,* the forfeiture order in this case imposes no legal impediment to—no prior restraint on—petitioner's ability to engage in any expressive activity he chooses. He is perfectly free to open an adult bookstore or otherwise engage in the production and distribution of erotic materials; he just cannot finance these enterprises with assets derived from his prior racketeering offenses.

"The constitutional infirmity in nearly all of our prior restraint cases involving obscene material ... was that Government had seized or otherwise restrained materials suspected of being obscene without a prior judicial determination that they were in fact so.... In this case, however, the assets in question were not ordered forfeited because they were believed to be obscene, but because they were directly related to petitioner's past racketeering violations. The RICO forfeiture statute calls for the forfeiture of assets because of the financial role they play in the operation of the racketeering enterprise. The statute is oblivious to the expressive or nonexpressive nature of the assets forfeited; books, sports cars, narcotics, and cash are all forfeitable alike under RICO. Indeed, a contrary scheme would be disastrous from a policy standpoint, enabling racketeers to evade forfeiture by investing the proceeds of their crimes in businesses engaging in expressive activity.

"Nor were the assets in question ordered forfeited without according petitioner the requisite procedural safeguards, another recurring theme in our prior restraint cases.... [T]he seizure was not premature, because the Government established beyond a reasonable doubt the basis for the forfeiture[—] ... that the ... forfeited assets were directly linked to petitioner's commission of racketeering offenses.

"... [T]he time-honored distinction between ... prior restraints and subsequent punishments ... is critical to our First Amendment jurisprudence. Because we have interpreted the First Amendment as providing greater protection from prior restraints than from subsequent punishments, ... it is important for us to delineate with some precision the defining characteristics of a prior restraint. To hold that the forfeiture order in this case constituted a prior restraint would have the exact opposite effect: it would blur the line separating prior restraints from subsequent punishments to such a degree that it would be impossible to determine with any certainty whether a particular measure is a prior restraint or not."

Analyzing the forfeiture "under normal First Amendment standards," the Chief Justice noted the Court's past rejection of "First Amendment challenges to statutes that impose severe prison sentences and fines as punishment for obscenity offenses" and found "the threat of forfeiture" to have "no more of a chilling effect on free expression than the threat of a prison term or a large fine." The case was remanded, however, for a determination whether the forfeiture here violated "the Eighth Amendment's Excessive Fines Clause."

Justice Kennedy dissented from the First Amendment ruling. Joined by Justices Blackmun and Stevens, he thought the Court's prior restraint precedents should apply to forfeitures based on a "speech offense" and involving "the destruction of protected titles and the facilities for their distribution or publication." He faulted the Court for not confronting "the pervasive danger of government censorship" arising from the 1984 amendment to RICO adding "obscenity as a predicate offense," because that "went far beyond the imposition of severe penalties for obscenity offenses" and "render[ed] vulnerable to government destruction any business daring to deal in sexually explicit materials." As he saw it:

> ". . . The admitted design and the overt purpose of the forfeiture in this case are to destroy an entire speech business and all its protected titles, thus depriving the public of access to lawful expression. This is restraint in more than theory. It is censorship all too real."

In particular, the "distinction between prior restraints and subsequent punishments . . . is neither so rigid nor so precise that it can bear the weight the Court places upon it to sustain the destruction of a speech business and its inventory as a punishment for past expression." Analyzing the development and previous extensions of prior restraint law, Justice Kennedy said in part:

> "In one sense the injunctive order [in *Near*], which paralleled the nuisance statute, did nothing more than announce the conditions under which some later punishment might be imposed, for one presumes that contempt could not be found until there was a further violation in contravention of the order. But in *Near* the publisher, because of past wrongs, was subjected to active state intervention for the control of future speech. We found that the scheme was a prior restraint because it embodied 'the essence of censorship.' . . . [T]he Court has been consistent in adopting a speech-protective definition of prior restraint when the state attempts to attack future speech in retribution for a speaker's past transgressions. See Vance v. Universal Amusement Co., 445 U.S. 308 (1980)(per curiam)(invalidating as a prior restraint procedure authorizing state courts to abate as a nuisance an adult theater which had exhibited obscene films in the past because the effect of the procedure was to prevent future exhibitions of pictures not yet found to be obscene). It is a flat misreading of our precedents to declare as the majority does that the definition of a prior restraint includes only those measures which impose a 'legal impediment' on a speaker's ability to engage in future expressive activity. Bantam Books, Inc. v. Sullivan, 372 U.S. 58, 70 (1963), best illustrates the point. There a state commission did nothing more than warn book sellers that certain titles could be obscene, implying that criminal prosecutions could follow if their warnings were not heeded. The commission had no formal enforcement powers and failure to heed

its warnings was not a criminal offense. Although the commission could impose no legal impediment on a speaker's ability to engage in future expressive activity, we held that scheme was an impermissible 'system of prior administrative restraints.' ... If mere warning against sale of certain materials was a prior restraint, I fail to see why the physical destruction of a speech enterprise and its protected inventory is not condemned by the same doctrinal principles."

Thus, that "forfeiture follows a lawful conviction for obscenity offenses ... does not suffice" to avoid prior restraint analysis "because in some instances the operation and effect of a particular enforcement scheme, though not in the form of a traditional prior restraint, may be to raise the same concerns which inform all of our prior restraint cases: the evils of state censorship and the unacceptable chilling of protected speech." Regarding these concerns, Justice Kennedy concluded:

> "The operation and effect of RICO's forfeiture remedies is different from a heavy fine or a severe jail sentence because RICO's forfeiture provisions are different in purpose and kind from ordinary criminal sanctions. The government's stated purpose under RICO, to destroy or incapacitate the offending enterprise, bears a striking resemblance to the motivation for the state nuisance statute the Court struck down as an impermissible prior restraint in *Near*.... Under the principle the Court adopts, any bookstore or press enterprise could be forfeited as punishment for even a single obscenity conviction.

> " . . .

> "What is at work in this case is not the power to punish an individual for his past transgressions but the authority to suppress a particular class of disfavored speech. The forfeiture provisions accomplish this in a direct way by seizing speech presumed to be protected along with the instruments of its dissemination, and in an indirect way by threatening all who engage in the business of distributing adult or sexually explicit materials with the same disabling measures....

> " ... Though perhaps not in the form of a classic prior restraint, the application of the forfeiture statute here bears its censorial cast.

> " ... Where ... RICO forfeiture stems from a previous speech offense, the punishment serves not only the government's interest in purging organized-crime taint, but also its interest in deterring the activities of the speech-related business itself. The threat of a censorial motive and of ongoing speech supervision by the state justifies the imposition of First Amendment protection."

In a final portion of his opinion, Justice Kennedy also argued that "[q]uite apart from the direct bearing that our prior restraint cases have on the entire forfeiture that was ordered in this case, the destruction of books and films that were not obscene and not adjudged to be so is a remedy with no parallel in our cases." In a separate statement, Justice Souter agreed with this point, but he otherwise agreed with the majority that the forfeiture was not "a prior restraint as we have traditionally understood that term."

SECTION 3. SPEECH CONFLICTING WITH OTHER COMMUNITY VALUES: GOVERNMENT CONTROL OF THE CONTENT OF SPEECH

C. CONTROL OF "FIGHTING WORDS" AND OFFENSIVE SPEECH

Page 1302. Replace Federal Communications Commission v. Pacifica Foundation with the following:

DENVER AREA EDUCATIONAL TELECOMMUNICATIONS CONSORTIUM, INC. v. FEDERAL COMMUNICATIONS COMMISSION

___ U.S. ___, 116 S.Ct. 2374, ___ L.Ed.2d ___ (1996).

Justice Breyer announced the judgment of the Court and delivered the opinion of the Court with respect to Part III, an opinion with respect to Parts I, II, and V, in which Justice Stevens, Justice O'Connor, and Justice Souter join, and an opinion with respect to Parts IV and VI, in which Justice Stevens and Justice Souter join.

These cases present First Amendment challenges to three statutory provisions that seek to regulate the broadcasting of "patently offensive" sex-related material on cable television. Cable Television Consumer Protection and Competition Act of 1992 (1992 Act or Act), 106 Stat. 1486, §§ 10(a), 10(b), and 10(c), 47 U.S.C. §§ 532(h), 532(j), and note following § 531. The provisions apply to programs broadcast over cable on what are known as "leased access channels" and "public, educational, or governmental channels." Two of the provisions essentially permit a cable system operator to prohibit the broadcasting of "programming" that the "operator reasonably believes describes or depicts sexual or excretory activities or organs in a patently offensive manner." 1992 Act, § 10(a); see § 10(c). ... The remaining provision requires cable system operators to segregate certain "patently offensive" programming, to place it on a single channel, and to block that channel from viewer access unless the viewer requests access in advance and in writing. 1992 Act, § 10(b); 47 CFR § 76.701(g)(1995).

We conclude that the first provision—that permits the operator to decide whether or not to broadcast such programs on leased access channels—is consistent with the First Amendment. The second provision, that requires leased channel operators to segregate and to block that programming, and the third provision, applicable to public, educational, and governmental channels, violate the First Amendment, for they are not appropriately tailored to achieve the basic, legitimate objective of protecting children from exposure to "patently offensive" material.

I

Cable operators typically own a physical cable network used to convey programming over several dozen cable channels into subscribers' houses. Program sources vary from channel to channel. Most channels carry programming produced by independent firms, including "many national and regional cable programming networks that have emerged in recent years," Turner Broadcasting System, Inc. v. FCC, 512 U.S. ___, ___ (1994), as well as some programming that the system operator itself (or an operator affiliate) may provide. Other channels may simply retransmit through cable the signals of over-the-air broadcast stations. Certain special channels here at issue, called "leased channels" and "public, educational, or governmental channels," carry programs provided by those to whom the law gives special cable system access rights.

A "leased channel" is a channel that federal law requires a cable system operator to reserve for commercial lease by unaffiliated third parties. About 10 to 15 percent of a cable system's channels would typically fall into this category.... "[P]ublic, educational, or governmental channels" (which we shall call "public access" channels) are channels that, over the years, local governments have required cable system operators to set aside for public, educational, or governmental purposes as part of the consideration an operator gives in return for permission to install cables under city streets and to use public rights-of-way. ... Between 1984 and 1992 federal law (as had much pre–1984 state law, in respect to public access channels) prohibited cable system operators from exercising any editorial control over the content of any program broadcast over either leased or public access channels. ...

In 1992, in an effort to control sexually explicit programming conveyed over access channels, Congress enacted the three provisions before us. The first two provisions relate to leased channels. The first says: "This subsection shall permit a cable operator to enforce prospectively a written and published policy of prohibiting programming that the cable operator reasonably believes describes or depicts sexual or excretory activities or organs in a patently offensive manner as measured by contemporary community standards." 1992 Act, § 10(a)(2), 106 Stat. 1486.

The second provision applicable only to leased channels requires cable operators to segregate and to block similar programming if they decide to permit, rather than to prohibit, its broadcast. The provision tells the Federal Communications Commission (FCC or Commission) to promulgate regulations that will (a) require "programmers to inform cable operators if the program[ming] would be indecent as defined by Commission regulations"; (b) require "cable operators to place" such material "on a single channel"; and (c) require "cable operators to block such single channel unless the subscriber requests access to such channel in writing." 1992 Act, § 10(b)(1). ...

The third provision is similar to the first provision, but applies only to public access channels. The relevant statutory section instructs the FCC to promulgate regulations that will "enable a cable operator of a cable system to prohibit the use, on such system, of any channel capacity of any public, educational, or governmental access facility for any programming which contains obscene material, sexually explicit conduct, or material soliciting or promoting unlawful conduct." 1992 Act, § 10(c), . . .

The upshot is, as we said at the beginning, that the federal law before us . . . now permits cable operators either to allow or to forbid the transmission of "patently offensive" sex-related materials over both leased and public access channels, and requires those operators, at a minimum, to segregate and to block transmission of that same material on leased channels.

Petitioners, claiming that the three statutory provisions, as implemented by the Commission regulations, violate the First Amendment, sought judicial review of [FCC orders implementing them.] A panel of that Circuit agreed with petitioners that the provisions violated the First Amendment. The entire Court of Appeals, however, heard the case *en banc* and reached the opposite conclusion. . . .

II

We turn initially to the provision that permits cable system operators to prohibit "patently offensive" (or "indecent") programming transmitted over leased access channels. 1992 Act, § 10(a). . . .

We recognize that the First Amendment, the terms of which apply to governmental action, ordinarily does not itself throw into constitutional doubt the decisions of private citizens to permit, or to restrict, speech—and this is so ordinarily even where those decisions take place within the framework of a regulatory regime such as broadcasting. Were that not so, courts might have to face the difficult, and potentially restrictive, practical task of deciding which, among any number of private parties involved in providing a program (for example, networks, station owners, program editors, and program producers), is the "speaker" whose rights may not be abridged, and who is the speech-restricting "censor." Furthermore, as this Court has held, the editorial function itself is an aspect of "speech," see *Turner*, 512 U.S., at ___, and a court's decision that a private party, say, the station owner, is a "censor," could itself interfere with that private "censor's" freedom to speak as an editor. Thus, not surprisingly, this Court's First Amendment broadcasting cases have dealt with governmental efforts to restrict, not governmental efforts to provide or to maintain, a broadcaster's freedom to pick and to choose programming. . . .

Nonetheless, petitioners, while conceding that this is ordinarily so, point to circumstances that, in their view, make the analogy with private broadcasters inapposite and make this case a special one, warranting a different constitutional result. As a practical matter, they say, cable system operators have considerably more power to "censor" program viewing than do broadcasters, for individual communities typically have only one cable system, linking broadcasters and other program providers with each community's many subscribers. ... Moreover, concern about system operators' exercise of this considerable power originally led government—local and federal—to insist that operators provide leased and public access channels free of operator editorial control. ... To permit system operators to supervise programming on leased access channels will create the very private-censorship risk that this anticensorship effort sought to avoid. At the same time, petitioners add, cable systems have two relevant special characteristics. They are unusually involved with government, for they depend upon government permission and government facilities (streets, rights-of-way) to string the cable necessary for their services. And in respect to leased channels, their speech interests are relatively weak because they act less like editors, such as newspapers or television broadcasters, than like common carriers, such as telephone companies.

Under these circumstances, petitioners conclude, Congress' "permissive" law, in actuality, will "abridge" their free speech. And this Court should treat that law as a congressionally imposed, content-based, restriction unredeemed as a properly tailored effort to serve a "compelling interest." ... And, finally, petitioners say that the legal standard the law contains (the "patently offensive" standard) is unconstitutionally vague. ...

Like the petitioners, Justices Kennedy and Thomas would have us decide this case simply by transferring and applying literally categorical standards this Court has developed in other contexts. For Justice Kennedy, leased access channels are like a common carrier, cablecast is a protected medium, strict scrutiny applies, § 10(a) fails this test, and, therefore, § 10(a) is invalid. For Justice Thomas, the case is simple because the cable operator who owns the system over which access channels are broadcast, like a bookstore owner with respect to what it displays on the shelves, has a predominant First Amendment interest. Both categorical approaches suffer from the same flaws: they import law developed in very different contexts into a new and changing environment, and they lack the flexibility necessary to allow government to respond to very serious practical problems without sacrificing the free exchange of ideas the First Amendment is designed to protect.

. . .

Over the years, this Court has restated and refined ... basic First Amendment principles, adopting them more particularly to the balance of competing interests and the special circumstances of each field of application. ...

This tradition teaches that the First Amendment embodies an overarching commitment to protect speech from Government regulation through close judicial scrutiny, thereby enforcing the Constitution's constraints, but without imposing judicial formulae so rigid that they become a straightjacket that disables Government from responding to serious problems. ... [N]o definitive choice among competing analogies (broadcast, common carrier, bookstore) allows us to declare a rigid single standard, good for now and for all future media and purposes. That is not to say that we reject all the more specific formulations of the standard—they appropriately cover the vast majority of cases involving Government regulation of speech. Rather, aware as we are of the changes taking place in the law, the technology, and the industrial structure, related to telecommunications, ... we believe it unwise and unnecessary definitively to pick one analogy or one specific set of words now. ... We therefore think it premature to answer the broad questions that Justices Kennedy and Thomas raise in their efforts to find a definitive analogy, deciding, for example, the extent to which private property can be designated a public forum ...; whether public access channels are a public forum ...; whether the Government's viewpoint neutral decision to limit a public forum is subject to the same scrutiny as a selective exclusion from a pre-existing public forum ...; whether exclusion from common carriage must for all purposes be treated like exclusion from a public forum ...; and whether the interests of the owners of communications media always subordinate the interests of all other users of a medium....

Rather than decide these issues, we can decide this case more narrowly, by closely scrutinizing § 10(a) to assure that it properly addresses an extremely important problem, without imposing, in light of the relevant interests, an unnecessarily great restriction on speech. The importance of the interest at stake here—protecting children from exposure to patently offensive depictions of sex; the accommodation of the interests of programmers in maintaining access channels and of cable operators in editing the contents of their channels; the similarity of the problem and its solution to those at issue in [Federal Communications Commission v.] Pacifica [Foundation, 438 U.S. 726 (1978)]; and the flexibility inherent in an approach that permits private cable operators to make editorial decisions, lead us to conclude that § 10(a) is a sufficiently tailored response to an extraordinarily important problem.

First, the provision before us comes accompanied with an extremely important justification, one that this Court has often found compelling—the need to protect children from exposure to patently offensive sex-related material. ...

Second, the provision arises in a very particular context—congressional permission for cable operators to regulate programming that, but for a previous Act of Congress, would have had no path of access to cable channels free of an operator's control. The First Amendment interests involved are therefore complex, and involve a balance between those interests served by the access requirements themselves ..., and the disadvantage to the First Amendment interests of cable operators and other programmers ...

Third, the problem Congress addressed here is remarkably similar to the problem addressed by the FCC in *Pacifica*, and the balance Congress struck is commensurate with the balance we approved there. In *Pacifica* this Court considered a governmental ban of a radio broadcast of "indecent" materials, defined in part, like the provisions before us, to include " 'language that describes, in terms patently offensive as measured by contemporary community standards for the broadcast medium, sexual or excretory activities and organs, at times of the day when there is a reasonable risk that children may be in the audience.' " . . . The Court found this ban constitutionally permissible primarily because "broadcasting is uniquely accessible to children" and children were likely listeners to the program there at issue—an afternoon radio broadcast. . . . In addition, the Court wrote, "the broadcast media have established a uniquely pervasive presence in the lives of all Americans," . . . "[p]atently offensive, indecent material . . . confronts the citizen, not only in public, but also in the privacy of the home," generally without sufficient prior warning to allow the recipient to avert his or her eyes or ears, ibid.; and "[a]dults who feel the need may purchase tapes and records or go to theaters and nightclubs" to hear similar performances. . . .

All these factors are present here. Cable television broadcasting, including access channel broadcasting, is as "accessible to children" as over-the-air broadcasting, if not more so. . . . Cable television systems, including access channels, "have established a uniquely pervasive presence in the lives of all Americans." . . . "Patently offensive" material from these stations can "confron[t] the citizen" in the "privacy of the home," . . . with little or no prior warning. . . . There is nothing to stop "adults who feel the need" from finding similar programming elsewhere, say, on tape or in theaters. In fact, the power of cable systems to control home program viewing is not absolute. Over-the-air broadcasting and direct broadcast satellites already provide alternative ways for programmers to reach the home, and are likely to do so to a greater extent in the near future. . . .

Fourth, the permissive nature of § 10(a) means that it likely restricts speech less than, not more than, the ban at issue in *Pacifica*. The provision removes a restriction as to some speakers—namely, cable operators. Moreover, although the provision does create a risk that a program will not appear, that risk is not the same as the certainty that accompanies a governmental ban. In fact, a glance at the programming that cable operators allow on their own (nonaccess) channels suggests that this distinction is not theoretical, but real. . . . Finally, the provision's permissive nature brings with it a flexibility that allows cable operators, for example, not to ban broadcasts, but, say, to rearrange broadcast times, better to fit the desires of adult audiences while lessening the risks of harm to children. . . .

Of course, cable system operators may not always rearrange or reschedule patently offensive programming. Sometimes, as petitioners fear, they may ban the programming instead. But the same may be said of *Pacifica*'s ban. . . .

. . .

Our basic disagreement with Justice Kennedy is narrow. . . . While we cannot agree with Justice Thomas that everything turns on the rights of the cable owner, we also cannot agree with Justice Kennedy that we must ignore the expressive interests of cable operators altogether. Second, . . . [r]ather than seeking an analogy to [the public forum cases], . . . we found that *Pacifica* provides the closest analogy and lends considerable support to our conclusion.

Petitioners, and Justice Kennedy, argue that the opposite result is required by two other cases: Sable Communications of Cal., Inc. v. FCC, 492 U.S. 115 (1989), a case in which this Court found unconstitutional a statute that banned "indecent" telephone messages, and *Turner*, in which this Court stated that cable broadcast receives full First Amendment protection. The ban at issue in *Sable*, however, was not only a total governmentally imposed ban on a category of communications, but also involved a communications medium, telephone service, that was significantly less likely to expose children to the banned material, was less intrusive, and allowed for significantly more control over what comes into the home than either broadcasting or the cable transmission system before us. ... The Court's distinction in *Turner*, furthermore, between cable and broadcast television, relied on the inapplicability of the spectrum scarcity problem to cable. ... While that distinction was relevant in *Turner* to the justification for structural regulations at issue there (the "must carry" rules), it has little to do with a case that involves the effects of television viewing on children. Those effects are the result of how parents and children view television programming, and how pervasive and intrusive that programming is. In that respect, cable and broadcast television differ little, if at all....

The petitioners also rely on this Court's "public forum" cases. ...Justice Kennedy adds by analogy that the decision to exclude certain content from common carriage is similarly subject to strict scrutiny ....

For three reasons, however, it is unnecessary, indeed, unwise, for us definitively to decide whether or how to apply the public forum doctrine to leased access channels. First, while it may be that content-based exclusions from the right to use common carriers could violate the First Amendment, it is not at all clear that the public forum doctrine should be imported wholesale into the area of common carriage regulation. ... Second, it is plain from this Court's cases that a public forum "may be created for a limited purpose." ... Our cases have not yet determined, however, that the Government's decision to dedicate a public forum to one type of content or another is necessarily subject to the highest level of scrutiny. Must a local government, for example, show a compelling state interest if it builds a band shell in the park and dedicates it solely to classical music (but not to jazz)? The answer is not obvious. ... But, at a minimum, this case does not require us to answer it. Finally, and most important, the effects of Congress' decision on the interests of programmers, viewers, cable operators, and children are the same, whether we characterize Congress' decision as one that limits access to a public forum, discriminates in common carriage, or constrains speech because of its content. If we consider this particular limitation of indecent television programming acceptable as a constraint on speech, we must no less accept the limitation it places on access to the claimed public forum or on use of a common carrier.

. . .

Finally, petitioners argue that the definition of the materials subject to the challenged provisions is too vague, thereby granting cable system operators too broad a program-screening authority. ...

The provisions, as augmented by FCC regulations, permit cable system operators to prohibit "programming that the cable operator reasonably believes describes or depicts sexual or excretory activities or organs in a patently offensive manner as measured by contemporary community standards." ... This language is similar to language adopted by this Court in Miller v. California, 413 U.S. 15, 24 (1973), as a "guidelin[e]" for identifying materials that states may constitutionally regulate as obscene. ...In § 10(a) and the FCC regulations, ... the language would seem to refer to material that would be offensive enough to [be obscene] but for the fact that the material also has "serious literary, artistic, political or scientific value" or nonprurient purposes.

This history suggests that the statute's language aims at the kind of programming to which its sponsors referred—pictures of oral sex, bestiality, and rape ...—and not at scientific or educational programs (at least unless done with a highly unusual lack of concern for viewer reaction). Moreover, as this Court pointed out in *Pacifica*, what is "patently offensive" depends on context (the kind of program on which it appears), degree (not "an occasional expletive"), and time of broadcast (a "pig" is offensive in "the parlor" but not the "barnyard"). ...

Further, the statute protects against overly broad application of its standards insofar as it permits cable system operators to screen programs only pursuant to a "written and published policy." ... A cable system operator would find it difficult to show that a leased access program prohibition reflects a rational "policy" if the operator permits similarly "offensive" programming to run elsewhere on its system at comparable times or in comparable ways. ...

For the reasons discussed, we conclude that § 10(a) is consistent with the First Amendment.

III

The statute's second provision significantly differs from the first, for it does not simply permit, but rather requires, cable system operators to restrict speech—by segregating and blocking "patently offensive" sex-related material appearing on leased channels (but not on other channels). 1992 Act, § 10(b). ...

These requirements have obvious restrictive effects. The several up-to–30–day delays, along with single channel segregation, mean that a subscriber cannot decide to watch a single program without considerable advance planning and without letting the "patently offensive" channel in its entirety invade his household for days, perhaps weeks, at a time. ... Moreover, the "written notice" requirement will further restrict viewing by subscribers who fear for their reputations should the operator, advertently or inadvertently, disclose the list of those who wish to watch the "patently offensive" channel. ... Further, the added costs and burdens that these requirements impose upon a cable system operator may encourage that operator to ban programming that the operator would otherwise permit to run, even if only late at night.

The Government argues that, despite these adverse consequences, the "segregate and block" requirements are lawful because they are "the least restrictive means of realizing" a "compelling interest," namely "protecting the physical and psychological well-being of minors." It adds that, in any event, the First Amendment, as applied in *Pacifica,* "does not require that regulations of indecency on television be subject to the strictest" First Amendment "standard of review."

We ... do not agree that the "segregate and block" requirements properly accommodate the speech restrictions they impose and the legitimate objective they seek to attain. Nor need we here determine whether, or the extent to which, *Pacifica* does, or does not, impose some lesser standard of review where indecent speech is at issue .... That is because once one examines this governmental restriction, it becomes apparent that, not only is it not a "least restrictive alternative," and is not "narrowly tailored" to meet its legitimate objective, it also seems considerably "more extensive than necessary." ...

Several circumstances lead us to this conclusion. For one thing, the law, as recently amended, uses other means to protect children from similar "patently offensive" material broadcast on unleased cable channels, i.e., broadcast over any of a system's numerous ordinary, or public access, channels. The law, as recently amended, requires cable operators to "scramble or ... block" such programming on any (unleased) channel "primarily dedicated to sexually-oriented programming." ... In addition, cable operators must honor a subscriber's request to block any, or all, programs on any channel to which he or she does not wish to subscribe. ... And manufacturers, in the future, will have to make television sets with a so-called "V-chip"—a device that will be able automatically to identify and block sexually explicit or violent programs. ...

Although we cannot, and do not, decide whether the new provisions are themselves lawful (a matter not before us), we note that they are significantly less restrictive than the provision here at issue. ... [I]f these provisions do not adequately protect children from "patently offensive" material broadcast on ordinary channels, how could one justify more severe leased channel restrictions when (given ordinary channel programming) they would yield so little additional protection for children?

. . .

... We have no empirical reason to believe, for example, that sex-dedicated channels are all (or mostly) leased channels, or that "patently offensive" programming on non-sex-dedicated channels is found only (or mostly) on leased channels. ...

. . .

The record's description and discussion of a different alternative—the "lockbox"—leads, through a different route, to a similar conclusion. The Cable Communications Policy Act of 1984 required cable operators to provide "upon the request of a subscriber, a device by which the subscriber can prohibit viewing of a particular cable service during periods selected by the subscriber."... This device ... would help

protect children by permitting their parents to "lock out" those programs or channels that they did not want their children to see.   . . .

. . .

No provision, we concede, short of an absolute ban, can offer certain
protection against assault by a determined child.   We have not, however,
generally allowed this fact alone to justify " 'reduc[ing] the adult population . . . to . . . only what is fit for children.' "   . . . But, . . . the . . .
practical difficulties would seem to call, not for "segregate and block"
requirements, but, rather, for informational requirements, for a simple
coding system, for readily available blocking equipment (perhaps accessible by telephone), for imposing cost burdens upon system operators (who
may spread them through subscription fees); or perhaps even for a
system that requires lockbox defaults to be set to block certain channels
(say, sex-dedicated-channels).   These kinds of requirements resemble
those that Congress has recently imposed upon all but leased channels.
. . .

. . .

Consequently, we cannot find that the "segregate and block" restrictions on speech are a narrowly, or reasonably, tailored effort to
protect children.   . . .

IV

The statute's third provision, as implemented by FCC regulation, is
similar to its first provision, in that it too permits a cable operator to
prevent transmission of "patently offensive" programming, in this case
on public access channels.   1992 Act, § 10(c) . . . But there are four
important differences.

The first is the historical background.   . . . [C]able operators have
traditionally agreed to reserve channel capacity for public, governmental,
and educational channels as part of the consideration they give municipalities that award them cable franchises.   . . . Significantly, these are
channels over which cable operators have not historically exercised
editorial control.   . . . Unlike § 10(a) therefore, § 10(c) does not restore
to cable operators editorial rights that they once had, and the countervailing First Amendment interest is nonexistent, or at least much
diminished. . . .

The second difference is the institutional background that has
developed as a result of the historical difference.   When a "leased
channel" is made available by the operator to a private lessee, the lessee
has total control of programming during the leased time slot.   . . . Public
access channels, on the other hand, are normally subject to complex
supervisory systems of various sorts, often with both public and private
elements.   . . . Municipalities generally provide in their cable franchising
agreements for an access channel manager, who is most commonly a
nonprofit organization, but may also be the municipality, or, in some
instances, the cable system owner.   . . . Access channel activity and
management are partly financed with public funds—through franchise
fees or other payments pursuant to the franchise agreement, or from

general municipal funds—and are commonly subject to supervision by a local supervisory board. ...

This system of public, private, and mixed nonprofit elements, through its supervising boards and nonprofit or governmental access managers, can set programming policy and approve or disapprove particular programming services. ... [T]here is a locally accountable body capable of addressing the problem, should it arise, of patently offensive programming broadcast to children, making it unlikely that many children will in fact be exposed to programming considered patently offensive in that community. ...

Third, the existence of a system aimed at encouraging and securing programming that the community considers valuable strongly suggests that a "cable operator's veto" is less likely necessary to achieve the statute's basic objective, protecting children, than a similar veto in the context of leased channels....

Finally, our examination of the legislative history and the record before us is consistent with what common sense suggests, namely that the public/nonprofit programming control systems now in place would normally avoid, minimize, or eliminate any child-related problems concerning "patently offensive" programming.

. . .

The upshot, in respect to the public access channels, is a law that could radically change present programming-related relationships among local community and nonprofit supervising boards and access managers, which relationships are established through municipal law, regulation, and contract. In doing so, it would not significantly restore editorial rights of cable operators, but would greatly increase the risk that certain categories of programming (say, borderline offensive programs) will not appear. At the same time, given present supervisory mechanisms, the need for this particular provision, aimed directly at public access channels, is not obvious. ...

V

Finally, we must ask whether § 10(a) is severable from the two other provisions. ...

. . .

... [W]e believe the valid provision is severable from the others.

VI

For these reasons, the judgment of the Court of Appeals is affirmed insofar as it upheld § 10(a); the judgment of the Court of Appeals is reversed insofar as it upheld § 10(b) and § 10(c).

It is so ordered.

Justice Stevens, concurring.

The difference between § 10(a) and § 10(c) is the difference between a permit and a prohibition. ...While I join the Court's opinion, I add these comments to emphasize the difference between the two provisions and to endorse the analysis in Part III–B of Justice Kennedy's opinion even though I do not think it necessary to characterize the public access channels as public fora.   ...

I

... [Section] 10(a) constitutes a reasonable, viewpoint neutral limitation on a federally-created access right for certain cable programmers.

II

... [T]he public, educational and governmental access channels that are regulated by § 10(c) are not creations of the Federal Government. ...

As their name reflects, so-called PEG channels are subject to a variety of local governmental controls and regulations....

What is of critical importance to me ... is that if left to their own devices, those authorities may choose to carry some programming that the Federal Government has decided to restrict. As I read § 10(c), the federal statute would disable local governments from making that choice. ...

Section 10(c) operates as a direct restriction on speech that, in the absence of federal intervention, might flow freely. ...

. . .

Justice Souter, concurring.

Justice Kennedy's separate opinion stresses the worthy point that First Amendment values generally are well-served by categorizing speech protection.... Reviewing speech regulations under fairly strict categorical rules keeps the starch in the standards for those moments when the daily politics cries loudest for limiting what may be said. ... The value of the categorical approach generally to First Amendment security prompts a word to explain why I join the Court's unwillingness to announce a definitive categorical analysis in this case.

. . .

All of the relevant characteristics of cable are presently in a state of technological and regulatory flux. Recent and far-reaching legislation not only affects the technical feasibility of parental control over children's access to undesirable material, ... but portends fundamental changes in the competitive structure of the industry and, therefore, the ability of individual entities to act as bottlenecks to the free flow of information.... As cable and telephone companies begin their competition for control over the single wire that will carry both their services, we can hardly settle rules for review of regulation on the assumption that cable will remain a separable and useful category of First Amendment scrutiny. And as broadcast, cable, and the cyber-technology of the Internet and the World Wide Web approach the day of using a common receiver, we can hardly assume that standards for judging the regulation of one of them will not have immense, but now unknown and unknowable, effects on the others.

Accordingly, in charting a course that will permit reasonable regulation in light of the values in competition, we have to accept the likelihood that the media of communication will become less categorical and more protean. Because we cannot be confident that for purposes of judging speech restrictions it will continue to make sense to distinguish cable from other technologies, and because we know that changes in these regulated technologies will enormously alter the structure of regulation itself, we should be shy about saying the final word today about what will be accepted as reasonable tomorrow. In my own ignorance I have to accept the real possibility that "if we had to decide today ... just what the First Amendment should mean in cyberspace, ... we would get it fundamentally wrong." Lessig, The Path of Cyberlaw, 104 Yale L.J. 1743, 1745 (1995).

The upshot of appreciating the fluidity of the subject that Congress must regulate is simply to accept the fact that not every nuance of our old standards will necessarily do for the new technology, and that a proper choice among existing doctrinal categories is not obvious. Rather than definitively settling the issue now, Justice Breyer wisely reasons by direct analogy rather than by rule. . . .

. . .

Justice O'Connor, concurring in part and dissenting in part.

I agree that § 10(a) is constitutional and that § 10(b) is unconstitutional, and I join Parts I, II, III, and V, and the judgment in part. I am not persuaded, however, that the asserted "important differences" between §§ 10(a) and 10(c) are sufficient to justify striking down § 10(c). I find the features shared by § 10(a), which covers leased access channels, and § 10(c), which covers public access channels, to be more significant than the differences. For that reason, I would find that § 10(c) too withstands constitutional scrutiny.

. . .

. . . I am not persuaded that the difference in the origin of the access channels is sufficient to justify upholding § 10(a) and striking down § 10(c). The interest in protecting children remains the same, whether on a leased access channel or a public access channel, and allowing the cable operator the option of prohibiting the transmission of indecent speech seems a constitutionally permissible means of addressing that interest. Nor is the fact that public access programming may be subject to supervisory systems in addition to the cable operator sufficient in my mind to render § 10(c) so ill-tailored to its goal as to be unconstitutional.

. . .

Justice Kennedy, with whom Justice Ginsburg joins, concurring in part, concurring in the judgment in part, and dissenting in part.

The plurality opinion, insofar as it upholds § 10(a) of the 1992 Cable Act, is adrift. The opinion treats concepts such as public forum, broadcaster, and common carrier as mere labels rather than as categories with settled legal significance; it applies no standard, and by this omission loses sight of existing First Amendment doctrine.   When confronted with a threat to free speech in the context of an emerging technology, we ought to have the discipline to analyze the case by reference to existing elaborations of constant First Amendment principles.   ... Although I join Part III of the opinion (there for the Court) striking down § 10(b) of the Act, and concur in the judgment that § 10(c) is unconstitutional, with respect I dissent from the remainder.

I

. . .

Though the two provisions differ in significant respects, [§§ 10(a) and 10(c)] have common flaws.   In both instances, Congress singles out one sort of speech for vulnerability to private censorship in a context where content-based discrimination is not otherwise permitted.   ...

. . .

... As a general matter, a private person may exclude certain speakers from his or her property without violating the First Amendment, ... and if §§ 10(a) and (c) were no more than affirmations of this principle they might be unremarkable.   Access channels, however, are property of the cable operator dedicated or otherwise reserved for programming of other speakers or the government.   A public access channel is a public forum, and laws requiring leased access channels create common carrier obligations.   When the government identifies certain speech on the basis of its content as vulnerable to exclusion from a common carrier or public forum, strict scrutiny applies.   These laws cannot survive this exacting review.   However compelling Congress' interest in shielding children from indecent programming, the provisions in this case are not drawn with enough care to withstand scrutiny under our precedents.

II

. . .

... I have expressed misgivings about judicial balancing under the First Amendment, ... but strict scrutiny at least confines the balancing process in a manner protective of speech ...

... [T]he creation of standards and adherence to them, even when it means affording protection to speech unpopular or distasteful, is the central achievement of our First Amendment jurisprudence.   Standards are the means by which we state in advance how to test a law's validity, rather than letting the height of the bar be determined by the apparent exigencies of the day.   They also provide notice and fair warning to those who must predict how the courts will respond to attempts to suppress their speech.   Yet formulations like strict scrutiny, used in a number of constitutional settings to ensure that the inequities of the moment are subordinated to commitments made for the long run, ... mean little if they can be watered down whenever they seem too strong. They mean still less if they can be ignored altogether when considering a case not on all fours with what we have seen before.

The plurality seems distracted by the many changes in technology and competition in the cable industry. ... The laws challenged here, however, do not retool the structure of the cable industry or (with the exception of § 10(b)) involve intricate technologies. The straightforward issue here is whether the Government can deprive certain speakers, on the basis of the content of their speech, of protections afforded all others. There is no reason to discard our existing First Amendment jurisprudence in answering this question.

While it protests against standards, the plurality does seem to favor one formulation of the question in this case: namely, whether the Act "properly addresses an extremely important problem, without imposing, in light of the relevant interests, an unnecessarily great restriction on speech." ... This description of the question accomplishes little, save to clutter our First Amendment case law by adding an untested rule with an uncertain relationship to the others we use to evaluate laws restricting speech. ...

... The words end up being a legalistic cover for an ad hoc balancing of interests.... [C]omparisons and analogies to other areas of our First Amendment case law ... provide discipline to the Court and guidance for others, and give clear content to our standards—all the things I find missing in the plurality's opinion. ...

Another troubling aspect of the plurality's approach is its suggestion that Congress has more leeway than usual to enact restrictions on speech where emerging technologies are concerned, because we are unsure what standard should be used to assess them. ...

I turn now to the issues presented, and explain why strict scrutiny is warranted.

III

A

. . .

My principal concern is with public access channels.... These are the channels open to programming by members of the public. ... No local governmental entity or school system has petitioned for relief in this case, and none of the petitioners who are viewers has asserted an interest in viewing educational or governmental programming or briefed the relevant issues.

B

The public access channels established by franchise agreements tend to have certain traits. They are available at low or no cost to members of the public, often on a first-come, first-served basis. ... The programmer on one of these channels most often has complete control over, as well as liability for, the content of its show. ... The entity managing the technical aspects of public access, such as scheduling and transmission, is not always the cable operator; it may be the local government or a third party that runs the access centers, which are facilities made available for the public to produce programs and transmit them on the access channels. . . .

. . .

. . . Required by the franchise authority as a condition of the franchise and open to all comers, [public access channels] are a designated public forum of unlimited character. . . .

It is important to understand that public access channels are public forums created by local or state governments in the cable franchise. Section § 10(c) does not, as the Court of Appeals thought, just return rightful First Amendment discretion to the cable operator. . . .   The cable operator may own the cables transmitting the signal, but it is the franchise . . . that allocates some channels to the full discretion of the cable operator while reserving others for public access.

In providing public access channels under their franchise agreements, cable operators therefore are not exercising their own First Amendment rights. They serve as conduits for the speech of others. . . . Section 10(c) thus restores no power of editorial discretion over public access channels that the cable operator once had; the discretion never existed. . . . By enacting a law in 1992 excluding indecent programming from protection but retaining the prohibition on cable operators' editorial control over all other protected speech, the Federal Government at the same time ratified the public-forum character of public access channels but discriminated against certain speech based on its content.

. . .

C

. . . . In my view, strict scrutiny also applies to § 10(a)'s authorization to cable operators to exclude indecent programming from [leased access] channels.

. . .

Before 1992, cable operators were forbidden editorial control over any video programming on leased access channels, and could not consider the content of the programming except to set the price of access. . . . Section 10(a) of the 1992 Act modifies the no-discretion rule. . . .

. . .

The constitutionality under *Turner Broadcasting* . . . of requiring a cable operator to set aside leased access channels is not before us. For purposes of this case, we should treat the cable operator's rights in these channels as extinguished, and address the issue these petitioners present: namely, whether the Government can discriminate on the basis of content in affording protection to certain programmers. I cannot agree with Justice Thomas that the cable operator's rights inform this analysis.

Laws requiring cable operators to provide leased access are the practical equivalent of making them common carriers, analogous in this respect to telephone companies: They are obliged to provide a conduit for the speech of others. . . .

. . .

Laws removing common-carriage protection from a single form of speech based on its content should be reviewed under the same standard as content-based restrictions on speech in a public forum. Making a cable operator a common carrier does not create a public forum in the sense of taking property from private control and dedicating it to public use; rather, regulations of a common carrier dictate the manner in which private control is exercised. A common-carriage mandate, nonetheless, serves the same function as a public forum. It ensures open, nondiscriminatory access to the means of communication. . . . The functional equivalence of designating a public forum and mandating common carriage suggests the same scrutiny should be applied to attempts in either setting to impose content discrimination by law. Under our precedents, the scrutiny is strict. . . .

In Police Dept. of Chicago v. Mosley, 408 U.S. 92 (1972), we made clear that selective exclusions from a public forum were unconstitutional. Invoking the First and Fourteenth Amendments to strike down a city ordinance allowing only labor picketing on any public way near schools, we held the "government may not grant the use of a forum to people whose views it finds acceptable, but deny use to those wishing to express less favored or more controversial views." . . . [T]here is no reason the kind of selective exclusion we condemned in *Mosley* should be tolerated here.

. . .

I do not foreclose the possibility that the Government could create a forum limited to certain topics or to serving the special needs of certain speakers or audiences without its actions being subject to strict scrutiny. This possibility seems to trouble the plurality, which wonders if a local government must "show a compelling state interest if it builds a band shell in the park and dedicates it solely to classical music (but not to jazz)." This is not the correct analogy. Our case is more akin to the Government's creation of a band shell in which all types of music might be performed except for rap music. The provisions here are content-based discriminations in the strong sense of suppressing a certain form of expression that the Government dislikes, or otherwise wishes to exclude on account of its effects, and there is no justification for anything but strict scrutiny here.

Giving government free rein to exclude speech it dislikes by delimiting public forums (or common carriage provisions) would have pernicious effects in the modern age. Minds are not changed in streets and parks as they once were. To an increasing degree, the more significant interchanges of ideas and shaping of public consciousness occur in mass

and electronic media. ... The extent of public entitlement to participate in those means of communication may be changed as technologies
change; and in expanding those entitlements the Government has no
greater right to discriminate on suspect grounds than it does when it
effects a ban on speech against the backdrop of the entitlements to
which we have been more accustomed. It contravenes the First Amendment to give Government a general license to single out some categories
of speech for lesser protection so long as it stops short of viewpoint
discrimination.

D

The Government advances a different argument for not applying
strict scrutiny in this case. The nature of access channels to one side, it
argues the nature of the speech in question—indecent broadcast (or
cablecast)—is subject to the lower standard of review it contends was
applied in FCC v. Pacifica Foundation, 438 U.S. 726, 748 (1978)....

Pacifica did not purport, however, to apply a special standard for
indecent broadcasting. Emphasizing the narrowness of its holding, the
Court in *Pacifica* conducted a context-specific analysis of the FCC's
restriction on indecent programming during daytime hours. ...It relied
on the general rule that "broadcasting ... has received the most limited
First Amendment protection." ... We already have rejected the application of this lower broadcast standard of review to infringements on the
liberties of cable operators, even though they control an important
communications medium. Turner Broadcasting, 512 U.S., at ___.
There is even less cause for a lower standard here.

Pacifica did identify two important considerations relevant to the
broadcast of objectionable material. ...

These concerns are weighty and will be relevant to whether the law
passes strict scrutiny. They do not justify, however, a blanket rule of
lesser protection for indecent speech. Other than the few categories of
expression which can be proscribed, ... we have been reluctant to mark
off new categories of speech for diminished constitutional protection.
Our hesitancy reflects skepticism about the possibility of courts' drawing
principled distinctions to use in judging governmental restrictions on
speech and ideas, ... a concern heightened here by the inextricability of
indecency from expression. ... In artistic or political settings, indecency may have strong communicative content, protesting conventional
norms or giving an edge to a work by conveying "otherwise inexpressible
emotions,".... In scientific programs, the more graphic the depiction
(even if to the point of offensiveness), the more accurate and comprehensive the portrayal of the truth may be. Indecency often is inseparable
from the ideas and viewpoints conveyed, or separable only with loss of
truth or expressive power. Under our traditional First Amendment
jurisprudence, factors perhaps justifying some restriction on indecent
cable programming may all be taken into account without derogating
this category of protected speech as marginal.

IV

. . .

The Government has no compelling interest in restoring a cable operator's First Amendment right of editorial discretion. As to § 10(c), Congress has no interest at all, since under most franchises operators had no rights of editorial discretion over PEG access channels in the first place. As to § 10(a), any governmental interest in restoring operator discretion over indecent programming on leased access channels is too minimal to justify the law. First, the transmission of indecent programming over leased access channels is not forced speech of the operator. . . . Second, the discretion conferred by the law is slight. The operator is not authorized to place programs of its own liking on the leased access channels, nor to remove other speech (racist or violent, for example) that might be offensive to it or to viewers. The operator is just given a veto over the one kind of lawful speech Congress disdains.

Congress does have, however, a compelling interest in protecting children from indecent speech. . . . This interest is substantial enough to justify some regulation of indecent speech even under, I will assume, the indecency standard used here.

Sections 10(a) and (c) nonetheless are not narrowly tailored to protect children from indecent programs on access channels. First, to the extent some operators may allow indecent programming, children in localities those operators serve will be left unprotected. Partial service of a compelling interest is not narrow tailoring. . . . Put another way, the interest in protecting children from indecency only at the caprice of the cable operator is not compelling. . . .

Second, to the extent cable operators prohibit indecent programming on access channels, not only children but adults will be deprived of it. . . . When applying strict scrutiny, we will not assume plausible alternatives will fail to protect compelling interests. . . .

Sections 10(a) and (c) present a classic case of discrimination against speech based on its content. There are legitimate reasons why the Government might wish to regulate or even restrict the speech at issue here, but §§ 10(a) and 10(c) are not drawn to address those reasons with the precision the First Amendment requires.

. . .

VI

In agreement with the plurality's analysis of § 10(b) of the Act, insofar as it applies strict scrutiny, I join Part III of its opinion. Its position there, however, cannot be reconciled with upholding § 10(a). . . .

Justice Thomas, joined by the Chief Justice and Justice Scalia, concurring in the judgment in part and dissenting in part.

I agree with the plurality's conclusion that § 10(a) is constitutionally permissible, but I disagree with its conclusion that §§ 10(b) and (c) violate the First Amendment. For many years, we have failed to articulate how and to what extent the First Amendment protects cable operators, programmers, and viewers from state and federal regulation. I think it is time we did so, and I cannot go along with the plurality's assiduous attempts to avoid addressing that issue openly.

I

The text of the First Amendment makes no distinction between print, broadcast, and cable media, but we have done so. In *Red Lion Broadcasting Co. v. FCC*, 395 U.S. 367 (1969), we held that, in light of the scarcity of broadcasting frequencies, the Government may require a broadcast licensee "to share his frequency with others and to conduct himself as a proxy or fiduciary with obligations to present those views and voices which are representative of his community and which would otherwise, by necessity, be barred from the airwaves." . . .

In contrast, we have not permitted that level of government interference in the context of the print media. . . .

Our First Amendment distinctions between media, dubious from their infancy, placed cable in a doctrinal wasteland in which regulators and cable operators alike could not be sure whether cable was entitled to the substantial First Amendment protections afforded the print media or was subject to the more onerous obligations shouldered by the broadcast media. . . . Over time, however, we have drawn closer to recognizing that cable operators should enjoy the same First Amendment rights as the nonbroadcast media.

. . .

In *Turner*, by adopting much of the print paradigm, and by rejecting *Red Lion*, we adopted with it a considerable body of precedent that governs the respective First Amendment rights of competing speakers. In *Red Lion*, we had legitimized consideration of the public interest and emphasized the rights of viewers, at least in the abstract. . . . After *Turner*, however, that view can no longer be given any credence in the cable context. It is the operator's right that is preeminent. . . .

By recognizing the general primacy of the cable operator's editorial rights over the rights of programmers and viewers, *Turner* raises serious questions about the merits of petitioners' claims. None of the petitioners in these cases are cable operators; they are all cable viewers or access programmers or their representative organizations. . . . It is not intuitively obvious that the First Amendment protects the interests petitioners assert, and neither petitioners nor the plurality have adequately explained the source or justification of those asserted rights.

. . .

. . . [L]eased and public access are a type of forced speech. Though the constitutionality of leased and public access channels is not directly at issue in these cases, the position adopted by the Court in *Turner* ineluctably leads to the conclusion that the federal access requirements are subject to some form of heightened scrutiny. . . .

Petitioners must concede that cable access is not a constitutionally required entitlement and that the right they claim to leased and public access has, by definition, been governmentally created at the expense of cable operators' editorial discretion. Just because the Court has apparently accepted, for now, the proposition that the Constitution permits some degree of forced speech in the cable context does not mean that the beneficiaries of a government-imposed forced speech program enjoy additional First Amendment protections beyond those normally afforded to purely private speakers.

. . .

It is one thing to compel an operator to carry leased and public access speech, in apparent violation of *Tornillo*, but it is another thing altogether to say that the First Amendment forbids Congress to give back part of the operators' editorial discretion, which all recognize as fundamentally protected, in favor of a broader access right. It is no answer to say that leased and public access are content neutral and that §§ 10(a) and (c) are not, for that does not change the fundamental fact, which petitioners never address, that it is the operators' journalistic freedom that is infringed, whether the challenged restrictions be content neutral or content based.

. . .

B

. . . Labeling leased access a common carrier scheme has no real First Amendment consequences. It simply does not follow from common carrier status that cable operators may not, with Congress' blessing, decline to carry indecent speech on their leased access channels. Common carriers are private entities and may, consistent with the First Amendment, exercise editorial discretion in the absence of a specific statutory prohibition. . . .

. . . [T]he fact that the leased access provisions impose a form of common carrier obligation on cable operators does not alter my view that Congress' leased access scheme burdens the constitutionally protected speech rights of cable operators in order to expand the speaking opportunities of access programmers, but does not independently burden the First Amendment rights of programmers or viewers.

C

. . . I do not agree with petitioners' . . . assertion that public access channels are public fora.

. . .

. . . The public forum doctrine is a rule governing claims of "a right of access to public property," . . . and has never been thought to extend beyond property generally understood to belong to the government. . . .

. . .

. . . Our public forum cases have involved property in which the government has held at least some formal easement or other property interest permitting the government to treat the property as its own in designating the property as a public forum. . . .

. . .

. . . [E]ven were I inclined to view public access channels as public property, which I am not, the numerous additional obligations imposed on the cable operator in managing and operating the public access channels convince me that these channels share few, if any, of the basic characteristics of a public forum. As I have already indicated, public access requirements, in my view, are a regulatory restriction on the exercise of cable operators' editorial discretion, not a transfer of a sufficient property interest in the channels to support a designation of that property as a public forum. . . .

III

Most sexually oriented programming appears on premium or pay-per-view channels that are naturally blocked from nonpaying customers by market forces, and it is only governmental intervention in the first instance that requires access channels, on which indecent programming may appear, to be made part of the basic cable package. Section 10(b) does nothing more than adjust the nature of government-imposed leased access requirements in order to emulate the market forces that keep indecent programming primarily on premium channels (without permitting the operator to charge subscribers for that programming).

Unlike §§ 10(a) and (c), § 10(b) clcarly implicates petitioners' free speech rights. Though § 10(b) by no means bans indecent speech, it clearly places content-based restrictions on the transmission of private speech by requiring cable operators to block and segregate indecent programming that the operator has agreed to carry. Consequently, § 10(b) must be subjected to strict scrutiny. . . . The parties agree that Congress has a "compelling interest in protecting the physical and psychological well-being of minors" and that its interest "extends to shielding minors from the influence of [indecent speech] that is not obscene by adult standards." . . . Because § 10(b) is narrowly tailored to achieve that well-established compelling interest, I would uphold it. I therefore dissent from the Court's decision to the contrary.

. . .

The Court strikes down § 10(b) by pointing to alternatives, such as reverse-blocking and lockboxes, that it says are less restrictive than segregation and blocking. Though these methods attempt to place in parents' hands the ability to permit their children to watch as little, or as much, indecent programming as the parents think proper, they do not effectively support parents' authority to direct the moral upbringing of their children. . . . The FCC recognized that leased-access programming comes "from a wide variety of independent sources, with no single editor controlling [its] selection and presentation." . . . Thus, indecent programming on leased access channels is "especially likely to be shown randomly or intermittently between non-indecent programs." Rather than being able to simply block out certain channels at certain times, a subscriber armed with only a lockbox must carefully monitor all leased-access programming and constantly reprogram the lockbox to keep out undesired programming.   Thus, even assuming that cable subscribers generally have the technical proficiency to properly operate a lockbox, by no means a given, this distinguishing characteristic of leased access channels makes lockboxes and reverse-blocking largely ineffective.

. . .

The segregation and blocking requirement was not intended to be a replacement for lockboxes, V-chips, reverse-blocking, or other subscriber-initiated measures.   ... Once a subscriber requests access to blocked programming, however, the subscriber remains free to use other methods, such as lockboxes, to regulate the kind of programming shown on those channels in that home.   ... Given the limited scope of § 10(b) as a default setting, I see nothing constitutionally infirm about Congress' decision to permit the cable operator 30 days to unblock or reblock the segregated channel.

. . .

In arguing that Congress could not impose a blocking requirement without also imposing that requirement on public access and nonaccess channels, petitioners fail to allege, much less argue, that doing so would further Congress' compelling interest.   While it is true that indecent programming appears on nonaccess channels, that programming appears almost exclusively on "per-program or per channel services that subscribers must specifically request in advance, in the same manner as under the blocking approach mandated by section 10(b)."   ... In contrast to these premium services, leased access channels are part of the basic cable package, and the segregation and blocking scheme Congress imposed does nothing more than convert sexually oriented leased access programming into a free "premium service." ...

The United States has carried its burden of demonstrating that § 10(b) and its implementing regulations are narrowly tailored to satisfy a compelling governmental interest.   Accordingly, I would affirm the judgment of the Court of Appeals in its entirety.   I therefore concur in the judgment upholding § 10(a) and respectfully dissent from that portion of the judgment striking down §§ 10(b) and (c).

Page 1331.   Add at end of subsection:

WISCONSIN v. MITCHELL, 508 U.S. 476 (1993).   A Wisconsin statute enhances the penalty for an offense whenever the defendant "[i]ntentionally selects the person against whom the crime ... is committed ... because of the race, religion, color, disability, sexual orientation, national origin or ancestry of that person ...."   Mitchell's maximum possible sentence for aggravated battery was enhanced from two to seven years because a jury found that he had selected his victim because of race.   The Wisconsin Supreme Court concluded that the penalty enhancement statute violated the First Amendment, relying on R.A.V. v. St. Paul.   The Supreme Court reversed.

Chief Justice Rehnquist wrote for a unanimous court. Traditionally, a defendant's motive for committing a crime has been a factor in fixing sentences. "[M]otive plays the same role under the Wisconsin statute as it does under federal and state antidiscrimination laws ..." The Court distinguished *R.A.V.* "[W]hereas the ordinance struck down in *R.A.V.* was explicitly directed at expression ..., the statute in this case is aimed at conduct unprotected by the First Amendment." In addition, the "statute singles out for enhancement bias-inspired conduct because this conduct is thought to inflict greater individual and societal harm"—such as "provok[ing] retaliatory crimes, inflict[ing] distinct emotional harms on their victims, and incit[ing] community unrest." "The State's desire to redress these perceived harms provides an adequate explanation for its penalty-enhancement provision over and above mere disagreement with offenders' beliefs or biases."

D. REGULATION OF COMMERCIAL SPEECH

Page 1338. Add before last paragraph of note, "Attorney Advertising":

The Court distinguished *Shapero* in Florida Bar v. Went For It, Inc., 115 S.Ct. 2371 (1995). *Shapero* had dealt with a rule imposing a ban on direct mail solicitation "whatever the time frame and whoever the recipient." Justice O'Connor's opinion for the Court concluded that a rule forbidding solicitation of accident victims during a 30-day period after the accident met the three-part *Central Hudson* test. "The Bar has substantial interest both in protecting injured Floridians from invasive conduct by lawyers and in preventing the erosion of confidence in the profession that such repeated invasions have engendered.... The palliative devised by the Bar to address these harms is narrow both in scope and in duration." Justice Kennedy's dissent, joined by Justices Stevens, Souter and Ginsburg, argued that the rule prejudiced accident victims "to vindicate the State's purported desire for more dignity in the legal profession."

Page 1338. Add at end of note, "Attorney Advertising":

In Ibanez v. Florida Department of Business and Professional Regulation, Board of Accountancy, 114 S.Ct. 2084 (1994), a lawyer was also a state-licensed Certified Public Accountant and was authorized to use the designation "Certified Financial Planner" by the Certified Financial Planner Board of Standards, a private organization. The Court held that she could not be disciplined for referring to those two credentials in her yellow pages listing, on her business cards, and on her law offices stationery, because neither was false or misleading.

The Court distinguished CPAs from attorneys in Edenfield v. Fane, 507 U.S. 761 (1993). As noted, the Court had held in *Ohralik* that in-person solicitation by attorneys could be prohibited. In *Edenfield,* the Court concluded that a ban on in-person solicitation by accountants violated the First Amendment. While lawyers are trained in the art of persuasion, accountants are trained to emphasize independence and objectivity. Moreover, an accountant's typical potential client is an experienced business executive. Therefore, CPA solicitation is not "inherently conducive to overreaching."

Page 1346. Delete note, "Time, Place, and Manner Regulation of Commercial Speech"

Page 1347. Add after note, "The Definition of Commercial Speech":

CITY OF CINCINNATI v. DISCOVERY NETWORK, INC.

507 U.S. 410, 113 S.Ct. 1505, 123 L.Ed.2d 99 (1993).

Justice Stevens delivered the opinion of the Court.

Motivated by its interest in the safety and attractive appearance of its streets and sidewalks, the city of Cincinnati has refused to allow respondents to distribute their commercial publications through freestanding newsracks located on public property. The question presented is whether this refusal is consistent with the First Amendment. In agreement with the District Court and the Court of Appeals, we hold that it is not.

I

Respondent, Discovery Network, Inc., is engaged in the business of providing adult educational, recreational, and social programs to individuals in the Cincinnati area. It advertises those programs in a free magazine that it publishes nine times a year. Although these magazines consist primarily of promotional material pertaining to Discovery's courses, they also include some information about current events of general interest. Approximately one third of these magazines are distributed through the 38 newsracks that the city authorized Discovery to place on public property in 1989.

Respondent, Harmon Publishing Company, Inc., publishes and distributes a free magazine that advertises real estate for sale at various locations throughout the United States. The magazine contains listings and photographs of available residential properties in the greater Cincinnati area, and also includes some information about interest rates, market trends, and other real estate matters. In 1989 Harmon received the city's permission to install 24 newsracks at approved locations. About 15% of its distribution in the Cincinnati area is through those devices.

In March 1990, the city's Director of Public Works notified each of the respondents that its permit to use dispensing devices on public property was revoked, and ordered the newsracks removed within 30 days. Each notice explained that respondent's publication was a "commercial handbill" within the meaning of § 714–1–C of the Municipal Code [2] and therefore § 714–23 of the Code [3] prohibited its distribution on public property. Respondents were granted administrative hearings and review by the Sidewalk Appeals Committee. Although the Committee did not modify the city's position, it agreed to allow the dispensing devices to remain in place pending a judicial determination of the constitutionality of its prohibition. Respondents then commenced this litigation in the United States District Court for the Southern District of Ohio.

After an evidentiary hearing the District Court concluded that "the regulatory scheme advanced by the City of Cincinnati completely prohibiting the distribution of commercial handbills on the public right of way violates the First Amendment." ...

... [T]he Court of Appeals agreed with the District Court that the burden placed on speech "cannot be justified by the paltry gains in safety and beauty achieved by the ordinance." Ibid....

II

There is no claim in this case that there is anything unlawful or misleading about the contents of respondents' publications. Moreover, respondents do not challenge their characterization as "commercial speech." Nor do respondents question the substantiality of the city's interest in safety and esthetics. It was, therefore, proper for the District Court and the Court of Appeals to judge the validity of the city's prohibition under the standard we set forth in Central Hudson [Gas & Electric Corp. v. Public Service Commission of New York, 447 U.S. 557 (1980)] and [Board of Trustees of State Univ. of New York v.] Fox[, 492 U.S. 469 (1989)].[11] It was the city's burden to establish a "reasonable

[2] That section provides:

" 'Commercial Handbill' shall mean any printed or written matter, dodger, circular, leaflet, pamphlet, paper, booklet or any other printed or otherwise reproduced original or copies of any matter of literature:

"(a) Which advertises for sale any merchandise, product, commodity or thing; or

"(b) Which directs attention to any business or mercantile or commercial establishment, or other activity, for the purpose of directly promoting the interest thereof by sales; or

"(c) Which directs attention to or advertises any meeting, theatrical performance, exhibition or event of any kind for which an admission fee is charged for the purpose of private gain or profit." Cincinnati Municipal Code § 714–1–C (1992).

[3] That section provides:

"No person shall throw or deposit any commercial or non-commercial handbill in or upon any sidewalk, street or other public place within the city. Nor shall any person hand out or distribute or sell any commercial handbill in any public place. Provided, however, that it shall not be unlawful on any sidewalk, street or other public place within the city for any person to hand out or distribute, without charge to the receiver thereof, any non-commercial handbill to any person willing to accept it, except within or around the city hall building." § 714.23.

[11] While the Court of Appeals ultimately applied the standards set forth in Central Hudson and Fox, its analysis at least suggested that those standards might not apply to the type of regulation at issue in this case. For if commercial speech is entitled to "lesser protection" only when the regulation is aimed at either the content of the speech or the

fit" between its legitimate interests in safety and esthetics and its choice of a limited and selective prohibition of newsracks as the means chosen to serve those interests.

There is ample support in the record for the conclusion that the city did not "establish the reasonable fit we require." ... The ordinance on which it relied was an outdated prohibition against the distribution of any commercial handbills on public property. It was enacted long before any concern about newsracks developed. Its apparent purpose was to prevent the kind of visual blight caused by littering, rather than any harm associated with permanent, freestanding dispensing devices. The fact that the city failed to address its recently developed concern about newsracks by regulating their size, shape, appearance, or number indicates that it has not "carefully calculated" the costs and benefits associated with the burden on speech imposed by its prohibition.[13] The benefit to be derived from the removal of 62 newsracks while about 1,500–2,000 remain in place was considered "minute" by the District Court and "paltry" by the Court of Appeals. We share their evaluation of the "fit" between the city's goal and its method of achieving it.

In seeking reversal, the city argues that it is wrong to focus attention on the relatively small number of newsracks affected by its prohibition, because the city's central concern is with the overall number of newsracks on its sidewalks, rather than with the unattractive appearance of a handful of dispensing devices. It contends, first, that a categorical prohibition on the use of newsracks to disseminate commercial messages burdens no more speech than is necessary to further its interest in limiting the number of newsracks; and, second, that the prohibition is a valid "time, place, and manner" regulation because it is content-neutral and leaves open ample alternative channels of communication. We consider these arguments in turn.

III

The city argues that there is a close fit between its ban on newsracks dispensing "commercial handbills" and its interest in safety and esthetics because every decrease in the number of such dispensing devices necessarily effects an increase in safety and an improvement in

---

particular adverse effects stemming from that content, it would seem to follow that a regulation that is not so directed should be evaluated under the standards applicable to regulations on fully protected speech, not the more lenient standards by which we judge regulations on commercial speech. Because we conclude that Cincinnati's ban on commercial newsracks cannot withstand scrutiny under *Central Hudson* and *Fox*, we need not decide whether that policy should be subjected to more exacting review.

[13] We reject the city's argument that the lower courts' and our consideration of alternative, less drastic measures by which the city could effectuate its interests in safety and esthetics somehow violates *Fox*'s holding that regulations on commercial speech are not subject to "least-restrictive-means" analysis.... [W]hile we have rejected the "least-restrictive-means" test for judging restrictions on commercial speech, so too have we rejected mere rational basis review. A regulation need not be "absolutely the least severe that will achieve the desired end," *Fox*, supra, at 480, but if there are numerous and obvious less-burdensome alternatives to the restriction on commercial speech, that is certainly a relevant consideration in determining whether the "fit" between ends and means is reasonable.

the attractiveness of the cityscape. In the city's view, the prohibition is thus entirely related to its legitimate interests in safety and esthetics.

We accept the validity of the city's proposition, but consider it an insufficient justification for the discrimination against respondents' use of newsracks that are no more harmful than the permitted newsracks, and have only a minimal impact on the overall number of newsracks on the city's sidewalks. The major premise supporting the city's argument is the proposition that commercial speech has only a low value. Based on that premise, the city contends that the fact that assertedly more valuable publications are allowed to use newsracks does not undermine its judgment that its esthetic and safety interests are stronger than the interest in allowing commercial speakers to have similar access to the reading public.

We cannot agree. In our view, the city's argument attaches more importance to the distinction between commercial and noncommercial speech than our cases warrant and seriously underestimates the value of commercial speech.

This very case illustrates the difficulty of drawing bright lines that will clearly cabin commercial speech in a distinct category. For respondents' publications share important characteristics with the publications that the city classifies as "newspapers." Particularly, they are "commercial handbills" within the meaning of § 714–1–C of the city's Code because they contain advertising, a feature that apparently also places ordinary newspapers within the same category. Separate provisions in the code specifically authorize the distribution of "newspapers" on the public right of way, but that term is not defined. Presumably, respondents' publications do not qualify as newspapers because an examination of their content discloses a higher ratio of advertising to other text, such as news and feature stories, than is found in the exempted publications. Indeed, Cincinnati's City Manager has determined that publications that qualify as newspapers and therefore can be distributed by newsrack are those that are published daily and or weekly and "primarily presen[t] coverage of, and commentary on, current events."

The absence of a categorical definition of the difference between "newspapers" and "commercial handbills" in the city's Code is also a characteristic of our opinions considering the constitutionality of regulations of commercial speech. Fifty years ago, we concluded that the distribution of a commercial handbill was unprotected by the First Amendment, even though half of its content consisted of political protest. Valentine v. Chrestensen, 316 U.S. 52 (1942). A few years later, over Justice Black's dissent, we held that the "commercial feature" of door-to-door solicitation of magazine subscriptions was a sufficient reason for denying First Amendment protection to that activity. Breard v. Alexandria, 341 U.S. 622 (1951). Subsequent opinions, however, recognized that important commercial attributes of various forms of communication do not qualify their entitlement to constitutional protection. . . .

. . .

In later opinions we have stated that speech proposing a commercial transaction is entitled to lesser protection than other constitutionally guaranteed expression, see Ohralik v. Ohio State Bar Assn., 436 U.S. 447, 455–456 (1978). We have also suggested that such lesser protection was appropriate for a somewhat larger category of commercial speech— "that is, expression related solely to the economic interests of the speaker and its audience." Central Hudson Gas & Elec. Corp. v. Public Service Comm'n of New York, 447 U.S., at 561. We did not, however, use that definition in either Bolger v. Youngs Drug Products, 463 U.S. 60 (1983), or in Board of Trustees of State Univ. of New York v. Fox, 492 U.S. 469 (1989).

In the *Bolger* case we held that a federal statute prohibiting the mailing of unsolicited advertisements for contraceptives could not be applied to the appellee's promotional materials. Most of the appellee's mailings consisted primarily of price and quantity information, and thus fell "within the core notion of commercial speech—'speech which does "no more than propose a commercial transaction." ' " ... In *Fox,* we described the category even more narrowly, by characterizing the proposal of a commercial transaction as "the test for identifying commercial speech." ...

Under the *Fox* test it is clear that much of the material in ordinary newspapers is commercial speech and, conversely, that the editorial content in respondents' promotional publications is not what we have described as "core" commercial speech. There is no doubt a "common sense" basis for distinguishing between the two, but under both the city's Code and our cases the difference is a matter of degree.

Nevertheless, for the purpose of deciding this case, we assume that all of the speech barred from Cincinnati's sidewalks is what we have labeled "core" commercial speech and that no such speech is found in publications that are allowed to use newsracks. We nonetheless agree with the Court of Appeals that Cincinnati's actions in this case run afoul of the First Amendment. Not only does Cincinnati's categorical ban on commercial newsracks place too much importance on the distinction between commercial and noncommercial speech, but in this case, the distinction bears no relationship *whatsoever* to the particular interests that the city has asserted. It is therefore an impermissible means of responding to the city's admittedly legitimate interests.... The city has asserted an interest in esthetics, but respondent publishers' newsracks are no greater an eyesore than the newsracks permitted to remain on Cincinnati's sidewalks. Each newsrack, whether containing "newspapers" or "commercial handbills," is equally unattractive....

Cincinnati has not asserted an interest in preventing commercial harms by regulating the information distributed by respondent publishers' newsracks, which is, of course, the typical reason why commercial speech can be subject to greater governmental regulation than noncommercial speech....

A closer examination of ... Bolger v. Youngs Drug Products demonstrates the fallacy of the city's argument that a reasonable fit is established by the mere fact that the entire burden imposed on commercial speech by its newsrack policy may in some small way limit the total number of newsracks on Cincinnati's sidewalks. Here, the city contends that safety concerns and visual blight may be addressed by a prohibition that distinguishes between commercial and noncommercial publications that are equally responsible for those problems. In *Bolger,* however, in rejecting the Government's reliance on its interest in protecting the public from "offensive" speech, "[we] specifically declined to recognize a distinction between commercial and noncommercial speech that would render this interest a sufficient justification for a prohibition of commercial speech." ... Moreover, the fact that the regulation "provide[d] only the most limited incremental support for the interest asserted," ... — that it achieved only a "marginal degree of protection," ... for that interest—supported our holding that the prohibition was invalid. Finally, in *Bolger,* as in this case, the burden on commercial speech was imposed by denying the speaker access to one method of distribution— there the United States mails, and here the placement of newsracks on public property—without interfering with alternative means of access to the audience....

In the absence of some basis for distinguishing between "newspapers" and "commercial handbills" that is relevant to an interest asserted by the city, we are unwilling to recognize Cincinnati's bare assertion that the "low value" of commercial speech is a sufficient justification for its selective and categorical ban on newsracks dispensing "commercial handbills." Our holding, however, is narrow. As should be clear from the above discussion, we do not reach the question whether, given certain facts and under certain circumstances, a community might be able to justify differential treatment of commercial and noncommercial newsracks. We simply hold that on this record Cincinnati has failed to make such a showing. Because the distinction Cincinnati has drawn has absolutely no bearing on the interests it has asserted, we have no difficulty concluding, as did the two courts below, that the city has not established the "fit" between its goals and its chosen means that is required by our opinion in *Fox.* It remains to consider the city's argument that its prohibition is a permissible time, place, and manner regulation.

IV

... The city contends that its regulation of newsracks qualifies as [a time, place, and manner] restriction because the interests in safety and esthetics that it serves are entirely unrelated to the content of respondents' publications. Thus, the argument goes, the justification for the regulation is content neutral.

The argument is unpersuasive because the very basis for the regulation is the difference in content between ordinary newspapers and commercial speech. True, there is no evidence that the city has acted with animus toward the ideas contained within respondents' publications, but just last Term we expressly rejected the argument that "discriminatory ... treatment is suspect under the First Amendment only when the legislature intends to suppress certain ideas." Simon & Schuster v. Members of New York State Crime Victims Bd., 502 U.S., at

____. Regardless of the *mens rea* of the city, it has enacted a sweeping ban on the use of newsracks that distribute "commercial handbills," but not "newspapers." Under the city's newsrack policy, whether any particular newsrack falls within the ban is determined by the content of the publication resting inside that newsrack. Thus, by any common-sense understanding of the term, the ban in this case is "content-based."

Nor are we persuaded that our statements that the test for whether a regulation is content-based turns on the "justification" for the regulation ... compel a different conclusion. We agree with the city that its desire to limit the total number of newsracks is "justified" by its interest in safety and esthetics. The city has not, however, limited the number of newsracks; it has limited (to zero) the number of newsracks distributing commercial publications. As we have explained, there is no justification for that particular regulation other than the city's naked assertion that commercial speech has "low value." It is the absence of a neutral justification for its selective ban on newsracks that prevents the city from defending its newsrack policy as content-neutral.

. . .

In sum, the city's newsrack policy is neither content-neutral nor, as demonstrated in Part III, supra, "narrowly tailored." Thus, regardless of whether or not it leaves open ample alternative channels of communication, it cannot be justified as a legitimate time, place, or manner restriction on protected speech.

Cincinnati has enacted a sweeping ban that bars from its sidewalks a whole class of constitutionally protected speech. As did the District Court and the Court of Appeals, we conclude that Cincinnati has failed to justify that policy. The regulation is not a permissible regulation of commercial speech, for on this record it is clear that the interests that Cincinnati has asserted are unrelated to any distinction between "commercial handbills" and "newspapers." Moreover, because the ban is predicated on the content of the publications distributed by the subject newsracks, it is not a valid time, place, or manner restriction on protected speech. For these reasons, Cincinnati's categorical ban on the distribution, via newsrack, of "commercial handbills" cannot be squared with the dictates of the First Amendment.

The judgment of the Court of Appeals is

Affirmed.

Justice Blackmun, concurring.

... I continue to believe that the analysis set forth in *Central Hudson* and refined in *Fox* affords insufficient protection for truthful, noncoercive commercial speech concerning lawful activities.... The present case demonstrates that there is no reason to treat truthful commercial speech as a class that is less "valuable" than noncommercial speech....

. . .

... [I]t is little wonder that when the city of Cincinnati wanted to remove some newsracks from its streets, it chose to eliminate all the *commercial* newsracks first although its reasons had nothing to do with either the deceptiveness of particular commercial publications or the particular characteristics of commercial newsracks themselves. First, Cincinnati could rely on this Court's broad statements that commercial speech "is of less constitutional moment than other forms of speech," . . . and occupies a "subordinate position in the scale of First Amendment values," . . . . Second, it knew that under *Central Hudson* its restrictions on commercial speech would be examined with less enthusiasm and with less exacting scrutiny than any restrictions it might impose on other speech. Indeed, it appears that Cincinnati felt it had no choice under this Court's decisions but to burden commercial newsracks more heavily . . . .

. . .

. . . The Court expressly reserves the question whether regulations not directed at the content of commercial speech or adverse effects stemming from that content should be evaluated under the standards applicable to regulations of fully protected speech. Ante, n. 11. I believe the Court should answer that question in the affirmative and hold that truthful, noncoercive commercial speech concerning lawful activities is entitled to full First Amendment protection. . . .

The commercial publications at issue in this case illustrate the absurdity of treating all commercial speech as less valuable than all noncommercial speech. Respondent Harmon Publishing Company, Inc., publishes and distributes a free magazine containing listings and photographs of residential properties. Like the "For Sale" signs this Court, in Linmark Associates, Inc. v. Willingboro, 431 U.S. 85 (1977), held could not be banned, the information contained in Harmon's publication "bear[s] on one of the most important decisions [individuals] have a right to make: where to live and raise their families." Id., at 96. Respondent Discovery Network, Inc., advertises the availability of adult educational, recreational, and social programs. Our cases have consistently recognized the importance of education to the professional and personal development of the individual. See, e.g., Brown v. Board of Education, 347 U.S. 483, 493 (1954). The "value" of respondents' commercial speech, at least to those who receive it, certainly exceeds the value of the offensive, though political, slogan displayed on the petitioner's jacket in Cohen v. California, 403 U.S. 15 (1971).

I think it highly unlikely that according truthful, noncoercive commercial speech the full protection of the First Amendment will erode the level of that protection. . . . The very fact that government remains free, in my view, to ensure that commercial speech is not deceptive or coercive, to prohibit commercial speech proposing illegal activities, and to impose reasonable time, place, or manner restrictions on commercial speech greatly reduces the risk that protecting truthful commercial speech will dilute the level of First Amendment protection for speech generally.

. . .

Chief Justice Rehnquist, with whom Justice White and Justice Thomas join, dissenting.

. . .

... I agree with the Court that the city's prohibition against respondents' newsracks is properly analyzed under *Central Hudson,* but differ as to the result this analysis should produce.

... This case turns ... on the application of the last part of the *Central Hudson* analysis. Although the Court does not say so, there can be no question that Cincinnati's prohibition against respondents' newsracks "directly advances" its safety and esthetic interests because, if enforced, the city's policy will decrease the number of newsracks on its street corners. This leaves the question whether the city's prohibition is "more extensive than necessary" to serve its interests, or, as we elaborated in *Fox,* whether there is a "reasonable fit" between the city's desired ends and the means it has chosen to accomplish those ends.... Because the city's "commercial handbill" ordinance was not enacted specifically to address the problems caused by newsracks, and, if enforced, the city's prohibition against respondents' newsracks would result in the removal of only 62 newsracks from its street corners, the Court finds "ample support in the record for the conclusion that the city did not establish [a] reasonable fit." ... I disagree.

... As we observed in *Fox,* "almost all of the restrictions disallowed under Central Hudson's fourth prong have been substantially excessive, disregarding far less restrictive and more precise means." ... That there may be other—less restrictive—means by which Cincinnati could have gone about addressing its safety and esthetic concerns, then, does not render its prohibition against respondents' newsracks unconstitutional.

Nor does the fact that, if enforced, the city's prohibition would result in the removal of only 62 newsracks from its street corners. The Court attaches significance to the lower courts' findings that any benefit that would be derived from the removal of respondents' newsracks would be " 'minute' " or " 'paltry.' " The relevant inquiry, though, is not the degree to which the locality's interests are furthered in a particular case, but rather the relation that the challenged regulation of commercial speech bears to the "overall problem" the locality is seeking to alleviate. *Ward v. Rock Against Racism,* 491 U.S. 781, 801 (1989). This follows from our test for reviewing the validity of "time, place, or manner" restrictions on noncommercial speech, which we have said is "substantially similar" to the *Central Hudson* analysis. *Board of Trustees of State Univ. of New York v. Fox.* ... Properly viewed, then, the city's prohibition against respondents' newsracks is directly related to its efforts to alleviate the problems caused by newsracks, since every newsrack that is removed from the city's sidewalks marginally enhances the safety of its streets and esthetics of its cityscape. This conclusion is not altered by the fact that the city has chosen to address its problem by banning only those newsracks that disseminate commercial speech, rather than regulating all newsracks alike.

Our commercial speech cases establish that localities may stop short of fully accomplishing their objectives without running afoul of the First Amendment. In Posadas de Puerto Rico Associates v. Tourism Co. of Puerto Rico, 478 U.S. 328, 342 (1986), where we upheld Puerto Rico's ban on promotional advertising of casino gambling aimed at Puerto Rico residents, we rejected the appellant's argument that the ban was invalid under *Central Hudson* because other types of gambling (e.g., horse racing) were permitted to be advertised to local residents.... Thus, the fact that Cincinnati's regulatory scheme is underinclusive does not render its ban on respondents' newsracks unconstitutional.

The Court offers an alternative rationale for invalidating the city's policy: viz., the distinction Cincinnati has drawn (between commercial and noncommercial speech) in deciding which newsracks to regulate "bears no relationship *whatsoever* to the particular interests that the city has asserted." ...

Thus, despite the fact that we have consistently distinguished between commercial and noncommercial speech for the purpose of determining whether the regulation of speech is permissible, the Court holds that in attempting to alleviate its newsrack problem Cincinnati may not choose to proceed incrementally by burdening only commercial speech first. Based on the different levels of protection we have accorded commercial and noncommercial speech, we have previously said that localities may not favor commercial over noncommercial speech in addressing similar urban problems, ... but before today we have never even suggested that the converse holds true. It is not surprising, then, that the Court offers little in the way of precedent supporting its new rule. The cases it does cite involve challenges to the restriction of noncommercial speech in which we have refused to accept distinctions drawn between restricted and nonrestricted speech on the ground that they bore no relationship to the interests asserted for regulating the speech in the first place....

The Court's reliance on Bolger v. Youngs Drug Products Corp. is also misplaced. In that case we said that the State's interest in "shield[ing] recipients of mail from materials that they are likely to find offensive" was invalid regardless of the type of speech—commercial or noncommercial—involved.... By contrast, there can be no question here that the city's safety and esthetic interests justify its prohibition against respondents' newsracks....

If (as I am certain) Cincinnati may regulate newsracks that disseminate commercial speech based on the interests it has asserted, I am at a loss as to why its scheme is unconstitutional because it does not also regulate newsracks that disseminate noncommercial speech. One would have thought that the city, perhaps even following the teachings of our commercial speech jurisprudence, could have decided to place the burden of its regulatory scheme on less protected speech (i.e., commercial handbills) without running afoul of the First Amendment. Today's decision, though, places the city in the position of having to decide between restricting more speech—fully protected speech—and allowing the proliferation of newsracks on its street corners to continue unabated. It scarcely seems logical that the First Amendment compels such a result. In my view, the city may order the removal of all newsracks from its public right-of-ways if it so chooses.... But however it decides to address its newsrack problem, it should be allowed to proceed in the manner and scope it sees fit so long as it does not violate established First Amendment principles, such as the rule against discrimination on the basis of content....

... I see no reason to engage in a "time, place, or manner" analysis of the city's prohibition, which in any event strikes me as duplicative of the *Central Hudson* analysis.... Nor do I think it necessary or wise, on the record before us, to reach the question whether the city's regulatory scheme vests too much discretion in city officials to determine whether a particular publication constitutes a "commercial handbill." It is undisputed, by the parties at least, that respondents' magazines constitute commercial speech. I dissent.

Page 1347. Replace Posadas de Puerto Rico Associates v. Tourism Company of Puerto Rico with the following:

44 LIQUORMART, INC. v. RHODE ISLAND

___ U.S. ___, 116 S.Ct. 1495, 134 L.Ed.2d 711 (1996).

Justice Stevens announced the judgment of the Court and delivered the opinion of the Court with respect to Parts I, II, VII, and VIII, an opinion with respect to Parts III and V, in which Justice Kennedy, Justice Souter, and Justice Ginsburg join, an opinion with respect to Part VI, in which Justice Kennedy, Justice Thomas, and Justice Ginsburg join, and an opinion with respect to Part IV, in which Justice Kennedy and Justice Ginsburg join.

Last Term we held that a federal law abridging a brewer's right to provide the public with accurate information about the alcoholic content of malt beverages is unconstitutional. (Rubin v. Coors Brewing Co., 514 U.S. ___, ___ (1995)). We now hold that Rhode Island's statutory prohibition against advertisements that provide the public with accurate information about retail prices of alcoholic beverages is also invalid. Our holding rests on the conclusion that such an advertising ban is an abridgment of speech protected by the First Amendment and that it is not shielded from constitutional scrutiny by the Twenty-first Amendment.

I

In 1956, the Rhode Island Legislature enacted two separate prohibitions against advertising the retail price of alcoholic beverages. The first applies to vendors licensed in Rhode Island as well as to out-of-state manufacturers, wholesalers, and shippers. It prohibits them from "advertising in any manner whatsoever" the price of any alcoholic beverage offered for sale in the State; the only exception is for price tags or signs displayed with the merchandise within licensed premises and not visible from the street. The second statute applies to the Rhode Island news media. It contains a categorical prohibition against the publication or broadcast of any advertisements—even those referring to sales in other States—that "make reference to the price of any alcoholic beverages."

. . .

II

Petitioners 44 Liquormart, Inc. (44 Liquormart), and Peoples Super Liquor Stores, Inc. (Peoples), are licensed retailers of alcoholic beverages. Petitioner 44 Liquormart operates a store in Rhode Island and petitioner Peoples operates several stores in Massachusetts that are patronized by Rhode Island residents. Peoples uses alcohol price advertising extensively in Massachusetts, where such advertising is permitted, but Rhode Island newspapers and other media outlets have refused to accept such ads.

Complaints from competitors about an advertisement placed by 44 Liquormart in a Rhode Island newspaper in 1991 generated enforcement proceedings that in turn led to the initiation of this litigation. The advertisement did not state the price of any alcoholic beverages. Indeed, it noted that "State law prohibits advertising liquor prices." The ad did, however, state the low prices at which peanuts, potato chips, and Schweppes mixers were being offered, identify various brands of packaged liquor, and include the word "WOW" in large letters next to pictures of vodka and rum bottles. Based on the conclusion that the implied reference to bargain prices for liquor violated the statutory ban on price advertising, the Rhode Island Liquor Control Administrator assessed a $400 fine.

After paying the fine, 44 Liquormart, joined by Peoples, filed this action . . . in the Federal District Court seeking a declaratory judgment that the two statutes and the administrator's implementing regulations violate the First Amendment . . .

. . .

. . . [The District Court] concluded that the price advertising ban was unconstitutional . . . .

The Court of Appeals reversed. . . .

. . .

III

. . .

In Central Hudson Gas & Elec. Corp. v. Public Serv. Comm'n of N.Y., 447 U.S. 557 (1980), we took stock of our developing commercial speech jurisprudence. . . .

. . .

. . . [T]he majority explained that although the special nature of commercial speech may require less than strict review of its regulation, special concerns arise from "regulations that entirely suppress commercial speech in order to pursue a nonspeech-related policy." Id., at 566, n. 9. In those circumstances, "a ban on speech could screen from public view the underlying governmental policy." Ibid. As a result, the Court concluded that "special care" should attend the review of such blanket bans, and it pointedly remarked that "in recent years this Court has not approved a blanket ban on commercial speech unless the speech itself was flawed in some way, either because it was deceptive or related to unlawful activity." Ibid.

<h2 style="text-align:center">IV</h2>

As our review of the case law reveals, Rhode Island errs in concluding that all commercial speech regulations are subject to a similar form of constitutional review simply because they target a similar category of expression. The mere fact that messages propose commercial transactions does not in and of itself dictate the constitutional analysis that should apply to decisions to suppress them. . . .

When a State regulates commercial messages to protect consumers from misleading, deceptive, or aggressive sales practices, or requires the disclosure of beneficial consumer information, the purpose of its regulation is consistent with the reasons for according constitutional protection to commercial speech and therefore justifies less than strict review. However, when a State entirely prohibits the dissemination of truthful, nonmisleading commercial messages for reasons unrelated to the preservation of a fair bargaining process, there is far less reason to depart from the rigorous review that the First Amendment generally demands.

Sound reasons justify reviewing the latter type of commercial speech regulation more carefully. Most obviously, complete speech bans, unlike content-neutral restrictions on the time, place, or manner of expression, . . . are particularly dangerous because they all but foreclose alternative means of disseminating certain information.

. . .

The special dangers that attend complete bans on truthful, nonmisleading commercial speech cannot be explained away by appeals to the "commonsense distinctions" that exist between commercial and noncommercial speech. . . . Regulations that suppress the truth are no less troubling because they target objectively verifiable information, nor are they less effective because they aim at durable messages. As a result, neither the "greater objectivity" nor the "greater hardiness" of truthful, nonmisleading commercial speech justifies reviewing its complete suppression with added deference. . . .

It is the State's interest in protecting consumers from "commercial harms" that provides "the typical reason why commercial speech can be subject to greater governmental regulation than noncommercial speech." . . . Yet bans that target truthful, nonmisleading commercial messages rarely protect consumers from such harms. Instead, such bans often serve only to obscure an "underlying governmental policy" that could be implemented without regulating speech. . . . In this way, these commercial speech bans not only hinder consumer choice, but also impede debate over central issues of public policy. ...

Precisely because bans against truthful, nonmisleading commercial speech rarely seek to protect consumers from either deception or over-reaching, they usually rest solely on the offensive assumption that the public will respond "irrationally" to the truth. ... The First Amendment directs us to be especially skeptical of regulations that seek to keep people in the dark for what the government perceives to be their own good. That teaching applies equally to state attempts to deprive consumers of accurate information about their chosen products. ...

V

In this case, there is no question that Rhode Island's price advertising ban constitutes a blanket prohibition against truthful, nonmisleading speech about a lawful product. There is also no question that the ban serves an end unrelated to consumer protection. Accordingly, we must review the price advertising ban with "special care," *Central Hudson*, 447 U.S., at 566, n. 9, mindful that speech prohibitions of this type rarely survive constitutional review. Ibid.

The State argues that the price advertising prohibition should nevertheless be upheld because it directly advances the State's substantial interest in promoting temperance, and because it is no more extensive than necessary. ... Although there is some confusion as to what Rhode Island means by temperance, we assume that the State asserts an interest in reducing alcohol consumption.

In evaluating the ban's effectiveness in advancing the State's interest, we note that a commercial speech regulation "may not be sustained if it provides only ineffective or remote support for the government's purpose." *Central Hudson*, 447 U.S., at 564. For that reason, the State bears the burden of showing not merely that its regulation will advance its interest, but also that it will do so "to a material degree." ... The need for the State to make such a showing is particularly great given the drastic nature of its chosen means—the wholesale suppression of truthful, nonmisleading information. Accordingly, we must determine whether the State has shown that the price advertising ban will significantly reduce alcohol consumption.

We can agree that common sense supports the conclusion that a prohibition against price advertising, like a collusive agreement among competitors to refrain from such advertising, will tend to mitigate competition and maintain prices at a higher level than would prevail in a completely free market. Despite the absence of proof on the point, we can even agree with the State's contention that it is reasonable to assume that demand, and hence consumption throughout the market, is somewhat lower whenever a higher, noncompetitive price level prevails. However, without any findings of fact, or indeed any evidentiary support whatsoever, we cannot agree with the assertion that the price advertising ban will significantly advance the State's interest in promoting temperance.

Although the record suggests that the price advertising ban may have some impact on the purchasing patterns of temperate drinkers of modest means, the State has presented no evidence to suggest that its speech prohibition will significantly reduce market-wide consumption. Indeed, the District Court's considered and uncontradicted finding on this point is directly to the contrary. Moreover, the evidence suggests that the abusive drinker will probably not be deterred by a marginal price increase, and that the true alcoholic may simply reduce his purchases of other necessities.

In addition, as the District Court noted, the State has not identified what price level would lead to a significant reduction in alcohol consumption, nor has it identified the amount that it believes prices would decrease without the ban. Thus, the State's own showing reveals that any connection between the ban and a significant change in alcohol consumption would be purely fortuitous.

As is evident, any conclusion that elimination of the ban would significantly increase alcohol consumption would require us to engage in the sort of "speculation or conjecture" that is an unacceptable means of demonstrating that a restriction on commercial speech directly advances the State's asserted interest. ... Such speculation certainly does not suffice when the State takes aim at accurate commercial information for paternalistic ends.

The State also cannot satisfy the requirement that its restriction on speech be no more extensive than necessary. It is perfectly obvious that alternative forms of regulation that would not involve any restriction on speech would be more likely to achieve the State's goal of promoting temperance. As the State's own expert conceded, higher prices can be maintained either by direct regulation or by increased taxation. Per capita purchases could be limited as is the case with prescription drugs. Even educational campaigns focused on the problems of excessive, or even moderate, drinking might prove to be more effective.

As a result, even under the less than strict standard that generally applies in commercial speech cases, the State has failed to establish a "reasonable fit" between its abridgment of speech and its temperance goal. ... It necessarily follows that the price advertising ban cannot survive the more stringent constitutional review that *Central Hudson* itself concluded was appropriate for the complete suppression of truthful, nonmisleading commercial speech. ...

VI

The State responds by arguing that it merely exercised appropriate "legislative judgment" in determining that a price advertising ban would best promote temperance. Relying on the *Central Hudson* analysis set forth in Posadas de Puerto Rico Associates v. Tourism Co. of P. R., 478 U.S. 328 (1986), and United States v. Edge Broadcasting Co., 509 U.S. ___ (1993), Rhode Island first argues that, because expert opinions as to the effectiveness of the price advertising ban "go both ways," the Court of Appeals correctly concluded that the ban constituted a "reasonable choice" by the legislature. The State next contends that precedent

requires us to give particular deference to that legislative choice because
the State could, if it chose, ban the sale of alcoholic beverages outright.
See *Posadas*, 478 U.S., at 345–346.   Finally, the State argues that
deference is appropriate because alcoholic beverages are so-called "vice"
products.   See *Edge*, 509 U.S. at ___; *Posadas*, 478 U.S., at 346–347.
We consider each of these contentions in turn.

The State's first argument fails to justify the speech prohibition at
issue.   Our commercial speech cases recognize some room for the exercise of legislative judgment.   . . . However, Rhode Island errs in concluding that *Edge* and *Posadas* establish the degree of deference that its
decision to impose a price advertising ban warrants.

In *Edge*, we upheld a federal statute that permitted only those
broadcasters located in States that had legalized lotteries to air lottery
advertising.   The statute was designed to regulate advertising about an
activity that had been deemed illegal in the jurisdiction in which the
broadcaster was located.   . . . Here, by contrast, the commercial speech
ban targets information about entirely lawful behavior.

Posadas is more directly relevant.   There, a five-Member majority
held that, under the *Central Hudson* test, it was "up to the legislature"
to choose to reduce gambling by suppressing in-state casino advertising
rather than engaging in educational speech.   . . . Rhode Island argues
that this logic demonstrates the constitutionality of its own decision to
ban price advertising in lieu of raising taxes or employing some other
less speech-restrictive means of promoting temperance.

The reasoning in *Posadas* does support the State's argument, but,
on reflection, we are now persuaded that *Posadas* erroneously performed
the First Amendment analysis.   The casino advertising ban was designed
to keep truthful, nonmisleading speech from members of the public for
fear that they would be more likely to gamble if they received it.   As a
result, the advertising ban served to shield the State's antigambling
policy from the public scrutiny that more direct, nonspeech regulation
would draw.   See *Posadas*, 478 U.S., at 351 (Brennan, J., dissenting).

Given our longstanding hostility to commercial speech regulation of
this type, *Posadas* clearly erred in concluding that it was "up to the
legislature" to choose suppression over a less speech-restrictive policy.
The *Posadas* majority's conclusion on that point cannot be reconciled
with the unbroken line of prior cases striking down similarly broad
regulations on truthful, nonmisleading advertising when non-speech-
related alternatives were available.   . . .

Because the 5-to-4 decision in *Posadas* marked such a sharp break
from our prior precedent, and because it concerned a constitutional
question about which this Court is the final arbiter, we decline to give
force to its highly deferential approach.   Instead, in keeping with our
prior holdings, we conclude that a state legislature does not have the
broad discretion to suppress truthful, nonmisleading information for
paternalistic purposes that the *Posadas* majority was willing to tolerate.
    . . .

We also cannot accept the State's second contention, which is premised entirely on the "greater-includes-the-lesser" reasoning endorsed toward the end of the majority's opinion in *Posadas*. There, the majority stated that "the greater power to completely ban casino gambling necessarily includes the lesser power to ban advertising of casino gambling." 478 U.S., at 345–346. It went on to state that "because the government could have enacted a wholesale prohibition of [casino gambling] it is permissible for the government to take the less intrusive step of allowing the conduct, but reducing the demand through restrictions on advertising." Id., at 346. The majority concluded that it would "surely be a strange constitutional doctrine which would concede to the legislature the authority to totally ban a product or activity, but deny to the legislature the authority to forbid the stimulation of demand for the product or activity through advertising on behalf of those who would profit from such increased demand." Ibid. On the basis of these statements, the State reasons that its undisputed authority to ban alcoholic beverages must include the power to restrict advertisements offering them for sale.

In Rubin v. Coors Brewing Co., 514 U.S. ___ (1995), the United States advanced a similar argument as a basis for supporting a statutory prohibition against revealing the alcoholic content of malt beverages on product labels. We rejected the argument, noting that the statement in the *Posadas* opinion was made only after the majority had concluded that the Puerto Rican regulation "survived the *Central Hudson* test." ... Further consideration persuades us that the "greater-includes-the-lesser" argument should be rejected for the additional and more important reason that it is inconsistent with both logic and well-settled doctrine.

Although we do not dispute the proposition that greater powers include lesser ones, we fail to see how that syllogism requires the conclusion that the State's power to regulate commercial activity is "greater" than its power to ban truthful, nonmisleading commercial speech. Contrary to the assumption made in *Posadas*, we think it quite clear that banning speech may sometimes prove far more intrusive than banning conduct. ... [W]e reject the assumption that words are necessarily less vital to freedom than actions, or that logic somehow proves that the power to prohibit an activity is necessarily "greater" than the power to suppress speech about it.

As a matter of First Amendment doctrine, the *Posadas* syllogism is even less defensible. The text of the First Amendment makes clear that the Constitution presumes that attempts to regulate speech are more dangerous than attempts to regulate conduct. That presumption accords with the essential role that the free flow of information plays in a democratic society. As a result, the First Amendment directs that government may not suppress speech as easily as it may suppress conduct, and that speech restrictions cannot be treated as simply another means that the government may use to achieve its ends.

These basic First Amendment principles clearly apply to commercial speech; indeed, the *Posadas* majority impliedly conceded as much by applying the *Central Hudson* test. Thus, it is no answer that commercial speech concerns products and services that the government may freely regulate. ...

. . .

Thus, just as it is perfectly clear that Rhode Island could not ban all obscene liquor ads except those that advocated temperance, we think it equally clear that its power to ban the sale of liquor entirely does not include a power to censor all advertisements that contain accurate and nonmisleading information about the price of the product. As the entire Court apparently now agrees, the statements in the *Posadas* opinion on which Rhode Island relies are no longer persuasive.

Finally, we find unpersuasive the State's contention that, under *Posadas* and *Edge*, the price advertising ban should be upheld because it targets commercial speech that pertains to a "vice" activity. The appellees premise their request for a so-called "vice" exception to our commercial speech doctrine on language in *Edge* which characterized gambling as a "vice".... The respondents misread our precedent. Our decision last Term striking down an alcohol-related advertising restriction effectively rejected the very contention respondents now make. See Rubin v. Coors Brewing Co., 514 U.S., at ___, ___, n. 2.

Moreover, the scope of any "vice" exception to the protection afforded by the First Amendment would be difficult, if not impossible, to define. Almost any product that poses some threat to public health or public morals might reasonably be characterized by a state legislature as relating to "vice activity". Such characterization, however, is anomalous when applied to products such as alcoholic beverages, lottery tickets, or playing cards, that may be lawfully purchased on the open market. The recognition of such an exception would also have the unfortunate consequence of either allowing state legislatures to justify censorship by the simple expedient of placing the "vice" label on selected lawful activities, or requiring the federal courts to establish a federal common law of vice. ... For these reasons, a "vice" label that is unaccompanied by a corresponding prohibition against the commercial behavior at issue fails to provide a principled justification for the regulation of commercial speech about that activity.

VII

. . .

... [T]he text of the Twenty-first Amendment supports the view that, while it grants the States authority over commerce that might otherwise be reserved to the Federal Government, it places no limit whatsoever on other constitutional provisions. Nevertheless, Rhode Island argues ... that in this case the Twenty-first Amendment tilts the First Amendment analysis in the State's favor.

In reaching its conclusion, the Court of Appeals relied on our decision in California v. LaRue, 409 U.S. 109 (1972). In *LaRue*, five Members of the Court relied on the Twenty-first Amendment to buttress the conclusion that the First Amendment did not invalidate California's prohibition of certain grossly sexual exhibitions in premises licensed to serve alcoholic beverages. Specifically, the opinion stated that the Twenty-first Amendment required that the prohibition be given an added presumption in favor of its validity. ... We are now persuaded that the Court's analysis in *LaRue* would have led to precisely the same result if it had placed no reliance on the Twenty-first Amendment.

Entirely apart from the Twenty-first Amendment, the State has ample power to prohibit the sale of alcoholic beverages in inappropriate locations. Moreover, in subsequent cases the Court has recognized that the States' inherent police powers provide ample authority to restrict the kind of "bacchanalian revelries" described in the *LaRue* opinion regardless of whether alcoholic beverages are involved. ... As we recently noted: "*LaRue* did not involve commercial speech about alcohol, but instead concerned the regulation of nude dancing in places where alcohol was served." Rubin v. Coors Brewing Co., 514 U.S., at ___, n. 2.

Without questioning the holding in *LaRue*, we now disavow its reasoning insofar as it relied on the Twenty-first Amendment. As we explained in a case decided more than a decade after *LaRue*, although the Twenty-first Amendment limits the effect of the dormant Commerce Clause on a State's regulatory power over the delivery or use of intoxicating beverages within its borders, "the Amendment does not license the States to ignore their obligations under other provisions of the Constitution." Capital Cities Cable, Inc. v. Crisp, 467 U.S. 691, 712 (1984). ... The Twenty-first Amendment, therefore, cannot save Rhode Island's ban on liquor price advertising.

VIII

Because Rhode Island has failed to carry its heavy burden of justifying its complete ban on price advertising, we conclude that R.I. Gen. Laws §§ 3–8–7 and 3–8–8.1, as well as Regulation 32 of the Rhode Island Liquor Control Administration, abridge speech in violation of the First Amendment as made applicable to the States by the Due Process Clause of the Fourteenth Amendment. The judgment of the Court of Appeals is therefore reversed.

It is so ordered.

Justice Scalia, concurring in part and concurring in the judgment.

I share Justice Thomas's discomfort with the *Central Hudson* test, which seems to me to have nothing more than policy intuition to support it. I also share Justice Stevens' aversion towards paternalistic governmental policies that prevent men and women from hearing facts that might not be good for them. On the other hand, it would also be paternalism for us to prevent the people of the States from enacting laws that we consider paternalistic, unless we have good reason to believe that the Constitution itself forbids them. I will take my guidance as to what the Constitution forbids, with regard to a text as indeterminate as the First Amendment's preservation of "the freedom of speech," and where the core offense of suppressing particular political ideas is not at issue, from the long accepted practices of the American people. ...

The briefs and arguments of the parties in the present case provide no illumination on that point; understandably so, since both sides accepted *Central Hudson*. ... I consider ... relevant the state legislative practices prevalent at the time the First Amendment was adopted, since almost all of the States had free-speech constitutional guarantees of their own, whose meaning was not likely to have been different from the federal constitutional provision derived from them. Perhaps more relevant still are the state legislative practices at the time the Fourteenth Amendment was adopted, since it is most improbable that that adoption was meant to overturn any existing national consensus regarding free speech. ... The parties and their amici provide no evidence on these points.

Since I do not believe we have before us the wherewithal to declare *Central Hudson* wrong—or at least the wherewithal to say what ought to replace it—I must resolve this case in accord with our existing jurisprudence, which all except Justice Thomas agree would prohibit the challenged regulation. I am not disposed to develop new law, or reinforce old, on this issue, and accordingly I merely concur in the judgment of the Court. ...

Justice Thomas, concurring in Parts I, II, VI, and VII, and concurring in the judgment.

In cases such as this, in which the government's asserted interest is to keep legal users of a product or service ignorant in order to manipulate their choices in the marketplace, the balancing test adopted in Central Hudson Gas & Elec. Corp. v. Public Serv. Comm'n of N.Y., 447 U.S. 557 (1980), should not be applied, in my view. Rather, such an "interest" is per se illegitimate and can no more justify regulation of "commercial" speech than it can justify regulation of "noncommercial" speech.

. . .

II

I do not join the principal opinion's application of the *Central Hudson* balancing test because I do not believe that such a test should be applied to a restriction of "commercial" speech, at least when, as here, the asserted interest is one that is to be achieved through keeping would-be recipients of the speech in the dark. Application of the advancement-of-state-interest prong of *Central Hudson* makes little sense to me in such circumstances. Faulting the State for failing to show that its price advertising ban decreases alcohol consumption "significantly," as Justice Stevens does, seems to imply that if the State had been more successful at keeping consumers ignorant and thereby decreasing their consumption, then the restriction might have been upheld. This contradicts *Virginia Pharmacy Bd.*'s rationale for protecting "commercial" speech in the first instance.

Both Justice Stevens and Justice O'Connor appear to adopt a stricter, more categorical interpretation of the fourth prong of *Central Hudson* than that suggested in some of our other opinions, one that could, as a practical matter, go a long way toward the position I take.

... In their application of the fourth prong, both ... hold that because the State can ban the sale of lower priced alcohol altogether by instituting minimum prices or levying taxes, it cannot ban advertising regarding lower priced liquor. Although the tenor of Justice O'Connor's opinion (and, to a lesser extent, that of Justice Stevens's opinion) might suggest that this is just another routine case-by-case application of *Central Hudson*'s fourth prong, the Court's holding will in fact be quite sweeping if applied consistently in future cases. The opinions would appear to commit the courts to striking down restrictions on speech whenever a direct regulation (i.e., a regulation involving no restriction on speech regarding lawful activity at all) would be an equally effective method of dampening demand by legal users. But it would seem that directly banning a product (or rationing it, taxing it, controlling its price, or otherwise restricting its sale in specific ways) would virtually always be at least as effective in discouraging consumption as merely restricting advertising regarding the product would be, and thus virtually all restrictions with such a purpose would fail the fourth prong of the *Central Hudson* test. This would be so even if the direct regulation is, in one sense, more restrictive of conduct generally. In this case, for example, adoption of minimum prices or taxes will mean that those who, under the current legal system, would have happened across cheap liquor or would have sought it out, will be forced to pay more. Similarly, a State seeking to discourage liquor sales would have to ban sales by convenience stores rather than banning convenience store liquor advertising; it would have to ban liquor sales after midnight, rather than banning advertising by late-night liquor sellers; and so on.

The upshot of the application of the fourth prong in the opinions of Justice Stevens and of Justice O'Connor seems to be that the government may not, for the purpose of keeping would-be consumers ignorant and thus decreasing demand, restrict advertising regarding commercial transactions—or at least that it may not restrict advertising regarding commercial transactions except to the extent that it outlaws or otherwise directly restricts the same transactions within its own borders. I welcome this outcome; but, rather than "applying" the fourth prong of *Central Hudson* to reach the inevitable result that all or most such advertising restrictions must be struck down, I would [hold] that all attempts to dissuade legal choices by citizens by keeping them ignorant are impermissible.

. . . .

Justice O'Connor, with whom the Chief Justice, Justice Souter, and Justice Breyer join, concurring in the judgment.

... I agree with the Court that Rhode Island's price-advertising ban is invalid. I would resolve this case more narrowly, however, by applying our established *Central Hudson* test to determine whether this commercial-speech regulation survives First Amendment scrutiny.

Under that test, we first determine whether the speech at issue concerns lawful activity and is not misleading, and whether the asserted governmental interest is substantial. If both these conditions are met, we must decide whether the regulation "directly advances the governmental interest asserted, and whether it is not more extensive than is necessary to serve that interest." ...

. . .

Both parties agree that the first two prongs of the *Central Hudson* test are met. Even if we assume arguendo that Rhode Island's regulation also satisfies the requirement that it directly advance the governmental interest, Rhode Island's regulation fails the final prong; that is, its ban is more extensive than necessary to serve the State's interest.

. . .

... Rhode Island says that the ban is intended to keep alcohol prices high as a way to keep consumption low. ...

The fit between Rhode Island's method and this particular goal is not reasonable. If the target is simply higher prices generally to discourage consumption, the regulation imposes too great, and unnecessary, a prohibition on speech in order to achieve it. The State has other methods at its disposal—methods that would more directly accomplish this stated goal without intruding on sellers' ability to provide truthful, nonmisleading information to customers. Indeed, Rhode Island's own expert conceded that " 'the objective of lowering consumption of alcohol by banning price advertising could be accomplished by establishing minimum prices and/or by increasing sales taxes on alcoholic beverages.' " ... The ready availability of such alternatives—at least some of which would far more effectively achieve Rhode Island's only professed goal, at comparatively small additional administrative cost—demonstrates that the fit between ends and means is not narrowly tailored. ...

Respondents point for support to Posadas de Puerto Rico Associates v. Tourism Co. of P. R., 478 U.S. 328 (1986), where, applying the *Central Hudson* test, we upheld the constitutionality of a Puerto Rico law that prohibited the advertising of casino gambling aimed at residents of Puerto Rico, but permitted such advertising aimed at tourists.

. . .

It is true that *Posadas* accepted as reasonable, without further inquiry, Puerto Rico's assertions that the regulations furthered the government's interest and were no more extensive than necessary to serve that interest. Since *Posadas*, however, this Court has examined more searchingly the State's professed goal, and the speech restriction put into place to further it, before accepting a State's claim that the speech restriction satisfies First Amendment scrutiny. ... The closer look that we have required since *Posadas* comports better with the purpose of the analysis set out in *Central Hudson*, by requiring the State to show that the speech restriction directly advances its interest and is narrowly tailored. Under such a closer look, Rhode Island's price-advertising ban clearly fails to pass muster.

Because Rhode Island's regulation fails even the less stringent standard set out in *Central Hudson*, nothing here requires adoption of a new analysis for the evaluation of commercial speech regulation. ... I would not here undertake the question whether the test we have employed since *Central Hudson* should be displaced.

. . .

... While I agree with the Court's finding that the regulation is invalid, I would decide that issue on narrower grounds. I therefore concur in the judgment.

Chapter 14

RESTRICTIONS ON TIME, PLACE, OR MANNER OF EXPRESSION

SECTION 1. THE TRADITIONAL PUBLIC FORUM: SPEECH ACTIVITIES IN STREETS AND PARKS

Page 1365. Add after Burson v. Freeman:

MADSEN v. WOMEN'S HEALTH CENTER, INC.

___ U.S. ___, 114 S.Ct. 2516, 129 L.Ed.2d 593 (1994).

Chief Justice Rehnquist delivered the opinion of the Court.

Petitioners challenge the constitutionality of an injunction entered by a Florida state court which prohibits antiabortion protestors from demonstrating in certain places and in various ways outside of a health clinic that performs abortions. We hold that the establishment of a 36–foot buffer zone on a public street from which demonstrators are excluded passes muster under the First Amendment, but that several other provisions of the injunction do not.

I

Respondents operate abortion clinics throughout central Florida. Petitioners and other groups and individuals are engaged in activities near the site of one such clinic in Melbourne, Florida. They picketed and demonstrated where the public street gives access to the clinic. In September 1992, a Florida state court permanently enjoined petitioners from blocking or interfering with public access to the clinic, and from physically abusing persons entering or leaving the clinic. Six months later, respondents sought to broaden the injunction, complaining that access to the clinic was still impeded by petitioners' activities and that such activities had also discouraged some potential patients from entering the clinic, and had deleterious physical effects on others. The trial court thereupon issued a broader injunction, which is challenged here.

The court found that, despite the initial injunction, protesters continued to impede access to the clinic by congregating on the paved portion of the street—Dixie Way—leading up to the clinic, and by marching in front of the clinic's driveways. It found that as vehicles heading toward the clinic slowed to allow the protesters to move out of the way, "sidewalk counselors" would approach and attempt to give the vehicle's occupants antiabortion literature. The number of people

264

congregating varied from a handful to 400, and the noise varied from singing and chanting to the use of loudspeakers and bullhorns.

The protests, the court found, took their toll on the clinic's patients. A clinic doctor testified that, as a result of having to run such a gauntlet to enter the clinic, the patients "manifested a higher level of anxiety and hypertension causing those patients to need a higher level of sedation to undergo the surgical procedures, thereby increasing the risk associated with such procedures." The noise produced by the protestors could be heard within the clinic, causing stress in the patients both during surgical procedures and while recuperating in the recovery rooms. And those patients who turned away because of the crowd to return at a later date, the doctor testified, increased their health risks by reason of the delay.

Doctors and clinic workers, in turn, were not immune even in their homes. Petitioners picketed in front of clinic employees' residences; shouted at passersby; rang the doorbells of neighbors and provided literature identifying the particular clinic employee as a "baby killer." Occasionally, the protestors would confront minor children of clinic employees who were home alone. This and similar testimony led the state court to conclude that its original injunction had proved insufficient "to protect the health, safety and rights of women in Brevard and Seminole County, Florida, and surrounding counties seeking access to [medical and counseling] services." Id., at 5. The state court therefore amended its prior order, enjoining a broader array of activities. The amended injunction prohibits petitioners from engaging in the following acts:

"(1) At all times on all days, from entering the premises and property of the Aware Woman Center for Choice [the Melbourne clinic]...

"(2) At all times on all days, from blocking, impeding, inhibiting, or in any other manner obstructing or interfering with access to, ingress into and egress from any building or parking lot of the Clinic.

"(3) At all times on all days, from congregating, picketing, patrolling, demonstrating or entering that portion of public right-of-way or private property within [36] feet of the property line of the Clinic.... An exception to the 36 foot buffer zone is the area immediately adjacent to the Clinic on the east.... The [petitioners] ... must remain at least [5] feet from the Clinic's east line. Another exception to the 36 foot buffer zone relates to the record title owners of the property to the north and west of the Clinic. The prohibition against entry into the 36 foot buffer zones does not apply to such persons and their invitees. The other prohibitions contained herein do apply, if such owners and their invitees are acting in concert with the [petitioners]....

"(4) During the hours of 7:30 a.m. through noon, on Mondays through Saturdays, during surgical procedures and recovery periods, from singing, chanting, whistling, shouting, yelling, use of bullhorns, auto horns, sound amplification equipment or other sounds or images observable to or within earshot of the patients inside the Clinic.

"(5) At all times on all days, in an area within [300] feet of the Clinic, from physically approaching any person seeking the services of the Clinic unless such person indicates a desire to communicate by approaching or by inquiring of the [petitioners]. . . .

"(6) At all times on all days, from approaching, congregating, picketing, patrolling, demonstrating or using bullhorns or other sound amplification equipment within [300] feet of the residence of any of the [respondents'] employees, staff, owners or agents, or blocking or attempting to block, barricade, or in any other manner, temporarily or otherwise, obstruct the entrances, exits or driveways of the residences of any of the [respondents'] employees, staff, owners or agents. The [petitioners] and those acting in concert with them are prohibited from inhibiting or impeding or attempting to impede, temporarily or otherwise, the free ingress or egress of persons to any street that provides the sole access to the street on which those residences are located.

"(7) At all times on all days, from physically abusing, grabbing, intimidating, harassing, touching, pushing, shoving, crowding or assaulting persons entering or leaving, working at or using services at the [respondents'] Clinic or trying to gain access to, or leave, any of the homes of owners, staff or patients of the Clinic.

"(8) At all times on all days, from harassing, intimidating or physically abusing, assaulting or threatening any present or former doctor, health care professional, or other staff member, employee or volunteer who assists in providing services at the [respondents'] Clinic.

"(9) At all times on all days, from encouraging, inciting, or securing other persons to commit any of the prohibited acts listed herein."

The Florida Supreme Court upheld the constitutionality of the trial court's amended injunction. . . .

Shortly before the Florida Supreme Court's opinion was announced, the United States Court of Appeals for the Eleventh Circuit heard a separate challenge to the same injunction. The Court of Appeals struck down the injunction . . . We granted certiorari to resolve the conflict between the Florida Supreme Court and the Court of Appeals over the constitutionality of the state court's injunction.

II

We begin by addressing petitioners' contention that the state court's order, because it is an injunction that restricts only the speech of antiabortion protesters, is necessarily content or viewpoint based. Accordingly, they argue, we should examine the entire injunction under the strictest standard of scrutiny. . . . We disagree. To accept petitioners' claim would be to classify virtually every injunction as content or viewpoint based. An injunction, by its very nature, applies only to a particular group (or individuals) and regulates the activities, and perhaps the speech, of that group. It does so, however, because of the group's past actions in the context of a specific dispute between real parties. The parties seeking the injunction assert a violation of their rights; the court hearing the action is charged with fashioning a remedy for a specific deprivation, not with the drafting of a statute addressed to the general public.

The fact that the injunction in the present case did not prohibit activities of those demonstrating in favor of abortion is justly attributable to the lack of any similar demonstrations by those in favor of abortion, and of any consequent request that their demonstrations be regulated by injunction. There is no suggestion in this record that Florida law would not equally restrain similar conduct directed at a target having nothing to do with abortion; none of the restrictions imposed by the court were directed at the contents of petitioner's message.

Our principal inquiry in determining content neutrality is whether the government has adopted a regulation of speech "without reference to the content of the regulated speech." ... We thus look to the government's purpose as the threshold consideration. Here, the state court imposed restrictions on petitioners incidental to their antiabortion message because they repeatedly violated the court's original order. That petitioners all share the same viewpoint regarding abortion does not in itself demonstrate that some invidious content or viewpoint-based purpose motivated the issuance of the order. It suggests only that those in the group whose conduct violated the court's order happen to share the same opinion regarding abortions being performed at the clinic. In short, the fact that the injunction covered people with a particular viewpoint does not itself render the injunction content or viewpoint based....[2] Accordingly, the injunction issued in this case does not demand the level of heightened scrutiny set forth in Perry Education Assn., 460 U.S., at 45. And we proceed to discuss the standard which does govern.

III

If this were a content-neutral, generally applicable statute, instead of an injunctive order, its constitutionality would be assessed under the standard set forth in Ward v. Rock Against Racism, [491 U.S.] at 791,

---

[2] We also decline to adopt the prior restraint analysis urged by petitioners. Prior restraints do often take the form of injunctions. See, e.g., New York Times Co. v. United States, 403 U.S. 713 (1971) (refusing to enjoin publications of the "Pentagon Papers"); Vance v. Universal Amusement Co., 445 U.S. 308 (1980)(per curiam)(holding that Texas public nuisance statute which authorized state judges, on the basis of a showing that a theater had exhibited obscene films in the past, to enjoin its future exhibition of films not yet found to be obscene was unconstitutional as authorizing an invalid prior restraint.) Not all injunctions which may incidentally affect expression, however, are "prior restraints" in the sense that that term was used in *New York Times Co.,* supra, or *Vance,* supra. Here petitioners are not prevented from expressing their message in any one of several different ways; they are simply prohibited from expressing it within the 36–foot buffer zone. Moreover, the injunction was issued not because of the content of petitioners' expression, as was the case in *New York Times Co.* and *Vance,* but because of their prior unlawful conduct.

and similar cases. Given that the forum around the clinic is a tradition-al public forum ... we would determine whether the time, place, and manner regulations were "narrowly tailored to serve a significant gov-ernmental interest." ...

There are obvious differences, however, between an injunction and a generally applicable ordinance. Ordinances represent a legislative choice regarding the promotion of particular societal interests. Injunctions, by contrast, are remedies imposed for violations (or threatened violations) of a legislative or judicial decree.... Injunctions also carry greater risks of censorship and discriminatory application than do general ordinances. Injunctions, of course, have some advantages over generally applicable statutes in that they can be tailored by a trial judge to afford more precise relief than a statute where a violation of the law has already occurred....

We believe that these differences require a somewhat more stringent application of general First Amendment principles in this context. In past cases evaluating injunctions restricting speech ... we have relied upon such general principles while also seeking to ensure that the injunction was no broader than necessary to achieve its desired goals.... Our close attention to the fit between the objectives of an injunction and the restrictions it imposes on speech is consistent with the general rule, quite apart from First Amendment considerations, "that injunctive relief should be no more burdensome to the defendants than necessary to provide complete relief to the plaintiffs." ... Accordingly, when evalu-ating a content-neutral injunction, we think that our standard time, place, and manner analysis is not sufficiently rigorous. We must ask instead whether the challenged provisions of the injunction burden no more speech than necessary to serve a significant government inter-est....

Both Justice Stevens and Justice Scalia disagree with the standard we announce, for policy reasons. Justice Stevens believes that "injunc-tive relief should be judged by a more lenient standard than legislation," because injunctions are imposed on individuals or groups who have engaged in illegal activity. Justice Scalia, by contrast, believes that content-neutral injunctions are "at least as deserving of strict scrutiny as a statutory, content-based restriction." Justice Scalia bases his belief on the danger that injunctions, even though they might not "attack content as content," may be used to suppress particular ideas; that individual judges should not be trusted to impose injunctions in this context; and that an injunction is procedurally more difficult to chal-lenge than a statute. We believe that consideration of all of the differences and similarities between statutes and injunctions supports, as a matter of policy, the standard we apply here.

Justice Scalia ... cites a number of cases in which we have struck down, with little or no elaboration, prior restraints on free expression. As we have explained, however, we do not believe that this injunction constitutes a prior restraint, and we therefore believe that the "heavy presumption" against its constitutionality does not obtain here. See n. 2, supra.

. . .

The Florida Supreme Court concluded that numerous significant government interests are protected by the injunction. It noted that the State has a strong interest in protecting a woman's freedom to seek lawful medical or counseling services in connection with her pregnancy. The State also has a strong interest in ensuring the public safety and order, in promoting the free flow of traffic on public streets and side-walks, and in protecting the property rights of all its citizens. In addition, the court believed that the State's strong interest in residential privacy, acknowledged in Frisby v. Schultz, 487 U.S. 474 (1988), applied by analogy to medical privacy. The court observed that while targeted picketing of the home threatens the psychological well-being of the "captive" resident, targeted picketing of a hospital or clinic threatens not only the psychological, but the physical well-being of the patient held "captive" by medical circumstance. We agree with the Supreme Court of Florida that the combination of these governmental interests is quite sufficient to justify an appropriately tailored injunction to protect them. We now examine each contested provision of the injunction to see if it burdens more speech than necessary to accomplish its goal.

A

1

We begin with the 36–foot buffer zone. The state court prohibited petitioners from "congregating, picketing, patrolling, demonstrating or entering" any portion of the public right-of-way or private property within 36 feet of the property line of the clinic as a way of ensuring access to the clinic. This speech-free buffer zone requires that petition-ers move to the other side of Dixie Way and away from the driveway of the clinic, where the state court found that they repeatedly had inter-fered with the free access of patients and staff.... The buffer zone also applies to private property to the north and west of the clinic property. We examine each portion of the buffer zone separately.

We have noted a distinction between the type of focused picketing banned from the buffer zone and the type of generally disseminated communication that cannot be completely banned in public places, such as handbilling and solicitation.... Here the picketing is directed pri-marily at patients and staff of the clinic.

The 36–foot buffer zone protecting the entrances to the clinic and the parking lot is a means of protecting unfettered ingress to and egress from the clinic, and ensuring that petitioners do not block traffic on Dixie Way....

The need for a complete buffer zone near the clinic entrances and driveway may be debatable, but some deference must be given to the state court's familiarity with the facts and the background of the dispute between the parties even under our heightened review.... On balance, we hold that the 36–foot buffer zone around the clinic entrances and driveway burdens no more speech than necessary to accomplish the governmental interest at stake.

. . .

2

The inclusion of private property on the back and side of the clinic in the 36–foot buffer zone raises different concerns. The accepted purpose of the buffer zone is to protect access to the clinic and to facilitate the orderly flow of traffic on Dixie Way. Patients and staff wishing to reach the clinic do not have to cross the private property abutting the clinic property on the north and west, and nothing in the record indicates that petitioners' activities on the private property have obstructed access to the clinic. . . . We hold that on the record before us the 36–foot buffer zone as applied to the private property to the north and west of the clinic burdens more speech than necessary to protect access to the clinic.

B

In response to high noise levels outside the clinic, the state court restrained the petitioners from "singing, chanting, whistling, shouting, yelling, use of bullhorns, auto horns, sound amplification equipment or other sounds or images observable to or within earshot of the patients inside the [c]linic" during the hours of 7:30 a.m. through noon on Mondays through Saturdays. . . . Noise control is particularly important around hospitals and medical facilities during surgery and recovery periods . . .

We hold that the limited noise restrictions imposed by the state court order burden no more speech than necessary to ensure the health and well-being of the patients at the clinic. The First Amendment does not demand that patients at a medical facility undertake Herculean efforts to escape the cacophony of political protests. . . .

C

The same, however, cannot be said for the "images observable" provision of the state court's order. Clearly, threats to patients or their families, however communicated, are proscribable under the First Amendment. But rather than prohibiting the display of signs that could be interpreted as threats or veiled threats, the state court issued a blanket ban on all "images observable." This broad prohibition on all "images observable" burdens more speech than necessary to achieve the purpose of limiting threats to clinic patients or their families. Similarly, if the blanket ban on "images observable" was intended to reduce the level of anxiety and hypertension suffered by the patients inside the clinic, it would still fail. The only plausible reason a patient would be bothered by "images observable" inside the clinic would be if the patient found the expression contained in such images disagreeable. But it is much easier for the clinic to pull its curtains than for a patient to stop up her ears, and no more is required to avoid seeing placards through the windows of the clinic. This provision of the injunction violates the First Amendment.

D

The state court ordered that petitioners refrain from physically approaching any person seeking services of the clinic "unless such person indicates a desire to communicate" in an area within 300 feet of the clinic. The state court was attempting to prevent clinic patients and staff from being "stalked" or "shadowed" by the petitioners as they approached the clinic....

But it is difficult, indeed, to justify a prohibition on all uninvited approaches of persons seeking the services of the clinic, regardless of how peaceful the contact may be, without burdening more speech than necessary to prevent intimidation and to ensure access to the clinic. Absent evidence that the protesters' speech is independently proscribable (i.e., "fighting words" or threats), or is so infused with violence as to be indistinguishable from a threat of physical harm, ... this provision cannot stand.... The "consent" requirement alone invalidates this provision; it burdens more speech than is necessary to prevent intimidation and to ensure access to the clinic.

E

The final substantive regulation challenged by petitioners relates to a prohibition against picketing, demonstrating, or using sound amplification equipment within 300 feet of the residences of clinic staff. The prohibition also covers impeding access to streets that provide the sole access to streets on which those residences are located. The same analysis applies to the use of sound amplification equipment here as that discussed above: the government may simply demand that petitioners turn down the volume if the protests overwhelm the neighborhood....

As for the picketing, our prior decision upholding a law banning targeted residential picketing remarked on the unique nature of the home, as " 'the last citadel of the tired, the weary, and the sick.' " *Frisby,* 487 U.S., at 484....

But the 300–foot zone around the residences in this case is much larger than the zone provided for in the ordinance which we approved in *Frisby.* The ordinance at issue there ... was limited to "focused picketing taking place solely in front of a particular residence." ... By contrast, the 300–foot zone would ban "[g]eneral marching through residential neighborhoods, or even walking a route in front of an entire block of houses." ... The record before us does not contain sufficient justification for this broad a ban on picketing; it appears that a limitation on the time, duration of picketing, and number of pickets outside a smaller zone could have accomplished the desired result.

IV

Petitioners also challenge the state court's order as being vague and overbroad. They object to the portion of the injunction making it applicable to those acting "in concert" with the named parties. But petitioners themselves are named parties in the order, and they therefore lack standing to challenge a portion of the order applying to persons who are not parties. Nor is that phrase subject, at the behest of petitioners, to a challenge for "overbreadth"; the phrase itself does not prohibit any conduct, but is simply directed at unnamed parties who might later be found to be acting "in concert" with the named parties....

. . .

V

In sum, we uphold the noise restrictions and the 36–foot buffer zone around the clinic entrances and driveway because they burden no more speech than necessary to eliminate the unlawful conduct targeted by the state court's injunction. We strike down as unconstitutional the 36–foot buffer zone as applied to the private property to the north and west of the clinic, the "images observable" provision, the 300–foot no-approach zone around the clinic, and the 300–foot buffer zone around the residences, because these provisions sweep more broadly than necessary to accomplish the permissible goals of the injunction. Accordingly, the judgment of the Florida Supreme Court is

Affirmed in part, and reversed in part.*

Justice Stevens, concurring in part and dissenting in part.

... I ... join Parts II and IV of the Court's opinion ... I part company with the Court, however, on its ... enunciation of the applicable standard of review.

I

I agree with the Court that a different standard governs First Amendment challenges to generally applicable legislation than the standard that measures such challenges to judicial remedies for proven wrongdoing. .... Unlike the Court, however, I believe that injunctive relief should be judged by a more lenient standard than legislation. As the Court notes, legislation is imposed on an entire community, regardless of individual culpability. By contrast, injunctions apply solely to an individual or a limited group of individuals who, by engaging in illegal conduct, have been judicially deprived of some liberty—the normal consequence of illegal activity. Given this distinction, a statute prohibiting demonstrations within 36 feet of an abortion clinic would probably violate the First Amendment, but an injunction directed at a limited group of persons who have engaged in unlawful conduct in a similar zone might well be constitutional.

The standard governing injunctions has two obvious dimensions. On the one hand, the injunction should be no more burdensome than necessary to provide complete relief, ... In a First Amendment context, as in any other, the propriety of the remedy depends almost entirely on the character of the violation and the likelihood of its recurrence. For this reason, standards fashioned to determine the constitutionality of statutes should not be used to evaluate injunctions.

---

* A brief concurring opinion by Justice Souter, who also joined the Court's opinion, is omitted.

On the other hand, even when an injunction impinges on constitutional rights, more than "a simple proscription against the precise conduct previously pursued" may be required ... [R]epeated violations may justify sanctions that might be invalid if applied to a first offender or if enacted by the legislature....

In this case, the trial judge heard three days of testimony and found that petitioners not only had engaged in tortious conduct, but also had repeatedly violated an earlier injunction. The injunction is thus twice removed from a legislative proscription applicable to the general public and should be judged by a standard that gives appropriate deference to the judge's unique familiarity with the facts.

II

The second question presented by the certiorari petition asks whether the "consent requirement before speech is permitted" within a 300-foot buffer zone around the clinic unconstitutionally infringes on free speech.... [T]he Court seems to suggest that, even in a more narrowly defined zone, such a consent requirement is constitutionally impermissible....

That paragraph does not purport to prohibit speech; it prohibits a species of conduct. Specifically, it prohibits petitioners "from physically approaching any person seeking the services of the Clinic unless such person indicates a desire to communicate by approaching or by inquiring" of petitioners. The meaning of the term "physically approaching" is explained by the detailed prohibition that applies when the patient refuses to converse with, or accept delivery of literature from, petitioners. Absent such consent, the petitioners "shall not accompany such person, encircle, surround, harass, threaten or physically or verbally abuse those individuals who choose not to communicate with them." As long as petitioners do not physically approach patients in this manner, they remain free not only to communicate with the public but also to offer verbal or written advice on an individual basis to the clinic's patients through their "sidewalk counseling."

Petitioners' "counseling" of the clinic's patients is a form of expression analogous to labor picketing. It is a mixture of conduct and communication.... Just as it protects picketing, the First Amendment protects the speaker's right to offer "sidewalk counseling" to all passersby. That protection, however, does not encompass attempts to abuse an unreceptive or captive audience, at least under the circumstances of this case....

The "physically approaching" prohibition entered by the trial court is no broader than the protection necessary to provide relief for the violations it found. The trial judge entered this portion of the injunction only after concluding that the injunction was necessary to protect the clinic's patients and staff from "uninvited contacts, shadowing and stalking" by petitioners. The protection is especially appropriate for the clinic patients given that the trial judge found that petitioners' prior conduct caused higher levels of "anxiety and hypertension" in the patients ...

... I thus conclude that, under the circumstances of this case, the prohibition against "physically approaching" in the 300–foot zone around the clinic withstands petitioners' First Amendment challenge. I therefore dissent from Part III–D.

III

. . .

IV

For the reasons stated, I concur in Parts I, II, III–E, and IV of the Court's opinion, and respectfully dissent from the remaining portions.

Justice Scalia, with whom Justice Kennedy and Justice Thomas join, concurring in the judgment in part and dissenting in part.

The judgment in today's case has an appearance of moderation and Solomonic wisdom, upholding as it does some portions of the injunction while disallowing others. That appearance is deceptive. The entire injunction in this case departs so far from the established course of our jurisprudence that in any other context it would have been regarded as a candidate for summary reversal.

But the context here is abortion.... Today's decision ... makes it painfully clear that no legal rule or doctrine is safe from ad hoc nullification by this Court when an occasion for its application arises in a case involving state regulation of abortion.... Today the ad hoc nullification machine claims its latest, greatest, and most surprising victim: the First Amendment.

Because I believe that the judicial creation of a 36–foot zone in which only a particular group, which had broken no law, cannot exercise its rights of speech, assembly, and association, and the judicial enactment of a noise prohibition, applicable to that group and that group alone, are profoundly at odds with our First Amendment precedents and traditions, I dissent.

I

. . .

The videotape and the rest of the record, including the trial court's findings, show that a great many forms of expression and conduct occurred in the vicinity of the clinic. These include singing, chanting, praying, shouting, the playing of music both from the clinic and from handheld boom boxes, speeches, peaceful picketing, communication of familiar political messages, handbilling, persuasive speech directed at opposing groups on the issue of abortion, efforts to persuade individuals not to have abortions, personal testimony, interviews with the press, and media efforts to report on the protest. What the videotape, the rest of the record, and the trial court's findings do not contain is any suggestion of violence near the clinic, nor do they establish any attempt to prevent entry or exit.

II

A

. . .

... The Court begins, in Part II of the opinion, by considering petitioners' contention that, since the restriction is content based, strict scrutiny should govern. It rejects the premise, and hence rejects the conclusion. It then proceeds, in Part III, to examination of respondents' contention that plain old intermediate scrutiny should apply. It says no to that, too, because of the distinctive characteristics of injunctions that it discusses, and hence decides to supplement intermediate scrutiny with intermediate-intermediate scrutiny. But this neatly staged progression overlooks an obvious option. The real question in this case is not whether intermediate scrutiny, which the Court assumes to be some kind of default standard, should be supplemented because of the distinctive characteristics of injunctions; but rather whether those distinctive characteristics are not, for reasons of both policy and precedent, fully as good a reason as "content-basis" for demanding strict scrutiny....

... [A] restriction upon speech imposed by injunction (whether nominally content based or nominally content neutral) is at least as deserving of strict scrutiny as a statutory, content-based restriction.

That is so for several reasons: The danger of content-based statutory restrictions upon speech is that they may be designed and used precisely to suppress the ideas in question rather than to achieve any other proper governmental aim. But that same danger exists with injunctions. Although a speech-restricting injunction may not attack content as content (in the present case, as I shall discuss, even that is not true), it lends itself just as readily to the targeted suppression of particular ideas. When a judge, on the motion of an employer, enjoins picketing at the site of a labor dispute, he enjoins (and he knows he is enjoining) the expression of pro-union views. Such targeting of one or the other side of an ideological dispute cannot readily be achieved in speech-restricting general legislation except by making content the basis of the restriction; it is achieved in speech-restricting injunctions almost invariably. The proceedings before us here illustrate well enough what I mean. The injunction was sought against a single-issue advocacy group by persons and organizations with a business or social interest in suppressing that group's point of view.

The second reason speech-restricting injunctions are at least as deserving of strict scrutiny is obvious enough: they are the product of individual judges rather than of legislatures—and often of judges who have been chagrined by prior disobedience of their orders. The right to free speech should not lightly be placed within the control of a single man or woman. And the third reason is that the injunction is a much more powerful weapon than a statute, and so should be subjected to greater safeguards. Normally, when injunctions are enforced through contempt proceedings, only the defense of factual innocence is available.... Thus, persons subject to a speech-restricting injunction who have not the money or not the time to lodge an immediate appeal face a Hobson's choice: they must remain silent, since if they speak their First

Amendment rights are no defense in subsequent contempt proceedings. This is good reason to require the strictest standard for issuance of such orders.

. . . [T]he Court errs in thinking that the vice of content-based statutes is that they necessarily have the invidious purpose of suppressing particular ideas. . . .   The vice of content-based legislation—what renders it deserving of the high standard of strict scrutiny—is not that it is always used for invidious, thought-control purposes, but that it lends itself to use for those purposes.   And, because of the unavoidable "targeting" discussed above, precisely the same is true of the speech-restricting injunction.

Finally, though I believe speech-restricting injunctions are dangerous enough to warrant strict scrutiny even when they are not technically content based, I think the injunction in the present case was content based (indeed, viewpoint based) to boot.   The Court claims that it was directed, not at those who spoke certain things (anti-abortion sentiments), but at those who did certain things (violated the earlier injunction).   If that were true, then the injunction's residual coverage of "all persons acting in concert or participation with [the named individuals and organizations], or on their behalf" would not include those who merely entertained the same beliefs and wished to express the same views as the named defendants.   But the construction given to the injunction by the issuing judge, which is entitled to great weight . . . is to the contrary . . .

. . .

. . . [T]he revised injunction here is tailored to restrain persons distinguished, not by proscribable conduct, but by proscribable views.

. . .

III

. . .

B

I turn now to the Court's performance in the present case.   I am content to evaluate it under the lax (intermediate-intermediate scrutiny) standard that the Court has adopted, because even by that distorted light it is inadequate.

. . .

According to the Court, the state court imposed the later injunction's "restrictions on petitioner[s'] . . . anti-abortion message because they repeatedly violated the court's original order."   Surprisingly, the Court accepts this reason as valid, without asking whether the court's findings of fact support it—whether, that is, the acts of which the petitioners stood convicted were violations of the original injunction.

The Court simply takes this on faith—even though violation of the original injunction is an essential part of the reasoning whereby it approves portions of the amended injunction, even though petitioners denied any violation of the original injunction, even though the utter lack of proper basis for the other challenged portions of the injunction hardly inspires confidence that the lower courts knew what they were doing, and even though close examination of the factual basis for essential conclusions is the usual practice in First Amendment cases . . .

. . . .

If the original injunction is read as it must be, there is nothing in the trial court's findings to suggest that it was violated. . . .   There was no sitting down, no linking of arms, no packing en masse in the driveway; the most that can be alleged (and the trial court did not even make this a finding) is that on one occasion protestors "took their time to get out of the way."   If that is enough to support this one-man proscription of free speech, the First Amendment is in grave peril.

. . . [N]either the Florida courts *nor this Court* makes the slightest attempt to link [the no-noise-within-earshot-of-patients provision] to prior violations of law. . . .   Part II–B simply reasons that hospital patients should not have to be bothered with noise, from political protests or anything else (which is certainly true), and that therefore the noise restrictions could be imposed *by injunction* (which is certainly false).   Since such a law is reasonable, in other words, it can be enacted by a single man to bind only a single class of social protesters.   The pro-abortion demonstrators who were often making (if respondents' video-tape is accurate) more noise than the petitioners, can continue to shout their chants at their opponents exiled across the street to their hearts' content. . . .

Perhaps there is a local ordinance in Melbourne, Florida, prohibiting loud noise in the vicinity of hospitals and abortion clinics.   Or perhaps even a Florida common-law prohibition applies, rendering such noise-making tortious.   But the record in this case shows (and, alas, the Court's opinion today demands) neither indication of the existence of any such law nor a finding that it had been violated.   The fact that such a law would be reasonable is enough, according to the Court, to justify a single judge in imposing it upon these protesters alone.   The First Amendment . . . reels in disbelief.

. . . .

To sum up: The interests assertedly protected by the supplementary injunction did not include any interest whose impairment was a violation of Florida law or of a Florida-court injunction.   Unless the Court intends today to overturn long-settled jurisprudence, that means that the interests cannot possibly qualify as "significant interests" under the Court's new standard.

C

Finally, I turn to the Court's application of the second part of its test: whether the provisions of the injunction "burden no more speech than necessary" to serve the significant interest protected.

... With regard to the 36–foot speech-free zone, ... the test which the Court sets for itself has not been met.

Assuming a "significant state interest" of the sort cognizable for injunction purposes (i.e., one protected by a law that has been or is threatened to be violated) in both (1) keeping pedestrians off the paved portion of Dixie Way, and (2) enabling cars to cross the public sidewalk at the clinic's driveways without having to slow down or come to even a "momentary" stop, there are surely a number of ways to protect those interests short of banishing the entire protest demonstration from the 36–foot zone....

But I need not engage in such precise analysis, since the Court itself admits that the requirement is not to be taken seriously. "The need for a complete buffer zone," it says, "may be debatable, but some deference must be given to the state court's familiarity with the facts and the background of the dispute between the parties even under our heightened review." Ibid. (emphasis added). In application, in other words, the "burden no more speech than is necessary" test has become an "arguably burden no more speech than is necessary" test. This renders the Court's intermediate-intermediate scrutiny not only no more stringent than plain old intermediate scrutiny, but considerably less stringent.

. . .

What we have decided seems to be, and will be reported by the media as, an abortion case. But it will go down in the lawbooks, it will be cited, as a free-speech injunction case—and the damage its novel principles produce will be considerable. The proposition that injunctions against speech are subject to a standard indistinguishable from (unless perhaps more lenient in its application than) the "intermediate scrutiny" standard we have used for "time, place, and manner" legislative restrictions; the notion that injunctions against speech need not be closely tied to any violation of law, but may simply implement sound social policy; and the practice of accepting trial-court conclusions permitting injunctions without considering whether those conclusions are supported by any findings of fact—these latest by-products of our abortion jurisprudence ought to give all friends of liberty great concern.

For these reasons, I dissent from that portion of the judgment upholding parts of the injunction.

CAPITOL SQUARE REVIEW AND ADVISORY BOARD v. PINETTE

___ U.S. ___, 115 S.Ct. 2440, 132 L.Ed.2d 650 (1995).

[The report in this case appears infra, page 351.]

SECTION 3. SPEECH ON PRIVATE PREMISES

Page 1384. Add at beginning of section:

CITY OF LADUE v. GILLEO
___ U.S. ___, 114 S.Ct. 2038, 129 L.Ed.2d 36 (1994).

Justice Stevens delivered the opinion of the Court.

An ordinance of the City of Ladue prohibits homeowners from displaying any signs on their property except "residence identification" signs, "for sale" signs, and signs warning of safety hazards. The ordinance permits commercial establishments, churches, and nonprofit organizations to erect certain signs that are not allowed at residences. The question presented is whether the ordinance violates a Ladue resident's right to free speech.

I

Respondent Margaret P. Gilleo owns one of the 57 single-family homes in the Willow Hill subdivision of Ladue. On December 8, 1990, she placed on her front lawn a 24 by 36 inch sign printed with the words "Say No to War in the Persian Gulf, Call Congress Now." After that sign disappeared, Gilleo put up another but it was knocked to the ground. When Gilleo reported these incidents to the police, they advised her that such signs were prohibited in Ladue. The City Council denied her petition for a variance. Gilleo then filed this action under 42 U.S.C. § 1983 against the City, the Mayor, and members of the City Council, alleging that Ladue's sign ordinance violated her First Amendment right of free speech.

The District Court issued a preliminary injunction against enforcement of the ordinance. Gilleo then placed an 8.5 by 11 inch sign in the second story window of her home stating, "For Peace in the Gulf." The Ladue City Council responded to the injunction by repealing its ordinance and enacting a replacement. Like its predecessor, the new ordinance contains a general prohibition of "signs" and defines that term broadly. The ordinance prohibits all signs except those that fall within one of ten exemptions. Thus, "residential identification signs" no larger than one square foot are allowed, as are signs advertising "that the property is for sale, lease or exchange" and identifying the owner or agent. Also exempted are signs "for churches, religious institutions, and schools," "[c]ommercial signs in commercially or industrial zoned districts," and on-site signs advertising "gasoline filling stations." Unlike its predecessor, the new ordinance contains a lengthy "Declaration of Findings, Policies, Interests, and Purposes," part of which recites that the "proliferation of an unlimited number of signs in private, residential, commercial, industrial, and public areas of the City of Ladue would create ugliness, visual blight and clutter, tarnish the natural beauty of the landscape as well as the residential and commercial architecture, impair property values, substantially impinge upon the privacy and special ambience of the community, and may cause safety and traffic hazards to motorists, pedestrians, and children[.]"

Gilleo amended her complaint to challenge the new ordinance, which explicitly prohibits window signs like hers. The District Court held the ordinance unconstitutional, and the Court of Appeals affirmed....

We ... affirm.

II

While signs are a form of expression protected by the Free Speech Clause, they pose distinctive problems that are subject to municipalities' police powers. Unlike oral speech, signs take up space and may obstruct views, distract motorists, displace alternative uses for land, and pose other problems that legitimately call for regulation. It is common ground that governments may regulate the physical characteristics of signs—just as they can, within reasonable bounds and absent censorial purpose, regulate audible expression in its capacity as noise....

In Linmark Associates, Inc. v. Willingboro, 431 U.S. 85 (1977), we addressed an ordinance that sought to maintain stable, integrated neighborhoods by prohibiting homeowners from placing "For Sale" or "Sold" signs on their property. Although we recognized the importance of Willingboro's objective, we held that the First Amendment prevented the township from "achieving its goal by restricting the free flow of truthful information." Id., at 95. In some respects Linmark is the mirror image of this case. For instead of prohibiting "For Sale" signs without banning any other signs, Ladue has exempted such signs from an otherwise virtually complete ban. Moreover, whereas in Linmark we noted that the ordinance was not concerned with the promotion of aesthetic values unrelated to the content of the prohibited speech, id., at 93–94, here Ladue relies squarely on that content-neutral justification for its ordinance.

. . .

[There are] two analytically distinct grounds for challenging the constitutionality of a municipal ordinance regulating the display of signs. One is that the measure in effect restricts too little speech because its exemptions discriminate on the basis of the signs' messages.... Alternatively, such provisions are subject to attack on the ground that they simply prohibit too much protected speech.... The City of Ladue contends, first, that the Court of Appeals' reliance on the former rationale was misplaced because the City's regulatory purposes are content-neutral, and, second, that those purposes justify the comprehensiveness of the sign prohibition. A comment on the former contention will help explain why we ultimately base our decision on a rejection of the latter.

III

While surprising at first glance, the notion that a regulation of speech may be impermissibly underinclusive is firmly grounded in basic

First Amendment principles. Thus, an exemption from an otherwise permissible regulation of speech may represent a governmental "attempt to give one side of a debatable public question an advantage in expressing its views to the people." First Nat. Bank of Boston v. Bellotti, 435 U.S. 765, 785–786 (1978). Alternatively, through the combined operation of a general speech restriction and its exemptions, the government might seek to select the "permissible subjects for public debate" and thereby to "control ... the search for political truth." Consolidated Edison Co. of N.Y. v. Public Service Comm'n of N.Y., 447 U.S. 530, 538 (1980).

The City argues that its sign ordinance implicates neither of these concerns, and that the Court of Appeals therefore erred in demanding a "compelling" justification for the exemptions. The mix of prohibitions and exemptions in the ordinance, Ladue maintains, reflects legitimate differences among the side effects of various kinds of signs. These differences are only adventitiously connected with content, and supply a sufficient justification, unrelated to the City's approval or disapproval of specific messages, for carving out the specified categories from the general ban. Thus, according to the Declaration of Findings, Policies, Interests, and Purposes supporting the ordinance, the permitted signs, unlike the prohibited signs, are unlikely to contribute to the dangers of "unlimited proliferation" associated with categories of signs that are not inherently limited in number. Because only a few residents will need to display "for sale" or "for rent" signs at any given time, permitting one such sign per marketed house does not threaten visual clutter. Because the City has only a few businesses, churches, and schools, the same rationale explains the exemption for on-site commercial and organizational signs. Moreover, some of the exempted categories (e.g., danger signs) respond to unique public needs to permit certain kinds of speech. Even if we assume the validity of these arguments, the exemptions in Ladue's ordinance nevertheless shed light on the separate question of whether the ordinance prohibits too much speech.

Exemptions from an otherwise legitimate regulation of a medium of speech may be noteworthy for a reason quite apart from the risks of viewpoint and content discrimination: they may diminish the credibility of the government's rationale for restricting speech in the first place. In this case, at the very least, the exemptions from Ladue's ordinance demonstrate that Ladue has concluded that the interest in allowing certain messages to be conveyed by means of residential signs outweighs the City's aesthetic interest in eliminating outdoor signs. Ladue has not imposed a flat ban on signs because it has determined that at least some of them are too vital to be banned.

Under the Court of Appeals' content discrimination rationale, the City might theoretically remove the defects in its ordinance by simply repealing all of the exemptions. If, however, the ordinance is also vulnerable because it prohibits too much speech, that solution would not save it. Moreover, if the prohibitions in Ladue's ordinance are impermissible, resting our decision on its exemptions would afford scant relief for respondent Gilleo. She is primarily concerned not with the scope of the exemptions available in other locations, such as commercial areas and on church property. She asserts a constitutional right to display an antiwar sign at her own home. Therefore, we first ask whether Ladue may properly prohibit Gilleo from displaying her sign, and then, only if necessary, consider the separate question whether it was improper for the City simultaneously to permit certain other signs. In examining the propriety of Ladue's near-total prohibition of residential signs, we will assume, arguendo, the validity of the City's submission that the various exemptions are free of impermissible content or viewpoint discrimination.

IV

In *Linmark* we held that the City's interest in maintaining a stable, racially integrated neighborhood was not sufficient to support a prohibition of residential "For Sale" signs. We recognized that even such a narrow sign prohibition would have a deleterious effect on residents' ability to convey important information because alternatives were "far from satisfactory." 431 U.S., at 93. Ladue's sign ordinance is supported principally by the City's interest in minimizing the visual clutter associated with signs, an interest that is concededly valid but certainly no more compelling than the interests at stake in *Linmark*. Moreover, whereas the ordinance in *Linmark* applied only to a form of commercial speech, Ladue's ordinance covers even such absolutely pivotal speech as a sign protesting an imminent governmental decision to go to war.

The impact on free communication of Ladue's broad sign prohibition, moreover, is manifestly greater than in *Linmark*. Gilleo and other residents of Ladue are forbidden to display virtually any "sign" on their property. The ordinance defines that term sweepingly....

... Ladue has almost completely foreclosed a venerable means of communication that is both unique and important. It has totally foreclosed that medium to political, religious, or personal messages. Signs that react to a local happening or express a view on a controversial issue both reflect and animate change in the life of a community. Often placed on lawns or in windows, residential signs play an important part in political campaigns, during which they are displayed to signal the resident's support for particular candidates, parties, or causes. They may not afford the same opportunities for conveying complex ideas as do other media, but residential signs have long been an important and distinct medium of expression.

Our prior decisions have voiced particular concern with laws that foreclose an entire medium of expression. Thus, we have held invalid ordinances that completely banned the distribution of pamphlets within the municipality, Lovell v. Griffin, 303 U.S. 444, 451–452 (1938); handbills on the public streets, Jamison v. Texas, 318 U.S. 413, 416 (1943); the door-to-door distribution of literature, Martin v. Struthers, 319 U.S. 141, 145–149 (1943); Schneider v. State, 308 U.S. 147, 164–165 (1939), and live entertainment, Schad v. Mount Ephraim, 452 U.S. 61, 75–76 (1981).... Although prohibitions foreclosing entire media may be completely free of content or viewpoint discrimination, the danger they pose to the freedom of speech is readily apparent—by eliminating a common means of speaking, such measures can suppress too much speech.

Ladue contends, however, that its ordinance is a mere regulation of the "time, place, or manner" of speech because residents remain free to convey their desired messages by other means, such as hand-held signs, "letters, handbills, flyers, telephone calls, newspaper advertisements, bumper stickers, speeches, and neighborhood or community meetings." However, even regulations that do not foreclose an entire medium of expression, but merely shift the time, place, or manner of its use, must "leave open ample alternative channels for communication." Clark v. Community for Creative Non–Violence, 468 U.S. 288, 293 (1984). In this case, we are not persuaded that adequate substitutes exist for the important medium of speech that Ladue has closed off.

Displaying a sign from one's own residence often carries a message quite distinct from placing the same sign someplace else, or conveying the same text or picture by other means. Precisely because of their location, such signs provide information about the identity of the "speaker." As an early and eminent student of rhetoric observed, the identity of the speaker is an important component of many attempts to persuade. A sign advocating "Peace in the Gulf" in the front lawn of a retired general or decorated war veteran may provoke a different reaction than the same sign in a 10–year–old child's bedroom window or the same message on a bumper sticker of a passing automobile. An espousal of socialism may carry different implications when displayed on the grounds of a stately mansion than when pasted on a factory wall or an ambulatory sandwich board.

Residential signs are an unusually cheap and convenient form of communication. Especially for persons of modest means or limited mobility, a yard or window sign may have no practical substitute. Even for the affluent, the added costs in money or time of taking out a newspaper advertisement, handing out leaflets on the street, or standing in front of one's house with a hand-held sign may make the difference between participating and not participating in some public debate. Furthermore, a person who puts up a sign at her residence often intends to reach neighbors, an audience that could not be reached nearly as well by other means.

A special respect for individual liberty in the home has long been part of our culture and our law ...; that principle has special resonance when the government seeks to constrain a person's ability to speak there.... Most Americans would be understandably dismayed, given that tradition, to learn that it was illegal to display from their window an 8 by 11 inch sign expressing their political views. Whereas the government's need to mediate among various competing uses, including expressive ones, for public streets and facilities is constant and unavoidable, ... its need to regulate temperate speech from the home is surely much less pressing....

Our decision that Ladue's ban on almost all residential signs violates the First Amendment by no means leaves the City powerless to address the ills that may be associated with residential signs. It bears mentioning that individual residents themselves have strong incentives to keep their own property values up and to prevent "visual clutter" in their own yards and neighborhoods—incentives markedly different from those of persons who erect signs on others' land, in others' neighborhoods, or on public property. Residents' self-interest diminishes the danger of the "unlimited" proliferation of residential signs that concerns the City of Ladue. We are confident that more temperate measures could in large part satisfy Ladue's stated regulatory needs without harm to the First Amendment rights of its citizens. As currently framed, however, the ordinance abridges those rights.

Accordingly, the judgment of the Court of Appeals is Affirmed.

Justice O'Connor, concurring.

It is unusual for us, when faced with a regulation that on its face draws content distinctions, to "assume, arguendo, the validity of the City's submission that the various exemptions are free of impermissible content or viewpoint discrimination." With rare exceptions, content discrimination in regulations of the speech of private citizens on private property or in a traditional public forum is presumptively impermissible, and this presumption is a very strong one.... The normal inquiry that our doctrine dictates is, first, to determine whether a regulation is content-based or content-neutral, and then, based on the answer to that question, to apply the proper level of scrutiny....

Over the years, some cogent criticisms have been leveled at our approach. See, e.g., ... Farber, Content Regulation and the First Amendment: A Revisionist View, 68 Geo.L.J. 727 (1980); Stephan, The First Amendment and Content Discrimination, 68 Va.L.Rev. 203 (1982). And it is quite true that regulations are occasionally struck down because of their content-based nature, even though common sense may suggest that they are entirely reasonable. The content distinctions present in this ordinance may, to some, be a good example of this.

But though our rule has flaws, it has substantial merit as well. It is a rule, in an area where fairly precise rules are better than more discretionary and more subjective balancing tests.... On a theoretical level, it reflects important insights into the meaning of the free speech principle—for instance, that content-based speech restrictions are especially likely to be improper attempts to value some forms of speech over others, or are particularly susceptible to being used by the government to distort public debate.... On a practical level, it has in application generally led to seemingly sensible results. And, perhaps most importantly, no better alternative has yet come to light.

I would have preferred to apply our normal analytical structure in this case, which may well have required us to examine this law with the scrutiny appropriate to content-based regulations. Perhaps this would have forced us to confront some of the difficulties with the existing doctrine; perhaps it would have shown weaknesses in the rule, and led us to modify it to take into account the special factors this case presents. But such reexamination is part of the process by which our rules evolve and improve.

Nonetheless, I join the Court's opinion, because I agree with its conclusion in Part IV that even if the restriction were content-neutral, it would still be invalid, and because I do not think Part III casts any doubt on the propriety of our normal content discrimination inquiry.

———

SECTION 5. GOVERNMENT SUBSIDIES TO SPEECH

———

Page 1428. Add at end of chapter:

ROSENBERGER v. RECTOR and VISITORS OF THE UNIVERSITY OF VIRGINIA

___ U.S. ___, 115 S.Ct. 2510, 132 L.Ed.2d 700 (1995).

[The report in this case appears infra, page 391.]

Chapter 15

PROTECTION OF PENUMBRAL FIRST AMENDMENT RIGHTS

SECTION 3. FREEDOM OF ASSOCIATION

E. COMPULSORY SPEECH ACCESS FOR THIRD PARTIES

Page 1478. Add at end of Section:

HURLEY v. IRISH–AMERICAN GAY, LESBIAN AND BISEXUAL GROUP OF BOSTON

___ U.S. ___, 115 S.Ct. 2338, 132 L.Ed.2d 487 (1995).

Justice Souter delivered the opinion of the Court.

The issue in this case is whether Massachusetts may require private citizens who organize a parade to include among the marchers a group imparting a message the organizers do not wish to convey. We hold that such a mandate violates the First Amendment.

I

March 17 is set aside for two celebrations in South Boston. As early as 1737, some people in Boston observed the feast of the apostle to Ireland, and since 1776 the day has marked the evacuation of royal troops and Loyalists from the city, prompted by the guns captured at Ticonderoga and set up on Dorchester Heights under General Washington's command. . . . Although the General Court of Massachusetts did not officially designate March 17 as Evacuation Day until 1938, . . . the City Council of Boston had previously sponsored public celebrations of Evacuation Day, including notable commemorations on the centennial in 1876, and on the 125th anniversary in 1901, with its parade, salute, concert, and fireworks display. . . .

The tradition of formal sponsorship by the city came to an end in 1947, however, when Mayor James Michael Curley himself granted authority to organize and conduct the St. Patrick's Day–Evacuation Day Parade to the petitioner South Boston Allied War Veterans Council, an unincorporated association of individuals elected from various South Boston veterans groups. Every year since that time, the Council has applied for and received a permit for the parade, which at times has included as many as 20,000 marchers and drawn up to 1 million watchers. No other applicant has ever applied for that permit.

Through 1992, the city allowed the Council to use the city's official seal, and provided printing services as well as direct funding.

1992 was the year that a number of gay, lesbian, and bisexual descendants of the Irish immigrants joined together with other supporters to form the respondent organization, GLIB, to march in the parade as a way to express pride in their Irish heritage as openly gay, lesbian, and bisexual individuals, to demonstrate that there are such men and women among those so descended, and to express their solidarity with like individuals who sought to march in New York's St. Patrick's Day Parade. Although the Council denied GLIB's application to take part in the 1992 parade, GLIB obtained a state-court order to include its contingent, which marched "uneventfully" among that year's 10,000 participants and 750,000 spectators.

In 1993, after the Council had again refused to admit GLIB to the upcoming parade, the organization and some of its members filed this suit against the Council, the individual petitioner John J. "Wacko" Hurley, and the City of Boston, alleging violations of the State and Federal Constitutions and of the state public accommodations law, which prohibits "any distinction, discrimination or restriction on account of . . . sexual orientation . . . relative to the admission of any person to, or treatment in any place of public accommodation, resort or amusement." . . .

. . .

. . . [The state trial court] ruled that "GLIB is entitled to participate in the Parade on the same terms and conditions as other participants."

The Supreme Judicial Court of Massachusetts affirmed, seeing nothing clearly erroneous in the trial judge's findings that GLIB was excluded from the parade based on the sexual orientation of its members, that it was impossible to detect an expressive purpose in the parade, that there was no state action, and that the parade was a public accommodation . . .

. . .

We granted certiorari to determine whether the requirement to admit a parade contingent expressing a message not of the private organizers' own choosing violates the First Amendment. We hold that it does and reverse.

II

Given the scope of the issues as originally joined in this case, it is worth noting some that have fallen aside in the course of the litigation, before reaching us. Although the Council presents us with a First Amendment claim, respondents do not. Neither do they press a claim that the Council's action has denied them equal protection of the laws in violation of the Fourteenth Amendment. . . . In this Court, then, their claim for inclusion in the parade rests solely on the Massachusetts public accommodations law.

There is no corresponding concession from the other side, however, and certainly not to the state courts' characterization of the parade as lacking the element of expression for purposes of the First Amendment. Accordingly, our review of petitioners' claim that their activity is indeed in the nature of protected speech carries with it a constitutional duty to conduct an independent examination of the record as a whole, without deference to the trial court. See Bose Corp. v. Consumers Union of United States, Inc., 466 U.S. 485, 499 (1984)....

III

A

If there were no reason for a group of people to march from here to there except to reach a destination, they could make the trip without expressing any message beyond the fact of the march itself. Some people might call such a procession a parade, but it would not be much of one. Real "[p]arades are public dramas of social relations, and in them performers define who can be a social actor and what subjects and ideas are available for communication and consideration." S. Davis, Parades and Power: Street Theatre in Nineteenth–Century Philadelphia 6 (1986). Hence, we use the word "parade" to indicate marchers who are making some sort of collective point, not just to each other but to bystanders along the way. Indeed a parade's dependence on watchers is so extreme that nowadays, as with Bishop Berkeley's celebrated tree, "if a parade or demonstration receives no media coverage, it may as well not have happened." Id., at 171. Parades are thus a form of expression, not just motion, and the inherent expressiveness of marching to make a point explains our cases involving protest marches. In Gregory v. Chicago, 394 U.S. 111, 112 (1969), for example, petitioners had taken part in a procession to express their grievances to the city government, and we held that such a "march, if peaceful and orderly, falls well within the sphere of conduct protected by the First Amendment." Similarly, in Edwards v. South Carolina, 372 U.S. 229, 235 (1963), where petitioners had joined in a march of protest and pride, carrying placards and singing The Star Spangled Banner, we held that the activities "reflect an exercise of these basic constitutional rights in their most pristine and classic form." ...

The protected expression that inheres in a parade is not limited to its banners and songs, however, for the Constitution looks beyond written or spoken words as mediums of expression. Noting that "[s]ymbolism is a primitive but effective way of communicating ideas," West Virginia Bd. of Ed. v. Barnette, 319 U.S. 624, 632 (1943), our cases have recognized that the First Amendment shields such acts as saluting a flag (and refusing to do so), id., at 632, 642, wearing an arm band to protest a war, Tinker v. Des Moines Independent Community School Dist., 393 U.S. 503, 505–506 (1969), displaying a red flag, Stromberg v. California, 283 U.S. 359, 369 (1931), and even "[m]arching, walking or parading" in uniforms displaying the swastika, National Socialist Party of America v. Skokie, 432 U.S. 43 (1977). As some of these examples show, a narrow, succinctly articulable message is not a condition of constitutional protection ...

Not many marches, then, are beyond the realm of expressive parades, and the South Boston celebration is not one of them. . . .   To be sure, we agree with the state courts that in spite of excluding some applicants, the Council is rather lenient in admitting participants.   But a private speaker does not forfeit constitutional protection simply by combining multifarious voices, or by failing to edit their themes to isolate an exact message as the exclusive subject matter of the speech. Nor, under our precedent, does First Amendment protection require a speaker to generate, as an original matter, each item featured in the communication.   Cable operators, for example, are engaged in protected speech activities even when they only select programming originally produced by others.   Turner Broadcasting System, Inc. v. FCC, 512 U.S. ___, ___ (1994). . . .

Respondents' participation as a unit in the parade was equally expressive. . . .   GLIB understandably seeks to communicate its ideas as part of the existing parade, rather than staging one of its own.

. . . .

C

In the case before us, . . . the Massachusetts [public accommodations] law has been applied in a peculiar way.   Its enforcement does not address any dispute about the participation of openly gay, lesbian, or bisexual individuals in various units admitted to the parade.   The petitioners disclaim any intent to exclude homosexuals as such, and no individual member of GLIB claims to have been excluded from parading as a member of any group that the Council has approved to march. Instead, the disagreement goes to the admission of GLIB as its own parade unit carrying its own banner.   Since every participating unit affects the message conveyed by the private organizers, the state courts' application of the statute produced an order essentially requiring petitioners to alter the expressive content of their parade.   Although the state courts spoke of the parade as a place of public accommodation, once the expressive character of both the parade and the marching GLIB contingent is understood, it becomes apparent that the state courts' application of the statute had the effect of declaring the sponsors' speech itself to be the public accommodation.   Under this approach any contingent of protected individuals with a message would have the right to participate in petitioners' speech, so that the communication produced by the private organizers would be shaped by all those protected by the law who wished to join in with some expressive demonstration of their own.   But this use of the State's power violates the fundamental rule of protection under the First Amendment, that a speaker has the autonomy to choose the content of his own message.

"Since all speech inherently involves choices of what to say and what to leave unsaid," Pacific Gas & Electric Co. v. Public Utilities Comm'n of Cal., 475 U.S. 1, 11 (1986)(plurality opinion)(emphasis in original), one important manifestation of the principle of free speech is that one who chooses to speak may also decide "what not to say," id., at 16. . . .   [T]he State . . . may not compel affirmance of a belief with which the speaker disagrees, see Barnette, 319 U.S., at 642.   Indeed this general rule, that the speaker has the right to tailor the speech, applies not only to expressions of value, opinion, or endorsement, but equally to statements of fact the speaker would rather avoid, McIntyre v. Ohio Elections Comm'n, 514 U.S. ___, ___ (1995) .... Nor is the rule's benefit restricted to the press, being enjoyed by business corporations generally and by ordinary people engaged in unsophisticated expression as well as by professional publishers. Its point is simply the point of all speech protection, which is to shield just those choices of content that in someone's eyes are misguided, or even hurtful....

Petitioners' claim to the benefit of this principle of autonomy to control one's own speech is as sound as the South Boston parade is expressive. Rather like a composer, the Council selects the expressive units of the parade from potential participants, and though the score may not produce a particularized message, each contingent's expression in the Council's eyes comports with what merits celebration on that day. Even if this view gives the Council credit for a more considered judgment than it actively made, the Council clearly decided to exclude a message it did not like from the communication it chose to make, and that is enough to invoke its right as a private speaker to shape its expression by speaking on one subject while remaining silent on another. The message it disfavored is not difficult to identify. Although GLIB's point (like the Council's) is not wholly articulate, a contingent marching behind the organization's banner would at least bear witness to the fact that some Irish are gay, lesbian, or bisexual, and the presence of the organized marchers would suggest their view that people of their sexual orientations have as much claim to unqualified social acceptance as heterosexuals and indeed as members of parade units organized around other identifying characteristics. The parade's organizers may not believe these facts about Irish sexuality to be so, or they may object to unqualified social acceptance of gays and lesbians or have some other reason for wishing to keep GLIB's message out of the parade. But whatever the reason, it boils down to the choice of a speaker not to propound a particular point of view, and that choice is presumed to lie beyond the government's power to control.

Respondents argue that any tension between this rule and the Massachusetts law falls short of unconstitutionality, citing the most recent of our cases on the general subject of compelled access for expressive purposes, *Turner Broadcasting*, 512 U.S. ___. There we reviewed regulations requiring cable operators to set aside channels for designated broadcast signals, and applied only intermediate scrutiny.... Respondents contend on this authority that admission of GLIB to the parade would not threaten the core principle of speaker's autonomy because the Council, like a cable operator, is merely "a conduit" for the speech of participants in the parade "rather than itself a speaker." But this metaphor is not apt here, because GLIB's participation would likely be perceived as having resulted from the Council's customary determination about a unit admitted to the parade, that its message was worthy of presentation and quite possibly of support as well.... Indeed, in *Pacific Gas & Electric*, we invalidated coerced access to the envelope of a private utility's bill and newsletter because the utility "may be forced either to appear to agree with [the intruding leaflet] or to respond." 475 U.S., at 15 (plurality)(citation omitted). The plurality made the further point that if "the government [were] freely able to compel ... speakers to propound political messages with which they disagree, ... protection [of a speaker's freedom] would be empty, for the government could require speakers to affirm in one breath that which they deny in the next." Id., at 16. Thus, when dissemination of a view contrary to one's own is forced upon a speaker intimately connected with the communication advanced, the speaker's right to autonomy over the message is compromised.

In *Turner Broadcasting*, we found this problem absent in the cable context, because "[g]iven cable's long history of serving as a conduit for broadcast signals, there appears little risk that cable viewers would assume that the broadcast stations carried on a cable system convey ideas or messages endorsed by the cable operator." 512 U.S., at ____. ...

Parades and demonstrations, in contrast, are not understood to be so neutrally presented or selectively viewed. Unlike the programming offered on various channels by a cable network, the parade does not consist of individual, unrelated segments that happen to be transmitted together for individual selection by members of the audience. Although each parade unit generally identifies itself, each is understood to contribute something to a common theme, and accordingly there is no customary practice whereby private sponsors disavow "any identity of viewpoint" between themselves and the selected participants. Practice follows practicability here, for such disclaimers would be quite curious in a moving parade. Cf. PruneYard Shopping Center v. Robins, 447 U.S. 74, 87 (1980)(owner of shopping mall "can expressly disavow any connection with the message by simply posting signs in the area where the speakers or handbillers stand"). Without deciding on the precise significance of the likelihood of misattribution, it nonetheless becomes clear that in the context of an expressive parade, as with a protest march, the parade's overall message is distilled from the individual presentations along the way, and each unit's expression is perceived by spectators as part of the whole.

An additional distinction between *Turner Broadcasting* and this case points to the fundamental weakness of any attempt to justify the state court order's limitation on the Council's autonomy as a speaker. A cable is not only a conduit for speech produced by others and selected by cable operators for transmission, but a franchised channel giving monopolistic opportunity to shut out some speakers. This power gives rise to the government's interest in limiting monopolistic autonomy in order to allow for the survival of broadcasters who might otherwise be silenced and consequently destroyed. The government's interest in *Turner Broadcasting* was not the alteration of speech, but the survival of speakers. In thus identifying an interest going beyond abridgment of speech itself, the defenders of the law at issue in *Turner Broadcasting* addressed the threshold requirement of any review under the Speech Clause, whatever the ultimate level of scrutiny, that a challenged restriction on speech serve a compelling, or at least important, governmental object. ...

In this case, of course, there is no assertion comparable to the *Turner Broadcasting* claim that some speakers will be destroyed in the absence of the challenged law. True, the size and success of petitioners' parade makes it an enviable vehicle for the dissemination of GLIB's views, but that fact, without more, would fall far short of supporting a claim that petitioners enjoy an abiding monopoly of access to spectators. Considering that GLIB presumably would have had a fair shot (under neutral criteria developed by the city) at obtaining a parade permit of its own, respondents have not shown that petitioners enjoy the capacity to "silence the voice of competing speakers," as cable operators do with respect to program providers who wish to reach subscribers, *Turner Broadcasting*, supra, at ___. Nor has any other legitimate interest been identified in support of applying the Massachusetts statute in this way to expressive activity like the parade.

The statute ... is a piece of protective legislation that announces no purpose beyond the object both expressed and apparent in its provisions, which is to prevent any denial of access to (or discriminatory treatment in) public accommodations on proscribed grounds, including sexual orientation. On its face, the object of the law is to ensure by statute for gays and lesbians desiring to make use of public accommodations what the old common law promised to any member of the public wanting a meal at the inn, that accepting the usual terms of service, they will not be turned away merely on the proprietor's exercise of personal preference. When the law is applied to expressive activity in the way it was done here, its apparent object is simply to require speakers to modify the content of their expression to whatever extent beneficiaries of the law choose to alter it with messages of their own. But in the absence of some further, legitimate end, this object is merely to allow exactly what the general rule of speaker's autonomy forbids.

It might, of course, have been argued that a broader objective is apparent: that the ultimate point of forbidding acts of discrimination toward certain classes is to produce a society free of the corresponding biases. Requiring access to a speaker's message would thus be not an end in itself, but a means to produce speakers free of the biases, whose expressive conduct would be at least neutral toward the particular classes, obviating any future need for correction. But if this indeed is the point of applying the state law to expressive conduct, it is a decidedly fatal objective. Having availed itself of the public thoroughfares "for purposes of assembly [and] communicating thoughts between citizens," the Council is engaged in a use of the streets that has "from ancient times, been a part of the privileges, immunities, rights, and liberties of citizens." Hague v. Committee for Industrial Organization, 307 U.S. 496, 515 (1939)(opinion of Roberts, J.). Our tradition of free speech commands that a speaker who takes to the street corner to express his views in this way should be free from interference by the State based on the content of what he says.... The very idea that a noncommercial speech restriction be used to produce thoughts and statements acceptable to some groups or, indeed, all people, grates on the First Amendment, for it amounts to nothing less than a proposal to limit speech in the service of orthodox expression. The Speech Clause has no more certain antithesis.... While the law is free to promote all sorts of conduct in place of harmful behavior, it is not free to interfere with speech for no better reason than promoting an approved message or discouraging a disfavored one, however enlightened either purpose may strike the government.

Far from supporting GLIB, then, *Turner Broadcasting* points to the reasons why the present application of the Massachusetts law can not be sustained. So do the two other principal authorities GLIB has cited. In *PruneYard*, ... to be sure, we sustained a state law requiring the proprietors of shopping malls to allow visitors to solicit signatures on political petitions without a showing that the shopping mall owners would otherwise prevent the beneficiaries of the law from reaching an audience. But we found in that case that the proprietors were running "a business establishment that is open to the public to come and go as they please," that the solicitations would "not likely be identified with those of the owner," and that the proprietors could "expressly disavow any connection with the message by simply posting signs in the area where the speakers or handbillers stand." ... Also, in *Pacific Gas & Electric*, we noted that *PruneYard* did not involve "any concern that access to this area might affect the shopping center owner's exercise of his own right to speak: the owner did not even allege that he objected to the content of the pamphlets...." The principle of speaker's autonomy was simply not threatened in that case.

New York State Club Association is also instructive by the contrast it provides. There, we turned back a facial challenge to a state antidiscrimination statute on the assumption that the expressive associational character of a dining club with over 400 members could be sufficiently attenuated to permit application of the law even to such a private organization, but we also recognized that the State did not prohibit exclusion of those whose views were at odds with positions espoused by the general club memberships.... In other words, although the association provided public benefits to which a State could ensure equal access, it was also engaged in expressive activity; compelled access to the benefit, which was upheld, did not trespass on the organization's message itself. If we were to analyze this case strictly along those lines, GLIB would lose. Assuming the parade to be large enough and a source of benefits (apart from its expression) that would generally justify a mandated access provision, GLIB could nonetheless be refused admission as an expressive contingent with its own message just as readily as a private club could exclude an applicant whose manifest views were at odds with a position taken by the club's existing members.

IV

Our holding today rests not on any particular view about the Council's message but on the Nation's commitment to protect freedom of speech. Disapproval of a private speaker's statement does not legitimize use of the Commonwealth's power to compel the speaker to alter the message by including one more acceptable to others. Accordingly, the judgment of the Supreme Judicial Court is reversed and the case remanded for proceedings not inconsistent with this opinion.

It is so ordered.

———

SECTION 4. APPLICATION OF THE FIRST AMENDMENT TO GOVERNMENT REGULATION OF ELECTIONS

———

A.   CHOOSING AND ELECTING CANDIDATES FOR PUBLIC OFFICE

———

Page 1487.   Add at end of subsection:

U.S. TERM LIMITS, INC. v. THORNTON
__ U.S. __, 115 S.Ct. 1842, 131 L.Ed.2d 881 (1995).

Justice Stevens delivered the opinion of the Court.

The Constitution sets forth qualifications for membership in the Congress of the United States. Article I, § 2, cl. 2, which applies to the House of Representatives, provides:

> "No Person shall be a Representative who shall not have attained to the Age of twenty five Years, and been seven Years a Citizen of the United States, and who shall not, when elected, be an Inhabitant of that State in which he shall be chosen."

Article I, § 3, cl. 3, which applies to the Senate, similarly provides:

> "No Person shall be a Senator who shall not have attained to the Age of thirty Years, and been nine Years a Citizen of the United States, and who shall not, when elected, be an Inhabitant of that State for which he shall be chosen."

Today's cases present a challenge to an amendment to the Arkansas State Constitution that prohibits the name of an otherwise-eligible candidate for Congress from appearing on the general election ballot if that candidate has already served three terms in the House of Representatives or two terms in the Senate. The Arkansas Supreme Court held that the amendment violates the Federal Constitution. We agree with that holding. Such a state-imposed restriction is contrary to the "fundamental principle of our representative democracy," embodied in the Constitution, that "the people should choose whom they please to govern them." Powell v. McCormack, 395 U.S. 486, 547 (1969)(internal quotation marks omitted). Allowing individual States to adopt their own qualifications for congressional service would be inconsistent with the Framers' vision of a uniform National Legislature representing the people of the United States. If the qualifications set forth in the text of the Constitution are to be changed, that text must be amended.

I

At the general election on November 3, 1992, the voters of Arkansas adopted Amendment 73 to their State Constitution. Proposed as a "Term Limitation Amendment," its preamble stated:

"The people of Arkansas find and declare that elected officials who remain in office too long become preoccupied with reelection and ignore their duties as representatives of the people. Entrenched incumbency has reduced voter participation and has led to an electoral system that is less free, less competitive, and less representative than the system established by the Founding Fathers. Therefore, the people of Arkansas, exercising their reserved powers, herein limit the terms of the elected officials."

... Section 3, the provision at issue in these cases, applies to the Arkansas Congressional Delegation. It provides:

"(a) Any person having been elected to three or more terms as a member of the United States House of Representatives from Arkansas shall not be certified as a candidate and shall not be eligible to have his/her name placed on the ballot for election to the United States House of Representatives from Arkansas.

"(b) Any person having been elected to two or more terms as a member of the United States Senate from Arkansas shall not be certified as a candidate and shall not be eligible to have his/her name placed on the ballot for election to the United States Senate from Arkansas." ...

On November 13, 1992, respondent Bobbie Hill, on behalf of herself, similarly situated Arkansas "citizens, residents, taxpayers and registered voters," and the League of Women Voters of Arkansas, filed a complaint in the Circuit Court for Pulaski County, Arkansas, seeking a declaratory judgment that § 3 of Amendment 73 is "unconstitutional and void." Her complaint named as defendants then-Governor Clinton, other state officers, the Republican Party of Arkansas, and the Democratic Party of Arkansas. The State of Arkansas, through its Attorney General, petitioner Winston Bryant, intervened as a party defendant in support of the amendment. Several proponents of the amendment also intervened, including petitioner U.S. Term Limits, Inc.

On cross-motions for summary judgment, the Circuit Court held that § 3 of Amendment 73 violated Article I of the Federal Constitution.

... [T]he Arkansas Supreme Court affirmed ...

. . .

The State of Arkansas, by its Attorney General, and the intervenors petitioned for writs of certiorari. Because of the importance of the issues, we granted both petitions and consolidated the cases for argument. We now affirm.

II

... [T]he constitutionality of Amendment 73 depends critically on the resolution of two distinct issues. The first is whether the Constitution forbids States from adding to or altering the qualifications specifically enumerated in the Constitution. The second is, if the Constitution does so forbid, whether the fact that Amendment 73 is formulated as a ballot access restriction rather than as an outright disqualification is of constitutional significance. Our resolution of these issues draws upon our prior resolution of a related but distinct issue: whether Congress has the power to add to or alter the qualifications of its Members.

Twenty-six years ago, in Powell v. McCormack, 395 U.S. 486 (1969), we reviewed the history and text of the Qualifications Clauses in a case involving an attempted exclusion of a duly elected Member of Congress. The principal issue was whether the power granted to each House in Art. I, § 5, to judge the "Qualifications of its own Members" includes the power to impose qualifications other than those set forth in the text of the Constitution. In an opinion by Chief Justice Warren for eight Members of the Court, we held that it does not. Because of the obvious importance of the issue, the Court's review of the history and meaning of the relevant constitutional text was especially thorough. We therefore begin our analysis today with a full statement of what we decided in that case.

THE ISSUE IN *POWELL*

In November 1966, Adam Clayton Powell, Jr., was elected from a District in New York to serve in the United States House of Representatives for the 90th Congress. Allegations that he had engaged in serious misconduct while serving as a committee chairman during the 89th Congress led to the appointment of a Select Committee to determine his eligibility to take his seat. That Committee found that Powell met the age, citizenship, and residency requirements set forth in Art. I, § 2, cl. 2. The Committee also found, however, that Powell had wrongfully diverted House funds for the use of others and himself and had made false reports on expenditures of foreign currency. Based on those findings, the House after debate adopted House Resolution 278, excluding Powell from membership in the House, and declared his seat vacant. . . .

Powell and several voters of the District from which he had been elected filed suit seeking a declaratory judgment that the House Resolution was invalid because Art. I, § 2, cl. 2, sets forth the exclusive qualifications for House membership. We ultimately accepted that contention, concluding that the House of Representatives has no "authority to *exclude* any person, duly elected by his constituents, who meets all the requirements for membership expressly prescribed in the Constitution." . . . In reaching that conclusion, we undertook a detailed historical review to determine the intent of the Framers. Though recognizing that the Constitutional Convention debates themselves were inconclusive, . . . we determined that the "relevant historical materials" reveal that Congress has no power to alter the qualifications in the text of the Constitution . . . .

POWELL'S RELIANCE ON HISTORY

. . . [W]e concluded in *Powell* that "on the eve of the Constitutional Convention, English precedent stood for the proposition that 'the law of the land had regulated the qualifications of members to serve in parliament' and those qualifications were 'not occasional but fixed.'" . . .

Against this historical background, we viewed the Convention debates as manifesting the Framers' intent that the qualifications in the Constitution be fixed and exclusive. We found particularly revealing the debate concerning a proposal made by the Committee of Detail that would have given Congress the power to add property qualifications. James Madison argued that such a power would vest " 'an improper & dangerous power in the Legislature,' " by which the Legislature " 'can by degrees subvert the Constitution.' " ...

The Framers further revealed their concerns about congressional abuse of power when Gouverneur Morris suggested modifying the proposal of the Committee of Detail to grant Congress unfettered power to add qualifications.... We found significant that the Convention rejected both Morris' modification and the Committee's proposal.

We also recognized in *Powell* that the post-Convention ratification debates confirmed that the Framers understood the qualifications in the Constitution to be fixed and unalterable by Congress. For example, we noted that in response to the antifederalist charge that the new Constitution favored the wealthy and well-born, Alexander Hamilton wrote: " 'The truth is that there is no method of securing to the rich the preference apprehended but by prescribing qualifications of property either for those who may elect or be elected. But this forms no part of the power to be conferred upon the national government.... The qualifications of the persons who may choose or be chosen, as has been remarked upon other occasions, are defined and fixed in the Constitution, and are unalterable by the legislature.' " ... quoting The Federalist No. 60 ... We thus attached special significance to "Hamilton's express reliance on the immutability of the qualifications set forth in the Constitution." ...

The exercise by Congress of its power to judge the qualifications of its Members further confirmed this understanding. We concluded that, during the first 100 years of its existence, "Congress strictly limited its power to judge the qualifications of its members to those enumerated in the Constitution." ...

As this elaborate summary reveals, our historical analysis in *Powell* was both detailed and persuasive. We thus conclude now, as we did in *Powell*, that history shows that, with respect to Congress, the Framers intended the Constitution to establish fixed qualifications.

POWELL 'S RELIANCE ON DEMOCRATIC PRINCIPLES

In *Powell*, of course, we ... noted that allowing Congress to impose additional qualifications would violate that "fundamental principle of our representative democracy ... 'that the people should choose whom they please to govern them.' " ...

Our opinion made clear that this broad principle incorporated at least two fundamental ideas. First, we emphasized the egalitarian concept that the opportunity to be elected was open to all. We noted in particular Madison's statement in The Federalist that " '[u]nder these reasonable limitations [enumerated in the Constitution], the door of this part of the federal government is open to merit of every description, whether native or adoptive, whether young or old, and without regard to poverty or wealth, or to any particular profession of religious faith.' " ...

Second, we recognized the critical postulate that sovereignty is vested in the people, and that sovereignty confers on the people the right to choose freely their representatives to the National Government. For example, we noted that "Robert Livingston ... endorsed this same fundamental principle: 'The people are the best judges who ought to represent them. To dictate and control them, to tell them whom they shall not elect, is to abridge their natural rights.' " ...

. . .

POWELL 'S HOLDING

Petitioners argue somewhat half-heartedly that the narrow holding in *Powell*, which involved the power of the House to exclude a member pursuant to Art. I, § 5, does not control the more general question whether Congress has the power to add qualifications. *Powell*, however, is not susceptible to such a narrow reading. Our conclusion that Congress may not alter or add to the qualifications in the Constitution was integral to our analysis and outcome....

. . .

III

Our reaffirmation of *Powell* does not necessarily resolve the specific questions presented in these cases. For petitioners argue that whatever the constitutionality of additional qualifications for membership imposed by Congress, the historical and textual materials discussed in *Powell* do not support the conclusion that the Constitution prohibits additional qualifications imposed by States. In the absence of such a constitutional prohibition, petitioners argue, the Tenth Amendment and the principle of reserved powers require that States be allowed to add such qualifications.

Before addressing these arguments, we find it appropriate to take note of the striking unanimity among the courts that have considered the issue. None of the overwhelming array of briefs submitted by the parties and amici has called to our attention even a single case in which a state court or federal court has approved of a State's addition of qualifications for a member of Congress. To the contrary, an impressive number of courts have determined that States lack the authority to add qualifications.... Courts have struck down state-imposed qualifications in the form of term limits.... Prior to *Powell*, the commentators were similarly unanimous. See, e. g., ... 1 Story § 627 (each member of Congress is "an officer of the union, deriving his powers and qualifications from the constitution, and neither created by, dependent upon, nor controllable by, the states");.... This impressive and uniform body of judicial decisions and learned commentary indicates that the obstacles confronting petitioners are formidable indeed.

Petitioners argue that the Constitution contains no express prohibition against state-added qualifications, and that Amendment 73 is therefore an appropriate exercise of a State's reserved power to place additional restrictions on the choices that its own voters may make. We disagree for two independent reasons. First, we conclude that the power to add qualifications is not within the "original powers" of the States, and thus is not reserved to the States by the Tenth Amendment. Second, even if States possessed some original power in this area, we conclude that the Framers intended the Constitution to be the exclusive source of qualifications for members of Congress, and that the Framers thereby "divested" States of any power to add qualifications.

The "plan of the convention" ... draws a basic distinction between the powers of the newly created Federal Government and the powers retained by the pre-existing sovereign States. As Chief Justice Marshall explained, "it was neither necessary nor proper to define the powers retained by the States. These powers proceed, not from the people of America, but from the people of the several States; and remain, after the adoption of the constitution, what they were before, except so far as they may be abridged by that instrument." Sturges v. Crowninshield, 4 Wheat. 122, 193 (1819).

This classic statement by the Chief Justice endorsed Hamilton's reasoning in The Federalist No. 32 that the plan of the Constitutional Convention did not contemplate "[a]n entire consolidation of the States into one complete national sovereignty," but only a partial consolidation in which "the State governments would clearly retain all the rights of sovereignty which they before had, and which were not, by that act, exclusively delegated to the United States." The Federalist No. 32.... The text of the Tenth Amendment unambiguously confirms this principle....

As we have frequently noted, "[t]he States unquestionably do retain a significant measure of sovereign authority. They do so, however, only to the extent that the Constitution has not divested them of their original powers and transferred those powers to the Federal Government." Garcia v. San Antonio Metropolitan Transit Authority, 469 U.S. 528, 549 (1985)....

SOURCE OF THE POWER

Contrary to petitioners' assertions, the power to add qualifications is not part of the original powers of sovereignty that the Tenth Amendment reserved to the States. Petitioners' Tenth Amendment argument misconceives the nature of the right at issue because that Amendment could only "reserve" that which existed before. As Justice Story recognized, "the states can exercise no powers whatsoever, which exclusively spring out of the existence of the national government, which the constitution does not delegate to them.... No state can say, that it has reserved, what it never possessed." 1 Story § 627.

Justice Story's position thus echoes that of Chief Justice Marshall in McCulloch v. Maryland, 4 Wheat. 316 (1819). In *McCulloch*, the Court rejected the argument that the Constitution's silence on the subject of state power to tax corporations chartered by Congress implies that the States have "reserved" power to tax such federal instrumentalities. As Chief Justice Marshall pointed out, an "original right to tax" such federal entities "never existed, and the question whether it has been surrendered, cannot arise." ... In language that presaged Justice Story's argument, Chief Justice Marshall concluded: "This opinion does not deprive the States of any resources which they originally possessed."

With respect to setting qualifications for service in Congress, no such right existed before the Constitution was ratified.... [T]he Framers envisioned a uniform national system, rejecting the notion that the Nation was a collection of States, and instead creating a direct link between the National Government and the people of the United States.... As Justice Story observed, each Member of Congress is "an officer of the union, deriving his powers and qualifications from the constitution, and neither created by, dependent upon, nor controllable by, the states.... Those officers owe their existence and functions to the united voice of the whole, not of a portion, of the people." 1 Story § 627. Representatives and Senators are as much officers of the entire union as is the President. States thus "have just as much right, and no more, to prescribe new qualifications for a representative, as they have for a president.... It is no original prerogative of state power to appoint a representative, a senator, or president for the union." Ibid.

We believe that the Constitution reflects the Framers' general agreement with the approach later articulated by Justice Story. For example, Art. I, § 5, cl. 1 provides: "Each House shall be the Judge of the Elections, Returns and Qualifications of its own Members." The text of the Constitution thus gives the representatives of all the people the final say in judging the qualifications of the representatives of any one State. For this reason, the dissent falters when it states that "the people of Georgia have no say over whom the people of Massachusetts select to represent them in Congress." ...

Two other sections of the Constitution further support our view of the Framers' vision. First, consistent with Story's view, the Constitution provides that the salaries of representatives should "be ascertained by Law, and paid out of the Treasury of the United States," Art. I, § 6, rather than by individual States.... Second, the provisions governing elections reveal the Framers' understanding that powers over the election of federal officers had to be delegated to, rather than reserved by, the States. It is surely no coincidence that the context of federal elections provides one of the few areas in which the Constitution expressly requires action by the States, namely that "[t]he Times, Places and Manner of holding Elections for Senators and Representatives, shall be prescribed in each State by the legislature thereof." This duty parallels the duty under Article II that "Each State shall appoint, in such Manner as the Legislature thereof may direct, a Number of Electors." Art II., § 1, cl. 2. These Clauses are express delegations of power to the States to act with respect to federal elections.

This conclusion is consistent with our previous recognition that, in certain limited contexts, the power to regulate the incidents of the federal system is not a reserved power of the States, but rather is delegated by the Constitution. Thus, we have noted that "[w]hile, in a loose sense, the right to vote for representatives in Congress is sometimes spoken of as a right derived from the states, ... this statement is true only in the sense that the states are authorized by the Constitution, to legislate on the subject as provided by § 2 of Art. I." United States v. Classic, 313 U.S. 299, 315 (1941)....

In short, as the Framers recognized, electing representatives to the National Legislature was a new right, arising from the Constitution itself. The Tenth Amendment thus provides no basis for concluding that the States possess reserved power to add qualifications to those that are fixed in the Constitution. Instead, any state power to set the qualifications for membership in Congress must derive not from the reserved powers of state sovereignty, but rather from the delegated powers of national sovereignty. In the absence of any constitutional delegation to the States of power to add qualifications to those enumerated in the Constitution, such a power does not exist.

THE PRECLUSION OF STATE POWER

Even if we believed that States possessed as part of their original powers some control over congressional qualifications, the text and structure of the Constitution, the relevant historical materials, and, most importantly, the "basic principles of our democratic system" all demonstrate that the Qualifications Clauses were intended to preclude the States from exercising any such power and to fix as exclusive the qualifications in the Constitution.

Much of the historical analysis was undertaken by the Court in *Powell*. There is, however, additional historical evidence that pertains directly to the power of States. That evidence, though perhaps not as extensive as that reviewed in *Powell*, leads unavoidably to the conclusion that the States lack the power to add qualifications.

The Convention and Ratification Debates

The available affirmative evidence indicates the Framers' intent that States have no role in the setting of qualifications. In Federalist Paper No. 52, dealing with the House of Representatives, ... Madison ... explicitly contrasted the state control over the qualifications of electors with the lack of state control over the qualifications of the elected:

> "The qualifications of the elected, being less carefully and properly defined by the State constitutions, and being at the same time more susceptible of uniformity, have been very properly considered and regulated by the convention. A representative of the United States must be of the age of twenty-five years; must have been seven years a citizen of the United States; must, at the time of his election be an inhabitant of the State he is to represent; and, during the time of his service must be in no office under the United States. Under these reasonable limitations, the door of this part of the federal government is open to merit of every description, whether native or adoptive, whether young or old, and without regard to poverty or wealth, or to any particular profession of religious faith."
> ...

. . . .

In light of the Framers' evident concern that States would try to undermine the National Government, they could not have intended States to have the power to set qualifications. . . .

. . .

We find further evidence of the Framers' intent in Art. 1, § 5, cl. 1, which provides: "Each House shall be the Judge of the Elections, Returns and Qualifications of its own Members." . . . If the States had the right to prescribe additional qualifications—such as property, educational, or professional qualifications—for their own representatives, state law would provide the standard for judging a Member's eligibility. . . . The judging of questions concerning rights which depend on state law is not, however, normally assigned to federal tribunals. . . .

We also find compelling the complete absence in the ratification debates of any assertion that States had the power to add qualifications. . . .

. . .

In short, if it had been assumed that States could add additional qualifications, that assumption would have provided the basis for a powerful rebuttal to the arguments being advanced. The failure of intelligent and experienced advocates to utilize this argument must reflect a general agreement that its premise was unsound, and that the power to add qualifications was one that the Constitution denied the States.

Congressional Experience

Congress' subsequent experience with state-imposed qualifications provides further evidence of the general consensus on the lack of state power in this area. In *Powell*, we examined that experience and noted that during the first 100 years of its existence, "Congress strictly limited its power to judge the qualifications of its members to those enumerated in the Constitution." . . .

. . .

We recognize, as we did in *Powell*, that "congressional practice has been erratic" and that the precedential value of congressional exclusion cases is "quite limited." . . .

Democratic Principles

Our conclusion that States lack the power to impose qualifications vindicates the same "fundamental principle of our representative democracy" that we recognized in *Powell*, namely that "the people should choose whom they please to govern them." . . .

As we noted earlier, the *Powell* Court recognized that an egalitarian ideal—that election to the National Legislature should be open to all people of merit—provided a critical foundation for the Constitutional structure. This egalitarian theme echoes throughout the constitutional debates. In The Federalist No. 57, for example, Madison wrote:

"Who are to be the objects of popular choice? Every citizen whose merit may recommend him to the esteem and confidence of his country. No qualification of wealth, of birth, of religious faith, or of civil profession is permitted to fetter the judgment or disappoint the inclination of the people." . . .

. . .

Similarly, we believe that state-imposed qualifications, as much as congressionally imposed qualifications, would undermine the second critical idea recognized in *Powell*: that an aspect of sovereignty is the right of the people to vote for whom they wish. Again, the source of the qualification is of little moment in assessing the qualification's restrictive impact.

Finally, state-imposed restrictions, unlike the congressionally imposed restrictions at issue in *Powell*, violate a third idea central to this basic principle: that the right to choose representatives belongs not to the States, but to the people. . . . [T]he Framers, in perhaps their most important contribution, conceived of a Federal Government directly responsible to the people, possessed of direct power over the people, and chosen directly, not by States, but by the people. The Framers implemented this ideal most clearly in the provision, extant from the beginning of the Republic, that calls for the Members of the House of Representatives to be "chosen every second Year by the People of the several States." Art. I, § 2, cl. 1. Following the adoption of the 17th Amendment in 1913, this ideal was extended to elections for the Senate. The Congress of the United States, therefore, is not a confederation of nations in which separate sovereigns are represented by appointed delegates, but is instead a body composed of representatives of the people. As Chief Justice John Marshall observed: "The government of the union, then, . . . is, emphatically, and truly, a government of the people. In form and in substance it emanates from them. Its powers are granted by them, and are to be exercised directly on them, and for their benefit." McCulloch v. Maryland, 4 Wheat., at 404–405. . . .

The Framers deemed this principle critical when they discussed qualifications. For example, during the debates on residency requirements, Morris noted that in the House, "the people at large, not the States, are represented." . . . Similarly, George Read noted that the Framers "were forming a Nati[ona]l Gov[ernmen]t and such a regulation would correspond little with the idea that we were one people." . . .

Consistent with these views, the constitutional structure provides for a uniform salary to be paid from the national treasury, allows the States but a limited role in federal elections, and maintains strict checks on state interference with the federal election process. The Constitution also provides that the qualifications of the representatives of each State will be judged by the representatives of the entire Nation. The Constitution thus creates a uniform national body representing the interests of a single people.

Permitting individual States to formulate diverse qualifications for their representatives would result in a patchwork of state qualifications, undermining the uniformity and the national character that the Framers envisioned and sought to ensure. . . .

State Practice

Petitioners attempt to overcome this formidable array of evidence against the States' power to impose qualifications by arguing that the practice of the States immediately after the adoption of the Constitution demonstrates their understanding that they possessed such power. One may properly question the extent to which the States' own practice is a reliable indicator of the contours of restrictions that the Constitution imposed on States, especially when no court has ever upheld a state-imposed qualification of any sort. But petitioners' argument is unpersuasive even on its own terms. At the time of the Convention, "[a]lmost all the State Constitutions required members of their Legislatures to possess considerable property." . . . Despite this near uniformity, only one State, Virginia, placed similar restrictions on members of Congress, requiring that a representative be, inter alia, a "freeholder." . . . Just 15 years after imposing a property qualification, Virginia replaced that requirement with a provision requiring that representatives be only "qualified according to the constitution of the United States." . . . Moreover, several States, including New Hampshire, Georgia, Delaware, and South Carolina, revised their Constitutions at around the time of the Federal Constitution. In the revised Constitutions, each State retained property qualifications for its own state elected officials yet placed no property qualification on its congressional representatives.

The contemporaneous state practice with respect to term limits is similar. At the time of the Convention, States widely supported term limits in at least some circumstances. . . . Despite this wide spread support, no State sought to impose any term limits on its own federal representatives. Thus, a proper assessment of contemporaneous state practice provides further persuasive evidence of a general understanding that the qualifications in the Constitution were unalterable by the States.

In sum, the available historical and textual evidence, read in light of the basic principles of democracy underlying the Constitution and recognized by this Court in Powell, reveal the Framers' intent that neither Congress nor the States should possess the power to supplement the exclusive qualifications set forth in the text of the Constitution.

IV

Petitioners argue that, even if States may not add qualifications, Amendment 73 is constitutional because it is not such a qualification, and because Amendment 73 is a permissible exercise of state power to regulate the "Times, Places and Manner of Holding Elections." We reject these contentions.

Unlike §§ 1 and 2 of Amendment 73, which create absolute bars to service for long-term incumbents running for state office, § 3 merely provides that certain Senators and Representatives shall not be certified as candidates and shall not have their names appear on the ballot. They may run as write-in candidates and, if elected, they may serve. Petitioners contend that only a legal bar to service creates an impermissible qualification, and that Amendment 73 is therefore consistent with the Constitution.

Petitioners support their restrictive definition of qualifications with language from Storer v. Brown, 415 U.S. 724 (1974), in which we faced a constitutional challenge to provisions of the California Elections Code that regulated the procedures by which both independent candidates and candidates affiliated with qualified political parties could obtain ballot position in general elections. The Code required candidates affiliated with a qualified party to win a primary election, and required independents to make timely filing of nomination papers signed by at least 5% of the entire vote cast in the last general election. The Code also denied ballot position to independents who had voted in the most recent primary election or who had registered their affiliation with a qualified party during the previous year.

In *Storer*, we rejected the argument that the challenged procedures created additional qualifications.... Petitioners maintain that, under *Storer*, Amendment 73 is not a qualification.

We need not decide whether petitioners' narrow understanding of qualifications is correct because, even if it is, Amendment 73 may not stand....

In our view, Amendment 73 is an indirect attempt to accomplish what the Constitution prohibits Arkansas from accomplishing directly. As the plurality opinion of the Arkansas Supreme Court recognized, Amendment 73 is an "effort to dress eligibility to stand for Congress in ballot access clothing," because the "intent and the effect of Amendment 73 are to disqualify congressional incumbents from further service." We must, of course, accept the State Court's view of the purpose of its own law: we are thus authoritatively informed that the sole purpose of § 3 of Amendment 73 was to attempt to achieve a result that is forbidden by the Federal Constitution. Indeed, it cannot be seriously contended that the intent behind Amendment 73 is other than to prevent the election of incumbents. The preamble of Amendment 73 states explicitly: "[T]he people of Arkansas ... herein limit the terms of elected officials." Sections 1 and 2 create absolute limits on the number of terms that may be served. There is no hint that § 3 was intended to have any other purpose.

Petitioners do, however, contest the Arkansas Supreme Court's conclusion that the Amendment has the same practical effect as an absolute bar. They argue that the possibility of a write-in campaign creates a real possibility for victory, especially for an entrenched incumbent. One may reasonably question the merits of that contention.... But even if petitioners are correct that incumbents may occasionally win reelection as write-in candidates, there is no denying that the ballot restrictions will make it significantly more difficult for the barred candidate to win the election. In our view, an amendment with the avowed purpose and obvious effect of evading the requirements of the Qualifications Clauses by handicapping a class of candidates cannot stand.... Petitioners' argument treats the Qualifications Clauses not as the embodiment of a grand principle, but rather as empty formalism....

Petitioners make the related argument that Amendment 73 merely regulates the "Manner" of elections, and that the Amendment is therefore a permissible exercise of state power under Article I, § 4, cl. 1 (the Elections Clause) to regulate the "Times, Places and Manner" of elections. We cannot agree.

A necessary consequence of petitioners' argument is that Congress itself would have the power to "make or alter" a measure such as Amendment 73.... That the Framers would have approved of such a result is unfathomable.... Petitioners would have us believe, however, that even as the Framers carefully circumscribed congressional power to set qualifications, they intended to allow Congress to achieve the same result by simply formulating the regulation as a ballot access restriction under the Elections Clause. We refuse to adopt an interpretation of the Elections Clause that would so cavalierly disregard what the Framers intended to be a fundamental constitutional safeguard.

Moreover, petitioners' broad construction of the Elections Clause is fundamentally inconsistent with the Framers' view of that Clause. The Framers intended the Elections Clause to grant States authority to create procedural regulations, not to provide States with license to exclude classes of candidates from federal office....

.   .   .

The provisions at issue in *Storer* and our other Elections Clause cases were thus constitutional because they regulated election procedures and did not even arguably impose any substantive qualification rendering a class of potential candidates ineligible for ballot position. They served the state interest in protecting the integrity and regularity of the election process, an interest independent of any attempt to evade the constitutional prohibition against the imposition of additional qualifications for service in Congress. And they did not involve measures that exclude candidates from the ballot without reference to the candidates' support in the electoral process. Our cases upholding state regulations of election procedures thus provide little support for the contention that a state-imposed ballot access restriction is constitutional when it is undertaken for the twin goals of disadvantaging a particular class of candidates and evading the dictates of the Qualifications Clauses.

.   .   .

V

The merits of term limits ... have been the subject of debate since the formation of our Constitution, when the Framers unanimously rejected a proposal to add such limits to the Constitution. The cogent arguments on both sides of the question that were articulated during the process of ratification largely retain their force today. Over half the States have adopted measures that impose such limits on some offices either directly or indirectly, and the Nation as a whole, notably by constitutional amendment, has imposed a limit on the number of terms that the President may serve. Term limits, like any other qualification for office, unquestionably restrict the ability of voters to vote for whom they wish. On the other hand, such limits may provide for the infusion of fresh ideas and new perspectives, and may decrease the likelihood that representatives will lose touch with their constituents. It is not our province to resolve this longstanding debate.

We are, however, firmly convinced that allowing the several States to adopt term limits for congressional service would effect a fundamental change in the constitutional framework. Any such change must come not by legislation adopted either by Congress or by an individual State, but rather—as have other important changes in the electoral process— the Amendment procedures set forth in Article V. . . .

The judgment is affirmed.

It is so ordered.

Justice Kennedy, concurring.

I join the opinion of the Court.

. . . [I]t is well settled that the whole people of the United States asserted their political identity and unity of purpose when they created the federal system. The dissent's course of reasoning suggesting other-wise might be construed to disparage the republican character of the National Government, and it seems appropriate to add these few re-marks to explain why that course of argumentation runs counter to fundamental principles of federalism.

. . .

A distinctive character of the National Government, the mark of its legitimacy, is that it owes its existence to the act of the whole people who created it. It must be remembered that the National Government too is republican in essence and in theory. . . .

. . .

It might be objected that because the States ratified the Constitu-tion, the people can delegate power only through the States or by acting in their capacities as citizens of particular States. But in McCulloch v. Maryland, the Court set forth its authoritative rejection of this idea: "The Convention which framed the constitution was indeed elected by the State legislatures. But the instrument . . . was submitted to the people. . . . It is true, they assembled in their several States—and where else should they have assembled? No political dreamer was ever wild enough to think of breaking down the lines which separate the States, and of compounding the American people into one common mass. Of consequence, when they act, they act in their States. But the measures they adopt do not, on that account, cease to be the measures of the people themselves, or become the measures of the State governments." 4 Wheat., at 403.

The political identity of the entire people of the Union is reinforced by the proposition, which I take to be beyond dispute, that, though limited as to its objects, the National Government is and must be controlled by the people without collateral interference by the States....

Of course, because the Framers recognized that state power and identity were essential parts of the federal balance, ... the Constitution is solicitous of the prerogatives of the States, even in an otherwise sovereign federal province.... The Constitution uses state boundaries to fix the size of congressional delegations, U.S. Const., Art. I, § 2, cl. 3, ensures that each State shall have at least one representative, ibid., grants States certain powers over the times, places, and manner of federal elections (subject to congressional revision), Art. I, § 4, cl. 1, requires that when the President is elected by the House of Representatives, the delegations from each State have one vote, Art. II, § 1, cl. 3, and Amdt. 12, and allows States to appoint electors for the President, Art. II, § 1, cl. 2. Nothing in the Constitution or The Federalist Papers, however, supports the idea of state interference with the most basic relation between the National Government and its citizens, the selection of legislative representatives. Indeed, even though the Constitution uses the qualifications for voters of the most numerous branch of the States' own legislatures to set the qualifications of federal electors, Art. I, § 2, cl. 1, when these electors vote, we have recognized that they act in a federal capacity and exercise a federal right.... We made the ... point in United States v. Classic, 313 U.S. 299, 315 (1941), when we said, "[T]he right of qualified voters within a state to cast their ballots and have them counted at Congressional elections ... is a right secured by the Constitution" and "is secured against the action of individuals as well as of states."

The federal character of congressional elections flows from the political reality that our National Government is republican in form and that national citizenship has privileges and immunities protected from state abridgement by the force of the Constitution itself. Even before the passage of the Fourteenth Amendment, the latter proposition was given expression in Crandall v. Nevada where the Court recognized the right of the Federal Government to call "any or all of its citizens to aid in its service, as members of the Congress, of the courts, of the executive departments, and to fill all its other offices," and further recognized that "this right cannot be made to depend upon the pleasure of a State over whose territory they must pass to reach the point where these services must be rendered." 6 Wall., at 43....

In the Slaughter–House Cases, 16 Wall. 36, 78–80 (1873), the Court was careful to hold that federal citizenship in and of itself suffices for the assertion of rights under the Constitution, rights that stem from sources other than the States....

. . .

... [T]here exists a federal right of citizenship, a relationship between the people of the Nation and their National Government, with which the States may not interfere. Because the Arkansas enactment intrudes upon this federal domain, it exceeds the boundaries of the Constitution.

Justice Thomas, with whom the Chief Justice, Justice O'Connor, and Justice Scalia join, dissenting.

. . .

I dissent. Nothing in the Constitution deprives the people of each State of the power to prescribe eligibility requirements for the candidates who seek to represent them in Congress. The Constitution is simply silent on this question. And where the Constitution is silent, it raises no bar to action by the States or the people.

I

Because the majority fundamentally misunderstands the notion of "reserved" powers, I start with some first principles. Contrary to the majority's suggestion, the people of the States need not point to any affirmative grant of power in the Constitution in order to prescribe qualifications for their representatives in Congress, or to authorize their elected state legislators to do so.

A

Our system of government rests on one overriding principle: all power stems from the consent of the people. To phrase the principle in this way, however, is to be imprecise about something important to the notion of "reserved" powers. The ultimate source of the Constitution's authority is the consent of the people of each individual State, not the consent of the undifferentiated people of the Nation as a whole.

The ratification procedure erected by Article VII makes this point clear. The Constitution took effect once it had been ratified by the people gathered in convention in nine different States. But the Constitution went into effect only "between the States so ratifying the same," . . . .

When they adopted the Federal Constitution, of course, the people of each State surrendered some of their authority to the United States (and hence to entities accountable to the people of other States as well as to themselves) . . . .

In each State, the remainder of the people's powers—"[t]he powers not delegated to the United States by the Constitution, nor prohibited by it to the States," Amdt. 10—are either delegated to the state government or retained by the people. The Federal Constitution does not specify which of these two possibilities obtains; it is up to the various state constitutions to declare which powers the people of each State have delegated to their state government. As far as the Federal Constitution is concerned, then, the States can exercise all powers that the Constitution does not withhold from them. The Federal Government and the States thus face different default rules: where the Constitution is silent about the exercise of a particular power—that is, where the Constitution does not speak either expressly or by necessary implication—the Federal Government lacks that power and the States enjoy it.

These basic principles are enshrined in the Tenth Amendment. . . .

To be sure, when the Tenth Amendment uses the phrase "the people," it does not specify whether it is referring to the people of each State or the people of the Nation as a whole.... [I]t would make no sense to speak of powers as being reserved to the undifferentiated people of the Nation as a whole, because the Constitution does not contemplate that those people will either exercise power or delegate it. The Constitution simply does not recognize any mechanism for action by the undifferentiated people of the Nation. Thus, the amendment provision of Article V calls for amendments to be ratified not by a convention of the national people, but by conventions of the people in each State or by the state legislatures elected by those people. Likewise, the Constitution calls for Members of Congress to be chosen State by State, rather than in nationwide elections. Even the selection of the President—surely the most national of national figures—is accomplished by an electoral college made up of delegates chosen by the various States, and candidates can lose a Presidential election despite winning a majority of the votes cast in the Nation as a whole. See also Art. II, § 1, cl. 3 (providing that when no candidate secures a majority of electoral votes, the election of the President is thrown into the House of Representatives, where "the Votes shall be taken by States, the Representatives from each State having one Vote"); Amdt. 12 (same).

In short, the notion of popular sovereignty that undergirds the Constitution does not erase state boundaries, but rather tracks them.... As Chief Justice Marshall put it, "[n]o political dreamer was ever wild enough to think of breaking down the lines which separate the States, and of compounding the American people into one common mass." McCulloch v. Maryland, 4 Wheat. 316, 403 (1819).

... [I]f we are to invalidate Arkansas' Amendment 73, we must point to something in the Federal Constitution that deprives the people of Arkansas of the power to enact such measures.

B

The majority disagrees that it bears this burden. But its arguments are unpersuasive.

1

The majority begins by announcing an enormous and untenable limitation on the principle expressed by the Tenth Amendment. According to the majority, the States possess only those powers that the Constitution affirmatively grants to them or that they enjoyed before the Constitution was adopted ...

The majority's essential logic is that the state governments could not "reserve" any powers that they did not control at the time the Constitution was drafted. But it was not the state governments that were doing the reserving. The Constitution derives its authority instead from the consent of the people of the States. Given the fundamental principle that all governmental powers stem from the people of the States, it would simply be incoherent to assert that the people of the

States could not reserve any powers that they had not previously controlled.

. . .

The majority ... seeks support for its view of the Tenth Amendment in McCulloch v. Maryland, 4 Wheat. 316 (1819). But this effort is misplaced. *McCulloch* did make clear that a power need not be "expressly" delegated to the United States or prohibited to the States in order to fall outside the Tenth Amendment's reservation; delegations and prohibitions can also arise by necessary implication. True to the text of the Tenth Amendment, however, *McCulloch* indicated that all powers as to which the Constitution does not speak (whether expressly or by necessary implication) are "reserved" to the state level. Thus, in its only discussion of the Tenth Amendment, *McCulloch* observed that the Amendment "leav[es] the question, whether the particular power which may become the subject of contest has been delegated to the one government, or prohibited to the other, to depend on a fair construction of the whole [Constitution]." ... *McCulloch* did not qualify this observation by indicating that the question also turned on whether the States had enjoyed the power before the framing. To the contrary, *McCulloch* seemed to assume that the people had "conferred on the general government the power contained in the constitution, and on the States the whole residuum of power." ...

. . .

For the past 175 years, *McCulloch* has been understood to rest on the proposition that the Constitution affirmatively barred Maryland from imposing its tax on the Bank's operations.... For the majority, however, *McCulloch* apparently turned on the fact that before the Constitution was adopted, the States had possessed no power to tax the instrumentalities of the governmental institutions that the Constitution created. This understanding of *McCulloch* makes most of Chief Justice Marshall's opinion irrelevant; according to the majority, there was no need to inquire into whether federal law deprived Maryland of the power in question, because the power could not fall into the category of "reserved" powers anyway.

... [T]he only true support for its view of the Tenth Amendment comes from Joseph Story's 1833 treatise on constitutional law.... Justice Story was a brilliant and accomplished man, and one cannot casually dismiss his views. On the other hand, he was not a member of the Founding generation, and his Commentaries on the Constitution were written a half century after the framing. Rather than representing the original understanding of the Constitution, they represent only his own understanding....

2

The majority also sketches out what may be an alternative (and narrower) argument. Again citing Story, the majority suggests that it would be inconsistent with the notion of "national sovereignty" for the States or the people of the States to have any reserved powers over the selection of Members of Congress. The majority apparently reaches this conclusion in two steps. First, it asserts that because Congress as a whole is an institution of the National Government, the individual Members of Congress "owe primary allegiance not to the people of a State, but to the people of the Nation." Second, it concludes that because each Member of Congress has a nationwide constituency once he takes office, it would be inconsistent with the Framers' scheme to let a single State prescribe qualifications for him.

Political scientists can debate about who commands the "primary allegiance" of Members of Congress once they reach Washington.... But the selection of representatives in Congress is indisputably an act of the people of each State, not some abstract people of the Nation as a whole.

The concurring opinion suggests that this cannot be so, because it is the Federal Constitution that guarantees the right of the people of each State (so long as they are qualified electors under state law) to take part in choosing the Members of Congress from that State. But the presence of a federally guaranteed right hardly means that the selection of those representatives constitutes "the exercise of federal authority." When the people of Georgia pick their representatives in Congress, they are acting as the people of Georgia, not as the corporate agents for the undifferentiated people of the Nation as a whole. [W]hen one strips away its abstractions, the concurring opinion is simply saying that the people of Arkansas cannot be permitted to inject themselves into the process by which they themselves select Arkansas' representatives in Congress.

The concurring opinion attempts to defend this surprising proposition by pointing out that Americans are "citizens of the United States" as well as "of the State wherein they reside," ... and that national citizenship ... "has privileges and immunities protected from state abridgement by the force of the Constitution itself." These facts ... do not contradict anything that I have said. Although the United States obviously is a Nation, and although it obviously has citizens, the Constitution does not call for Members of Congress to be elected by the undifferentiated national citizenry; indeed, it does not recognize any mechanism at all (such as a national referendum) for action by the undifferentiated people of the Nation as a whole. Even at the level of national politics, then, there always remains a meaningful distinction between someone who is a citizen of the United States and of Georgia and someone who is a citizen of the United States and of Massachusetts. The Georgia citizen who is unaware of this distinction will have it pointed out to him as soon as he tries to vote in a Massachusetts congressional election.

. . .

II

I take it to be established, then, that the people of Arkansas do enjoy "reserved" powers over the selection of their representatives in Congress.... [W]e may not override the decision of the people of Arkansas unless something in the Federal Constitution deprives them of the power to enact such measures.

The majority settles on "the Qualifications Clauses" as the constitutional provisions that Amendment 73 violates. Because I do not read those provisions to impose any unstated prohibitions on the States, it is unnecessary for me to decide whether the majority is correct to identify Arkansas' ballot-access restriction with laws fixing true term limits or otherwise prescribing "qualifications" for congressional office. As I discuss in Part A below, the Qualifications Clauses are merely straightforward recitations of the minimum eligibility requirements that the Framers thought it essential for every Member of Congress to meet. They restrict state power only in that they prevent the States from abolishing all eligibility requirements for membership in Congress.

Because the text of the Qualifications Clauses does not support its position, the majority turns instead to its vision of the democratic principles that animated the Framers. But the majority's analysis goes to a question that is not before us: whether Congress has the power to prescribe qualifications for its own members. As I discuss in Part B, the democratic principles that contributed to the Framers' decision to withhold this power from Congress do not prove that the Framers also deprived the people of the States of their reserved authority to set eligibility requirements for their own representatives.

In Part C, I review the majority's more specific historical evidence. To the extent that they bear on this case, the records of the Philadelphia Convention affirmatively support my unwillingness to find hidden meaning in the Qualifications Clauses, while the surviving records from the ratification debates help neither side. As for the postratification period, five States supplemented the constitutional disqualifications in their very first election laws. The historical evidence thus refutes any notion that the Qualifications Clauses were generally understood to be exclusive. Yet the majority must establish just such an understanding in order to justify its position that the Clauses impose unstated prohibitions on the States and the people. In my view, the historical evidence is simply inadequate to warrant the majority's conclusion that the Qualifications Clauses mean anything more than what they say.

A

. . .

The majority is quite correct that the "negative phrasing" of [the Qualifications] Clauses has little relevance.... At least on their face, ... the Qualifications Clauses do nothing to prohibit the people of a State from establishing additional eligibility requirements for their own representatives.

Joseph Story thought that such a prohibition was nonetheless implicit in the constitutional list of qualifications ... When the Framers decided which qualifications to include in the Constitution, they also decided not to include any other qualifications in the Constitution....

To spell out the logic underlying this argument is to expose its weakness. Even if one were willing to ignore the distinction between requirements enshrined in the Constitution and other requirements that the Framers were content to leave within the reach of ordinary law, Story's application of the expressio unius maxim takes no account of federalism. At most, the specification of certain nationwide disqualifications in the Constitution implies the negation of other nationwide disqualifications; it does not imply that individual States or their people are barred from adopting their own disqualifications on a state-by-state basis. . . .

The Qualifications Clauses do prevent the individual States from abolishing all eligibility requirements for Congress. . . .

If the people of a State decide that they would like their representatives to possess additional qualifications, however, they have done nothing to frustrate the policy behind the Qualifications Clauses. Anyone who possesses all of the constitutional qualifications, plus some qualifications required by state law, still has all of the federal qualifications. Accordingly, the fact that the Constitution specifies certain qualifications that the Framers deemed necessary to protect the competence of the National Legislature does not imply that it strips the people of the individual States of the power to protect their own interests by adding other requirements for their own representatives.

. . .

This conclusion is buttressed by our reluctance to read constitutional provisions to preclude state power by negative implication. The very structure of the Constitution counsels such hesitation. After all, § 10 of Article I contains a brief list of express prohibitions on the States. . . . Many of the prohibitions listed in § 10, moreover, might have been thought to be implicit in other constitutional provisions or in the very nature of our federal system. Compare, e.g., Art. II, § 2, cl. 2 ("[The President] shall have Power, by and with the Advice and Consent of the Senate, to make Treaties") and Art. I, § 8, cl. 5 ("The Congress shall have Power . . . [t]o coin Money") with Art. I, § 10, cl. 1 ("No State shall enter into any Treaty" and "No State shall . . . coin Money"); see also Art. VI, cl. 2 (explicitly declaring that state law cannot override the Constitution). The fact that the Framers nonetheless made these prohibitions express confirms that one should not lightly read provisions like the Qualifications Clauses as implicit deprivations of state power. . . .

The majority responds that "a patchwork of state qualifications" would "undermin[e] the uniformity and the national character that the Framers envisioned and sought to ensure." Yet the Framers thought it perfectly consistent with the "national character" of Congress for the Senators and Representatives from each State to be chosen by the legislature or the people of that State. The majority never explains why Congress' fundamental character permits this state-centered system, but nonetheless prohibits the people of the States and their state legislatures from setting any eligibility requirements for the candidates who seek to represent them.

. . .

B

Although the Qualifications Clauses neither state nor imply the prohibition that it finds in them, the majority infers from the Framers' "democratic principles" that the Clauses must have been generally understood to preclude the people of the States and their state legislatures from prescribing any additional qualifications for their representatives in Congress. But the majority's evidence on this point establishes only two more modest propositions: (1) the Framers did not want the Federal Constitution itself to impose a broad set of disqualifications for congressional office, and (2) the Framers did not want the Federal Congress to be able to supplement the few disqualifications that the Constitution does set forth. The logical conclusion is simply that the Framers did not want the people of the States and their state legislatures to be constrained by too many qualifications imposed at the national level. The evidence does not support the majority's more sweeping conclusion that the Framers intended to bar the people of the States and their state legislatures from adopting additional eligibility requirements to help narrow their own choices.

I agree with the majority that Congress has no power to prescribe qualifications for its own Members. This fact, however, does not show that the Qualifications Clauses contain a hidden exclusivity provision. The reason for Congress' incapacity is not that the Qualifications Clauses deprive Congress of the authority to set qualifications, but rather that nothing in the Constitution grants Congress this power. In the absence of such a grant, Congress may not act. But deciding whether the Constitution denies the qualification-setting power to the States and the people of the States requires a fundamentally different legal analysis.

. . . [T]his explanation for Congress' incapacity to supplement the Qualifications Clauses is perfectly consistent with the reasoning of *Powell v. McCormack*, 395 U.S. 486 (1969). . . . [T]he critical question in *Powell* was whether § 5 conferred a qualification-setting power—not whether the Qualifications Clauses took it away. . . .

. . .

As the majority argues, democratic principles also contributed to the Framers' decision to withhold the qualification-setting power from Congress. But the majority is wrong to suggest that the same principles must also have led the Framers to deny this power to the people of the States and the state legislatures. In particular, it simply is not true that "the source of the qualification is of little moment in assessing the qualification's restrictive impact." There is a world of difference between a self-imposed constraint and a constraint imposed from above.

Congressional power over qualifications would have enabled the representatives from some States, acting collectively in the National

Legislature, to prevent the people of another State from electing their preferred candidates....

. . .

... [T]he authority to narrow the field of candidates ... may be part and parcel of the right to elect Members of Congress. That is, the right to choose may include the right to winnow....

. . .

C

In addition to its arguments about democratic principles, the majority asserts that more specific historical evidence supports its view that the Framers did not intend to permit supplementation of the Qualifications Clauses. But when one focuses on the distinction between congressional power to add qualifications for congressional office and the power of the people or their state legislatures to add such qualifications, one realizes that this assertion has little basis.

. . .

1

To the extent that the records from the Philadelphia Convention itself shed light on this case, they tend to hurt the majority's case....

. . .

2

Unable to glean from the Philadelphia Convention any direct evidence that helps its position, the majority seeks signs of the Framers' unstated intent in the Framers' comments about four other constitutional provisions.... But even if the majority's reading of its evidence were correct, the most that one could infer is that the Framers did not want state legislatures to be able to prescribe qualifications that would narrow the people's choices. However wary the Framers might have been of permitting state legislatures to exercise such power, there is absolutely no reason to believe that the Framers feared letting the people themselves exercise this power....

In any event, none of the provisions cited by the majority is inconsistent with state power to add qualifications for congressional office.

. . .

3

In discussing the ratification period, the majority stresses two principal data. One of these pieces of evidence is no evidence at all—literally. The majority devotes considerable space to the fact that the recorded ratification debates do not contain any affirmative statement that the States can supplement the constitutional qualifications....

But the majority's argument cuts both ways. The recorded ratification debates also contain no affirmative statement that the States cannot supplement the constitutional qualifications....

If one concedes that the absence of relevant records from the ratification debates is not strong evidence for either side, then the majority's only significant piece of evidence from the ratification period is Federalist No. 52. Contrary to the majority's assertion, however, this essay simply does not talk about "the lack of state control over the qualifications of the elected," whether "explicitly" or otherwise....

It is true that Federalist No. 52 contrasts the Constitution's treatment of the qualifications of voters in elections for the House of Representatives with its treatment of the qualifications of the Representatives themselves.... But while Madison did say that the qualifications of the elected were "more susceptible of uniformity" than the qualifications of electors, ... he did not say that the Constitution prescribes anything but uniform minimum qualifications for congressmen. That, after all, is more than it does for congressional electors.

. . .

4

. . .

... [S]tate practice immediately after the ratification of the Constitution refutes the majority's suggestion that the Qualifications Clauses were commonly understood as being exclusive. Five States supplemented the constitutional disqualifications in their very first election laws, and the surviving records suggest that the legislatures of these States considered and rejected the interpretation of the Constitution that the majority adopts today.

As the majority concedes, the first Virginia election law erected a property qualification for Virginia's contingent in the Federal House of Representatives.... What is more, while the Constitution merely requires representatives to be inhabitants of their State, the legislatures of five of the seven States that divided themselves into districts for House elections added that representatives also had to be inhabitants of the district that elected them. Three of these States adopted durational residency requirements too, insisting that representatives have resided within their districts for at least a year (or, in one case, three years) before being elected.

. . .

... [W]hatever the explanation, the fact remains that five of the election laws enacted immediately after ratification of the Constitution imposed additional qualifications that would clearly be unconstitutional under today's holding. This history of state practice ... refutes the majority's position that the Qualifications Clauses were generally understood to include an unstated exclusivity provision.

5

The same is true of the final category of historical evidence discussed by the majority: controversies in the House and the Senate over seating candidates who were duly elected but who arguably failed to satisfy qualifications imposed by state law.

As the majority concedes, " 'congressional practice has been erratic' " and is of limited relevance anyway. . . .

. . .

III

It is radical enough for the majority to hold that the Constitution implicitly precludes the people of the States from prescribing any eligibility requirements for the congressional candidates who seek their votes. This holding, after all, does not stop with negating the term limits that many States have seen fit to impose on their Senators and Representatives. Today's decision also means that no State may disqualify congressional candidates whom a court has found to be mentally incompetent, . . . who are currently in prison, . . . or who have past vote-fraud convictions. . . . Likewise, after today's decision, the people of each State must leave open the possibility that they will trust someone with their vote in Congress even though they do not trust him with a vote in the election for Congress. . . .

In order to invalidate § 3 of Amendment 73, however, the majority must go farther. The bulk of the majority's analysis . . . addresses the issues that would be raised if Arkansas had prescribed "genuine, unadulterated, undiluted term limits." But . . . Amendment 73 does not actually create this kind of disqualification. . . . It does not say that covered candidates may not serve any more terms in Congress if reelected, and it does not indirectly achieve the same result by barring those candidates from seeking reelection. It says only that if they are to win reelection, they must do so by write-in votes.

. . .

. . . As the majority notes, the plurality below asserted that "[t]he intent" of Amendment 73 was "to disqualify congressional incumbents from further service." . . .

I am not sure why the intent behind a law should affect our analysis under the Qualifications Clauses. If a law does not in fact add to the constitutional qualifications, the mistaken expectations of the people who enacted it would not seem to affect whether it violates the alleged exclusivity of those Clauses. But in any event, the majority is wrong about what "the State Court" has told us. Even the plurality below did not flatly assert that the desire to "disqualify" congressional incumbents was the sole purpose behind § 3 of Amendment 73. More important, neither of the Justices who concurred in the plurality's holding said anything at all about the intent behind Amendment 73. As a result, we cannot attribute any findings on this issue to the Arkansas Supreme Court.

. . .

. . . One of petitioners' central arguments is that congressionally conferred advantages have artificially inflated the pre-existing electoral chances of the covered candidates, and that Amendment 73 is merely designed to level the playing field on which challengers compete with them.

. . .

The voters of Arkansas evidently believe that incumbents would not enjoy such overwhelming success if electoral contests were truly fair— that is, if the government did not put its thumb on either side of the scale. The majority offers no reason to question the accuracy of this belief. Given this context, petitioners portray § 3 of Amendment 73 as an effort at the state level to offset the electoral advantages that congressional incumbents have conferred upon themselves at the federal level.

. . .

I do not mean to suggest that States have unbridled power to handicap particular classes of candidates, even when those candidates enjoy federally conferred advantages that may threaten to skew the electoral process. But laws that allegedly have the purpose and effect of handicapping a particular class of candidates traditionally are reviewed under the First and Fourteenth Amendments rather than the Qualifications Clauses. . . .

To analyze such laws under the Qualifications Clauses may open up whole new vistas for courts. If it is true that "the current congressional campaign finance system . . . has created an electoral system so stacked against challengers that in many elections voters have no real choices," . . . are the Federal Election Campaign Act Amendments of 1974 unconstitutional under (of all things) the Qualifications Clauses? . . . If it can be shown that nonminorities are at a significant disadvantage when they seek election in districts dominated by minority voters, would the intentional creation of "majority-minority districts" violate the Qualifications Clauses even if it were to survive scrutiny under the Fourteenth Amendment? . . . More generally, if "[d]istrict lines are rarely neutral phenomena" and if "districting inevitably has and is intended to have substantial political consequences," . . . will plausible Qualifications Clause challenges greet virtually every redistricting decision? . . .

The majority's opinion may not go so far, although it does not itself suggest any principled stopping point. No matter how narrowly construed, however, today's decision reads the Qualifications Clauses to impose substantial implicit prohibitions on the States and the people of the States. I would not draw such an expansive negative inference from the fact that the Constitution requires Members of Congress to be a certain age, to be inhabitants of the States that they represent, and to have been United States citizens for a specified period. Rather, I would read the Qualifications Clauses to do no more than what they say. I respectfully dissent.

———

B. POLITICAL FUNDRAISING AND EXPENDITURES

Page 1512. Add at end of subsection:

COLORADO REPUBLICAN FEDERAL CAMPAIGN COM-MITTEE v. FEDERAL ELECTION COMMISSION, 116 S.Ct. 2309 (1996). The "Party Expenditure Provision" of the Federal Election Campaign Act of 1971 imposes dollar limits on "expenditure[s] in connection with the general election campaign of a [congressional] candidate." 2 U.S.C. § 441a(d)(3). After the Colorado Republican Party selected its 1986 candidate for United States Senate, it bought radio advertisements attacking the likely Democratic Party candidate. While seven Justices agreed that the Constitution precluded enforcement of the Act in this case, there was no opinion for the Court. Three Justices (Breyer, O'Connor and Souter) concluded that the Party Expenditure Provision was unconstitutional as applied to"independent" party expenditures that were not an "indirect campaign contribution" to a candidate. Justice Breyer's opinion took no position concerning the validity of party expenditure limitations as applied to a party expenditure "in cooperation, consultation, or concert with ... a candidate." Four Justices (Kennedy, Rehnquist, Scalia and Thomas) would have held the Party Expenditure Provision unconstitutional on its face, even in the latter context. Justice Kennedy (joined by the Chief Justice and Justice Scalia) argued that all party expenditures fell within the rationale of Buckley v. Valeo, which forbids limitation on spending money on one's own speech. Justice Thomas (also joined by the Chief Justice and Justice Scalia) argued that *Buckley*'s corruption rationale was inapplicable to contributions by a party to its own candidate.[1] Justice Stevens (joined by Justice Ginsburg) dissented, arguing that spending limits on political parties were constitutional, serving "an important interest in leveling the electoral field by constraining the cost of federal campaigns."

C. DISCLOSURE REQUIREMENTS

Page 1517. Add at end of section:

McINTYRE v. OHIO ELECTIONS COMMISSION
___ U.S. ___, 115 S.Ct. 1511, 131 L.Ed.2d 426 (1995).

Justice Stevens delivered the opinion of the Court.

The question presented is whether an Ohio statute that prohibits the distribution of anonymous campaign literature is a "law ... abridging the freedom of speech" within the meaning of the First Amendment.

---

[1] In a portion of his opinion where he spoke only for himself, Justice Thomas argued that *Buckley*'s distinction between contribution limits and spending limits should be rejected.

I

On April 27, 1988, Margaret McIntyre distributed leaflets to persons attending a public meeting at the Blendon Middle School in Westerville, Ohio. At this meeting, the superintendent of schools planned to discuss an imminent referendum on a proposed school tax levy. The leaflets expressed Mrs. McIntyre's opposition to the levy. There is no suggestion that the text of her message was false, misleading, or libelous. She had composed and printed it on her home computer and had paid a professional printer to make additional copies. Some of the handbills identified her as the author; others merely purported to express the views of "CONCERNED PARENTS AND TAX PAYERS." Except for the help provided by her son and a friend, who placed some of the leaflets on car windshields in the school parking lot, Mrs. McIntyre acted independently.

While Mrs. McIntyre distributed her handbills, an official of the school district, who supported the tax proposal, advised her that the unsigned leaflets did not conform to the Ohio election laws. Undeterred, Mrs. McIntyre appeared at another meeting on the next evening and handed out more of the handbills.

The proposed school levy was defeated at the next two elections, but it finally passed on its third try in November 1988. Five months later, the same school official filed a complaint with the Ohio Elections Commission charging that Mrs. McIntyre's distribution of unsigned leaflets violated § 3599.09(A) of the Ohio Code. The Commission agreed and imposed a fine of $100.

The Franklin County Court of Common Pleas reversed. Finding that Mrs. McIntyre did not "mislead the public nor act in a surreptitious manner," the court concluded that the statute was unconstitutional as applied to her conduct. The Ohio Court of Appeals, by a divided vote, reinstated the fine. . . .

The Ohio Supreme Court affirmed by a divided vote. . . .

Mrs. McIntyre passed away during the pendency of this litigation. Even though the amount in controversy is only $100, petitioner, as the executor of her estate, has pursued her claim in this Court. Our grant of certiorari reflects our agreement with his appraisal of the importance of the question presented.

II

Ohio maintains that the statute under review is a reasonable regulation of the electoral process. The State does not suggest that all anonymous publications are pernicious or that a statute totally excluding them from the marketplace of ideas would be valid. This is a wise (albeit implicit) concession, for the anonymity of an author is not ordinarily a sufficient reason to exclude her work product from the protections of the First Amendment.

"Anonymous pamphlets, leaflets, brochures and even books have played an important role in the progress of mankind." Talley v. California, 362 U.S. 60, 64 (1960). Great works of literature have frequently been produced by authors writing under assumed names. Despite readers' curiosity and the public's interest in identifying the creator of a work of art, an author generally is free to decide whether or not to disclose her true identity. The decision in favor of anonymity may be motivated by fear of economic or official retaliation, by concern about social ostracism, or merely by a desire to preserve as much of one's privacy as possible. Whatever the motivation may be, at least in the field of literary endeavor, the interest in having anonymous works enter the marketplace of ideas unquestionably outweighs any public interest in requiring disclosure as a condition of entry. Accordingly, an author's decision to remain anonymous, like other decisions concerning omissions or additions to the content of a publication, is an aspect of the freedom of speech protected by the First Amendment.

The freedom to publish anonymously extends beyond the literary realm. In *Talley*, the Court held that the First Amendment protects the distribution of unsigned handbills urging readers to boycott certain Los Angeles merchants who were allegedly engaging in discriminatory employment practices.... Writing for the Court, Justice Black noted that "[p]ersecuted groups and sects from time to time throughout history have been able to criticize oppressive practices and laws either anonymously or not at all." Justice Black recalled England's abusive press licensing laws and seditious libel prosecutions, and he reminded us that even the arguments favoring the ratification of the Constitution advanced in the Federalist Papers were published under fictitious names.... On occasion, quite apart from any threat of persecution, an advocate may believe her ideas will be more persuasive if her readers are unaware of her identity. Anonymity thereby provides a way for a writer who may be personally unpopular to ensure that readers will not prejudge her message simply because they do not like its proponent. Thus, even in the field of political rhetoric, where "the identity of the speaker is an important component of many attempts to persuade," City of Ladue v. Gilleo, 512 U.S. ___, ___ (1994), the most effective advocates have sometimes opted for anonymity. The specific holding in *Talley* related to advocacy of an economic boycott, but the Court's reasoning embraced a respected tradition of anonymity in the advocacy of political causes. This tradition is perhaps best exemplified by the secret ballot, the hard-won right to vote one's conscience without fear of retaliation.

III

California had defended the Los Angeles ordinance at issue in *Talley* as a law "aimed at providing a way to identify those responsible for fraud, false advertising and libel." ... We rejected that argument because nothing in the text or legislative history of the ordinance limited its application to those evils.... We then made clear that we did "not pass on the validity of an ordinance limited to prevent these or any other supposed evils." ... The Ohio statute likewise contains no language limiting its application to fraudulent, false, or libelous statements; to the extent, therefore, that Ohio seeks to justify § 3599.09(A) as a means to prevent the dissemination of untruths, its defense must fail for the same reason given in *Talley*. As the facts of this case demonstrate, the ordinance plainly applies even when there is no hint of falsity or libel.

Ohio's statute does, however, contain a different limitation: It applies only to unsigned documents designed to influence voters in an election. In contrast, the Los Angeles ordinance prohibited all anonymous handbilling "in any place under any circumstances." ... For that reason, Ohio correctly argues that *Talley* does not necessarily control the disposition of this case. We must, therefore, decide whether and to what extent the First Amendment's protection of anonymity encompasses documents intended to influence the electoral process.

Ohio places its principal reliance on cases such as Anderson v. Celebrezze, 460 U.S. 780 (1983); Storer v. Brown, 415 U.S. 724 (1974); and Burdick v. Takushi, 504 U.S. 428 (1992), in which we reviewed election code provisions governing the voting process itself.... In those cases we refused to adopt "any 'litmus-paper test' that will separate valid from invalid restrictions." ... Instead, we pursued an analytical process comparable to that used by courts "in ordinary litigation": we considered the relative interests of the State and the injured voters, and we evaluated the extent to which the State's interests necessitated the contested restrictions....

The "ordinary litigation" test does not apply here. Unlike the statutory provisions challenged in *Storer* and *Anderson*, § 3599.09(A) of the Ohio Code does not control the mechanics of the electoral process. It is a regulation of pure speech. Moreover, even though this provision applies evenhandedly to advocates of differing viewpoints, it is a direct regulation of the content of speech. Every written document covered by the statute must contain "the name and residence or business address of the chairman, treasurer, or secretary of the organization issuing the same, or the person who issues, makes, or is responsible therefor." Ohio Rev.Code Ann. § 3599.09(A)(1988). Furthermore, the category of covered documents is defined by their content—only those publications containing speech designed to influence the voters in an election need bear the required markings.... Consequently, we are not faced with an ordinary election restriction ...

Indeed, as we have explained on many prior occasions, the category of speech regulated by the Ohio statute occupies the core of the protection afforded by the First Amendment ...

Of course, core political speech need not center on a candidate for office. The principles ... extend equally to issue-based elections such as the school-tax referendum that Mrs. McIntyre sought to influence through her handbills.... Indeed, the speech in which Mrs. McIntyre engaged—handing out leaflets in the advocacy of a politically controversial viewpoint—is the essence of First Amendment expression.... That this advocacy occurred in the heat of a controversial referendum vote only strengthens the protection afforded to Ms. McIntyre's expression: urgent, important, and effective speech can be no less protected than impotent speech, lest the right to speak be relegated to those instances when it is least needed....

When a law burdens core political speech, we apply "exacting scrutiny," and we uphold the restriction only if it is narrowly tailored to serve an overriding state interest.... Our precedents thus make abundantly clear that the Ohio Supreme Court applied a significantly more lenient standard than is appropriate in a case of this kind.

IV

Nevertheless, the State argues that even under the strictest standard of review, the disclosure requirement in § 3599.09(A) is justified by two important and legitimate state interests. Ohio judges its interest in preventing fraudulent and libelous statements and its interest in providing the electorate with relevant information to be sufficiently compelling to justify the anonymous speech ban. These two interests necessarily overlap to some extent, but it is useful to discuss them separately.

Insofar as the interest in informing the electorate means nothing more than the provision of additional information that may either buttress or undermine the argument in a document, we think the identity of the speaker is no different from other components of the document's content that the author is free to include or exclude.... The simple interest in providing voters with additional relevant information does not justify a state requirement that a writer make statements or disclosures she would otherwise omit. Moreover, in the case of a handbill written by a private citizen who is not known to the recipient, the name and address of the author adds little, if anything, to the reader's ability to evaluate the document's message. Thus, Ohio's informational interest is plainly insufficient to support the constitutionality of its disclosure requirement.

The state interest in preventing fraud and libel stands on a different footing. We agree with Ohio's submission that this interest carries special weight during election campaigns when false statements, if credited, may have serious adverse consequences for the public at large. Ohio does not, however, rely solely on § 3599.09(A) to protect that interest. Its Election Code includes detailed and specific prohibitions against making or disseminating false statements during political campaigns.... These regulations apply both to candidate elections and to issue-driven ballot measures. Thus, Ohio's prohibition of anonymous leaflets plainly is not its principal weapon against fraud. Rather, it serves as an aid to enforcement of the specific prohibitions and as a deterrent to the making of false statements by unscrupulous prevaricators. Although these ancillary benefits are assuredly legitimate, we are not persuaded that they justify § 3599.09(A)'s extremely broad prohibition.

As this case demonstrates, the prohibition encompasses documents that are not even arguably false or misleading. It applies not only to the activities of candidates and their organized supporters, but also to individuals acting independently and using only their own modest resources. It applies not only to elections of public officers, but also to ballot issues that present neither a substantial risk of libel nor any potential appearance of corrupt advantage. It applies not only to leaflets distributed on the eve of an election, when the opportunity for reply is limited, but also to those distributed months in advance. It applies no matter what the character or strength of the author's interest in anonymity. Moreover, as this case also demonstrates, the absence of the author's name on a document does not necessarily protect either that person or a distributor of a forbidden document from being held responsible for compliance with the election code. Nor has the State explained why it can more easily enforce the direct bans on disseminating false documents against anonymous authors and distributors than against wrongdoers who might use false names and addresses in an attempt to avoid detection. We recognize that a State's enforcement interest might justify a more limited identification requirement, but Ohio has shown scant cause for inhibiting the leafletting at issue here.

V

Finally, Ohio vigorously argues that our opinions in First Nat. Bank of Boston v. Bellotti, 435 U.S. 765 (1978), and Buckley v. Valeo, 424 U.S. 1 (1976), amply support the constitutionality of its disclosure requirement. Neither case is controlling: the former concerned the scope of First Amendment protection afforded to corporations; the relevant portion of the latter concerned mandatory disclosure of campaign-related expenditures. Neither case involved a prohibition of anonymous campaign literature.

In *Bellotti*, we ... made it perfectly clear that we were not deciding whether the First Amendment's protection of corporate speech is coextensive with the protection it affords to individuals. Accordingly, although we commented in dicta on the prophylactic effect of requiring identification of the source of corporate advertising, that footnote did not necessarily apply to independent communications by an individual like Mrs. McIntyre.

Our reference in the *Bellotti* footnote to the "prophylactic effect" of disclosure requirements cited a portion of our earlier opinion in *Buckley*, in which we stressed the importance of providing "the electorate with information 'as to where political campaign money comes from and how it is spent by the candidate.'" ... We observed that the "sources of a candidate's financial support also alert the voter to the interests to which a candidate is most likely to be responsive and thus facilitate predictions of future performance in office." ... Those comments concerned contributions to the candidate or expenditures authorized by the candidate or his responsible agent. They had no reference to the kind of independent activity pursued by Mrs. McIntyre. Required disclosures about the level of financial support a candidate has received from various sources are supported by an interest in avoiding the appearance of corruption that has no application to this case.

True, in another portion of the *Buckley* opinion we expressed approval of a requirement that even "independent expenditures" in excess of a threshold level be reported to the Federal Election Commission.... But that requirement entailed nothing more than an identification to the Commission of the amount and use of money expended in support of a candidate.... Though such mandatory reporting undeniably impedes protected First Amendment activity, the intrusion is a far cry from compelled self-identification on all election-related writings. A written election-related document—particularly a leaflet—is often a personally crafted statement of a political viewpoint. Mrs. McIntyre's handbills surely fit that description. As such, identification of the author against her will is particularly intrusive; it reveals unmistakably the content of her thoughts on a controversial issue. Disclosure of an expenditure and its use, without more, reveals far less information. It may be information that a person prefers to keep secret, and undoubtedly it often gives away something about the spender's political views. Nonetheless, even though money may "talk," its speech is less specific, less personal, and less provocative than a handbill—and as a result, when money supports an unpopular viewpoint it is less likely to precipitate retaliation.

Not only is the Ohio statute's infringement on speech more intrusive than the *Buckley* disclosure requirement, but it rests on different and less powerful state interests. The Federal Election Campaign Act of 1971, at issue in *Buckley*, regulates only candidate elections, not referenda or other issue-based ballot measures; and we construed "independent expenditures" to mean only those expenditures that "expressly advocate the election or defeat of a clearly identified candidate." ... In candidate elections, the Government can identify a compelling state interest in avoiding the corruption that might result from campaign expenditures. Disclosure of expenditures lessens the risk that individuals will spend money to support a candidate as a quid pro quo for special treatment after the candidate is in office. Curriers of favor will be deterred by the knowledge that all expenditures will be scrutinized by the Federal Election Commission and by the public for just this sort of abuse. Moreover, the federal Act contains numerous legitimate disclosure requirements for campaign organizations; the similar requirements for independent expenditures serve to ensure that a campaign organization will not seek to evade disclosure by routing its expenditures through individual supporters.... In short, although *Buckley* may permit a more narrowly drawn statute, it surely is not authority for upholding Ohio's open-ended provision.

VI

Under our Constitution, anonymous pamphleteering is not a pernicious, fraudulent practice, but an honorable tradition of advocacy and of dissent. Anonymity is a shield from the tyranny of the majority.... It thus exemplifies the purpose behind the Bill of Rights, and of the First Amendment in particular: to protect unpopular individuals from retaliation—and their ideas from suppression—at the hand of an intolerant society. The right to remain anonymous may be abused when it shields fraudulent conduct. But political speech by its nature will sometimes have unpalatable consequences, and, in general, our society accords greater weight to the value of free speech than to the dangers of its misuse.... Ohio has not shown that its interest in preventing the misuse of anonymous election-related speech justifies a prohibition of all uses of that speech. The State may, and does, punish fraud directly. But it cannot seek to punish fraud indirectly by indiscriminately outlawing a category of speech, based on its content, with no necessary relationship to the danger sought to be prevented. One would be hard pressed to think of a better example of the pitfalls of Ohio's blunderbuss approach than the facts of the case before us.

The judgment of the Ohio Supreme Court is reversed.

It is so ordered.

Justice Ginsburg, concurring.

The dissent is stirring in its appreciation of democratic values. But I do not see the Court's opinion as unguided by "bedrock principle," tradition, or our case law. . . .

In for a calf is not always in for a cow. The Court's decision finds unnecessary, overintrusive, and inconsistent with American ideals the State's imposition of a fine on an individual leafleteer who, within her local community, spoke her mind, but sometimes not her name. We do not thereby hold that the State may not in other, larger circumstances, require the speaker to disclose its interest by disclosing its identity. Appropriately leaving open matters not presented by McIntyre's handbills, the Court recognizes that a State's interest in protecting an election process "might justify a more limited identification requirement." . . .

Justice Thomas, concurring in the judgment.

I agree with the majority's conclusion that Ohio's election law, Ohio Rev.Code Ann. § 3599.09(A), is inconsistent with the First Amendment. I would apply, however, a different methodology to this case. Instead of asking whether "an honorable tradition" of anonymous speech has existed throughout American history, or what the "value" of anonymous speech might be, we should determine whether the phrase "freedom of speech, or of the press," as originally understood, protected anonymous political leafletting. I believe that it did.

. . .

III

The historical record is not as complete or as full as I would desire. For example, there is no evidence that, after the adoption of the First Amendment, the Federal Government attempted to require writers to attach their names to political documents. Nor do we have any indication that the federal courts of the early Republic would have squashed such an effort as a violation of the First Amendment. The understanding described above, however, when viewed in light of the Framers' universal practice of publishing anonymous articles and pamphlets, indicates that the Framers shared the belief that such activity was firmly part of the freedom of the press. It is only an innovation of modern times that has permitted the regulation of anonymous speech.

. . .

IV

This evidence leads me to agree with the majority's result, but not its reasoning. The majority fails to seek the original understanding of the First Amendment. . . .

I cannot join the majority's analysis because it deviates from our settled approach to interpreting the Constitution and because it superimposes its modern theories concerning expression upon the constitutional text. . . . And although the majority faithfully follows our approach to "content-based" speech regulations, we need not undertake this analysis when the original understanding provides the answer.

While, like Justice Scalia, I am loath to overturn a century of practice shared by almost all of the States, I believe the historical evidence from the framing outweighs recent tradition. When interpreting other provisions of the Constitution, this Court has believed itself bound by the text of the Constitution and by the intent of those who drafted and ratified it. It should hold itself to no less a standard when interpreting the Speech and Press Clauses. After reviewing the weight of the historical evidence, it seems that the Framers understood the First Amendment to protect an author's right to express his thoughts on political candidates or issues in an anonymous fashion. Because the majority has adopted an analysis that is largely unconnected to the Constitution's text and history, I concur only in the judgment.

Justice Scalia, with whom The Chief Justice joins, dissenting.

At a time when both political branches of Government and both political parties reflect a popular desire to leave more decisionmaking authority to the States, today's decision moves in the opposite direction, adding to the legacy of inflexible central mandates (irrevocable even by Congress) imposed by this Court's constitutional jurisprudence. In an opinion which reads as though it is addressing some peculiar law like the Los Angeles municipal ordinance at issue in Talley v. California, 362 U.S. 60 (1960), the Court invalidates a species of protection for the election process that exists, in a variety of forms, in every State except California, and that has a pedigree dating back to the end of the 19th century. . . . I dissent from this imposition of free-speech imperatives that are demonstrably not those of the American people today, and that there is inadequate reason to believe were those of the society that begat the First Amendment or the Fourteenth.

I

The question posed by the present case is not the easiest sort to answer for those who adhere to the Court's (and the society's) traditional view that the Constitution bears its original meaning and is unchanging. Under that view, "[o]n every question of construction, [we should] carry ourselves back to the time when the Constitution was adopted; recollect the spirit manifested in the debates; and instead of trying [to find] what meaning may be squeezed out of the text, or invented against it, conform to the probable one in which it was passed." T. Jefferson, Letter to William Johnson (June 12, 1823), in 15 Writings of Thomas

Jefferson 439, 449 (A. Lipscomb ed. 1904). That technique is simple of application when government conduct that is claimed to violate the Bill of Rights or the Fourteenth Amendment is shown, upon investigation, to have been engaged in without objection at the very time the Bill of Rights or the Fourteenth Amendment was adopted. There is no doubt, for example, that laws against libel and obscenity do not violate "the freedom of speech" to which the First Amendment refers; they existed and were universally approved in 1791. Application of the principle of an unchanging Constitution is also simple enough at the other extreme, where the government conduct at issue was not engaged in at the time of adoption, and there is ample evidence that the reason it was not engaged in is that it was thought to violate the right embodied in the constitutional guarantee. Racks and thumbscrews, well known instruments for inflicting pain, were not in use because they were regarded as cruel punishments.

The present case lies between those two extremes. Anonymous electioneering was not prohibited by law in 1791 or in 1868. In fact, it was widely practiced at the earlier date, an understandable legacy of the revolutionary era in which political dissent could produce governmental reprisal. I need not dwell upon the evidence of that, since it is described at length in today's concurrence....

But to prove that anonymous electioneering was used frequently is not to establish that it is a constitutional right....

Evidence that anonymous electioneering was regarded as a constitutional right is sparse, and as far as I am aware evidence that it was generally regarded as such is nonexistent....

. . .

What we have, then, is the most difficult case for determining the meaning of the Constitution. No accepted existence of governmental restrictions of the sort at issue here demonstrates their constitutionality, but neither can their nonexistence clearly be attributed to constitutional objections. In such a case, constitutional adjudication necessarily involves not just history but judgment: judgment as to whether the government action under challenge is consonant with the concept of the protected freedom (in this case, the freedom of speech and of the press) that existed when the constitutional protection was accorded. In the present case, absent other indication I would be inclined to agree with the concurrence that a society which used anonymous political debate so regularly would not regard as constitutional even moderate restrictions made to improve the election process. (I would, however, want further evidence of common practice in 1868, since I doubt that the Fourteenth Amendment time-warped the post-Civil War States back to the Revolution.)

But there is other indication, of the most weighty sort: the widespread and longstanding traditions of our people. Principles of liberty fundamental enough to have been embodied within constitutional guarantees are not readily erased from the Nation's consciousness. A governmental practice that has become general throughout the United

States, and particularly one that has the validation of long, accepted usage, bears a strong presumption of constitutionality. And that is what we have before us here. Section 3599.09(A) was enacted by the General Assembly of the State of Ohio almost 80 years ago.... Even at the time of its adoption, there was nothing unique or extraordinary about it. The earliest statute of this sort was adopted by Massachusetts in 1890, little more than 20 years after the Fourteenth Amendment was ratified. No less than 24 States had similar laws by the end of World War I, and today every State of the Union except California has one, as does the District of Columbia, see D.C.Code Ann. § 1–1420 (1992), and as does the Federal Government where advertising relating to candidates for federal office is concerned, see 2 U.S.C. § 441d(a). Such a universal and long established American legislative practice must be given precedence, I think, over historical and academic speculation regarding a restriction that assuredly does not go to the heart of free speech.

It can be said that we ignored a tradition as old, and almost as widespread, in Texas v. Johnson, 491 U.S. 397 (1989), where we held unconstitutional a state law prohibiting desecration of the United States flag. See also United States v. Eichman, 496 U.S. 310 (1990). But those cases merely stand for the proposition that post-adoption tradition cannot alter the core meaning of a constitutional guarantee....

II

The foregoing analysis suffices to decide this case for me. Where the meaning of a constitutional text (such as "the freedom of speech") is unclear, the widespread and long-accepted practices of the American people are the best indication of what fundamental beliefs it was intended to enshrine. Even if I were to close my eyes to practice, however, and were to be guided exclusively by deductive analysis from our case law, I would reach the same result.

Three basic questions must be answered to decide this case. Two of them are readily answered by our precedents; the third is readily answered by common sense and by a decent regard for the practical judgment of those more familiar with elections than we are. The first question is whether protection of the election process justifies limitations upon speech that cannot constitutionally be imposed generally. (If not, Talley v. California, which invalidated a flat ban on all anonymous leafletting, controls the decision here.) Our cases plainly answer that question in the affirmative—indeed, they suggest that no justification for regulation is more compelling than protection of the electoral process....

The second question relevant to our decision is whether a "right to anonymity" is such a prominent value in our constitutional system that even protection of the electoral process cannot be purchased at its expense. The answer, again, is clear: no. Several of our cases have held that in peculiar circumstances the compelled disclosure of a person's identity would unconstitutionally deter the exercise of First Amendment associational rights.... But those cases did not acknowledge any general right to anonymity, or even any right on the part of all citizens to ignore the particular laws under challenge.... Anonymity can still be enjoyed by those who require it, without utterly destroying useful disclosure laws. The record in this case contains not even a hint that Mrs. McIntyre feared "threats, harassment, or reprisals"; indeed, she placed her name on some of her fliers and meant to place it on all of them.

.   .   .

   The Court's unprecedented protection for anonymous speech does not even have the virtue of establishing a clear (albeit erroneous) rule of law.   For after having announced that this statute, because it "burdens core political speech," requires "exacting scrutiny" and must be "narrowly tailored to serve an overriding state interest," (ordinarily the kiss of death), the opinion goes on to proclaim soothingly (and unhelpfully) that "a State's enforcement interest might justify a more limited identification requirement."   ... Perhaps, then, not all the State statutes I have alluded to are invalid, but just some of them; or indeed maybe all of them remain valid in "larger circumstances"! It may take decades to work out the shape of this newly expanded right-to-speak-incognito, even in the elections field.   And in other areas, of course, a whole new boutique of wonderful First Amendment litigation opens its doors. Must a parade permit, for example, be issued to a group that refuses to provide its identity, or that agrees to do so only under assurance that the identity will not be made public? Must a municipally owned theater that is leased for private productions book anonymously sponsored presentations? Must a government periodical that has a "letters to the editor" column disavow the policy that most newspapers have against the publication of anonymous letters? Must a public university that makes its facilities available for a speech by Louis Farrakhan or David Duke refuse to disclose the on-campus or off-campus group that has sponsored or paid for the speech? Must a municipal "public-access" cable channel permit anonymous (and masked) performers? The silliness that follows upon a generalized right to anonymous speech has no end.

   The third and last question relevant to our decision is whether the prohibition of anonymous campaigning is effective in protecting and enhancing democratic elections.   In answering this question no, the Justices of the majority set their own views—on a practical matter that bears closely upon the real-life experience of elected politicians and not upon that of unelected judges—up against the views of 49 ... state legislatures and the federal Congress. We might also add to the list on the other side the legislatures of foreign democracies: Australia, Canada, and England, for example, all have prohibitions upon anonymous campaigning....   How is it, one must wonder, that all of these elected legislators, from around the country and around the world, could not see what six Justices of this Court see so clearly that they are willing to require the entire Nation to act upon it: that requiring identification of the source of campaign literature does not improve the quality of the campaign?

   The Court says that the State has not explained "why it can more easily enforce the direct bans on disseminating false documents against anonymous authors and distributors than against wrongdoers who might use false names and addresses in an attempt to avoid detection." I am not sure what this complicated comparison means. I am sure, however, that (1) a person who is required to put his name to a document is much less likely to lie than one who can lie anonymously, and (2) the distributor of a leaflet which is unlawful because it is anonymous runs much more risk of immediate detection and punishment than the distributor of a leaflet which is unlawful because it is false. Thus, people will be more likely to observe a signing requirement than a naked "no falsity" requirement; and, having observed that requirement, will then be significantly less likely to lie in what they have signed.

But the usefulness of a signing requirement lies not only in promoting observance of the law against campaign falsehoods (though that alone is enough to sustain it). It lies also in promoting a civil and dignified level of campaign debate—which the State has no power to command, but ample power to encourage by such undemanding measures as a signature requirement. Observers of the past few national elections have expressed concern about the increase of character assassination—"mudslinging" is the colloquial term—engaged in by political candidates and their supporters to the detriment of the democratic process. Not all of this, in fact not much of it, consists of actionable untruth; most is innuendo, or demeaning characterization, or mere disclosure of items of personal life that have no bearing upon suitability for office. Imagine how much all of this would increase if it could be done anonymously. The principal impediment against it is the reluctance of most individuals and organizations to be publicly associated with uncharitable and uncivil expression. Consider, moreover, the increased potential for "dirty tricks." It is not unheard-of for campaign operatives to circulate material over the name of their opponents or their opponents' supporters (a violation of election laws) in order to attract or alienate certain interest groups.... How much easier—and sanction-free!—it would be to circulate anonymous material (for example, a really tasteless, though not actionably false, attack upon one's own candidate) with the hope and expectation that it will be attributed to, and held against, the other side.

. . .

We have approved much more onerous disclosure requirements in the name of fair elections. In Buckley v. Valeo, 424 U.S. 1 (1976), we upheld provisions of the Federal Election Campaign Act that required private individuals to report to the Federal Election Commission independent expenditures made for communications advocating the election or defeat of a candidate for federal office.... Our primary rationale for upholding this provision was that it served an "informational interest" by "increas[ing] the fund of information concerning those who support the candidates,"... The provision before us here serves the same informational interest, as well as more important interests, which I have discussed above....

* * *

I do not know where the Court derives its perception that "anonymous pamphleteering is not a pernicious, fraudulent practice, but an honorable tradition of advocacy and of dissent." I can imagine no reason why an anonymous leaflet is any more honorable, as a general matter, than an anonymous phone call or an anonymous letter. It facilitates wrong by eliminating accountability, which is ordinarily the very purpose of the anonymity. There are of course exceptions, and where anonymity is needed to avoid "threats, harassment, or reprisals" the First Amendment will require an exemption from the Ohio law. Cf. NAACP v. Alabama ex rel. Patterson, 357 U.S. 449 (1958). But to strike down the Ohio law in its general application—and similar laws of 48 other States and the Federal Government—on the ground that all anonymous communication is in our society traditionally sacrosanct, seems to me a distortion of the past that will lead to a coarsening of the future.

I respectfully dissent.

SECTION 5. SPEECH AND ASSOCIATION RIGHTS OF GOVERNMENT EMPLOYEES

Page 1536. Add at end of chapter:

SPEECH AND ASSOCIATION RIGHTS OF GOVERNMENT CONTRACTORS

In Board of County Commissioners v. Umbeher, 116 S.Ct. 2342 (1996), the Court extended Pickering v. Board of Education to the case of a government contractor whose trash hauling contract was terminated after he publicly criticized the county's governing board. On the same day, in O'Hare v. City of Northlake, 116 S.Ct. 2353 (1996), the Court extended Elrod v. Burns and Branti v. Finkel to a person whose towing service was removed from a city list of available towing companies after he refused to contribute to the mayor's re-election campaign and instead supported the mayor's opponent. In *Umbeher*, Justice O'Connor's opinion for the Court reserved the question whether the First Amendment would be implicated by government's speech-motivated refusal to contract in the first instance. The opinion further stated that once the plaintiff had proved that termination was motivated by speech on a matter of public concern, the defendant might still prevail even if it failed to prove that it would have terminated the contract regardless of the speech. An additional defense would be that government's legitimate interests as a contractor outweighed the plaintiff's free speech interests. That additional defense would not be available in *O'Hare*. Justice Kennedy's opinion for the Court in *O'Hare* explained that where a contract was terminated because of the plaintiff's political affiliation, the reasonableness inquiry was confined to the question whether political affiliation was an appropriate requirement for the effective performance of the contracted work. Justices Scalia and Thomas dissented in both cases.

UNITED STATES v. NATIONAL TREASURY EMPLOYEES UNION
___ U.S. ___, 115 S.Ct. 1003, 130 L.Ed.2d 964 (1995).

Justice Stevens delivered the opinion of the Court.

In 1989 Congress enacted a law that broadly prohibits federal employees from accepting any compensation for making speeches or writing articles. The prohibition applies even when neither the subject of the speech or article nor the person or group paying for it has any connection with the employee's official duties. We must decide whether that statutory prohibition comports with the Constitution's command that "Congress shall make no law ... abridging the freedom of speech." We hold that it does not.

I

In 1967 Congress authorized the appointment every four years of a special Commission on Executive, Legislative, and Judicial Salaries, whose principal function would be to recommend appropriate levels of compensation for the top positions in all three branches of the Federal Government. Each of the first five quadrennial commissions recommended significant salary increases, but those recommendations went largely ignored. The Report of the 1989 Quadrennial Commission, however, was instrumental in leading to the enactment of the Ethics Reform Act of 1989, which contains the provision challenged in this case.

The 1989 Quadrennial Commission's report noted that inflation had decreased the salary levels for senior Government officials, measured in constant dollars, by approximately 35% since 1969. The report "also found that because their salaries are so inadequate, many members of Congress are supplementing their official compensation by accepting substantial amounts of 'honoraria' for meeting with interest groups which desire to influence their votes. Albeit to a less troubling extent, the practice of accepting honoraria also extends to top officials of the Executive and Judicial branches." ... Accordingly, the Commission recommended that "salary levels for top officials be set at approximately the same amount in constant dollars" as those in effect in 1969 and further that "Congress enact legislation abolishing the practice of accepting honoraria in all three branches." ...

The President's Commission on Federal Ethics Law Reform subsequently issued a report that endorsed the Quadrennial Commission's views....

Although not adopted in their entirety, the two Commissions' recommendations echo prominently in the Ethics Reform Act of 1989.

Section 703 of that Act provided a 25% pay increase to Members of Congress, federal judges, and Executive Branch employees above the salary grade GS–15.... Another section—the one at issue here— amended § 501(b) of the Ethics in Government Act of 1978 to create an "Honoraria Prohibition," which reads: "An individual may not receive any honorarium while that individual is a Member, officer or employee."

Section 505 of the Ethics Reform Act defined "officer or employee" to include nearly all employees of the Federal Government and "Member" to include any Representative, Delegate, or Resident Commissioner to Congress. The Congressional Operations Appropriations Act, 1992, extended both the salary increase and the prohibition against honoraria to the Senate. The 1989 Act defined "honorarium" to encompass any compensation paid to a Government employee for "an appearance, speech or article." The 1992 Appropriations Act amended that definition to exclude any series of appearances, speeches, or articles unrelated to the employee's official duties or status. The definition now reads as follows:

> "(3) The term 'honorarium' means a payment of money or any thing of value for an appearance, speech or article (including a series of appearances, speeches, or articles if the subject matter is directly related to the individual's official duties or the payment is made because of the individual's status with the Government) by a Member, officer or employee, excluding any actual and necessary travel expenses incurred by such individual (and one relative) to the extent that such expenses are paid or reimbursed by any other person, and the amount otherwise determined shall be reduced by the amount of any such expenses to the extent that such expenses are not paid or reimbursed." . . .

. . .

II

Two unions and several career civil servants employed full-time by various Executive departments and agencies filed suit in the United States District Court for the District of Columbia to challenge the constitutionality of the honoraria ban....

. . .

The District Court granted respondents' motion for summary judgment, held the statute "unconstitutional insofar as it applies to Executive Branch employees of the United States government," and enjoined the Government from enforcing the statute against any Executive Branch employee....

The Court of Appeals affirmed....

. . .

III

Federal employees who write for publication in their spare time have made significant contributions to the marketplace of ideas. They include literary giants like Nathaniel Hawthorne and Herman Melville, who were employed by the Customs Service; Walt Whitman, who worked for the Departments of Justice and Interior; and Bret Harte, an employee of the Mint. Respondents have yet to make comparable contributions to American culture, but they share with these great artists important characteristics that are relevant to the issue we confront.

Even though respondents work for the Government, they have not relinquished "the First Amendment rights they would otherwise enjoy as citizens to comment on matters of public interest." Pickering v. Board of Ed. of Township High School Dist., 391 U.S. 563, 568 (1968). They seek compensation for their expressive activities in their capacity as citizens, not as Government employees. They claim their employment status has no more bearing on the quality or market value of their literary output than it did on that of Hawthorne or Melville. With few exceptions, the content of respondents' messages has nothing to do with their jobs and does not even arguably have any adverse impact on the efficiency of the offices in which they work. They do not address audiences composed of co-workers or supervisors; instead, they write or speak for segments of the general public. Neither the character of the authors, the subject matter of their expression, the effect of the content of their expression on their official duties, nor the kind of audiences they address has any relevance to their employment.

In *Pickering* and a number of other cases we have recognized that Congress may impose restraints on the job-related speech of public employees that would be plainly unconstitutional if applied to the public at large.... When a court is required to determine the validity of such a restraint, it must "arrive at a balance between the interests of the [employee], as a citizen, in commenting upon matters of public concern and the interest of the State, as an employer, in promoting the efficiency of the public services it performs through its employees." *Pickering,* 391 U.S., at 568.

In such cases, which usually have involved disciplinary actions taken in response to a government employee's speech, we have applied *Pickering*'s balancing test only when the employee spoke "as a citizen upon matters of public concern" rather than "as an employee upon matters only of personal interest." ... Thus, private speech that involves nothing more than a complaint about a change in the employee's own duties may give rise to discipline without imposing any special burden of justification on the government employer.... If, however, the speech does involve a matter of public concern, the Government bears the burden of justifying its adverse employment action.... Respondents' expressive activities in this case fall within the protected category of citizen comment on matters of public concern rather than employee comment on matters related to personal status in the workplace. The speeches and articles for which they received compensation in the past were addressed to a public audience, were made outside the workplace, and involved content largely unrelated to their government employment.

The sweep of § 501(b) makes the Government's burden heavy. Unlike *Pickering* and its progeny, this case does not involve a post hoc analysis of one employee's speech and its impact on that employee's public responsibilities.... Rather, the Government asks us to apply *Pickering* to Congress' wholesale deterrent to a broad category of expression by a massive number of potential speakers. In Civil Service Comm'n v. Letter Carriers, 413 U.S. 548 (1973), we established that the Government must be able to satisfy a balancing test of the *Pickering* form to maintain a statutory restriction on employee speech. Because the discussion in that case essentially restated in balancing terms our approval of the Hatch Act in Public Workers v. Mitchell, 330 U.S. 75 (1947), we did not determine how the components of the *Pickering* balance should be analyzed in the context of a sweeping statutory impediment to speech.

We normally accord a stronger presumption of validity to a congressional judgment than to an individual executive's disciplinary action.... The widespread impact of the honoraria ban, however, gives rise to far more serious concerns than could any single supervisory decision. In addition, unlike an adverse action taken in response to actual speech, this ban chills potential speech before it happens. Cf. Near v. Minnesota ex rel. Olson, 283 U.S. 697 (1931). For these reasons, the Government's burden is greater with respect to this statutory restriction on expression than with respect to an isolated disciplinary action. The Government must show that the interests of both potential audiences and a vast group of present and future employees in a broad range of present and future expression are outweighed by that expression's "necessary impact on the actual operation" of the Government. *Pickering*, 391 U.S., at 571.

Although § 501(b) neither prohibits any speech nor discriminates among speakers based on the content or viewpoint of their messages, its prohibition on compensation unquestionably imposes a significant burden on expressive activity.... Publishers compensate authors because compensation provides a significant incentive toward more expression. By denying respondents that incentive, the honoraria ban induces them to curtail their expression if they wish to continue working for the Government.

The ban imposes a far more significant burden on respondents than on the relatively small group of lawmakers whose past receipt of honoraria motivated its enactment. The absorbing and time-consuming responsibilities of legislators and policymaking executives leave them little opportunity for research or creative expression on subjects unrelated to their official responsibilities. Such officials often receive invitations to appear and talk about subjects related to their work because of their official identities. In contrast, invitations to rank-and-file employees usually depend only on the market value of their messages. The honoraria ban is unlikely to reduce significantly the number of appearances by high-ranking officials as long as travel expense reimbursement for the speaker and one relative is available as an alternative form of remuneration. In contrast, the denial of compensation for lower-paid, nonpolicymaking employees will inevitably diminish their expressive output.

The large-scale disincentive to Government employees' expression also imposes a significant burden on the public's right to read and hear what the employees would otherwise have written and said.... We have no way to measure the true cost of that burden, but we cannot ignore the risk that it might deprive us of the work of a future Melville or Hawthorne. The honoraria ban imposes the kind of burden that abridges speech under the First Amendment.

IV

Because the vast majority of the speech at issue in this case does not involve the subject matter of government employment and takes place outside the workplace, the Government is unable to justify § 501(b) on the grounds of immediate workplace disruption asserted in *Pickering* and the cases that followed it. Instead, the Government submits that the ban comports with the First Amendment because the prohibited honoraria were "reasonably deemed by Congress to interfere with the efficiency of the public service." United Public Workers v. Mitchell, 330 U.S. 75, 101 (1947).

In *Mitchell* we upheld the prohibition of the Hatch Act, 5 U.S.C. § 7324(a)(2), on partisan political activity by all classified federal employees, including, for example, a skilled mechanic at the Mint named Poole who had no policymaking authority. We explained that "[t]here are hundreds of thousands of United States employees with positions no more influential upon policy determination than that of Mr. Poole. Evidently what Congress feared was the cumulative effect on employee morale of political activity by all employees who could be induced to participate actively." 330 U.S., at 101. In Civil Service Commn. v. Letter Carriers, 413 U.S. 548 (1973), we noted that enactment of the Hatch Act in 1939 reflected "the conviction that the rapidly expanding Government work force should not be employed to build a powerful, invincible, and perhaps corrupt political machine." ... An equally important concern was "to further serve the goal that employment and advancement in the Government service not depend on political performance, and at the same time to make sure that Government employees would be free from pressure and from express or tacit invitation to vote in a certain way or perform political chores in order to curry favor with their superiors rather than to act out their own beliefs." ...

Thus, the Hatch Act aimed to protect employees' rights, notably their right to free expression, rather than to restrict those rights. Like the Hatch Act, the honoraria ban affects hundreds of thousands of federal employees. Unlike partisan political activity, however, honoraria hardly appear to threaten employees' morale or liberty. Moreover, Congress effectively designed the Hatch Act to combat demonstrated ill effects of Government employees' partisan political activities. In contrast, the Government has failed to show how it serves the interests it asserts by applying the honoraria ban to respondents.

The Government's underlying concern is that federal officers not misuse or appear to misuse power by accepting compensation for their unofficial and nonpolitical writing and speaking activities. This interest is undeniably powerful, but the Government cites no evidence of misconduct related to honoraria in the vast rank and file of federal employees below grade GS–16.... [T]he Government relies here on limited evidence of actual or apparent impropriety by legislators and high-level executives, together with the purported administrative costs of avoiding or detecting lower-level employees' violations of established policies.

... [T]he Government has based its defense of the ban on abuses of honoraria by Members of Congress. Congress reasonably could assume that payments of honoraria to judges or high-ranking officials in the Executive Branch might generate a similar appearance of improper influence. Congress could not, however, reasonably extend that assumption to all federal employees below Grade GS–16, an immense class of workers with negligible power to confer favors on those who might pay to hear them speak or to read their articles. A federal employee, such as a supervisor of mechanics at the Mint, might impair efficiency and morale by using political criteria to judge the performance of his or her staff. But one can envision scant harm, or appearance of harm, resulting from the same employee's accepting pay to lecture on the Quaker religion or to write dance reviews.

Although operational efficiency is undoubtedly a vital governmental interest, ... several features of the honoraria ban's text cast serious doubt on the Government's submission that Congress perceived honoraria as so threatening to the efficiency of the entire federal service as to render the ban a reasonable response to the threat.... The first is the rather strange parenthetical reference to "a series of appearances, speeches, or articles" that the 1991 amendment inserted in the definition of the term "honorarium." The amended definition excludes such a series from the prohibited category unless "the subject matter is directly related to the individual's official duties or the payment is made because of the individual's status with the Government." In other words, accepting pay for a series of articles is prohibited if and only if a nexus exists between the author's employment and either the subject matter of the expression or the identity of the payor. For an individual article or speech, in contrast, pay is taboo even if neither the subject matter nor the payor bears any relationship at all to the author's duties.

Congress' decision to provide a total exemption for all unrelated series of speeches undermines application of the ban to individual speeches and articles with no nexus to Government employment. Absent such a nexus, no corrupt bargain or even appearance of impropriety appears likely. The Government's only argument against a general nexus limitation is that a wholesale prophylactic rule is easier to enforce than one that requires individual nexus determinations. The nexus limitation for series, however, unambiguously reflects a congressional judgment that agency ethics officials and the OGE can enforce the statute when it includes a nexus test. A blanket burden on the speech of nearly 1.7 million federal employees requires a much stronger justification than the Government's dubious claim of administrative convenience.

The definition's limitation of "honoraria" to expressive activities also undermines the Government's submission that the breadth of § 501 is reasonably necessary to protect the efficiency of the public service. Both Commissions that recommended the ban stressed the importance of defining honoraria in a way that would close "potential loopholes such as receipt of consulting, professional or similar fees; payments for serving on boards; travel; sport, or other entertainment expenses not reasonably necessary for the appearance involved; or any other benefit that is the substantial equivalent of an honorarium." Those recommendations reflected a considered judgment that compensation for "an appearance, speech or article" poses no greater danger than compensation for other services that a Government employee might perform in his or her spare time. Congress, however, chose to restrict only expressive activities. One might reasonably argue that expressive activities, because they occupy a favored position in the constitutional firmament, should be exempt from even a comprehensive ban on outside income. Imposing a greater burden on speech than on other off-duty activities assumed to pose the same threat to the efficiency of the federal service is, at best, anomalous.

The fact that § 501 singles out expressive activity for special regulation heightens the Government's burden of justification.... The Government has not persuaded us that § 501(b) is a reasonable response to the posited harms.

We also attach significance to the OGE regulations that limit the coverage of the statutory terms "appearance, speech or article." 5 CFR § 2636.203 (1994). The regulations exclude a wide variety of performances and writings that would normally appear to have no nexus with an employee's job, such as sermons, fictional writings, and athletic competitions, countermanding the Commissions' recommendation that an even more inclusive honoraria ban would be appropriate. The exclusions, of course, make the task of the OGE and agency ethics officials somewhat easier, but they "diminish the credibility of the government's rationale" that paying lower-level employees for speech entirely unrelated to their work jeopardizes the efficiency of the entire federal service. We recognize our obligation to defer to considered congressional judgments about matters such as appearances of impropriety, but on the record of this case we must attach greater weight to the powerful and realistic presumption that the federal work force consists of dedicated and honorable civil servants. The exclusions in the OGE regulations are more consistent with that presumption than with the honoraria ban's dubious application not merely to policymakers, whose loss of honoraria was offset by a salary increase, but to all Executive Branch employees below Grade GS–16 as well.

These anomalies in the text of the statute and regulations underscore our conclusion: the speculative benefits the honoraria ban may provide the Government are not sufficient to justify this crudely crafted burden on respondents' freedom to engage in expressive activities. Section 501(b) violates the First Amendment.

V

After holding § 501(b) invalid because it was not as carefully tailored as it should have been, the Court of Appeals approved a remedy that is itself arguably overinclusive. The relief granted by the District Court and upheld by the Court of Appeals enjoined enforcement of the entire honoraria ban as applied to the entire Executive Branch of the

Government. That injunction provides relief to senior executives who are not parties to this case. It also prohibits enforcement of the statute even when an obvious nexus exists between the employee's job and either the subject matter of his or her expression or the interest of the person paying for it. As an alternative to its request for outright reversal, the Government asks us to modify the judgment by upholding the statute as it applies, first, to employees not party to this action and, second, to situations in which a nexus is present.

For three reasons, we agree with the Government's first suggestion—that the relief should be limited to the parties before the Court. First, although the occasional case requires us to entertain a facial challenge in order to vindicate a party's right not to be bound by an unconstitutional statute, ... we neither want nor need to provide relief to nonparties when a narrower remedy will fully protect the litigants.... In this case, granting full relief to ... Executive Branch employees below Grade GS–16 does not require passing on the applicability of § 501(b) to the senior executives who received a 25 percent salary increase that offsets the honoraria ban's disincentive to speak and write. Second, the Government conceivably might advance a different justification for an honoraria ban limited to more senior officials, thus presenting a different constitutional question than the one we decide today. Third, as the Court of Appeals recognized, its remedy required it to tamper with the text of the statute, a practice we strive to avoid.

Our obligation to avoid judicial legislation also persuades us to reject the Government's second suggestion—that we modify the remedy by crafting a nexus requirement for the honoraria ban. We cannot be sure that our attempt to redraft the statute to limit its coverage to cases involving an undesirable nexus between the speaker's official duties and either the subject matter of the speaker's expression or the identity of the payor would correctly identify the nexus Congress would have adopted in a more limited honoraria ban. We cannot know whether Congress accurately reflected its sense of an appropriate nexus in the terse, 33–word parenthetical statement with which it exempted series of speeches and articles from the definition of honoraria in the 1991 amendment; in an elaborate, nearly 600–word provision with which it later exempted Department of Defense military school faculty and students from the ban; or in neither. The process of drawing a proper nexus, even more than the defense of the statute's application to senior employees, would likely raise independent constitutional concerns whose adjudication is unnecessary to decide this case. We believe the Court of Appeals properly left to Congress the task of drafting a narrower statute.

Insofar as the judgment of the Court of Appeals affirms the injunction against enforcement of § 501(b) against respondents, it is affirmed; insofar as it grants relief to parties not before the Court, it is reversed. The case is remanded for further proceedings consistent with this opinion.

It is so ordered.

Justice O'Connor, concurring in the judgment in part and dissenting in part.

Although I agree that aspects of the honoraria ban run afoul of the First Amendment, I write separately for two reasons. First, I wish to emphasize my understanding of how our precedents ... direct the Court's conclusion. Second, I write to express my disagreement with the Court's remedy, which in my view paints with too broad a brush.

I

. . .

The Government, when it acts as employer, possesses substantial leeway; in appropriate circumstances, it may restrain speech that the Constitution would otherwise protect.... In this case, however, the Government has exceeded the limits of its latitude. The bare assertion of interest in a wide-ranging prophylactic ban here, without any showing that Congress considered empirical or anecdotal data pertaining to abuses by lower-echelon executive employees, cannot suffice to outweigh the substantial burden on the 1.7 million affected employees. I agree with the Court that § 501 is unconstitutional to the extent that it bars this class of employees from receiving honoraria for expressive activities that bear no nexus to government employment.

II

The class before us is defined by pay scale, not by its members' propensity to write articles without nexus to government employment. As to any member of the class, the honoraria ban may have unconstitutional applications. But the ban may be susceptible of constitutional application to every member of the class, as well. We do not decide the question—a far harder case for respondents, in my view—whether it is constitutional to apply the honoraria ban to speech by this class that bears a relationship to government employment. I believe that the Court overlooks this nuance when it enjoins all enforcement of § 501 against the class, any one of whose members may, in the future, receive honoraria for work-related activities. I would give respondents relief tailored to what they request: invalidation of the statute insofar as it applies to honoraria they receive for speech without nexus to government employment....

. . .

The Court assumes that it would venture into judicial legislation were it to invalidate the provision as it applies to no-nexus speech. But it is equally if not more inconsistent with congressional intent to strike a greater portion of the statute than is necessary to remedy the problem at hand....

. . .

In sum, I agree with the Court that § 501 is unconstitutional insofar as it bars the respondent class of Executive Branch employees from receiving honoraria for nonwork-related speeches, appearances, and articles. In contrast to the Court, I would hold § 501 invalid only to that extent.

Chief Justice Rehnquist, with whom Justice Scalia and Justice Thomas join, dissenting.

I believe that the Court's opinion is seriously flawed in two respects. First, its application of the First Amendment understates the weight which should be accorded to the governmental justifications for the honoraria ban and overstates the amount of speech which actually will be deterred. Second, its discussion of the impact of the statute which it strikes down is carefully limited to only a handful of the most appealing individual situations, but when it deals with the remedy it suddenly shifts gears and strikes down the statute as applied to the entire class of Executive Branch employees below grade GS–16. I therefore dissent.

I

. . .

. . . In Public Workers v. Mitchell, 330 U.S. 75 (1947), we examined § 9(a) of the Hatch Act. . . . Despite the fact that § 9(a) barred three-million public employees from taking "effective part in campaigns that may bring about changes in their lives, their fortunes, and their happiness," id., at 107 (Black, J., dissenting), we held that if in Congress' judgment "efficiency may be best obtained by prohibiting active participation by classified employees in politics as party officers or workers," there was no constitutional objection. . . .

More than 25 years later, we again addressed the constitutionality of § 9(a) of the Hatch Act. In Civil Service Comm'n v. Letter Carriers, 413 U.S. 548 (1973), we "unhesitatingly reaffirm[ed] the *Mitchell* holding," . . . because "neither the First Amendment nor any other provision of the Constitution invalidate[d] a law barring this kind of partisan political conduct by federal employees," . . . . We applied the balancing approach set forth in *Pickering* to the Hatch Act's sweeping limitation on partisan political activity, and determined that the balance struck by Congress was "sustainable by the obviously important interests sought to be served by the limitations on partisan political activities now contained in the Hatch Act." . . . We concluded that "[p]erhaps Congress at some time w[ould] come to a different view of the realities of political life and Government service," but we were in no position to dispute Congress' current view of the matter. . . .

. . .

Applying these standards to the honoraria ban, I cannot say that the balance that Congress has struck between its interests and the interests of its employees to receive compensation for their First Amendment expression is unreasonable. . . .

The Court largely ignores the Government's foremost interest— prevention of impropriety and the appearance of impropriety—by focusing solely on the burdens of the statute as applied to several carefully selected Executive Branch employees whose situations present the application of the statute where the Government's interests are at their lowest ebb....

        . . .

The Court concedes that in light of the abuses of honoraria by its Members, Congress could reasonably assume that "payments of honoraria to judges or highranking officials in the Executive Branch might generate a similar appearance of improper influence," but it concludes that Congress could not extend this presumption to federal employees below grade GS–16. The theory underlying the Court's distinction— that federal employees below grade GS–16 have negligible power to confer favors on those who might pay to hear them speak or to read their articles—is seriously flawed. Tax examiners, bank examiners, enforcement officials, or any number of federal employees have substantial power to confer favors even though their compensation level is below Grade GS–16.

Furthermore, we rejected the same distinction in Public Workers v. Mitchell....

The Court dismisses the Hatch Act experience as irrelevant, because it aimed to protect employees' rights, notably their right to free expression, rather than to restrict those rights. This is, indeed, a strange characterization of § 9(a) of the Hatch Act.... [I]t can hardly be said that the Act protected the rights of workers who wished to engage in partisan political activity. One of the purposes of the Act was assuredly to free employees who did not wish to become engaged in politics from requests by their superiors to contribute money or time, but to the extent the Act protected these employees it undoubtedly limited the First Amendment rights of those who did wish to take an active part in politics.

The Government's related concern regarding the difficulties that would attach in administering a case-by-case analysis of the propriety of particular honoraria also supports the honoraria ban's validity....

The Court observes that because a nexus limitation is retained for a series of speeches, it cannot be that difficult to enforce. The exception which the honoraria ban makes for a "series of appearances, speeches, or articles," far from undermining the statute's basic purpose, demonstrates that Congress was sensitive to the need for inhibiting as little speech consistent with its responsibility of ensuring that its employees perform their duties impartially and that there is no appearance of impropriety. One is far less likely to undertake a "series" of speeches or articles without being paid than he is to make a single speech or write a single article without being paid. Congress reasonably could have concluded that the number of cases where an employee wished to deliver a "series" of speeches would be much smaller than the number of requests to give individual speeches or write individual articles.

Unlike our prototypical application of *Pickering* which normally involves a response to the content of employee speech, the honoraria ban prohibits no speech and is unrelated to the message or the viewpoint expressed by the government employee.... Furthermore, the honoraria ban exempts from its prohibition travel and other expenses related to employee speech.... Because there is only a limited burden on respondents' First Amendment rights, Congress reasonably could have determined that its paramount interests in preventing impropriety and the appearance of impropriety in its work force justified the honoraria ban....

There is a special irony to the Court's decision. In order to combat corruption and to regain the public's trust, the Court essentially requires Congress to resurrect a bureaucracy that it previously felt compelled to replace and to equip it with resources sufficient to conduct case-by-case determinations regarding the actual and apparent propriety of honoraria by all Executive Branch employees below grade GS–16. I believe that a proper application of the *Pickering* test to this content-neutral restriction on the receipt of compensation compels the conclusion that the honoraria ban is consistent with the First Amendment....

II

... Even if I agreed that application of the honoraria ban to expressive activity unrelated to an employee's Government employment violated the First Amendment, I could not agree with the Court's remedy.

. . .

Although the Court limits its analysis to only those applications of the honoraria ban where there is no nexus between the honoraria and Government employment, the Court prohibits application of the honoraria ban to all Executive Branch employees below grade GS–16 even where there is a nexus between the honoraria and the employees' Government employment....

... I would affirm the Court of Appeals only insofar as its judgment affirmed the injunction against the enforcement of § 501(b) as applied to Executive Branch employees below grade GS–16 who seek honoraria that are unrelated to their Government employment.

Chapter 16

FREEDOM OF THE PRESS

SECTION 6. SPECIAL PROBLEMS OF THE ELECTRONIC MEDIA

Page 1586. Replace Federal Communications Commission v. Pacifica Foundation with the following:

DENVER AREA EDUCATIONAL TELECOMMUNICATIONS CONSORTIUM, INC. v. FEDERAL COMMUNICATIONS COMMISSION

___ U.S. ___, 116 S.Ct. 2374, ___ L.Ed.2d ___ (1996).

[The report in this case appears supra, page 217.]

Page 1587. Delete City of Los Angeles v. Preferred Communications, Inc.

Chapter 17

RELIGION AND THE CONSTITUTION

SECTION 1.   THE ESTABLISHMENT CLAUSE

B.   GOVERNMENT RELIGIOUS EXERCISES, CEREMONIES, AND PRACTICES

Page 1635.   Add before Edwards v. Aguillard:

LAMB'S CHAPEL v. CENTER MORICHES UNION FREE SCHOOL DISTRICT

508 U.S. 384, 113 S.Ct. 2141, 124 L.Ed.2d 352 (1993).

Justice White delivered the opinion of the Court.

Section 414 of the New York Education Law ... authorizes local school boards to adopt reasonable regulations for the use of school property for 10 specified purposes when the property is not in use for school purposes. Among the permitted uses is the holding of "social, civic and recreational meetings and entertainments, and other uses pertaining to the welfare of the community; but such meetings, entertainment and uses shall be non-exclusive and open to the general public." § 414(c). The list of permitted uses does not include meetings for religious purposes, and a New York appellate court ... ruled that local boards could not allow student bible clubs to meet on school property ...

Pursuant to § 414's empowerment of local school districts, the Board of Center Moriches Union Free School District (District) has issued rules and regulations with respect to the use of school property when not in use for school purposes. The rules allow only 2 of the 10 purposes authorized by § 414: social, civic, or recreational uses (Rule 10) and use by political organizations if secured in compliance with § 414 (Rule 8). Rule 7, however, consistent with the judicial interpretation of state law, provides that "[t]he school premises shall not be used by any group for religious purposes."

The issue in this case is whether, against this background of state law, it violates the Free Speech Clause of the First Amendment, made applicable to the States by the Fourteenth Amendment, to deny a church access to school premises to exhibit for public viewing and for assertedly religious purposes, a film dealing with family and child-rearing issues faced by parents today.

I

Petitioners (Church) are Lamb's Chapel, an evangelical church in the community of Center Moriches, and its pastor John Steigerwald. Twice the Church applied to the District for permission to use school facilities to show a six-part film series containing lectures by Doctor James Dobson. A brochure provided on request of the District identified Dr. Dobson as a licensed psychologist, former associate clinical professor of pediatrics at the University of Southern California, best-selling author, and radio commentator. The brochure stated that the film series would discuss Dr. Dobson's views on the undermining influences of the media that could only be counterbalanced by returning to traditional, Christian family values instilled at an early stage. The brochure went on to describe the contents of each of the six parts of the series. The District denied the first application, saying that "[t]his film does appear to be church related and therefore your request must be refused." The second application for permission to use school premises for showing the film, which described it as a "Family oriented movie—from the Christian perspective," was denied using identical language.

The Church brought suit in District Court, challenging the denial as a violation of the Freedom of Speech and Assembly Clauses, the Free Exercise Clause, and the Establishment Clause of the First Amendment, as well as the Equal Protection Clause of the Fourteenth Amendment.... The District Court granted summary judgment for respondents, rejecting all of the Church's claims....

The Court of Appeals affirmed the judgment of the District Court ... Because the holding below was questionable under our decisions, we granted the petition for certiorari, which in principal part challenged the holding below as contrary to the Free Speech Clause of the First Amendment.

II

. . .

With respect to public property that is not a designated public forum open for indiscriminate public use for communicative purposes, we have said that "[c]ontrol over access to a nonpublic forum can be based on subject matter and speaker identity so long as the distinctions drawn are reasonable in light of the purpose served by the forum and are viewpoint neutral." ... Rule 7 was unconstitutionally applied in this case.

... That all religions and all uses for religious purposes are treated alike under Rule 7 ... does not answer the critical question whether it discriminates on the basis of viewpoint to permit school property to be used for the presentation of all views about family issues and child-rearing except those dealing with the subject matter from a religious standpoint.

... [A] lecture or film about child-rearing and family values would ... be a use for social or civic purposes otherwise permitted by Rule 10. That subject matter is not one that the District has placed off limits to any and all speakers. Nor is there any indication in the record before us that the application to exhibit the particular film involved here was or would have been denied for any reason other than the fact that the presentation would have been from a religious perspective.... The principle that has emerged from our cases "is that the First Amendment forbids the government to regulate speech in ways that favor some viewpoints or ideas at the expense of others." City Council of Los Angeles v. Taxpayers for Vincent, 466 U.S. 789, 804 (1984). That principle applies in the circumstances of this case ...

The District, as a respondent, would save its judgment below on the ground that to permit its property to be used for religious purposes would be an establishment of religion forbidden by the First Amendment. This Court suggested in Widmar v. Vincent, 454 U.S. 263, 271 (1981), that the interest of the State in avoiding an Establishment Clause violation "may be [a] compelling" one justifying an abridgment of free speech otherwise protected by the First Amendment; but the Court went on to hold that permitting use of University property for religious purposes under the open access policy involved there would not be incompatible with the Court's Establishment Clause cases.

We have no more trouble than did the *Widmar* Court in disposing of the claimed defense on the ground that the posited fears of an Establishment Clause violation are unfounded. The showing of this film would not have been during school hours, would not have been sponsored by the school, and would have been open to the public, not just to church members. The District property had repeatedly been used by a wide variety of private organizations. Under these circumstances, as in *Widmar*, there would have been no realistic danger that the community would think that the District was endorsing religion or any particular creed, and any benefit to religion or to the Church would have been no more than incidental. As in *Widmar*, ... permitting District property to be used to exhibit the film involved in this case would not have been an establishment of religion under the three-part test articulated in Lemon v. Kurtzman, 403 U.S. 602 (1971): The challenged governmental action has a secular purpose, does not have the principal or primary effect of advancing or inhibiting religion, and does not foster an excessive entanglement with religion.[7]

.   .   .

For the reasons stated in this opinion, the judgment of the Court of Appeals is

Reversed.

Justice Scalia, with whom Justice Thomas joins, concurring in the judgment.

I join the Court's conclusion that the District's refusal to allow use of school facilities for petitioners' film viewing, while generally opening the schools for community activities, violates petitioners' First Amendment free speech rights (as does N.Y.Educ.Law § 414 (McKinney 1988

---

[7] While we are somewhat diverted by Justice Scalia's evening at the cinema, we return to the reality that there is a proper way to inter an established decision and *Lemon*, however frightening it might be to some, has not been overruled. . . .

and Supp.1993)), to the extent it compelled the District's denial. I also agree with the Court that allowing Lamb's Chapel to use school facilities poses "no realistic danger" of a violation of the Establishment Clause, but I cannot accept most of its reasoning in this regard. . . .

As to the Court's invocation of the *Lemon* test: Like some ghoul in a late-night horror movie that repeatedly sits up in its grave and shuffles abroad, after being repeatedly killed and buried, *Lemon* stalks our Establishment Clause jurisprudence once again, frightening the little children and school attorneys of Center Moriches Union Free School District. Its most recent burial, only last Term, was, to be sure, not fully six-feet under: our decision in Lee v. Weisman, 505 U.S. ___, ___ (1992), conspicuously avoided using the supposed "test" but also declined the invitation to repudiate it. Over the years, however, no fewer than five of the currently sitting Justices have, in their own opinions, personally driven pencils through the creature's heart (the author of today's opinion repeatedly), and a sixth has joined an opinion doing so. See, e.g., *Weisman,* supra, at ___ (Scalia, J., joined by, inter alios, Thomas, J., dissenting); Allegheny County v. American Civil Liberties Union, Greater Pittsburgh Chapter, 492 U.S. 573, 655–657 (1989)(Kennedy, J., concurring in judgment in part and dissenting in part); Corporation of Presiding Bishop of Church of Jesus Christ of Latter-Day Saints v. Amos, 483 U.S. 327, 346–349 (1987)(O'Connor, J., concurring); Wallace v. Jaffree, 472 U.S. 38, 107–113 (1985)(Rehnquist, J., dissenting); id., at 90–91 (White, J., dissenting); School Dist. of Grand Rapids v. Ball, 473 U.S. 373, 400 (1985)(White, J., dissenting); Widmar v. Vincent, 454 U.S. 263, 282 (1981)(White, J., dissenting); New York v. Cathedral Academy, 434 U.S. 125, 134–135 (1977)(White, J., dissenting); Roemer v. Maryland Bd. of Public Works, 426 U.S. 736, 768 (1976)(White, J., concurring in judgment); Committee for Public Education & Religious Liberty v. Nyquist, 413 U.S. 756, 820 (1973)(White, J., dissenting).

The secret of the *Lemon* test's survival, I think, is that it is so easy to kill. It is there to scare us (and our audience) when we wish it to do so, but we can command it to return to the tomb at will. See, e.g., Lynch v. Donnelly, 465 U.S. 668, 679 (1984)(noting instances in which Court has not applied *Lemon* test). When we wish to strike down a practice it forbids, we invoke it, see, e.g., Aguilar v. Felton, 473 U.S. 402 (1985)(striking down state remedial education program administered in part in parochial schools); when we wish to uphold a practice it forbids, we ignore it entirely, see Marsh v. Chambers, 463 U.S. 783 (1983)(upholding state legislative chaplains). Sometimes, we take a middle course, calling its three prongs "no more than helpful signposts," Hunt v. McNair, 413 U.S. 734, 741 (1973). Such a docile and useful monster is worth keeping around, at least in a somnolent state; one never knows when one might need him.

For my part, I agree with the long list of constitutional scholars who have criticized *Lemon* and bemoaned the strange Establishment Clause geometry of crooked lines and wavering shapes its intermittent use has produced. See, e.g., Choper, The Establishment Clause and Aid to Parochial Schools—An Update, 75 Cal.L.Rev. 5 (1987); Marshall, "We

Know It When We See It": The Supreme Court and Establishment, 59 S.Cal.L.Rev. 495 (1986); McConnell, Accommodation of Religion, 1985 S.Ct.Rev. 1; Kurland, The Religion Clauses and the Burger Court, 34 Cath.U.L.Rev. 1 (1984); R. Cord, Separation of Church and State (1982); Choper, The Religion Clauses of the First Amendment: Reconciling the Conflict, 41 U.Pitt.L.Rev. 673 (1980). I will decline to apply *Lemon*— whether it validates or invalidates the government action in question— and therefore cannot join the opinion of the Court today.

I cannot join for yet another reason: the Court's statement that the proposed use of the school's facilities is constitutional because (among other things) it would not signal endorsement of religion in general. What a strange notion, that a Constitution which itself gives "religion in general" preferential treatment (I refer to the Free Exercise Clause) forbids endorsement of religion in general. The Attorney General of New York not only agrees with that strange notion, he has an explanation for it: "Religious advocacy," he writes, "serves the community only in the eyes of its adherents and yields a benefit only to those who already believe." That was not the view of those who adopted our Constitution, who believed that the public virtues inculcated by religion are a public good. It suffices to point out that during the summer of 1789, when it was in the process of drafting the First Amendment, Congress enacted the famous Northwest Territory Ordinance of 1789, Article III of which provides, "Religion, morality, and knowledge, being necessary to good government and the happiness of mankind, schools and the means of education shall forever be *encouraged*." 1 Stat. 52 (emphasis added). Unsurprisingly, then, indifference to "religion in general" is not what our cases, both old and recent, demand. . . .

. . .

Justice Kennedy, concurring in part and concurring in the judgment.

. . . I agree with Justice Scalia that the Court's citation of Lemon v. Kurtzman . . . is unsettling and unnecessary. The same can be said of the Court's use of the phrase "endorsing religion," which, as I have indicated elsewhere, cannot suffice as a rule of decision consistent with our precedents and our traditions in this part of our jurisprudence. See Allegheny County v. American Civil Liberties Union, Greater Pittsburgh Chapter, 492 U.S. 573, 655 (Kennedy, J., concurring in judgment in part and dissenting in part). With these observations, I concur in part and concur in the judgment.

————

CAPITOL SQUARE REVIEW AND ADVISORY BOARD v. PINETTE
___ U.S. ___, 115 S.Ct. 2440, 132 L.Ed.2d 650 (1995).

Justice Scalia announced the judgment of the Court and delivered the opinion of the Court with respect to Parts I, II, and III, and an opinion with respect to Part IV, in which the Chief Justice, Justice Kennedy and Justice Thomas join.

... The question in this case is whether a State violates the Establishment Clause when, pursuant to a religiously neutral state policy, it permits a private party to display an unattended religious symbol in a traditional public forum located next to its seat of government.

I

Capitol Square is a 10–acre, state-owned plaza surrounding the Statehouse in Columbus, Ohio. For over a century the square has been used for public speeches, gatherings, and festivals advocating and celebrating a variety of causes, both secular and religious. Ohio Admin.Code Ann. § 128–4–02(A)(1994) makes the square available "for use by the public ... for free discussion of public questions, or for activities of a broad public purpose," and Ohio Rev. Code Ann. § 105.41 (1994), gives the Capitol Square Review and Advisory Board responsibility for regulating public access. To use the square, a group must simply fill out an official application form and meet several criteria, which concern primarily safety, sanitation, and non-interference with other uses of the square, and which are neutral as to the speech content of the proposed event. . . .

It has been the Board's policy "to allow a broad range of speakers and other gatherings of people to conduct events on the Capitol Square." Such diverse groups as homosexual rights organizations, the Ku Klux Klan and the United Way have held rallies. The Board has also permitted a variety of unattended displays on Capitol Square: a State-sponsored lighted tree during the Christmas season, a privately-sponsored menorah during Chanukah, a display showing the progress of a United Way fundraising campaign, and booths and exhibits during an arts festival. Although there was some dispute in this litigation regarding the frequency of unattended displays, the District Court found, with ample justification, that there was no policy against them.

In November 1993, after reversing an initial decision to ban unattended holiday displays from the square during December 1993, the Board authorized the State to put up its annual Christmas tree. On November 29, 1993, the Board granted a rabbi's application to erect a menorah. That same day, the Board received an application from respondent Donnie Carr, an officer of the Ohio Ku Klux Klan, to place a cross on the square from December 8, 1993, to December 24, 1993. The Board denied that application on December 3, informing the Klan by letter that the decision to deny "was made upon the advice of counsel, in a good faith attempt to comply with the Ohio and United States Constitutions, as they have been interpreted in relevant decisions by the Federal and State Courts."

... [T]he Ohio Klan, through its leader Vincent Pinette, filed the present suit in the United States District Court for the Southern District of Ohio, seeking an injunction requiring the Board to issue the requested permit. The Board defended on the ground that the permit would violate the Establishment Clause. The District Court issued the injunction and, after the Board's application for an emergency stay was denied, (Stevens, J., in chambers), the Board permitted the Klan to erect its cross. The Board then received, and granted, several additional applications to erect crosses on Capitol Square during December 1993 and January 1994.

On appeal by the Board, the United States Court of Appeals for the Sixth Circuit affirmed the District Court's judgment....

II

First, a preliminary matter: Respondents contend that we should treat this as a case in which freedom of speech (the Klan's right to present the message of the cross display) was denied because of the State's disagreement with that message's political content, rather than because of the State's desire to distance itself from sectarian religion. They suggest in their merits brief and in their oral argument that Ohio's genuine reason for disallowing the display was disapproval of the political views of the Ku Klux Klan. Whatever the fact may be, the case was not presented and decided that way. The record facts before us and the opinions below address only the Establishment Clause issue; that is the question upon which we granted certiorari; and that is the sole question before us to decide.

Respondents' religious display in Capitol Square was private expression. Our precedent establishes that private religious speech, far from being a First Amendment orphan, is as fully protected under the Free Speech Clause as secular private expression. Lamb's Chapel v. Center Moriches Union Free School Dist., 508 U.S. __ (1993).... Indeed, in Anglo–American history, at least, government suppression of speech has so commonly been directed precisely at religious speech that a free-speech clause without religion would be Hamlet without the prince. Accordingly, we have not excluded from free-speech protections religious proselytizing, ... or even acts of worship. Petitioners do not dispute that respondents, in displaying their cross, were engaging in constitutionally protected expression. They do contend that the constitutional protection does not extend to the length of permitting that expression to be made on Capitol Square.

It is undeniable, of course, that speech which is constitutionally protected against state suppression is not thereby accorded a guaranteed forum on all property owned by the State.... The right to use government property for one's private expression depends upon whether the property has by law or tradition been given the status of a public forum, or rather has been reserved for specific official uses.... If the former, a State's right to limit protected expressive activity is sharply circumscribed: it may impose reasonable, content-neutral time, place and manner restrictions (a ban on all unattended displays, which did not exist here, might be one such), but it may regulate expressive content only if such a restriction is necessary, and narrowly drawn, to serve a compelling state interest.... These strict standards apply here, since the District Court and the Court of Appeals found that Capitol Square was a traditional public forum. Petitioners do not claim that their denial of respondents' application was based upon a content-neutral time, place, or manner restriction. To the contrary, they concede— indeed it is the essence of their case—that the Board rejected the display precisely because its content was religious. Petitioners advance a single justification for closing Capitol Square to respondents' cross: the State's interest in avoiding official endorsement of Christianity, as required by the Establishment Clause.

III

There is no doubt that compliance with the Establishment Clause is a state interest sufficiently compelling to justify content-based restrictions on speech. . . .   Whether that interest is implicated here, however, is a different question. And we do not write on a blank slate in answering it. We have twice previously addressed the combination of private religious expression, a forum available for public use, content-based regulation, and a State's interest in complying with the Establishment Clause. Both times, we have struck down the restriction on religious content. . . .

In *Lamb's Chapel*, a school district allowed private groups to use school facilities during off-hours for a variety of civic, social and recreational purposes, excluding, however, religious purposes. We held that even if school property during off-hours was not a public forum, the school district violated an applicant's free-speech rights by denying it use of the facilities solely because of the religious viewpoint of the program it wished to present. 508 U.S., at ___. We rejected the district's compelling-state-interest Establishment Clause defense (the same made here) because the school property was open to a wide variety of uses, the district was not directly sponsoring the religious group's activity, and "any benefit to religion or to the Church would have been no more than incidental." . . . .   The *Lamb's Chapel* reasoning applies a fortiori here, where the property at issue is not a school but a full-fledged public forum.

Lamb's Chapel followed naturally from our decision in Widmar [v. Vincent, 454 U.S. 263 (1981)], in which we examined a public university's exclusion of student religious groups from facilities available to other student groups. There also we addressed official discrimination against groups who wished to use a "generally open forum" for religious speech. . . .   And there also the State claimed that its compelling interest in complying with the Establishment Clause justified the content-based restriction. We rejected the defense because the forum created by the State was open to a broad spectrum of groups and would provide only incidental benefit to religion. . . .   We stated categorically that "an open forum in a public university does not confer any imprimatur of state approval on religious sects or practices." . . .

Quite obviously, the factors that we considered determinative in *Lamb's Chapel* and *Widmar* exist here as well. The State did not sponsor respondents' expression, the expression was made on government property that had been opened to the public for speech, and permission was requested through the same application process and on the same terms required of other private groups.

IV

Petitioners argue that one feature of the present case distinguishes it from *Lamb's Chapel* and *Widmar*: the forum's proximity to the seat of government, which, they contend, may produce the perception that the cross bears the State's approval. They urge us to apply the so-called "endorsement test," see, e.g., Allegheny County v. American Civil Liberties Union, Greater Pittsburgh Chapter, 492 U.S. 573 (1989); Lynch v. Donnelly, 465 U.S. 668 (1984), and to find that, because an observer might mistake private expression for officially endorsed religious expression, the State's content-based restriction is constitutional.

We must note, to begin with, that it is not really an "endorsement test" of any sort, much less the "endorsement test" which appears in our more recent Establishment Clause jurisprudence, that petitioners urge upon us. "Endorsement" connotes an expression or demonstration of approval or support.... Our cases have accordingly equated "endorsement" with "promotion" or "favoritism." ... We find it peculiar to say that government "promotes" or "favors" a religious display by giving it the same access to a public forum that all other displays enjoy. And as a matter of Establishment Clause jurisprudence, we have consistently held that it is no violation for government to enact neutral policies that happen to benefit religion.... Where we have tested for endorsement of religion, the subject of the test was either expression by the government itself, *Lynch*, supra, or else government action alleged to discriminate in favor of private religious expression or activity, Board of Ed. of Kiryas Joel Village School Dist. v. Grumet, 512 U.S. ___ (1994), *Allegheny County*, supra. The test petitioners propose, which would attribute to a neutrally behaving government private religious expression, has no antecedent in our jurisprudence, and would better be called a "transferred endorsement" test.

Petitioners rely heavily on *Allegheny County* and *Lynch*, but each is easily distinguished. In *Allegheny County* we held that the display of a privately-sponsored creche on the "Grand Staircase" of the Allegheny County Courthouse violated the Establishment Clause. That staircase was not, however, open to all on an equal basis, so the County was favoring sectarian religious expression.... We expressly distinguished that site from the kind of public forum at issue here, and made clear that if the staircase were available to all on the same terms, "the presence of the creche in that location for over six weeks would then not serve to associate the government with the creche." ... In *Lynch* we held that a city's display of a creche did not violate the Establishment Clause because, in context, the display did not endorse religion.... The opinion does assume, as petitioners contend, that the government's use of religious symbols is unconstitutional if it effectively endorses sectarian religious belief. But the case neither holds nor even remotely assumes that the government's neutral treatment of private religious expression can be unconstitutional.

Petitioners argue that absence of perceived endorsement was material in *Lamb's Chapel* and *Widmar*. We did state in *Lamb's Chapel* that there was "no realistic danger that the community would think that the District was endorsing religion or any particular creed,".... But that conclusion was not the result of empirical investigation; it followed directly, we thought, from the fact that the forum was open and the religious activity privately sponsored.... [W]e in effect said, given an open forum and private sponsorship, erroneous conclusions do not count. So also in *Widmar*. Once we determined that the benefit to religious groups from the public forum was incidental and shared by other groups, we categorically rejected the State's Establishment Clause defense....

What distinguishes *Allegheny County* and the dictum in *Lynch* from *Widmar* and *Lamb's Chapel* is the difference between government speech and private speech.... Petitioners assert, in effect, that that distinction disappears when the private speech is conducted too close to the symbols of government. But that, of course, must be merely a subpart of a more general principle: that the distinction disappears whenever private speech can be mistaken for government speech. That proposition cannot be accepted, at least where, as here, the government has not fostered or encouraged the mistake.

Of course, giving sectarian religious speech preferential access to a forum close to the seat of government (or anywhere else for that matter) would violate the Establishment Clause (as well as the Free Speech Clause, since it would involve content discrimination). And one can conceive of a case in which a governmental entity manipulates its administration of a public forum close to the seat of government (or within a government building) in such a manner that only certain religious groups take advantage of it, creating an impression of endorsement that is in fact accurate. But those situations, which involve governmental favoritism, do not exist here. Capitol Square is a genuinely public forum, is known to be a public forum, and has been widely used as a public forum for many, many years. Private religious speech cannot be subject to veto by those who see favoritism where there is none.

The contrary view, most strongly espoused by Justice Stevens, but endorsed by Justice Souter and Justice O'Connor as well, exiles private religious speech to a realm of less-protected expression heretofore inhabited only by sexually explicit displays and commercial speech.... It will be a sad day when this Court casts piety in with pornography, and finds the First Amendment more hospitable to private expletives, see Cohen v. California, 403 U.S. 15, 26 (1971), than to private prayers. This would be merely bizarre were religious speech simply as protected by the Constitution as other forms of private speech; but it is outright perverse when one considers that private religious expression receives preferential treatment under the Free Exercise Clause. It is no answer to say that the Establishment Clause tempers religious speech. By its terms that Clause applies only to the words and acts of government. It was never meant, and has never been read by this Court, to serve as an impediment to purely private religious speech connected to the State only through its occurrence in a public forum.

Since petitioners' "transferred endorsement" principle cannot possibly be restricted to squares in front of state capitols, the Establishment Clause regime that it would usher in is most unappealing. To require (and permit) access by a religious group in *Lamb's Chapel*, it was sufficient that the group's activity was not in fact government sponsored, that the event was open to the public, and that the benefit of the facilities was shared by various organizations. Petitioners' rule would require school districts adopting similar policies in the future to guess whether some undetermined critical mass of the community might nonetheless perceive the district to be advocating a religious viewpoint. Similarly, state universities would be forced to reassess our statement that "an open forum in a public university does not confer any imprimatur of state approval on religious sects or practices." *Widmar*, 454 U.S., at 274. Whether it does would henceforth depend upon immediate appearances. Policy makers would find themselves in a vise between the Establishment Clause on one side and the Free Speech and Free Exercise Clauses on the other. Every proposed act of private, religious expression in a public forum would force officials to weigh a host of imponderables. How close to government is too close? What kind of building, and in what context, symbolizes state authority? If the State guessed wrong in one direction, it would be guilty of an Establishment Clause violation; if in the other, it would be liable for suppressing free exercise or free speech (a risk not run when the State restrains only its own expression).

The "transferred endorsement" test would also disrupt the settled principle that policies providing incidental benefits to religion do not contravene the Establishment Clause. That principle is the basis for the constitutionality of a broad range of laws, not merely those that implicate free-speech issues, see, e.g., *Witters*, supra; *Mueller*, supra. It has radical implications for our public policy to suggest that neutral laws are invalid whenever hypothetical observers may—even reasonably—confuse an incidental benefit to religion with state endorsement.

If Ohio is concerned about misperceptions, nothing prevents it from requiring all private displays in the Square to be identified as such. That would be a content-neutral "manner" restriction which is assuredly constitutional.... But the State may not, on the claim of misperception of official endorsement, ban all private religious speech from the public square, or discriminate against it by requiring religious speech alone to disclaim public sponsorship.

* * *

Religious expression cannot violate the Establishment Clause where it (1) is purely private and (2) occurs in a traditional or designated public forum, publicly announced and open to all on equal terms. Those conditions are satisfied here, and therefore the State may not bar respondents' cross from Capitol Square.

The judgment of the Court of Appeals is

Affirmed.

Justice Thomas, concurring.

. . .

Although the Klan might have sought to convey a message with some religious component, I think that the Klan had a primarily nonreligious purpose in erecting the cross. The Klan simply has appropriated one of the most sacred of religious symbols as a symbol of hate. In my mind, this suggests that this case may not have truly involved the Establishment Clause, although I agree with the Court's disposition because of the manner in which the case has come before us. In the end, there may be much less here than meets the eye.

Justice O'Connor, with whom Justice Souter and Justice Breyer join, concurring in part and concurring in the judgment.

I join Parts I, II, and III of the Court's opinion and concur in the judgment. . . . I see no necessity to carve out, as the plurality opinion would today, an exception to the endorsement test for the public forum context.

For the reasons given by Justice Souter, whose opinion I also join, I conclude on the facts of this case that there is "no realistic danger that the community would think that the [State] was endorsing religion or any particular creed," . . . . I write separately, however, to emphasize that . . . the endorsement test necessarily focuses upon the perception of a reasonable, informed observer.

I

. . .

While the plurality would limit application of the endorsement test . . . , I believe that an impermissible message of endorsement can be sent in a variety of contexts, not all of which involve direct government speech or outright favoritism. It is true that neither *Allegheny* nor *Lynch*, our two prior religious display cases, involved the same combination of private religious speech and a public forum that we have before us today. Nonetheless, as Justice Souter aptly demonstrates, we have on several occasions employed an endorsement perspective in Establishment Clause cases where private religious conduct has intersected with a neutral governmental policy providing some benefit in a manner that parallels the instant case. Thus, while I join the discussion of *Lamb's Chapel* and Widmar v. Vincent, . . . in Part III of the Court's opinion, I do so with full recognition that the factors the Court properly identifies ultimately led in each case to the conclusion that there was no endorsement of religion by the State. . . .

. . .

None of this is to suggest that I would be likely to come to a different result from the plurality where truly private speech is allowed on equal terms in a vigorous public forum that the government has administered properly. . . . Indeed, many of the factors the plurality identifies are some of those I would consider important in deciding cases like this one where religious speakers seek access to public spaces. . . . And, as I read the plurality opinion, a case is not governed by its proposed per se rule where such circumstances are otherwise—that is, where preferential placement of a religious symbol in a public space or government manipulation of the forum is involved.

To the plurality's consideration of the open nature of the forum and the private ownership of the display, however, I would add the presence of a sign disclaiming government sponsorship or endorsement on the Klan cross, which would make the State's role clear to the community. This factor is important because, as Justice Souter makes clear, certain aspects of the cross display in this case arguably intimate government approval of respondents' private religious message—particularly that the cross is an especially potent sectarian symbol which stood unattended in close proximity to official government buildings. In context, a disclaimer helps remove doubt about State approval of respondents' religious message. . . .

Our agreement as to the outcome of this case, however, cannot mask the fact that I part company with the plurality on a fundamental point: I disagree that "[i]t has radical implications for our public policy to suggest that neutral laws are invalid whenever hypothetical observers may—even reasonably—confuse an incidental benefit to religion with State endorsement." On the contrary, when the reasonable observer would view a government practice as endorsing religion, I believe that it is our duty to hold the practice invalid. The plurality today takes an exceedingly narrow view of the Establishment Clause that is out of step both with the Court's prior cases and with well-established notions of what the Constitution requires. The Clause is more than a negative prohibition against certain narrowly defined forms of government favoritism; it also imposes affirmative obligations that may require a State, in some situations, to take steps to avoid being perceived as supporting or endorsing a private religious message. That is, the Establishment Clause forbids a State from hiding behind the application of formally neutral criteria and remaining studiously oblivious to the effects of its actions. Governmental intent cannot control, and not all state policies are permissible under the Religion Clauses simply because they are neutral in form.

Where the government's operation of a public forum has the effect of endorsing religion, even if the governmental actor neither intends nor actively encourages that result, . . . the Establishment Clause is violated. . . .

In the end, I would recognize that the Establishment Clause inquiry cannot be distilled into a fixed, per se rule. . . .

II

Today, Justice Stevens reaches a different conclusion regarding whether the Board's decision to allow respondents' display on Capitol Square constituted an impermissible endorsement of the cross' religious message. Yet I believe it is important to note that we have not simply arrived at divergent results after conducting the same analysis. Our fundamental point of departure, it appears, concerns the knowledge that is properly attributed to the test's "reasonable observer [who] evaluates whether a challenged governmental practice conveys a message of endorsement of religion." In my view, proper application of the endorsement test requires that the reasonable observer be deemed more informed than the casual passerby postulated by the dissent.

. . .

I therefore disagree that the endorsement test should focus on the actual perception of individual observers, who naturally have differing degrees of knowledge. Under such an approach, a religious display is necessarily precluded so long as some passersby would perceive a governmental endorsement thereof. In my view, however, the endorsement test creates a more collective standard.... In this respect, the applicable observer is similar to the "reasonable person" in tort law.... Saying that the endorsement inquiry should be conducted from the perspective of a hypothetical observer who is presumed to possess a certain level of information that all citizens might not share neither chooses the perceptions of the majority over those of a "reasonable nonadherent," ... nor invites disregard for the values the Establishment Clause was intended to protect. It simply recognizes the fundamental difficulty inherent in focusing on actual people: there is always someone who, with a particular quantum of knowledge, reasonably might perceive a particular action as an endorsement of religion. A State has not made religion relevant to standing in the political community simply because a particular viewer of a display might feel uncomfortable.

. . .

The dissent's property-based argument fails to give sufficient weight to the fact that the cross at issue here was displayed in a forum traditionally open to the public.... The reasonable observer would recognize the distinction between speech the government supports and speech that it merely allows in a place that traditionally has been open to a range of private speakers accompanied, if necessary, by an appropriate disclaimer.

In this case, I believe, the reasonable observer would view the Klan's cross display fully aware that Capitol Square is a public space in which a multiplicity of groups, both secular and religious, engage in expressive conduct.... On the facts of this case, therefore, I conclude that the reasonable observer would not interpret the State's tolerance of the Klan's private religious display in Capitol Square as an endorsement of religion.

. . .

Justice Souter, with whom Justice O'Connor and Justice Breyer join, concurring in part and concurring in the judgment.

I concur in Parts I, II, and III of the Court's opinion. I also want to note specifically my agreement with the Court's suggestion that the State of Ohio could ban all unattended private displays in Capitol Square if it so desired. The fact that the Capitol lawn has been the site of public protests and gatherings, and is the location of any number of the government's own unattended displays, such as statues, does not disable the State from closing the square to all privately owned, unattended structures....

Otherwise, however, I limit my concurrence to the judgment. Although I agree in the end that, in the circumstances of this case, petitioners erred in denying the Klan's application for a permit to erect a cross on Capitol Square, my analysis of the Establishment Clause issue differs from Justice Scalia's, and I vote to affirm in large part because of the possibility of affixing a sign to the cross adequately disclaiming any government sponsorship or endorsement of it.

The plurality's opinion declines to apply the endorsement test to the Board's action, in favor of a per se rule: religious expression cannot violate the Establishment Clause where it (1) is private and (2) occurs in a public forum, even if a reasonable observer would see the expression as indicating state endorsement. This per se rule would be an exception to the endorsement test, not previously recognized and out of square with our precedents.

I

My disagreement with the plurality on the law may receive some focus from attention to a matter of straight fact that we see alike: in some circumstances an intelligent observer may mistake private, unattended religious displays in a public forum for government speech endorsing religion....

... Given the domination of the square by the government's own displays, one would not be a dimwit as a matter of law to think that an unattended religious display there was endorsed by the government, even though the square has also been the site of three privately sponsored, unattended displays over the years (a menorah, a United Way "thermometer," and some artisans' booths left overnight during an arts festival), ... and even though the square meets the legal definition of a public forum and has been used "[f]or over a century" as the site of "speeches, gatherings, and festivals." When an individual speaks in a public forum, it is reasonable for an observer to attribute the speech, first and foremost, to the speaker, while an unattended display (and any message it conveys) can naturally be viewed as belonging to the owner of the land on which it stands.

In sum, I do not understand that I am at odds with the plurality when I assume that in some circumstances an intelligent observer would reasonably perceive private religious expression in a public forum to imply the government's endorsement of religion. My disagreement with the plurality is simply that I would attribute these perceptions of the intelligent observer to the reasonable observer of Establishment Clause analysis under our precedents, where I believe that such reasonable perceptions matter.

II

. . .

Allegheny County's endorsement test cannot be dismissed, as Justice Scalia suggests, as applying only to situations in which there is an allegation that the Establishment Clause has been violated through "expression by the government itself" or "government action ... discriminat[ing] in favor of private religious expression." ... Unless we are to retreat entirely to government intent and abandon consideration of effects, it makes no sense to recognize a public perception of endorsement as a harm only in that subclass of cases in which the government owns the display. . . .

. . .

Even if precedent and practice were otherwise, however, and there were an open question about applying the endorsement test to private speech in public forums, I would apply it in preference to the plurality's view, which creates a serious loophole in the protection provided by the endorsement test. In Justice Scalia's view, as I understand it, the Establishment Clause is violated in a public forum only when the government itself intentionally endorses religion or willfully "foster[s]" a misperception of endorsement in the forum, or when it "manipulates" the public forum "in such a manner that only certain religious groups take advantage of it." If the list of forbidden acts is truly this short, then governmental bodies and officials are left with generous scope to encourage a multiplicity of religious speakers to erect displays in public forums. As long as the governmental entity does not "manipulat[e]" the forum in such a way as to exclude all other speech, the plurality's opinion would seem to invite such government encouragement, even when the result will be the domination of the forum by religious displays and religious speakers. By allowing government to encourage what it can not do on its own, the proposed per se rule would tempt a public body to contract out its establishment of religion, by encouraging the private enterprise of the religious to exhibit what the government could not display itself.

Something of the sort, in fact, may have happened here. Immediately after the District Court issued the injunction ordering petitioners to grant the Klan's permit, a local church council applied for a permit, apparently for the purpose of overwhelming the Klan's cross with other crosses. The council proposed to invite all local churches to erect crosses, and the Board granted "blanket permission" for "all churches friendly to or affiliated with" the council to do so. The end result was that a part of the square was strewn with crosses, and while the effect in this case may have provided more embarrassment than suspicion of endorsement, the opportunity for the latter is clear.

III

As for the specifics of this case, one must admit that a number of facts known to the Board, or reasonably anticipated, weighed in favor of upholding its denial of the permit. For example, the Latin cross the Klan sought to erect is the principal symbol of Christianity around the world, and display of the cross alone could not reasonably be taken to have any secular point. It was displayed immediately in front of the Ohio Statehouse, with the government's flags flying nearby, and the government's statues close at hand. For much of the time the cross was supposed to stand on the square, it would have been the only private display on the public plot (the menorah's permit expired several days before the cross actually went up). There was nothing else on the Statehouse lawn that would have suggested a forum open to any and all private, unattended religious displays.

Based on these and other factors, the Board was understandably concerned about a possible Establishment Clause violation if it had granted the permit. But a flat denial of the Klan's application was not the Board's only option to protect against an appearance of endorsement, and the Board was required to find its most "narrowly drawn" alternative.... The Board ... could have granted the application subject to the condition that the Klan attach a disclaimer.... In the alternative, the Board could have instituted a policy of restricting all private, unattended displays to one area of the square, with a permanent sign marking the area as a forum for private speech carrying no endorsement from the State.

With such alternatives available, the Board cannot claim that its flat denial was a narrowly tailored response to the Klan's permit application and thus cannot rely on that denial as necessary to ensure that the State did not "appea[r] to take a position on questions of religious belief." ... For these reasons, I concur in the judgment.

Justice Stevens, dissenting.

The Establishment Clause should be construed to create a strong presumption against the installation of unattended religious symbols on public property. Although the State of Ohio has allowed Capitol Square, the area around the seat of its government, to be used as a public forum, and although it has occasionally allowed private groups to erect other sectarian displays there, neither fact provides a sufficient basis for rebutting that presumption. On the contrary, the sequence of sectarian displays disclosed by the record in this case illustrates the importance of rebuilding the "wall of separation between church and State" that Jefferson envisioned.

.   .   .

II

The plurality does not disagree with the proposition that the State may not espouse a religious message. It concludes, however, that the State has not sent such a message; it has merely allowed others to do so on its property....

.   .   .

In determining whether the State's maintenance of the Klan's cross in front of the Statehouse conveyed a forbidden message of endorsement, we should be mindful of the power of a symbol standing alone and unexplained. Even on private property, signs and symbols are generally understood to express the owner's views. The location of the sign is a significant component of the message it conveys.

... [T]he location of a stationary, unattended sign generally is both a component of its message and an implicit endorsement of that message by the party with the power to decide whether it may be conveyed from that location.

So it is with signs and symbols left to speak for themselves on public property. The very fact that a sign is installed on public property implies official recognition and reinforcement of its message. That implication is especially strong when the sign stands in front of the seat of the government itself. The "reasonable observer" of any symbol placed unattended in front of any capitol in the world will normally assume that the sovereign—which is not only the owner of that parcel of real estate but also the lawgiver for the surrounding territory—has sponsored and facilitated its message.

That the State may have granted a variety of groups permission to engage in uncensored expressive activities in front of the capitol building does not, in my opinion, qualify or contradict the normal inference of endorsement that the reasonable observer would draw from the unattended, freestanding sign or symbol. Indeed, parades and demonstrations at or near the seat of government are often exercises of the right of the people to petition their government for a redress of grievances—exercises in which the government is the recipient of the message rather than the messenger. Even when a demonstration or parade is not directed against government policy, but merely has made use of a particularly visible forum in order to reach as wide an audience as possible, there usually can be no mistake about the identity of the messengers as persons other than the State. But when a statue or some other free-standing, silent, unattended, immoveable structure—regardless of its particular message—appears on the lawn of the Capitol building, the reasonable observer must identify the State either as the messenger, or, at the very least, as one who has endorsed the message. Contrast, in this light, the image of the cross standing alone and unattended, and the image the observer would take away were a hooded Klansman holding, or standing next to, the very same cross.

This Court has never held that a private party has a right to place an unattended object in a public forum. Today the Court correctly recognizes that a State may impose a ban on all private unattended displays in such a forum. This is true despite the fact that our cases have condemned a number of laws that foreclose an entire medium of expression, even in places where free speech is otherwise allowed....

Because structures on government property—and, in particular, in front of buildings plainly identified with the state—imply state approval of their message, the Government must have considerable leeway, outside of the religious arena, to choose what kinds of displays it will allow and what kinds it will not. Although the First Amendment requires the Government to allow leafletting or demonstrating outside its buildings, the state has greater power to exclude unattended symbols when they convey a type of message with which the state does not wish to be identified. I think it obvious, for example, that Ohio could prohibit certain categories of signs or symbols in Capitol Square—erotic exhibits, commercial advertising, and perhaps campaign posters as well—without violating the Free Speech Clause. Moreover, our "public forum" cases do not foreclose public entities from enforcing prohibitions against all unattended displays in public parks, or possibly even limiting the use of such displays to the communication of non-controversial messages. Such a limitation would not inhibit any of the traditional forms of expression that have been given full constitutional protection in public fora.

The State's general power to restrict the types of unattended displays does not alone suffice to decide this case, because Ohio did not profess to be exercising any such authority. Instead, the Capitol Square Review Board denied a permit for the cross because it believed the Establishment Clause required as much, and we cannot know whether the Board would have denied the permit on other grounds. Accordingly, we must evaluate the State's rationale on its own terms. But in this case, the endorsement inquiry under the Establishment Clause follows from the State's power to exclude unattended private displays from public property. Just as the Constitution recognizes the State's interest in preventing its property from being used as a conduit for ideas it does not wish to give the appearance of ratifying, the Establishment Clause prohibits government from allowing, and thus endorsing, unattended displays that take a position on a religious issue. If the State allows such stationary displays in front of its seat of government, viewers will reasonably assume that it approves of them.... Even if the disclaimer at the foot of the cross (which stated that the cross was placed there by a private organization) were legible, that inference would remain, because a property owner's decision to allow a third party to place a sign on her property conveys the same message of endorsement as if she had erected it herself.

When the message is religious in character, it is a message the state can neither send nor reinforce without violating the Establishment Clause. Accordingly, I would hold that the Constitution generally forbids the placement of a symbol of a religious character in, on, or before a seat of government.

III

. . .

... For a religious display to violate the Establishment Clause, I think it is enough that some reasonable observers would attribute a religious message to the State.

The plurality appears to rely on the history of this particular public forum—specifically, it emphasizes that Ohio has in the past allowed three other private unattended displays. Even if the State could not reasonably have been understood to endorse the prior displays, I would not find this argument convincing, because it assumes that all reasonable viewers know all about the history of Capitol Square—a highly unlikely supposition. But the plurality's argument fails on its own terms, because each of the three previous displays conveyed the same message of approval and endorsement that this one does.

Most significant, of course, is the menorah that stood in Capitol Square during Chanukah. The display of that religious symbol should be governed by the same rule as the display of the cross. In my opinion, both displays are equally objectionable. Moreover, the fact that the State has placed its stamp of approval on two different religions instead of one only compounds the constitutional violation. The Establishment Clause does not merely prohibit the State from favoring one religious sect over others. It also proscribes state action supporting the establishment of a number of religions, as well as the official endorsement of religion in preference to nonreligion....

The record identifies two other examples of free-standing displays that the State previously permitted in Capitol Square: a "United Way Campaign 'thermometer,' " and "craftsmen's booths and displays erected during an Arts Festival." Both of those examples confirm the proposition that a reasonable observer should infer official approval of the message conveyed by a structure erected in front of the Statehouse. Surely the thermometer suggested that the State was encouraging passersby to contribute to the United Way. It seems equally clear that the State was endorsing the creativity of artisans and craftsmen by permitting their booths to occupy a part of the Square. Nothing about either of those freestanding displays contradicts the normal inference that the State has endorsed whatever message might be conveyed by permitting an unattended symbol to adorn the Capitol grounds....

This case is therefore readily distinguishable from Widmar v. Vincent, 454 U.S. 263 (1981), and Lamb's Chapel v. Center Moriches Union Free School Dist., 508 U.S. ___ (1993). In both of those cases, as we made perfectly clear, there was no danger of incorrect identification of the speakers and no basis for inferring that their messages had been endorsed by any public entity....

.   .   .

IV

.   .   .

... The Court's decision today is unprecedented. It entangles two sovereigns in the propagation of religion, and it disserves the principle of tolerance that underlies the prohibition against state action "respecting an establishment of religion."

I respectfully dissent.

Justice Ginsburg, dissenting.

We confront here ... a large Latin cross that stood alone and unattended in close proximity to Ohio's Statehouse.... Near the stationary cross were the government's flags and the government's statues. No human speaker was present to disassociate the religious symbol from the State. No other private display was in sight. No plainly visible sign informed the public that the cross belonged to the Klan and that Ohio's government did not endorse the display's message.

If the aim of the Establishment Clause is genuinely to uncouple government from church, ... a State may not permit, and a court may not order, a display of this character.... Justice Souter, in the final paragraphs of his opinion, suggests two arrangements that might have distanced the State ...: a sufficiently large and clear disclaimer,; or an area reserved for unattended displays carrying no endorsement from the State, a space plainly and permanently so marked. Neither arrangement is even arguably present in this case. The District Court's order did not mandate a disclaimer. And the disclaimer the Klan appended to the foot of the cross was unsturdy: it did not identify the Klan as sponsor; it failed to state unequivocally that Ohio did not endorse the display's message; and it was not shown to be legible from a distance. The relief ordered by the District Court thus violated the Establishment Clause.

Whether a court order allowing display of a cross, but demanding a sturdier disclaimer, could withstand Establishment Clause analysis is a question more difficult than the one this case poses. I would reserve that question for another day and case. But I would not let the prospect of what might have been permissible control today's decision on the constitutionality of the display the District Court's order in fact authorized.

C. FINANCIAL AID TO CHURCH–RELATED SCHOOLS AND CHURCH–RELATED INSTRUCTION

1. ELEMENTARY AND SECONDARY SCHOOLS

Page 1656. Add at end of subsection:

ZOBREST v. CATALINA FOOTHILLS SCHOOL DISTRICT

509 U.S. 1, 113 S.Ct. 2462, 125 L.Ed.2d 1 (1993).

Chief Justice Rehnquist delivered the opinion of the Court.

Petitioner James Zobrest, who has been deaf since birth, asked respondent school district to provide a sign-language interpreter to accompany him to classes at a Roman Catholic high school in Tucson, Arizona, pursuant to the Individuals with Disabilities Education Act (IDEA), 20 U.S.C. § 1400 et seq., and its Arizona counterpart, Ariz.Rev. Stat.Ann. § 15–761 et seq. (1991 and Supp.1992). The United States Court of Appeals for the Ninth Circuit decided, however, that provision of such a publicly employed interpreter would violate the Establishment Clause of the First Amendment. We hold that the Establishment Clause does not bar the school district from providing the requested interpreter.

. . .

Respondent has raised . . . several issues unrelated to the Establishment Clause question. . . .

. . .

Here, in contrast to . . . cases applying the prudential rule of avoiding constitutional questions, only First Amendment questions were pressed in the Court of Appeals. . . .

Given this posture of the case, we think the prudential rule of avoiding constitutional questions has no application. The fact that there may be buried in the record a nonconstitutional ground for decision is not by itself enough to invoke this rule.... We therefore turn to the merits of the constitutional claim.

We have never said that "religious institutions are disabled by the First Amendment from participating in publicly sponsored social welfare programs." Bowen v. Kendrick, 487 U.S. 589, 609 (1988).... [W]e have consistently held that government programs that neutrally provide benefits to a broad class of citizens defined without reference to religion are not readily subject to an Establishment Clause challenge just because sectarian institutions may also receive an attenuated financial benefit. Nowhere have we stated this principle more clearly than in Mueller v. Allen, 463 U.S. 388 (1983), and Witters v. Washington Dept. of Services for Blind, 474 U.S. 481 (1986), two cases dealing specifically with government programs offering general educational assistance.

In *Mueller,* we rejected an Establishment Clause challenge to a Minnesota law allowing taxpayers to deduct certain educational expenses in computing their state income tax, even though the vast majority of those deductions (perhaps over 90%) went to parents whose children attended sectarian schools....

... In [*Witters*] we upheld against an Establishment Clause challenge the State of Washington's extension of vocational assistance, as part of a general state program, to a blind person studying at a private Christian college to become a pastor, missionary, or youth director. Looking at the statute as a whole, we observed that "[a]ny aid provided under Washington's program that ultimately flows to religious institutions does so only as a result of the genuinely independent and private choices of aid recipients." 474 U.S., at 487....

That same reasoning applies with equal force here. The service at issue in this case is part of a general government program that distributes benefits neutrally to any child qualifying as "handicapped" under the IDEA, without regard to the "sectarian-nonsectarian, or public-nonpublic nature" of the school the child attends. By according parents freedom to select a school of their choice, the statute ensures that a government-paid interpreter will be present in a sectarian school only as a result of the private decision of individual parents. In other words, because the IDEA creates no financial incentive for parents to choose a sectarian school, an interpreter's presence there cannot be attributed to state decisionmaking. Viewed against the backdrop of *Mueller* and *Witters,* then, the Court of Appeals erred in its decision. When the government offers a neutral service on the premises of a sectarian school as part of a general program that "is in no way skewed towards religion," *Witters,* supra, at 488, it follows under our prior decisions that provision of that service does not offend the Establishment Clause. Indeed, this is an even easier case than *Mueller* and *Witters* in the sense that, under the IDEA, no funds traceable to the government ever find their way into sectarian schools' coffers. The only indirect economic benefit a sectarian school might receive by dint of the IDEA is the handicapped child's tuition—and that is, of course, assuming that the school makes a profit on each student; that, without an IDEA interpreter, the child would have gone to school elsewhere; and that the school, then, would have been unable to fill that child's spot.

Respondent contends, however, that this case differs from *Mueller* and *Witters,* in that petitioners seek to have a public employee physically present in a sectarian school to assist in James' religious education. In light of this distinction, respondent argues that this case more closely resembles Meek v. Pittenger, 421 U.S. 349 (1975), and School Dist. of Grand Rapids v. Ball, 473 U.S. 373 (1985). In *Meek,* we struck down a statute that, inter alia, provided "massive aid" to private schools—more than 75% of which were church related—through a direct loan of teaching material and equipment. 421 U.S., at 364–365. The material and equipment covered by the statute included maps, charts, and tape recorders. Id., at 355. According to respondent, if the government could not place a tape recorder in a sectarian school in *Meek,* then it surely cannot place an interpreter in Salpointe. The statute in *Meek* also authorized state-paid personnel to furnish "auxiliary services"— which included remedial and accelerated instruction and guidance counseling—on the premises of religious schools. We determined that this part of the statute offended the First Amendment as well. Id., at 372. *Ball* similarly involved two public programs that provided services on private school premises; there, public employees taught classes to students in private school classrooms. 473 U.S., at 375.... According to respondent, if the government could not provide educational services on the premises of sectarian schools in *Meek* and *Ball,* then it surely cannot provide James with an interpreter on the premises of Salpointe.

Respondent's reliance on *Meek* and *Ball* is misplaced for two reasons. First, the programs ... relieved sectarian schools of costs they otherwise would have borne in educating their students.... For example, the religious schools in *Meek* received teaching material and equipment from the State, relieving them of an otherwise necessary cost of performing their educational function.... So, too, was the case in *Ball:* The programs challenged there, which provided teachers in addition to instructional equipment and material, "in effect subsidize[d] the religious functions of the parochial schools by taking over a substantial portion of their responsibility for teaching secular subjects." 473 U.S., at 397.... The extension of aid to petitioners, however, does not amount to "an impermissible 'direct subsidy'" of Salpointe. *Witters,* 474 U.S., at 487. For Salpointe is not relieved of an expense that it otherwise would have assumed in educating its students. And, as we noted above, any attenuated financial benefit that parochial schools do ultimately receive from the IDEA is attributable to "the private choices of individual parents." *Mueller,* 463 U.S., at 400. Handicapped children, not sectarian schools, are the primary beneficiaries of the IDEA; to the extent sectarian schools benefit at all from the IDEA, they are only incidental beneficiaries. Thus, the function of the IDEA is hardly " 'to provide desired financial support for nonpublic, sectarian institutions.' " Id., at 488 (quoting *Nyquist,* 413 U.S., at 783).

Second, the task of a sign-language interpreter seems to us quite different from that of a teacher or guidance counselor.... [T]he Establishment Clause lays down no absolute bar to the placing of a public employee in a sectarian school. Such a flat rule, smacking of antiquated notions of "taint," would indeed exalt form over substance.[11]   Nothing in this record suggests that a sign-language interpreter would do more than accurately interpret whatever material is presented to the class as a whole.   In fact, ethical guidelines require interpreters to "transmit everything that is said in exactly the same way it was intended." James' parents have chosen of their own free will to place him in a pervasively sectarian environment.   The sign-language interpreter they have requested will neither add to nor subtract from that environment, and hence the provision of such assistance is not barred by the Establishment Clause.

The IDEA creates a neutral government program dispensing aid not to schools but to individual handicapped children.   If a handicapped child chooses to enroll in a sectarian school, we hold that the Establishment Clause does not prevent the school district from furnishing him with a sign-language interpreter there in order to facilitate his education.   The judgment of the Court of Appeals is therefore

Reversed.

Justice Blackmun, with whom Justice Souter joins, and with whom Justice Stevens and Justice O'Connor join as to Part I, dissenting.

Today, the Court unnecessarily addresses an important constitutional issue, disregarding longstanding principles of constitutional adjudication.   In so doing, the Court holds that placement in a parochial school classroom of a public employee whose duty consists of relaying religious messages does not violate the Establishment Clause of the First Amendment.   I disagree both with the Court's decision to reach this question and with its disposition on the merits.   I therefore dissent.

I

. . .

. . . The obligation to avoid unnecessary adjudication of constitutional questions does not depend upon the parties' litigation strategy, but rather is a "self-imposed limitation on the exercise of this Court's jurisdiction [that] has an importance to the institution that transcends the significance of particular controversies."   City of Mesquite v. Aladdin's Castle, Inc., 455 U.S. 283, 294 (1982). . . .

. . . Prudence counsels that the Court [vacate and remand] this case for consideration of the nonconstitutional questions, rather than proceeding directly to the merits of the constitutional claim. . . .

II

. . . Until now, the Court never has authorized a public employee to participate directly in religious indoctrination.   Yet that is the consequence of today's decision.

. . .

---

[11] Indeed, respondent readily admits, as it must, that there would be no problem under the Establishment Clause if the IDEA funds instead went directly to James' parents, who, in turn, hired the interpreter themselves.

... [G]overnmental assistance to the educational function of the school necessarily entails governmental participation in the school's inculcation of religion. A state-employed sign-language interpreter would be required to communicate the material covered in religion class, the nominally secular subjects that are taught from a religious perspective, and the daily Masses at which Salpointe encourages attendance for Catholic students. In an environment so pervaded by discussions of the divine, the interpreter's every gesture would be infused with religious significance....

The majority ... offer[s] three reasons why this sort of aid to petitioners survives Establishment Clause scrutiny. First, the majority observes that provision of a sign-language interpreter occurs as "part of a general government program that distributes benefits neutrally to any child qualifying as 'handicapped' under the IDEA, without regard to the 'sectarian-nonsectarian, or public-nonpublic' nature of the school the child attends." Second, the majority finds significant the fact that aid is provided to pupils and their parents, rather than directly to sectarian schools. As a result, " '[a]ny aid ... that ultimately flows to religious institutions does so only as a result of the genuinely independent and private choices of aid recipients.' " And, finally, the majority opines that "the task of a sign-language interpreter seems to us quite different from that of a teacher or guidance counselor."

But the majority's arguments are unavailing. As to the first two, even a general welfare program may have specific applications that are constitutionally forbidden under the Establishment Clause.... For example, a general program granting remedial assistance to disadvantaged schoolchildren attending public and private, secular and sectarian schools alike would clearly offend the Establishment Clause insofar as it authorized the provision of teachers. See Aguilar v. Felton, 473 U.S. 402, 410 (1985) ... Such a program would not be saved simply because it supplied teachers to secular as well as sectarian schools. Nor would the fact that teachers were furnished to pupils and their parents, rather than directly to sectarian schools, immunize such a program from Establishment Clause scrutiny.... The majority's decision must turn, then, upon the distinction between a teacher and a sign-language interpreter.

... [O]ur cases consistently have rejected the provision by government of any resource capable of advancing a school's religious mission. Although the Court generally has permitted the provision of "secular and nonideological services unrelated to the primary, religion-oriented educational function of the sectarian school," *Meek,* 421 U.S., at 364, it has always proscribed the provision of benefits that afford even "the opportunity for the transmission of sectarian views," *Wolman,* 433 U.S., at 244.

. . .

... [O]ur cases make clear that government crosses the boundary when it furnishes the medium for communication of a religious message. If petitioners receive the relief they seek, it is beyond question that a state-employed sign-language interpreter would serve as the conduit for petitioner's religious education, thereby assisting Salpointe in its mission of religious indoctrination. . . .

Witters, supra, and Mueller v. Allen, 463 U.S. 388 (1983), are not to the contrary. Those cases dealt with the payment of cash or a tax deduction, where governmental involvement ended with the disbursement of funds or lessening of tax. This case, on the other hand, involves ongoing, daily, and intimate governmental participation in the teaching and propagation of religious doctrine. When government dispenses public funds to individuals who employ them to finance private choices, it is difficult to argue that government is actually endorsing religion. But the graphic symbol of the concert of church and state that results when a public employee or instrumentality mouths a religious message is likely to "enlis[t]—at least in the eyes of impressionable youngsters—the powers of government to the support of the religious denomination operating the school." *Grand Rapids,* 473 U.S., at 385. And the union of church and state in pursuit of a common enterprise is likely to place the imprimatur of governmental approval upon the favored religion, conveying a message of exclusion to all those who do not adhere to its tenets.

Moreover, this distinction between the provision of funds and the provision of a human being is not merely one of form. . . . As Amicus Council on Religious Freedom points out, the provision of a state-paid sign-language interpreter may pose serious problems for the church as well as for the state. Many sectarian schools impose religiously based rules of conduct, as Salpointe has in this case. A traditional Hindu school would be likely to instruct its students and staff to dress modestly, avoiding any display of their bodies. And an orthodox Jewish yeshiva might well forbid all but kosher food upon its premises. To require public employees to obey such rules would impermissibly threaten individual liberty, but to fail to do so might endanger religious autonomy. . . .

.   .   .

BOARD OF EDUCATION OF KIRYAS JOEL VILLAGE SCHOOL DISTRICT v. GRUMET

___ U.S. ___, 114 S.Ct. 2481, 129 L.Ed.2d 546 (1994).

Justice Souter delivered the opinion of the Court.

The Village of Kiryas Joel in Orange County, New York, is a religious enclave of Satmar Hasidim, practitioners of a strict form of Judaism. The village fell within the Monroe–Woodbury Central School District until a special state statute passed in 1989 carved out a separate district, following village lines, to serve this distinctive population. . . . The question is whether the Act creating the separate school district violates the Establishment Clause of the First Amendment, binding on the States through the Fourteenth Amendment. Because this unusual act is tantamount to an allocation of political power on a religious criterion and neither presupposes nor requires governmental impartiality toward religion, we hold that it violates the prohibition against establishment.

I

The Satmar Hasidic sect takes its name from the town near the Hungarian and Romanian border where, in the early years of this century, Grand Rebbe Joel Teitelbaum molded the group into a distinct community. After World War II and the destruction of much of European Jewry, the Grand Rebbe and most of his surviving followers moved to the Williamsburg section of Brooklyn, New York. Then, 20 years ago, the Satmars purchased an approved but undeveloped subdivision in the town of Monroe and began assembling the community that has since become the Village of Kiryas Joel. When a zoning dispute arose in the course of settlement, the Satmars presented the Town Board of Monroe with a petition to form a new village within the town, a right that New York's Village Law gives almost any group of residents who satisfy certain procedural niceties..... Neighbors who did not wish to secede with the Satmars objected strenuously, and after arduous negotiations the proposed boundaries of the Village of Kiryas Joel were drawn to include just the 320 acres owned and inhabited entirely by Satmars. The village, incorporated in 1977, has a population of about 8,500 today. Rabbi Aaron Teitelbaum, eldest son of the current Grand Rebbe, serves as the village rov (chief rabbi) and rosh yeshivah (chief authority in the parochial schools).

The residents of Kiryas Joel are vigorously religious people who make few concessions to the modern world and go to great lengths to avoid assimilation into it. They interpret the Torah strictly; segregate the sexes outside the home; speak Yiddish as their primary language; eschew television, radio, and English-language publications; and dress in distinctive ways that include headcoverings and special garments for boys and modest dresses for girls. Children are educated in private religious schools, most boys at the United Talmudic Academy where they receive a thorough grounding in the Torah and limited exposure to secular subjects, and most girls at Bais Rochel, an affiliated school with a curriculum designed to prepare girls for their roles as wives and mothers. . . .

These schools do not, however, offer any distinctive services to handicapped children, who are entitled under state and federal law to special education services even when enrolled in private schools.... Starting in 1984 the Monroe–Woodbury Central School District provided such services for the children of Kiryas Joel at an annex to Bais Rochel, but a year later ended that arrangement in response to our decisions in Aguilar v. Felton, 473 U.S. 402 (1985), and School Dist. of Grand Rapids v. Ball, 473 U.S. 373 (1985). Children from Kiryas Joel who needed special education (including the deaf, the mentally retarded, and others suffering from a range of physical, mental, or emotional disorders) were then forced to attend public schools outside the village, which their families found highly unsatisfactory. Parents of most of these children withdrew them from the Monroe–Woodbury secular schools, citing "the panic, fear and trauma [the children] suffered in leaving their own community and being with people whose ways were so different,"....

. . .

By 1989, only one child from Kiryas Joel was attending Monroe–Woodbury's public schools; the village's other handicapped children received privately funded special services or went without. It was then that the New York Legislature passed the statute at issue in this litigation, which provided that the Village of Kiryas Joel "is constituted a separate school district, ... and shall have and enjoy all the powers and duties of a union free school district...." 1989 N.Y.Laws, ch. 748. The statute thus empowered a locally elected board of education to take such action as opening schools and closing them, hiring teachers, prescribing textbooks, establishing disciplinary rules, and raising property taxes to fund operations....

Although it enjoys plenary legal authority over the elementary and secondary education of all school-aged children in the village, ... the Kiryas Joel Village School District currently runs only a special education program for handicapped children. The other village children have stayed in their parochial schools, relying on the new school district only for transportation, remedial education, and health and welfare services. If any child without handicap in Kiryas Joel were to seek a public-school education, the district would pay tuition to send the child into Monroe–Woodbury or another school district nearby. Under like arrangements, several of the neighboring districts send their handicapped Hasidic children into Kiryas Joel, so that two thirds of the full-time students in the village's public school come from outside. In all, the new district serves just over 40 full-time students, and two or three times that many parochial school students on a part-time basis.

Several months before the new district began operations, the New York State School Boards Association and respondents Grumet and Hawk brought this action ..., challenging Chapter 748 under the national and state constitutions as an unconstitutional establishment of religion.... [T]he trial court ruled for the plaintiffs (respondents here), finding that the statute failed all three prongs of the test in Lemon v. Kurtzman, 403 U.S. 602 (1971), and was thus unconstitutional under both the National and State Constitutions.

A divided Appellate Division affirmed on the ground that Chapter 748 had the primary effect of advancing religion, in violation of both constitutions, and the state Court of Appeals affirmed on the federal question ...

. . .

II

"A proper respect for both the Free Exercise and the Establishment Clauses compels the State to pursue a course of 'neutrality' toward religion," Committee for Public Ed. & Religious Liberty v. Nyquist, 413 U.S. 756, 792–793 (1973), favoring neither one religion over others nor religious adherents collectively over nonadherents.... Chapter 748, the statute creating the Kiryas Joel Village School District, departs from this constitutional command by delegating the State's discretionary authority over public schools to a group defined by its character as a religious community, in a legal and historical context that gives no assurance that governmental power has been or will be exercised neutrally.

Larkin v. Grendel's Den, Inc., 459 U.S. 116 (1982), provides an instructive comparison with the litigation before us. There, the Court was requested to strike down a Massachusetts statute granting religious bodies veto power over applications for liquor licenses. Under the statute, the governing body of any church, synagogue, or school located within 500 feet of an applicant's premises could, simply by submitting written objection, prevent the Alcohol Beverage Control Commission from issuing a license.... [T]he Court found that in two respects the statute violated "the wholesome 'neutrality' of which this Court's cases speak".... The Act brought about a " 'fusion of governmental and religious functions' " ... by delegating "important, discretionary govern-mental powers" to religious bodies, thus impermissibly entangling gov-ernment and religion.... And it lacked "any 'effective means of guar-anteeing' that the delegated power '[would] be used exclusively for secular, neutral, and nonideological purposes,' " ...; this, along with the "significant symbolic benefit to religion" associated with "the mere appearance of a joint exercise of legislative authority by Church and State," led the Court to conclude that the statute had a " 'primary' and 'principal' effect of advancing religion,".... Comparable constitutional problems inhere in the statute before us.

A

Larkin presented an example of united civic and religious authority, an establishment rarely found in such straightforward form in modern America....

The Establishment Clause problem presented by Chapter 748 is more subtle, but it resembles the issue raised in *Larkin* to the extent that the earlier case teaches that a State may not delegate its civic authority to a group chosen according to a religious criterion.... What makes this litigation different from *Larkin* is the delegation here of civic power to the "qualified voters of the village of Kiryas Joel," ... as distinct from a religious leader such as the village rov, or an institution of religious government like the formally constituted parish council in *Larkin*. In light of the circumstances of this case, however, this distinc-tion turns out to lack constitutional significance.

It is, first, not dispositive that the recipients of state power in this case are a group of religious individuals united by common doctrine, not the group's leaders or officers. Although some school district franchise is common to all voters, the State's manipulation of the franchise for this district limited it to Satmars, giving the sect exclusive control of the political subdivision.... If New York were to delegate civic authority to "the Grand Rebbe," *Larkin* would obviously require invalidation ..., and the same is true if New York delegates political authority by reference to religious belief. Where "fusion" is an issue, the difference lies in the distinction between a government's purposeful delegation on the basis of religion and a delegation on principles neutral to religion, to individuals whose religious identities are incidental to their receipt of civic authority.

Of course, Chapter 748 delegates power not by express reference to the religious belief of the Satmar community, but to residents of the "territory of the village of Kiryas Joel." ... Thus, the second (and arguably more important) distinction between this case and *Larkin* is the identification here of the group to exercise civil authority in terms not expressly religious. But our analysis does not end with the text of the statute at issue, ... and the context here persuades us that Chapter 748 effectively identifies these recipients of governmental authority by reference to doctrinal adherence, even though it does not do so expressly. We find this to be the better view of the facts because of the way the boundary lines of the school district divide residents according to religious affiliation, under the terms of an unusual and special legislative act.

It is undisputed that those who negotiated the village boundaries when applying the general village incorporation statute drew them so as to exclude all but Satmars, and that the New York Legislature was well aware that the village remained exclusively Satmar in 1989 when it adopted Chapter 748. The significance of this fact to the state legislature is indicated by the further fact that carving out the village school district ran counter to customary districting practices in the State. Indeed, the trend in New York is not toward dividing school districts but toward consolidating them.... The object of the State's practice of consolidation is the creation of districts large enough to provide a comprehensive education at affordable cost, which is thought to require at least 500 pupils for a combined junior-senior high school.... The Kiryas Joel Village School District, in contrast, has only 13 local, full-time students in all (even including out-of-area and part-time students leaves the number under 200), and in offering only special education and remedial programs it makes no pretense to be a full-service district.

The origin of the district in a special act of the legislature, rather than the State's general laws governing school district reorganization, is likewise anomalous..... [T]he Kiryas Joel Village School District is exceptional to the point of singularity, as the only district coming to our notice that the legislature carved from a single existing district to serve local residents....

Because the district's creation ran uniquely counter to state practice, following the lines of a religious community where the customary and neutral principles would not have dictated the same result, we have good reasons to treat this district as the reflection of a religious criterion for identifying the recipients of civil authority. Not even the special needs of the children in this community can explain the legislature's unusual Act, for the State could have responded to the concerns of the Satmar parents without implicating the Establishment Clause, as we explain in some detail further on. We therefore find the legislature's Act to be substantially equivalent to defining a political subdivision and hence the qualification for its franchise by a religious test, resulting in a purposeful and forbidden "fusion of governmental and religious functions." Larkin v. Grendel's Den....[6]

B

The fact that this school district was created by a special and unusual Act of the legislature also gives reason for concern whether the benefit received by the Satmar community is one that the legislature will provide equally to other religious (and nonreligious) groups. This is the second malady the *Larkin* Court identified in the law before it, the absence of an "effective means of guaranteeing" that governmental power will be and has been neutrally employed.... But whereas in *Larkin* it was religious groups the Court thought might exercise civic power to advance the interests of religion (or religious adherents), here the threat to neutrality occurs at an antecedent stage.

The fundamental source of constitutional concern here is that the legislature itself may fail to exercise governmental authority in a religiously neutral way. The anomalously case-specific nature of the legislature's exercise of state authority in creating this district for a religious community leaves the Court without any direct way to review such state action for the purpose of safeguarding a principle at the heart of the Establishment Clause, that government should not prefer one religion to another, or religion to irreligion.... Because the religious community of Kiryas Joel did not receive its new governmental authority simply as one of many communities eligible for equal treatment under a general law, we have no assurance that the next similarly situated group seeking a school district of its own will receive one; unlike an administrative agency's denial of an exemption from a generally applicable law, which "would be entitled to a judicial audience," ... a legislature's failure to enact a special law is itself unreviewable.... The general principle that civil power must be exercised in a manner neutral to religion is one the *Larkin* Court recognized, although it did not discuss the specific possibility of legislative favoritism along religious lines ... But the principle is well grounded in our case law, as we have frequently relied explicitly on the general availability of any benefit provided religious groups or individuals in turning aside Establishment Clause challenges. In Walz v. Tax Comm'n of New York City, 397 U.S. 664, 673 (1970), for example, the Court sustained a property tax exemption for religious properties in part because the State had "not singled out one particular church or religious group or even churches as such," but had exempted "a broad class of property owned by nonprofit, quasi-public corporations." ... And Bowen v. Kendrick, 487 U.S. 589, 608 (1988), upheld a statute enlisting a "wide spectrum of organizations" in addressing adolescent sexuality because the law was "neutral with respect to the grantee's status as a sectarian or purely secular institution." ... Here the benefit flows only to a single sect, but aiding this single, small religious group

---

[6] Because it is the unusual circumstances of this district's creation that persuade us the State has employed a religious criterion for delegating political power, this conclusion does not imply that any political subdivision that is coterminous with the boundaries of a religiously homogeneous community suffers the same constitutional infirmity. The district in this case is distinguishable from one whose boundaries are derived according to neutral historical and geographic criteria, but whose population happens to comprise coreligionists.

causes no less a constitutional problem than would follow from aiding a sect with more members or religion as a whole, ... and we are forced to conclude that the State of New York has violated the Establishment Clause.

C

In finding that Chapter 748 violates the requirement of governmental neutrality by extending the benefit of a special franchise, we do not deny that the Constitution allows the state to accommodate religious needs by alleviating special burdens. Our cases leave no doubt that in commanding neutrality the Religion Clauses do not require the government to be oblivious to impositions that legitimate exercises of state power may place on religious belief and practice....

But accommodation is not a principle without limits, and what petitioners seek is an adjustment to the Satmars' religiously grounded preferences that our cases do not countenance. Prior decisions have allowed religious communities and institutions to pursue their own interests free from governmental interference, ... but we have never hinted that an otherwise unconstitutional delegation of political power to a religious group could be saved as a religious accommodation. Petitioners' proposed accommodation singles out a particular religious sect for special treatment, and whatever the limits of permissible legislative accommodations may be, ... it is clear that neutrality as among religions must be honored....

This conclusion does not, however, bring the Satmar parents, the Monroe–Woodbury school district, or the State of New York to the end of the road in seeking ways to respond to the parents' concerns. Just as the Court in *Larkin* observed that the State's interest in protecting religious meeting places could be "readily accomplished by other means," ... there are several alternatives here for providing bilingual and bicultural special education to Satmar children. Such services can perfectly well be offered to village children through the Monroe–Woodbury Central School District. Since the Satmars do not claim that separatism is religiously mandated, their children may receive bilingual and bicultural instruction at a public school already run by the Monroe–Woodbury district. Or if the educationally appropriate offering by Monroe–Woodbury should turn out to be a separate program of bilingual and bicultural education at a neutral site near one of the village's parochial schools, ... no Establishment Clause difficulty would inhere in such a scheme, administered in accordance with neutral principles that would not necessarily confine special treatment to Satmars....

. . .

III

Justice Cardozo once cast the dissenter as "the gladiator making a last stand against the lions." B. Cardozo, Law and Literature 34 (1931). Justice Scalia's dissent is certainly the work of a gladiator, but he thrusts at lions of his own imagining. We do not disable a religiously homogeneous group from exercising political power conferred on it without regard to religion. Unlike the states of Utah and New Mexico (which were laid out according to traditional political methodologies taking account of lines of latitude and longitude and topographical features), . . . the reference line chosen for the Kiryas Joel Village School District was one purposely drawn to separate Satmars from non-Satmars. Nor do we impugn the motives of the New York Legislature, which no doubt intended to accommodate the Satmar community without violating the Establishment Clause; we simply refuse to ignore that the method it chose is one that aids a particular religious community, . . . rather than all groups similarly interested in separate schooling. The dissent protests it is novel to insist "up front" that a statute not tailor its benefits to apply only to one religious group. . . . [U]nder the dissent's theory, if New York were to pass a law providing school buses only for children attending Christian day schools, we would be constrained to uphold the statute against Establishment Clause attack until faced by a request from a non-Christian family for equal treatment under the patently unequal law. . . . And to end on the point with which Justice Scalia begins, the license he takes in suggesting that the Court holds the Satmar sect to be New York's established church, is only one symptom of his inability to accept the fact that this Court has long held that the First Amendment reaches more than classic, 18th century establishments. . . .

Our job, of course, would be easier if the dissent's position had prevailed with the Framers and with this Court over the years. An Establishment Clause diminished to the dimensions acceptable to Justice Scalia could be enforced by a few simple rules, and our docket would never see cases requiring the application of a principle like neutrality toward religion as well as among religious sects. But that would be as blind to history as to precedent, and the difference between Justice Scalia and the Court accordingly turns on the Court's recognition that the Establishment Clause does comprehend such a principle and obligates courts to exercise the judgment necessary to apply it.

In this case we are clearly constrained to conclude that the statute before us fails the test of neutrality. It delegates a power . . . to an electorate defined by common religious belief and practice, in a manner that fails to foreclose religious favoritism. It therefore crosses the line from permissible accommodation to impermissible establishment. The judgment of the Court of Appeals of the State of New York is accordingly

Affirmed.

Justice Blackmun, concurring.

For the reasons stated by Justice Souter and Justice Stevens, whose opinions I join, I agree that the New York statute under review violates the Establishment Clause of the First Amendment. I write separately only to note my disagreement with any suggestion that today's decision signals a departure from the principles described in Lemon v. Kurtzman, 403 U.S. 602 (1971). . . .

I have no quarrel with the observation of Justice O'Connor, that the application of constitutional principles, including those articulated in *Lemon,* must be sensitive to particular contexts. But I remain convinced of the general validity of the basic principles stated in *Lemon,* which have guided this Court's Establishment Clause decisions in over 30 cases. . . .

Justice Stevens with whom Justice Blackmun and Justice Ginsburg join, concurring.

New York created a special school district for the members of the Satmar religious sect in response to parental concern that children suffered "panic, fear and trauma" when "leaving their own community and being with people whose ways were so different." To meet those concerns, the State could have taken steps to alleviate the children's fear by teaching their schoolmates to be tolerant and respectful of Satmar customs. Action of that kind would raise no constitutional concerns and would further the strong public interest in promoting diversity and understanding in the public schools.

Instead, the State responded with a solution that affirmatively supports a religious sect's interest in segregating itself and preventing its children from associating with their neighbors. The isolation of these children, while it may protect them from "panic, fear and trauma," also unquestionably increased the likelihood that they would remain within the fold, faithful adherents of their parents' religious faith. By creating a school district that is specifically intended to shield children from contact with others who have "different ways," the State provided official support to cement the attachment of young adherents to a particular faith. It is telling, in this regard, that two thirds of the school's full-time students are Hasidic handicapped children from outside the village; the Kiryas Joel school thus serves a population far wider than the village—one defined less by geography than by religion.

Affirmative state action in aid of segregation of this character is unlike the evenhanded distribution of a public benefit or service, a "release time" program for public school students involving no public premises or funds, or a decision to grant an exemption from a burdensome general rule. It is, I believe, fairly characterized as establishing, rather than merely accommodating, religion. For this reason, as well as the reasons set out in Justice Souter's opinion, I am persuaded that the New York law at issue in these cases violates the Establishment Clause of the First Amendment.

Justice O'Connor, concurring in part and concurring in the judgment.

I

The question at the heart of this case is: What may the government do, consistently with the Establishment Clause, to accommodate people's religious beliefs? . . .

. . .

II

. . . Religious needs can be accommodated through laws that are neutral with regard to religion. The Satmars' living arrangements were accommodated by their right—a right shared with all other communities, religious or not, throughout New York—to incorporate themselves as a village. From 1984 to 1985, the Satmar handicapped children's educational needs were accommodated by special education programs like those available to all handicapped children, religious or not....

We have time and again held that the government generally may not treat people differently based on the God or gods they worship, or don't worship....

This emphasis on equal treatment is, I think, an eminently sound approach. In my view, the Religion Clauses ... all speak with one voice on this point: Absent the most unusual circumstances, one's religion ought not affect one's legal rights or duties or benefits....

That the government is acting to accommodate religion should generally not change this analysis. What makes accommodation permissible, even praiseworthy, is not that the government is making life easier for some particular religious group as such. Rather, it is that the government is accommodating a deeply held belief. Accommodations may thus justify treating those who share this belief differently from those who do not; but they do not justify discriminations based on sect. A state law prohibiting the consumption of alcohol may exempt sacramental wines, but it may not exempt sacramental wine use by Catholics but not by Jews. A draft law may exempt conscientious objectors, but it may not exempt conscientious objectors whose objections are based on theistic belief (such as Quakers) as opposed to nontheistic belief (such as Buddhists) or atheistic belief.... The Constitution permits "nondiscriminatory religious-practice exemption[s]," ... not sectarian ones.

III

I join Parts I, II–B, II–C, and III of the Court's opinion because I think this law, rather than being a general accommodation, singles out a particular religious group for favorable treatment. The Court's analysis of the history of this law and of the surrounding statutory scheme, persuades me of this.

On its face, this statute benefits one group—the residents of Kiryas Joel. Because this benefit was given to this group based on its religion, it seems proper to treat it as a legislatively drawn religious classification....

Our invalidation of this statute in no way means that the Satmars' needs cannot be accommodated. There is nothing improper about a legislative intention to accommodate a religious group, so long as it is implemented through generally applicable legislation. New York may, for instance, allow all villages to operate their own school districts. If it does not want to act so broadly, it may set forth neutral criteria that a village must meet to have a school district of its own; these criteria can then be applied by a state agency, and the decision would then be reviewable by the judiciary. A district created under a generally applicable scheme would be acceptable even though it coincides with a village which was consciously created by its voters as an enclave for their religious group. I do not think the Court's opinion holds the contrary.

I also think there is one other accommodation that would be entirely permissible: the 1984 scheme, which was discontinued because of our decision in *Aguilar*. The Religion Clauses prohibit the government from favoring religion, but they provide no warrant for discriminating against religion.... If the government provides this education on-site at public schools and at nonsectarian private schools, it is only fair that it provide it on-site at sectarian schools as well.

I thought this to be true in *Aguilar,* see 473 U.S. at 421–431 (O'Connor, J., dissenting), and I still believe it today.... It is the Court's insistence on disfavoring religion in *Aguilar* that led New York to favor it here. The court should, in a proper case, be prepared to reconsider *Aguilar,* in order to bring our Establishment Clause jurisprudence back to what I think is the proper track—government impartiality, not animosity, towards religion.

IV

One aspect of the Court's opinion in this case is worth noting: Like the opinions in two recent cases, Lee v. Weisman, 505 U.S. (1992); Zobrest v. Catalina Foothills School Dist., 509 U.S. (1993), and the case I think is most relevant to this one, Larson v. Valente, 456 U.S. 228 (1982), the Court's opinion does not focus on the Establishment Clause test we set forth in Lemon v. Kurtzman, 403 U.S. 602 (1971).

It is always appealing to look for a single test, a Grand Unified Theory that would resolve all the cases that may arise under a particular clause....

But the same constitutional principle may operate very differently in different contexts. ...

And setting forth a unitary test for a broad set of cases may sometimes do more harm than good. Any test that must deal with widely disparate situations risks being so vague as to be useless....

Moreover, shoehorning new problems into a test that does not reflect the special concerns raised by those problems tends to deform the language of the test. Relatively simple phrases like "primary effect ... that neither advances nor inhibits religion" and "entanglement," *Lemon,* supra, at 612–613, acquire more and more complicated definitions which stray ever further from their literal meaning.... Alternatives to *Lemon* suffer from a similar failing when they lead us to find "coercive pressure" to pray when a school asks listeners—with no threat of legal sanctions—to stand or remain silent during a graduation prayer. Lee v. Weisman ... Some of the results and perhaps even some of the reasoning in these cases may have been right. I joined two of the cases cited above, *Larkin* and *Lee,* and continue to believe they were correctly decided. But I think it is more useful to recognize the relevant concerns in each case on their own terms, rather than trying to squeeze them into language that does not really apply to them.

Finally, another danger to keep in mind is that the bad test may drive out the good. Rather than taking the opportunity to derive narrower, more precise tests from the case law, courts tend to continually try to patch up the broad test, making it more and more amorphous and distorted. This, I am afraid, has happened with *Lemon.*

Experience proves that the Establishment Clause, like the Free Speech Clause, cannot easily be reduced to a single test. There are different categories of Establishment Clause cases, which may call for different approaches. Some cases, like this one, involve government actions targeted at particular individuals or groups, imposing special duties or giving special benefits. Cases involving government speech on religious topics ... seem to me to fall into a different category and to require an analysis focusing on whether the speech endorses or disapproves of religion, rather than on whether the government action is neutral with regard to religion....

Another category encompasses cases in which the government must make decisions about matters of religious doctrine and religious law. See Serbian Eastern Orthodox Diocese v. Milivojevich, 426 U.S. 696 (1976) (which also did not apply *Lemon*). These cases, which often arise in the application of otherwise neutral property or contract principles to religious institutions, involve complicated questions not present in other situations.... Government delegations of power to religious bodies may make up yet another category. As *Larkin* itself suggested, government impartiality towards religion may not be enough in such situations: A law that bars all alcohol sales within some distance of a church, school, or hospital may be valid, but an equally even-handed law that gives each institution discretionary power over the sales may not be.... Of course, there may well be additional categories, or more opportune places to draw the lines between the categories.

As the Court's opinion today shows, the slide away from *Lemon's* unitary approach is well under way. A return to *Lemon,* even if possible, would likely be futile, regardless of where one stands on the substantive Establishment Clause questions. I think a less unitary approach provides a better structure for analysis.... [A]bandoning the *Lemon* framework need not mean abandoning some of the insights that the test reflected, nor the insights of the cases that applied it.

. . .

Justice Kennedy, concurring in the judgment.

The Court's ruling that the Kiryas Joel Village School District violates the Establishment Clause is in my view correct, but my reservations about what the Court's reasoning implies for religious accommodations in general are sufficient to require a separate writing. As the Court recognizes, a legislative accommodation that discriminates among religions may become an establishment of religion. But the Court's opinion can be interpreted to say that an accommodation for a particular religious group is invalid because of the risk that the legislature will not grant the same accommodation to another religious group suffering some similar burden. This rationale seems to me without grounding in our precedents and a needless restriction upon the legislature's ability to respond to the unique problems of a particular religious group. The real vice of the school district, in my estimation, is that New York created it by drawing political boundaries on the basis of religion. I would decide the issue we confront upon this narrower theory, though in accord with many of the Court's general observations about the State's actions in this case.

I

This is not a case in which the government has granted a benefit to a general class of recipients of which religious groups are just one part.... But for the forbidden manner in which the New York Legislature sought to go about it, the State's attempt to accommodate the special needs of the handicapped Satmar children would have been valid.

. . .

New York's object in creating the Kiryas Joel Village School District—to accommodate the religious practices of the handicapped Satmar children—is validated by the principles that emerge from ... precedents. First, by creating the district, New York sought to alleviate a specific and identifiable burden on the Satmars' religious practice.... New York was entitled to relieve these significant burdens, even though mainstream public schooling does not conflict with any specific tenet of the Satmars' religious faith....

Second, by creating the district, New York did not impose or increase any burden on non-Satmars, compared to the burden it lifted from the Satmars, that might disqualify the District as a genuine accommodation....

Third, the creation of the school district to alleviate the special burdens born by the handicapped Satmar children cannot be said, for that reason alone, to favor the Satmar religion to the exclusion of any other. "The clearest command of the Establishment Clause," of course, "is that one religious denomination cannot be officially preferred over another." Larson v. Valente, 456 U.S. 228, 244 (1982) ... I disagree, however, with the Court's conclusion that the school district breaches this command. The Court insists that religious favoritism is a danger here, because the "anomalously case-specific nature of the legislature's exercise of state authority in creating this district for a religious community leaves the Court without any direct way to review such state action" to ensure interdenominational neutrality....

This reasoning reverses the usual presumption that a statute is constitutional and, in essence, adjudges the New York Legislature guilty until it proves itself innocent. No party has adduced any evidence that the legislature has denied another religious community like the Satmars its own school district under analogous circumstances. The legislature, like the judiciary, is sworn to uphold the Constitution, and we have no reason to presume that the New York Legislature would not grant the same accommodation in a similar future case. The fact that New York singled out the Satmars for this special treatment indicates nothing other than the uniqueness of the handicapped Satmar children's plight. It is normal for legislatures to respond to problems as they arise—no less so when the issue is religious accommodation....

Nor is it true that New York's failure to accommodate another religious community facing similar burdens would be insulated from challenge in the courts. The burdened community could sue the State of New York, contending that New York's discriminatory treatment of the two religious communities violated the Establishment Clause....

II

The Kiryas Joel Village School District thus does not suffer any of the typical infirmities that might invalidate an attempted legislative accommodation. In the ordinary case, the fact that New York has chosen to accommodate the burdens unique to one religious group would raise no constitutional problems. Without further evidence that New York has denied the same accommodation to religious groups bearing similar burdens, we could not presume from the particularity of the accommodation that the New York Legislature acted with discriminatory intent.

This particularity takes on a different cast, however, when the accommodation requires the government to draw political or electoral boundaries.... Whether or not the purpose is accommodation and whether or not the government provides similar gerrymanders to people of all religious faiths, the Establishment Clause forbids the government to use religion as a line-drawing criterion. In this respect, the Establishment Clause mirrors the Equal Protection Clause. Just as the government may not segregate people on account of their race, so too it may not segregate on the basis of religion. The danger of stigma and stirred animosities is no less acute for religious line-drawing than for racial. Justice Douglas put it well in a statement this Court quoted with approval just last Term: "When racial or religious lines are drawn by the State, the multiracial, multireligious communities that our Constitution seeks to weld together as one become separatist; antagonisms that relate to race or to religion rather than to political issues are generated; communities seek not the best representative but the best racial or religious partisan...." ... I agree with the Court insofar as it invalidates the school district for being drawn along religious lines. As the plurality observes, the New York Legislature knew that everyone within the village was Satmar when it drew the school district along the village lines, and it determined who was to be included in the district by imposing, in effect, a religious test. There is no serious question that the legislature configured the school district, with purpose and precision, along a religious line. This explicit religious gerrymandering violates the First Amendment Establishment Clause.

It is important to recognize the limits of this principle. We do not confront the constitutionality of the Kiryas Joel Village itself, and the formation of the village appears to differ from the formation of the school district in one critical respect.... [T]he Kiryas Joel Village School District was created by state legislation. The State of New York had complete discretion not to enact it. The State thus had a direct hand in accomplishing the religious segregation.

... [T]he village was formed pursuant to a religion-neutral self-incorporation scheme.... People who share a common religious belief or lifestyle may live together without sacrificing the basic rights of self-governance that all American citizens enjoy, so long as they do not use those rights to establish their religious faith. . . .   There is more than a fine line, however, between the voluntary association that leads to a political community comprised of people who share a common religious faith, and the forced separation that occurs when the government draws explicit political boundaries on the basis of peoples' faith. In creating the Kiryas Joel Village School District, New York crossed that line, and so we must hold the district invalid.

III

This is an unusual case, for it is rare to see a State exert such documented care to carve out territory for people of a particular religious faith. It is also unusual in that the problem to which the Kiryas Joel Village School District was addressed is attributable in no small measure to what I believe were unfortunate rulings by this Court.

Before 1985, the handicapped Satmar children of Kiryas Joel attended the private religious schools within the village that the other Satmar children attended. Because their handicaps were in some cases acute (ranging from mental retardation and deafness to spina bifida and cerebral palsy), the State of New York provided public funds for special education of these children at annexes to the religious schools. Then came the companion cases of School Dist. of Grand Rapids v. Ball, 473 U.S. 373 (1985), and Aguilar v. Felton, 473 U.S. 402 (1985). In *Grand Rapids,* the Court invalidated a program in which public school teachers would offer supplemental classes at private schools, including religious schools, at the end of the regular school day. And in *Aguilar,* the Court invalidated New York City's use of Title I funding to pay the salaries of public school teachers who taught educationally deprived children of low-income families at parochial schools in the city. After these cases, the Monroe–Woodbury School District suspended its special education program at the Kiryas Joel religious schools. . . .

The decisions in *Grand Rapids* and *Aguilar* may have been erroneous. In light of the case before us, and in the interest of sound elaboration of constitutional doctrine, it may be necessary for us to reconsider them at a later date. . . .

One misjudgment is no excuse, however, for compounding it with another. We must confront this case as it comes before us, without bending rules to free the Satmars from a predicament into which we put them. The Establishment Clause forbids the government to draw political boundaries on the basis of religious faith. For this reason, I concur in the judgment of the Court.

Justice Scalia, with whom The Chief Justice and Justice Thomas join, dissenting.

The Court today finds that the Powers That Be, up in Albany, have conspired to effect an establishment of the Satmar Hasidim. I do not know who would be more surprised at this discovery: the Founders of our Nation or Grand Rebbe Joel Teitelbaum, founder of the Satmar. The Grand Rebbe would be astounded to learn that after escaping brutal persecution and coming to America with the modest hope of religious toleration for their ascetic form of Judaism, the Satmar had become so powerful, so closely allied with Mammon, as to have become an "establishment" of the Empire State. And the Founding Fathers would be astonished to find that the Establishment Clause ... has been employed to prohibit characteristically and admirably American accommodation of the religious practices (or more precisely, cultural peculiarities) of a tiny minority sect. I, however, am not surprised. Once this Court has abandoned text and history as guides, nothing prevents it from calling religious toleration the establishment of religion.

I

Unlike most of our Establishment Clause cases involving education, these cases involve no public funding, however slight or indirect, to private religious schools. They do not involve private schools at all. The school under scrutiny is a public school.... The only thing distinctive about the school is that all the students share the same religion.

None of our cases has ever suggested that there is anything wrong with that.... There is no danger in educating religious students in a public school.

For these very good reasons, Justice Souter's opinion does not focus upon the school, but rather upon the school district and the New York Legislature that created it. His arguments, though sometimes intermingled, are two: that reposing governmental power in the Kiryas Joel School District is the same as reposing governmental power in a religious group; and that in enacting the statute creating the district, the New York State Legislature was discriminating on the basis of religion, i.e., favoring the Satmar Hasidim over others. I shall discuss these arguments in turn.

II

For his thesis that New York has unconstitutionally conferred governmental authority upon the Satmar sect, Justice Souter relies extensively, and virtually exclusively, upon Larkin v. Grendel's Den, Inc., 459 U.S. 116 (1982)....

... The uniqueness of the case stemmed from the grant of governmental power directly to a religious institution.... Justice Souter dismisses the difference between a transfer of government power to citizens who share a common religion as opposed to "the officers of its sectarian organization"—the critical factor that made *Grendel's Den* unique and "rar[e]"—as being "one of form, not substance."

Justice Souter's steamrolling of the difference between civil authority held by a church, and civil authority held by members of a church, is breathtaking. To accept it, one must believe that large portions of the civil authority exercised during most of our history were unconstitutional, and that much more of it than merely the Kiryas Joel School District is unconstitutional today.... If the conferral of governmental power upon a religious institution as such (rather than upon American citizens who belong to the religious institution) is not the test of *Grendel's Den* invalidity, there is no reason why giving power to a body that is overwhelmingly dominated by the members of one sect would not suffice to invoke the Establishment Clause. That might have made the entire States of Utah and New Mexico unconstitutional at the time of their admission to the Union, and would undoubtedly make many units of local government unconstitutional today.

. . .

Perhaps appreciating the startling implications for our constitutional jurisprudence of collapsing the distinction between religious institutions and their members, Justice Souter tries to limit his "unconstitutional conferral of civil authority" holding by pointing out several features supposedly unique to the present case: that the "boundary lines of the school district divide residents according to religious affiliation,"; that the school district was created by "a special act of the legislature,"; and that the formation of the school district ran counter to the legislature's trend of consolidating districts in recent years. Assuming all these points to be true (and they are not), they would certainly bear upon whether the legislature had an impermissible religious motivation in creating the district (which is Justice Souter's next point, in the discussion of which I shall reply to these arguments). But they have nothing to do with whether conferral of power upon a group of citizens can be the conferral of power upon a religious institution. It can not. Or if it can, our Establishment Clause jurisprudence has been transformed.

III

I turn, next, to Justice Souter's second justification for finding an establishment of religion: his facile conclusion that the New York Legislature's creation of the Kiryas Joel School District was religiously motivated. But in the Land of the Free, democratically adopted laws are not so easily impeached by unelected judges....

There is of course no possible doubt of a secular basis here. The New York Legislature faced a unique problem in Kiryas Joel: a community in which all the non-handicapped children attend private schools, and the physically and mentally disabled children who attend public school suffer the additional handicap of cultural distinctiveness....

Since the obvious presence of a neutral, secular basis renders the asserted preferential effect of this law inadequate to invalidate it, Justice Souter is required to come forward with direct evidence that religious preference was the objective. His case could scarcely be weaker....

. . .

Justice Souter's case against the statute comes down to nothing more ... than ... the fact that all the residents of the Kiryas Joel Village School District are Satmars. But all its residents also wear unusual dress, have unusual civic customs, and have not much to do with people who are culturally different from them. ... On what basis does Justice Souter conclude that it is the theological distinctiveness rather than the cultural distinctiveness that was the basis for New York State's decision? The normal assumption would be that it was the latter, since it was not theology but dress, language, and cultural alienation that posed the educational problem for the children....

. . .

At various times Justice Souter intimates, though he does not precisely say, that the boundaries of the school district were intentionally drawn on the basis of religion.... What happened in the creation of the village is in fact precisely what happened in the creation of the school district, so that the former cannot possibly infect the latter, as Justice Souter tries to suggest. Entirely secular reasons (zoning for the village, cultural alienation of students for the school district) produced a political unit whose members happened to share the same religion. There is no evidence (indeed, no plausible suspicion) of the legislature's desire to favor the Satmar religion, as opposed to meeting distinctive secular needs or desires of citizens who happened to be Satmars. If there were, Justice Souter would say so; instead, he must merely insinuate.

IV

But even if Chapter 748 were intended to create a special arrangement for the Satmars because of their religion ..., it would be a permissible accommodation....

When a legislature acts to accommodate religion, particularly a minority sect, "it follows the best of our traditions." *Zorach,* supra, at 314. The Constitution itself contains an accommodation of sorts. Article VI, cl. 3, prescribes that executive, legislative and judicial officers of the Federal and State Governments shall bind themselves to support the Constitution "by Oath or Affirmation." Although members of the most populous religions found no difficulty in swearing an oath to God, Quakers, Moravians, and Mennonites refused to take oaths based on Matthew 5:34's injunction "swear not at all." The option of affirmation was added to accommodate these minority religions and enable their members to serve in government....

. . .

The ... reason the Court finds accommodation impermissible is, astoundingly, the mere risk that the State will not offer accommodation to a similar group in the future, and that neutrality will therefore not be preserved. ...

At bottom, the Court's "no guarantee of neutrality" argument is an assertion of this Court's inability to control the New York Legislature's future denial of comparable accommodation ....

The Court's demand for "up front" assurances of a neutral system is at war with both traditional accommodation doctrine and the judicial role. ... [M]ost efforts at accommodation seek to solve a problem that applies to members of only one or a few religions. Not every religion uses wine in its sacraments, but that does not make an exemption from

Prohibition for sacramental wine-use impermissible, ... nor does it require the State granting such an exemption to explain in advance how it will treat every other claim for dispensation from its controlled-substances laws. Likewise, not every religion uses peyote in its services, but we have suggested that legislation which exempts the sacramental use of peyote from generally applicable drug laws is not only permissible, but desirable, ... without any suggestion that some "up front" legislative guarantee of equal treatment for sacramental substances used by other sects must be provided. The record is clear that the necessary guarantee can and will be provided, after the fact, by the courts. . . .

Contrary to the Court's suggestion, I do not think that the Establishment Clause prohibits formally established "state" churches and nothing more. I have always believed, and all my opinions are consistent with the view, that the Establishment Clause prohibits the favoring of one religion over others. In this respect, it is the Court that attacks lions of straw. What I attack is the Court's imposition of novel "up front" procedural requirements on state legislatures. Making law (and making exceptions) one case at a time, whether through adjudication or through highly particularized rulemaking or legislation, violates, ex ante, no principle of fairness, equal protection, or neutrality, simply because it does not announce in advance how all future cases (and all future exceptions) will be disposed of. . . .

V

A few words in response to the separate concurrences: Justice Stevens adopts, for these cases, a rationale that is almost without limit. The separate Kiryas Joel school district is problematic in his view because "[t]he isolation of these children, while it may protect them from 'panic, fear and trauma,' also unquestionably increased the likelihood that they would remain within the fold, faithful adherents of their parents' religious faith." So much for family values. . . .

Justice Kennedy's "political-line-drawing" approach founders on its own terms. He concedes that the Constitution does not prevent people who share a faith from forming their own villages and towns, and suggests that the formation of the village of Kiryas Joel was free from defect. . . . I do not see, then, how a school district drawn to mirror the boundaries of an existing village (an existing geographic line), which itself is not infirm, can violate the Constitution. . . .

Justice Kennedy expresses the view that School Dist. of Grand Rapids v. Ball, 473 U.S. 373 (1985), and Aguilar v. Felton, 473 U.S. 402 (1985) ... "may have been erroneous," and he suggests that "it may be necessary for us to reconsider them at a later date." Justice O'Connor goes even further and expresses the view that *Aguilar* should be overruled .. I heartily agree that these cases ... should be overruled at the earliest opportunity; but meanwhile, today's opinion causes us to lose still further ground, and in the same anti-accommodationist direction.

Finally, Justice O'Connor observes that the Court's opinion does not focus on the so-called *Lemon* test, ... and she urges that that test be abandoned, at least as a "unitary approach" to all Establishment Clause claims.... I no longer take any comfort in the Court's failure to rely on it in any particular case, as I once mistakenly did, see Lee v. Weisman ... (Scalia, J., dissenting). But the Court's snub of *Lemon* today (it receives only two "see also" citations, in the course of the opinion's description of *Grendel's Den*) is particularly noteworthy because all three courts below (who are not free to ignore Supreme Court precedent at will) relied on it, and the parties (also bound by our case law) dedicated over 80 pages of briefing to the application and continued vitality of the *Lemon* test. ... [I]t seems quite inefficient for this Court, which in reaching its decisions relies heavily on the briefing of the parties and, to a lesser extent, the opinions of lower courts, to mislead lower courts and parties about the relevance of the *Lemon* test....

Unlike Justice O'Connor, however, I would not replace *Lemon* with nothing, and let the case law "evolve" into a series of situation-specific rules.... The problem with (and the allure of) *Lemon* has not been that it is "rigid," but rather that in many applications it has been utterly meaningless, validating whatever result the Court would desire.... The foremost principle I would apply is fidelity to the longstanding traditions of our people, which surely provide the diversity of treatment that Justice O'Connor seeks, but do not leave us to our own devices.

. . .

2. HIGHER EDUCATION

Page 1664. Add at end of subsection:

ROSENBERGER v. RECTOR and VISITORS OF THE UNIVERSITY OF VIRGINIA

___ U.S. ___, 115 S.Ct. 2510, 132 L.Ed.2d 700 (1995).

Justice Kennedy delivered the opinion of the Court.

The University of Virginia, [a state university] ... , authorizes the payment of outside contractors for the printing costs of a variety of student publications. It withheld any authorization for payments on behalf of petitioners for the sole reason that their student paper "primarily promotes or manifests a particular belie[f] in or about a deity or an ultimate reality." That the paper did promote or manifest views within the defined exclusion seems plain enough. The challenge is to the University's regulation and its denial of authorization, the case raising issues under the Speech and Establishment Clauses of the First Amendment.

I

. . .

Before a student group is eligible to submit bills from its outside contractors for payment by the fund described below, it must become a "Contracted Independent Organization" (CIO). CIO status is available to any group the majority of whose members are students, whose managing officers are fulltime students, and that complies with certain procedural requirements. .A CIO must file its constitution with the University; must pledge not to discriminate in its membership; and must include in dealings with third parties and in all written materials a disclaimer, stating that the CIO is independent of the University and that the University is not responsible for the CIO.…

All CIOs may exist and operate at the University, but some are also entitled to apply for funds from the Student Activities Fund (SAF). Established and governed by University Guidelines, the purpose of the SAF is to support a broad range of extracurricular student activities that "are related to the educational purpose of the University." … The SAF receives its money from a mandatory fee of $14 per semester assessed to each full-time student. The Student Council, elected by the students, has the initial authority to disburse the funds, but its actions are subject to review by a faculty body chaired by a designee of the Vice President for Student Affairs.

Some, but not all, CIOs may submit disbursement requests to the SAF. The Guidelines recognize 11 categories of student groups that may seek payment to third-party contractors because they "are related to the educational purpose of the University of Virginia." One of these is "student news, information, opinion, entertainment, or academic communications media groups." The Guidelines also specify, however, that the costs of certain activities of CIOs that are otherwise eligible for funding will not be reimbursed by the SAF. The student activities which are excluded from SAF support are religious activities, philanthropic contributions and activities, political activities, activities that would jeopardize the University's tax exempt status, those which involve payment of honoraria or similar fees, or social entertainment or related expenses. The prohibition on "political activities" is defined so that it is limited to electioneering and lobbying. The Guidelines provide that "[t]hese restrictions on funding political activities are not intended to preclude funding of any otherwise eligible student organization which … espouses particular positions or ideological viewpoints, including those that may be unpopular or are not generally accepted." A "religious activity," by contrast, is defined as any activity that "primarily promotes or manifests a particular belie[f] in or about a deity or an ultimate reality."

. . .

Petitioners' organization, Wide Awake Productions (WAP), qualified as a CIO. Formed by petitioner Ronald Rosenberger and other undergraduates in 1990, WAP was established "[t]o publish a magazine of philosophical and religious expression," "[t]o facilitate discussion which fosters an atmosphere of sensitivity to and tolerance of Christian viewpoints," and "[t]o provide a unifying focus for Christians of multicultural backgrounds." WAP publishes Wide Awake: A Christian Perspective at the University of Virginia. The paper's Christian viewpoint was evident from the first issue, in which its editors wrote that the journal "offers a Christian perspective on both personal and community issues, especially those relevant to college students at the University of Virginia." The editors committed the paper to a two-fold mission: "to challenge Christians to live, in word and deed, according to the faith they proclaim and to encourage students to consider what a personal relationship with Jesus Christ means." The first issue had articles about racism, crisis pregnancy, stress, prayer, C.S. Lewis' ideas about evil and free will, and reviews of religious music. In the next two issues, Wide Awake featured stories about homosexuality, Christian missionary work, and eating disorders, as well as music reviews and interviews with University professors. Each page of Wide Awake, and the end of each article or review, is marked by a cross. The advertisements carried in Wide Awake also reveal the Christian perspective of the journal. For the most part, the advertisers are churches, centers for Christian study, or Christian bookstores. By June 1992, WAP had distributed about 5,000 copies of Wide Awake to University students, free of charge.

WAP had acquired CIO status soon after it was organized. This is an important consideration in this case, for had it been a "religious organization," WAP would not have been accorded CIO status. As defined by the Guidelines, a "religious organization" is "an organization whose purpose is to practice a devotion to an acknowledged ultimate reality or deity." At no stage in this controversy has the University contended that WAP is such an organization.

A few months after being given CIO status, WAP requested the SAF to pay its printer $5,862 for the costs of printing its newspaper. The Appropriations Committee of the Student Council denied WAP's request on the ground that Wide Awake was a "religious activity" within the meaning of the Guidelines, i.e., that the newspaper "promote[d] or manifest[ed] a particular belie[f] in or about a deity or an ultimate reality." ... WAP appealed to ... the Student Activities Committee. In a letter signed by the Dean of Students, the committee sustained the denial of funding.

Having no further recourse within the University structure, WAP, Wide Awake, and three of its editors and members filed suit in the United States District Court for the Western District of Virginia, challenging the SAF's action as violative of ... 42 U.S.C. § 1983. They alleged that refusal to authorize payment of the printing costs of the publication, solely on the basis of its religious editorial viewpoint, violated their rights to freedom of speech and press, to the free exercise of religion, and to equal protection of the law.... The suit sought damages for the costs of printing the paper, injunctive and declaratory relief, and attorney's fees.

On cross-motions for summary judgment, the District Court ruled for the University, holding that denial of SAF support was not an impermissible content or viewpoint discrimination against petitioners' speech, and that the University's Establishment Clause concern over its "religious activities" was a sufficient justification for denying payment to third-party contractors....

The United States Court of Appeals for the Fourth Circuit, in disagreement with the District Court, held that the Guidelines did discriminate on the basis of content.... The Court of Appeals affirmed the judgment of the District Court nonetheless, concluding that the discrimination by the University was justified by the "compelling interest in maintaining strict separation of church and state."

II

It is axiomatic that the government may not regulate speech based on its substantive content or the message it conveys....

... [T]he State [is forbidden] from exercising viewpoint discrimination, even when the limited public forum is one of its own creation. In a case involving a school district's provision of school facilities for private uses, we declared that "[t]here is no question that the District, like the private owner of property, may legally preserve the property under its control for the use to which it is dedicated." Lamb's Chapel v. Center Moriches Union Free School Dist., 508 U.S. ___, ___ (1993). The necessities of confining a forum to the limited and legitimate purposes for which it was created may justify the State in reserving it for certain groups or for the discussion of certain topics.... Once it has opened a limited forum, however, the State must respect the lawful boundaries it has itself set.... Thus, in determining whether the State is acting to preserve the limits of the forum it has created so that the exclusion of a class of speech is legitimate, we have observed a distinction between, on the one hand, content discrimination, which may be permissible if it preserves the purposes of that limited forum, and, on the other hand, viewpoint discrimination, which is presumed impermissible when directed against speech otherwise within the forum's limitations....

The SAF is a forum more in a metaphysical than in a spatial or geographic sense, but the same principles are applicable.... The most recent and most apposite case is our decision in *Lamb's Chapel*, supra. There, a school district had opened school facilities for use after school hours by community groups for a wide variety of social, civic, and recreational purposes. The district, however, had enacted a formal policy against opening facilities to groups for religious purposes. Invoking its policy, the district rejected a request from a group desiring to show a film series addressing various child-rearing questions from a "Christian perspective." There was no indication in the record in Lamb's Chapel that the request to use the school facilities was "denied for any reason other than the fact that the presentation would have been from a religious perspective." 508 U.S., at ___. Our conclusion was unanimous: "[I]t discriminates on the basis of viewpoint to permit school property to be used for the presentation of all views about family issues and child-rearing except those dealing with the subject matter from a religious standpoint." Ibid.

The University does acknowledge (as it must in light of our precedents) that "ideologically driven attempts to suppress a particular point of view are presumptively unconstitutional in funding, as in other contexts," but insists that this case does not present that issue because the Guidelines draw lines based on content, not viewpoint. As we have noted, discrimination against one set of views or ideas is but a subset or particular instance of the more general phenomenon of content discrimination. . . . And, it must be acknowledged, the distinction is not a precise one. It is, in a sense, something of an understatement to speak of religious thought and discussion as just a viewpoint, as distinct from a comprehensive body of thought. The nature of our origins and destiny and their dependence upon the existence of a divine being have been subjects of philosophic inquiry throughout human history. We conclude, nonetheless, that here, as in *Lamb's Chapel*, viewpoint discrimination is the proper way to interpret the University's objections to Wide Awake. By the very terms of the SAF prohibition, the University does not exclude religion as a subject matter but selects for disfavored treatment those student journalistic efforts with religious editorial viewpoints. Religion may be a vast area of inquiry, but it also provides, as it did here, a specific premise, a perspective, a standpoint from which a variety of subjects may be discussed and considered. The prohibited perspective, not the general subject matter, resulted in the refusal to make third-party payments, for the subjects discussed were otherwise within the approved category of publications.

The dissent's assertion that no viewpoint discrimination occurs because the Guidelines discriminate against an entire class of viewpoints reflects an insupportable assumption that all debate is bipolar and that anti-religious speech is the only response to religious speech. Our understanding of the complex and multifaceted nature of public discourse has not embraced such a contrived description of the marketplace of ideas. If the topic of debate is, for example, racism, then exclusion of several views on that problem is just as offensive to the First Amendment as exclusion of only one. It is as objectionable to exclude both a theistic and an atheistic perspective on the debate as it is to exclude one, the other, or yet another political, economic, or social viewpoint. The dissent's declaration that debate is not skewed so long as multiple voices are silenced is simply wrong; the debate is skewed in multiple ways.

The University's denial of WAP's request for third-party payments in the present case is based upon viewpoint discrimination not unlike the discrimination the school district relied upon in Lamb's Chapel and that we found invalid. The church group in *Lamb's Chapel* would have been qualified as a social or civic organization, save for its religious purposes. Furthermore, just as the school district in *Lamb's Chapel* pointed to nothing but the religious views of the group as the rationale for excluding its message, so in this case the University justifies its denial of SAF participation to WAP on the ground that the contents of Wide Awake reveal an avowed religious perspective. . . . [T]he dissent seems to argue that we found viewpoint discrimination in that case because the government excluded Christian, but not atheistic, viewpoints from being expressed in the forum there. The Court relied on no such distinction. . . .

The University tries to escape the consequences of our holding in *Lamb's Chapel* by urging that this case involves the provision of funds rather than access to facilities. . . . Were the reasoning of Lamb's Chapel to apply to funding decisions as well as to those involving access to facilities, it is urged, its holding "would become a judicial juggernaut, constitutionalizing the ubiquitous content-based decisions that schools, colleges, and other government entities routinely make in the allocation of public funds."

To this end the University relies on our assurance in Widmar v. Vincent, [454 U.S. 263 (1981).] There, in the course of striking down a public university's exclusion of religious groups from use of school facilities made available to all other student groups, we stated: "Nor do we question the right of the University to make academic judgments as to how best to allocate scarce resources." 454 U.S., at 276. The quoted language in *Widmar* was but a proper recognition of the principle that when the State is the speaker, it may make content-based choices. When the University determines the content of the education it provides, it is the University speaking, and we have permitted the government to regulate the content of what is or is not expressed when it is the speaker or when it enlists private entities to convey its own message.... When the government disburses public funds to private entities to convey a governmental message, it may take legitimate and appropriate steps to ensure that its message is neither garbled nor distorted by the grant- ee....

It does not follow, however, and we did not suggest in *Widmar*, that viewpoint-based restrictions are proper when the University does not itself speak or subsidize transmittal of a message it favors but instead expends funds to encourage a diversity of views from private speakers. A holding that the University may not discriminate based on the viewpoint of private persons whose speech it facilitates does not restrict the University's own speech, which is controlled by different princi- ples....

The distinction between the University's own favored message and the private speech of students is evident in the case before us.... The University declares that the student groups eligible for SAF support are not the University's agents, are not subject to its control, and are not its responsibility. Having offered to pay the third-party contractors on behalf of private speakers who convey their own messages, the Universi- ty may not silence the expression of selected viewpoints.

The University urges that, from a constitutional standpoint, funding of speech differs from provision of access to facilities because money is scarce and physical facilities are not. Beyond the fact that in any given case this proposition might not be true as an empirical matter, the underlying premise that the University could discriminate based on viewpoint if demand for space exceeded its availability is wrong as well. The government cannot justify viewpoint discrimination among private speakers on the economic fact of scarcity. Had the meeting rooms in Lamb's Chapel been scarce, had the demand been greater than the supply, our decision would have been no different. It would have been incumbent on the State, of course, to ration or allocate the scarce resources on some acceptable neutral principle; but nothing in our decision indicated that scarcity would give the State the right to exercise viewpoint discrimination that is otherwise impermissible.

. .. .

The Guideline invoked by the University to deny third-party contractor payments on behalf of WAP effects a sweeping restriction on student thought and student inquiry in the context of University sponsored publications. The prohibition on funding on behalf of publications that "primarily promot[e] or manifes[t] a particular belie[f] in or about a deity or an ultimate reality," in its ordinary and commonsense meaning, has a vast potential reach. The term "promotes" as used here would comprehend any writing advocating a philosophic position that rests upon a belief in a deity or ultimate reality.... And the term "manifests" would bring within the scope of the prohibition any writing that is explicable as resting upon a premise which presupposes the existence of a deity or ultimate reality....

Based on the principles we have discussed, we hold that the regulation invoked to deny SAF support, both in its terms and in its application to these petitioners, is a denial of their right of free speech guaranteed by the First Amendment. It remains to be considered whether the violation following from the University's action is excused by the necessity of complying with the Constitution's prohibition against state establishment of religion. We turn to that question.

III

Before its brief on the merits in this Court, the University had argued at all stages of the litigation that inclusion of WAP's contractors in SAF funding authorization would violate the Establishment Clause. Indeed, that is the ground on which the University prevailed in the Court of Appeals. We granted certiorari on this question: "Whether the Establishment Clause compels a state university to exclude an otherwise eligible student publication from participation in the student activities fund, solely on the basis of its religious viewpoint, where such exclusion would violate the Speech and Press Clauses if the viewpoint of the publication were nonreligious." The University now seems to have abandoned this position.... That the University itself no longer presses the Establishment Clause claim is some indication that it lacks force; but as the Court of Appeals rested its judgment on the point and our dissenting colleagues would find it determinative, it must be addressed.

. . .

If there is to be assurance that the Establishment Clause retains its force in guarding against those governmental actions it was intended to prohibit, we must in each case inquire first into the purpose and object of the governmental action in question and then into the practical details of the program's operation. Before turning to these matters, however, we can set forth certain general principles that must bear upon our determination.

A central lesson of our decisions is that a significant factor in upholding governmental programs in the face of Establishment Clause attack is their neutrality towards religion. We have decided a series of cases addressing the receipt of government benefits where religion or religious views are implicated in some degree.... More than once have we rejected the position that the Establishment Clause even justifies, much less requires, a refusal to extend free speech rights to religious speakers who participate in broad-reaching government programs neutral in design. See *Lamb's Chapel*, 508 U.S., at ____ . . . .

The governmental program here is neutral toward religion. There is no suggestion that the University created it to advance religion or adopted some ingenious device with the purpose of aiding a religious cause. The object of the SAF is to open a forum for speech and to support various student enterprises, including the publication of newspapers, in recognition of the diversity and creativity of student life. The University's SAF Guidelines have a separate classification for, and do not make third-party payments on behalf of, "religious organizations," which are those "whose purpose is to practice a devotion to an acknowledged ultimate reality or deity." The category of support here is for "student news, information, opinion, entertainment, or academic communications media groups," of which Wide Awake was 1 of 15 in the 1990 school year. WAP did not seek a subsidy because of its Christian editorial viewpoint; it sought funding as a student journal, which it was.

The neutrality of the program distinguishes the student fees from a tax levied for the direct support of a church or group of churches. A tax of that sort, of course, would run contrary to Establishment Clause concerns dating from the earliest days of the Republic. The apprehensions of our predecessors involved the levying of taxes upon the public for the sole and exclusive purpose of establishing and supporting specific sects. The exaction here, by contrast, is a student activity fee designed to reflect the reality that student life in its many dimensions includes the necessity of wide-ranging speech and inquiry and that student expression is an integral part of the University's educational mission. The fee is mandatory, and we do not have before us the question whether an objecting student has the First Amendment right to demand a pro rata return to the extent the fee is expended for speech to which he or she does not subscribe. See Keller v. State Bar of California, 496 U.S. 1, 15–16 (1990); Abood v. Detroit Board of Ed., 431 U.S. 209, 235–236 (1977). We must treat it, then, as an exaction upon the students. But the $14 paid each semester by the students is not a general tax designed to raise revenue for the University. . . . The SAF cannot be used for unlimited purposes, much less the illegitimate purpose of supporting one religion. Much like the arrangement in *Widmar*, the money goes to a special fund from which any group of students with CIO status can draw for purposes consistent with the University's educational mission; and to the extent the student is interested in speech, withdrawal is permitted to cover the whole spectrum of speech, whether it manifests a religious view, an antireligious view, or neither. Our decision, then, cannot be read as addressing an expenditure from a general tax fund. Here, the disbursements from the fund go to private contractors for the cost of printing that which is protected under the Speech Clause of the First Amendment. This is a far cry from a general public assessment designed and effected to provide financial support for a church.

Government neutrality is apparent in the State's overall scheme in a further meaningful respect. The program respects the critical difference "between government speech endorsing religion, which the Establishment Clause forbids, and private speech endorsing religion, which the Free Speech and Free Exercise Clauses protect." ... The University has taken pains to disassociate itself from the private speech involved in this case. The Court of Appeals' apparent concern that Wide Awake's religious orientation would be attributed to the University is not a plausible fear, and there is no real likelihood that the speech in question is being either endorsed or coerced by the State....

The Court of Appeals (and the dissent) are correct to extract from our decisions the principle that we have recognized special Establishment Clause dangers where the government makes direct money payments to sectarian institutions ... The error is not in identifying the principle but in believing that it controls this case. Even assuming that WAP is no different from a church and that its speech is the same as the religious exercises conducted in *Widmar* (two points much in doubt), the Court of Appeals decided a case that was, in essence, not before it, and the dissent would have us do the same. We do not confront a case where, even under a neutral program that includes nonsectarian recipients, the government is making direct money payments to an institution or group that is engaged in religious activity. Neither the Court of Appeals nor the dissent, we believe, takes sufficient cognizance of the undisputed fact that no public funds flow directly to WAP's coffers.

It does not violate the Establishment Clause for a public university to grant access to its facilities on a religion-neutral basis to a wide spectrum of student groups, including groups which use meeting rooms for sectarian activities, accompanied by some devotional exercises.... This is so even where the upkeep, maintenance, and repair of the facilities attributed to those uses is paid from a student activities fund to which students are required to contribute. *Widmar*, supra, at 265. The government usually acts by spending money. Even the provision of a meeting room, as in ... *Widmar*, involved governmental expenditure, if only in the form of electricity and heating or cooling costs. The error made by the Court of Appeals, as well as by the dissent, lies in focusing on the money that is undoubtedly expended by the government, rather than on the nature of the benefit received by the recipient. If the expenditure of governmental funds is prohibited whenever those funds pay for a service that is, pursuant to a religion-neutral program, used by a group for sectarian purposes, then *Widmar* ... and *Lamb's Chapel* would have to be overruled. Given our holdings in these cases, it follows that a public university may maintain its own computer facility and give student groups access to that facility, including the use of the printers, on a religion neutral, say first-come-first-served, basis. If a religious student organization obtained access on that religion-neutral basis and used a computer to compose or a printer or copy machine to print speech with a religious content or viewpoint, the State's action in providing the group with access would no more violate the Establishment Clause than would giving those groups access to an assembly hall.... There is no difference in logic or principle, and no difference of constitutional significance, between a school using its funds to operate a facility to which students have access, and a school paying a third-party contractor to operate the facility on its behalf. The latter occurs here. The University provides printing services to a broad spectrum of student newspapers qualified as CIOs by reason of their officers and membership. Any benefit to religion is incidental to the government's provision of secular services for secular purposes on a religion-neutral basis. Printing is a routine, secular, and recurring attribute of student life.

By paying outside printers, the University in fact attains a further degree of separation from the student publication, for it avoids the duties of supervision, escapes the costs of upkeep, repair, and replacement attributable to student use, and has a clear record of costs. As a result, and as in *Widmar*, the University can charge the SAF, and not the taxpayers as a whole, for the discrete activity in question. It would be formalistic for us to say that the University must forfeit these advantages and provide the services itself in order to comply with the Establishment Clause. It is, of course, true that if the State pays a church's bills it is subsidizing it, and we must guard against this abuse. That is not a danger here, based on the considerations we have advanced and for the additional reason that the student publication is not a religious institution, at least in the usual sense of that term as used in our case law, and it is not a religious organization as used in the University's own regulations. It is instead a publication involved in a pure forum for the expression of ideas, ideas that would be both incomplete and chilled were the Constitution to be interpreted to require that state officials and courts scan the publication to ferret out views that principally manifest a belief in a divine being.

Were the dissent's view to become law, it would require the University, in order to avoid a constitutional violation, to scrutinize the content of student speech, lest the expression in question-speech otherwise protected by the Constitution-contain too great a religious content. The dissent, in fact, anticipates such censorship as "crucial" in distinguishing between "works characterized by the evangelism of Wide Awake and writing that merely happens to express views that a given religion might approve." That eventuality raises the specter of governmental censorship, to ensure that all student writings and publications meet some baseline standard of secular orthodoxy. To impose that standard on student speech at a university is to imperil the very sources of free speech and expression. As we recognized in *Widmar*, official censorship would be far more inconsistent with the Establishment Clause's dictates than would governmental provision of secular printing services on a religion-blind basis.... Merely to draw the distinction would require the university—and ultimately the courts—to inquire into the significance of words and practices to different religious faiths, and in varying circumstances by the same faith. Such inquiries would tend inevitably to entangle the State with religion in a manner forbidden by our cases....

* * *

To obey the Establishment Clause, it was not necessary for the University to deny eligibility to student publications because of their viewpoint. The neutrality commanded of the State by the separate Clauses of the First Amendment was compromised by the University's course of action.   The viewpoint discrimination inherent in the University's regulation required public officials to scan and interpret student publications to discern their underlying philosophic assumptions respecting religious theory and belief.   That course of action was a denial of the right of free speech and would risk fostering a pervasive bias or hostility to religion, which could undermine the very neutrality the Establishment Clause requires.   There is no Establishment Clause violation in the University's honoring its duties under the Free Speech Clause.

The judgment of the Court of Appeals must be, and is, reversed.   It is so ordered.

Justice O'Connor, concurring.

.   .   .

This case lies at the intersection of the principle of government neutrality and the prohibition on state funding of religious activities. . . . Not to finance Wide Awake, according to petitioners, violates the principle of neutrality by sending a message of hostility toward religion.   To finance Wide Awake, argues the University, violates the prohibition on direct state funding of religious activities.

When two bedrock principles so conflict, understandably neither can provide the definitive answer.   Reliance on categorical platitudes is unavailing. Resolution instead depends on the hard task of judging-sifting through the details and determining whether the challenged program offends the Establishment Clause.   Such judgment requires courts to draw lines, sometimes quite fine, based on the particular facts of each case. . . .

.   .   .

So it is in this case.   The nature of the dispute does not admit of categorical answers, nor should any be inferred from the Court's decision today.   Instead, certain considerations specific to the program at issue lead me to conclude that by providing the same assistance to Wide Awake that it does to other publications, the University would not be endorsing the magazine's religious perspective.

First, the student organizations, at the University's insistence, remain strictly independent of the University. . . .   Any reader of Wide Awake would be on notice of the publication's independence from the University. . . .

Second, financial assistance is distributed in a manner that ensures its use only for permissible purposes.   A student organization seeking assistance must submit disbursement requests; if approved, the funds are paid directly to the third-party vendor and do not pass through the organization's coffers.   This safeguard accompanying the University's financial assistance, when provided to a publication with a religious viewpoint such as Wide Awake, ensures that the funds are used only to further the University's purpose in maintaining a free and robust marketplace of ideas, from whatever perspective.   This feature also makes this case analogous to a school providing equal access to a generally available printing press (or other physical facilities), and unlike a block grant to religious organizations.

Third, assistance is provided to the religious publication in a context that makes improbable any perception of government endorsement of the religious message. Wide Awake does not exist in a vacuum. It competes with 15 other magazines and newspapers for advertising and readership. The widely divergent viewpoints of these many purveyors of opinion, all supported on an equal basis by the University, significantly diminishes the danger that the message of any one publication is perceived as endorsed by the University. . . .

Finally, although the question is not presented here, I note the possibility that the student fee is susceptible to a Free Speech Clause challenge by an objecting student that she should not be compelled to pay for speech with which she disagrees. See, e. g., Keller v. State Bar of California, 496 U.S. 1, 15 (1990); Abood v. Detroit Board of Education, 431 U.S. 209, 236 (1977). There currently exists a split in the lower courts as to whether such a challenge would be successful. . . . While the Court does not resolve the question here, the existence of such an opt-out possibility not available to citizens generally . . . provides a potential basis for distinguishing proceeds of the student fees in this case from proceeds of the general assessments in support of religion that lie at the core of the prohibition against religious funding. Unlike monies dispensed from state or federal treasuries, the Student Activities Fund is collected from students who themselves administer the fund and select qualifying recipients only from among those who originally paid the fee. The government neither pays into nor draws from this common pool, and a fee of this sort appears conducive to granting individual students proportional refunds. The Student Activities Fund, then, represents not government resources, whether derived from tax revenue, sales of assets, or otherwise, but a fund that simply belongs to the students.

The Court's decision today therefore neither trumpets the supremacy of the neutrality principle nor signals the demise of the funding prohibition in Establishment Clause jurisprudence. . . . When bedrock principles collide, they test the limits of categorical obstinacy and expose the flaws and dangers of a Grand Unified Theory that may turn out to be neither grand nor unified. The Court today does only what courts must do in many Establishment Clause cases—focus on specific features of a particular government action to ensure that it does not violate the Constitution. By withholding from Wide Awake assistance that the University provides generally to all other student publications, the University has discriminated on the basis of the magazine's religious viewpoint in violation of the Free Speech Clause. And particular features of the University's program—such as the explicit disclaimer, the disbursement of funds directly to third-party vendors, the vigorous nature of the forum at issue, and the possibility for objecting students to opt out—convince me that providing such assistance in this case would not carry the danger of impermissible use of public funds to endorse Wide Awake's religious message.

Subject to these comments, I join the opinion of the Court.

Justice Thomas, concurring.

I agree with the Court's opinion and join it in full, but I write separately to express my disagreement with the historical analysis put forward by the dissent. . . .

Even assuming that the Virginia debate on the so-called "Assessment Controversy" was indicative of the principles embodied in the Establishment Clause, this incident hardly compels the dissent's conclusion that government must actively discriminate against religion. The dissent's historical discussion glosses over the fundamental characteristic of the Virginia assessment bill that sparked the controversy: The assessment was to be imposed for the support of clergy in the performance of their function of teaching religion. . . .

James Madison's Memorial and Remonstrance Against Religious Assessments (hereinafter Madison's Remonstrance) must be understood in this context. Contrary to the dissent's suggestion, Madison's objection to the assessment bill did not rest on the premise that religious entities may never participate on equal terms in neutral government programs. Nor did Madison embrace the argument that forms the linchpin of the dissent: that monetary subsidies are constitutionally different from other neutral benefits programs. Instead, Madison's comments are more consistent with the neutrality principle that the dissent inexplicably discards. . . .

Legal commentators have disagreed about the historical lesson to take from the Assessment Controversy. For some, the experience in Virginia is consistent with the view that the Framers saw the Establishment Clause simply as a prohibition on governmental preferences for some religious faiths over others. See R. Cord, Separation of Church and State: Historical Fact and Current Fiction 20–23 (1982); Smith, Getting Off on the Wrong Foot and Back on Again: A Reexamination of the History of the Framing of the Religion Clauses of the First Amendment and a Critique of the Reynolds and Everson Decisions, 20 Wake Forest L. Rev. 569, 590–591 (1984). Other commentators have rejected this view, concluding that the Establishment Clause forbids not only government preferences for some religious sects over others, but also government preferences for religion over irreligion. See, e.g., Laycock, "Nonpreferential" Aid to Religion: A False Claim About Original Intent, 27 Wm. & Mary L. Rev. 875, 875 (1986).

I find much to commend the former view. . . .

But resolution of this debate is not necessary to decide this case. Under any understanding of the Assessment Controversy, the history cited by the dissent cannot support the conclusion that the Establishment Clause "categorically condemn[s] state programs directly aiding religious activity" when that aid is part of a neutral program available to a wide array of beneficiaries. Even if Madison believed that the principle of nonestablishment of religion precluded government financial support for religion per se (in the sense of government benefits specifically targeting religion), there is no indication that at the time of the framing he took the dissent's extreme view that the government must discrimi-

ainst religious adherents by excluding them from more generally ole financial subsidies.

. . .

Though our Establishment Clause jurisprudence is in hopeless disarray, this case provides an opportunity to reaffirm one basic principle that has enjoyed an uncharacteristic degree of consensus: The Clause does not compel the exclusion of religious groups from government benefits programs that are generally available to a broad class of participants. . . .

. . .

Thus, history provides an answer for the constitutional question posed by this case, but it is not the one given by the dissent. The dissent identifies no evidence that the Framers intended to disable religious entities from participating on neutral terms in evenhanded government programs. The evidence that does exist points in the opposite direction and provides ample support for today's decision.

Justice Souter, with whom Justice Stevens, Justice Ginsburg, and Justice Breyer join, dissenting.

The Court today, for the first time, approves direct funding of core religious activities by an arm of the State. It does so, however, only after erroneous treatment of some familiar principles of law implementing the First Amendment's Establishment and Speech Clauses, and by viewing the very funds in question as beyond the reach of the Establishment Clause's funding restrictions as such. Because there is no warrant for distinguishing among public funding sources for purposes of applying the First Amendment's prohibition of religious establishment, I would hold that the University's refusal to support petitioners' religious activities is compelled by the Establishment Clause. I would therefore affirm.

I

The central question in this case is whether a grant from the Student Activities Fund to pay Wide Awake's printing expenses would violate the Establishment Clause. Although the Court does not dwell on the details of Wide Awake's message, it recognizes something sufficiently religious in the publication to demand Establishment Clause scrutiny. Although the Court places great stress on the eligibility of secular as well as religious activities for grants from the Student Activities Fund, it recognizes that such evenhanded availability is not by itself enough to satisfy constitutional requirements for any aid scheme that results in a benefit to religion. . . . Some members of the Court, at least, may think the funding permissible on a view that it is indirect, since the money goes to Wide Awake's printer, not through Wide Awake's own checking account. The Court's principal reliance, however, is on an argument that providing religion with economically valuable services is permissible on the theory that services are economically indistinguishable from religious access to governmental speech forums, which sometimes is permissible. But this reasoning would commit the Court to approving direct religious aid beyond anything justifiable for the sake of access to speaking forums. The Court implicitly recognizes this in its further attempt to circumvent the clear bar to direct governmental aid to religion. Different members of the Court seek to avoid this bar in different ways. The opinion of the Court makes the novel assumption that only direct aid financed with tax revenue is barred, and draws the erroneous conclusion that the involuntary Student Activities Fee is not a tax. I do not read Justice O'Connor's opinion as sharing that assumption; she places this Student Activities Fund in a category of student funding enterprises from which religious activities in public universities may benefit, so long as there is no consequent endorsement of religion. The resulting decision is in unmistakable tension with the accepted law that the Court continues to avow.

A

The Court's difficulties will be all the more clear after a closer look at Wide Awake than the majority opinion affords. . . .

. . .

Using public funds for the direct subsidization of preaching the word is categorically forbidden under the Establishment Clause, and if the Clause was meant to accomplish nothing else, it was meant to bar this use of public money. Evidence on the subject antedates even the Bill of Rights itself, as may be seen in the writings of Madison. . . . Four years before the First Congress proposed the First Amendment, Madison gave his opinion on the legitimacy of using public funds for religious purposes, in the Memorial and Remonstrance Against Religious Assessments, which played the central role in ensuring the defeat of the Virginia tax assessment bill in 1786 and framed the debate upon which the Religion Clauses stand. . . .

Madison wrote against a background in which nearly every Colony had exacted a tax for church support. . . . Madison's Remonstrance captured the colonists' "conviction that individual religious liberty could be achieved best under a government which was stripped of all power to tax, to support, or otherwise to assist any or all religions, or to interfere with the beliefs of any religious individual or group." . . . Their sentiment as expressed by Madison in Virginia, led not only to the defeat of Virginia's tax assessment bill, but also directly to passage of the Virginia Bill for Establishing Religious Freedom, written by Thomas Jefferson. That bill's preamble declared that "to compel a man to furnish contributions of money for the propagation of opinions which he disbelieves, is sinful and tyrannical," . . . and its text provided "[t]hat no man shall be compelled to frequent or support any religious worship, place, or ministry whatsoever . . . ," . . . .

The principle against direct funding with public money is patently violated by the contested use of today's student activity fee. . . . The University exercises the power of the State to compel a student to pay it, . . . and the use of any part of it for the direct support of religious activity thus strikes at what we have repeatedly held to be the heart of the prohibition on establishment. . . .

The Court, accordingly, has never before upheld direct state funding of the sort of proselytizing published in Wide Awake and, in fact, has

cally condemned state programs directly aiding religious activi-

. . .

B

. . . [I]t is easy for the Court to lose sight of what the University students and the Court of Appeals found so obvious, and to blanch the patently and frankly evangelistic character of the magazine by unrevealing allusions to religious points of view.

Nevertheless, even without the encumbrance of detail from Wide Awake's actual pages, the Court finds something sufficiently religious about the magazine to require examination under the Establishment Clause, and one may therefore ask why the unequivocal prohibition on direct funding does not lead the Court to conclude that funding would be unconstitutional. The answer is that the Court focuses on a subsidiary body of law, which it correctly states but ultimately misapplies. That subsidiary body of law accounts for the Court's substantial attention to the fact that the University's funding scheme is "neutral," in the formal sense that it makes funds available on an evenhanded basis to secular and sectarian applicants alike. While this is indeed true and relevant under our cases, it does not alone satisfy the requirements of the Establishment Clause, as the Court recognizes when it says that evenhandedness is only a "significant factor" in certain Establishment Clause analysis, not a dispositive one.... This recognition reflects the Court's appreciation of two general rules: that whenever affirmative government aid ultimately benefits religion, the Establishment Clause requires some justification beyond evenhandedness on the government's part; and that direct public funding of core sectarian activities, even if accomplished pursuant to an evenhanded program, would be entirely inconsistent with the Establishment Clause and would strike at the very heart of the Clause's protection.

. . . At the heart of the Establishment Clause stands the prohibition against direct public funding, but that prohibition does not answer the questions that occur at the margins of the Clause's application. Is any government activity that provides any incidental benefit to religion likewise unconstitutional? Would it be wrong to put out fires in burning churches, wrong to pay the bus fares of students on the way to parochial schools, wrong to allow a grantee of special education funds to spend them at a religious college? These are the questions that call for drawing lines, and it is in drawing them that evenhandedness becomes important.... In the doubtful cases (those not involving direct public funding), where there is initially room for argument about a law's effect, evenhandedness serves to weed out those laws that impermissibly advance religion by channelling aid to it exclusively. Evenhandedness is therefore a prerequisite to further enquiry into the constitutionality of a doubtful law, but evenhandedness goes no further. It does not guarantee success under Establishment Clause scrutiny.

. . .

C

Since conformity with the marginal or limiting principle of even-handedness is insufficient of itself to demonstrate the constitutionality of providing a government benefit that reaches religion, the Court must identify some further element in the funding scheme that does demonstrate its permissibility. For one reason or another, the Court's chosen element appears to be the fact that under the University's Guidelines, funds are sent to the printer chosen by Wide Awake, rather than to Wide Awake itself.

1

... Here there is no third party standing between the government and the ultimate religious beneficiary to break the circuit by its independent discretion to put state money to religious use. The printer, of course, has no option to take the money and use it to print a secular journal instead of Wide Awake. It only gets the money because of its contract to print a message of religious evangelism at the direction of Wide Awake, and it will receive payment only for doing precisely that. The formalism of distinguishing between payment to Wide Awake so it can pay an approved bill and payment of the approved bill itself cannot be the basis of a decision of Constitutional law....

2

It is more probable, however, that the Court's reference to the printer goes to a different attempt to justify the payment. On this purported justification, the payment to the printer is significant only as the last step in an argument resting on the assumption that a public university may give a religious group the use of any of its equipment or facilities so long as secular groups are likewise eligible.... The Court reasons that the availability of a forum has economic value (the government built and maintained the building, while the speakers saved the rent for a hall); and that economically there is no difference between the University's provision of the value of the room and the value, say, of the University's printing equipment; and that therefore the University must be able to provide the use of the latter. Since it may do that, the argument goes, it would be unduly formalistic to draw the line at paying for an outside printer, who simply does what the magazine's publishers could have done with the University's own printing equipment. The argument is as unsound as it is simple, and the first of its troubles emerges from an examination of the cases relied upon to support it. The common factual thread running through *Widmar* and *Lamb's Chapel*, is that a governmental institution created a limited forum for the use of students in a school or college, or for the public at large, but sought to exclude speakers with religious messages.... [E]ach case drew ultimately on unexceptionable Speech Clause doctrine treating the evangelist, the Salvation Army, the millennialist or the Hare Krishna like any other speaker in a public forum. It was the preservation of free speech on the model of the street corner that supplied the justification going beyond the requirement of evenhandedness.

. . . The analogy breaks down entirely, however, if the cases are read more broadly than the Court wrote them, to cover more than forums for literal speaking. There is no traditional street corner printing provided by the government on equal terms to all comers, and the forum cases cannot be lifted to a higher plane of generalization without admitting that new economic benefits are being extended directly to religion in clear violation of the principle barring direct aid. The argument from economic equivalence thus breaks down on recognizing that the direct state aid it would support is not mitigated by the street corner analogy in the service of free speech. Absent that, the rule against direct aid stands as a bar to printing services as well as printers.

3

It must, indeed, be a recognition of just this point that leads the Court to take a third tack. . . . The opinion of the Court concludes . . . that the activity fee is not a tax, and then proceeds to find the aid permissible on the legal assumption that the bar against direct aid applies only to aid derived from tax revenue. . . .

Although it was a taxation scheme that moved Madison to write in the first instance, the Court has never held that government resources obtained without taxation could be used for direct religious support, and our cases on direct government aid have frequently spoken in terms in no way limited to tax revenues. . . .

Allowing non-tax funds to be spent on religion would, in fact, fly in the face of clear principle. Leaving entirely aside the question whether public non-tax revenues could ever be used to finance religion without violating the endorsement test, . . . any such use of them would ignore one of the dual objectives of the Establishment Clause, which was meant not only to protect individuals and their republics from the destructive consequences of mixing government and religion, but to protect religion from a corrupting dependence on support from the Government. . . . Since the corrupting effect of government support does not turn on whether the Government's own money comes from taxation or gift or the sale of public lands, the Establishment Clause could hardly relax its vigilance simply because tax revenue was not implicated. Accordingly, in the absence of a forthright disavowal, one can only assume that the Court does not mean to eliminate one half of the Establishment Clause's justification.

D

Nothing in the Court's opinion would lead me to end this enquiry into the application of the Establishment Clause any differently from the way I began it. The Court is ordering an instrumentality of the State to support religious evangelism with direct funding. This is a flat violation of the Establishment Clause.

II

Given the dispositive effect of the Establishment Clause's bar to funding the magazine, there should be no need to decide whether in the absence of this bar the University would violate the Free Speech Clause by limiting funding as it has done.... But the Court's speech analysis may have independent application, and its flaws should not pass unremarked.

The Court acknowledges the necessity for a university to make judgments based on the content of what may be said or taught when it decides, in the absence of unlimited amounts of money or other resources, how to honor its educational responsibilities.... Accordingly, the Court recognizes that the relevant enquiry in this case is not merely whether the University bases its funding decisions on the subject matter of student speech; if there is an infirmity in the basis for the University's funding decision, it must be that the University is impermissibly distinguishing among competing viewpoints....

The issue whether a distinction is based on viewpoint does not turn simply on whether a government regulation happens to be applied to a speaker who seeks to advance a particular viewpoint; the issue, of course, turns on whether the burden on speech is explained by reference to viewpoint....

Accordingly, the prohibition on viewpoint discrimination serves that important purpose of the Free Speech Clause, which is to bar the government from skewing public debate. Other things being equal, viewpoint discrimination occurs when government allows one message while prohibiting the messages of those who can reasonably be expected to respond.... It is precisely this element of taking sides in a public debate that identifies viewpoint discrimination and makes it the most pernicious of all distinctions based on content. Thus, if government assists those espousing one point of view, neutrality requires it to assist those espousing opposing points of view, as well.

There is no viewpoint discrimination in the University's application of its Guidelines to deny funding to Wide Awake. Under those Guidelines, a "religious activit[y]," which is not eligible for funding, is "an activity which primarily promotes or manifests a particular belief(s) in or about a deity or an ultimate reality." It is clear that this is the basis on which Wide Awake Productions was denied funding....

If the Guidelines were written or applied so as to limit only such Christian advocacy and no other evangelical efforts that might compete with it, the discrimination would be based on viewpoint. But that is not what the regulation authorizes; it applies to Muslim and Jewish and Buddhist advocacy as well as to Christian. And since it limits funding to activities promoting or manifesting a particular belief not only "in" but "about" a deity or ultimate reality, it applies to agnostics and atheists as well as it does to deists and theists.... The Guidelines, and their application to Wide Awake, thus do not skew debate by funding one position but not its competitors. As understood by their application to Wide Awake, they simply deny funding for hortatory speech that "primarily promotes or manifests" any view on the merits of religion; they deny funding for the entire subject matter of religious apologetics.

   . . . .

The Guidelines are thus substantially different from the access restriction considered in *Lamb's Chapel*....

... [I]n *Lamb's Chapel* we unanimously determined that the access restriction, as applied to a speaker wishing to discuss family values from a Christian perspective, impermissibly distinguished between speakers on the basis of viewpoint.... Equally obvious is the distinction between that case and this one, where the regulation is being applied, not to deny funding for those who discuss issues in general from a religious viewpoint, but to those engaged in promoting or opposing religious conversion and religious observances as such. If this amounts to viewpoint discrimination, the Court has all but eviscerated the line between viewpoint and content.

To put the point another way, the Court's decision equating a categorical exclusion of both sides of the religious debate with viewpoint discrimination suggests the Court has concluded that primarily religious and antireligious speech, grouped together, always provides an opposing (and not merely a related) viewpoint to any speech about any secular topic. Thus, the Court's reasoning requires a university that funds private publications about any primarily nonreligious topic also to fund publications primarily espousing adherence to or rejection of religion. But a university's decision to fund a magazine about racism, and not to fund publications aimed at urging repentance before God does not skew the debate either about racism or the desirability of religious conversion. The Court's contrary holding amounts to a significant reformulation of our viewpoint discrimination precedents and will significantly expand access to limited-access forums....

III

Since I cannot see the future I cannot tell whether today's decision portends much more than making a shambles out of student activity fees in public colleges. Still, my apprehension is whetted by Chief Justice Burger's warning in Lemon v. Kurtzman, 403 U.S. 602, 624 (1971): "in constitutional adjudication some steps, which when taken were thought to approach 'the verge,' have become the platform for yet further steps. A certain momentum develops in constitutional theory and it can be a 'downhill thrust' easily set in motion but difficult to retard or stop."

I respectfully dissent.

———

SECTION 2. THE FREE EXERCISE OF RELIGION

———

Page 1692. Add at end of chapter:

CHURCH OF THE LUKUMI BABALU AYE, INC. v. CITY OF HIALEAH, 508 U.S. 520 (1993). The church practices the Santeria religion, whose services include animal sacrifices. When the church proposed to build a house of worship in Hialeah, the city enacted ordinances that targeted the practice of animal sacrifice by the church. One ordinance provided that "[i]t shall be unlawful for any person, persons, corporations or associations to sacrifice any animal within the corporate limits of the City of Hialeah, Florida." "Sacrifice" was defined as "to unnecessarily kill, torment, torture, or mutilate an animal in a public or private ritual or ceremony not for the primary purpose of food consumption." The ordinance contained an exemption for slaughtering by "licensed establishment[s]" of animals "specifically raised for food purposes." The Court held that the ordinances violated the free exercise clause since they were neither "neutral" nor "of general applicability." The ordinances were drafted so that "almost the only conduct subject to [them] is the religious exercise of Santeria church members." All of the asserted governmental purposes (protecting public health and preventing cruelty to animals) were only pursued in the context of Santeria religious practices. "A law that targets religious conduct for distinctive treatment or advances legitimate governmental interests only against conduct with a religious motivation will survive strict scrutiny only in rare cases."

THE RELIGIOUS FREEDOM RESTORATION ACT

On November 16, 1993, President Clinton signed into law the Religious Freedom Restoration Act, PL 103–141. The Act provides, in relevant part:

SEC. 2. CONGRESSIONAL FINDINGS AND DECLARATION OF PURPOSES.

(a) FINDINGS.—The Congress finds that—

(1) the framers of the Constitution, recognizing free exercise of religion as an unalienable right, secured its protection in the First Amendment to the Constitution;

(2) laws "neutral" toward religion may burden religious exercise as surely as laws intended to interfere with religious exercise;

(3) governments should not substantially burden religious exercise without compelling justification;

(4) in Employment Division v. Smith, 494 U.S. 872 (1990) the Supreme Court virtually eliminated the requirement that the government justify burdens on religious exercise imposed by laws neutral toward religion; and

(5) the compelling interest test as set forth in prior Federal court rulings is a workable test for striking sensible balances between religious liberty and competing prior governmental interests.

(b) PURPOSES.—The purposes of this Act are—

(1) to restore the compelling interest test as set forth in Sherbert v. Verner, 374 U.S. 398 (1963) and Wisconsin v. Yoder, 406 U.S.

205 (1972) and to guarantee its application in all cases where free exercise of religion is substantially burdened; and

(2) to provide a claim or defense to persons whose religious exercise is substantially burdened by government.

SEC. 3. FREE EXERCISE OF RELIGION PROTECTED.

(a) IN GENERAL.—Government shall not substantially burden a person's exercise of religion even if the burden results from a rule of general applicability, except as provided in subsection (b).

(b) EXCEPTION.—Government may substantially burden a person's exercise of religion only if it demonstrates that application of the burden to the person—

(1) is in furtherance of a compelling governmental interest; and

(2) is the least restrictive means of furthering that compelling governmental interest.

(c) JUDICIAL RELIEF.—A person whose religious exercise has been burdened in violation of this section may assert that violation as a claim or defense in a judicial proceeding and obtain appropriate relief against a government. Standing to assert a claim or defense under this section shall be governed by the general rules of standing under article III of the Constitution.

SEC. 5. DEFINITIONS.

As used in this Act—

(1) the term "government" includes a branch, department, agency, instrumentality, and official (or other person acting under color of law) of the United States, a State, or a subdivision of a State;

(2) the term "State" includes the District of Columbia, the Commonwealth of Puerto Rico, and each territory and possession of the United States;

(3) the term "demonstrates" means meets the burdens of going forward with the evidence and of persuasion; and

(4) the term "exercise of religion" means the exercise of religion under the First Amendment to the Constitution.

SEC. 6. APPLICABILITY.

(a) IN GENERAL.—This Act applies to all Federal and State law, and the implementation of that law, whether statutory or otherwise, and whether adopted before or after the enactment of this Act.

(b) RULE OF CONSTRUCTION.—Federal statutory law adopted after the date of the enactment of this Act is subject to this Act unless such law explicitly excludes such application by reference to this Act.

(c) RELIGIOUS BELIEF UNAFFECTED.—Nothing in this Act shall be construed to authorize any government to burden any religious belief.

†